Communications in Computer and Information Science 1057

Commenced Publication in 2007
Founding and Former Series Editors:
Phoebe Chen, Alfredo Cuzzocrea, Xiaoyong Du, Orhun Kara, Ting Liu,
Krishna M. Sivalingam, Dominik Ślęzak, Takashi Washio, Xiaokang Yang,
and Junsong Yuan

Editorial Board Members

More information about this series at http://www.springer.com/series/7899

Emmanouel Garoufallou · Francesca Fallucchi ·
Ernesto William De Luca (Eds.)

Metadata and Semantic Research

13th International Conference, MTSR 2019
Rome, Italy, October 28–31, 2019
Revised Selected Papers

 Springer

Editors
Emmanouel Garoufallou (iD)
International Hellenic University
Thessaloniki, Greece

Francesca Fallucchi (iD)
Guglielmo Marconi University
Rome, Italy

Ernesto William De Luca (iD)
Georg Eckert Institute – Leibniz Institute
for International Textbook Research
Braunschweig, Germany

ISSN 1865-0929   ISSN 1865-0937   (electronic)
Communications in Computer and Information Science
ISBN 978-3-030-36598-1   ISBN 978-3-030-36599-8   (eBook)
https://doi.org/10.1007/978-3-030-36599-8

This Springer imprint is published by the registered company Springer Nature Switzerland AG
The registered company address is: Gewerbestrasse 11, 6330 Cham, Switzerland

Preface

Metadata and semantics are integral to any information system and important to the sphere of Web data. Research and development addressing metadata and semantics is crucial to advancing how we effectively discover, use, archive, and repurpose information. In response to this need, researchers are actively examining methods for generating, reusing, and interchanging metadata. Integrated with these developments is research on the application of computational methods, linked data, and data analytics. A growing body of literature also targets conceptual and theoretical designs providing foundational frameworks for metadata and semantic applications. There is no doubt that metadata weaves its way through nearly every aspect of our information ecosystem, and there is great motivation for advancing the current state of understanding in the fields of metadata and semantics. To this end, it is vital that scholars and practitioners convene and share their work.

Since 2005, the International Metadata and Semantics Research Conference (MTSR) has served as a significant venue for dissemination and sharing of metadata and semantic-driven research and practices. 2019 marked the 13th MTSR, drawing scholars, researchers, and practitioners who are investigating and advancing our knowledge on a wide range of metadata and semantic-driven topics. The 13th International Conference on Metadata and Semantics Research (MTSR 2019) was held at the Guglielmo Marconi University in Rome, Italy, October 28–31, 2019.

MTSR conferences have grown in number of participants and paper submission rates over the past decade, marking it as a leading, international research conference. Continuing in the successful legacy of previous MTSR conferences (MTSR 2005, MTSR 2007, MTSR 2009, MTSR 2010, MTSR 2011, MTSR 2012, MTSR 2013, MTSR 2014, MTSR 2015, MTSR 2016, MTSR 2017, and MTSR 2018), MTSR 2019 brought together scholars and practitioners who share a common interest in the interdisciplinary field of metadata, linked data, and ontologies.

The MTSR 2019 program and the proceedings show a rich diversity of research and practices from metadata and semantically focused tools and technologies, linked data, cross-language semantics, ontologies, metadata models, semantic systems, and metadata standards. The general session of the conference included 18 papers covering a broad spectrum of topics, proving the interdisciplinary view of metadata. Metadata as a research topic is maturing, and the conference supported the following eight tracks: Digital Libraries, Information Retrieval, Big, Linked, Social and Open Data; Cultural Collections and Applications; European and National Projects; Open Repositories, Research Information Systems, and Data Infrastructures; Digital Humanities and Digital Curation; Agriculture, Food, and Environment; and Knowledge IT Artifacts in Professional Communities and Aggregations. The new eight track that MTSR 2019 introduced was on Metadata, Identifiers, and Semantics in Decentralized Applications, Blockchains, and P2P Systems. Each of these tracks had a rich selection of short and full research papers, in total 24, giving broader diversity to MTSR, and enabling deeper exploration of significant topics.

All the papers underwent a thorough and rigorous peer-review process. The review and selection for this year was highly competitive and only papers containing significant research results, innovative methods, or novel and best practices were accepted for publication. From the general session, only 14 submissions were accepted as full research papers, representing 41.1% of the total number of submissions, and 4 as short papers. An additional 13 contributions from tracks covering noteworthy and important results were accepted as full research papers, representing 36.1% of the total number of submissions, and 11 as short papers, bringing the total of MTSR 2019 accepted contributions to 42. The acceptance rate of full research papers for both the general session and tracks was 38.6% of the total number of submissions.

Guglielmo Marconi University (GMU) is the first Italian Open University which has been recognized by the Ministry of Education (MIUR) in Italy and provides innovative high-quality degree programs in the fields of humanities, social sciences, law, business, and engineering. The GMU's mission is to promote interdisciplinary research and innovation. In its activities, the university adheres to the following pillars: openness, quality, professionalism, and international vocation.

MTSR 2019 was pleased to host a remarkable keynote presentation held by Dr. Alfio M. Gliozzo, Research Manager - Knowledge Induction at IBM T.J. Watson Research (New York, USA). In his presentation "Extending Knowledge Graphs Using Distantly Supervised Deep Nets" Dr. Gliozzo shared his extensive experience and insights about how to train deep nets for relation extraction using distant supervision able to induce taxonomies directly from text provided as input in any domain, thus enabling SMEs to easily customize them to their needs.

Furthermore, in a round table titled "The Digital World 2030", three keynote speakers from different disciplines discussed challenges and future developments for the next decade.

The first keynote in the field of Industry 4.0 was held by Professor Gabriele Arcidiacono, Full Professor of Machine Design and Head of Department of Innovation and Information Engineering (DIIE) at Guglielmo Marconi University (Rome, Italy). His presentation "Lean Education and Society 5.0: the Global Excellence" described the need for a cultural revolution which would go hand in hand with the technological one: the human technology oriented model of the Society 5.0.

The second presenter from the telecommunications research field was Professor Romeo Giuliano, Associate Professor in the Department of Innovation and Information Engineering (DIIE) at Guglielmo Marconi University (Rome, Italy). In his presentation "The 6-th Generation Network (6G): Drivers, Services and Requirements" Professor Giuliano explained how the forthcoming 6-th generation network will be, what services it will provide, and how it will be organized. 6G will be immersive in the environment we live in, equipped with artificial intelligence, providing social services worldwide.

The last presentation given by Professor Fabio Massimo Zanzotto, Associate Professor in the Department of Enterprise Engineering - University of Rome Tor Vergata was focused on computer science. In his talk "Hey, Merry Men! Robin-Hood Artificial Intelligence is Calling You!" Professor Zanzotto explained how the innovations of artificial intelligence are changing the future job market. Artificial intelligence is exploiting human knowledge stored in personal data to replace workers owning this knowledge. A real research challenge for the future is how to constantly repay workers for their knowledge as these workers are contributing to the construction of the artificial intelligence that will replace them. Without a clear agenda, the artificial intelligence revolution will be a step of no return.

MTSR 2019 hosted a tutorial on "VocBench 3: Collaborative Development of Thesauri, Ontologies, Lexicons and RDF Datasets for the Sematic Web" organized by a remarkable team of Professionals and Professors as Armando Stellato, Manuel Fiorelli, Tiziano Lorenzetti, Willem van Gemert, Denis Dechandon, Christine Laaboudi-Spoiden, Anikó Gerencsér, Anne Waniart, Eugeniu Costetchi, and Andrea Turbati.

We conclude this preface by thanking the many people who contributed their time and efforts to MTSR 2019 and made this year's conference possible. We also thank all the organizations that supported this conference. We thank all institutions and universities that co-organized MTSR 2019. We extend a sincere gratitude to members of the Program Committees both main and special tracks, the Steering Committee and the Organizing Committees (both general and local), and the conference reviewers who invested their time generously to ensure the timely review of the submitted manuscripts. A special thanks to local organization chair Professor Francesca Fallucchi from Guglielmo Marconi University, Italy; to program chair Professor Noemi Scarpato from San Raffaele Roma Open University, Italy; to workshop, tutorial, and demonstration chair Professor Ivo Keller from TH Brandenburg, Germany; and to all special track chairs of MTSR 2019. A special thank you to Francesca Fallucchi and Anxhela Dani for supporting us throughout this event, to Iro Sotiriadou and Anxhela Dani who assisted us with the preparation of proceedings, and to Vasiliki, Nikoleta, and Stavroula for their endless support and patience. Our thanks go to our sponsors Elsevier, Springer Nature, EBSCO, IEEE, and Reasonable Graph, and our best paper and best student paper sponsor euroCRIS. Finally, our deepest thank you go to all authors and participants of MTSR 2019 for making the event a great success.

September 2019

Emmanouel Garoufallou
Francesca Fallucchi
Ernesto William De Luca

Organization

General Chairs

Emmanouel Garoufallou   International Hellenic University, Greece
Ernesto William De Luca   Georg Eckert Institute – Leibniz Institute for
                                    International Textbook Research, Germany

Program Chair

Noemi Scarpato   San Raffaele Roma Open University, Italy

Local Organization Chair

Francesca Fallucchi   Guglielmo Marconi University, Italy

Workshop, Tutorial, and Demonstration Chair

Ivo Keller   TH Brandenburg, Germany

Special Track Chairs

Miguel-Ángel Sicilia	University of Alcalá, Spain
Francesca Fallucchi	Guglielmo Marconi University, Italy
Riem Spielhaus	Georg Eckert Institute for International Textbook Research, Germany
Ernesto William De Luca	Georg Eckert Institute – Leibniz Institute for International Textbook Research, Germany
Armando Stellato	University of Rome Tor Vergata, Italy
Nikos Houssos	IRI, Greece
Michalis Sfakakis	Ionian University, Greece
Lina Bountouri	EU Publications Office, Luxembourg
Emmanouel Garoufallou	International Hellenic University, Greece
Jane Greenberg	Drexel University, USA
R. J. Hartley	Manchester Metropolitan University, UK
Stavroula Antonopoulou	Perrotis College, American Farm School, Greece
Rob Davies	Cyprus University of Technology, Cyprus
Fabio Sartori	University of Milano-Bicocca, Italy
Angela Locoro	Università Carlo Cattaneo – LIUC, Italy
Arlindo Flavio da Conceição	Federal University of São Paulo (UNIFESP), Brazil

Steering Committee

Juan Manuel Dodero	University of Cádiz, Spain
Emmanouel Garoufallou	International Hellenic University, Greece
Nikos Manouselis	AgroKnow, Greece
Fabio Santori	University of Milano-Bicocca, Italy
Miguel-Ángel Sicilia	University of Alcalá, Spain

Organizing Committee

Anxhela Dani	National Library of Greece, Greece
Athina Evagorou	Cyprus University of Technology, Cyprus
Fotini Nikolaidou	Cyprus University of Technology, Cyprus
Chrysanthi Chatzopoulou	European Publishing, Greece
Pavlos Metaxas	Cyprus University of Technology, Cyprus
Stephani Liasi	Cyprus University of Technology, Cyprus
Maria Haraki	Cyprus University of Technology, Cyprus
Nasia Panagiotou	Cyprus University of Technology, Cyprus
Marina Antoniou	Cyprus University of Technology, Cyprus
Iro Sotiriadou	American Farm School, Greece

Technical Support Staff

Ilias Nitsos	International Hellenic University, Greece
Petros Artemi	Cyprus University of Technology, Cyprus

Programme Committee

Trond Aalberg	Oslo Metropolitan University, Norway
Rajendra Akerkar	Western Norway Research Institute, Norway
Getaneh Alemu	Southampton Solent University, UK
Arif Altun	Hacettepe University, Turkey
Stavroula Antonopoulou	Perrotis College, American Farm School, Greece
Ioannis N. Athanasiadis	Wageningen University, The Netherlands
Sophie Aubin	INRA, France
Thomas Baker	Sungkyunkwan University, South Korea
Panos Balatsoukas	King's College London, UK
Wolf-Tilo Balke	TU Braunschweig, Germany
Tomaz Bartol	University of Ljubljana, Slovenia
Hugo Besemer	Wageningen UR Library, The Netherlands
Ina Bluemel	German National Library of Science and Technology TIBm, Germany
Lina Bountouri	EU Publications Office, Luxembourg
Derek Bousfield	Manchester Metropolitan University, UK
Karin Bredenberg	The National Archives of Sweden, Sweden
Patrice Buche	INRA, France

Gerhard Budin	University of Vienna, Austria
Federico Cabitza	University of Milano-Bicocca, Italy
Özgü Can	Ege University, Turkey
Caterina Caracciolo	Food and Agriculture Organization (FAO) of the United Nations, Italy
Christian Cechinel	Federal University of Santa Catarina, Brazil
Artem Chebotko	University of Texas - Pan American, USA
Philip Cimiano	Bielefeld University, Germany
Sissi Closs	Karlsruhe University of Applied Sciences, Germany
Ricardo Colomo-Palacios	Universidad Carlos III, Spain
Mike Conway	University of North Carolina at Chapel Hill, USA
Phil Couch	The University of Manchester, UK
Sally Jo Cunningham	Waikato University, New Zealand
Constantina Costopoulou	Agricultural University of Athens, Greece
Ernesto William De Luca	Georg Eckert Institute – Leibniz Institute for International Textbook Research, Germany
Milena Dobreva	UCL, Qatar
Juan Manuel Dodero	University of Cádiz, Spain
Erdogan Dogdu	Cankaya University, Turkey
Gordon Dunshire	University of Strathclyde, UK
Biswanath Dutta	Documentation Research and Training Centre (DRTC), Indian Statistical Institute, India
Jan Dvorak	Charles University of Prague, Czech Republic
Ali Emrouznejad	Aston University, UK
Juan José Escribano Otero	Universidad Europea de Madrid, Spain
Francesca Fallucchi	Guglielmo Marconi University, Italy
Arlindo Flavio da Conceição	Federal University of São Paulo (UNIFESP), Brazil
Muriel Foulonneau	Knowledge Engineer, Amazon.com
Enrico Francesconi	EU Publications Office, Luxembourg
Panorea Gaitanou	Ministry of Justice, Transparency and Human Rights, Greece
Ana Garcia-Serrano	ETSI Informatica – UNED, Spain
Emmanouel Garoufallou	International Hellenic University, Greece
Manolis Gergatsoulis	Ionian University, Greece
Elena González-Blanco	Universidad Nacional de Educación a Distancia, Spain
Jorge Gracia	University of Zaragoza, Spain
Jane Greenberg	Drexel University, USA
Jill Griffiths	Manchester Metropolitan University, UK
Siddeswara Guru	University of Queensland, Australia
R. J. Hartley	Manchester Metropolitan University, UK
Steffen Hennicke	Georg Eckert Institute – Leibniz Institute for International Textbook Research, Germany
Nikos Houssos	IRI, Greece
Carlos A. Iglesias	Universidad Politécnica de Madrid, Spain
Antoine Isaac	Vrije Universiteit, Amsterdam, The Netherlands

Keith Jeffery	Keith G. Jeffery Consultants, UK
Frances Johnson	Manchester Metropolitan University, UK
Dimitris Kanellopoulos	University of Patras, Greece
Pinar Karagöz	Middle East Technical University (METU), Turkey
Pythagoras Karampiperis	AgroKnow, Greece
Johannes Keizer	Food and Agriculture Organization (FAO) of the United Nations, Italy
Ivo Keller	Food and Agriculture Organization (FAO) of the United Nations, Italy
Maret Keller	Georg Eckert Institute – Leibniz Institute for International Textbook Research, Germany
Brian Kelly	CETIS, University of Bolton, UK
Nikolaos Konstantinou	The University of Manchester, UK
Stasinos Konstantopoulos	NCSR Demokritos, Greece
Christian Kop	University of Klagenfurt, Austria
Rebecca Koskela	University of New Mexico, USA
Jessica Lindholm	Malmö University, Sweden
Angela Locoro	University of Milano-Bicocca, Italy
Andreas Lommatzsch	TU Berlin, Germany
Daniela Luzi	National Research Council, Italy
Paolo Manghi	Institute of Information Science and Technologies (ISTI), National Research Council (CNR), Italy
Brian Matthews	Science and Technology Facilities Council, UK
Philipp Mayr	GESIS, Germany
John McCrae	National University of Ireland Galway, Ireland
Peter McKinney	National Library of New Zealand Te Puna Mātauranga o Aotearoa, New Zealand
Riccardo Melen	University of Milano-Bicocca, Italy
Claire Nédellec	INRA, France
Ilias Nitsos	International Hellenic University, Greece
Xavier Ochoa	Centro de Tecnologías de Información Guayaquil, Ecuador
Mehmet C. Okur	Yaşar University, Turkey
Gabriela Ossenbach	UNED, Spain
Matteo Palmonari	University of Milano-Bicocca, Italy
Laura Papaleo	University of Genova, Italy
Christos Papatheodorou	Ionian University, Greece
Marios Poulos	Ionian University, Greece
T. V. Prabhakar	Indian Institute of Technology Kanpur, India
Aurelio Ravarini	Università Carlo Cattaneo – LIUC, Italy
Maria Cláudia Reis Cavalcanti	Military Institute of Engineering, Brazil
Cristina Ribeiro	INESC TEC, University of Porto, Portugal
Eva Mendez Rodriguez	Universidad Carlos III of Madrid, Spain
Dimitris Rousidis	International Hellenic University, Greece
Athena Salaba	Kent State University, USA

Salvador Sánchez-Alonso	University of Alcalá, Spain
Fabio Sartori	University of Milano-Bicocca, Italy
Noemi Scarpato	San Raffaele Roma Open University, Italy
Christian Scheel	Georg Eckert Institute – Leibniz Institute for International Textbook Research, Germany
Jochen Schirrwagen	University of Bielefeld, Germany
Birgit Schmidt	University of Göttingen, Germany
Joachim Schöpfel	University of Lille, France
Michalis Sfakakis	Ionian University, Greece
Cleo Sgouropoulou	University of West Attica, Greece
Kathleen Shearer	Confederation of Open Access Repositories (COAR), Germany
Rania Siatri	International Hellenic University, Greece
Miguel-Ángel Sicilia	University of Alcalá, Spain
Carla Simone	University of Siegen, Germany
Flávio Soares Corrêa da Silva	University of São Paulo, Brazil
Ahmet Soylu	Norwegian University of Science and Technology, Norway
Riem Spielhaus	Georg Eckert Institute – Leibniz Institute for International Textbook Research, Germany
Lena-Luise Stahn	Georg Eckert Institute – Leibniz Institute for International Textbook Research, Germany
Armando Stellato	University of Rome Tor Vergata, Italy
Imma Subirats	Food and Agriculture Organization (FAO) of the United Nations, Italy
Shigeo Sugimoto	University of Tsukuba, Japan
Maguelonne Teisseire	Irstea Montpellier, France
Jan Top	Wageningen Food & Biobased Research, The Netherlands
Robert Trypuz	John Paul II Catholic University of Lublin, Poland
Giannis Tsakonas	University of Patras, Greece
Chrisa Tsinaraki	Joint Research Centre, European Commission, Italy
Andrea Turbati	University of Rome Tor Vergata, Italy
Yannis Tzitzikas	University of Crete and ICS-FORTH, Greece
Christine Urquhart	Aberystwyth University, UK
Evangelia Vassilakaki	National Library of Greece, Greece
Sirje Virkus	Tallinn University, Estonia
Andreas Vlachidis	University College London, UK
Zhong Wang	Sun-Yat-Sen University, China
Andreas Weiß	Georg Eckert Institute – Leibniz Institute for International Textbook Research, Germany
Katherine Wisser	Graduate School of Library and Information Science, Simmons College, USA
Georgia Zafeiriou	University of Macedonia, Greece
Cecilia Zanni-Merk	Insa Rouen Normandie, France

Fabio Massimo Zanzotto	University of Rome Tor Vergata, Italy
Marcia Zeng	Kent State University, USA
Marios Zervas	Cyprus University of Technology, Cyprus
Thomas Zschocke	World Agroforestry Centre (ICRAF), Kenya
Maja Žumer	University of Ljubljana, Slovenia

Special Track on Metadata and Semantics for Open Repositories, Research Information Systems, and Data Infrastructures

Special Track Chairs

Nikos Houssos	IRI, Greece
Armando Stellato	University of Rome Tor Vergata, Italy

Honorary Track Chair

Imma Subirats	Food and Agriculture Organization (FAO) of the United Nations, Italy

Program Committee

Sophie Aubin	INRA, France
Thomas Baker	Sungkyunkwan University, South Korea
Hugo Besemer	Wageningen UR Library, The Netherlands
Gordon Dunshire	University of Strathclyde, UK
Jan Dvorak	Charles University of Prague, Czech Republic
Jane Greenberg	Drexel University, USA
Siddeswara Guru	The University of Queensland, Australia
Keith Jeffery	Keith G Jeffery Consultants, UK
Nikolaos Konstantinou	The University of Manchester, UK
Rebecca Koskela	University of New Mexico, USA
Jessica Lindholm	Malmö University, Sweden
Paolo Manghi	Institute of Information Science and Technologies (ISTI), National Research Council, Italy
Brian Matthews	Science and Technology Facilities Council, UK
Eva Mendez Rodriguez	University of Carlos III of Madrid, Spain
Joachim Schöpfel	University of Lille, France
Kathleen Shearer	Confederation of Open Access Repositories (COAR), Germany
Jochen Schirrwagen	University of Göttingen, Germany
Chrisa Tsinaraki	European Commission, Joint Research Centre, Italy
Yannis Tzitzikas	University of Crete and ICS-FORTH, Greece
Zhong Wang	Sun-Yat-Sen University, China
Marcia Zeng	Kent State University, USA

Track on Metadata and Semantics for Digital Libraries, Information Retrieval, Big, Linked, Social, and Open Data

Special Track Chairs

Emmanouel Garoufallou	International Hellenic University, Greece
Jane Greenberg	Drexel University, USA

Program Committee

Panos Balatsoukas	King's College London, UK
Özgü Can	Ege University, Turkey
Sissi Closs	Karlsruhe University of Applied Sciences, Germany
Mike Conway	University of North Carolina at Chapel Hill, USA
Phil Couch	The University of Manchester, UK
Milena Dobreva	UCL, Qatar
Ali Emrouznejad	Aston University, UK
Panorea Gaitanou	Ministry of Justice, Transparency and Human Rights, Greece
Stamatios Giannoulakis	Cyprus University of Technology, Cyprus
Jane Greenberg	Drexel University, USA
R. J. Hartley	Manchester Metropolitan University, UK
Nikos Korfiatis	University of East Anglia, UK
Rebecca Koskela	University of New Mexico, USA
Dimitris Rousidis	International Hellenic University, Greece
Athena Salaba	Kent State University, USA
Miguel-Ángel Sicilia	University of Alcalá, Spain
Christine Urquhart	Aberystwyth University, UK
Evgenia Vassilakaki	National Library of Greece, Greece
Sirje Virkus	Tallinn University, Estonia
Georgia Zafeiriou	University of Macedonia, Greece
Marios Zervas	Cyprus University of Technology, Cyprus

Track on Metadata and Semantics for Agriculture, Food, and Environment (AgroSEM 2019)

Special Track Chair

Miguel-Ángel Sicilia	University of Alcalá, Spain

Program Committee

Ioannis Athanasiadis	Wageningen University, The Netherlands
Patrice Buche	INRA, France
Caterina Caracciolo	Food and Agriculture Organization (FAO) of the United Nations, Italy
Johannes Keizer	Food and Agriculture Organization (FAO) of the United Nations, Italy

Stasinos Konstantopoulos	NCSR Demokritos, Greece
Claire Nédellec	INRA, France
Ivo Pierozzi	Embrapa Agricultural Informatics, Brazil
Armando Stellato	University of Rome Tor Vergata, Italy
Maguelonne Teisseire	Irstea Montpellier, France
Jan Top	Wageningen Food, and Biobased Research, The Netherlands
Robert Trypuz	John Paul II Catholic University of Lublin, Poland

Track on Metadata and Semantics for Digital Humanities and Digital Curation (DHC2019)

Special Track Chairs

Ernesto William De Luca	Georg Eckert Institute – Leibniz Institute for International Textbook Research, Germany
Francesca Fallucchi	Guglielmo Marconi University, Italy
Riem Spielhaus	Georg Eckert Institute – Leibniz Institute for International Textbook Research, Germany

Program Committee

Maret Keller	Georg Eckert Institute – Leibniz Institute for International Textbook Research, Germany
Elena González-Blanco	Universidad Nacional de Educación a Distancia, Spain
Steffen Hennicke	Georg Eckert Institute – Leibniz Institute for International Textbook Research, Germany
Ana García-Serrano	ETSI Informatica – UNED, Spain
Philipp Mayr	GESIS, Germany
Noemi Scarpato	San Raffaele Roma Open University, Italy
Lena-Luise Stahn	Georg Eckert Institute – Leibniz Institute for International Textbook Research, Germany
Andrea Turbati	University of Rome Tor Vergata, Italy
Christian Scheel	Georg Eckert Institute – Leibniz Institute for International Textbook Research, Germany
Armando Stellato	University of Rome Tor Vergata, Italy
Wolf-Tilo Balke	TU Braunschweig, Germany
Andreas Lommatzsch	TU Berlin, Germany
Ivo Keller	TH Brandenburg, Germany
Gabriela Ossenbach	UNED, Spain
Francesca Fallucchi	Guglielmo Marconi University, Italy

Track on Metadata and Semantics for Cultural Collections and Applications

Special Track Chairs

Michalis Sfakakis	Ionian University, Greece
Lina Bountouri	EU Publications Office, Luxembourg

Program Committee

Trond Aalberg	Oslo Metropolitan University, Norway
Karin Bredenberg	The National Archives of Sweden, Sweden
Enrico Francesconi	EU Publications Office, Luxembourg, and Consiglio Nazionale delle Recerche, Italy
Manolis Gergatsoulis	Ionian University, Greece
Antoine Isaac	Vrije Universiteit Amsterdam, The Netherlands
Sarantos Kapidakis	Ionian University, Greece
Christos Papatheodorou	Ionian University and Digital Curation Unit, IMIS, Athena RC, Greece
Chrisa Tsinaraki	European Commission, Joint Research Centre, Italy
Andreas Vlachidis	University College London, UK
Katherine Wisser	Graduate School of Library and Information Science, Simmons College, USA
Maja Žumer	University of Ljubljana, Slovenia

Track on Metadata and Semantics for European and National Projects

Special Track Chairs

R. J. Hartley	Manchester Metropolitan University, UK
Stavroula Antonopoulou	Perrotis College, American Farm School, Greece
Robert Davies	Cyprus University of Technology, Cyprus

Program Committee

Panos Balatsoukas	King's College London, UK
Mike Conway	University of North Carolina at Chapel Hill, USA
Emmanouel Garoufallou	International Hellenic University, Greece
Jane Greenberg	Drexel University, USA
Nikos Houssos	IRI, Greece
Nikos Korfiatis	University of East Anglia, UK
Damiana Koutsomiha	American Farm School, Greece
Paolo Manghi	Institute of Information Science and Technologies (ISTI), National Research Council, Italy
Dimitris Rousidis	International Hellenic University, Greece
Rania Siatri	International Hellenic University, Greece
Miguel-Ángel Sicilia	University of Alcalá, Spain

Armando Stellato   University of Rome Tor Vergata, Italy
Sirje Virkus   Tallinn University, Estonia

Track on Metadata and Semantics for Metadata, Identifiers and Semantics in Decentralized Applications, Blockchains and P2P Systems

Special Track Chair

Miguel-Ángel Sicilia   University of Alcalá, Spain

Program Committee

Sissi Closs   Karlsruhe University of Applied Sciences, Germany
Ernesto William De Luca   Georg Eckert Institute – Leibniz Institute for
                             International Textbook Research, Germany
Juan Manuel Dodero   University of Cádiz, Spain
Francesca Fallucchi   Guglielmo Marconi University, Italy
Jane Greenberg   Drexel University, USA
Nikos Houssos   IRI, Greece
Nikos Korfiatis   University of East Anglia, UK
Dimitris Rousidis   International Hellenic University, Greece
Salvador Sánchez-Alonso   University of Alcalá, Spain
Michalis Sfakakis   Ionian University, Greece
Rania Siatri   International Hellenic University, Greece
Armando Stellato   University of Rome Tor Vergata, Italy
Robert Trypuz   John Paul II Catholic University of Lublin, Poland
Sirje Virkus   Tallinn University, Estonia

MTSR 2019 Reviewers

Sina Ahmadi   National University of Ireland Galway, Ireland
Ana Garcia-Serrano   Spanish Open University, Spain
Andrés Felipe Pineda   Federal University of Santa Catarina, Brazil
  Corcho
Blerina Spahiu   University of Milano-Bicocca, Italy
Sotiris Konstantinidis   AgroKnow, Greece
Alessandro Ligi   Georg Eckert Institute – Leibniz Institute for
                             International Textbook Research, Germany
Andreas Lommatzsch   TU Berlin, Germany
Sergey Parinov   CEMI RAS, Russia
Petito Michele   University of Pisa, Italy
Noemi Scarpato   San Raffaele Roma Open University, Italy

Co-organized MTSR 2019 Conference by

GEOЯG ECKERT
INSTITUTE

for International Textbook Research

Department of Informatics, Systems and Communication
University of Milano-Bicocca, Italy

DIPARTIMENTO
DI INFORMATICA
SISTEMISTICA
E COMUNICAZIONE

 School of Information

International Hellenic University, Greece

 Department of Library Science
Archives and Information Systems

Università degli Studi
Guglielmo Marconi

 Cyprus
University of
Technology

Sponsors Supporting MTSR 2019 Conference

Gold

Silver

Awards Sponsored By

Contents

Track on Metadata and Semantics for Open Repositories, Research Information Systems, and Data Infrastructures

Track on Metadata and Semantics for Digital Libraries, Information Retrieval, Big, Linked, Social and Open Data

Track on Metadata and Semantics for Agriculture, Food and Environment (AgroSEM 2019)

Track on Metadata and Semantics for Digital Humanities and Digital Curation (DHC2019)

**Track on Metadata and Semantics for Cultural Collections
and Applications**

**Track on Metadata and Semantics for European
and National Projects**

**Track on Metadata, Identifiers and Semantics in Decentralized
Applications, Blockchains and P2P Systems**

Metadata, Linked Data, Semantics and Ontologies – General Session

CLaRO: A Controlled Language for Authoring Competency Questions

C. Maria Keet$^{(\boxtimes)}$ (iD), Zola Mahlaza (iD), and Mary-Jane Antia (iD)

Department of Computer Science, University of Cape Town, Cape Town, South Africa
{mkeet,zmahlaza,mjantia}@cs.uct.ac.za

Abstract. Competency Questions (CQs) assist in the development and maintenance of ontologies and similar knowledge organisation systems. The absence of tools to support the authoring of CQs has hampered their effective use. The few existing question templates have limited coverage of sentence constructions and are restricted to OWL. We aim to address this by proposing the CLaRO template-based CNL to author CQs. For its design, we exploited a new dataset of 234 CQs that had been processed automatically into 106 patterns, which we analysed and used to design a template-based CNL, with an additional CNL model and XML serialisation. The CNL was evaluated, showing coverage of about 90% with the 93 templates and their 41 variants. CLaRO has the potential to facilitate streamlining formalising ontology content requirements and, given that about one third of the CQs in the test sets turned out to be invalid questions, assist in writing good questions.

1 Introduction

The specification of Competency Questions (CQ) is a step in the process of the development of ontologies and similar artefacts—called "OMS" in [16], for Ontologies, Models and Specifications that also comprises knowledge organisation systems (KOSs). CQs aim to provide insights into the contents of an OMS, to demarcate its scope, and, ideally, are to be used in the verification step during testing of the model [10,20,22]. They function alike requirements in the traditional requirements engineering setting, but then are formulated as questions that such an OMS should be able to answer. For instance, Do lions eat grass? that some wildlife ontology may have to be able to answer, Which software can perform clustering? for a structured controlled vocabulary about software, and What are the related terms of propaganda? for the ERIC thesaurus. However, CQs are rarely published at all or in full except in a few cases, notably, [5,14]. Two main reasons put forward for their low uptake are, firstly, the lack of guidance for formalising them—be this in SPARQL, SPARQL-OWL, OWL or another language—which affects testing of the OMS, and, secondly, the 'free text' nature of CQs makes operationalising them difficult.

A well-known solution direction to such problems is to constrain the natural language so as to streamline the input, which facilitate their formalisation

© Springer Nature Switzerland AG 2019
E. Garoufallou et al. (Eds.): MTSR 2019, CCIS 1057, pp. 3–15, 2019.
https://doi.org/10.1007/978-3-030-36599-8_1

into the desired target logic or query language. A few CQ types, patterns, and "archetypes" have been proposed based on a manual analysis of a small set of CQs [4,17], which go in the direction of a controlled natural language (CNL) that constrains a full language to a subset of its vocabulary and grammar. However, their 19 resp. 14 patterns are merged with types of ontology elements, therewith constraining its usage to OWL and a particular modelling style, and their adequacy, or coverage, is unknown. Currently, no CNL exists for CQs that has been shown to be adequate in coverage and be at the natural language layer.

In this paper, we seek to address these shortcomings by developing a CNL for CQs. We reuse the novel CQ and CQ pattern dataset of [24] and based on the analysis of the patterns and other design decisions, we convert them into a template-based CNL, called CLaRO: Competency question Language for specifying Requirements for an Ontology, model, or specification. CLaRO is evaluated against a random selection of CQs from the CQ dataset [24] for verification, two newly collected set of CQs that were not part of the training set, and related work. CLaRO's coverage was found to range from good to excellent and substantially outperforming the related work. Overall, this resulted in 93 core templates and 41 variants, which cover about 90% of the CQs of the test sets. We have created a proof-of-concept CQ tool to assist authoring CQs with CLaRO. All data, results, CLaRO, the tool, and a screencast thereof are available as supplementary material at https://github.com/mkeet/CLaRO.

The remainder of this paper is structured as follows. Related work is discussed in Sect. 2. The CNL design and evaluation are described in Sects. 3 and 4, respectively. We discuss in Sect. 6 and conclude in Sect. 7.

2   Related Work

CQs have been proposed for use in several fields, such as education and law (e.g., [12,23]). In ontology engineering, CQs are deemed important for demarcation of the scope of an ontology and alignment of source and target ontologies [21,22], and verification and evaluation [1–3,10]. In spite of their acknowledged importance, few CQs are available publicly [24].

CNLs for CQ specifically do not exist, but there are four contributions in that direction. Wisniewski et al. [24] recently compiled 234 CQs from 5 ontologies into a freely available dataset[1], and analysed the questions with NLP to chunk it and replace nouns and verbs with variables for entities and predicates, resulting in 106 CQ patterns. Earlier work [4,6,17] incorporate ontology elements explicitly, using 1:1 mappings between noun or noun phrase in the CQ and OWL class ("[CE]") and verb and OWL object property ("[OPE]") in an "archetype" that is template-like; e.g., "Which [CE1] [OPE] [CE2]?". However, a CQ, in general, does not need to be for OWL nor does a verb need to become an object property in the ontology. Limited in number of templates, they have limited coverage for CQ patterns; e.g., a simple subclass request, like DemCare_CQ_8.What are the types of diagnosis? [5] has no applicable pattern in [17].

---

[1] https://github.com/CQ2SPARQLOWL/Dataset.

A difficulty with CQs is that they may require different formalisations to query the OMS depending on the usage scenario, such as SPARQL-OWL or SPARQL [24,25] and others. In addition, given that a CNL for CQs is supposed to function for specifying requirements for any ontology, the logic-based knowledge representation must be decoupled from the natural language. At the same time, it is well-known that the other extreme—free-form sentences—is hard to formalise, be this for query or axiom generation; e.g., most recently, Salgueiro et al.'s system allows free-text as input, but only four types of questions may generate answers [19]. A middle way to bridge this gap is to design a CNL.

CNLs for computation have been proposed as a solution for various information management aspects [11,18], yet all systems surveyed focus on assertions for ontology authoring, even those for queries (e.g., "give me all writers who ..." rather than "which writers...?"). When there are CNL questions, they are for instances in databases or RDF stores, rather than the TBox-level of typical CQs, hence, take a different form, and/or require the ontology to already exist so as to assist in query formulation [7]. Thus, to the best of our knowledge, there is no CNL for CQs for ontologies that is technology- and KOS-independent.

3 CNL Design

The approach to the design of the CNL for CQs is a semi-automated and data-driven bottom-up. The input data is taken from the novel dataset of CQ patterns [24]; this is summarised first so as to keep the paper self-contained. We analysed those CQ patterns, which informed the CNL design and specification that is described in Sect. 3.2.

3.1 Preliminaries: CQ Patterns

The automated CQ pattern creation process—described in detail in [24]—uses 234 CQs that were collected from five publicly available CQ sets for publicly available ontologies (SWO, Dam@care, OntoDT, AWO, and Stuff), which is the largest data set of type-level CQs for ontologies. These CQs were used to create *domain-independent CQ patterns*, which are the general structures of the CQs that is shared among more than one CQ and thus irrespective of an ontology's vocabulary. The following process was applied for each CQ in the dataset [24]:

1. *Entity Chunk (EC) and Predicate Chunk (PC) identification*, where ECs contain nouns and noun phrases and PCs are verbs and may contain adpositions/particles and they may have an auxiliary part that may be located in a different place of the question than the main part of PC. This was computed automatically with SpaCy (https://spacy.io/) and algorithms developed by [24]. Subsequently, it was manually verified and, if accepted, a sequential number was added to distinguish different ECs and PCs. For instance, the CQ Which country do I have to visit to see elephants? would be chunked into *Which EC1 PC1 I PC1 to PC2 EC2?*, as "do" and "have to visit" belong together, and "see" is a second PC.

2. *Generalisable pattern selection*: The resultant domain-independent form of every CQ was a "candidate pattern". To determine whether it would be added to the list of patterns, it made use of the notions of "dematerialized" and "materialised" CQs:
   - Dematerialised CQ: the CQ has 'replaceable' content already. For instance, SWO's What software can perform task x? is meant to be used such that the user fills in a real task from the ontology for the placeholder "task x", and thus there would be multiple instances of such questions, and therefore it produced a CQ pattern.
   - Materialised CQ: each entity is mentioned in the CQ. If a candidate pattern based on such a CQ was unique, it was rejected as CQ pattern.

This procedure resulted in the list of 106 subject domain-independent patterns.

Analysis of the CQ Patterns. We analyse these 106 patterns on both structural features and their meanings, such as the use of synonyms, and other aspects that may emerge on closer manual analysis of the patterns.

Considering the anatomy of the CQ patterns: text chunks can appear anywhere in the pattern and have between 0 and 4 text chunks; a pattern has at most 4 EC and 2 PC variables, and an overall of at most 5 variables. Because a PC variable can be split up into different chunks (e.g., a "do we need" is chunked as *PC1 we PC1*), the highest number of slots for the variables is 6. Split PCs either have another variable, text, or a single space between the slots, and there are at most 3 chunks for a PC variable.

There are common sources of variation in the patterns. Illustrative examples for each type of variation are as follows.

1. Singular/plural; e.g., pattern *82.What type of EC1 is EC2?* and *83.What types of EC1 are EC2?*.
2. Superfluous words in the sentence. For instance, the "or not" in *27.Is EC1 EC2 or not?* and "possible" in *51.What are the possible types of EC1?*.
3. Impersonal and personal sentences and patterns. A CQ alike swo37.Can we collaborate with developers of [software x]? could also have been written as, say, "Is it possible to collaborate with developers of [software x]?".
4. Synonym usage in the text chunks, of which there are few; e.g., "kind of" and "type of" are used synonymously in CQs (cf. *79.What kind of EC1 is EC2?* and *82.What type of EC1 is EC2?*).
5. The same information request can be formulated in different ways, such that it would need/use a different pattern; e.g., the CQ swo15.What software can I use [my data] with to support [my task]? can be rewritten as, e.g., "Which software can use [my data] to support [my task]?" as well as "Which software can support [my task] with [my data]?" and corresponding different patterns.

Personal pronouns only appear in the SWO CQ set, "kind of" appears only in the AWO and Stuff CQ sets that were authored by the same author, "type of" appears only in the SWO CQ set, and "types of" appears only in the Dem@Care CQ set. This suggests there might be either author preference or some (un)conscious authoring choice to generate more questions in the same way.

Finally, negation—in the sense of both disjointness among classes and for a class' properties—is present in the CQs, but only once each and thus did not result in a pattern in [24]. It appears in Ren et al.'s and Bezerra et al's Pizza example CQs, but not in the original Pizza CQ set. Nonetheless, one may expect also negative CQs to be posed.

3.2 The CLaRO CNL

Design Considerations. There are two extreme design options for a CNL, which is often template-based: (1) minimalist with the fewest amount of templates that are shortest and (2) including variants to allow flexibility and have better flowing text. The latter approach has been proposed elsewhere for a CNL for temporal conceptual modelling [9], which was based on a user evaluation on template preferences. Also, since different formulation habits were detected in the dataset, we will keep all CQ patterns and convert them into templates, but also generate a 'default' CQ template, where applicable. Because there is a limited number of CQ patterns, a template-based approach will be taken for the CNL at this stage, rather than specification of a grammar.

Finally, while there is no negation in any of the patterns of [24], there is in the CQ set and elsewhere; therefore, we deem it reasonable to add a few templates to cover these cases. Even though that hiding the negation makes it less cumbersome for a CNL, it will make it harder for processing it automatically into a query over the resource, whereas it is an easy signal in a template.

Specification. The generation of the 'default' templates applies to those CQ patterns of [24] where there were issues or commonalities regarding, mainly: (1) singular/plural forms, (2) the personal pronouns in a pattern, (3) removing redundant words in text chunks, and (4) synonym usage. To illustrate some of these changes (see github repo for details), consider CQ pattern *1. Are there any EC1 for EC2?*: it is in the plural and has the redundant "any" word, which therefore results in a template of *Is there [EC1] for [EC2]?*, which turned out to be identical to CQ pattern 30, and thus removed so as to obtain a list of unique sentences. Regarding synonyms, 'type of' was selected over 'kind' and 'category' for the defaults. This resulted in the merger of, e.g., CQ pattern 79 and 82 into template *70. What type of [EC1] is [EC2]?*.

Applying these transformations manually and removing any duplicates that were generated during this process resulted in 89 templates with 40 variants, where the variants have an additional letter designation; e.g., *22. Is [EC1] [EC2]?* and variant *22a. Is [EC1] [EC2] or not?*. Fourteen of the 89 templates are fragments of others; e.g., *22. Is [EC1] [EC2]?* is a template fragment of *23. Is [EC1] [EC2] for [EC3]*. This may be of interest to further reduce the number of templates as well as be of interest for a predictive editor in tool design.

To cater for the negations, three basic templates were attached, so as to cover the cases of 'does not PCi', 'PCi no ECi', and class disjointness (numbers 90–92).

Storing Templates and CQs. While CQ templates can be stored in a simple txt file, it serves to store them in a structured way so that multiple tools can use and analyse them in the same manner. To the best of our knowledge, there is no standard for storing a CNL. Therefore, we designed our own data model for storing CQ templates, which is depicted in Fig. 1 in UML Class Diagram notation. To permit extensions to CLaRO, there may be CQs that do not instantiate a template (hence, the 0..* on instantiates). Also, users should be permitted to author CQs without an ontology being present already, as this activity may happen before the OMS development; hence, the 0..* on the for association end.

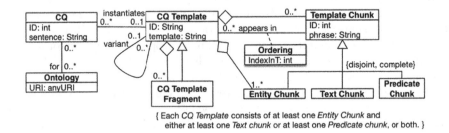

Fig. 1. Data model for storing CQ templates.

4   Evaluation

We conduct an evaluation of CLaRO to answer the following two questions:

RQ1: Does CLaRO cover the CQs from the training set?
RQ2: Is CLaRO sufficiently comprehensive for unseen CQs?

CLaRO should be able to deal with the CQs of the original data set of [24], but may not, because not all CQs resulted in a pattern. Also, the CQ patterns were obtained automatically and a verification was not performed. In addition, for the time being that there is no advanced CQ tool, authors will author a question manually and thus may need to do the chunking of a CQ themselves.

The second question aims to assess whether CLaRO provides a broad enough coverage of possible sentence templates to be adequate beyond the training data.

Finally, we compare CLaRO to the templates of Ren et al. and Bezerra et al.

4.1   Design

Methods. To answer Question 1, we take a random selection of 10% of the CQs in the dataset and test them on authorability with the CNL. This set is called SetA. Each sentence is manually chunked into ECs and PCs by one of the authors and then checked against CLaRO's templates. For each CQ in SetA, record whether it can be authored in the CNL and, if not, why not, then compute percent coverage. Afterward, the manual chunking was compared against the mapping of CQs to CQ patterns that was kindly provided by D. Wisniewski.

To answer Question 2, we collect a new set of CQs that are at least for a different ontology, are authored by people other than those who authored the CQs in the data set, and are ideally also in a different domain. The target is 20 type-level CQs. This set is called SetB. A second test set, SetC, is created from half of the Pizza ontology CQs so that it is about the same size as SetB; they are kept separate, as there is some overlap in CQ authors of the SWO and Pizza CQs. For each CQ in SetB and SetC, record whether it can be authored in the CNL. If it cannot be authored directly, attempt to manually reformulate it into a sentence with equivalent meaning that does fit with one of the templates. Compute percent coverage for both the original set and the set with reformulations (if any). Compare the outcomes of SetA, SetB, and SetC.

The comparison with Ren et al. and Bezerra et al.'s templates is two-fold. First, we compare their respective templates to the CLaRO templates, with the alignment that their CE maps to CLaRO's EC and their OP/OPE/DP to CLaRO's PC. Second, from this comparison follows at least part, if not fully, the coverage of their template sets for the CQs in SetA, SetB, and SetC. If there is no equivalent template, then Ren et al.'s, respectively, Bezerra et al.'s template, is checked against the CQ in question, and tested against the CQs for which CLaRO does not have a fitting template (if applicable). Second, assess the coverage of their template sets for the CQs in SetA, SetB, and SetC.

Materials. To construct SetA, we take every 10th CQ from the list of [24], being: swo01, ...swo81, stuff_03, awo_2, awo_12, DemCare_CQ_9, ..., DemCare_CQ_99, ontodt_02, and ontodt_12, resulting in a set of 24 CQs. For SetB, we assess CQs from a recent [15] and a related paper [25] and filling it up to 20 with the CQ set of the Vicinity project[2]. The scopes of the ontologies that the CQs relate to are at least partially different from those in the dataset and, to the best of our knowledge, there is no overlap in CQ authors. The CQs are different from those in Wisniewski et al. [24]'s CQ set. The Pizza ontology CQs are sourced from R. Stevens' slides[3]. Every other CQ in the list is selected, resulting in 21 sentences. The templates of Bezerra et al. and Ren et al. are taken as published in [4,17].

4.2   Results and Discussion

Verification with Training set CQs. Manual chunking of the CQs in SetA and testing against CLaRO yielded a 70.8% initial success rate. Further analysis on alternative ways of chunking the sentences increased it to 83.3%. The four remaining cases demonstrate challenges with bottom-up approaches to designing a CNL. For instance, we chunked swo11.Which visualisation software is there for [this

---

[2] http://vicinity.iot.linkeddata.es/vicinity/; last accessed: 20 Dec. 2018.

[3] page 4 of http://studentnet.cs.manchester.ac.uk/pgt/2014/COMP60421/slides/ Week2-CQ.pdf; last accessed: 9-1-2019.

data] and what will it cost? as Which [visualisation software]$_{EC1}$ is there for [this data]$_{EC2}$ and what [will]$_{PC1}$ [it]$_{EC1}$ [cost]$_{PC1}$?, because of the referring expression "it" that the automated chunker had not recognised and allocated the consecutive EC3 variable label. Another issue is the (mis)use of 'What..." vs "Which..." in the question formulation that affected first-hit matching but passed after grammar correction.

The automatically chunked CQs had a 91.7% initial success rate, and 100% upon further analysis. The two that failed initially, DemCare_CQ_29 and Dem-Care_CQ_89, were sentences with unique sentence structures in the CQ set, and therefore did not qualify to become a CQ pattern, hence, did not enter CLaRO as such. The manual chunking of DemCare_CQ_89—different from the way the algorithm had done it—did match template 42.

Overall, RQ1 can thus be answered in the affirmative, but noting the challenges to chunk it in the 'right' way.

Coverage of CLaRO. The results for SetB are mixed. 25% of the sentences were not CQs for OMSs, such as hero5.Why universities are organized into departments? Of the remaining 15, five had a direct match with a CLaRO template. Three more matched after rewording the plural into the singular (What are ... into What is ...) and a grammar rephrasing. Given that the 'What are/is' also appeared in SetA, hence, twice now, we add the following template as variant to CLaRO: *60a. What are [EC1] of [EC2]?*.

The remaining seven did not have a match, of which six would match a template of *What is [EC1]?*, such as vic1.What is an organization?. Such simple definition request CQs appeared only once as a materialised CQ in the original dataset (DemCare_CQ_4). When we extend CLaRO with the template *93. What is [EC1]?*, then the coverage for SetB is 93.3% out of the 15 valid CQs (splitting up CQ hero3, it reaches 100% of the valid CQs).

Nine sentences of SetC were invalid as CQ, due to, among others, imperatives and an extra-ontological modelling discussion question. Of the remaining 12, four were successfully matched in the first round and six more after rewording, reaching 83.3% coverage. Rewriting the imperatives into questions, all five passed immediately, totalling to a coverage of 88.2% of the valid CQs in SetC.

Overall, CLaRO's 134 templates can process unseen CQs with a good level of coverage, thereby answering RQ2 in the positive. Given that 34.1% of the questions in SetB and SetC turned out not to be CQs for ontologies and the different levels of coverage for SetB and SetC, this evaluation has to be considered preliminary. The percentage of improper CQs suggests that a CNL for CQs may be a welcome addition, so that CQ authors may be encouraged more to write grammatically better and answerable questions.

Comparison of CLaRO *Against Related Work.* Regarding Ren et al.'s 19 templates, one is not a question (R1b."Find [CE1] with [CE2]."), two match after rewriting the template into grammatically correct English (from "Be there ..." into "Is there..."), and two are ambiguous of which one does not have a match. The one that does not match, R12. "Do [CE1] have [QM] values of [DP]?", is based on a CQ "Do pizzas have different values of size?", which is not in the

Table 1. Aggregate results for coverage of the test sets; best values of the comparison are highlighted in italics. The CLaRO data is for the complete set of 134 templates.

		Set A	Set B	Set C	Combined
	|Total CQs|	24	20	21	65
	|Valid CQs|	24	15	12	51
Match	Ren et al.	6	5	6	17
	Bezerra et al.	3	3	4	10
	CLaRO	*20*	*14*	*11*	*45*
Pct. coverage (valid CQs)	Ren et al.	25	33	50	33
	Bezerra et al.	13	20	33	20
	CLaRO	*83*	*93*	*92*	*88*

Pizza QC set. The Pizza CQ set does have "Do pizzas come in different sizes?", which can be chunked into *PC1 EC1 PC1 EC2?*, which does match template number 29.

Three of Bezerra et al's 14 templates do not have a matching CLaRO template. The first one, B3 "From which + <property> + <class>?" is based on the sample sentence "From which nation is American pizza?", which is not in the Pizza CQ set and with that sample sentence, the template should have had two classes. B10, also has a pizza example, but it is also not in the Pizza CQ set. The B9 mismatch is a variant with negation, "Are + <class> + <class>disjoint?", which can be reworded into the disjointness template 92 repeatedly.

While CLaRO does not fully encompass the other two sets of templates, it substantially outperforms them on coverage for actual CQs; as can be seen from the aggregate data included in Table 1.

5   CQ Authoring Tool

We developed a tool to aid domain experts and CQ authors in writing questions so that they do not have to start from scratch.

The main components of the tool are the user interface, template processing module, and storage module. The user interface is responsible for accepting the user's input, displaying user-friendly template suggestions, and listing all the user-defined CQs. The template processing module is responsible for generating possible template suggestions given some user input and associating the final user input with a CLaRO template. When the user provides input, the system suggests a set of user-friendly forms of CLaRO templates, which are generated within the autocomplete module by replacing all instances of the numbered abbreviations ECi and PCi (for $i \in \mathbb{N}$) with the English full form "noun phrase" and "verb phrase", respectively, from CLaRO's templates. For instance, CLaRO's template 1 is transformed from *Is there [EC1] for [EC2]?* to "Is there [noun phrase] for [noun phrase]?". The auto-complete function filters out non-relevant suggestions among the set of all possible ones for some given user input. A suggestion is considered relevant by the tool either if it starts with or contains the user input, which is configurable in the tool. For instance, when the user types "What type", then templates 70, 70a, and 71 are retrieved and rendered in their user-friendly form. Once the user selects a suggestion, they can edit the verb and noun phrase slots to finalise the CQ. They can also edit the selected template and write a question that does not fit within any CLaRO template. The CQs and their corresponding CLaRO templates, if any, are then saved to disk. The storage module is responsible for loading CLaRO templates from disk and loading/saving the user defined questions to disk. The storage module serialises the set of user defined CQs according to an XML schema that implements the model described in Sect. 3.2.

Since the CQs may be created also for artefacts similar to ontologies (e.g., thesauri) and ontologies not formalised in OWL, we deemed it best to create a stand-alone tool that is not tightly coupled with an existing KOS editor. The source code and a screencast of the tool are available as supplementary material.

6   Discussion

CLaRO is, to the best of our knowledge, the first CNL for competency questions for ontologies, surpassing the previously published archetypes and patterns [4, 13,17] principally on the following aspects: (i) decoupling of the language and cognition from the ontology artefact layer where design decision already have been taken, (ii) more variants in sentences structures to accommodate for several question formulation preferences, and therewith (iii) better coverage for CQs.

Trying to find new CQs was a non-trivial endeavour, and of those we could find that were listed as CQs, it turned out that about a third of the questions were invalid as CQ. It is unclear what the main reason for that is, but it is certainly clear that CLaRO can assist with reducing that percentage for newly created CQs. Wisniewski's et al.'s dataset [24] does not have invalid CQs, which means they either have been curated upfront (not described to be the case in [24]), or all the good CQ sets available went into that dataset.

It was expected that the Pizza CQs (SetC) would yield a higher percentage of coverage than the other newly sourced CQs (SetB), due to the overlap in people involved in Pizza and SWO. This turned out to be the case in the strict sense: the original coverage for SetB before adding template 93 to CLaRO was 53.3% whereas for SetC it was 83.3%. With the required manual interventions—a new template and rephrasing the imperatives—this increased the coverage to 93.3% and 88.2%, respectively, which is similar.

The model for storing the CQ templates (Fig. 1) may appear straightforward. To the best of our knowledge, however, there is no other model as precursor to an XML schema for storage of any CNL, even though there are template-based CNLs that are stored in XML notation. This model, therefore, may contribute toward the development of a *de facto* standard for storing template-based CNLs, not only for CQs, but generally for any CNL. This then may perhaps be wrapped in an extended version of, e.g., the NIF for NLP tool exchange of text annotations [8] when linked to a chunker for analysis free text CQs.

While the templates of CLaRO cover more sentence structures than the earlier proposed patterns and archetypes, the evaluation also has shown that more sentence structures may be possible than currently are covered with CLaRO. Therefore, the CLaRO editor allows also new free-form CQs. A planned extension is to have the editor learn from the input given. Also, it could be integrated in ontology authoring methods, such as TDD [10] and iterative development [13], and other activities, such as CQs for validation [25] and alignment [21].

7 Conclusions

The paper presented the, to the best of our knowledge, first Controlled Natural Language for competency questions: **C**ompetency question **La**nguage for specifying **R**equirements for an **O**ntology, model, or specification (CLaRO). It was designed in a bottom-up way, availing of a new dataset of questions and their patterns. Those patterns were analysed, and converted into a template-based Controlled Natural Language, CLaRO. The language was evaluated with questions from the training set and a small new set of competency questions, which demonstrated good to excellent coverage. Overall, the process resulted in 93 core templates and 41 variants, which cover over 90% of the CQs of the test sets. CLaRO also comes with a basic CQ authoring tool, where the CQs are stored in XML format for possible further processing.

We are currently working on an intelligent editor for CLaRO in order to offer more effective software-support for authoring competency questions, such as automated chunking and self-learning of new templates.

References

1. Azzaoui, K., Jacoby, E., Senger, S., et al.: Scientific competency questions as the basis for semantically enriched open pharmacological space development. Drug Discov. Today **18**(17), 843–852 (2013)
2. Bezerra, C., Freitas, F.: Verifying description logic ontologies based on competency questions and unit testing. In: ONTOBRAS, pp. 159–164 (2017)
3. Bezerra, C., Freitas, F., Santana, F.: Evaluating ontologies with competency questions. In: Proceedings of IEEE/WIC/ACM International Joint Conferences on Web Intelligence (WI) and Intelligent Agent Technologies (IAT) 2013, pp. 284–285. IEEE Computer Society, Washington, DC (2013)
4. Bezerra, C., Santana, F., Freitas, F.: CQChecker: a tool to check ontologies in OWL-DL using competency questions written in controlled natural language. Learn. Nonlinear Models **12**(2), 4 (2014)
5. Dasiopoulou, S., Meditskos, G., Efstathiou, V.: Semantic knowledge structures and representation. Technical report. D5.1, FP7-288199 Dem@Care: Dementia Ambient Care: Multi-Sensing Monitoring for Intelligence Remote Management and Decision Support. http://www.demcare.eu/downloads/D5.1SemanticKnowledgeStructures_andRepresentation.pdf

6. Dennis, M., van Deemter, K., Dell'Aglio, D., Pan, J.Z.: Computing authoring tests from competency questions: experimental validation. In: d'Amato, C., et al. (eds.) ISWC 2017. LNCS, vol. 10587, pp. 243–259. Springer, Cham (2017). https://doi.org/10.1007/978-3-319-68288-4_15

7. Hallett, C., Power, R., Scott, D.: Composing questions through conceptual authoring. Comput. Linguist. **33**(1), 105–133 (2007)

8. Hellmann, S., Lehmann, J., Auer, S., Brümmer, M.: Integrating NLP using linked data. In: Alani, H., et al. (eds.) ISWC 2013. LNCS, vol. 8219, pp. 98–113. Springer, Heidelberg (2013). https://doi.org/10.1007/978-3-642-41338-4_7

9. Keet, C.M.: Natural language template selection for temporal constraints. In: CREOL, JOWO 2017, vol. 2050, p. 12, Bolzano, Italy, 21–23 September 2017. CEUR-WS (2017)

10. Keet, C.M., Ławrynowicz, A.: Test-driven development of ontologies. In: Sack, H., Blomqvist, E., d'Aquin, M., Ghidini, C., Ponzetto, S.P., Lange, C. (eds.) ESWC 2016. LNCS, vol. 9678, pp. 642–657. Springer, Cham (2016). https://doi.org/10.1007/978-3-319-34129-3_39

11. Kuhn, T.: A survey and classification of controlled natural languages. Comput. Linguist. **40**(1), 121–170 (2014)

12. Lyon, T.D., Saywitz, K.J., Kaplan, D.L., Dorado, J.S.: Reducing maltreated children's reluctance to answer hypothetical oath-taking competency questions. Law Hum Behav. **25**(1), 81–92 (2001)

13. Malheiros, Y., Freitas, F.: A method to develop description logic ontologies iteratively based on competency questions: an implementation. In: ONTOBRAS, pp. 142–153 (2013)

14. Malone, J., et al.: The software ontology (SWO): a resource for reproducibility in biomedical data analysis, curation and digital preservation. J. Biomed. Sem. **5**(1), 25 (2014)

15. Moreira, J., Pires, L.F., van Sinderen, M., Daniele, L.: SAREF4health: IoT standard-based ontology-driven healthcare systems. In: Proceedings of FOIS 2018. FAIA, vol. 306, pp. 239–252. IOS Press (2018)

16. Mossakowski, T., Codescu, M., Neuhaus, F., Kutz, O.: The distributed ontology, modeling and specification language – DOL. In: Koslow, A., Buchsbaum, A. (eds.) The Road to Universal Logic. SUL, pp. 489–520. Birkhäuser, Cham (2015). https://doi.org/10.1007/978-3-319-15368-1_21

17. Ren, Y., Parvizi, A., Mellish, C., Pan, J.Z., van Deemter, K., Stevens, R.: Towards competency question-driven ontology authoring. In: Presutti, V., d'Amato, C., Gandon, F., d'Aquin, M., Staab, S., Tordai, A. (eds.) ESWC 2014. LNCS, vol. 8465, pp. 752–767. Springer, Cham (2014). https://doi.org/10.1007/978-3-319-07443-6_50

18. Safwat, H., Davis, B.: CNLs for the semantic web: a state of the art. Lang. Resour. Eval. **51**(1), 191–220 (2017)

19. Salgueiro, A.M., Alves, C.B., Balsa, J.: Querying an ontology using natural language. In: Villavicencio, A., et al. (eds.) PROPOR 2018. LNCS (LNAI), vol. 11122, pp. 164–169. Springer, Cham (2018). https://doi.org/10.1007/978-3-319-99722-3_17

20. Suarez-Figueroa, M.C., de Cea, G.A., Buil, C., et al.: NeOn methodology for building contextualized ontology networks. NeOn Deliverable D5.4.1, NeOn Project (2008)

21. Thiéblin, E., Haemmerlé, O., Trojahn, C.: Complex matching based on competency questions for alignment: a first sketch. In: 13th International Workshop on Ontology Matching (OM 2018), pp. 66–70. CEUR-WS, Monterey (2018)

22. Uschold, M., Gruninger, M.: Ontologies: principles, methods and applications. Knowl. Eng. Rev. **11**(2), 93–136 (1996)
23. Williams, P.: Resourcing for the future? Information technology provision and competency questions for school-based initial teacher education. J. Inf. Technol. Teach. Educ. **5**(3), 271–282 (1996)
24. Wisniewski, D., Potoniec, J., Lawrynowicz, A., Keet, C.M.: Competency questions and SPARQL-OWL queries dataset and analysis. Technical report 1811.09529, November 2018. https://arxiv.org/abs/1811.09529
25. Zemmouchi-Ghomari, L., Ghomari, A.R.: Translating natural language competency questions into SPARQL queries: a case study. In: First International Conference on Building and Exploring Web Based Environments, pp. 81–86. IARIA (2013)

Metadata-Driven Semantic Coordination

Manuel Fiorelli[1] , Armando Stellato[1(✉)] , Tiziano Lorenzetti[1],
Peter Schmitz[2], Enrico Francesconi[2], Najeh Hajlaoui[2],
and Brahim Batouche[2]

[1] Department of Enterprise Engineering, University of Rome Tor Vergata,
via del Politecnico 1, 00133 Rome, Italy
fiorelli@info.uniroma2.it, stellato@uniroma2.it,
tiziano.lorenzetti@gmail.com
[2] Publications Office of the European Union, Luxembourg, Luxembourg
{Peter.SCHMITZ,
Enrico.FRANCESCONI}@publications.europa.eu,
{Najeh.HAJLAOUI,
Brahim.BATOUCHE}@ext.publications.europa.eu

Abstract. Reuse and combination of disparate datasets on the Semantic Web require semantic coordination, i.e. the ability to match heterogeneous semantic models. Systematic evaluations raised the performance of matching systems in terms of compliance and resource consumption. However, it is equally important to be able to identify diverse matching scenarios, covering a range of variations in the datasets such as different modeling languages, heterogeneous lexicalizations, structural differences and to be able to properly handle these scenarios through dedicated techniques and the exploitation of external resources. Furthermore, this should be achieved without requiring manual tinkering of low-level configuration knobs. As of the Semantic Web vision, machines should be able to coordinate and talk to each other to solve problems. To that end, we propose a system that automates most decisions by leveraging explicit metadata regarding the datasets to be matched and potentially useful support datasets. This system uses established metadata vocabularies such as VoID, Dublin Core and the LIME module of OntoLex-Lemon. Consequently, the system can work on real-world cases, leveraging metadata already published alongside self-describing datasets.

Keywords: Ontology matching · Metadata · OntoLex-Lemon

1 Introduction

The Semantic Web [1, 2] and, followingly, Linked Open Data (LOD) best-practices [3] brought knowledge representation, sharing and reuse to the web scale. At such scale, proliferation of different semantic models for overlapping domains is inevitable and even positive, being connected to autonomy and diversity, and to the complementary needs for specialization and experimentation [4]. Moreover, traditional data integration based on the upfront definition of a mediated schema fails on the web, as the web deals with any domain, while a mediated schema about everything is impossible to construct

© Springer Nature Switzerland AG 2019
E. Garoufallou et al. (Eds.): MTSR 2019, CCIS 1057, pp. 16–27, 2019.
https://doi.org/10.1007/978-3-030-36599-8_2

and in any case very brittle [5]. Integration on the web should be afforded in a pay-as-you-go manner [5], only when tighter integration between some data sources appears necessary. This lazy approach to integration marks a departure from consolidated databases towards the novel concept of dataspace [6]. Indeed, Linked Open Data has been evolving the web into a global dataspace [7].

Initially conceived in the context of distributed systems using a game theoretic perspective, semantic coordination is conceptually close to ontology matching [8]: the problem of finding a set of correspondences (i.e. an alignment) between semantically related concepts in two (or more) ontologies. The innumerous approaches to ontology[1] matching can be classified according to different criteria [9]. An important distinction is then between approaches that rely solely on the content of the input ontologies (internal) and those that benefit from other information sources (external). Indeed, matching with background knowledge was identified as one of the future challenges for ontology matching [10], together with – to mention just another example – matcher selection, combination and tuning.

Annual campaigns for the evaluation of ontology matching systems have greatly sustained the improvement of matching techniques, especially for what concerns compliance to the task (measured in terms of precision and recall) and resource consumption (e.g. limiting the amount of time and memory required to solve large matching problems). However, these campaigns are strongly targeted at evaluating the approaches, often allowing data to be cleaned, uniformed and made generally "more easily processable" [11, 12]. It is thus equally important that matching systems are flexible enough to identify diverse matching scenarios, covering a range of variations in the datasets such as different modeling languages, heterogeneous lexicalizations, structural differences and that are able to properly handle these scenarios through dedicated techniques and the exploitation of external resources.

While configurability is a necessary condition for flexibility, we contend that a usable matching system should be smart enough to do most configuration decisions on its own. Furthermore, as the assessment of an alignment scenario should be based upon the combined analysis of resources' characteristics, we believe that these characteristics should be made evident a priori, in the form of exploitable metadata.

In this paper, we propose a platform for semantic coordination that aims to achieve this goal, by relying on metadata about the input ontologies and potentially relevant third-party resources. We extended our previous work on MAPLE [11], such semantic coordination system, improving its architecture and providing a use case inside the VocBench 3 [13] collaborative RDF editor.

The paper is structured as follows. Section 2 discusses related work focusing on setup of matching processes. Section 3 presents our framework, while Sect. 4 provides

---

[1] The expression "ontology matching" is often used in a broader sense than the one the first word of the term would suggest. "Ontology" is in this case a synecdoche for ontologies, thesauri, lexicons and any sort of knowledge resources modeled according to core knowledge modeling languages for the Semantic Web. The expression ontology matching thus defines the task of discovering and assessing alignments between ontologies and other data models of the RDF family; alternative expressions are ontology mapping or ontology alignment. In the RDF jargon, and following the terminology adopted in the VoID metadata vocabulary [29], a set of alignments is also called a Linkset.

a use case within a real collaborative editor of ontologies, thesauri and lexicons. Section 5 discusses our work. Finally, Sect. 6 concludes the paper.

2 Related Work

Nowadays, most matching systems use an ensemble of matching techniques, often relying on different features of the input ontologies, and combined according to varying topologies. As pointed out in the introduction, there is a need for automating the selection, tuning and combination of these approaches. Hereafter, we report some works to showcase the main approaches: weighting, rule-based systems, and machine learning.

RiMOM [14], a multi-strategy ontology matching system, relies on automatically computed metrics about a given matching task to decide the relative weight of lexical and structural approaches, to tune the construction of some representations (in particular, the inclusion of structural features in the virtual documents associated with the ontology concepts) and to decide which edges are considered for similarity propagation. These decisions are based on two metrics about the matching task that are computed jointly against the input ontologies: lexical similarity and structural similarity.

MOMA [15] uses a rule-based approach to select the appropriate matcher for the given match task from a repository of matchers. A set of rules (implemented in SWRL) captures the correspondence between characteristics of the matchers and characteristics of the input ontologies. Both characteristics are modeled through dedicated ontologies: metadata about the input ontologies are computed automatically, whereas metadata about the matchers were obtained through an online survey.

Cruz *et al.* [16] framed the selection of a matcher configuration as a classification problem, evaluating a number of supervised learning algorithms, and eventually concluding that k-NN performs best (given the limited amount of training data). In their formulation, the class to predict is the appropriate configuration (among a few of them), while the features are derived from the profiles of the input ontologies. They extended the OntoQA [17] metrics originally developed for ontology evaluation.

MOMA is surely close to our framework because of its use of explicit metadata about the input ontologies and (differently from us) about the available matchers. Like us, MOMA addresses the diversity of the core models (e.g. OWL ontology vs SKOS thesaurus); however, while we strive to support the adaptation of the same matcher to different models, the primary aim of MOMA is to check the compatibility between matchers and models.

Our work focuses on characterizing a matching task to enable the exploitation of information in the input ontologies and, if available, in external resources. Indeed, our work is propaedeutic to matcher selection, combination and tuning, which were dealt with in detail in the above-mentioned works. Moreover, those works disregard the selection of support resources (e.g. ontologies, thesauri, lexicons) that may provide additional clue for the creation of mappings.

As we already pointed out, RiMOM computes metrics about the matching task, by taking into consideration the pair of ontologies. Our framework, instead, is primarily

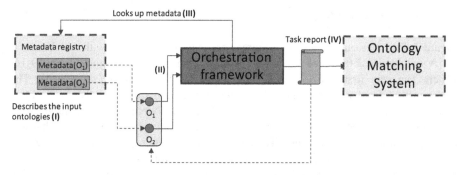

Fig. 1. Overall architecture of the framework. The picture shows dependencies (dashed rectangles) and how components interact (solid arrows).

concerned with metrics computed on the input ontologies, took into isolation. The metadata model used in MOMA has probably the widest coverage of syntactic (i.e. modelling constructs) and semantic features (e.g. subject domain, level of formality, natural language). Conversely, OntoQA provides a very detailed picture of the structure of an ontology, while offering just a metric, called "readability", telling the existence of rdfs:labels and rdfs:comments. This metric is bound to one lexicalization model (RDFS) and disregards the language in which information is expressed.

External resources can be useful because they may provide background knowledge that didn't find its way into the ontologies being matched. Following Faria *et al.* [18], external resources include ontologies or thesauri, lexical databases, textual corpora and websites. There are a lot of works that focus on some (wide coverage) resource, while – in the best cases – describing it a specific instance of a generic oracle. Mascardi *et al.* ran some experiments [19] of indirect matching using SUMO-OWL, OpenCyc and DOLCE, mining some rules for the use of upper ontologies as background knowledge in ontology matching. BLOOMS [20] uses the categories associated with Wikipedia pages to compare the results found with different class names. WikiMatch [21] also uses Wikipedia, but it only compares the search results as sets. Princeton WordNet [22] is a notable lexico-semantic resource used in several systems. Actually, relying on Princeton WordNet alone bounds the system to the English language, ignoring the opportunities offered by similarly modeled resources for other languages [23]. Furthermore, the publication of language resources on the web increasingly uses the linked data paradigm [24], and often relies on OntoLex-Lemon [25]. Following again Faria *et al.* [18], we report on a few attempts at discovering (or at least automating the choice of) suitable background ontologies. Sabou *et al.* [26] do element-level ontology matching by recursive search of class names using semantic search engines. Other works identify relevant ontologies by looking at the input ontologies as a whole, and trying to optimize different metrics, such as similarity between the input ontologies and the background ontology [27], effectiveness of the background ontology [28] (i.e. the mapping overlap between each input ontology and the background ontology), and mapping gain (i.e. fraction of new mappings generated using the background ontology) [18].

3 Our Framework

Figure 1 illustrates our orchestration framework and its interactions with collaborators.

A *matching task* (rounded rectangle) is defined by a pair of ontologies (O_1 and O_2) to match. The very first step is to add their metadata into the *metadata registry*. The *orchestration framework* depends on an implementation of this registry, to obtain metadata about the input ontologies and third-party resources that may support the matching task. In Sect. 4, we discuss a specific implementation of the registry that was developed as a part of a use case. The framework is independent from the implementation of the registry and, moreover, from the strategy for the generation of metadata (e.g. manual insertion, automatic profiling, etc.); nonetheless, it mandates a specific metadata profile, based on popular standards (DCAT [29], VoID [30], OntoLex-Lemon LIME [31], Dublin Core [32]).

Our *orchestration framework* looks up metadata about the input ontologies in the *metadata registry* and by analyzing the discovered metadata becomes aware of the characteristics of the *matching task* (e.g. knowledge/lexicalization models, overlap between supported natural languages, potentially useful external resources, etc.) and produces a *task report* to transfer such awareness to an *ontology matching system*. While the choice of a specific *matching approach* is delegated to the downstream matching system, our framework makes general assumptions, such as the use of lexicalizations to seed the matching process or looking for synonyms or translations within language resources.

Figure 2 contains a sample *task report* for the alignment of TESEO[2] and EuroVoc[3], respectively, the thesaurus of the Italian Senate of the Republic and the thesaurus of the European Union. A preliminary observation is that this report conforms to the JSON-LD standard, and consequently, can be mapped quite easily to RDF. Specifically, most properties in the JSON object correspond to properties with the same name in the metadata vocabularies just mentioned. A notable exception is the property `languageTag` that should be mapped to `lime:language`.

At the beginning of the report, we can find the description of the datasets to be matched as values of the properties `sourceDataset` and `targetDataset`, respectively. The description contains the identifier of the dataset (`@id`) in the *metadata registry*, which provides a consistent name to reference that dataset unambiguously. The metadata (`dcterms:`)`conformsTo` tells the nature of the dataset, e.g. to distinguish between an ontology, a thesaurus (as in this case), etc. Obviously, this is important in order to interpret the input, to establish the goal of the alignment (in the example, establish correspondences between `skos:Concepts`), and to fine tune the matching strategy (in the example, hierarchy-based techniques should consider the property `skos:broader` rather than `rdfs:subClassOf` as it happens with ontologies). The property (`void:`)`sparqlEndpoint` holds the address of a SPARQL endpoint where the actual content of the dataset can be found, which is, clearly, a must-have for an ontology matching system.

---

[2] http://www.senato.it/3235?testo_generico=745.

[3] http://eurovoc.europa.eu/.

```
{
"sourceDataset": { "@type": "Dataset",
    "@id": "http://.../void.ttl#TESEO",
    "conformsTo": "http://www.w3.org/2004/02/skos/core",
    "uriSpace": "http://www.senato.it/teseo/tes/",
    "sparqlEndpoint": http://localhost:7200/repositories/TESEO_core },
"targetDataset": {"@id": "http://.../void.ttl#EuroVoc", ... },
"supportDatasets": [{
    "@id": "http://.../omw/MultiWordNet-it-lexicon",
    "@type": "http://www.w3.org/ns/lemon/lime#Lexicon",
    "sparqlEndpoint": "http://localhost:7200/repositories/OMW_core",
    "languageTag": "43011", "lexicalEntries": 43011
}, {
    "@id": "http://.../omw/pwn30-conceptset",
    "@type": "http://www.w3.org/ns/lemon/ontolex#ConceptSet",
    "sparqlEndpoint": "http://localhost:7200/repositories/OMW_core",
    "concepts": 117659
}, {
    "@id": "http://.../void.ttl#OMW_ConceptualizationSet
    "@type": "http://www.w3.org/ns/lemon/lime#ConceptualizationSet",
    "sparqlEndpoint": "http://localhost:7200/repositories/OMW_core",
    "lexiconDataset": "http://.../omw/MultiWordNet-it-lexicon",
    "conceptualDataset": "http://.../omw/pwn30-conceptset",
    "conceptualizations": 63133, "concepts": 35001, "lexicalEntries": 43011,
    "avgSynonymy": 0.537, "avgAmbiguity": 1.468
}, {
    "@id": "http://.../void.ttl#TESEO_it_lexicalization_set",
    "@type": "http://www.w3.org/ns/lemon/lime#LexicalizationSet"
    "sparqlEndpoint": "http://localhost:7200/repositories/EuroVoc_core",
    "referenceDataset": "http://.../void.ttl#TESEO",
    "lexicalizationModel": "http://www.w3.org/2008/05/skos-xl",
    "lexicalizations": 18545, "references": 7282, "avgNumOfLexicalizations": 2.546,
    "percentage": 1.0,
    "languageTag": "it",
    },{ "@id": "http://.../void.ttl#EuroVoc_it_lexicalization_set", ...} ],
"pairings": [{
    "score": 0.7836831074710862,
    "source": {
        "lexicalizationSet": "http://.../void.ttl#TESEO_it_lexicalization_set",
        "synonymizer": {
            "lexicon": "http://.../omw/MultiWordNet-it-lexicon",
            "conceptualizationSet":        "http://.../void.ttl#MultiWordNet-it-lexicon_pwn30-
conceptset_conceptualization_set"
        }
    },
    "target": {
        "lexicalizationSet": "http://.../void.ttl#EuroVoc_it_lexicalization_set",
        "synonymizer": { ... }
    }
}]
}
```

Fig. 2. Task report for the alignment of TESEO and EuroVoc

The property `supportDatasets` contains other datasets that are referenced elsewhere in the report as they may be useful to solve the matching task. The description of these datasets is, in general, an extension of the one already discussed for the input datasets, including additional properties depending on the type of the dataset (`@type`). The dataset typology as well as the properties providing various metrics are defined by the LIME module of the OntoLex-Lemon vocabulary.

The `pairings` property contains an ordered list, the items of which contain a pair of lexicalization sets, respectively, for the source and target datasets. The underlying assumption made by our framework is that an important, if not primary, source of evidence for ontology matching is represented by the labels, which are grouped into lexicalization sets. Referenced through its identifier, the description of a lexicalization set includes useful information. First, the property `languageTag` identifies the natural language in which the labels are provided. This information is important for two reasons: (i) to apply language-specific processes (e.g. lemmatization requires the lexicon of a given language), (ii) to distinguish between a mono-lingual pairing (as in the example) and a cross-lingual one (currently under development).

In the example, the framework suggests working on labels in Italian, the sole language in common between the two thesauri. Furthermore, the framework instructs the matcher to extract them by applying the pattern for the SKOS-XL lexicalization model. In the case of a monolingual pairing, the framework also suggests a *synonymizer*, which can be understood as a wordnet-like assembly of a *lime:Lexicon* (providing the words) and a *lime:ConceptualizationSet* (linking words to lexical concepts): synonyms are words that share at least one lexical concept. Moreover, we assume that these lexical datasets conform to OntoLex-Lemon, which is gaining momentum for the representation of lexical resources. The score of a paring is computed through an empirical formula combining the metrics of the lexicalization sets and these optional resources.

$$
score = \left(\prod_{x \in \{source,target\}} percentage_{lexicalizationSet_x} \right) \left(1 - \alpha e^{-\beta \max\left(expr_{source},expr_{target}\right)} \right)
$$

where

$$
expr_x = \frac{avgNumOfLexicalizations_{lexicalizationSet_x}}{percentage_{lexicalizationSet_x}} (1 + lrContribution)
$$

and

$$
lrContribution
$$
$$
= \frac{conceptualizations_{conceptualizationSet}}{\max\limits_{x \in \{source,target\}} (lexicalizations_{lexicalizationSet_x})} avgAmbiguity_{conceptualizationSet}
$$
$$
\cdot avgSynonymy_{conceptualizationSet} \frac{lexicalEntries_{conceptualizationSet}}{lexicalEntries_{lexicon}}
$$

Looking at the *score*, the first factor means that the *score* increases as the *percentage* (expressed as a number between 0 and 1) of each input dataset covered by the

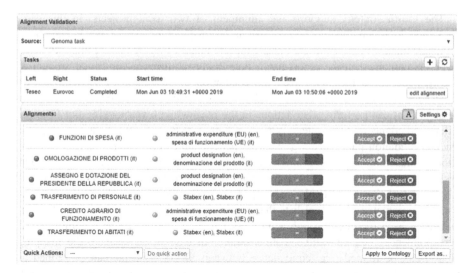

Fig. 3. Alignment validation panel in VocBench 3. It supports the interaction with external ontology matching systems that understand the task report generated by our framework.

paired lexicalization sets increases. The other factor is a number between 0 and 1 that tends to 1 as the expressivity ($expr_x$) of any of the paired lexicalization sets increases. α and β are parameters that were set during development. Here, expressivity is intended as the mean number of labels for entities that have at least one $\left(\dfrac{avgNumOfLexicalizations_{lexicalizationSet_x}}{percentage_{lexicalizationSet_x}}\right)$, possibly boosted with a factor depending on the synonymizer, *lrContribution*. If no *synonymizer* is suggested, then *lrContribution* = 0. It is important to observe that the addition of a synonymizer can only increase the expressivity of each hand of a pairing. The first factor in the definition of *lrContribution* correlates to the chance that a given sense of either lexicalization set matches one in the conceptualization set. The subsequent two factors boost language resources with high ambiguity and synonymy, since they are more representative of the actual linguistic problems (i.e. it is better to be aware that dog is ambiguous rather than to believe that it has just one sense). The last factor weights how much the conceptualization set covers the underlying lexicon.

4   Use Case: VocBench 3

We showed the usefulness of our framework by integrating it into VocBench 3. With respect to Fig. 1, VocBench 3 implements the *metadata registry* and consumes the *task report* or delivers it to a matching system. It can obtain metadata as follows:

1. Manual addition of a (remote) dataset description
2. Discovery of a (remote) dataset description using the VoID backlink mechanism
3. Limited profiling of (remote) dataset SPARQL endpoints
4. Harvesting of (automatically generated) metadata about local projects.

The fourth strategy supports the alignment of two local projects. In this case, VocBench 3 delivers the *task report* to an *ontology matching system*, which can obtain the actual data (input ontologies and support datasets) by means of the SPARQL endpoints contained in the report itself. Potentially requiring a non-trivial amount of time (depending on the input size), the generation of the alignment is treated as an asynchronous task, which does not block the user interface, so that the user requesting the alignment can perform other actions in the meanwhile (even logging out from the system and connecting to it later). When the alignment is ready, it is possible to open it inside a validation panel (see Fig. 3). This panel enables the interaction with external ontology matching systems, orchestrating the matching process using the task report produced by our framework. We collaborated with the team that worked on GENOMA [33], so that their system could understand our *task report*. Once the process is successfully completed, the panel lists the generated correspondences, showing the confidence on each of them through a progress bar (and, optionally, as a number). The correspondences can be validated individually: in case of acceptance, the mapping relation can be refined (e.g. equivalence between SKOS concepts can be refined as skos:exactMatch or skos:closeMatch). Bulk validation is also supported: e.g., it is possible to accept all correspondences scored above a user-supplied threshold. The alignment can be exported in the Alignment API format [34] or can be applied to the source dataset (i.e. adding the triples for the accepted correspondences).

5   Discussion

The use case presented in Sect. 4 validates our framework, showing that it can be instantiated in a real application. Indeed, this application can be regarded as another contribution on its own, since it is freely available and not restricted to an experiment.

The separation between the *metadata registry* and the *orchestration framework* isolates the latter from the generation of metadata, enabling several, interchangeable strategies. Most strategies might rely on facilities provided by the framework or ancillary libraries, for example, to profile datasets automatically. In the proposed use case, however, the harvesting of metadata about the datasets managed by the editing tool integrating the framework surely goes beyond what is offered by the framework itself.

Many works on ontology matching rely on predefined support resources (e.g. language-specific lexicons, domain terminologies, etc.), sometimes replaceable by a power-user. Conversely, our framework suggests the use of a (language) resource, if the *metadata registry* includes one that is compatible with the matching task at hand.

Another important observation is that the *lexicalization sets* in the *pairings* contained in the *task report* (see Sect. 3) are really *support datasets*, just like the language resources mentioned before. This means that the lexicalizations used by the ontology matcher may not come from either input dataset, but rather obtained from a third-party one. Indeed, this is a distinctive feature among ontology matching systems, which particularly fits the vision behind OntoLex-Lemon, which foresaw the possibility for the lexicalization of some dataset to be published independently from the dataset itself.

Adopting a data warehouse approach, our framework assumes that metadata about every potentially useful dataset has been collected beforehand. However, our methodology is compatible with the dynamic discovery of useful datasets. Indeed, our reliance on explicit metadata makes querying easy and efficient. Furthermore, since we use standard metadata vocabularies, we might use almost unmodified metadata published by existing repositories or by publishers alongside their datasets. Our use case has already achieved a similar goal through the discovery of online VoID descriptors.

In the related work, background ontologies were selected by optimizing some metric (similarity, effectiveness, mapping gain) defined in relation to one or both input datasets. Our methodology for selecting language resources is different and based on a two-step process. The first step is to identify language resources that are compatible with the given matching task, comparing their metadata (mostly the natural language) to the ones of the input datasets. However, the subsequent ranking is determined by intrinsic metrics on language resources, preferring essentially the large ones. This selection criterion clearly presupposes that candidate resources are homogenous, so that the chances that relevant information can be found increase with the size of the resource. For example, this assumption holds between general vocabularies for some natural language. Conversely, our approach can't accurately discriminate domain-specific terminologies. An interesting future development is whether we can address this issue with additional metadata (e.g. telling the domain of a resource) or whether we can incorporate some lexical overlap metrics. Indeed, it is probable that the latter remains confined to purposed vocabularies oriented at supporting the orchestration task, as this sort of metadata is unlikely to be published together with their described datasets, involving two datasets, and being very specific for a given matching task.

6 Conclusions

We discussed an orchestration framework addressing the need for robustness and adaptation in ontology matching. The framework analyzes metadata about the input ontologies and external resources, compiling a report that summarizes the matching scenario at hand. This report can thus guide the selection of the appropriate matching strategy, exploiting information contained in the input ontologies and in external resources. We validated our approach applying this framework to the knowledge editing platform VocBench 3, in order to satisfy its requirements on sematic coordination.

Acknowledgements. This work has been drafted under the 2016.16 action of the ISA2 Programme (https://ec.europa.eu/isa2).

References

1. Berners-Lee, T., Hendler, J.A., Lassila, O.: The Semantic Web: A new form of Web content that is meaningful to computers will unleash a revolution of new possibilities. Sci. Am. **284**(5), 34–43 (2001)
2. Shadbolt, N., Berners-Lee, T., Hall, W.: The semantic web revisited. IEEE Intell. Syst. **21**(3), 96–101 (2006)

3. Berners-Lee, T.: Linked data. In: Design Issues. https://www.w3.org/DesignIssues/LinkedData.html. Accessed 2006
4. Wiederhold, G.: Interoperation, mediation and ontologies. In: Proceedings International Symposium on Fifth Generation Computer Systems (FGCS 1994), Workshop on Heterogeneous Cooperative Knowledge Bases, Tokyo, Japan, pp. 33–48 (1994)
5. Madhavan, J., et al.: Web-scale data integration: you can only afford to pay as you go. In: Proceedings of CIDR 2007, pp. 342–350 (2007)
6. Halevy, A., Franklin, M., Maier, D.: Principles of dataspace systems. In: Proceedings of the Twenty-Fifth ACM SIGMOD-SIGACT-SIGART Symposium on Principles of Database Systems, pp. 1–9 (2006)
7. Heath, T., Bizer, C.: Linked data: evolving the web into a global data space. Synth. Lect. Semant. Web: Theory Technol. 1(1), 1–136 (2011)
8. Euzenat, J., Shvaiko, P.: Ontology Matching, 2nd edn. Springer, Heidelberg (2013). https://doi.org/10.1007/978-3-642-38721-0
9. Euzenat, J., Shvaiko, P.: Classifications of ontology matching techniques. In: Ontology Matching, pp. 61–72. Springer, Heidelberg (2007). https://doi.org/10.1007/978-3-540-49612-0_4
10. Shvaiko, P., Euzenat, J.: Ontology matching: state of the art and future challenges. IEEE Trans. Knowl. Data Eng. 25(1), 158–176 (2013)
11. Fiorelli, M., Pazienza, M.T., Stellato, A.: A meta-data driven platform for semi-automatic configuration of ontology mediators. In: Calzolari, N., et al. (eds.) Proceedings of the Ninth International Conference on Language Resources and Evaluation (LREC 2014), Reykjavik, Iceland, May 2014
12. Stellato, A.: A language-aware web will give us a bigger and better semantic web. In: Proceedings of the 4th Workshop on the Multilingual Semantic Web, co-located with the 12th Extended Semantic Web Conference – ESWC 2015, Portoroz, Slovenia (2015)
13. Stellato, A., et al.: Towards VocBench 3: pushing collaborative development of thesauri and ontologies further beyond. In: Mayr, P., Tudhope, D., Golub, K., Wartena, C., De Luca, E. W. (eds.) 17th European Networked Knowledge Organization Systems (NKOS) Workshop. Thessaloniki, Greece, 21 September 2017, pp. 39–52 (2017)
14. Li, J., Tang, J., Li, Y., Luo, Q.: RiMOM: a dynamic multistrategy ontology alignment framework. IEEE Trans. Knowl. Data Eng. 21(8), 1218–1232 (2009)
15. Mochol, M., Jentzsch, A.: Towards a rule-based matcher selection. In: Gangemi, A., Euzenat, J. (eds.) EKAW 2008. LNCS, vol. 5268, pp. 109–119. Springer, Heidelberg (2008). https://doi.org/10.1007/978-3-540-87696-0_12
16. Cruz, I.F., Fabiani, A., Caimi, F., Stroe, C., Palmonari, M.: Automatic configuration selection using ontology matching task profiling. In: Simperl, E., Cimiano, P., Polleres, A., Corcho, O., Presutti, V. (eds.) ESWC 2012. LNCS, vol. 7295, pp. 179–194. Springer, Heidelberg (2012). https://doi.org/10.1007/978-3-642-30284-8_19
17. Tartir, S., Arpinar, I.B.: Ontology evaluation and ranking using OntoQA. In: International Conference on Semantic Computing (ICSC 2007), pp. 185–192. IEEE (2007)
18. Faria, D., Pesquita, C., Santos, E., Cruz, I.F., Couto, F.M.: Automatic background knowledge selection for matching biomedical ontologies. PLoS ONE 9(11), 1–9 (2014)
19. Mascardi, V., Locoro, A., Rosso, P.: Automatic ontology matching via upper ontologies: a systematic evaluation. IEEE Trans. Knowl. Data Eng. 22(5), 609–623 (2010)
20. Jain, P., Hitzler, P., Sheth, A.P., Verma, K., Yeh, P.Z.: Ontology alignment for linked open data. In: Patel-Schneider, P.F., et al. (eds.) ISWC 2010. LNCS, vol. 6496, pp. 402–417. Springer, Heidelberg (2010). https://doi.org/10.1007/978-3-642-17746-0_26

21. Hertling, S., Paulheim, H.: WikiMatch: using wikipedia for ontology matching. In: Proceedings of the 7th International Conference on Ontology Matching, vol. 946, pp. 37–48 (2012)
22. Fellbaum, C.: WordNet: An Electronic Lexical Database. WordNet Pointers. MIT Press, Cambridge (1998)
23. Bond, F., Paik, K.: A survey of WordNets and their licenses. In: Proceedings of the 6th Global WordNet Conference (GWC 2012), Matsue, Japan, 9–13 January 2012, pp. 64–71 (2012)
24. Chiarcos, C., Nordhoff, S., Hellmann, S. (eds.): Linked Data in Linguistics. Springer, Heidelberg (2012). https://doi.org/10.1007/978-3-642-28249-2
25. McCrae, J.P., Bosque-Gil, J., Gracia, J., Buitelaar, P., Cimiano, P.: The OntoLex-Lemon model: development and applications. In: Kosem, I., Tiberius, C., Jakubíček, M., Kallas, J., Krek, S., Baisa, V. (eds.) Electronic Lexicography in the 21st Century. Proceedings of eLex 2017 Conference, pp. 587–597 (2017)
26. Sabou, M., d'Aquin, M., Motta, E.: Exploring the semantic web as background knowledge for ontology matching. In: Spaccapietra, S., et al. (eds.) Journal on Data Semantics XI. LNCS, vol. 5383, pp. 156–190. Springer, Heidelberg (2008). https://doi.org/10.1007/978-3-540-92148-6_6
27. Quix, C., Roy, P., Kensche, D.: Automatic selection of background knowledge for ontology matching. In: Proceedings of the International Workshop on Semantic Web Information Management, pp. 5:1–5:7. ACM, New York (2011)
28. Hartung, M., Groß, A., Kirsten, T., Rahm, E.: Effective mapping composition for biomedical ontologies. In: Workshop on Semantic Interoperability in Medical Informatics (SIMI)
29. World Wide Web Consortium (W3C): Data Catalog Vocabulary (DCAT). In: World Wide Web Consortium (W3C). http://www.w3.org/TR/vocab-dcat/. Accessed 16 Jan 2014
30. Alexander, K., Cyganiak, R., Hausenblas, M., Zhao, J.: Describing Linked Datasets with the VoID Vocabulary (W3C Interest Group Note). In: World Wide Web Consortium (W3C). http://www.w3.org/TR/void/. Accessed 3 Mar 2011
31. Fiorelli, M., Stellato, A., McCrae, J.P., Cimiano, P., Pazienza, M.T.: LIME: the metadata module for OntoLex. In: Gandon, F., Sabou, M., Sack, H., d'Amato, C., Cudré-Mauroux, P., Zimmermann, A. (eds.) ESWC 2015. LNCS, vol. 9088, pp. 321–336. Springer, Cham (2015). https://doi.org/10.1007/978-3-319-18818-8_20
32. DCMI Usage Board: DCMI Metadata Terms. In: Dublin Core Metadata Initiative (DCMI). http://dublincore.org/documents/dcmi-terms/. Accessed 14 June 2012
33. Enea, R., Pazienza, M.T., Turbati, A.: GENOMA: GENeric ontology matching architecture. In: Gavanelli, M., Lamma, E., Riguzzi, F. (eds.) AI*IA 2015. LNCS, vol. 9336, pp. 303–315. Springer, Cham (2015). https://doi.org/10.1007/978-3-319-24309-2_23
34. David, J., Euzenat, J., Scharffe, F., Trojahn dos Santos, C.: The alignment API 4.0. Semant. Web J. 2(1), 3–10 (2011)

Training Biomedical Researchers in Metadata with a MIBBI-Based Ontology

Marcelo Sampaio⬛, Ana Luís Ferreira⬛, João Aguiar Castro^(✉)⬛,
and Cristina Ribeiro⬛

INESC TEC, Faculdade de Engenharia, Universidade do Porto,
Rua Dr. Roberto Frias, 4200-465 Porto, Portugal
joaoaguiarcastro@gmail.com

Abstract. Recent initiatives in data management recognize that involving the researchers is one of the more problematic issues and that taking into account the practices of each domain can ease this process. We describe here an experiment in the adoption of data description by researchers in the biomedical domain. We started with a generic lightweight ontology based on the Minimum Information for Biological and Biomedical Investigations (MIBBI) standard and presented it to researchers from the Institute of Innovation and Investigation in Health (I3S) in Porto. This resulted in seven interviews and four data description sessions using a RDM platform. The feedback from researchers shows that this intentionally restricted ontology favours an easy entry point into RDM but does not prevent them from identifying the limitations of the model and pinpointing their specific domain requirements. To complete the experiment, we collected the extra descriptors suggested by the researchers and compared them to the full MIBBI. Part of these new descriptors can be obtained from the standard, reinforcing the importance of common metadata models for broad domains such as biomedical research.

Keywords: Research data management · Metadata · MIBBI · Biomedical research · FAIR

1 Introduction

Driven by new methods and advanced computing capacity, the importance and complexity of data in the research activity is growing [8]. The European Commission put forward the Guidelines on FAIR Data Management in Horizon 2020 to promote a set of principles to make data Findable, Accessible, Interoperable and Reusable [18]. The application of the FAIR principles depends critically on rich metadata, yet domain vocabularies are mostly underused. Therefore, the Action Plan to put the FAIR principles into practice [6] recommends the development

© Springer Nature Switzerland AG 2019
E. Garoufallou et al. (Eds.): MTSR 2019, CCIS 1057, pp. 28–39, 2019.
https://doi.org/10.1007/978-3-030-36599-8_3

of use cases to further engage communities and the provision of tools to make data description as easy as possible and promote its adoption by researchers.

In this exploratory study, we aim to facilitate the adoption of metadata tools by researchers from the biomedical domain. Our case study took place in I3S, a large institute for health sciences and technologies in Porto, bringing together researchers from different backgrounds in the biomedical sciences. We were motivated by the fact that research data management (RDM) is not yet a concern for most researchers and by the diversity of disciplinary requirements in I3S.

Our approach was designed with a focus on training researchers by means of tools for the production of metadata, and involved the adoption of a simple, yet comprehensive, ontology for the biomedical domain. This led to the consideration of existing domain metadata standards, namely the Minimum Information for Biological and Biomedical Investigations (MIBBI) [15] that can take into account the metadata requirements of groups at I3S. A subset of the standard was selected to account for the recognized difficulty of researchers in adopting complex standards [11]. This is intended as a motivation for researchers to engage in RDM, while the experiment provides them room to identify further metadata requirements.

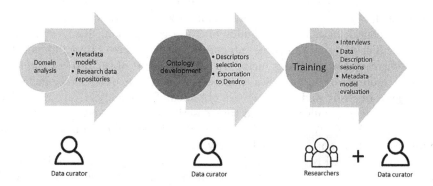

Fig. 1. General approach to train researchers in metadata

Figure 1 shows that we start with an analysis of metadata standards and their adoption in data repositories in the biomedical domain. Section 2 elaborates on the selection of a suitable set of descriptors for our case study. In Sect. 3 we briefly describe the creation of a lightweight ontology based on the MIBBI and its implementation in Dendro, a data description tool being developed at the University of Porto [14]. Our approach to train researchers included interviews to assess RDM perspectives and feedback regarding metadata elements, as presented in Sect. 4, and data description sessions described in Sect. 5.

2   Metadata Models for Biomedical Data

The research endeavour in biomedical sciences involves a multidisciplinary app-roach to the understanding of human health and diseases. This domain includes the study of human anatomy and physiology, cell biology, biochemistry, genetics and genomics, pharmacology and molecular biology [5]. With the current diver-sity of experimental and analytical techniques, the management of experimental data is not straightforward and to understand its context one must have access to a range of background information [15]. Hence, in recent years, recommenda-tions regarding metadata for different kinds of experiments in this domain have appeared and several community-developed standards and recommendations are available [13].

The Research Data Alliance Metadata Directory Working Group provides a community-maintained page of disciplinary metadata[1], which is featured as a recommended resource by the Digital Curation Centre[2]. Searching for an appro-priate standard to train I3S researchers in metadata production, we started with the directory list corresponding to standards in the life sciences, where the Genome Metadata, ISA-Tab and the MIBBI stood out as the more suitable ones. The Genome Metadata consists of 61 metadata fields with a focus in Genetics and Genomics[3], while ISA-Tab is a general metadata tracking framework that facilitates standards-compliant collection, curation, visualisation, storage and sharing of datasets [7]. The ISA-Tab framework focuses on the description of the experimental metadata and builds on the Investigation, Study and Assay categories. The metadata in these categories is kept in three tab-delimited files. An Investigation file maintains metadata on the context of the project and links to one or more study files. A Study file describes a unit of research, including the subjects of study and how they are obtained. Those subjects are then used in one or more Assay files, which in turn describe analytical measurements.

Checking the alternatives, MIBBI was considered more promising for the requirements of I3S and an accessible entry point for researchers to get into meta-data creation. MIBBI consists of a set of guidelines for reporting data derived by current methods in the biology and biomedical domains [15]. Following MIBBI ensures that the data can be easily verified, analysed and clearly interpreted by the wider scientific community and promotes transparency in experimental reporting.

There are 39 checklists in the MIBBI Portal[4], divided according to the exper-iment and its related biological science—e.g. the Minimum Information About a Microarray Experiment (MIAME) checklist is related to the use of (micro)arrays and analysis of the data they generate [3] and The Minimum Information About a Proteomics Experiment (MIAPE) checklist comprises modules for reporting the use and interpretation of data from various analytical techniques, such as

---

[1] http://rd-alliance.github.io/metadata-directory/standards/.

[2] http://www.dcc.ac.uk/resources/standards/.

[3] https://docs.patricbrc.org/user_guides/organisms_taxon/genome_metadata.html.

[4] https://fairsharing.org/collection/MIBBI.

mass spectrometry, gel electrophoresis or liquid chromatography [16]. Therefore, this metadata standard covers a wide range of disciplines, such as Genetics, Proteomics, Cell Biology and Bioengineering.

Table 1. Research data repositories in the biological sciences

Repository name	Metadata standards
European Nucleotide Archive (ENA)	Minimum Information about any (x) Sequence (MiXs)
Array Express	Minimum Information about an ENVironmental transcriptomic experiment (MIAME/Env), Minimal Information about a high throughput SEQuencing Experiment (MINSEQE) and Minimum Information About a Microarray Experiment (MIAME)
PRoteomics IDEntifications database (PRIDE)	Minimum Information about a Proteomics Experiment (MIAPE)
PubChem	Minimum Information about a RNAi Experiment (MIARE)
FlowRepository	Minimum Information about Flow Cytometry (MIFlowCyt)
European Genome-Phenome Archive (EGA)	Minimum Information about any (x) Sequence (MiXs)
Metabolights (MTBLS)	Core Information for Metabolomics Reporting (CIMR) and ISA-TAB
Sequence Read Archive (SRA)	Minimum Information about a MARKer gene Sequence (MIxS- MIMARKS) and Minimal Information about a high throughput SEQuencing Experiment (MINSEQE)

Table 1, based on the FAIRSharing community standards, shows that MIBBI checklists have been widely adopted by data repositories specialized in the biological sciences [13]. The number of FAIRSharing repositories is more extensive so we chose to make a broad coverage of disciplines corresponding to the research groups in I3S.

3   Ontology Development

Given the usefulness of ontologies in resource description, a number of scientific communities have been working to establish domain-oriented ontologies [10]. For example, ontologies are widely used in biological and biomedical research where their success lies in the combination of four features: standard identifiers for classes and relations that represent the phenomena within a domain, vocabulary for the domain, metadata describing the intended meaning of classes and the machine-readable axioms and definitions [9]. An example of a widely used ontology is the Ontology for Biomedical Investigations (OBI) that provides terms with precisely defined meaning to describe all aspects of research in the biological and biomedical domains [2]. The OBO[5] and BioPortal repositories[6] provide an overview of ontologies in the biomedical sciences domain.

In previous work at the University of Porto we have connected with domain experts to define lightweight ontologies and provide a set of meaningful descriptors to engage them in data description [4]. We mostly reused concepts from ontologies or metadata standards and often researchers were involved in the process of choosing appropriate descriptors. In this case, considering the research diversity at I3S and the availability of domain standards, we decided to start with a domain analysis by a data curator, selecting the descriptors that will most likely be common to the disciplinary requirements. The criterion was to have a set of descriptors aligned with the principles of simplicity and sufficiency identified as metadata goals for scientific data [19]. Moreover, we wanted to ensure that the proposed set of descriptors would allow any researcher, regardless of the type of experiment or data produced, to engage in data description.

Table 2. Selected descriptors from the MIBBI checklists

Category	Descriptors
Sample	Organism, Disease, Organism Part, Age, Sex, Ethnicity, Developmental Stage, Tissue, Cell Line, Cell Type, Sample Size, Molecule, Sample Type
Methods	Assay Type, Collection Date, Measurement, Method, Sample Collection Protocol, Treatment Protocol, Temperature, Study Design
Materials	Material, Drug Usage, Reagent
Technology	Instrument Name, Instrument Type, Software
Others	Experimental Factor, Environmental Factor, Study Domain

The analysis of biomedical metadata standards and their adoption by data repositories has led us to select a set of 30 descriptors and to include them as data properties in a lightweight ontology, MIBBIUP, using Protégé[7]. The selection of the descriptors was based on the frequency of each one (related to samples, experiments or equipment) in the MIBBI checklists and their use to catalog datasets in the biomedical data repositories [12]. Table 2 provides the list of descriptors captured in the ontology and their MIBBI categories.

The ontology is operationalized in Dendro, a collaborative RDM tool that promotes data description early in the research workflow. Figure 2 depicts the data description interface in Dendro and part of the MIBBIUP ontology.

---

[5] http://www.obofoundry.org/.

[6] http://bioportal.bioontology.org/.

[7] http://protege.stanford.edu/.

Although MIBBI checklists also propose the use of metadata for the title, date and people affiliated with the research, we did not include these to avoid duplication of concepts in Dendro. Descriptors for this purpose are already present in more generic ontologies, namely the Dublin Core element set[8], also included in Dendro.

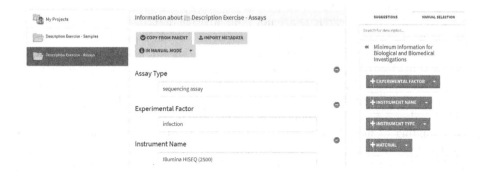

Fig. 2. MIBBIUP ontology implemented in Dendro

Dendro complies with FAIR guidelines by assigning persistent identifiers and enabling the combination of descriptors from multiple ontologies. For each dataset, researchers select the descriptors they consider appropriate. Yet, when researchers start a new project they are required to fill some generic descriptors, for the sake of interoperability with the documentation required by mainstream repositories [1]. The project creation form can also include conditions of access and use for the data.

4   The Perspectives of Researchers on RDM

By assessing researchers' perspectives on data sharing and reuse, it has been observed that although researchers see the benefits of and support data sharing, they do not engage much in this practice [17]. The same is true for the participants of this study. Between March and May 2019, we have interviewed seven researchers, from four research groups: three researchers from Genetic Diversity, two from Epithelial Interactions in Cancer, one from Glial Cell Biology and one from Differentiation & Cancer.

Sharing is mostly done with members of the group or external collaborators. Although the participants visit data repositories regularly and are interested in accessing data from other projects, they are still reluctant in doing it themselves. All the interviewees are familiar with data repositories and have positive experiences, occasionally resulting in data reuse. Although most researchers seem content with their present organization and storage of data, most believe their

---

[8] http://www.dublincore.org/specifications/dublin-core/dces/.

current methods can be improved. Moreover, they are aware that the risk of data loss increases as the number of files grows. The lack of established methods to manage data, even simple ones as systematic file naming, is regarded as an extra effort. From the collected feedback, it seems that there is room to improve the organization practices. Saving their time can be an encouraging factor to further the engagement of researchers in RDM.

When it comes to data description, the concept of metadata is not common knowledge and researchers are not familiar with descriptors, except for two who are in charge of data deposit in repositories. This lack of knowledge about metadata was also verified in a study on user behavior and patterns of metadata usage within electronic laboratory notebooks [20]. Furthermore, data description is perceived as a burden and is not a priority for some. The concept of metadata was equated with database by one of them and with meta-analysis by another. However, after a short background explanation, the participants showed a better understanding of metadata benefits and were more open to considering them, even mentioning themselves some advantages of their use, such as facilitating the search for data. The researcher from the Differentiation and Cancer group is used to describing the sample and techniques adopted to produce their data and showed preference for a small number of descriptors. During the meeting, the researcher from the Glial Cell Biology group opened a disciplinary data repository to facilitate the discussion about metadata.

We also introduced researchers to the concepts captured in the MIBBIUP ontology and most descriptors were unanimously accepted, except for Drug Usage and Development Stage, which got the agreement of only one of the researchers. Other descriptors were considered redundant: one researcher mentioned the Environmental Factor as a synonym for Experimental Factor, while many assumed that Tissue has the same use as Organism Part. Moreover, none of them would use a descriptor for the Temperature and Reagent, considering them part of the Method and Material descriptors.

5   Data Description Sessions

Data description sessions were carried out between April and May 2019, using the Dendro platform with 4 participants, two from the Genetic Diversity group and two from the Epithelial Interactions in Cancer group.

After a brief demonstration of Dendro, we advised participants to use domain-specific descriptors from MIBBIUP, but they were also told that they could pick any other of the available descriptors. Moreover, we suggested the use of Dublin Core descriptors to enrich the metadata, although these were not considered useful by the researchers. Figure 3 shows an example of some descriptors selected and filled by one of the researchers.

Participants from the Genetic Diversity group are PhD students involved in the study of human population and diseases. Researcher 1 is involved in a project focused on gastric cancer, while researcher 2 is analysing the exoma, microbiome and metabolome of african samples. Both researchers had no difficulty in exploring the Dendro interface or selecting the appropriate descriptors

Fig. 3. Data description session in Dendro

for their data. Both have selected metadata elements to contextualize biological samples used in their experiments. They also provided detailed information regarding the descriptors selected for the experiments, namely study design, materials and all the equipment used to generate the data. Overall, researcher 1 selected 21 descriptors, whereas researcher 2 selected 18 descriptors.

The Epithelial Interactions in Cancer group researchers are PhD students involved in different projects—researcher 3 studies the functional and molecular characterization of gastric cancer cells with stem-like cells, while researcher 4 is focused on the cellular and molecular mechanisms by which the Helicobacter pylori bacteria promotes the development of gastric cancer. Researcher 3 was particularly comfortable exploring the Dendro interface and selected a total of 16 descriptors from MIBBIUP. Researcher 4 found description more difficult and asked for help from the data curator. Nevertheless, this researcher filled in a total of 20 descriptors.

All 4 researchers stated that depending on the type of experiment and data they are likely to need a different set of descriptors, some of them not yet available on MIBBIUP. Moreover, researchers 2 and 4 would be interested in having the flexibility to create a descriptor on the fly. However, they understood the importance of adopting normalized descriptors and agreed that the generic experimental metadata elements selected would be enough to help other researchers contextualize their data.

5.1 Overview of Results

Results from the data description sessions showed that researchers understood the descriptors presented to them, although they suggested some new ones. The number of descriptors used ranged between 16 and 21 with an average of 18. The average duration of the experiments was 24 min. Table 3 shows the 9 descriptors that were used in all the data description experiments. They are mainly generic ones about the technology used to generate data (Instrument Names and Software), methods and materials used in the assays as well as information about the samples of the studies and the diseases they were targeting.

Table 3. Overview of the metadata created during the sessions

Descriptor	Researcher 1	Researcher 2	Researcher 3	Researcher 4
Disease	Gastric carcinoma	Hypertension	Gastric cancer	Cancer
Instrument name	Illumina HISEQ (2500)	Illumina	Ion Torrent Sequencer (Thermofischer, City, Country)	Flow Cytometer
Material	Trueseq	Whatmann paper	RPMI and Bovine Serum	Collection tubes
Method	Protocol Reference	Protocol Reference	Stop infection Remove medium Wash 2x with RPMI medium Add new medium - 200 uL R10 Add RTK inhibitors - 2uL per each 96 well (dil 1:1000)	Staining for immunofluo-rescence
Organism	Homo sapiens	Homo sapiens	Homo Sapiens	Human
Organism Part	Stomach	Blood	Stomach	Gut
Software	GraphPad	Sequencher	GraphPad v8 (statistical analysis)—IDEAS software v3 (imaging analysis)	FlowJo
Study Domain	Disease susceptibility	Genetic Diversity	Oncology	Stem cells and cancer
Recommended descriptors	Replicate Count, Replicate Type, Country of Origin and Study Type	Sample Identifier, Instrument Manufacturer, Study Type and Protocol	Clinical Trial Description, Clinical Trial Phase, Clinical Trial Type, Collection Site	X

Given their studies about human population, Genetic Diversity researchers added more descriptors to the sample information such as the `Age`, `Ethnicity`, `Sex` and `Developmental Stage` of the subject. Other descriptors such as `Assay Type`, `Cell Line`, `Cell Type` and `Experimental Factor` were used by 3 researchers.

There were differences in the values for the descriptors used in common by the researchers. For instance, when referring to the `Instrument Name` used to produce data, researcher 1 and 2 named the same instrument, but researcher 1 also added its version. Also, researcher 3 pointed out it was important to record the instrument manufacturer, while researcher 4 misunderstood the `Instrument Name` and wrote its type. A similar situation was observed in the organism definition in which 3 researchers followed the NCBI taxonomy and wrote it in Latin, while one used English. Finally, the descriptor `Material` was interpreted by 3 researchers as auxiliary tools, while the other got it as mediums and chemical reagents used during an experiment.

After the data description sessions, we also asked the researchers for more descriptors they might consider useful to describe and contextualize their data. Except for researcher 4, all suggested some new descriptors. Overall, the recommended descriptors are already implemented in the metadata checklists of the MIBBI. Researcher 1 from Genetics group suggested two descriptors from the MIAME checklist [3] which provide additional information for the interpretation of a microarray experiment. Researcher 2 suggested a descriptor named `Protocol`, which value can either be a name or a reference to an external object, according to the MIBBI. To the best of our knowledge, the recommended descriptors by researcher 3 are not available in the MIBBI checklists. They seem to be motivated by the repository that the researcher uses to deposit their clinical trial studies.

During the data description sessions, it was observed that researchers may have preferences regarding the interface to enter the metadata. The unstructured metadata representation in Dendro was valued by researchers for making data organization easier during a project, yet with limitations if the goal is to deposit data in some disciplinary repository. Hence, researchers seem to prefer to record metadata in a tabular form. In this case, the ISA-TAB standard can be interesting to solve interoperability issues.

6   Conclusion and Future Work

The motivation for this work was the need to train biomedical researchers in RDM, particularly by increasing their metadata skills. To this end we adapted MIBBI as a top-down reference on our ontology-design approach, but we also consider a bottom-up component with the involvement of researchers that has the potential to make the MIBBIUP grow according to their specific needs. An iteration involving ontology design, test with researchers and check for additional descriptors was completed. The continuation with more case studies with researchers from this domain will provide new feedback to improve the ontology. The data description sessions were productive, resulting in detailed domain-specific metadata records in a short time period. With this work we laid the foundations for future work with more researchers, and addressing new issues such as the use of taxonomies and metadata quality.

As long as researchers are provided with adequate tools and have clear, practical examples of metadata goals, data description can become an intuitive task for them. Besides the disciplinary ontology proposed here, other vocabularies can be explored to improve metadata FAIRness, for instance the Dublin Core generic metadata on top of the domain-specific descriptors. Currently, researchers at I3S mostly capture metadata in an informal fashion, so the priority is to encourage them to adopt tools to make metadata creation more systematic. After that, the focus can shift to the next level, namely with actions to improve the overall quality of metadata.

Acknowledgements. This work is financed by the ERDF – European Regional Development Fund through the Operational Programme for Competitiveness and

Internationalisation - COMPETE 2020 Programme and by National Funds through the Portuguese funding agency, FCT - Fundação para a Ciência e a Tecnologia within project TAIL, POCI-01-0145-FEDER-016736. João Aguiar Castro is supported by research grant PD/BD/114143/2015, provided by the FCT - Fundação para a Ciência e a Tecnologia.

References

1. Assante, M., et al.: Are scientific data repositories coping with research data publishing? Data Sci. J. **15**(6), 1–24 (2016). https://doi.org/10.5334/dsj-2016-006. ISSN 1683-1470
2. Bandrowski, A., et al.: The ontology for biomedical investigations. PLoS ONE **11**(4), 1–19 (2016)
3. Brazma, A., et al.: Minimum information about a microarray experiment (MIAME)-toward standards for microarray data. Nat. Genet. **29**(4), 365 (2001)
4. Castro, J.A., et al.: Involving data creators in an ontology-based design process for metadata models. In: Developing Metadata Application Profiles, pp. 181–213 (2017).https://doi.org/10.1007/s00799-018-0238-x
5. Cech, T.R.: Fostering innovation and discovery in biomedical research. JAMA **294**(11), 1390–1393 (2005)
6. Directorate-General for Research and Innovation (European Commission). Turning FAIR into reality. Technical report, pp. 1–78 (2018). https://doi.org/10.2777/1524
7. González-Beltrán, A., et al.: linkedISA: semantic representation of ISA-Tab experimental metadata. BMC Bioinform. **15**(14), S4 (2014)
8. Hey, A.J.G., Tansley, S., Tolle, K.M., et al.: The Fourth Paradigm: Data-Intensive Scientific Discovery. Microsoft Research (2009). ISBN 978-0-9825442-0-4
9. Hoehndorf, R., Schofield, P.N., Gkoutos, G.V.: The role of ontologies in biological and biomedical research: a functional perspective. Brief. Bioinform. **16**(6), 1069–1080 (2015). https://doi.org/10.1093/bib/bbv011
10. Mayer, G., et al.: Controlled vocabularies and ontologies in proteomics: overview, principles and practice. Biochim. Biophys. Acta (BBA) - Proteins Proteomics **1844**(1), 98–107 (2014). https://doi.org/10.1016/j.bbapap.2013.02.017
11. Qin, J., Ball, A., Greenberg, J.: Functional and architectural requirements for metadata: supporting discovery and management of scientific data. In: Proceedings of the International Conference on Dublin Core and Metadata Applications, pp. 62–71 (2012). ISSN 1939-1366. https://doi.org/10.1007/s00799-013-0106-7
12. Read, K.: Common Metadata Elements for Cataloging Biomedical Datasets. https://doi.org/10.6084/m9.figshare.1496573.v1
13. Sansone, S.-A., et al.: FAIRsharing as a community approach to standards, repositories and policies. Nat. Biotechnol. **37**(4), 358 (2019)
14. da Silva, J.R., Ribeiro, C., Lopes, J.C.: Ranking Dublin Core descriptor lists from user interactions: a case study with Dublin Core terms using the Dendro platform. Int. J. Digit. Libr. **20**(2) (2019). https://doi.org/10.1007/s00799-018-0238-x
15. Taylor, C.F., et al.: Promoting coherent minimum reporting guidelines for biological and biomedical investigations: the MIBBI project. Nat. Biotechnol. **26**(8), 889–896 (2009). https://doi.org/10.1038/nbt.1411.Promoting
16. Taylor, C.F., et al.: The minimum information about a proteomics experiment (MIAPE). Nat. Biotechnol. **25**(8), 887–893 (2007)

17. Tenopir, C., et al.: Changes in data sharing and data reuse practices and perceptions among scientists worldwide. PLoS ONE **10**(8), 26–40 (2015). ISSN 1613-0073. https://doi.org/10.1371/journal.pone.0134826

18. Wilkinson, M.D., et al.: The FAIR guiding principles for scientific data management and stewardship. Sci. Data **3** (2016). https://doi.org/10.1038/sdata.2016.18

19. Willis, C., Greenberg, J., White, H.: Analysis and synthesis of metadata goals for scientific data. J. Am. Soc. Inf. Sci. Technol. **63**(8), 1505–1520 (2012). https://doi.org/10.1002/asi

20. Willoughby, C., et al.: Creating context for the experiment record. User-defined metadata: investigations into metadata usage in the LabTrove ELN. J. Chem. Inf. Model. **54**, 3268–3283 (2014). https://doi.org/10.1021/ci500469f

RAMP Shapes: Declarative RDF ↔ ADT Mapping

Alexey Morozov[1,2]($\boxtimes$) (iD), Gerhard Wohlgenannt[1] (iD), Dmitry Mouromtsev[1] (iD), Dmitry Pavlov[2], and Yury Emelyanov[2]

[1] Faculty of Software Engineering and Computer Systems, ITMO University, St. Petersburg, Russia
gwohlg@itmo.ru, mouromtsev@mail.ifmo.ru
[2] Vismart Ltd., St. Petersburg, Russia
{alexey.morozov,dmitry.pavlov,yury.emelyanov}@vismart.biz

Abstract. With the broad availability of Linked Data efficient and convenient programmatic access to semantic graph data within programming languages is important for using the data in applications. To this end, we present RAMP (RDF Algebraic Data Type Mapping), a type construction language, specification and an implementation of mapping operations between RDF graphs and structured data types. RAMP is based on algebraic data types, and aims to overcome limitations of existing approaches for example regarding the set of supported language constructs, or the ability to generalize over a different programming languages. At the same time, RAMP focuses on providing computationally efficient mapping operations.

Keywords: RDF · ADT · Data mapping · JSON-LD

1 Introduction

The idea of using semantic graphs to represent domain knowledge becomes more common in the recent years. However application developers who are actually trying to use them usually face the difficulty on how to conveniently access graph-based data as data structures in the programming language of choice. The typical solution involves either an ad-hoc approach or the adoption of an existing library for one- or two-way RDF mapping, e.g. JSON-LD. In this paper we investigate existing takes on the problem, describe their limitations and propose a novel solution that focuses more strongly on mapping language design.

The initial goal of the project was to overcome the limitations of JSON-LD, such as missing support for union constructs in the framing language (see Sect. 2). RAMP takes an algebraic data type (ADT) approach [3] to design a set of composable type constructors to simplify mapping to/from RDF graphs.

ADTs are composable data types, so using them allows to model complex data descriptions with a limited number of type constructors. Using only a

E. Garoufallou et al. (Eds.): MTSR 2019, CCIS 1057, pp. 40–51, 2019.
https://doi.org/10.1007/978-3-030-36599-8_4

small set of parametrizable types makes it easier to reason about the data mapping. The focus on functional programming in mainstream languages allows for straightforward ways to translate the types into native data structures. So our goal is to provide a mapping language which overcomes the limitations of existing implementations, and is computationally efficient on mapping operations.

A properly designed mapping language between semantic graphs and programming languages can be used in multiple different ways. Based on the supported operations (see Sect. 3.4) it is possible to:

– Map graph-based data to and from specific programming environment's data structures (referred to as domain structures later).
– Validate domain structures.
– Query necessary data directly from a graph database without another query language such as SPARQL.

These use cases are relevant to Semantic Web application developers in order to simplify consuming and producing Linked Data while keeping the native representation for the specific programming environment.

In summary, this paper addresses the problem of mapping between Semantic Web graphs and programming languages by introducing a new type construction language and operations for the described types. Unlike existing solutions, this allows to generalize over different programming languages. The proposed way of composing orthogonal types to model domain structures described in the paper allows to not only implement the core functionality of commonly used tools but to resolve other use cases such as constructing a query by a data shape without an explicit SPARQL request. The application of types for pattern matching in the language provides an easy to understand semantics for both specification implementers and end users, and also leads to a clear way to extend the language through new type constructors and operation types.

We evaluate the functionality of the proposed solution by comparing the set of supported operation types between mapping languages, and regarding computational performance by modelling the same data shapes with an existing library and quantitatively measuring performance in the selected programming environment. The evaluation results suggest that our approach describes real-world RDF data (on average) with higher operation performance than JSON-LD.

2   Related Work

As mentioned, we base our work on the concept of ADTs. The algebraic data type approach has been suggested to apply the method to marshal (serialize) application domain data from the OCaml programming environment [3].

There are various approaches to perform mapping, validation and querying of semantic data by using declarative languages. The basic idea is to describe the shape of the given data. Firstly, *Shape Expressions* [9] define a formal language similar to regular expressions for validating RDF graphs, which is extended with declarative mappings into XML and JSON documents. The Shape Expressions language describes matching patterns, rules and constraints specifically for graph validation. The approach is very flexible as it allows to define special annotations called semantic actions familiar to the users of parser generators like Yacc [5] to facilitate custom constraints and implement transformations into other formats. But it is also hard to debug and error-prone due to code generation.

SHACL (Shapes Constraint Language) [6] is a similar language for validating RDF graphs using shapes. Unlike the former, shapes are expressed in the form of an RDF graph and may be used for multiple purposes. Although SHACL shapes may be extended beyond RDF validation it requires significant model changes, e.g. representing property cardinality restrictions as collection types.

The *JSON-LD* [11] language represents RDF graphs as JSON documents, and allows various transformations on such representations. The specified operations include graph serialization, RDF lowering (frame), lifting (toRdf) and several format-specific transforms [8]. JSON-LD implementations allow to transform JSON-LD to RDF without out-of-band type descriptions like SHACL shapes by including a context document or URL within the document. The limitations of JSON-LD include the inability to represent union types and frame map types. A major drawback of JSON-LD contexts is the inability to bind predicates to specific object types which results in hard-to-ensure resulting value shapes, e.g. compacting inconsistencies between single property values or collections.

SPARQL Transformer [7] defines and implements a query language by extending the JSON-LD notation with query-specific constructs. The key idea is to use a single JSON document to define the query and expected shape of the object. The limitations include the extension of JSON-LD without a proper type system and encoding property restrictions with a custom grammar as strings, which hampers developing a proper tooling support.

STTL [4] is a language to solve various RDF transformation use cases. It closely resembles SPARQL in syntax and provides data transformation functionality through string concatenation templates on matched entities. The major drawback of the approach comes from string concatenation being unsafe and hard to use as it requires to always be aware of escaping rules.

Finally, *XSPARQL* [1] is a language constructed by merging XQuery [2] and SPARQL. The language allows to construct concise queries to lower RDF data into XML documents and lift them back. Limitations of the approach include the tight coupling to the XML document structure and a monolithic pattern matching syntax without the ability to extract and name shared query parts.

3   RAMP

In this section we provide an overview of the main concepts and their specification, as well as a use case example, for the proposed approach RAMP.

3.1 Existing Approaches

When application developers are faced with the task of consuming semantic data in graph form, then there are several approaches. Based on Cohen and Herrmann [3] we can loosely categorize them as:

1. Querying a graph with SPARQL (or another query language) to produce flat tuples. This requires keeping queries in sync with the target data structures and either complex de-serialization logic or separate queries for nested entities.
2. Ad-hoc matching from an RDF graph by iterating over the array of triples looking for specific predicates. This approach works for small homogeneous graphs but quickly deteriorates into combinatorial explosion with lists, recursive types or any other kind of deeply nested structures.
3. Data lifting with JSON-LD framing, or other tools. Although this works for many use cases, none of the existing tools have the necessary generality to describe data structures in mainstream programming languages. Another drawback of this approach is the technical burden to support separate descriptions for querying, lifting and other operations.

Our approach falls into the last category but at the same time remains free of described limitations due to its language design allowing RAMP to perform the whole data workflow (see Sect. 4.1) with a single schema description.

3.2 The Proposed Approach

Similar to other solutions, RAMP provides a set of types (called shapes) to match domain-specific RDF graphs. But unlike the type systems in other approaches, the types are designed to be orthogonal and closely resemble ADTs. This key difference allows for a wider range of applicable operations incl. but not limited to framing (lifting), flattening (lowering), validating and querying RDF data.

The strong similarity between the chosen set of type constructors and the common data structures in programming environments provides transparent mapping in both directions without an intermediate step like the compact operation in JSON-LD or the need for separate languages for lowering and lifting.

RAMP consists of three main building blocks, which are (i) a declarative language for describing structured data types (Sect. 3.3); (ii) a specification of useful operations on these types (Sect. 3.4); (iii) an implementation for the JavaScript programming environment (Sect. 3.6).

3.3 Type Constructors

The set of defined types forms a type construction language with RDF-based atomic terms and ADTs (Algebraic Data Types).

The language defines only a limited set of types to reach the following goals:

- Make it simple to understand for developers with a functional programming background by using the familiar set of type constructors

- Reuse the same types for different operations (e.g. frame and flatten)
- Offer to describe as many as possible of existing structured data types with a small amount of orthogonal concepts
- Have the ability to describe the language with itself, i.e. provide a complete description of any RAMP shape using only RAMP shapes.

The main type Shape is defined as a disjoint union of basic types:

$$\text{Shape} = \text{ResourceShape} \mid \text{LiteralShape} \mid \text{ObjectShape} \mid$$
$$\text{UnionShape} \mid \text{OptionalShape} \mid \text{SetShape} \mid \text{ListShape} \mid \text{MapShape}$$

The exact runtime representation of a value that matches a shape is left to the implementation, and leaves the possibility to extend described shapes with hints such as references to runtime types.

ResourceShape describes an RDF resource term, which is either an IRI or a blank node:

$$\text{ResourceShape}(\text{value?} : \text{NamedNode}|\text{BlankNode}, \text{vocab?} : \text{Map}[\text{String}, \text{Term}])$$

LiteralShape describes an RDF literal term with its specified datatype and language (if the datatype is rdf:langString):

$$\text{LiteralShape}(\text{datatype?} : \text{NamedNode}, \text{language?} : \text{string}, \text{value?} : \text{Literal})$$

ObjectShape describes a product type of heterogeneous types accessible through named properties. Each property is specified by its name string, property path and value shape. A property with zero-length path allows to embed a different representation of the same subject, e.g. the subject IRI itself.

$$\text{ObjectShape}(\text{type} : \text{List}[\text{Property}], \text{properties} : \text{List}[\text{Property}])$$
$$\text{Property}(\text{name} : \text{string}, \text{path} : \text{PathSequence}, \text{value} : \text{Shape})$$
$$\text{PathSequence} = \text{List}[\text{PathExpression}|\text{PathSegment}]$$
$$\text{PathExpression}(\text{operator} : \mid \mid \wedge \mid \, ! \mid * \mid + \mid \, ? \, , \text{path} : \text{PathSequence})$$
$$\text{PathSegment}(\text{predicate} : \text{NamedNode})$$

UnionShape describes a sum (coproduct) type of several types. The variants are unordered, which means matching operations may produce results in arbitrary order when the same subject matches multiple variant types. This shape is similar to SHACL union expressions[1] which has no equivalent in JSON-LD.

$$\text{UnionShape}(\text{variants} : \text{Set}[\text{Shape}])$$

OptionalShape describes a sum type of an empty unit type and a single type. Although this type could also be represented as a UnionShape by introducing a

---

[1] https://www.w3.org/TR/shacl-af/#union

"nothing" unit type like *null* in C-like languages, the optional type more closely resembles the semantics of programming languages with either no explicit "nothing" type or multiple such types instead (e.g. *null* and *undefined* in JavaScript).

OptionalShape(item : Shape)

SetShape describes an unordered set of a single type.

SetShape(item : Shape)

ListShape describes an ordered set (list) of a single type. By default a ListShape represents RDF list structures, however it is possible to override the **head**, or **tail** property paths and the **nil** term to describe other kinds of ordered structures.

ListShape(item : Shape, head?, tail? : PathSequence, nil? : NamedNode)

MapShape describes an unordered set of items indexed by a key. Any nested shape value, datatype or language may be chosen as the key. When MapShape includes a nested map value with the same key, the key always refers to the innermost map shape. A key shape may be limited to non-composite types depending on the implementation.

MapShape(item : Shape, key, value? : ShapeReference)

ShapeReference(target : Shape, part? : value|datatype|language)

In future work it is possible to consider extension, intersection, negation and other kinds of types.

3.4 Operations

The specification of operations on the described data types includes the following methods:

1. frame : $(g : Graph, s : Shape, S : Set[Shape]) \mapsto v : s$—frame type s from RDF graph g as value v.
   This operation is usually referred to as RDF **lowering** [1]. The method matches shapes starting with root s to form a corresponding shape instance.
2. flatten : $(v : s, s : Shape, S : Set[Shape]) \mapsto g : Graph$—generates an RDF graph g from a value v of type s. This operation is usually referred to as RDF **lifting** [1]. The method generates RDF triples/quads from all available data contained in a corresponding shape instance.
3. validate : $(v : s, s : Shape, S : Set[Shape]) \mapsto g : boolean$—validates that value v matches type s.
4. generateQuery : $(s : Shape, S : Set[Shape]) \mapsto v : s$—generates SPARQL query to fetch a subset of graph data necessary to frame shape s.

In the listing above, g is an RDF graph, v is a value of type s, $s \in S$ and S is a set of defined types. We chose the specific methods in order to generalize over existing tools, and to supply the wide variety of operations possible with the presented approach.

3.5   Example

The following example should help to get a better understanding of the described functionalities. In the example, the JavaScript implementation of RAMP allows us to map the graph data in Fig. 1 using the shapes in Fig. 2 into a resulting JSON object (Fig. 3). After framing the shapes may be reused to validate that a given JavaScript value matches them, to lift a value back into a set of RDF triples or to generate a SPARQL query to fetch only the necessary data to frame.

Figure 2 shows the shapes describing an object *ex:Annotation* which includes a nested shape *ex:Selector* and properties *start* and *end*. *ex:Selector* is a union shape which in this case means it could be either a *ex:Point* object with integer *position* property or a *ex:Path* shape which is an RDF list of strings.

```
@prefix ex: <http://example.com/schema/>.
@prefix : <http://example.com/data/>.
:anno1 a ex:Annotation;
    ex:start :point1;
    ex:end ("1" "2").
:point1 a ex:Point;
    ex:position 42.
```

Fig. 1. Example source graph data in Turtle format

3.6   Implementation

We implemented the specified language for JavaScript VMs, written in Type-Script. Implementations for other runtimes and/or languages are possible, incl. the ability to define and use the same types in multiple environments. It should be noted, however, that different environments may need to define their own data transformation handlers to represent RDF terms as native data types.

The implementation uses the RDF/JS data model[2] to represent RDF terms and graph quads. The library is written in TypeScript and includes interface definitions for all shape types, and *frame* and *flatten* methods. Furthermore, the library provides "shapes-for-shapes" set of shapes which describe shape interface types as shapes themselves.

The project is published[3] and available under an open source (MIT) license. The repository also includes additional practical usage examples.

4   Evaluation

The evaluation of RAMP includes a qualitative comparison with related languages by listing required data descriptions (shapes, queries, templates) to per-

---

[2] http://rdf.js.org/data-model-spec/.
[3] https://github.com/ramp-shapes/ramp-shapes.

```
@prefix : <http://ramp-shapes.github.io/schema#>.
@prefix ex: <http://example.com/schema/>.

ex:Annotation a :ObjectShape;
    :typeProperty [
        :name "type"; :path ([ :predicate rdf:type ]);
        :shape [ a :ResourceShape; :termValue ex:Annotation ]
    ];
    :property [
        :name "id"; :path (); :shape [ a :ResourceShape ]
    ];
    :property [
        :name "start"; :path ([ :predicate ex:start ]);
        :shape ex:Selector
    ];
    :property [
        :name "end"; :path ([ :predicate ex:end ]);
        :shape [ a :OptionalShape; :item ex:Selector ]
    ].

ex:Selector a :UnionShape; :variant ex:Point, ex:Path.

ex:Point a :ObjectShape;
    :typeProperty [
        :name "type"; :path ([ :predicate rdf:type ]);
        :shape [ a :ResourceShape; :termValue ex:Point ]
    ];
    :property [
        :name "position"; :path ([ :predicate ex:position ]);
        :shape [ a :LiteralShape; :termDatatype xsd:integer ]
    ].

ex:Path a :ListShape;
    :item [ a :LiteralShape; :termDatatype xsd:string ].
```

Fig. 2. Example RAMP shapes

```
{
  "type": "http://example.com/schema/Annotation",
  "id": "http://example.com/data/anno1",
  "start": {
    "type": "http://example.com/schema/Point",
    "position": 42
  },
  "end": ["1", "2"]
}
```

Fig. 3. Example RAMP frame result

Languages	Operation types			
	query[*]	lower from RDF	validate	flatten to RDF
RAMP	shape	shape	shape[**]	shape
JSON-LD	–	context+frame	–	context
XSPARQL	–	to-XML query[†]	–	to-RDF query[†]
SHACL	–	–	shape	–
ShEx	–	GenX/GenJ actions	JS/SPARQL actions	–
STTL	template[‡]	template[‡]	–	–
SPARQL Transformer	query[††]	query+context[††]	–	context

[*] This means the ability to describe and query a specific subgraph, e.g. by a CONSTRUCT query from a SPARQL endpoint.

[**] Currently implemented in limited form as part of the flatten operation.

[†] XSPARQL uses the same language to lower and lift data but requires to implement separate queries for each operation type.

[‡] STTL combines querying the graph and lowering in a single template.

[††] SPARQL Transformer uses modified JSON-LD context/frame syntax to query and lower graph data, the result is mapped into plain JSON based on a query.

Fig. 4. Data descriptions required to perform operations in different languages

form supported operations, and a quantitative performance comparison with JSON-LD as one of the widely known and closely related language.

4.1 Workflow Comparison

In this section we compare data description and mapping languages regarding their ability to perform operations – based on their current specification. For each language and operation type (functionality), Fig. 4 summarizes the required descriptions of the RDF graph, and of the transformed value structure. We chose the same four operation types specified earlier for this comparison, because together they form a usual data workflow for semantic data applications. An important operation type not covered in this comparison is data mutation – as it is currently not supported by either language. In future work, we evaluate and compare other features between mapping languages such as mapping quality, incl. but not limited to completeness, simplicity, consistency, easy of use, etc.

From Fig. 4 we conclude that only RAMP provides the means to perform all specified operation types using *shapes* as universal description. Other languages require multiple separate data descriptions for specific operations, eg. XSPARQL uses separate queries to map RDF data into XML documents and back.

4.2 Performance Evaluation

Here we compare the performance for lowering and lifting operations between RAMP and JSON-LD. We selected JSON-LD as the most widely used tool with similar goals. More specifically, we evaluated the performance on frame and flatten operations for the **jsonld.js**[4] and **ramp-shapes** implementations. Both libraries target the JavaScript execution environment, so garbage collection and other costs are roughly the same when tested using the same setup.

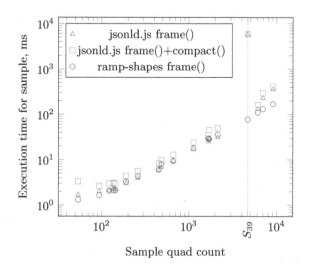

Fig. 5. RDF lowering (frame) performance comparison

Regarding **evaluation setup**, we use Node.js v8.12.0 on a 2.2 GHz CPU under Windows 10. The main metric is execution time for operations on the IIIF manifest [10] dataset provided by the Mirador project examples[5]. We restricted the manifests to the ones that use IIIF Presentation Context v2[6], as the majority of manifests in the dataset use the second (latest) revision. The Mirador dataset contains standardized JSON-LD frames which allow to compare performance on real-world data with a single set of shapes for every sample document.

In Fig. 5 we compare execution times for the frame() operation. We find similar performance for both, but ramp-shapes is about 15% faster on samples with higher quad count. Unexpectedly, sample S_{39} (Vatican Library[7]) takes a lot more time with jsonld.js, probably due to longer rdf:list structures for sc:hasCanvases and sc:hasRanges predicate values. Figure 6 suggests very close overall performance for the flatten() operation on ramp-shapes compared to jsonld.js.

---

[4] https://github.com/digitalbazaar/jsonld.js/.
[5] https://github.com/ProjectMirador/mirador-website.
[6] https://iiif.io/api/presentation/2.0/#linked-data-context-and-extensions.
[7] http://digi.vatlib.it/iiif/MSS_Vat.lat.3225/manifest.json.

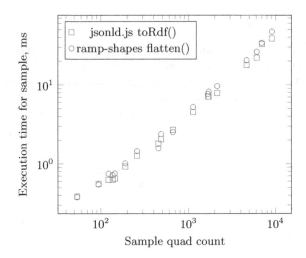

Fig. 6. RDF lifting (flatten) performance comparison

The source code and sample data for the evaluations are published[8] and available under an open source license. Overall, besides tackling conceptual and implementation limitations of existing approaches, the evaluations show that ramp-shapes is also very competitive, or faster, regarding execution times.

5   Conclusions

We present RAMP, a novel approach for mapping between data structures in programming languages and RDF (in both directions). RAMP is based on the algebraic data type (ADT) approach [3], and applies a set of composable type constructors to simplify the mapping process. After comparing to existing work in the field, we describe the main components of RAMP: the declarative language for structured data types, the specification of the main operations for those types, and a JS implementation. The evaluations show the benefits of RAMP regarding functionality in terms of supported operation types, and demonstrate equal or lower execution times for lowering and lifting operations than JSON-LD.

The contributions of this work include: (i) the specification of a mapping language including type constructors and operations – based on ADTs. (ii) its implementation for JS (which is available online), (iii) a comparative analysis of range of functionality of existing languages, (iv) experiments with a real-world dataset to evaluate the computational efficiency in comparison to JSON-LD.

Regarding future work, there are several potential directions for RAMP. As a language, it can add well-known type constructs such as type extension, intersection and negated types to extend a set of data structures, which RAMP can represent. As a specification, it can specify operation algorithms in a formal way.

---

[8] https://github.com/AlexeyMz/ramp-shapes-perf.

As a JS implementation, it can natively support or provide means to generate shapes from other languages, e.g. JSON-LD contexts, or SHACL shapes. Finally, the implementation can be ported to other platforms to reuse the same shapes across different programming languages.

Acknowledgements. This work was supported by the Government of the Russian Federation (Grant 074-U01) through the ITMO Fellowship and Professorship Program. Furthermore, the work is supported by Sputniq GmbH.

References

1. Akhtar, W., Kopecký, J., Krennwallner, T., Polleres, A.: XSPARQL: traveling between the XML and RDF worlds – and avoiding the XSLT pilgrimage. In: Bechhofer, S., Hauswirth, M., Hoffmann, J., Koubarakis, M. (eds.) ESWC 2008. LNCS, vol. 5021, pp. 432–447. Springer, Heidelberg (2008). https://doi.org/10.1007/978-3-540-68234-9_33
2. Boag, S., et al.: XQuery 1.0: an XML query language (2002)
3. Cohen, A., Herrmann, C.: Towards a high-productivity and high-performance marshaling library for compound data. In: 2nd MetaOCaml Workshop (2005)
4. Corby, O., Faron-Zucker, C., Gandon, F.: A generic RDF transformation software and its application to an online translation service for common languages of linked data. In: Arenas, M., et al. (eds.) ISWC 2015. LNCS, vol. 9367, pp. 150–165. Springer, Cham (2015). https://doi.org/10.1007/978-3-319-25010-6_9
5. Johnson, S.C., et al.: YACC: Yet Another Compiler-Compiler, vol. 32. Bell Laboratories, Murray Hill (1975)
6. Knublauch, H., Kontokostas, D.: Shapes constraint language (SHACL). W3C Candidate Recommendation, vol. 11, no. 8 (2017)
7. Lisena, P., Troncy, R.: Transforming the JSON output of SPARQL queries for linked data clients. In: Companion of the The Web Conference 2018 on The Web Conference 2018, pp. 775–780. International WWW Conferences Steering Committee (2018)
8. Longley, D., Kellogg, G., Lanthaler, M., Sporny, M.: JSON-LD 1.0 processing algorithms and API, vol. 18. WWW Consortium (2015). www.w3.org/TR/json-ld-api/
9. Prud'hommeaux, E., Labra Gayo, J.E., Solbrig, H.: Shape expressions: an RDF validation and transformation language. In: Proceedings of the 10th International Conference on Semantic Systems, pp. 32–40. ACM (2014)
10. Snydman, S., Sanderson, R., Cramer, T.: The international image interoperability framework (IIIF): a community & technology approach for web-based images. In: Archiving Conference, pp. 16–21. no. 1. Society for Imaging Science and Technology (2015)
11. Sporny, M., Longley, D., Kellogg, G., Lanthaler, M., Lindström, N.: JSON-LD 1.0, vol. 16, p. 41. W3C Recommendation (2014)

Emotional Concept Extraction Through Ontology-Enhanced Classification

Danilo Cavaliere$^{(\boxtimes)}$ and Sabrina Senatore

Dipartimento di Ingegneria dell'Informazione ed Elettrica e Matematica Applicata - DIEM, Universitá degli Studi di Salerno, Fisciano, SA, Italy
{dcavaliere,ssenatore}@unisa.it

Abstract. Capturing emotions affecting human behavior in social media bears strategic importance in many decision-making fields, such as business and public policy, health care, and financial services, or just social events. This paper introduces an emotion-based classification model to analyze the human behavior in reaction to some event described by a tweet trend. From tweets analysis, the model extracts terms expressing emotions, and then, it builds a topological space of emotion-based concepts. These concepts enable the training of the multi-class SVM classifier to identify emotions expressed in the tweets. Classifier results are "softly" interpreted as a blending of several emotional nuances which thoroughly depicts people's feeling. An ontology model captures the emotional concepts returned by classification, with respect to the tweet trends. The associated knowledge base provides human behavior analysis, in response to an event, by a tweet trend, by SPARQL queries.

Keywords: Sentiment analysis · Simplicial Complex · SVM · Ontology

1 Introduction

Nowadays, people share their ideas, feelings, and reactions via social networks to everyday-life events, politics, news, social issues, music, etc. Twitter seems to be the preferred popular social networks to express opinions and feelings about any kind of event, through tweets, generally composed of short sentences. There is a great interest in investigating human behavior in social networks, especially analyzing tweets, with the purpose to capture feelings, emotions expressed in natural language and study reactions about that specific event. Tweet analysis finds applications in many fields, such as business [7], marketing [3], political consensus analyses [10] and more.

Sentiment analysis has been widely used to interpret the sentiment polarity (positive, negative and neutral) from social media [8,11] and web documents [6]. Text mining [13] and Natural Language Processing (NLP) [12] have been widely used to extract feelings in the language structure, focusing on developing new text preprocessing methods including tokenization, stemming and other

© Springer Nature Switzerland AG 2019
E. Garoufallou et al. (Eds.): MTSR 2019, CCIS 1057, pp. 52–63, 2019.
https://doi.org/10.1007/978-3-030-36599-8_5

techniques to improve sentiment classification. The lexical analysis alone can not be enough to depict sentiments and opinions, because tweets and posts are written in colloquial language and strongly depend on context [1,4,5]. Therefore, tweet comprehension requires not only the analysis of the document and the paragraph, but also the sentence, clause and concept analysis. In fact, some trends in literature are aimed at concept extraction to better interpret text meaning and categorize tweets [4].

A thorough interpretation of the emotions and opinions from tweets requires knowledge from different fields, such as linguistic, psychology, cognitive science, sociology and ethics. To this purpose, Sentic computing is a multi-disciplinary approach which bridges computer as well as social sciences to better recognize and depict opinions and sentiments over the Web [9]. Therefore, affective ontologies and emotion-specific reasoner tools exploit social sciences knowledge for the opinion and sentiment interpretation [9], as well as the collective emotions influence human behavior [2].

In addition to emotion extraction difficulties, the main issue about tweet analysis is due to the continuous tweet stream, coming from people of different cultures, over all the world, expressing their opinions, sentiments on different topics [5]. The use of hashtags in tweets supports the detection of user behavior by the tweet trend analysis [8,13].

This paper presents an emotion-based classification system. The system also achieves a linguistic topological space of emotion-based concepts. These concepts characterize the emotional feelings expressed in a trend (associated with one or more hashtags) about an event, and supports the training of the multi-class Support Vector Machine (SVM) classifier to identify emotions expressed in tweets. The output of classifier is relaxed: not just the dominant feeling detected on the event, but nuances of emotions are returned, thanks to the intensity degree calculated by the classifier result. In order to improve the feeling analysis, an emotional concept ontology is also built and queried to provide meaningful views on the emotional reactions to events. For instance, let us consider the hashtag *#astarisborn*, the proposed approach depicts people reactions to the film in terms of feelings, such as love, open, angry, sad, etc.

The paper is organized as follows: Sect. 2 provides an overview of the system, while Sect. 3 discusses tweet collection and data preprocessing. Section 4 presents the emotional concept extraction from tweets. Then, Sects. 5 and 6, respectively, present soft classification in emotional classes and the ontology to model the collected data to return emotion-based views. System tests are presented in Sect. 7, then Sect. 8 concludes the paper.

2 Model Overview

Figure 1 shows the logical overview of the system as a data-flow through its main components. The collection of tweets is given as input to the *Tweet Analysis* component, that arranges the tweets into hashtag-based documents, to facilitate their processing. The component parses the document text by using the Natural

Language Processing (NLP) activities, to select emotional terms; these terms will form the feature space of the document-term (DT) matrix. The matrix is given as input to the *Emotional concept extraction* component, in charge of building a topological space of emotional terms. The Simplicial Complex method [4] is used to discover the strong correlation among terms in the multidimensional space. It generates emotion-based concepts with different term aggregation degrees: basic concepts (BCs) and extended concepts (CETs). The extracted BCs and CETs are provided to *Emotion classification* and *Ontology-based emotion view* components. *Emotion classification* component discovers the emotional BCs that are relevant to the hashtag-based documents. The found BCs are used to annotate the DT matrix for the classifier training. The *Ontology-based emotion view* analyses relations among BCs and CETs to automatically enrich the ontology model with new instances of the discovered emotional concepts. SPARQL queries on this ontology provide better insights on human behavior when a specific event described by hashtag is sought.

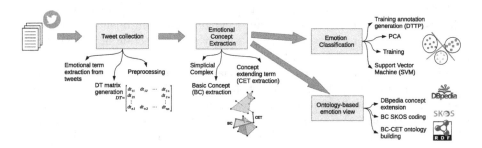

Fig. 1. System architecture.

3   Tweet Analysis

The tweet stream is analyzed and arranged in order to produce a document associated with the same hashtag. Thus, each document represents a social tweet trend associated with an event, described by a specific hashtag. The document collection is then parsed by NLP techniques in order to discard stop words, numbers, and then the remaining words are stemmed and further filtered according to a set of emotional term collection. The emotional terms are single terms that can be nouns, adjectives and adverbs expressing an emotional judgement about something, such as "thankful", "admiration", etc. or a particular mood triggered by something (i.e. "satisfied", "sad", "delighted"). Thus, the meaning can be positive as well as negative. Often, these terms are not meaningful of themselves, sometimes they need interpretation. For instance, "Good job" could not always be a compliment, in sarcastic sentences it could also be a negative remark about the action of somebody (i.e., "Good Job, Einstein!!!!"). These terms are, generally, related to specific classes of emotions. For instance, "devoted", "passionate" refer to love-related emotions, while terms such as "annoyed", "irritated" refer to angry-related emotions. The emotional terms are individual or atomic words, that in the natural language, are associated with a feeling, although they are not often enough to fully interpret the emotion expressed. In this approach, an Emotional Term List (ETL), describing a list of typical emotional terms[1], has been used. It is composed of sixteen emotional classes (also called *ETL emotional classes*), each one, in turn, composed of a set of words that are synonyms or words with similar meaning; a half of them include words expressing pleasant feelings ("open", "happy", "alive", "good", "love", "interest", "positive", "strong"), whereas the remaining classes are related to unpleasant feelings ("angry", "depressed", "confused", "helpless", "indifferent", "afraid", "hurt", "sad").

Terms in the ETL file are employed to detect and select the emotional terms in each (hashtag-based) document of tweets. The document-term matrix is indeed built considering all the documents, given the (stemmed) terms in the ETL. The cell (i, j) of matrix represents the importance of the emotional term i in the document j, and is valued by the TF-IDF (term frequency-inverse document frequency) metric. The metric offsets the frequency of a term in a document with the frequency of the same term in the whole corpus. The rationale behind the metric is to reduce the importance of the most frequent terms in general, which are often little significant.

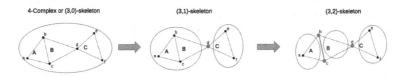

Fig. 2. The simplicial complex decomposition into simplexes A, B and C through skeleton definition

4   Emotional Concept Extraction via Simplicial Complex

The emotional terms are atomic terms, that can have emotional meaning, even though the proper meaning is often related to the context (surrounding words that make more explicit the intended sense) where the term appears. Understanding the actual sentiment expressed in the written language is not trivial, especially in tweets, whose reduced text length amplifies the difficulties in capturing sarcastic and ambiguous sentences. Thus, the same term could also assume different meanings depending on the context/situation. Our idea is to delineate a kind of context, by relating terms expressing emotions with other terms in sentences, with the purpose to outline an emotional concept accurately. The

---

[1] http://www.psychpage.com/learning/library/assess/feelings.html.

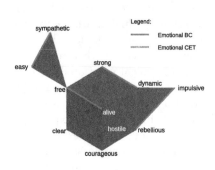

$$BCT = \begin{matrix} \text{terms} \\ BC \begin{bmatrix} 1 & 1 & \cdots & 0 \\ 1 & & & 1 \\ \vdots & & & \vdots \\ 0 & 1 & \cdots & 0 \end{bmatrix} \end{matrix} \quad \begin{aligned} BC_2 &= \{bct_{21}, bct_{2n}\} \\ BC_n &= \{bct_{n2}\} \end{aligned}$$

$$DT = \begin{matrix} \text{terms} \\ \text{Doc} \begin{bmatrix} 0.6 & 0 & \cdots & 0.7 \\ 0.7 & & & 0.2 \\ \vdots & & & \vdots \\ 0.9 & 0.8 & \cdots & 0.7 \end{bmatrix} \end{matrix} \Longleftrightarrow \begin{bmatrix} TP_1 \\ TP_1 \\ \vdots \\ TP_4 \end{bmatrix}$$

$$TP_1 = BC_2$$
$$TP_4 = BC_2 \cup BC_n$$

Fig. 3. BCs and CETs from simplicial complex structure

Fig. 4. DT and BCT matrices

Emotional Concept Extraction component is in charge of building the emotional concepts. It achieves the simplicial complex model, that is a geometric structure composed of several geometric figures, such as points, lines, triangles, squares, etc. More specifically, the simplicial complex is a finite collection of simpler geometric structures, called simplexes. Simplexes are a convex hull of $n+1$ independent vertices (i.e., 2-Simplex is a triangle). Simplexes could also be formed of sub-structures, called faces (i.e., triangles are composed of lines and points). The Simplicial Complex not only contains its simplexes, but also the faces connecting them. The connected simplexes in a Simplicial Complex could be separated by gradually removing faces connecting them at each step. This way, different complex skeletons are generated. Figure 2 shows this progressive decomposition of the initial simplicial complex. The two simplexes A and B are connected by the segment (b, c), while B and C are connected by the point (d). Firstly, the lowest dimension faces are removed, thus, points are removed generating the (3,1)-skeleton, d is removed and B and C are not yet connected. Then, the segments are removed, (a, b) included. Therefore, the (3,2)-skeleton is formed and A and B are no longer connected. This process is used to analyze the topological space (i.e., the whole simplicial complex), through its skeletons which represent different conceptualization levels. Since each point is a term, the simplicial complex of terms at skeleton k represents a linguistic topological space at the kth level of detail. The simplicial complex has been proved to be useful to analyze linguistic topological spaces and extract context-related conceptualization, called Basic Concepts (BCs) and Concept Extending Terms (CETs) [4]. BCs represent specific emotional concepts, composed as a simplexes of highly-related emotional terms. The CETs, extending the BC, add more general emotional terms to the BC, providing more complex context-based conceptualization. Figure 3 shows emotional BCs and CETs built on emotional words extracted from a corpus of documents. The most related terms in the text are grouped determining the emotional BCs, such as ("free", "alive"), ("strong", "dynamic"). These BCs represent the basic feelings expressed in the text. The CET ("sympathetic", "easy") better explains BC ("free", "alive"), while the CET ("impulsive", "rebellious") better describes BC ("strong", "dynamic"). Emotional BCs represent the emotional classes used in the training phase of our SVM classifier. The extracted BCs are arranged in a Basic Concept-emotional Term matrix (BCT). This matrix has the BCs, on the rows, and the emotional terms in the BCs, on the columns. A cell value (i, j) in BCT is 1 if the j-th emotional term belongs to the i-th BC, 0 otherwise. Let us notice that the emotional terms in each BCT are the same in the feature set of DT. An example of BCT definition is shown in Fig. 4.

5   Emotion-Driven Classification

This section presents the classification of the hashtag documents. The three following subsections present the training setting, the cross validation and the soft classification of the classifier outputs, respectively.

5.1   Target Class Generation by Emotional Conceptualizations

Since no prefixed emotion-based classes are available for the hashtag-based tweet stream, the emotional concepts (BCs), built via the simplicial complex, provide a way to compute the appropriate emotional class. Recall that each emotional class described in Sect. 3 is composed of emotional terms present in ETL; for instance, the ETL class identified by label *Happy* is composed of words like *ecstatic, joyous, gleeful*, etc. Since ETL is the feature set of the two matrices DT and BCT, the predominant classes to associate with each document are sought, taking the emotional terms in ETL in account. Specifically, the *Emotion-based Classification* component selects the BC terms that are also in a hashtag-based document. This way, a list of all the BCs (sharing terms with DT matrix) for each document is generated. The selected BCs, namely Hashtag-related BCs, describe the emotions related to the tweet trend, described by that hashtag (document). More formally,

Hashtag-Related BCs of a Document. Let $BC = \{x_1, x_2, ...x_n\}$ be a basic concept (BC) and $H = \{z_1, z_2, ...z_n\}$ a hashtag-based document, BC is related to H if and only if each emotional term t $(t \in ETL)$ in BC is also in H:

$$BC \subset H \leftrightarrow \forall t \in BC, t \in H \leftrightarrow x_t = 1 \ and \ z_t > 0 \tag{1}$$

where x_t and z_t are the values assumed by the term t in BC and H (a row of DT), respectively.

All the *Hashtag-related BCs* associated with a hashtag document form an *emotional topic*, which is composed of all the emotions expressed by the discovered concepts in that hashtag stream.

Emotional Topic of a Document. Let H be a hashtag document and BC the hashtag-related BC to H, the emotional topic T_H associated with the document H is defined as the union of each BC related to H:

$$T_H = \bigcup_{\forall BC \subset H} BC \tag{2}$$

The emotional topic is composed of all the terms in the union of all the *Hashtag-related BCs* of a document H. The topic enables the ETL class candidate selection to get the final annotation class for that hashtag document.

Hashtag Annotation Class. An ETL emotional class C_i of an emotional topic T_H is assigned to the hashtag document H if $|C_i \cap T| \geq |C_j \cap T|$, $\forall j = 1, ..., n$, (where n is the number of ETL emotional classes).

In other words, ETL class containing the largest common subset of terms (in BCs) with the topic T_H, associated to the document H, will be taken as the target class for H. The DT matrix with the class annotation is used to train the classifier.

5.2   Preprocessing, Cross Validation and Training

Our system employs Support Vector Machine (SVM) to classify the hashtag documents in ETL emotional classes.

As first step, the training and the test sets have been formed by dividing the annotated DT matrix in the 80% for the training and the 20% for the test. The DT division has been done by keeping the proportions among the classes. Then, the SVM parameters have been estimated by employing the k-fold method with k = 5. The high number of variables generally decreases classification performances and accuracy. In this case, the Principal Components Analysis (PCA) is applied to the dataset to detect the linearly independent variables at maximum variance. The number of the components to select is detected by cross-validation. The data reduced with PCA are also standardized in order to improve SVM accuracy. After cross validation, PCA-based data reduction and standardization have been performed, the model is trained.

5.3   Soft Classification

The human mood is often a blending of different emotion, with different intensity degrees. Sometimes, it is not possible to straightly label a feeling because it is come a mix of sensations, sentiments, there are not easy to recognize. Bearing this in mind, our system achieves a soft classification of the hashtags to better represent people's emotions and reactions to events, that in this case, are described by the relative hashtag trends. The multi-class SVM method employs the pairwise classification, which builds a classifier for each pair of classes. Therefore, given m classes, $m \cdot (m - 1)$ classifiers are employed. Each classifier chooses one class from the pair, which is assigned to. In a hard classification scheme, the most voted class on all the pairs is chosen to classify the hashtag (majority voting algorithm).

Our system, instead, does not only take the most voted class, but also the votes for each class over the $m \cdot (m - 1)$ pairs. Each vote number associated to each ETL emotional class normalized in the range $[0, 1]$, represents the intensity of that feeling. The degree of the feeling intensity allows a soft classification of the hashtag to ETL classes, which thoroughly expresses the wider nuances of people's mood to something (i.e., hashtag associated with an event, topiuc, etc.). An example of a classification of a tweet trend: (open 0.0), (happy 0.5), (alive 0.1), (good 0.0), (love 0.4), (interest 0.0), (positive 0.1), (strong 0.0), (angry 0.0), (depressed 0.0), (confused 0.0), (helpless 0.0), (indifferent 0.0), (afraid 0.0), (hurt 0.0), (sad 0.0). The value associated with each ETL emotional class describes the intensity degree of that emotion expressed in the tweet trend with a given hashtag. It is evident that the comprehensive feeling is pleasant since terms in the predominant emotional classes such as *happy*, *love* were discovered in the tweets with that hashtag. Also *alive* and *positive* contribute to completely depict the nuances of the human mood. The soft classification allows more accuracy in the description of the feeling, with respect to the crisp classification that would have expressed only happy emotion as people's mood. The soft classification better depicts all the people's feeling and emotional reaction to the hashtag/event.

6   Ontology-Based Emotion View

A semantic model encodes all the given and generated concepts, participating to the system pipeline shown in Fig. 1. The BCs and CETs are employed to build a concept ontology on the emotional concepts (Emotional Concept ontology). One of the first task of the *Ontology-based emotion view* component is indeed to link each generated BC to DBpedia[2], which is an online semantic dataset to extract structured content of Wikipedia resources, in order to enrich our ontology with the corresponding well defined DBpedia concepts. The modeling of BC is based on the *concept* class of SKOS[3] ontology. SKOS gives specifications and standards to support the use of Knowledge Organization Systems (i.e. thesauri, classification schemes, and taxonomies). It provides a knowledge model to represent and classify high-level concepts and the semantic relations among them. The concept of relations expresses how concepts are related to each other. Each BC is coded as a SKOS concept, and related to the other BCs defining RDF and SKOS properties. Three properties have been used to model the semantic relationships among the BCs: *skos:related, skos:narrower* and *rdfs:seeAlso*. These properties allow building a concept hierarchy based on relations among the BCs, and extend the BCs with the CETs and the DBpedia matching resources. The *skos:narrower* property is employed to model the relation between the hashtag document and its individual emotional topic (see Eq. (2)), which is in turn, the union of all the BCs present in the hashtag document. A hierarchy is built by the narrower property, that relates the hashtag documents to the emotional topics and their BCs. The *rdfs:seeAlso* property is employed to relate each BC (SKOS concept) to the DBpedia resource expressing the homonymous emotional concept. The DBpedia resource enriches the BC with additional information (i.e., definitions, related concepts, contexts in which BC is present).

Since each BC is also related to the CETs (that better contextualize the BCs), the *skos:related* property associates BC with CETs. This way, all the resources

---

[2] https://wiki.dbpedia.org/.

[3] https://www.w3.org/2004/02/skos/.

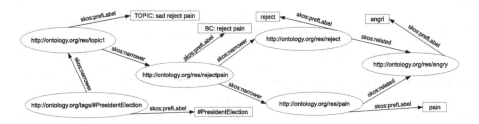

Fig. 5. Emotional concept ontology extract.

linked to a BC through *skos:related* provide a contextualized information about the BCs. The described ontology model is the basic skeleton of our emotional knowledge. The result from the classification provides a dynamic component of the ontology, viz., the population, composed of the actual terms, BCs, CETs, tweet trends, and the extracted emotional valences. Figure 5 shows an extract of the Emotional Concept ontology on (the documents generated by) the trend with the hashtag *#PresidentElection*. This hashtag is related to its emotional topic, labeled *topic1*, composed of two BCs: *sad* and *rejectpain*. The *rejectpain* BC is in turn, related to its terms: *reject* and *pain* terms. DBpedia resources, if present, are also related to the BCs; for instance, the BC *sad* is related to *Sadness* through *rdfs:seeAlso* property. BCs could also be related to their eventual CETs, such as *reject* and *pain* which are related to their common CET *angri*.

SPARQL queries can generate views on the knowledge base, that provide a better insight on the hashtag emotion classification, and better interpretations of the emotion-based human behavior in response to some events and tweet topics, through the continuous tweet streams. The ontology provides a simple representation of the emotional concepts, anyway, more refined semantics will be explored in the future.

7   Experimental Results

Tests have been conducted on tweets, selected according to hashtag in the top trends of the moment, from June to August, 2018. Hashtags have been extracted considering generic events related to week days (i.e. *#WednesdayWisdom*, *#ThursdayThoughts*, *#TBT*, *#FridayFeeling*) and important international events, such as *#PrimaryElection*, *#PMQs*, as well as to more frivolous events *#NationalBestFriendDay*, *#NationalChoccolateIceCreamDay*. Many hashtags refer to showbiz, music, sport and TV events, such as *#TonyAwards*, *#WMA*, *#loveisland*, *#astarisborn*, *#GNTM*, others to politics, social issues, news or religious events, such as *#Trump*, *#politicalcorrectness*, *#RSSTritiyaVarsh*, or even some initiatives or campaigns (i.e. *#FlirtWithYourCity*, *#GlobalRunningDay*).

Tweets related to the same hashtag have been collected and saved in a document. Tweets have been stored on a server employed for tests, which is equipped with 32 GB ram, 2 TB SATA HDD and 8 quadcores, that have speed up the

Table 1. Experimental results by varying configuration setting. Each row shows the experiment (Exp), document number (doc), feature number (Feats), pleasant (plF) and unpleasant features (unF), pleasant (plC) and unpleasant categories (unC), Accuracy (Acc)

Exp	Doc	Feats	plF	unF	plC	unC	Acc
1	5617	250	126	124	7	6	0.57
2	5617	75	38	37	6	5	0.58
3	5617	250	128	122	6	5	0.62
4	5061	100	100	0	6	0	**0.70**
5	5061	109	58	51	6	6	0.55
6	4000	105	54	51	6	5	**0.7**
7	4000	70	36	34	5	4	**0.7**
8	4000	46	16	30	2	3	**0.81**
9	4000	30	11	19	6	2	**0.89**
10	4000	30	11	19	2	3	**0.97**
11	3000	150	150	0	6	0	**0.68**
12	2000	30	16	14	6	4	**0.90**
13	2000	150	64	86	6	7	0.55

tweet collection and the execution of the overall system. The hashtag corpus contains 5617 documents, each one containing tweets with a specific hashtag. Each document is composed of about 2000 tweets, hence the dataset includes around 11,234,000 tweets.

Table 1 shows the results of the experimentation, we conducted, by varying the number of documents, features, and accordingly, the pleasant and unpleasant classes. Some classes have been discarded because their terms had a few occurrences in the document corpus. The experimentation shows the accuracy, by progressively varying some values. On average, the pleasant classes have more occurrences than unpleasant ones, due mainly to the tweet trend content, generally expressing positive emotions. Experiments namely *Exp 4* and *Exp 11* reveal better classification results when there are no unpleasant features in the corresponding classes. Most of emotional terms from the unpleasant classes are often rare in the tweet collection, indeed, on the whole document collection, unpleasant classes of features badly impact on accuracy (see *Exp 5*) as well as there are some ambiguous terms, e.g., *open* and *alive* related to some pleasant classes that could not refer to emotions. Some experiments provide considerable improvement in the classification results removing these terms, reducing consequently the emotional classes (*Exp 10*).

Additional experiments evidence meaningful performance rate of the classifiers after using PCA to reduce the number of features. For instance, by reducing the number of features from *Exp 6* to *Exp 9*, but keeping the same number of documents, the accuracy increases significantly. By increasing the number of

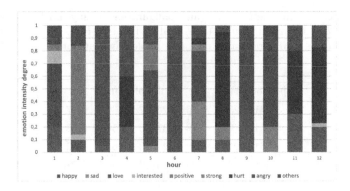

Fig. 6. Emotions associated with the hashtag #WorldCup2018 at each hour from the first appearance of the hashtag

documents as well, the selected features maintain high values of accuracy. Experiments *Exp 12* and *Exp 9* indeed, achieve an accuracy around the 90% passing through 2000 documents to 4000 documents, respectively.

The emotion analysis conducted via tweets also allows the evaluation of the reaction to events over time. Figure 6 shows people's reactions to the World Cup 2018, as emotional states on tweets with the hashtag #WorldCup2018. The tweets have been collected from streaming at each hour from the first appearance of the hashtag. The trend of the emotional reactions results from the hashtag-based document classification at each hour, which describes the evolution of the people feeling during the event time. Noticed that the *Love* and *Hurt* sentiments alternate as time goes by. This trend describes supporters' reactions to team matches, expressing positive feelings (i.e., *Love*) if their team won or negative (i.e., *Hurt*) if it lost. The stacked columns, present in figure, represent the soft emotional classification for the hashtag at each hour. The wider column portion at the hour h describes the highest ranked emotional class at that moment. The soft classification provides interesting insights on the reactions to the event. For instance, at some hour, even though the highest ranked feeling is pleasant, the second highest ranked one is unpleasant (e.g., *Love* and *Angry* at hour 6) and viceversa. In many cases, the first two highest ranked sentiments have also very close ranking values. This trend is quite common at several hours, such as *Love* and *Angry* at hour 6, *Love* and *Interested* at hour 7, *Love* and *Happy* at hour 9, etc.

8   Conclusion

The paper presented an emotion-based classification approach from stored tweet stream. Emotional terms are placed in a linguistic topological space that supports the detection of emotional concepts, used to train a Support Vector Machine (SVM) classifier. Final result is a "soft" classification that provides a complete description of people's reactions to the events represented by the hashtags over time. In addition, an emotional concept ontology provides views on the extracted emotional concepts and better support the analysis of people's behavior and reactions. Future works will further investigate the emotional concept extraction for mixed emotion detection.

References

1. AL-Sharuee, M.T., Liu, F., Pratama, M.: Sentiment analysis: an automatic contextual analysis and ensemble clustering approach and comparison. Data Knowl. Eng. **115**, 194–213 (2018). https://doi.org/10.1016/j.datak.2018.04.001
2. Alharbi, A.S.M., de Doncker, E.: Twitter sentiment analysis with a deep neural network: an enhanced approach using user behavioral information. Cogn. Syst. Res. **54**, 50–61 (2019). https://doi.org/10.1016/j.cogsys.2018.10.001
3. Çali, S., Balaman, Ş.Y.: Improved decisions for marketing, supply and purchasing: mining big data through an integration of sentiment analysis and intuitionistic fuzzy multi criteria assessment. Comput. Ind. Eng. **129**, 315–332 (2019). https://doi.org/10.1016/j.cie.2019.01.051
4. Cavaliere, D., Senatore, S., Loia, V.: Context-aware profiling of concepts from a semantic topological space. Knowl.-Based Syst. **130**, 102–115 (2017). https://doi.org/10.1016/j.knosys.2017.05.008
5. Cotelo, J., Cruz, F., Enríquez, F., Troyano, J.: Tweet categorization by combining content and structural knowledge. Inf. Fus. **31**, 54–64 (2016). https://doi.org/10.1016/j.inffus.2016.01.002
6. Hussein, D.M.E.D.M.: A survey on sentiment analysis challenges. J. King Saud Univ.-Eng. Sci. **30**(4), 330–338 (2018). https://doi.org/10.1016/j.jksues.2016.04.002
7. Li, X., Wu, C., Mai, F.: The effect of online reviews on product sales: a joint sentiment-topic analysis. Inf. Manag. **56**(2), 172–184 (2019). https://doi.org/10.1016/j.im.2018.04.007, social Commerce and Social Media: Behaviors in the New Service Economy
8. Öztürk, N., Ayvaz, S.: Sentiment analysis on Twitter: a text mining approach to the Syrian refugee crisis. Telemat. Inform. **35**(1), 136–147 (2018). https://doi.org/10.1016/j.tele.2017.10.006
9. Poria, S., Cambria, E., Winterstein, G., Huang, G.B.: Sentic patterns: dependency-based rules for concept-level sentiment analysis. Knowl.-Based Syst. **69**, 45–63 (2014). https://doi.org/10.1016/j.knosys.2014.05.005
10. Yaqub, U., Chun, S.A., Atluri, V., Vaidya, J.: Analysis of political discourse on Twitter in the context of the 2016 US presidential elections. Gov. Inf. Q. **34**(4), 613–626 (2017). https://doi.org/10.1016/j.giq.2017.11.001
11. Yoo, S., Song, J., Jeong, O.: Social media contents based sentiment analysis and prediction system. Expert Syst. Appl. **105**, 102–111 (2018). https://doi.org/10.1016/j.eswa.2018.03.055
12. Zeroual, I., Lakhouaja, A.: Data science in light of natural language processing: an overview. Procedia Comput. Sci. **127**, 82–91 (2018). https://doi.org/10.1016/j.procs.2018.01.101. Proceedings of the first international conference on intelligent computing in data sciences, ICDS 2017
13. Zhang, F., Fleyeh, H., Wang, X., Lu, M.: Construction site accident analysis using text mining and natural language processing techniques. Autom. Constr. **99**, 238–248 (2019). https://doi.org/10.1016/j.autcon.2018.12.016

A Classification of Grammar-Infused Templates for Ontology and Model Verbalisation

Zola Mahlaza[(⊠)] and C. Maria Keet

University of Cape Town, Cape Town, South Africa
{zmahlaza,mkeet}@cs.uct.ac.za

Abstract. Involving domain-experts in the development, maintenance, and use of knowledge organisation systems can be made easier through the introduction of easy-to-use interfaces that are based on natural language. Well resourced languages make use of natural language generation techniques to provide such interfaces. In particular, they often make use of templates combined with computational grammar rules to generate grammatically complex text. However, there is no model of pairing templates and computational grammar rules to ensure suitability for less-resourced languages. These languages require a modular design that ensures grammar detachability so as to allow grammar re-use across domains and applications. In this paper, we present a model and classification scheme for grammar-infused templates suited for less-resourced languages and classify existing systems that make use of them. We have found that of the 15 systems that pair templates and grammar rules, and their 11 distinct template types, 13 have support for detachable grammars.

1 Introduction

Involving domain experts in the construction, maintenance, and use of Knowledge Organisation Systems (KOS), such as ontologies, thesauri, and comprehensive metadata systems, requires end-user interaction with the system. A common approach to facilitate these interaction processes, is to verbalise—render in (pseudo-)natural language—the formally represented knowledge and to provide structured natural language for input to make the formalisation step easier. Examples of such systems include generating descriptions from ontologies in order to assist ontology experts in reaching a consensus about the scope and use of an ontology [31] and generating museum artefacts descriptions [1]. Such tools are developed mostly for English, but also other languages, such as Greek [1], Latvian [15], and isiZulu [19]. Technologically, this is typically achieved by using a Controlled Natural Language (CNL) or, more comprehensively, with Natural Language Generation (NLG) techniques [12,28] that predominantly choose a template-based approach. For instance, one could have an AGROVOC [26] template ... is used to make ..., where a domain expert could add, say, 'maize' and the

© Springer Nature Switzerland AG 2019
E. Garoufallou et al. (Eds.): MTSR 2019, CCIS 1057, pp. 64–76, 2019.
https://doi.org/10.1007/978-3-030-36599-8_6

drink 'chicha' or food 'mieliepap' in the open slots, respectively. This becomes a bit more involved with subsumption or broader-than relations, as then there are two template options, ... is a ... and ... is an ..., and thus needs a rule to select the correct template, being checking whether the first sound of the broader concept is a vowel sound or not. It faces increasing challenges—for both CNLs and NLG—with grammatically richer languages. For instance, an object property like *arbeitet für* 'works for' in some organisation ontology requires knowledge of the gender of the object so as to generate the correct article, and verb conjugation in most Bantu languages require the noun class of the subject to fire a rule to generate the verb in the sentence [8][1]. This so-called *surface realisation* step in generating textual descriptions thus may require multiple additional grammar rules to varying degrees so as to generate correct sentences. There are 'template-based' systems that address these limitations for well-resourced languages by combining templates with natural language Computational Grammar Rules (CGRs) [32]. However, most languages are not well-resourced. Therefore, the few grammar rules that are being, or have been, computerised for Less-Resourced Languages (LRLs) ideally should be reusable for other systems so as to reduce development efforts; e.g., the isiZulu grammar rules for ontology verbalisation [19] were reused for online language learning exercises [14]. This requires that template-based systems have a modular design in some way with detachable grammar rules that have no 'tactical generation' [13] function. To the best of our knowledge, this has not been assessed and categorised systematically. If known, however, it would provide insights that can assist with the design and deployment of multilingual CNLs and NLG for a broader range of languages spoken in the world.

We aim to address this gap by developing a model for pairing templates and natural language CGRs in different ways, which led to 7 different types of CNL or NLG systems that pair templates with CGRs. We analysed 41 previously published tools, identified a subset of 15 out of the 41 tools as making use of templates with CGRs, and classified the 15 tools into the different ways of pairing CGRs and templates. A majority, 8 out of 15, of the classified systems have support for languages other than English. This classification is a step toward simplifying the development of such grammar-enhanced template systems for LRLs.

The remainder of this paper is structured as follows: Sect. 2 presents the related work, Sect. 3 focuses of the developed the model of pairing templates and CGRs, Sect. 4 focuses on the classification of existing CNL and NLG systems, Sect. 6 presents the discussion, and Sect. 7 concludes the paper.

---

[1] e.g., when a person 'eats' something, it is *udla* in isiZulu (one of the 11 official languages of South Africa), but when a giraffe—a noun in a different noun class from person—eats something, then it is *idla*.

2   Related Work

Contemporary comparisons of surface realisation methods often feature hand-coded templates, hand-coded grammars, and statistical methods [12]. Substantial information is available pertaining to the appropriate conditions for which each of the methods can be used. For instance, templates are suitable "[w]hen application domains are small and variation is expected to be minimal, [and] realisation is a relatively easy task" [12, pg80], hand-coded grammars for "general-purpose, [and] domain-independent realisation systems" [12, pg80] where it is possible to provide "very detailed input" [12, pg80], and statical methods for when large corpora is available [12, pg81].

There are two types of templates, namely, the fill-in-the-slot templates [27] and the templates that make use of CGRs [32]. Templates of the first kind only have fixed words (including punctuation) and slots. An example is the template ... is a kind of ... for verbalising a simple super-class relation between two classes in an ontology so that when it is used to verbalise <*Benign hypertensive renal disease*> *SubClassOf* <*Hypertensive renal disease*>, we obtain Benign hypertensive renal disease is a kind of hypertensive renal disease [22]. The kind of values that can be inserted into the slots may differ based on the application; e.g. medical concepts [22] or soccer match information [33]. Despite their simplicity, these templates are used in a variety of applications including multilingual conceptual data model and application ontology verbalisation [16], tailored soccer summaries [33], etc. Templates of the second kind have CGRs that bestow them the ability to offer linguistic flexibility without necessarily having to build a complete grammar-based realiser like FUF/SURGE, MUMBLE, or RealPro [12, pg80]. For instance, syntax templates [32] introduce variation by attaching a syntax tree to each template. We will henceforth refer to templates of the second kind as *grammar-infused templates*.

To the best of our knowledge, there is no classification scheme that can be used to differentiate the systems that use templates. There only exists a classification of CNLs, named PENS, that may be used for the languages generated by the systems [21], which is based on four features of CNLs, namely: precision, expressiveness, naturalness, and simplicity. While PENS can be used to categorise the language generated by an ontology verbaliser, it is not suitable for differentiating the systems since it does not provide information pertaining to how templates and CGRs can be paired. A classification of the grammar-infused templates, as opposed to their resulting CNL, is important on its own because it can help when choosing an appropriate CNL or NLG system in cases where a modular design may be a priority.

A new method of differentiating NLG systems is required because the "in-depth vs. shallow generation" [6] differentiation is also insufficient for such as task. While it may be useful for a classification system whose sole purpose is to identify which grammar-infused template is suitable for small applications due to its "cost factor" [6], it is not informative regarding the grammar's detachability. We illustrate this using TEMSIS [6] and RoundTrip Ontology Authoring (ROA) [11]. While TEMSIS and ROA belong to the same class of shallow generators, they exhibit differences regarding grammar detachability. ROA's templates are designed to depend on an external grammar engine, SimpleNLG [13], for generating the third person singular forms of some words. On the other hand, TEMSIS's templates and associated CGRs are not separable because the deletion of the templates results in the deletion of the rules.

A new classification scheme that is based on the relationships between the templates and the natural language's CGRs and the detachability of the CGRs is required since existing schemes are insufficient. In the next section, we introduce two relationships for pairing templates templates with CGRs and the types of templates with CGRs that arise based on those relationships.

3   Pairing Templates and Grammar Rules

A pairing of CGR sets and templates to ensure suitability for LRLs exhibits two features:

(1) *detachability*: a modular design that facilitates grammar re-use across domains.
(2) *scaffolding*: the possibility to encode CGRs within the underlying templates since the existing grammar engines in some languages may be limited if they even exist.

The model is sketched graphically in Fig. 1. In this model, the CGR sets can be paired with the templates through two kinds of relationships: embedding and attachment where the latter can be compulsory or partial. The differentiation between partial and compulsory attachment allows one to specify that certain grammar rules must necessarily accompany a template (e.g. syntax trees in syntax templates [32]) or that certain grammar rules are compulsory only to a subset of the templates (e.g. noun pluralisation in patterns [8]).

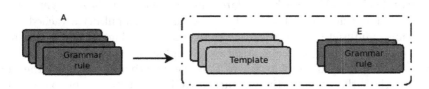

Fig. 1. Grammar-infused templates where templates are paired with CGR sets through two kinds of relationships; attachment and embedding. Attachment is illustrated through a directed arrow and embedding through a box whose border is a dotted line. The attached set is labelled with A and the embedded set is labelled with E.

In order to define embedding and the two kinds of attachment, we first introduce our definition of a natural language's grammar and its segmentation. Let a natural language grammar, denoted by G, be the set consisting of operations $O(W, \theta)$ whose arguments are words, W, and their features θ. The grammar can be segmented into portions using F, an ordered set of boolean predicate functions, $f : G \times G \rightarrow \{0, 1\}$ of any arbitrary size. The segmentation, and its subsets, govern the membership of operations to the grammar and its subsets. In particular, an operation's membership to the subsets labelled A and E in Fig. 1 is determined by two different subsets of F.

Embedding exists between templates and a CGR set if and only if the CGR set ceases to exist when the templates are destroyed. This relationship refers to the tight coupling of a small portion of grammar functions with the templates. Attachment exists between templates and CGR sets if the grammar rule sets continue to exist even after the deletion of the templates. A CGR set is compulsorily attached if every template must use at least one rule from it. A CGR set is partially attached if not all templates must use rules from it.

Examples of the embedding and two attachment relationships can be seen in the isiZulu verbaliser [20] and GoalGetter [32]. Embedding and partial attachment can be observed in the isiZulu verbaliser and compulsory attachment in GoalGetter. The isiZulu verbaliser's grammar-infused templates, the so-called patterns, responsible for verbalising subsumption and universal quantification use a separate noun pluralisation module. However since other grammar-infused templates from within the same verbaliser, such as those for existential quantification, do not make use of rules from that module, we can conclude that the noun pluralisation rules are partially attached. Embedding can be seen in how the verbaliser encodes agreement between words. IsiZulu requires quantifiers, verbs, and other parts of speech to be in agreement with their governing noun through one or two morphemes. The isiZulu verbaliser encodes the agreement explicitly within each pattern such that the deletion of pattern will result in the loss of that agreement rule hence we say that such rules are embedded. GoalGetter's syntax templates are defined as the tuple $\sigma = (S, E, C, T)$ "where S is a **syntax tree** (typically for a sentence) with open slots in it, E is a set of links to additional syntactic structures (typically NPs and PPs) which may be substituted in the gaps of S,C is a condition on the applicability of σ, and T is a set of **topics**" [32, pg18]. Each template must, by definition, have a syntax tree hence we can conclude that the set of syntax rules is compulsory attached.

Grammar-infused templates can be categorised into different kinds of families. In order to explain how categorisation is conducted, let $T_e = (T_b, A_p, A_c, E)$ be an grammar-infused template where T_b is the underlying basic fill-in-the-slot template, A_p is the set of partially attached CGRs, A_c is the set of compulsory attached CGRs, and E is the set of embedded CGRs. There are seven families of grammar-infused templates to which a set containing grammar-infused templates, T_e, can belong and they are shown in Fig. 2.

In the figure, each area denotes the pairing or lack thereof of two or three of the relationships; embedding, partial attachment, and compulsory attachment. In particular, a set of grammar-infused templates belong to one of the following families if all its grammar-infused templates meet the following criteria:

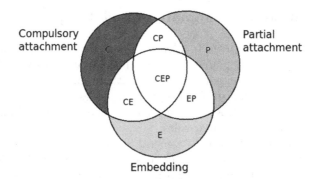

Embedding

Fig. 2. Seven different types of grammar-infused templates. The primary relations (and their abbreviations) that are used to define the family types are P = partial attachment, C = compulsory attachment, and E = Embedding. CP, CE, EP, and CEP are combinations of the primary three relations.

(1) *P* family: there is a set of CGRs that is attached to a subset of the templates, no set of CGR attached to all the templates, and no CGRs are embedded in the templates (i.e. $A_c = E = \emptyset$ and $A_p \neq \emptyset$ where $\emptyset$ denotes the empty set.)

(2) *C* family: there is a set of CGRs attached to all the templates, no set of CGRs attached only to a subset of the templates, and no CGRs are embedded in the templates (i.e. $A_p = E = \emptyset$ and $A_c \neq \emptyset$.)

(3) *E* family: there is a set of CGRs embedded in the templates, and no set of CGRs is attached to all or some of the templates (i.e. $A_c = A_p = \emptyset$ and $E \neq \emptyset$.)

(4) *CP* family: there is a set of CGRs that is attached to a subset of the templates and another set of CGRs attached to all the templates, but no CGRs are embedded in the templates (i.e. $A_c \neq \emptyset$ and $A_p \neq \emptyset$ and $E = \emptyset$.)

(5) *CE* family: there is a set of CGRs that is attached to all templates and another set of CGRs is embedded in the templates, but no CGRs are attached to a subset of the templates (i.e. $A_c \neq \emptyset$ and $E \neq \emptyset$ and $A_p = \emptyset$.)

(6) *EP* family: there is a set of CGRs embedded in the templates and a set of CGRs that is attached to a subset of the templates, but no set of CGRs that is attached to all the templates (i.e. $A_p \neq \emptyset$ and $E \neq \emptyset$ and $A_c = \emptyset$.)

(7) *CEP* family: family: there is a set of CGRs embedded in the templates, a set of CGRs that is attached to a subset of the templates, and another set of CGRs is attached to all the templates (i.e. $A_c \neq \emptyset$, $A_p \neq \emptyset$ and $E \neq \emptyset$.)

In order to illustrate a formalism's membership to one of the above families, we return to the running example of GoalGetter. Let us suppose that GoalGetter's syntax templates do not have any other rules besides the syntax trees. Then we can conclude that the formalism belongs to C family since it has compulsory attached rules but no embedded or partially attached rules.

4   Classification of Grammar-Infused Templates

The aim of the classification is to identify the different ways templates and natural language CGRs are paired in the template formalisms used by various NLG tools. The classification will provide us with an understanding of the conditions in which each formalism is used. This improves the task of selecting an appropriate existing CNL/NLG system for text generation based on the one's requirements or available grammar rules.

We collected a set of 41 tools: 7 general linguistic realisers [13], 5 systems from [32], and 29 systems and verbalisers based on both a recent review [4] and a search for systems with support for a language other than English explicitly. Each of the 41 tools was annotated with either:

(1) *templates*: systems that make use of traditional templates, be this for a single template per unit of information or offering a selection among equivalent alternates for variation purposes only;
(2) *grammar*: these systems use full fledged grammars and essentially manage the surface realisation by availing of the grammar only, rather than also a template to constrain the sentence;
(3) *statistical methods*: systems that generate text using probabilistic grammars learned from corpora and generators that make use of statistical models to rank the output of a grammar that is either hand-coded or learned from corpora.
(4) *template + grammar*: those systems that use 'grammar-infused templates', in some configuration to enhance the grammatical correctness of the generated sentences. These must not make use of statistical methods.
(5) *other*: systems that do not fall into any of the previous categories (which may be because insufficient information was presented in the documentation).

There were 9 systems annotated with *templates*, 6 *grammar*, 3 *statistical methods*, 15 *templates + grammar*, and 8 with *other*. The systems that do not belong to the *template + grammar* group were filtered out as out-of-scope, and the remaining 15 systems were categorised into their respective grammar-infused template family using the model introduced in Sect. 3. The list of all the 41 considered NLG tools is available as supplementary material at https://github. com/AdeebNqo/grammarinfusedtemplates.

The resulting classification of the formalisms from the systems is given in Table 1. We illustrate the classification process into the various families with a selection of the systems.

Davis et al.'s [10] Grammatical Framework (GF) verbaliser generates multilingual text from models of business processes. Its syntax templates have two layers, namely, the abstract and concrete. The abstract segment is application specific and language independent while the concrete segment is language specific. In particular, the concrete segment attaches a syntax tree to the basic text through GF's resource grammar. However, the function for creating such trees persists in GF even when Davis et al.'s templates are removed. Its set of compulsory rules is not empty as its made up of the syntax trees. Furthermore,

Table 1. Classification of grammar-infused templates for nine verbalisers, three NLG systems, and three realisers that have support for grammar-infused templates.

System/tool	Family	Language(s)	Formalism
Verbalisers			
Davis et al. [10]	C	English, Dutch	GF syntax template
Stevens et al. [31]	C	English	Definite Clause Grammar (DCG) template
Kaljurand [17]	C	English	DCG template
Lim and Halpin [23]	P	Malay, Mandarin	Logic pattern
Androutsopoulos et al. [1]	EC	English, Greek	Sentence plan
Gruzitis et al. [15]	EC	Latvian	GF syntax templates with synonymy
Davis et al. [11]	EP	English	XML template
Byamugisha et al. [7]	EP	Runyankore	Pattern
Keet et al. [20]	EP	IsiZulu	Pattern
NLG systems			
Stenzhorn [30]	EP	English, German, French, Italian, Russian, Bulgarian, Turkish	XML template
van Deemter [32]	EP	English, Dutch, German	Syntax template
Wilcock [34]	EP	–	Syntax template
Surface realisers			
McRoy et al. [25]	E	–	Template Specification Language (TSL)
Busemann [5]	E	–	Template Generation Language (TGL)
Bateman [2]	All[a]	Greek, English, German, Dutch, French, Japanese, Spanish	Extended Sentence Plan Language (SPL)

[a]grammar-infused templates created using the KPML environment may belong to any of the seven families.

since there are no other rules associated with the templates, we categorise the formalism as belonging to the C family (Compulsory attachment).

Androutsopoulos et al.'s [1] NaturalOWL verbaliser generates bilingual museum artefact descriptions from an ontology. NaturalOWL's sentence plans are defined such that they "completely specify the surface (final) form of each sentence" [1, p699]. A plan is a sequence of slots where each slot is filled either by verbs, nouns, or adjectives from its detailed lexicon. The lexicon items are tables that encode all their inflectional forms. NaturalOWL's set of embedded functions is not empty as it is made up of the rules specifying agreement between lexical items. NaturalOWL's inflection rules are not specified in the sentence plan. They are tightly coupled with the external lexicon and not provided through an actual grammar. Nonetheless, we can conclude that its set of compulsory attached rules is not empty because they are provided via the lexicon. Since it does not have any other CGRs besides those, we categorise it as belonging to the EC family.

Davis et al.'s [11] ROA verbaliser generates English text from an ontology. The ROA verbaliser's templates are made up of three parts, namely, the *in*, *out*, and *ignoreIf* elements. The *in* element specifies the template's input RDF triple. The *out* specifies the singular and plural form of the underlying traditional template. Each form of the traditional template makes use of items from the *in* element and they are annotated with a value for grammatical number. The *ignoreIf* element specifies that a template should be ignored if its conditions are met. The set of its embedded functions is not empty as it contains the rules for specifying the singular/plural forms of the phrases in the underlying template. The set of partially attached rules is also not empty as it contains SimpleNLG's [13] rules creating the third person singular inflection. Since the templates do not have any additional rules, we categorise the tool as being from the EP family.

Table 1 shows that there are three GF-based systems [10,15,29] that differ in how they pair templates with CGRs. In particular, one system's templates are either not grammar-infused [29] and the other two system's templates belong to different families [10,15].

5   Use Case: Model Verbalisation in IsiZulu

We illustrate the usefulness of the classification within the context of creating a model for a lexicon to be used for an ontology thereby support multilingual access to Semantic Web data (e.g. [3,24]). In particular, we show the use of the classification from Sect. 4 when verbalising the model to improve the participation of domain experts in the validation of the model.

IsiZulu does not have ontology lexicalisation support, which is mainly due to its complex grammar that RDFS's *label* and *comment* properties, and even declarative modes such as *lemon* [24], do not cater for sufficiently [9]. The Bantu Language Model (BLM) [3] that has been created to support isiXhosa may be suitable for isiZulu since the two languages are mutually intelligible and exhibit grammatical similarities. However, BLM's suitability for isiZulu has not been tested and the participation of domain experts in testing it may be impeded by their inability to understand the formal language in which the model is codified. This can be addressed through the verbalisation of the model in isiZulu using grammar-infused templates. Here, our proposed classification scheme can be used to choose an appropriate grammar-infused template language or tool.

We have identified two use cases where there are different requirements regarding grammar availability and re-use, and we illustrate how to choose a suitable template language or tool to verbalise the model under development in each case. *Case 1*: when CGR re-use is not a priority and few templates are sufficient, then a template approach that has the ability to embed CGRs (E/CE/EP/CEP families) may be suitable for use as-is or as a foundation for building an NLG tool. *Case 2*: when all CGRs must be reusable and the available noun pluralisation and verb conjugation rules [18,19] are sufficient, then a template approach that has the ability to attach CGRs—C/P/CP/CE/EP/CEP families—is appropriate. However, practically, since the only existing grammar-infused template formalism with support for isiZulu (i.e., patterns [20]) belongs to the EP family, then we conclude that all cases can be supported albeit in a limited manner for case 1. Support for case 1 is limited because those patterns [20] can only embed morphological agreement rules.

In summary, when building a natural language text generator and there are requirements regarding the availability and re-usability of the CGRs, then the classification could be useful in choosing an appropriate template formalism.

6   Discussion

We have developed the first classification scheme of grammar-infused templates. Our classification of existing NLG tools shows that most grammar-infused templates have detachable grammars, hence, support grammar re-use in some form. Nonetheless, we have observed that the technology used to create the templates does not guarantee a form of grammar-infusion.

The use of a complex grammar formalism to encode templates that are not grammar-infused can be observed by assessing the differences between the three verbalisers that make use of templates encoded in GF [10,15,29]. In the concrete layer, Sanby et al. [29] create a GF application grammar such that the concrete syntax is only responsible for inserting the values of the slots in the appropriate template. Essentially, their concrete 'grammar' is a basic fill-in-the-slot template despite using GF, as the rules in the Afrikaans resource grammar were deemed not usable. In contrast, Davis et al. [10] and Gruzitis et al. [15] make use of GF's resource grammar library thereby attaching syntax trees to their templates. This demonstrates that the technology used for encoding templates is not a reliable feature for classifying grammar-infused templates, but that our classification can bring afore.

The tools that we considered for the classification proposed are general purpose surface realisers, NLG systems, and verbalisers. There are systems that were not included due to insufficient information. There are CNLs reviewed by Safwat and Davis [28] that sound relevant by name, but they focus on the step of ontology authoring rather than verbalisation, that were not included because of the nine CNLs, five of them either "[do] not focus on bidirectionality", "sentences may look unnatural", or the CNL's sentences are "less readable than pure natural language" [28]. The remaining four systems do not present sufficient information pertaining to how they verbalise a conceptual data model or ontology. In particular, they either focus solely on document authoring and do not specify how they might be used to generate text or they make use of template-like language elements for authoring ontologies but it is unclear whether those same elements are used as-is for verbalisation. The only authoring and verbalisation system that is included in the scheme is ROA since its verbalisation procedure is well documented [11]. This lack of sufficient technical information makes it a challenge for one to decide whether such systems might be appropriate to re-use or as a base for new systems. Conversely, the classification scheme we developed could contribute to clarifying such matters for future tools, by means of succinctly specifying the nature of a system's template and CGR pairing thereby assist prospective re-use or repurposing.

7 Conclusions

We have developed a model of pairing templates with natural language CGRs, used it to develop a classification scheme where an grammar-infused template formalism may belong to one of 7 families, and classified existing grammar-infused templates. Most existing grammar-infused templates belong to the C/P/CE/EP families; hence support detachable CGRs.

We are currently working on devising modular architectures for NLG systems that have the capability to also process agglutinative languages.

References

1. Androutsopoulos, I., Lampouras, G., Galanis, D.: Generating natural language descriptions from OWL ontologies: the NaturalOWL system. J. Artif. Intell. Res. **48**, 671–715 (2013)
2. Bateman, J.A.: Enabling technology for multilingual natural language generation: the KPML development environment. Nat. Lang. Eng. **3**(1), 15–55 (1997)
3. Bosch, S.E., Eckart, T., Klimek, B., Goldhahn, D., Quasthoff, U.: Preparation and usage of Xhosa lexicographical data for a multilingual, federated environment. In: Proceedings of LREC 2018, Miyazaki, Japan, 7–12 May 2018 (2018)
4. Bouayad-Agha, N., Casamayor, G., Wanner, L.: Natural language generation in the context of the semantic web. Semant. Web **5**(6), 493–513 (2014)
5. Busemann, S.: Best-first surface realization. arXiv e-prints cmp-lg/9605010, May 1996
6. Busemann, S., Horacek, H.: A flexible shallow approach to text generation. In: Proceedings of INLG 1998, Ontario, Canada, 5–7 August 1998 (1998)
7. Byamugisha, J., Keet, C.M., DeRenzi, B.: Bootstrapping a Runyankore CNL from an isiZulu CNL. In: Davis, B., Pace, G.J.J., Wyner, A. (eds.) CNL 2016. LNCS (LNAI), vol. 9767, pp. 25–36. Springer, Cham (2016). https://doi.org/10.1007/978-3-319-41498-0_3
8. Byamugisha, J., Keet, C.M., Khumalo, L.: Pluralising nouns in isiZulu and related languages. In: Gelbukh, A. (ed.) CICLing 2016. LNCS, vol. 9623, pp. 271–283. Springer, Cham (2018). https://doi.org/10.1007/978-3-319-75477-2_18
9. Chavula, C., Keet, C.M.: Is *lemon* sufficient for building multilingual ontologies for Bantu languages? In: Proceedings of OWLED 2014, Riva Del Garda, Italy, 17–18 October 2014, pp. 61–72 (2014)

10. Davis, B., Enache, R., van Grondelle, J., Pretorius, L.: Multilingual verbalisation of modular ontologies using GF and *lemon*. In: Kuhn, T., Fuchs, N.E. (eds.) CNL 2012. LNCS (LNAI), vol. 7427, pp. 167–184. Springer, Heidelberg (2012). https://doi.org/10.1007/978-3-642-32612-7_12

11. Davis, B., et al.: RoundTrip ontology authoring. In: Sheth, A., et al. (eds.) ISWC 2008. LNCS, vol. 5318, pp. 50–65. Springer, Heidelberg (2008). https://doi.org/10.1007/978-3-540-88564-1_4

12. Gatt, A., Krahmer, E.: Survey of the state of the art in natural language generation: core tasks, applications and evaluation. J. Artif. Intell. Res. **61**, 65–170 (2018)

13. Gatt, A., Reiter, E.: SimpleNLG: a realisation engine for practical applications. In: ENLG 2009 - Proceedings of the 12th ENLG, Athens, Greece, 30–31 March 2009, pp. 90–93 (2009)

14. Gilbert, N., Keet, C.M.: Automating question generation and marking of language learning exercises for isiZulu. In: Proceedings of CNL 2018, Maynooth, Co., Kildare, Ireland, 27–28 August 2018, pp. 31–40 (2018)

15. Gruzitis, N., Nespore, G., Saulite, B.: Verbalizing ontologies in controlled Baltic languages. In: Human Language Technologies - The Baltic Perspective - Proceedings of the Fourth International Conference Baltic HLT 2010, Riga, Latvia, 7–8 October 2010, pp. 187–194 (2010)

16. Jarrar, M., Keet, C.M., Dongilli, P.: Multilingual verbalization of ORM conceptual models and axiomatized ontologies. Technical report, Starlab, Vrije Universiteit Brussel, Belgium, February 2006

17. Kaljurand, K.: Attempto controlled English as a semantic web language. Ph.D. thesis, Faculty of Mathematics and Computer Science, University of Tartu (2007)

18. Keet, C.M., Khumalo, L.: Grammar rules for the isiZulu complex verb. South. Afr. Linguist. Appl. Lang. Stud. **35**(2), 183–200 (2017)

19. Keet, C.M., Khumalo, L.: Toward a knowledge-to-text controlled natural language of isiZulu. Lang. Resour. Eval. **51**(1), 131–157 (2017)

20. Keet, C.M., Xakaza, M., Khumalo, L.: Verbalising OWL ontologies in IsiZulu with Python. In: Blomqvist, E., Hose, K., Paulheim, H., Ławrynowicz, A., Ciravegna, F., Hartig, O. (eds.) ESWC 2017. LNCS, vol. 10577, pp. 59–64. Springer, Cham (2017). https://doi.org/10.1007/978-3-319-70407-4_12

21. Kuhn, T.: A survey and classification of controlled natural languages. Comput. Linguist. **40**(1), 121–170 (2014)

22. Liang, S.F., Scott, D., Stevens, R., Rector, A.: Unlocking medical ontologies for non-ontology experts. In: Proceedings of BioNLP 2011 Workshop, Stroudsburg, PA, USA, pp. 174–181 (2011)

23. Lim, S.H., Halpin, T.A.: Automated verbalization of ORM models in Malay and Mandarin. IJISMD **7**(4), 1–16 (2016)

24. McCrae, J.P., Bosque-Gil, J., Gracia, J., Buitelaar, P., Cimiano, P.: The Ontolex-Lemon model: development and applications. In: Proceedings of eLex 2017, Leiden, The Netherlands, 19–21 September 2017, pp. 19–21 (2017)

25. McRoy, S.W., Channarukul, S., Ali, S.S.: YAG: a template-based generator for real-time systems. In: Proceedings of INLG 2000, Stroudsburg, PA, USA, pp. 264–267 (2000)

26. Rajbhandari, S., Keizer, J.: The AGROVOC concept scheme - a walkthrough. J. Integr. Agric. **11**(5), 694–699 (2012)

27. Reiter, E.: NLG vs. templates. CoRR cmp-lg/9504013 (1995). http://arxiv.org/abs/cmp-lg/9504013

28. Safwat, H., Davis, B.: CNLs for the semantic web: a state of the art. Lang. Resour. Eval. **51**(1), 191–220 (2017)

29. Sanby, L., Todd, I., Keet, C.M.: Comparing the template-based approach to GF: the case of Afrikaans. In: Proceedings of WebNLG 2016, Edinburgh, UK, 6 September 2016, pp. 50–53 (2016)
30. Stenzhorn, H.: Xtragen - a natural language generation system using XML and Java-technologies. In: Proceedings of NLPXML@COLING 2002, Taipei, Taiwan, 24 August–1 September 2002 (2002)
31. Stevens, R., Malone, J., Williams, S., Power, R., Third, A.: Automating generation of textual class definitions from OWL to English. J. Biomed. Semant. 2(S–2), S5 (2011)
32. van Deemter, K., Theune, M., Krahmer, E.: Real versus template-based natural language generation: a false opposition? Comput. Linguist. 31(1), 15–24 (2005)
33. van der Lee, C., Krahmer, E., Wubben, S.: PASS: a Dutch data-to-text system for soccer, targeted towards specific audiences. In: Proceedings of INLG 2017, Santiago de Compostela, Spain, 4–7 September 2017, pp. 95–104 (2017)
34. Wilcock, G.: Pipelines, templates and transformations: XML for natural language generation. In: Proceedings of NLPXML@NLPRS 2001, Hitotsubashi Memorial Hall, National Center of Sciences, Tokyo, Japan, 27–30 November 2001 (2001)

IoT Data Validation Using Spatial and Temporal Correlations

Fabio Sartori$^{(\boxtimes)}$, Riccardo Melen, and Fabio Giudici

Department of Informatics, Systems and Communication,
University of Milano-Bicocca, viale Sarca 336/14, 20126 Milan, Italy
fabio.sartori@unimib.it

Abstract. The Internet of Things (IoT) is the extension of Internet connectivity to physical devices and everyday objects. These devices composed by sensors, software and network connectivity can acquire, store and exchange data among them over the Internet. One of the main tasks of an IoT system consists in the continuous exchange of data and information of various kinds. The correctness of the value produced by the sensor is a crucial factor for the operation and reliability of the entire IoT system. This paper presents a centralized data validation algorithm which attempts to use *spatial* and *temporal* correlations to compensate for error on the data.

Keywords: Internet of Things · Wireless sensor networks · Data validation · Information fusion · Spatial and temporal correlation · Wireless sensor networks · kNN algorithm · Wearable devices

1 Introduction

One of the main tasks of an IoT system consists in the continuous exchange of data among sensors. A sensor is a device, module, or subsystem that detects some type of input from the physical environment and sends information to other electronics components. The output is generally a signal that is converted into human readable syntax and transmitted electronically over a network for future processing. The correctness of the values produced by each sensor is a crucial factor for the operation and reliability of the entire IoT system.

The sensors are susceptible to the environment in which they work: if such environment is not optimal their reliability decreases considerably, generating incorrect data (or faulty data). Therefore, the data produced by the sensors must be cleaned to obtain better results. A *data validation* procedure can be applied to sensor data to mitigate data defects and to improve system reliability.

There are several architectures for implementing data validation and data fault detection processes. These strategies differ from each other in terms of functional distribution and of the logical object they work on. It's possible to identify three different strategies: *centralized strategy*; *distributed strategy*; *hybrid strategy*.

All them apply data validation algorithms based on statistical, clustering, nearest neighbor, spectral decomposition approaches. This paper presents a centralized data validation algorithm which attempts to use *spatial* and *temporal* correlations to

© Springer Nature Switzerland AG 2019
E. Garoufallou et al. (Eds.): MTSR 2019, CCIS 1057, pp. 77–89, 2019.
https://doi.org/10.1007/978-3-030-36599-8_7

compensate for errors on the data. The proposed data validation process is based on the general idea that: *sensor faults are probable to be spatially unrelated while event measurements are likely to be spatially correlated* [1].

The algorithm tries to estimate the correct value when a missing data or an outlier error occurs in a regular series of measurements. To estimate the correct data as accurately as possible, the algorithm considers not only the temporal correlation of sensor data, but also the spatial correlation between nearby sensors.

The algorithm was tested using a very substantial dataset consisting of about 2.3 million measurements taken from 56 different sensors distributed in a laboratory. The tests carried out support the hypothesis that the measurements made by nearby sensors are correlated, while the failures that a sensor may have do not affect the nearby sensors. The algorithm is able to predict any missing measurements that is found within the data stream generated by the sensor or correct a possible wrong measurement produced by a sensor.

The rest of the paper is organized as follows: Sect. 2 briefly reviews the state of the art about data validation in the IoT field; Sect. 3 describes the proposed algorithm; Sect. 4 presents a case study and points out the results obtained; finally, conclusions and directions for future research are highlighted in Sect. 5.

2 Related Work

The design of an anomaly detection system is composed of two main stages: *design, development and calibration of the anomaly detection methods ensemble*; *its evaluation by the application to observed data streams*.

In the first phase we have two main approaches [2]. The first approach is based on the definition of threshold values. Threshold values represent the limit between valid and invalid data values and, if necessary, can be designed to change temporally. The second approach requires the modelling of expected anomaly signatures in a regular data series, together with the development of a classification algorithm that will determine the boundary between classes of regular and anomalous data.

Once a method is designed and developed the last step consists in providing a performance indicator. This step is difficult because anomaly detection method must provide results such as the estimation of missing values that cannot be verified by other methods or measurements and are usually not visually distinguishable, except for few major errors that can be readily identified by a human observer. There are two different approaches that can be used to overcome this problem: compare the new method/algorithm with existing ones, in order to *take advantage of the experience* and good knowledge about the methods and procedures used in anomaly detection and data preprocessing; *adjusting the selected anomaly detection methods* to the time series analyzed with already labelled anomalous data values. In the first approach the information produced by already well-tested methods or procedures is exploited in order to align the algorithm under test, while in the second one the algorithm is corrected by exploiting the known information present in the training set.

2.1 Data Validation Methods

According to [3], the data validation methods may be classified in several groups. The first group contains the *fault data detection* methods used during the data acquisition and processing phases to discover any incorrect values [4]. These methods, by analyzing some input values, can assign them a *valid*, *invalid* or *missing* label; simple test-based methods or physical/mathematical models are applied. The first subgroup includes various techniques such as local realistic range detection, physical range check, constant value detection, the tolerance band method and the signal's gradient test [5]. The other subgroup comprehends instead methods like extreme value using statistics, gross error detection, spatial consistency, data mining methods or the multivariate statistical test using PCA (Principal Component Analysis) [6].

To ensure the correct detection of anomalies, some methods can be run in parallel, but some have to be ordered in sequence to ensure the pre-processing effect for the following ones. According to [2], to get the best results it is necessary to apply different methods following a specific order: zero value detection, flat line detection, minimum and maximum values detection, minimum and maximum thresholds based on last values, statistical test that follow certain distributions, multivariate statistical test, ANNs (artificial neural networks), SVM (support vector machine), and classification and physical models.

The techniques in the second group, *data correction methods*, are applied to the incorrect values obtained during the data acquisition and processing steps [4].

The main approaches used by the data correction methods are:

- *Interpolation* = a method to identify new points in a cartesian plane using a set of known points. Examples of known points could be just the last measured value or all the previous series of measurements [7];
- *Smoothing* = consist in applying a filter function to acquire important patterns while ignoring noise or other non-useful phenomena. One example is the "moving average" algorithm which may be used to filter out the random noise and convert the data into a smooth curve that is relatively unbiased by outliers [5];
- *Data mining* = by exploiting the results of several data mining techniques, such as ANNs, it is possible to replace any faulty values [8];

The last of the three groups is composed of techniques or instruments that monitor the status of the sensors, the elapsed time after a maintenance session, the calibration of the measurement system and the consideration of uncertainty [4]. These techniques detect problems caused by the hardware components that make up the system or by the possible degeneration that may arise due to the system's working environment.

To improve the data validation process, *intelligent sensors* have been created that can perform data acquisition and validation. Such sensors take some predefined actions as part of their task or duty when a certain input occurs. Among these actions there are some procedures useful for the data validation process, for example: data compression, final compensation and digital information processing. According to many experts [9], intelligent sensor systems have a higher confidence level than systems built with normal sensors because they always use a functional validation process and a technology validation process [10].

The most sophisticated class of intelligent sensors is represented by SEVA (self-validating) sensors. These sensors take advantage of the internal processing for self-diagnostic, and employ digital communication to convey measurement and diagnostic data. For each measurement, a SEVA sensor generates a series of parameters that describe the quality of the measurement performed. The major parameters are: *Validated Measurement Value (VMV)*, that is the conventional measurement, or, in case of fault, an estimate of the correct value; *Validated Uncertainty (VU)*, that is the probably error of the VMV; *Measurement Value Status (MV Status)*: given the requirement to provide a measurement, even with a serious fault, the MV Status indicates the method by which the provided measurement has been calculated.

2.2 Data Validation for Wireless Sensor Network

The miniaturization of embedded computers and radio networking chips, led to the emergence in the early 2000s of *wireless sensor networks* (WSNn). WSNs are an embedded systems technology based on the cooperation of simple digital devices that collect information and possibly perform some actions [11].

A WSN is a network consisting of a set of nodes (called sensor nodes) with radio interconnections; each node runs concurrent and reactive programs that operate with severe memory and power constraints.

Those devices, being cheap and battery-powered, could be deployed in large areas to continuously monitor various physical environments or structures using a multitude of sensors. For example, WSNs were used to monitor agricultural crops for food-production [12], the structure of historical buildings like Torre Aquila in Italy [13], for military purposes [14] and healthcare [15].

Although early WSN deployments weren't connected to the internet, these systems influenced the IoT in many ways because this prolific research community gave birth to innovative ideas that shaped IoT technologies.

Sensor nodes are often distributed in natural and unpredictable environments, where human intervention for debugging or repairs is too expensive. To cope with this issue, it is necessary that the sensors can guarantee "exception-free" or unattended operations and above all that they are able to self-organize.

Losses and errors affecting sensor data decrease the efficiency of WSNs greatly. There are several techniques for validating data developed for WSN nodes. In addition to general purpose methods like statistical analysis, they exploit also the spatial information regarding the relative positioning of the network nodes, employing nearest neighbor algorithms, clustering and classification approaches.

The importance of the integration of spatial and temporal information has been stressed in [22], where a spatial-temporal ontology is employed to provide a semantic framework for data interpretation.

During a data validation process it is a good practice to execute a sequence of different data validation methods because often a single method is not sufficient to detect different types of errors. In the WSN infrastructures it is widely used the nearest neighbor approach, where different nodes of the network may perform the validation of the data collected for the neighborhood nodes [24]. The possibility of employing a network of fixed sensors to estimate background noise and improve the quality of all the measured data has been demonstrated in [21].

3 Our Approach

3.1 General Considerations

In many applications, the environment variables monitored by a collection of sensors, such as temperature and humidity, change continuously. When some data of a sensor node is missing, or it can be classified in one of the types of error described above (outlier, spike-fault, etc.), a naive method for estimating the missing data, based on the temporal correlation of sensor data, consists in using the correct data item whose collection time is closest to the fault to estimate.

However, this method works well only when the sensor data changes smoothly and the missing or the faulty data is placed in a short time period. In other cases, this method may cause large estimation errors. This is because the data measured by a sensor network may change sharply and irregularly, especially the data sensed in the natural environment, since too many uncertainty factors, such as environmental noise, will affect the variety of the data measured [16].

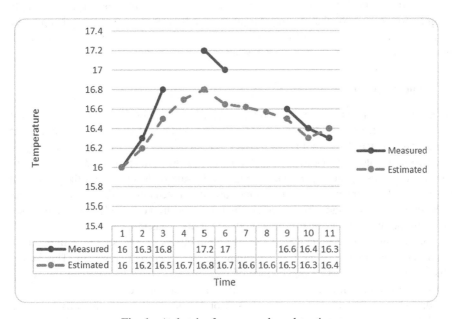

Fig. 1. A sketch of sensors values detection

Figure 1 represents a graph that highlights missing values in a time series. The blue series shows the temperature values read by an hypothetical sensor while the orange dotted line represents the estimated values.

As previously stated, the target of this paper is to present a centralized data validation algorithm in which the time domain estimation is combined with the approach based on the nearest neighbors.

The algorithm proposed tries to estimate the correct value when a missing data or an outlier error occurs in a regular series of measurements. It takes in consideration not only the temporal correlations, but also the spatial correlation of sensor data.

In general, it can be stated that the data detected by the sensor nodes whose positions are close together, are similar or have some well-defined relationship. Therefore, when a sensor provides a measurement affected by errors, it is possible to estimate the correct value from its neighboring nodes.

The algorithm presented here can be applied when the position of all sensors is known and when all the sensors do not change their position during their life cycle. Similar approaches have been proposed in [23] (where a-priori knowledge of effect of the sensor location is assumed) and more recently in [24].

The part of the proposed algorithm which deals with spatial vicinity relations is based on the k-nearest neighbor algorithm (kNN). kNN is one of many (supervised learning) algorithms used in data mining and machine learning; it is a classifier algorithm where the learning is based "how similar" is a data item from another one.

In kNN an object is classified by a plurality vote of its neighbors, with the object being assigned to the class most common among its k nearest neighbors. The parameter "k" is always a positive integer, typically small. If k = 1, then the object is simply assigned to the class of that nearest neighbor. The best choice of k depends upon the data; generally, larger values of k reduce the effect of the noise on the classification, but the parameter of choice for the class becomes more unstable [17].

3.2 The Algorithm

For each sensor, the proposed algorithm (see Fig. 2) calculates the distance from all the other sensors of the system and creates a cluster, composed of k sensors, taking the nearest ones. Once this initial phase is over, the algorithm processes, in chronological order, from the oldest to the most recent, all the measurements produced by the various sensors. The sensors are ordered according to a hierarchy dependent on the amount of new information carried by each one, therefore, if two sensors produce a measurement at the same time, the algorithm processes first the measurement produced by the sensor which in the more recent history has produced more measurements.

For each measurement analyzed, the algorithm inserts the measurement into a finite length buffer composed of the last measurements produced by that sensor. This buffer, which contains the most recent history of the sensor, is used to compare the sensor under examination with the other sensors that make up the cluster.

This phase of comparison between sensor histories allows to identify the relationships between sensors and to understand how much a sensor is related to another one. To do that, the algorithm uses the buffer containing the latest measurements for each sensor, to calculate the Pearson correlation coefficient between any two sensors (the possible missing data do not contribute to the calculation of the coefficient).

DATA VALIDATION ALGORITHM

1. read sensor configuration
2. group sensors in clusters of size k
3. **for all** time slices t **do**
4.   load all the measurements taken at t
5.   **for all** sensors s **do**
6.   **if** measurement is missing **then**
7.   search for the most strictly related sensor s^*
8.   **if** $PCC(s, s^*) > 0,3$ **then**
9.   estimate s value using s^*
10.   **else**
11.   estimate s value using linear regression
12.   **end if**
13.   **else**
14.   update $PCC(s, *)$ values
15.   **end if**
16.   add data point to history
17.   **end for**
18. **end for**

Fig. 2. The proposed algorithm.

The Pearson correlation coefficient (PCC) is a measure of the linear correlation between two different variables X and Y. The coefficient always assumes values between −1 and 1, in particular: $PCC > 0$: the two variables are directly correlated; $PCC = 0$: the two variables are uncorrelated; $PCC < 0$: the two variables are inversely correlated.

A further distinction can be made for direct correlation: $0 < PCC \le 0.3$: weak correlation; $0.3 < PCC \le 0.7$: moderate correlation; $PCC > 0.7$: strong correlation.

Once the Pearson Coefficient is calculated for a pair of sensors, the algorithm calculates the average of the last measurements on each buffer and compares them to each other. Comparing the two averages it is possible to establish how the correlation between the two sensors is reflected on average in their behaviors. The buffer containing the latest sensor measurements, as well as for calculating the Pearson coefficient, is also used to calculate the linear regression of the sensor. Linear regression is a valid approach to modelling the relationship between a scalar response (dependent variable) and one or more explanatory variables (independent variables). Like all forms of regression analysis, linear regression focuses on the conditional probability distribution of the response given the value of the predictors.

The algorithm, when identifying an outlier or a missing data on a particular sensor, tries to estimate the correct data. The estimation procedure for a missing or incorrect value of a particular sensor consists in searching, among the other sensors of the cluster, the sensor most strictly related to it (the one with the highest Pearson coefficient). Once the most correlated sensor has been identified, the algorithm uses the difference of two averages previously calculated to estimate the correct value. If the algorithm does not find any moderate or strongly correlated sensor inside the cluster, the estimation of the missing values is obtained using the linear regression formula previously calculated based on measurements made. Note that the PCC calculation performed again at each time step allows the algorithm to follow long-term variations of the sensor correlations (due for instance to some change in the physical environment).

4 Experiments and Results

The dataset used as a basis for the testing of this algorithm, contains data collected from 54 sensors deployed in the Intel Berkeley Research laboratory between February 28th and April 5th, 2004 [18]. The sensors were arranged in the laboratory according to the floorplan shown in Fig. 3. The dataset includes about 2.3 million readings collected from the sensors and stored in records according to the following schema: *Date*: the day on which measurement was taken; *Time*: the exact moment on which reading was taken; *Epoch*: monotonically increasing sequence number from each sensor; *Mote-Id*: the unique identifier of the sensor; *Temperature*: temperature measured in Celsius; *Humidity*: temperature corrected relative humidity, ranging from 0–100%; *Light*: light value measured in Lux; *Voltage*: the sensor battery expressed in volt, ranging from 2 V to 3 V.

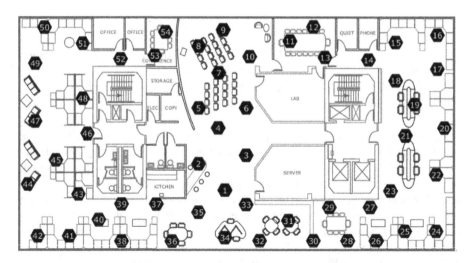

Fig. 3. Plan of the Intel Berkeley Research Laboratory

The dataset used for this experiment has been used in many other analytical studies on sensor data, like e.g. [19]. In order to exploit the spatial correlations, the algorithm identifies, among the sensors present in the cluster, the sensor with the greater Pearson coefficient having a real measurement in the time interval of the missing value or of the failure. Once the sensor most related to it is identified, it uses information from their stories to predict the new value. If no sensor correlated (with a Pearson correlation coefficient larger than 0,3) with the sensor in defect was found within the cluster sensors, then the algorithm uses the temporal correlation and, more in detail, uses linear regression of the sensor history in order to forecast the data. Once the measurement is predicted, the algorithm appends this to the sensor history by tagging the measurement with a particular flag indicating that a measurement was predicted and should not be counted for the purpose of calculating the sensor correlation with its nearby sensors.

A csv file is then created to store persistently the measurements/predictions of each sensor, with the following fields: DATETIME, i.e. the date and time of the measurement; EMPERATURE, i.e. the temperature value actually measured by the sensor; TEMPERATURE_CALCULATED, i.e. the predicted temperature value.

Figure 4 shows an example, with the values stored for sensor 25 in the dataset: red bullets are real measurements, while the other points are estimated. During the testing phase, a training set of 500 elements was analyzed (on average 10 measurement for sensor) and only one worker thread processed the various measurements. To process 500 measurements and create the related graphs, the application took about 9 s. The machine used to make these tests employs an Intel Core i7 processor, 8 GB of RAM DDR3 and a 256 GB SSD. At the end of the analysis of 500 measurements, only one value was classified as an outlier by the algorithm and about 150 missing values were found in the various sensor data streams. Analyzing the log file it was possible to deduce that about 70 values were predicted using the spatial correlations between sensors of the same cluster, while the remaining missing values were obtained using the linear regression. Moreover, it was observed how the spatial correlation is used in particular on the missing values present at the end of the data frame.

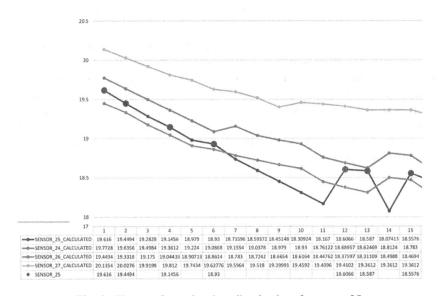

	1	2	3	4	5	6	7	8	9	10	11	12	13	14	15
SENSOR_25_CALCULATED	19.616	19.4494	19.2828	19.1456	18.979	18.93	18.73596	18.59372	18.45148	18.30924	18.167	18.6066	18.587	18.07413	18.5576
SENSOR_24_CALCULATED	19.7728	19.6356	19.4984	19.3612	19.224	19.0868	19.1554	19.0378	18.979	18.93	18.76122	18.68957	18.62469	18.8124	18.783
SENSOR_26_CALCULATED	19.4494	19.3318	19.175	19.04433	18.90713	18.8614	18.783	18.7242	18.6654	18.6164	18.44762	18.37597	18.31109	18.4988	18.4694
SENSOR_27_CALCULATED	20.1354	20.0276	19.9198	19.812	19.7434	19.62776	19.5964	19.518	19.39991	19.4592	19.4396	19.4102	19.3612	19.3612	19.3612
SENSOR_25	19.616	19.4494		19.1456		18.93					18.6066	18.587			18.5576

Fig. 4. The set of actual and predicted values for sensor 25.

Another test that was carried out, increasing the training set up to 1500 measurements. At the end of the execution about 1000 missing values were found within the various series of measurements: 620 of them were predicted using the linear regression, the rest using spatial correlation. Summarizing, tripling the training set the number of missing values has increased by about 10 times (form the initial value of 150 to the about 1000 value of the second test) and, the percentage of the predicted measurements using the spatial correlation has decreased from 46% to 38%. This decrease is mainly due to the enormous increase in the number of missing values.

With appropriate tuning, the algorithm performance has been improved, as demonstrated by the comparison of Figs. 5 and 6. The former contains the graph generated by the early version of the algorithm: the blue and the gray lines which respectively represent the behaviors of sensors 25 and 26 were intertwined with each other.

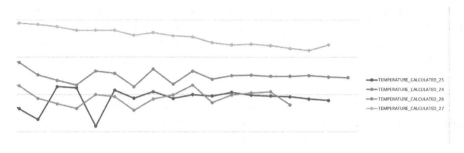

Fig. 5. Graphs generated by an early version of the software

Figure 6 instead refers to the current version of the algorithm, where the two lines intertwine with each other as little as possible, making the generated data more realistic. This improvement was achieved by ordering sensor measurements according to a precise criterion. As previously mentioned, the proposed tool first processes the measurements produced by the most reliable sensors (sensor ordering is performed after step 4 of the algorithm in Fig. 2). The reliability of the sensors is determined by the number of measurements made, therefore the more a sensor produces measurements, the more it is considered reliable.

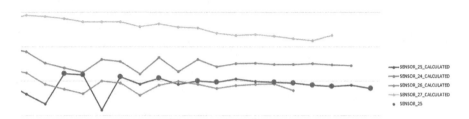

Fig. 6. Graph generated by the current software version

A last experiment consisted in a manual removal of a measurement from the database to understand how accurately the algorithm is able to reconstruct the missing data. The deleted measurement was produced by the sensor 25, on February 28th, 2004 at 01:10:10 AM and having a recorded temperature value equal to 18.44 °C.

Once the database was modified and the software was re-run it was possible to see that the value predicted by the algorithm is equal to 18,4739 °C. This value was obtained by exploiting the spatial correlation existing between the sensor 25 and the sensor 26.

5 Conclusions and Future Works

We have integrated the information concerning the location of devices with the history of their measurements in order to tackle some important problems concerning the quality of data collected from sensor networks, such as the presence of missing values and outliers.

We have identified the necessity of a correct ordering in the analysis of the measurement data points, driven by a careful evaluation of the current reliability of each sensor. The approach appears to be promising, having led to the reconstruction of complete measurement sequences by the estimation of missing data, and to very accurate estimations of data points which have been intentionally deleted from the sequence given to the algorithm.

There are many improvements and future developments that can be applied to the algorithm just discussed in order to better its performance and make it more adaptive and more general. The first improvement that could be implemented consists in identifying from the data stream not only the outlier values but also other types of errors such as spike-at-faults, etc. A further future development that could be implemented concerns the formula used in predicting missing or classified values as errors, e.g. combining the temporal correlation with all other spatial correlations between cluster sensors.

The proposed algorithm handles only sensors that have a fixed and known position; advanced versions dedicated to moving sensors could be the subject of a subsequent study. In this sense, the future developments will be planned to integrate the proposed algorithm within *WEAR-IT* [20], an innovative framework to provide mobile applications with APIs to select and query sensors distributed over a *wearable environment*, to extend the functionalities of wearable expert systems [25, 26].

References

1. Fawzy, A., Mokhtar, H.M., Hegazy, O.: Outliers detection and classification in wireless sensor networks. Egypt. Inform. J. **14**(2), 157–164 (2013)
2. Branisavljević, N., Kapelan, Z., Prodanović, D.: Improved real-time data anomaly detection using context classification. J. Hydroinformatics **13**, 307–323 (2011)
3. Brownlee, J.: A tour of machine learning algorithms. Mach. Learn. Mastery **1542**, 33–36 (2013)

4. Sun, S., Bertrand-Krajewski, J.L.: On calibration data selection: the case of stormwater quality regression models. Environ. Model Softw. **35**, 61–73 (2012)
5. Mourad, M., Bertrand-Krajewski, J.L.: A method for automatic validation of long time series of data in urban hydrology. Water Sci. Technol. **45**, 263–270 (2002)
6. Qin, S.J., Li, W.: Detection, identification, and reconstruction of faulty sensors with maximized sensitivity. AIChE J. **45**, 1963–1976 (1999)
7. Olsson, G., Nielsen, M., Yuan, Z., Lynggaard-Jensen, A., Steyer, J.-P.: Instrumentation, control and automation in wastewater systems. Water Intell. Online **4**, 9781780402680 (2015)
8. Kramer, M.A.: Nonlinear principal component analysis using autoassociative neural networks. AIChE J. **37**, 233–243 (1991)
9. Staroswiecki, M.: Intelligent sensors: a functional view. IEEE Trans. Ind. Inform. **1**, 238–249 (2005)
10. Ibargiengoytia, P.H., Sucar, L.E., Vadera, S.: Real time intelligent sensor validation. IEEE Trans. Power Syst. **16**, 770–775 (2001)
11. Srivastava, S., Singh, M., Gupta, S.: Wireless sensor network: a survey. In: 2018 International Conference on Automation and Computational Engineering, ICACE 2018, pp. 159–163. Institute of Electrical and Electronics Engineers Inc. (2019). https://doi.org/10.1109/icace.2018.8687059
12. Ruiz-Garcia, L., Lunadei, L., Barreiro, P., Robla, J.I.: A review of wireless sensor technologies and applications in agriculture and food industry: state of the art and current trends. Sensors (Switzerland) **9**, 4728–4750 (2009)
13. Zonta, D., et al.: Wireless sensor networks for permanent health monitoring of historic buildings. Smart Struct. Syst. **6**, 595–618 (2010)
14. Durisic, M.P., Tafa, Z., Dimic, G., Milutinovic, V.: A survey of military applications of wireless sensor networks. In: Mediterranean Conference on Embedded Computing (MECO), pp. 196–199 (2012)
15. Ko, J., et al.: Wireless sensor networks for healthcare. Proc. IEEE **98**, 1947–1960 (2010)
16. Pan, L., Li, J.: K-nearest neighbor based missing data estimation algorithm in wireless sensor networks. Wirel. Sens. Netw. **02**, 115–122 (2010)
17. Wilks, D.S.: Cluster analysis. Int. Geophys. **100**, 603–616 (2011)
18. Madden, S.: Intel Lab Data (2004). http://db.csail.mit.edu/labdata/labdata.html
19. Mollanoori, M., Hormati, M.M., Charkari, N.M.: An online prediction framework for sensor networks. In: 16th Iranian Conference on Electrical Engineering (2008)
20. Sartori, F., Melen, R.: An infrastructure for wearable environments acquisition and representation. In: Proceedings of the Twentieth ACM International Symposium on Mobile Ad Hoc Networking and Computing, pp. 371–372. ACM (2019)
21. Can, A., Guillaume, G., Picaut, J.: Cross-calibration of participatory sensor networks for environmental noise mapping. Appl. Acoust. **110**, 99–109 (2016)
22. Tran, B.H., Bouju, A., Plumejeaud-Perreau, C., Bretagnolle, V.: Towards a semantic framework for exploiting heterogeneous environmental data. Int. J. Metadata Semant. Ontol. **11**(3), 191–205 (2016)
23. Andrade, A.T.C., Montez, C., Moraes, R., Pinto, A.R., Vasques, F., da Silva, G.L.: Outlier detection using k-means clustering and lightweight methods for wireless sensor networks. In: IECON 2016-42nd Annual Conference of the IEEE Industrial Electronics Society, pp. 4683–4688. IEEE (2016)
24. Wang, Z.M., Song, G.H., Gao, C.: An isolation-based distributed outlier detection framework using nearest neighbor ensembles for wireless sensor networks. IEEE Access **7**, 96319–96333 (2019)

25. Melen, R., Sartori, F., Grazioli, L.: Modeling and understanding time-evolving scenarios. In: Proceedings of the 19th World Multiconference on Systemics, Cybernetics and Informatics (WMSCI 2015), vol. I, pp. 267–271 (2015)
26. Sartori, F., Melen, R.: Wearable expert system development: definitions, models and challenges for the future. Program **51**(3), 235–258 (2017)

Semantic Assistance System for Providing Smart Services and Reasoning in Aero-Engine Manufacturing

Sonika Gogineni[1(✉)], Konrad Exner[1], Rainer Stark[1,2], Jonas Nickel[3], Marian Oeler[3], and Heiko Witte[3]

[1] Fraunhofer Institute for Production Systems and Design Technology, Pascalstraße 8-9, 10587 Berlin, Germany
`Sonika.gogineni@ipk.fraunhofer.de`
[2] Technische Universität Berlin, Pascalstraße 8-9, 10587 Berlin, Germany
[3] Rolls-Royce Deutschland, Eschenweg 11, 15827 Blankenfelde-Mahlow, Germany

Abstract. Digitalization has led to creation and management of knowledge using information and communication technology tools (ICT) and systems. Implementing such tools and systems across the lifecycle is a tedious process and not to forget customizing them to the company's processes is an additional challenge. Hence, data in a company is spread across multiple ICT in heterogeneous data formats and are sparsely connected together. Connecting the various data sources to enable a single point of access of information in a company can improve performance, quality, reduce costs and time to market. The usage of semantic technologies enables meaningful and structured unification of these distributed data sources and therefore, is providing advantages such as reusability, interoperability, and information flow across the entire value chain. Extending these capabilities with smart services and intelligent algorithms, is advantageous for the user. The user will then receive context sensitive information and additional suggestions that increases the speed, quality and efficiency of work. This paper aims at describing the design, developing and validation of an assistance system for semantic product data, in cooperation with Rolls-Royce Deutschland, an aerospace manufacturing industry, using semantic technologies and machine learning.

Keywords: Semantic technologies · Ontology in manufacturing · Semantic product data · Information and knowledge management

1 Problem Statement

Along the product life cycle of durable capital goods, such as aircraft turbines, product data is generated across various phases and they are stored and managed using various information technology systems. This leads to the generation of a heterogeneous landscape with respect to data, processes and tools. Hence, in industries it is often a challenge to understand and obtain a big picture of the entire lifecycle, track changes, manage, collaborate and interoperate across processes [1–3]. This places a greater

© Springer Nature Switzerland AG 2019
E. Garoufallou et al. (Eds.): MTSR 2019, CCIS 1057, pp. 90–102, 2019.
https://doi.org/10.1007/978-3-030-36599-8_8

importance on availability and interconnectivity of product data across work processes such as production, assembly, maintenance or quality assurance, to improve efficiency of the processes and save costs and time. In general, the challenges faced in manufacturing industries trying to use the advantages of digitalization to improve product lifecycle processes can be classified as: 1. Diversity and complexity of IT tools and systems that are used for various activities. Hence, leading to lack of horizontal and vertical integration in a company; 2. As a consequence of usage of diverse tools, heterogeneous data is generated, which often leads to redundancy and inconsistency; 3. An increasing amount of data that is not being analyzed and managed to support decision making processes [4, 5].

These challenges are also faced in Rolls-Royce Deutschland similar to other industries. There are various IT systems and tools which generate heterogeneous data across the value stream. Not all information is fully transparent across the lifecycle of the product. As a consequence the designer is not always informed about the problems in manufacturing, assembly or supply chain. To tackle these challenges there are various approaches, such as, using a common IT-backbone, using internet technologies to make data easily available [5], using common information models and developing standard interfaces between various IT tools and systems [6]. However, these approaches are relatively static [7] and sometimes involve high levels of effort, time and money to restructure existing processes and infrastructure. Hence, an approach is required which minimizes these impacts and takes into consideration the intuitive communication of complex facts in which the interrelationships of information over the product life cycle and across system boundaries are connected and visualized. In this context, the approach of semantic product data linking is used [8]. This approach has achieved considerable progress in recent years through the development of efficient tools and the continuous further development of Semantic Web technologies [3, 9].

In this paper, we propose an ontology based assistant system to support activities in Rolls-Royce Deutschland by providing solutions to the above stated challenges. For this, a user- and task-specific information visualization is developed and implemented. The main objective of the research is the prototypical implementation of a semantic product data assistance system that serves the information needs in engineering and applies intelligent algorithms and machine learning for a reasoning system.

2 State of the Art

Semantic technologies are based on the World Wide Web Consortium (W3C) standards. They are widely used to interlink data stored on various systems, build vocabularies and handle data with rules [10]. They have already been utilized in structuring and managing complex and large amount of heterogeneous data in media and publishing, bio and medical informatics, life sciences and the World Wide Web design [11, 12]. Ontologies are a part of semantic technologies which enables the definition of data and their relationships [13]. In the manufacturing domain, ontologies have been developed for the purpose of knowledge management [14, 15], knowledge exploration [16] and manufacturability, verification and knowledge reuse [17]. In order to develop a complete application based on ontologies there are many elements to be considered. Referring to the basic architecture of Semantic Web [18] the elements are: the data to be connected or integrated into the ontology, the structure, format and size of data, rules which provide additional logic [19] and querying of the linked data. Additional interactive elements to be considered are the architecture of the user interface with which the user interacts and receives context sensitive information and its connection to the semantic layer. To support the development of such applications there are several commercial and non-commercial tools, languages and configurations available. Nonetheless, there is a lack of tools that support a complete end to end development and implementation of ontologies in an industrial environment [20]. This can be attributed to the fact that, developing solutions for corporate applications also involves the need to interface with existing infrastructure and tools such as databases and product design systems [21]. In addition, they also need to follow the policies and conventions of the company.

3   Research Approach

The research approach is based on the Design Science Research Methodology (DSRM) for Information Systems Research [22]. The steps conducted in this research are shown in Fig. 1.

1	Identify & define research questions based on state of the art and industrial requirements
2	Define objects of the solution by deriving use cases
3	Design and development of suitable architecture for the use cases
4	Experimenting with the developed demonstrator architecture
5	Evaluation of Demonstrator
6	Communication of research

Fig. 1. Research approach steps

This paper is addressing the complete set of steps from one to six, which is the initial cycle of defining the problem, analyzing, developing and evaluating the results. The main research questions in this research are:

1. How to integrate heterogeneous data sources from various ICT?
2. How can relevant context-sensitive knowledge be generated and presented to improve processes?
3. How to use intelligence in terms of algorithms to provide value added smart services along industrial processes?

4   Capturing Requirements by Deduction of Use Cases

To collect requirements, two workshops with twenty-five experts from different Rolls-Royce Deutschland departments were conducted. The focus groups were based on design, production planning and assembly. The workshop resulted in the derivation of seventy-nine user stories. The user stories consist of elements such as its name and description, the role of the user it refers to as well as the goal of the user and from which data sources it originates. In addition, the user stories were also clustered into groups based on their similarities and connections. An example of the user stories documented and structured is show in Table 1.

Table 1. A snippet of user stories generated

ID	Title	Perspective	Goal	Origin	Use-case	Group
WS1/01	Production data	Production	Production data in form of variation, capability, concessions of similarity	Geometric data	Statistical overview at component level	WS1.1
WS1/02	Visualization	Production	Visualization of production data on the part	Geometric data	Statistical overview at component level	WS1.2

From the user stories five use cases were derived and selected for further implementation, based on priority, availability of data and the ease of collaboration with Rolls-Royce Deutschland team. These five use cases are:

1. I am a designer and want to understand different variations of my component class in order to make better decisions about new designs (operational data, service data, manufacturing and assembly aspects, suppliers, configuration, ERP).
2. I am a designer and want to understand the production variability of the part in order to assess and optimize the ability of the manufacturing process in terms of tolerances.
3. I am an engineer and would like to view life cycle data to optimize the part.
4. I as an assembler, I want to give feedback to the engineers to improve the design (voice of the fitter, production planner).
5. I am an engineer and want to evaluate the activities around a component to identify important points.

To further detail these five use cases, ten interviews with representatives from the concerned departments were conducted. The questions to detail the use case were divided into four categories, namely "Description of the role", "Use case – Actual state", "Use case - Desired state" and "Business case". The same is outlined in the Fig. 2.

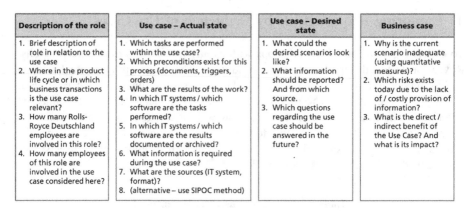

Description of the role	Use case – Actual state	Use case – Desired state	Business case
1. Brief description of role in relation to the use case 2. Where in the product life cycle or in which business transactions is the use case relevant? 3. How many Rolls-Royce Deutschland employees are involved in this role? 4. How many employees of this role are involved in the use case considered here?	1. Which tasks are performed within the use case? 2. Which preconditions exist for this process (documents, triggers, orders) 3. What are the results of the work? 4. In which IT systems / which software are the tasks performed? 5. In which IT systems / which software are the results documented or archived? 6. What information is required during the use case? 7. What are the sources (IT system, format)? 8. (alternative – use SIPOC method)	1. What could the desired scenarios look like? 2. What information should be reported? And from which source. 3. Which questions regarding the use case should be answered in the future?	1. Why is the current scenario inadequate (using quantitative measures)? 2. Which risks exists today due to the lack of / costly provision of information? 3. What is the direct / indirect benefit of the Use Case? And what is its impact?

Fig. 2. Key questions for use case description

The interviews results were transcribed, analyzed and integrated into five comprehensive use case descriptions, in the form of a document based on [23], with elements depicted in Fig. 3. The detailing of the use case helps in understanding the role of the user and the system, with the related IT systems and also the activities which take place.

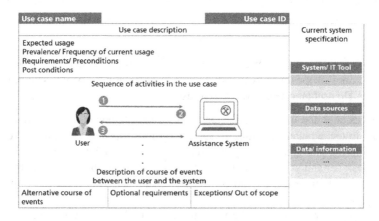

Fig. 3. Use case description (generic document form)

5 Development of Semantic Assistance System Demonstrator

In this section, the steps followed to design and develop the semantic assistance system are described. First, the derivation procedure for the system architecture requirements is discussed, followed by the derivation of the requirements of the use case, and finally the details about the design and development of the assistance system are detailed. For the design of the system architecture, it was important to identify the data flow paths in the company concerning the use cases. The data flow architecture tool developed by

Fraunhofer IPK [24] was used for this purpose. The tool aims at depicting the details of the data flow with process and organizations, virtual and digital models, and information tools and IT systems involved across the activities. Hence, the entire development environment can be idealized and the actual and target states can be compared. This enables the mapping and comparison of a wide variety of scenarios and their effects, which can be used to describe the target vision. With the help of the tool and additional workshops to integrate the new tool into the existing IT landscape at Rolls-Royce Deutschland, it was possible to extrapolate the essential information for fulfilling the requirements and the associated IT systems and artifacts for the use cases.

5.1 Implementation of a Use Case in the Assistance System

To be able to test and work with the architecture use case 3 (voice of the fitter, production planner), was selected. In particular, the voice of the fitter data was used for the demonstrator. This use case mainly consists of the problems fitters have on the assembly floor. These include issues like missing components, missing tools and potential quality problems on components and assembly to name a few. The fitter reports these issues to a voice of the fitter (VoF) team. The team tries to help the fitter to find a solution for their issue by searching various IT systems and sending emails to responsible colleagues, as well as tracking their responses. The issue resolution is a time consuming process, which requires a lot of expertise and effort. It is sometimes critical to assist the fitter as soon as possible, because there are situations in which these issues can lead to a stop in the assembly process, thus resulting in economic losses for the company. Hence, the assistance system was linked to a semantic network, which refers to three data sources. The data sources comprise relevant details about the parts of a particular engine model, VoF cases and concession decisions about reported non-conformances associated with the engine. The aim of the assistance system is to assist the VoF team by visualizing information about the VoF cases, concessions and the geometry of the part with an issue on the assistance system without having to check other tools and systems. In addition, through the semantic network the user can also check for previous cases with similar problems with their solutions on the assistance system. Hence, enabling the usage of previous knowledge and speeding up the solution finding and decision making processes.

5.2 Architecture Design

Based on the results of data flow analysis the components of the system architecture were identified. In addition, results from a series of workshops, literature research [25, 26] and iterative and agile development solutions the architecture for the demonstrator was derived. The architecture for the assistance system utilizes various components to provide context sensitive information to the user from various data sources, and supports integration of machine learning algorithms. These components involved are further organized into layers as shown in Fig. 4.

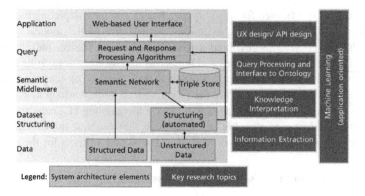

Fig. 4. System architecture and key research topics

The application layer hosts the web based user interface. The query layer facilitates the request and response functions. The semantic middleware layer consists the semantic network in the form of ontologies and the triple store. The data layer and the data structuring layer take care of accessing and structuring data sources in order to integrate them within the semantic network. The key research topics along these layers as show in Fig. 4 are user experience (UX) design and application programming interface (API) design, query processing and interfacing to the semantic network, knowledge interpretation and information extraction. The machine learning integration depends on the application, hence can be integrated on various layers.

The architecture formed the backbone for selection of suitable standards, tools, frameworks and software. The research aims at using primarily open source tools to ensure a cost efficient solution whilst keeping a maximum amount of adaptability for the development of the assistance system demonstrator. Eclipse was chosen as the integrated development environment (IDE). Apache Tomcat is used as the web server, which is compatible and interoperable with Eclipse. MariaDB was chosen as the buffer databank used to store the data required. The programming language used is Java Enterprise Edition as it provides the necessary support in the form of object-oriented programming for developing the demonstrator. To enable versioning management of the collaborative development Gitlab was used. The layers mentioned in the architecture and the associated software tools and structure are explained in the following paragraphs:

The application layer hosts the web based user interface. The interface acts as the front end of the assistance system with which the user interacts and receives context sensitive information as desired. It is important to note that the design has to be user and use case centric. Hence, the design of the web-based user interface contains several elements that should be considered during the development process. The elements considered are functional user requirements, user experience requirements, design of the information access and visualization, design of the user interaction and visual design. These key requirements were used as foundations to design the interface. Workshops with the end users were conducted to evaluate the alternatives and select the most suitable layout based on the ranking from the users and the use case needs. The chosen layout of the web interface is shown in the Fig. 7.

The query layer is responsible for the request and response activity which connects the web based front end with the semantic network. That is, based on the user's requests or interaction with the front end, request algorithms are triggered to receive the right information from the semantic network. This layer connects to the semantic network via a SPARQL endpoint [27]. The design of the requests is important to determine the SPARQL request to the semantic network. For example, when the user clicks on a button requesting for all the parts with similar problems, the ontology is queried for all parts with similar problems and the results of the query are pushed to the front end.

The semantic middleware layer hosts the semantic network. The semantic network consists of the ontology, the mapping files to map the ontology with the data instances, the rules and the derived triples. The triples generated from combining the ontology and the mapped data are stored in a triple store. The process of development of the semantic network began with the modelling of the ontology, Protégé is the tool used [28]. The model of the ontology was developed considering relationships in the original databank sources [29, 30] and the expected system queries [31]. The ontology is shown in Fig. 5, the main classes are based on the three main data sources, information about the physical part (Part_Phys), concessions and VoF case details (VoF_Case). The classes are assigned with data properties that link instances with further details about the instance, for example, the particular part has a "Part_name" data property which is assigned to the domain "Part_Phys" and range "xsd:string". To connect the individuals in the classes with relationships object properties are defined. For example, to determine which "Part_Phys" has a problem, the object property "Part_has_VoF" is defined with domain as "Part_Phys" and range as "VoF_Case". The corresponding mappings are shown in Fig. 6. The three object properties in the ontology are represented by the arrows between the classes as shown in Fig. 5.

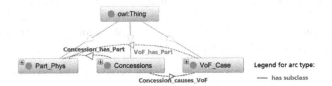

Fig. 5. Ontology modelled in Protégé

As the data from the three data sources could be easily converted and stored in a relational database, they were converted and added into the MariaDB databank. The next step was to map the ontology with data. An open source tool called *Ontop* was used for this purpose [32]. It is an ontology-based data access (OBDA) tool which comes as a plugin with Protégé and hence is compatible with the architecture. It also has performed well in comparison to other competitors on various benchmark tests [32]. *Ontop* is connected to the MariaDB using the Java DataBase Connectivity (JDBC) driver. Figure 6 shows the screenshot of the mappings created using the Mapping manager.

```
Part_DatatypeProperties
:part_table/{PART_NUM} a untitled-ontology-10:Part_Phys ; untitled-ontology-10:Part_num {PART_NUM} ;
untitled-ontology-10:Part_name {PART_NAME} ; untitled-ontology-10:Part_Supplier {SUPPLIER} .
select PART_NUM,SUPPLIER, PART_NAME from part_table

Part_has_VoF
:part_table/{PART_NUM} untitled-ontology-10:Part_has_VoF :table3/{VOF_CASE_ID}
select part_table.PART_NUM, table3.VOF_CASE_ID from part_table join table3 on part_table.PART_NUM=table3.VOF_PART_NBR
```

Fig. 6. Ontop plugin screenshots of mappings in the Mapping manager

Class axioms and relation-constraints, which are controlled by reasoning and serve knowledge interpretation, are now binding for the individuals. In this way, queries become simpler and easier to understand, but with the additional advantage that the data is still enriched with meaning, paving the way for context-based interpretation and knowledge discovery for e.g. learning algorithms or reasoning. In order to facilitate query answering, the generated files from *Ontop* and Protégé, namely, the owl file, mapping files, and properties files were added onto a tool called Eclipse RDF4 J. It is an open source framework for creating, parsing, storing, reasoning, interfacing and querying RDF data [33, 34]. The tool is compatible with *Ontop* and generates an *Ontop* virtual RDF store. This acts as SPARQL endpoint on the Apache Tomcat server for answering queries.

The data structuring and data layer consists of the work data generated by Rolls-Royce Deutschland processes. They are stored in different systems, with different formats and structures. In order to support the development of the semantic network the data for the use cases were structured and converted. The data associated with the physical part and concessions were extracted from the Product Data Management (PDM) system and concessions system respectively, into excel sheets, which were then loaded into the MariaDB in a relational database format. The VoF cases already exist as a set of relational database tables, these were also uploaded into the MariaDB database.

Machine learning algorithms can be integrated into the architecture based on application needs. It is important to determine the function of machine learning, the data sets to be used, the algorithm and the method of machine learning to be considered. The three applications considered for the given use cases were:

1. Visualization of context sensitive information based on user behavior, where the assistance system learns from the user interactions with the system, and reacts by providing context sensitive information on the next request.
2. Provision of suggestions based on previous problem solving history using machine learning algorithm assisting in decision making process.
3. Self-learning ontologies to enable addition of new data into ontologies without manual intervention.

Currently for the above mentioned second application the machine learning model is being developed by using a topic detection algorithm called Latent Dirichlet allocation. The possible integration of the model into the system is also being investigated.

6 Evaluation and Preliminary Results

The assistance system is developed to assist VoF team members with their daily tasks of solving problems faced by the fitters during assembly processes. The developed system presents the team with context sensitive information in the information field area, from various data sources, which provides relevant details to quickly carry out investigative work to solve problems. The assistance system demonstrator was evaluated with an expert VoF team member. The front end of the evaluated demonstrator is shown in Fig. 7. The user was instructed about the aim and general functions available in the assistance system. Then the user was allowed to interact with the tool. The tool testing stage ended with an interview to receive a qualitative feedback and suggestions with respect to the features and the functioning of the tool. This lead to the development of further requirements for improvement of the tool.

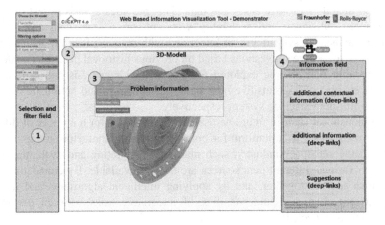

Fig. 7. Front of assistance system

The user was then asked to fill the questionnaire presented by F.D Davis to measure perceived usefulness, perceived ease of use, and user acceptance of the tool [35]. The rating was based on a five-stage scale with a total of ten questions with criteria ranging from "not at all" to "entirely", with a rating of 1 to 5 respectively. The answered questionnaire was evaluated, the perceived usefulness average was 4.75 out of 5, perceived ease of use was rated as 4.25 and user acceptance as 5. Hence, indicating that the user acknowledged the advantages of the tool to support daily work. However, the evaluation indicated that there is scope for improvement of the tool with respect to the user interface and additional features to integrate the tool into the work environment.

7 Conclusion and Outlook

By following a methodological research approach, the semantic assistance system demonstrator was analyzed and developed for a particular use case. It is a web based semantic system, which assists the user in accessing context sensitive data in an industrial scenario in which different information tools and heterogeneous data sources exist. This reduces the time taken to search for information in different tools and also helps in accessing historical knowledge to support decision making processes. The demonstrator is a step towards solving the current issues in the field of knowledge management and traceability of data across the value chain. The 3D models integrated into the tool were from the design phase stored in the PDM system, concessions and VoF data from production phase stored in SAP system and VoF tool respectively. The alpha version was tested for usability, which resulted in positive feedback to the tool and development of requirements for further improvement suggestions. Hence, enabling the realization of the use of semantic technologies in an industrial environment for providing context-sensitive information and services from various tools and formats.

In the future, the aim is to further develop the demonstrator by implementing the suggestions provided by the end users. The ontology and the assistance system will be scaled up to include more use cases and data. This provides a basis to test two main factors namely, efficiency and scalability with enterprise scale data and load. In addition, the assistance system will be integrated with machine learning results which enable the user to receive suggestions based on previous historical decisions made. The machine learning will also be explored for user behavior analysis and self-learning ontology to enable context-sensitive information presentation and automatic new data integration into the assistance system respectively.

The demonstrator shall in future be used as an incubator for a number of different and arising use cases – as a platform for both design and manufacturing engineers. In particular in the aerospace industry, such platforms integrating and evaluating information from various different data sources are not yet available. By connecting those different data sources together, and by applying intelligent algorithms and machine learning, a step change in understanding of integrative tasks between design and manufacturing is expected.

Acknowledgements. This project is funded by the Europäischer Fonds für regionale Entwicklung (EFRE).

References

1. Manuel, H., Falk, U., Walter, B.: Challenges in product lifecycle management. In: Australasian Conference on Information Systems (2016)
2. Lee, J., Chae, H., Kim, C.-H., Kim, K.: Design of product ontology architecture for collaborative enterprises. Expert Syst. Appl. **36**(2), 2300–2309 (2009)
3. Otte, J.N., et al.: An ontological approach to representing the product life cycle. AO **14**(2), 179–197 (2019)
4. Deloitte, A.G.: Industry 4.0: challenges and solutions for the digital transformation and use of exponential technologies. https://www2.deloitte.com/content/dam/Deloitte/ch/Documents/manufacturing/ch-en-manufacturing-industry-4-0-24102014.pdf
5. Kiritsis, D., Bufardi, A., Xirouchakis, P.: Research issues on product lifecycle management and information tracking using smart embedded systems. Adv. Eng. Inform. **17**(3–4), 189–202 (2003)

6. Franke, M., Klein, P., Schröder, L., Thoben, K.-D.: Ontological semantics of standards and PLM repositories in the product development phase. In: Proceedings of the 20th CIRP Design Conference, pp. 473–483 (2010)
7. Agarwal, S., Haase, P.: Process-based integration of heterogeneous information sources. In: GI Jahrestagung (2004)
8. Graube, M., Pfeffer, J., Ziegler, J., Urbas, L.: Linked data as integrating technology for industrial data. In: 14th International Conference on Network-Based Information Systems, Tirana, Albania, pp. 162–167 (2011)
9. Ferrara, A., Nikolov, A., Scharffe, F.: Data linking for the semantic web. Int. J. Semant. Web Inf. Syst. **7**(3), 46–76 (2011)
10. W3C, Linked Data. https://www.w3.org/standards/semanticweb/data#summary
11. Miah, S.J., Gammack, J., Kerr, D.: Ontology development for context-sensitive decision support. In: Third International Conference on Semantics, Knowledge and Grid (SKG 2007), Xi'an, Shan Xi, China, pp. 475–478, October 2007
12. The truth about triplestores. https://ontotext.com/wp-content/uploads/2014/07/The-Truth-About-Triplestores.pdf
13. Ontotext, What is Semantic Technology? https://www.ontotext.com/knowledgehub/funda mentals/semantic-web-technology/
14. Li, S.-T., Hsieh, H.-C., Sun, I.-W.: An ontology-based knowledge management system for the metal industry. In: WWW (2003)
15. Cheng, H., et al.: Manufacturing ontology development based on Industry 4.0 demonstration production line. In: 2016 Third International Conference on Trustworthy Systems and their Applications (TSA), Wuhan, China, pp. 42–47 (2016)
16. Ahonen, E.Q., Watson, D.P., Adams, E.L., McGuire, A.: Alpha test results for a housing first eLearning strategy: the value of multiple qualitative methods for intervention design. In: Pilot and Feasibility Studies, vol. 3, p. 46 (2017)
17. Li, Z., et al.: An ontology-based product design framework for manufacturability verification and knowledge reuse. Int. J. Adv. Manuf. Technol. **99**(9–12), 2121–2135 (2018). https:// link.springer.com/content/pdf/10.1007%2Fs00170-018-2099-2.pdf
18. Tim, B.-L.: Semantic Web - XML2000: Architecture. https://www.w3.org/2000/Talks/1206-xml2k-tbl/slide10-0.html
19. Eine, B., Jurisch, M., Quint, W.: Ontology-based big data management. Systems **5**(3), 45 (2017)
20. Holanda, O., Isotani, S., Bittencourt, I.I., Elias, E., Tenório, T.: JOINT: Java ontology integrated toolkit. Expert Syst. Appl. **40**(16), 6469–6477 (2013)
21. Hoppe, T., et al.: Corporate semantic web – applications, technology, methodology. Inform. Spektrum **39**(1), 57–63 (2016)
22. Peffers, K., Tuunanen, T., Rothenberger, M.A., Chatterjee, S.: A design science research methodology for information systems research. J. Manag. Inf. Syst. **24**(3), 45–77 (2007)
23. Hee, K.: Object-oriented modeling, simulation and automatic generation of PLC ladder logic. In: Affonso, L. (ed.) Programmable Logic Controller. InTech (2010)
24. Lindow, K., Riedelsheimer, T., Lünnemann, P., Stark, R.: Betrachtung des Entwicklungsumfeldes durch die methodische Datenflussanalyse. ProduktDaten J. **2**, 52–56 (2017)
25. Thangaraj, M., Sujatha, G.: An architectural design for effective information retrieval in semantic web. Expert Syst. Appl. **41**(18), 8225–8233 (2014)
26. Guermah, H., Tarik, F., Hafiddi, H., Nassar, M., Kriouile, A.: An ontology oriented architecture for context aware services adaptation. ArXiv abs/1404.3280 (2014)
27. Harris, S., Seaborne, A.: SPARQL 1.1 Query Language. W3C Recommendation, 21 March 2013. https://www.w3.org/TR/2013/REC-sparql11-query-20130321/

28. Horridge, M.: A practical guide to building OWL ontologies. http://mowl-power.cs.man.ac.uk/protegeowltutorial/resources/ProtegeOWLTutorialP4_v1_3.pdf
29. Telnarova, Z.: Relational database as a source of ontology creation. In: Proceedings of the International Multiconference on Computer Science and Information Technology, Wisla, pp. 135–139 (2010)
30. Louhdi, M.R.C., Behja, H., El Alaoui, S.O.: Transformation rules for building OWL ontologies from relational databases. In: Computer Science & Information Technology (CS & IT), pp. 271–283 (2013)
31. Chujai, P., Kerdprasop, N., Kerdprasop, K.: On transforming the ER model to ontology using Protégé OWL tool. IJCTE **6**(6), 484–489 (2014)
32. Calvanese, D., et al.: Ontop: answering SPARQL queries over relational databases. SW **8**(3), 471–487 (2016). http://www.semantic-web-journal.net/system/files/swj1004.pdf
33. rdf4j, Welcome to RDF4 J. https://rdf4j.org/
34. Oleksiy, K.: Lecture 5: Programming with Semantic Web (RDF4 J and Jena APIs). University of Jyväskylä (2018)
35. Davis, F.D.: Perceived usefulness, perceived ease of use, and user acceptance of information technology. MIS Q. **13**(3), 319 (1989)

Automated Subject Indexing of Domain Specific Collections Using Word Embeddings and General Purpose Thesauri

Michalis Sfakakis[1], Leonidas Papachristopoulos[2], Kyriaki Zoutsou[1], Giannis Tsakonas[3], and Christos Papatheodorou[1(✉)]

[1] Department of Archives, Library Science and Museology, Ionian University, Corfu, Greece
{sfakakis,papatheodor}@ionio.gr, k.zoutsou@gmail.com
[2] Hellenic Open University Distance Library and Information Center, Patras, Greece
lpapachristopoulos@eap.gr
[3] Library and Information Center, University of Patras, Patras, Greece
gtsak@upatras.gr

Abstract. In the era of enormous information production human capabilities have reached their limits. The need for automatic information processing which would not be incommensurate to human sophistication seems to be more than imperative. Information scientists have focused on the development of techniques and processes that would assist human contribution while improve, or at least guarantee, information quality. Automatic indexing techniques may lay on various approaches offering different results in information retrieval. In this paper we introduce an automated methodology for subject analysis, including both the determination of the aboutness of the documents and the translation of the related concepts to the terms of a knowledge organization system. Focusing on a corpus consisting of articles related to the Digital Library Evaluation domain, topic modeling algorithms are utilized for the aboutness of the documents, while the context of the words in topics, as captured by Word Embeddings, are used for the assignment of the extracted topics to the concepts of the EuroVoc thesaurus.

Keywords: Subject indexing · Similarity measures · Text classification · Machine learning · Word Embedding

1 Introduction

Indexing is considered to be one of the most tedious and debatable processes within the Library and Information Science domain. Indexer's difficulties are summarized in the determination of (a) a set of documents' indexing terms and (b) the degree of term representativeness [1]. According to Coates [2, p. 15] "the cognitive skills required for good term selection include reading comprehension, the ability to conceptualize, and the ability to articulate concepts in a concise and intelligible manner". Therefore, researchers and institutions attempted to identify and formalize the indexing process

© Springer Nature Switzerland AG 2019
E. Garoufallou et al. (Eds.): MTSR 2019, CCIS 1057, pp. 103–114, 2019.
https://doi.org/10.1007/978-3-030-36599-8_9

aiming at its optimization [3]. ISO 5963-1985 for example, indicates the necessary steps for indexing documents mentioning that indexers should firstly examine the document and establish the content and then they have to identify the main concepts and express these concepts according to controlled vocabulary [4].

Indexing quality affects documents' retrieval. In an overactive document producing environment, text mining techniques enhance information retrieval and ameliorate indexers' workload. The implementation of Topic Modeling on a corpus provides us both its subject overview and a categorization of its documents to a pre-defined set of topics [5, 6]. These topics are not actual indexing terms belonging to a controlled vocabulary, but bag-of-words lacking contextualization. Contextualization means the identification of a term from a controlled vocabulary indicating a specific knowledge area that these words would have significance.

This paper attempts to introduce an approach for document subject indexing based both on Topic Modeling and automated labeling processes, aiming to the improvement of the performance of the indexing and the quality of the indexing terms assigned to a document. Firstly, we identify "basic-level terms" via Topic Modeling and subsequently we attempt to upgrade them to a "significance level" by translating them to specific controlled vocabularies, according to Thellefsen, Brier and Thellefsen [7]. Topic Modeling was applied on a data set consisted of papers in the Digital Library (DL) Evaluation domain, published in the proceedings of the most significant conferences of the domain, namely JCDL, ICADL and ECDL/TPDL, during the period 2001–2013. The Topic Modeling process produced 13 sets of words (topics) needing interpretation and labels. The labelling process was based on the creation and collation of Word Embedding vectors for both the terms (words) describing the Topics, as produced by Topic Modeling, and the sets of words labeling and describing the EuroVoc Concepts. The computation of the similarity between the Word Embedding vectors of the Topics and the EuroVoc Concepts respectively will point to the most appropriate concept in EuroVoc, which will be considered as candidate subject term for a Topic.

In fact, this work aims to address the following question: given a domain specific corpus of documents, which is already thematically clustered, and a general purpose controlled vocabulary, how could we index the corpus utilizing the terms of the controlled vocabulary, so that the corpus could be interlinked and semantically interoperate with other collections indexed by the given controlled vocabulary? Thereafter, the challenge for indexing is to retain the thematic specificity, as it is expressed by the Topics to which the corpus has been already clustered. This research question reflects an ordinary problem of Libraries and Memory Organizations which manage heterogeneous collections, each one having its topical identification, but there is the need to provide seamless subject access services that integrates semantically all of them.

This article is organized as follows: Sect. 2 demonstrates the recent research on automatic indexing, as Topic Modeling and Word Embedding implementations. Section 3 presents the methodological steps of our experimental approach. Section 4 analyzes the outcomes of the research, while Sect. 5 debates the results of the study and signalizes points that future research should focus.

2   Literature Review

The vast amount of digital content productivity puts pressure to researchers' community for an analogous outcome on digital content handling and this is reflected to the steadily increase to a related scientific literature activity [8]. According to Brown and Barrière [9] "automatic indexing aims at the automatic creation of a list of index terms associated with a document often in the purpose of text retrieval. Two main approaches are Natural Language indexing and Controlled Vocabulary indexing, respectively extracting words from a text and assigning them from an external lexical resource". Our approach aims at the automatic controlled vocabulary indexing where the terms of a controlled vocabulary (thesaurus, subject headings, etc.) would be assigned to a document without human contribution.

Early attempts on the field of automatic indexing were applied on the diagnostic summaries of pathology reports which were attempted to automatically encode into the Systematized Nomenclature of Pathology (SNOP) via a morphosyntactic approach [10]. The authors admitted that their approach is a possible solution, although presented an important drawback the lack of semantic context.

The level of success for the outcomes of automatic subject indexing lies either on the assignment technique or the complexity of subject headings. Furthermore, the main issue that the experts of the field have to deal with is that the "performance measures need to be questioned and evaluation has to be dealt with in the broader contexts of users and their tasks" [11]. Many approaches have been applied in order to serve the purpose of automatic subject indexing satisfying performance measures but raising questions regarding in actual use level.

More specifically, Névéol et al. [12] applied various automatic indexing methods ("Jigsaw puzzle" methods, Rule-based methods, statistical) as a recommendation tool in order to assign MeSH terms to MEDLINE documents. These methods were evaluated as inconsistent and inadequate, as they were missing and erroneous recommendations. The whole experimentation highlighted the fact that complex subject headings need more sophisticated approaches. Joorabchi and Mahdi [13] introduced a concept matching-based approach in order to assigned subjects to DLs' content coming from DDC and FAST showing promising results. The specific approach is materialized through the detection of Wikipedia concepts within the documents which are sought to WorldCat database for MARC records retrieval. Accordingly, a dedicated algorithm undertakes the matching with DDC and FAST controlled vocabularies. A recent study attempted to compare the performance of two algorithms (Support Vector Machine with linear kernel and Multinomial Naïve Bayes) for automatic subject indexing of Swedish digital content with DDC classes proving the superiority of SVM [14]. Other attempts seem more simplistic as they try to exploit Table of Contents of printed books by extracting the keywords and assigning them to a specific classification system [15], while other are more sophisticated focusing on more demanding content and accordingly more complex subject heading systems [16].

On the other hand, the emergence of Topic Modelling with the invention of the Latent Dirichlet Allocation algorithm (LDA) induced the need for the reduction of human involvement in topic interpretation [17]. While Lau et al. [18] attempted to label the emerged topics by picking the most appropriate word from the word set of each topic, other researchers tried to develop mechanisms in order to flag these bags-of-words by dragging terms from external resources. For example, ALOT algorithm was applied on topics generated from Topic Modeling in order to map them to a topic hierarchy obtained from Google Directory Service and the OpenOffice English Thesaurus [19]. Another approach for automatic labeling was based on the exploitation of best term of each topic in order to be mapped with Wikipedia terms [20].

Lately, Mikolov et al. [21] managed to attach contextual, morphological, hierarchical and semantic information to each word in a document via a new method called "Word Embeddings". Some researchers attempted to make the most out of Topic Modeling and Word Embeddings methods by combining them under a new Topic Modeling approach called WE-LDA [22]. Word Embeddings will contribute to the materialization of automatic alignment and labeling of our topics derived from Topic Modeling with the labels used for the Concepts in EuroVoc.

The massive document production of EU's bodies led the EU Publication Office to develop a thesaurus for its better management [23]. EuroVoc is a multilingual tool (23 EU languages) aiming at the terminological standardization within various fields (finance, law, international relations, etc.), designed to cover the general needs of EU publications and not national specific needs. EuroVoc thesaurus is divided in 21 Domains (two-digit identification) and 127 Microthesauri (four-digit identification). EuroVoc's Concept relationships may be hierarchical (Broader (BT) or Narrower (NT) term) or associative (Related Term (RT)). Its current edition (v. 4.4) includes 6,883 concepts, 4,904 reciprocal hierarchical relationships and 6,922 reciprocal associative relationships.

Our study attempts to label Topics (sets of words) that have been generated by Topic Modelling with terms belonging to a controlled vocabulary. This rendering will accomplish effectively the first step of Topic extraction by assigning to them (Topics) established terms reflecting the analogous semantics.

3 Methodology

3.1 Corpus Formation

Conference proceedings are recognized as a credible channel for the dissemination of a state-of-the-art research. In the Digital Libraries (DL) domain, JCDL, ECDL/TPDL and ICADL conferences constitute historical venues, where anyone can follow the DL's evolution from its incunabulum to the latest advanced state. Accordingly, DL Evaluation domain is a crucial domain due to users' expectations for high quality services, content and performance [24], as challenging due to its interdisciplinarity which raise the level of complexity [6]. Our experimental study is based on a corpus of papers selected by the proceedings of JCDL (123 papers), ECDL/TPDL (147 papers) and ICADL (125 papers) for the period 2001–2013. A Bayesian classifier was trained to select the DL Evaluation oriented papers and three domain experts who worked independently validated its results [6, 25].

3.2   Topic Modeling Implementation

The selected papers were pre-processed to generate a "bag of words" (including abstracts and authors' keywords). We reduced the size of this bag of words removing the most frequent and rare words (above 2,100 or under 5 appearances) and stopwords included in Fox's list [26]. The outcome of the pre-processing was used as input to a web-based implementation of the Latent Dirichlet Allocation algorithm (LDA), called jsLDA [27], which generated a pre-defined number of Topics. A Topic is considered a set of words; the LDA algorithm computes the probability of a word to belong in a Topic. Moreover, it estimates the probability of a Topic to be included in each document of the corpus. We run the algorithm to produce various numbers of Topics (30, 25, 20, 15, 14, 13, 12, 11 and 10) and we concluded that 13 was the most well interpretable number of Topics that could be generated. The set of terms that describes each topic that derived from Topic modeling, were limited to those having probability greater than 0.004.

3.3   Topic and Concept Word Embeddings

Word embeddings are word representations extensively used in natural language processing [28, 29]. Each word is converted to a numerical vector which contains syntactic and semantic information [21, 29] in order to human language can be understood by computers. In this paper we used word representations from the pre-trained Word Vectors set,[1] trained using fastText[2] open-source library, according to [30]; Pre-trained word vectors set consists of one million word vectors trained on Wikipedia 2017, UMBC web-based corpus and statmt.org news datasets, while each word representation is a vector of 300 features.

Thereafter, each one of the words of each of the thirteen Topics generated by the LDA algorithm was represented by a Word Embedding, i.e. a word representation by a vector of 300 features. Then, for each Topic we calculated the weighted average of the Word Embedding of the words of the Topic to produce the word embedding of the topic, which is also a vector of 300 features and forms the Topic's Word Embedding. This process is represented by the formula (1):

$$eT = \sum_{i}^{n} p_i eW_i \qquad (1)$$

Where eT is the Topic's word embedding, eW_i is the vector for the Word Embedding of the i-th word in the Topic, p_i is the probability of the word to generate the Topic and n the number of words in the Topic. As already mentioned, a Topic is considered as a set of word-probability pairs, where the probability specifies how likely the word is to participate in the Topic. Therefore, the higher the probability of a word the higher the word's influence on the Topic, while a Topic consisting of high

---

[1] https://dl.fbaipublicfiles.com/fasttext/vectors-english/wiki-news-300d-1M.vec.zip.

[2] https://fasttext.cc/.

probability words considered as being more discrete and specific. Thereafter, the number n is topic specific and it depends on the threshold used to consider a word significant to the Topic. To select the most appropriate EuroVoc concepts, a number of alternative thresholds were evaluated, driving the study to focus on the values with probability greater than 0.0035, 0.0037 and 0.004. It is worth noting that lowering the probability threshold to zero, topics became more general and matched to even general concepts too.

Respectively, for each Concept of the EuroVoc thesaurus a Word Embedding vector is extracted using words either from the Concept description only or from the Concept description and its context. The context of a Concept is specified by the Microthesauri and the Domains it belongs to. It is worth mentioning that the SKOS version of EuroVoc was used for our experiments. Concretely, in order to calculate the Word Embedding vector for a Concept the following three alternative sources to select words from the concept description were evaluated:

1. the skos:prefLabel label only,
2. a wider set of labels consisting of the skos:prefLabel and skos:altLabel labels, and
3. the set of all concept's descriptive properties consisting of the skos:prefLabel, skos:altLabel, skos:hiddenLabel, rdfs:label, skos:scopeNote and skos:definition.

Furthermore, regarding the formulation of the Word Embedding vector of the context of a Concept we used the words in the skos:prefLabel of the Microthesaurus and the Domains the Concept belongs to.

For each EuroVoc Concept, either on its own or in its context a number of different word vectors of 300 features was calculated as follows:

$$eC = \frac{C_w}{N} \sum_i^n eW_i + \frac{MT_w}{M} \sum_j^m eW_m + \frac{D_w}{D} \sum_l^d eW_d \qquad (2)$$

As in the Topic Word Embedding formula, eC is the concept's Word Embedding, eW_i is the word embedding vector of the i-th word and C_w, MT_w and D_w are the weights for the words from the descriptions of the Concept, Microthesaurus and Domain respectively. N, M and D are the total number of words used for the Concept, Microthesauri and Domain respectively. C_w, MT_w and D_w are summing to one. It is worth noting that when C_w is one and the other weights are zeros, then the words from the Concepts' descriptions only are used, while the Microthesauri and Domains do not. Thereafter, for each studied case the word embeddings of the 7,247 EuroVoc's Concepts were calculated.

3.4 Labeling the Topics

In order to find the most suitable EuroVoc Concept for each Topic, we calculated the cosine similarity between the Word Embedding vector of each Topic and the Word Embedding vectors of the EuroVoc Concepts. When a Topic and a Concept are very similar, their Word Embedding vectors cosine similarity will be close to 1, while if they are dissimilar, their Word Embedding vectors cosine similarity will take a smaller value. The Concept with the highest cosine similarity to a topic was considered as the most suitable Concept to represent the Topic.

The rendering of the subjects we extracted from the Topic Modeling process to EuroVoc Concepts was done through a continuous testing process based on the optimal *average cosine similarity* between the topics and the qualitative evaluation of the Concepts attributed by a specialist who manages the dataset and utilized Topic Modeling algorithms to define the particular set of Topics. The latter initially examined the cases with a high *average cosine similarity*, since this was initially considered as the primary success marker. However, the results indicated that high *average cosine similarity* is not necessarily the only sign of success, as it can assign a Concept not so relevant to the space we look at (DL Evaluation) to a Topic.

4 Results

As already mentioned, the goal of this work is to index the documents of an already thematically clustered, domain specific corpus with terms from a general-purpose controlled vocabulary. Hence, we need to optimize the *average cosine similarity* between the Word Embeddings of the words in the EuroVoc Concepts and the Word Embeddings of the words in the Topics, under the constraint to preserve the meaning of the Topics revealed by the LDA algorithm. Thus, we need to identify a number of Concepts of EuroVoc that represent the meaning of the Topics. This number should be equal or close to the 13, since we had identified 13 Topics. Therefore, we need a combination of the weighting parameters of the Eq. (2) that preserve the meaning of the Topics.

However, the meaning of a Topic is revealed by its specificity, which is affected by the range of the word-probability pairs that describe the topic. Actually, Topic Specificity increases when the words that are included in the topic have a higher probability (p) to belong in the Topic. Obviously, Topic Specificity affects the Concepts that will be assigned to them; topics with smaller Specificity could be assigned to less specific and generic Concepts. The results exhibited an increase of the average cosine similarity between the Word Embeddings of the Topics and Concepts, for the Topics with smaller specificity. This is caused due to the increased number of the words in the Topics and hence the decrease of their specificity. Concluding, Topics with small Specificity exhibit higher values of average cosine similarity to generic and not specific Concepts.

Based on the aforementioned perspective, the cases using the Concepts' shortest descriptions (e.g. only the words in the skos:prefLabel property) within their context (Microthesaurus and Domain), combined with a small number of the most influential words of the Topics were better performed than the others. More specifically, for the EuroVoc Concepts' Word Embeddings created by weighting either the Concept's words 65% ($C_w = 0.65$), its Microthesaurus 17.5% ($MT_w = 0.175$) and its Domain 17.5% ($D_w = 0.175$), or $C_w = 0.70$, $MT_w = 0.15$, $D_w = 0.15$, 13 EuroVoc Concepts were identified to be used in place of the 13 Topics derived from the initial application of the LDA algorithm. These results were obtained when the Topics' words used for the Topics' Word Embeddings have a probability to belong to a Topic greater than 0.004 (p > 0.004). On the other hand, the more generalizing the topics by increasing the number of words (i.e. lowering the probability p threshold close to zero) the smaller the number of concepts assigned. Accordingly, the smaller the number of different concepts assigned to the Topics, the broader their meaning and resulting to higher *average cosine similarity*. This occurs because a smaller number of different Concepts signifies the merging of the meaning of the Topics to broader Concepts.

Figure 1 presents the number of different EuroVoc Concepts (vertical axis) that were assigned to the 13 Topics for the cases which only the words from the skos: prefLabel properties of the Concepts were used. The results for three weighting combinations are shown: (a) $C_w = 0.65$, $MT_w = 0.175$ and $D_w = 0.175$, represented by the magenta bullets, (b) $C_w = 0.70$, $MT_w = 0.15$ and $D_w = 0.15$, represented by the light green bullets and (c) $C_w = 0.80$, $MT_w = 0.10$ and $D_w = 0.10$, represented by the red bullets. Note that when a bullet does not appear in a case, it coincides with the bullet of a greater value of C_w. The figure verifies that only the weighting combinations (a) and (b) are assigned successfully to the 13 Topics when the latter exhibit a higher level of specificity (p > 0.0037 and p > 0.004). The rest cases lead to a smaller number of different Concepts meaning that the Topic Specificity is ignored and hence the corresponding Concepts are more generic and less than 13.

The quality of these results was further evaluated. An assiduous inspection on the words in each Topic by an expert on the DL evaluation field resulted to an interpretation of the topics. The columns of Table 1 present (a) a sample of words of each Topic with the highest probability p, (b) the EuroVoc Concepts assigned to the Topics, (c) the *average cosine similarity* between the Word Embeddings of the EuroVoc Concepts for the weighting parameters ($C_w = 0.65$, $MT_w = 0.175$, $D_w = 0.175$) and the Word Embeddings of the Topics' words with probability to belong in Topic greater that 0.004 (p > 0.004) and (d) the interpretation of the Topics provided by the expert.

The Table confirms that the expert's interpretation is very close to the Concepts resulted by the proposed automated approach of using Word Embeddings. There are cases where the human interpretation of the Topic and the automated assigned concept are the same or very close. The interpretation of Topic 9 is 'Search Engine', while the preferred label of the Concept is the same. The interpretation of Topic 6 is 'Metadata Quality', while the preferred label of the assigned Concept is 'Metadata'. The oxymoron in Topic 9 is the fact that it has one of the worst *average cosine similarities* in the list, but the result is ideal. Furthermore, in case of Topic 1 the human hermeneutic capability focused on the process of reading taking into account what 'participants, students' do with a book, while on the other hand the Word Embeddings revealed the features of the Concept's descriptions ('Exchange of publications') that describe the item of use ('publication'). Analogous cases are those of Topics 5 and 12. In both cases the produced Word Embeddings revealed features on the main tool ('Network server' and 'Database management system') that 'Distributed services' and 'Information retrieval' are based.

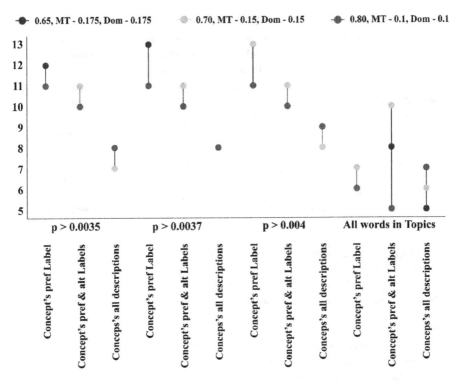

Fig. 1. Number of unique concepts

In the case of Topic 11, the system didn't understand its meaning. It is obvious from the words included in the Topic that music is a crucial part of it, but in the domain of DL Evaluation musical and sound issues are being studied under the 'Preservation' lens. However, the result is more than acceptable thus, as mentioned, EuroVoc is not a controlled vocabulary dedicated to DL Evaluation field. In the case of 'Open educational resources', the difference with human involvement is mainly an issue of expression. The expert used the word 'content' in his label while the system assigned the word 'resources'. However, the difference between 'Educational resources' and 'Educational content' is trivial.

On the other hand, in the cases of Topics 2 and 8 we can realize the human and machine capabilities. Human interpretation lied on the study of the 10 characteristic words of the Topic, while the system takes into consideration the total of the word with $p > 004$. This means that a human may possess a representative, but abstract view of the Topic, while the system has a holistic confrontation of the topic. As we can easily conjecture words 'similarity' and 'classification' have the specific dimension in their own cognitive system.

Table 1. Comparison of automatic and human indexing ($C_w = 0.65$, $MT_w = 0.175$, $D_w = 0.175$)

#	TopicWords	Related EuroVoc Concepts	Cosine Similarity (p > 0.004, Concept's prefLabels)	Human interpretation
1	Participants study text book students books reading paper	Exchange of publications	0.827169	Reading behavior
2	Similarity entities entity name names set data features	Geographical information system	0.850544	Similarity performance
3	Students resources learning design resource project educational teachers	Open educational resources	0.905495	Educational content
4	Data system server content service distributed node network	Network server	0.896054	Distributed services
5	User paper papers algorithm citation set recommendation cluster	Information technology user	0.855459	Recommending systems
6	Metadata data records resources content services objects elements	Metadata	0.918840	Metadata quality
7	Video image images videos task topics topic performance	Video display unit work	0.864785	Multimedia
8	Text words word performance method table classification data	On line data service	0.854793	Text classification
9	Search web results pages users relevance google engines	Search engine	0.843737	Search engines
10	Information users system evaluation user research process analysis	Information system	0.921446	Information seeking
11	Music preservation file data cluster sentiment files musical	Music	0.902214	Preservation
12	Query terms retrieval search using results relevant set	Database management system	0.814108	Information retrieval
13	User search interface task system tasks participants browsing	Information user	0.87754	Interface usability

5   Conclusions

The development of an effective workflow for automatic indexing seems not to be a 'chimera', but an issue of well-designed workflow, which will be based on the use of machine learning tools. Our proposed methodology includes tools for text clustering, classification, topic extraction and text representation, which were used either for the verification of human involvement (corpus selection and labeling), or for a complete automated workflow.

In general, the proposed process has given very promising results. The selection of a combination of weighting parameters for assigned concepts from a general-purpose thesaurus to a set of Topics that cluster a documents collection could provide similar results to human subject indexing workflow. Any differences appeared on the assigned labels of our experiment lie on the mismatch of the context between the general purpose controlled vocabulary and the very specific character of the document collection. In conclusion the current study managed effectively to balance the description of a very specific field with the potentials of a generic tool. In fact, that means that in case of absence of a more dedicated tool for indexing, a general purpose tool such as EuroVoc can cover the needs effectively.

Given the promising performance of the proposed method in the terms of average similarity between the Word Embeddings of the thesaurus concepts and the Word Embeddings of the words of the Topics, a future challenge is to test the performance of the proposed workflow using domain specific controlled vocabularies, such as ACM Taxonomy or the Computer Science Ontology (CSO).

References

1. Chu, C.M., Ajiferuke, I.: Quality of indexing in library and information science databases. Online Rev. **13**(1), 11–35 (1989)
2. Coates, S.: Teaching book indexing cognitive skills and term selection. The Indexer **23**(1), 15 (2002)
3. Hjørland, B.: Towards a theory of aboutness, subject, topicality, theme, domain, field, content ... and relevance. J. Am. Soc. Inf. Sci. Technol. **52**(9), 774–778 (2001)
4. International Organization for Standardization: ISO 5963-1985 Documentation - Methods for examining documents, determining their subjects, and selecting indexing terms. Geneva (1985)
5. Papachristopoulos, L., Kleidis, N., Sfakakis, M., Tsakonas, G., Papatheodorou, C.: Discovering the topical evolution of the digital library evaluation community. In: Garoufallou, E., Hartley, R., Gaitanou, P. (eds.) MTSR 2015. CCIS, vol. 544, pp. 101–112. Springer, Cham (2015). https://doi.org/10.1007/978-3-319-24129-6_9
6. Papachristopoulos, L., Tsakonas, G., Sfakakis, M., Kleidis, N., Papatheodorou, C.: The "Nomenclature of Multidimensionality" in the digital libraries evaluation domain. In: Fuhr, N., Kovács, L., Risse, T., Nejdl, W. (eds.) TPDL 2016. LNCS, vol. 9819, pp. 241–252. Springer, Cham (2016). https://doi.org/10.1007/978-3-319-43997-6_19
7. Thellefsen, T.L., Brier, S., Thellefsen, M.L.: Problems concerning the process of subject analysis and the practice of indexing. Semiotica **2003**(144), 177–218 (2003)
8. Pulgarín, A., Gil-Leiva, I.: Bibliometric analysis of the automatic indexing literature: 1956–2000. Inf. Process. Manag. **40**(2), 365–377 (2004)
9. Brown, K., Barrière, C.: Indexing, automatic. In: Encyclopedia of Language & Linguistics, pp. 603–610 (2006)
10. Dunham, G.S., Pacak, M.G., Pratt, A.W.: Automatic indexing of pathology data. J. Am. Soc. Inf. Sci. **29**(2), 81–90 (1978)
11. Golub, K.: Automated subject classification of textual web documents. J. Doc. **62**(3), 350–371 (2006)

12. Névéol, A., Shooshan, S.E., Humphrey, S.M., Mork, J.G., Aronson, A.R.: A recent advance in the automatic indexing of the biomedical literature. J. Biomed. Inform. **42**(5), 814–823 (2009)

13. Joorabchi, A., Mahdi, A.E.: Classification of scientific publications according to library controlled vocabularies. Libr. Hi Tech **31**(4), 725–747 (2013)

14. Golub, K., Hagelbäck, J., Ardö, A.: Automatic classification using DDC on the Swedish Union Catalogue. In: 18th European Networked Knowledge Organization Systems Workshop, NKOS 2018, Porto, Portugal, 13 September 2018, pp. 4–16 (2018)

15. Pokorny, J.: Automatic subject indexing and classification using text recognition and computer-based analysis of tables of contents. In: ELPUB 2018, Toronto, Canada, June 2018. https://hal.archives-ouvertes.fr/hal-01816705. Accessed 09 August 2019

16. Peng, S., You, R., Wang, H., Zhai, C., Mamitsuka, H., Zhu, S.: DeepMeSH: deep semantic representation for improving large-scale MeSH indexing. Bioinformatics **32**(12), i70–i79 (2016)

17. Blei, D.M., Ng, A.Y., Jordan, M.I.: Latent Dirichlet allocation. J. Mach. Learn. Res. **3**, 993–1022 (2003)

18. Lau, J.H., Newman, D., Karimi, S., Baldwin, T.: Best topic word selection for topic labelling, pp. 605–613 (2010)

19. Magatti, D., Calegari, S., Ciucci, D., Stella, F.: Automatic labeling of topics. In 2009 Ninth International Conference on Intelligent Systems Design and Applications, pp. 1227–1232 (2009)

20. Lau, J.H., Grieser, K., Newman, D., Baldwin, T.: Automatic labelling of topic models. In Proceedings of the 49th Annual Meeting of the Association for Computational Linguistics: Human Language Technologies-Volume 1, pp. 1536–1545 (2011)

21. Mikolov, T., Sutskever, I., Chen, K., Corrado, G.S., Dean, J.: Distributed representations of words and phrases and their compositionality. In: Advances in Neural Information Processing Systems, pp. 3111–3119 (2013)

22. Yao, L., Zhang, Y., Chen, Q., Qian, H., Wei, B., Hu, Z.: Mining coherent topics in documents using word embeddings and large-scale text data. Eng. Appl. Artif. Intell. **64**, 432–439 (2017)

23. Publications Office of the European Union: EuroVoc thesaurus Volume 1 Alphabetical version Part B. Luxembourg (2015)

24. Fuhr, N., et al.: Evaluation of digital libraries. Int. J. Digit. Libr. **8**(1), 21–38 (2007)

25. Afiontzi, E., Kazadeis, G., Papachristopoulos, L., Sfakakis, M., Tsakonas, G., Papatheodorou, C.: Charting the digital library evaluation domain with a semantically enhanced mining methodology. In: Proceedings of the 13th ACM/IEEECS Joint Conference on Digital Libraries, pp. 125–134. ACM Press (2013)

26. Fox, C.: A stop list for general text. ACM SIGIR Forum **24**(1–2), 19–21 (1989)

27. Mimno, D.: jsLDA: an implementation of Latent Dirichlet allocation in javascript (2018). https://github.com/mimno/jsLDA. Accessed 09 August 2019

28. Li, Y., Xu, L., Tian, F., Jiang, L., Zhong, X., Chen, E.: Word embedding revisited: a new representation learning and explicit matrix factorization perspective. In: Proceedings of the 24th International Conference on Artificial Intelligence, pp. 3650–3656. AAAI Press (2015)

29. Mikolov, T., Chen, K., Corrado, G., Dean, J.: Efficient estimation of word representations in vector space (2013). https://arxiv.org/abs/1301.3781. Accessed 09 August 2019

30. Mikolov, T., Grave, E., Bojanowski, P., Puhrsch, C., Joulin, A.: Learning word vectors for 157 languages. In: Proceedings of the International Conference on Language Resources and Evaluation (2018). http://www.lrec-conf.org/proceedings/lrec2018/pdf/627.pdf. Accessed 09 August 2019

An Ontology Based Approach for Data Leakage Prevention Against Advanced Persistent Threats

Emrah Kaya[1]([⊠])[iD], İbrahim Özçelik[1][iD], and Özgü Can[2][iD]

[1] Faculty of Computer and Information Sciences, Sakarya University,
Sakarya, Turkey
emrah.kaya@gmail.com, ozcelik@sakarya.edu.tr
[2] Department of Computer Engineering, Ege University, Bornova-Izmir, Turkey
ozgu.can@ege.edu.tr

Abstract. Advanced Persistent Threats (APTs) are increasingly being a risk for companies and institutions because of their distributed, complicated, multi-step and targeted behaviors. The amount of sensitive data in organizations are increasing and APTs threaten organizations by exfiltrating these data from the organization. The sensitive data not only include structured data such as credit card numbers but also unstructured data such as a private report created by the company. Although Data Leakage Prevention (DLP) systems are improving in terms of detecting the leakage of sensitive data, APTs' sophisticated methods are still successful against DLP systems. The characteristics of APTs require a prevention system that can semantically and hierarchically correlate basic elements and actions in the system with behaviors of an APT across the organization. Among many effort to classify APT behavior, MITRE's ATT&CK matrix for enterprise is widely accepted as an effective topology for the APT behavior. In this paper, an ontology based approach to achieve data leakage prevention against APTs is proposed. The proposed approach correlates low-level event details with APT techniques and tactics defined in MITRE's ATT&CK matrix.

Keywords: Data Leakage Prevention · Advanced Persistent Threat · Ontology · Semantic Web · MITRE ATT&CK

1 Introduction

In the cyber security domain, the most prevalent requirement is automatically detecting and preventing malicious actions while sharing information across systems in order to prevent same activity in those systems. Specifically, understandable rules have to be extracted for the computer in order to process them without human intervention. The solution for this problem is extracting a signature of the malware or extracting some specific features of the executable

© Springer Nature Switzerland AG 2019
E. Garoufallou et al. (Eds.): MTSR 2019, CCIS 1057, pp. 115–125, 2019.
https://doi.org/10.1007/978-3-030-36599-8_10

malware and classifying by using these features. The evasion tactics of malwares for these approaches vary from using different versions of the same malware via basic changes on the malware [1, 2] to using a virtual machine within the malware [3], which were successful. A better approach is monitoring operating system function calls (which we will refer as "system-calls" in this study) depending on the fact that all functions of a malware should call a corresponding system-call for executing the actual operation [4, 5]. Besides, APTs differ from malwares. APTs tend to exploit vulnerabilities within the core programs in a system like PDF readers, PowerShell and VBScript. They also execute steps of the attack using different programs. Therefore, a system wide and continuous detection and prevention mechanism is needed instead of a single process and executable based solution.

As the Intellectual Property values of companies increase, Data Leakage Prevention (DLP) systems are also widely used [6, 7] and gathering more importance. However, they still face challenges like dependency to human intervention, leakage over trusted applications and computers, lack of adaptability to different systems, lack of semantic inference from the content and lack of correlation of peripheral properties of documents like user, process, computer, etc. with the content.

In recent years, security practitioners use MITRE's "Adversarial Tactics, Techniques, and Common Knowledge" (ATT&CK)[1] matrix in order to develop and establish their security policies. The MITRE ATT&CK matrix divides an APT's attack into subsequent steps called as Tactic and defines behaviours for executing these steps as Techniques. In order to achieve a successful DLP against APT and to have a generic solution that doesn't depend on a specific system is attainable via describing the components in the system and their relationships correctly and independent of the system. For this purpose, an ontology for the DLP against APT is proposed in this study. Thus, MITRE's topology could be used and incorporated with event details such as operating system function calls. To the best of our knowledge, there's no ontology for the DLP against APT problem. In this study, the main components and their relationships of the proposed ontology are defined. The goal of the proposed approach is to interconnect the DLP solutions with the sophisticated risks of APTs and mitigate APTs' data exfiltration capabilities.

The paper is organized as follows: Sect. 2 presents the related work, Sect. 3 expresses the requirements and defines the main components of the ontology, and presents a use case, finally Sect. 4 contributes and outlines the vision for the future work.

2   Related Work

In the literature, current researches on APT are given in a general concept and do not directly related with DLP. Ontologies are used to describe attack vectors and APT related threats. In [8], attack behaviours of APTs are analyzed, an

---

[1] https://attack.mitre.org/.

attack ontology is proposed and ontology rules are defined in order to detect attacks. Also, it is shown that APTs execute attacks in phases and behaviours within the phases can be associated with certain system-calls. [9] discusses how sub-functions and actions of an attack can be defined, how these actions and the components (user, computer, data) that are affected in the action can be evaluated together, how an attack behaviour can be modelled using these details, and how an inference from function to behaviour to attack can be achieved. An attack ontology that is discussed in [10] shows the importance of the ontology both for the detection and prevention of attacks, and for the sharing of information within systems. A similar work that is presented in [1] is specific to intrusion detection. The related study defines the components of an attack and shows how those components can be used together in order to detect an attack. [11] discusses how to model process, system-call, source and target relationship in an ontology in order to detect a malicious behaviour. Also, the study shows how to calculate the risk of an unknown program using the proposed model by an implementation on a system. The research in [12] focuses on malwares and static analysis of executables, also shows how details like assembly instructions can be grouped as behaviours and a detection can be achieved by utilizing these behaviours.

The phases of APTs and malwares are generally studied in different works. In [13], different phases for malwares are suggested. Leveraging the attacks and describing behaviours for phases are also suggested in [14,15]. Among these studies, MITRE's ATT&CK matrix project is prominent as it proposes a topology for the attacks. The MITRE's ATT&CK matrix divides an attack into subsequent phases known as *Tactics* and each Tactic has behaviours known as *Techniques* for accomplishing the Tactic. Although MITRE's ATT&CK matrix is used to define the APT steps, to the best of our knowledge, MITRE's ATT&CK is not used as a part of an ontology in the literature. The study presented in [16] relates lower level details such as system audits with Techniques and Tactics, but it lacks of defining an ontology.

The literature study shows that although there are recent detailed studies on APTs and attack ontologies, none of them directly addresses the data leakage problem originated from APTs. Special studies are needed for data leakage detection on top of the APT attack awareness. Besides, it is important to incorporate the topologies like MITRE's ATT&CK with fine-grained details like system-calls. Therefore, an ontology based approach is needed, which not only binds higher level concepts like Techniques and Tactics with low-level events like operating system function calls, but also associates data leakage related properties with these events.

3   The DLP Ontology Against APT

In this section, firstly, requirements and components of the DLP ontology are explained respectively. Later, a case study of the proposed approach is presented.

3.1   Requirements of the DLP Ontology

The distinctive features of APT related DLP attacks are their diverse and non-trivial methods, their ability to upgrade their vectors and their tendency to hide and postpone the attack until the target is reached [15]. These features lead to the requirements of the DLP Ontology against APT. Therefore, the ontology should provide the following items:

- Include APT detection features that incorporate low level events such as system calls.
- To be able to maintain a hierarchical inferring mechanism that starts from system calls, merges systems calls into well defined functions, detect APT techniques with the presence of corresponding functions, and infer the APT tactics that took place.
- To be able to detect an APT event that is in the Initial Access state.
- To be aware of data collection and data exfiltration behaviours of an APT.
- To be aware of data hiding techniques of an APT.

System call is the basic element of any event in the operation system. Regardless of the tool or method being used, if an operation on a resource is needed, the only way to access the resource is through the corresponding system call. For instance, if a program needs to open a file for reading, the request will eventually end up with a *CreateFile* system call. As the toolkits that APTs utilize are very diverse, the DLP system needs inspecting basic elements like system calls for detecting suspicious actions. However, although system calls support finer details, most of the system calls are common for every process and there can be thousands of instances in a second. Thus, an inferring mechanism that incorporates both pattern matching and reasoning from system call up to the most general query for an APT presence is required.

APTs execute their attacks generally using the programs, scripts or tools that are already available in the operating system. However, they use special software or a compromised file especially in the first encounter with the target system for penetration into the system [7]. For that reason, during the "Initial Access" state, when there's not enough data for the assessment of the APT, a preventive static analysis of the executables or processes in the system is needed. In this study, this analysis is called as "Process Confidence Score". The result of Process Confidence Score should be merged with the other components of the ontology.

Specific to the DLP domain, data collection behaviours of an APT is distinctive. Thus, such an APT first needs to explore the important files and content for exfiltration. Otherwise, trying to upload every file in the system will result in higher data transfer rates, bigger footprints and eventually easy detection of the APT presence in the system. On top of that, data exfiltration behaviours are the final target for such an APT. Detection of these behaviours will help discovering the APT, even the previous steps of the attack couldn't be detected.

Most of the current DLP systems are able to detect keywords, regular expression, etc. For this reason, an APT cannot basically send the sensitive data that it finds in plain text. It requires to hide or to obfuscate such data for penetrating the DLP system. Although data hiding techniques like archiving, encoding using off the shelf libraries and tools are effective, they are detectable as usage of those libraries will be a distinctive feature. Therefore, a sophisticated APT might utilize customized in-memory methods that doesn't require a library usage or it may use benign tools or applications such as Calculator or Microsoft Excel for ciphering the data [17]. Even transfer of an encrypted data might be a distinctive feature for an attack. Hence, an APT might need to utilize Content Based Evasion Attacks [18] like transposition, substitution, synonymy, polysemy which are effective yet hard-to-detect. Thus, a DLP system against an APT should be aware of those techniques and detect an APT with the presence of these behaviours.

In order to meet the above criteria, a list of questions that the ontology should be able to answer for each system call are determined. The determined questions can be seen in Fig. 1. These questions aim to find the required components of the ontology. Thus, the question at each step gives a finer detail of the system in order to answer the most general question at the top of the Fig. 1.

3.2   Components of the DLP Ontology

After determining the questions that are listed in Fig. 1, the key components of the DLP Ontology are specified. The key components are SystemCall, Process, Function, APTTechnique, APTTactic, APTRisk, Content, ContentPrivacyLevel, ContentModification and DLPDecision:

- SystemCall is the main concept in the DLP ontology. hasCategory, hasAncestor, hasUser, calledBy, originatedAt are the object properties of the SystemCall. In the literature, system calls are grouped into categories [19,20]. Thus, further steps in the analysis and detecting patterns will be more robust. Therefore, hasCategory property is created. hasAncestor is used to determine the SystemCall sequences such as Functions. hasUser, calledBy and originatedAt determine the User, Process and the Host of the SystemCall correspondingly. SystemCall's data properties are systemCallName, systemCallParameters, dateTime.
- Process maps to a process in the system and has the hasReputation as data property. hasReputation stands for the confidence level acquired through the analysis of the executable.
- Function represents the pattern of system calls that any of the Techniques might utilize in the attack. It can be associated with the system call sequences in several ways. rdf:List [21] can be utilized, or regular expression matching capabilities of the modern inference engines can be used, or a machine learning method such as N-Gram [22] can be utilized. In order to store the system calls, Function uses hasSystemCalls object property and systemCallList data property.

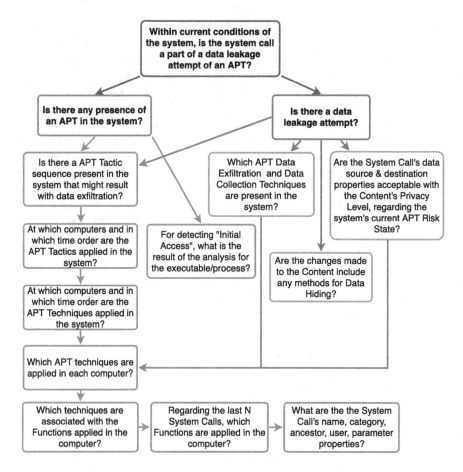

Fig. 1. Questions of the DLP ontology.

- APTTechnique associates the Function with more generic and reusable behaviour of an APT, so that a set of Functions will combine into an APTTechnique. The individuals of this class will be the Techniques of the MITRE ATT&CK Matrix. APTTechnique uses hasFunction and isUsedByTactic object properties for this association. Also, APTTechnique uses hasMinimumFunctionsExecuted data property in order to prevent false positives and provide a better risk assessment.
- APTTactic determines the behaviour of the APT and corresponds to the each Tactic column in the MITRE ATT&CK Matrix. APTTactic uses hasTechniques object property in order to associate with the corresponding APTTechnique.
- APTRisk represents the APT risk in the system. APTRiskMinimum, APTRiskMaximum, APTDataCollectionRisk and APTDataExfiltrationRisk are the sub-concepts of APTRisk. APTRiskMinimum and APTRiskMaximum

determine the risk in the system with the number of `APTTactics`
that are present in the system. `APTDataCollectionRisk` and `APTDataEx`
`filtrationRisk` specialize the risk with the presence of certain
`APTTechniques`.

- `Content` represents the content in use by the system call. `Content`
  uses the `hasContentPrivacyLevel` object property to associate it with
  `ContentPrivacyLevel`.
- `ContentPrivacyLevel` represents the structured content (such as credit card
  or security numbers) or unstructured content elements that are sensitive such
  as an report private to the organization. A machine learning algorithm will
  be utilized to extract this information from the text.
- `ContentModification` represents any in-memory data hiding methods that
  are used by the APT. As `APTTechnique` doesn't utilize any specific tool or
  library, an analysis on the content is needed. This analysis will compare
  pre and post content and determine if any content evasion method is used.
  `SubstitutionAttack` and `TranspositionAttack` are the sub-concepts of
  the `ContentModification` that are used to provide a better assessment of
  the risk. `ContentModification` uses `isContentAttack` data property that
  represents the presence of the content attack.
- `DLPDecision` represents the decision that should be done by the DLP
  ontology. DLP should decide whether the current system call is a part of an
  APT attack or not. `DLPAllow`, `DLPReject` and `DLPSuspect` are sub-concepts
  of the `DLPDecision` and represent the corresponding decisions of the DLP.
  The following rule defines the `DLPSuspect` decision:

$$\forall DLPDecision\ (hasAPTRisk\ some\ APTMinimumRisk)\ \sqcap$$
$$(hasAPTRisk\ some\ APTDataCollectionRisk)\ \sqcap$$
$$(\neg(hasAPTRisk\ some\ APTDataExfiltrationRisk))\ \sqcap$$
$$(isContentAttack\ value\ false)\ \sqcap$$
$$(hasContentPrivacyLevel\ some\ ConfidentalContent)\ \sqcap$$
$$(hasProcessReputation\ some\ xsd:double[>=\ "0.5"\ xsd:double])$$
$$\rightarrow \exists DLPDecisionSuspect$$

3.3 Case Study

In a standard scenario, an APT utilizes many techniques that are defined
in the MITRE ATT&CK matrix. APT3[2] is one of the APTs that is
referenced in MITRE ATT&CK topology. APT3 utilizes the "Data Compressed"
Technique (T1002). In the case study, data collection for this specific
APT Technique is accomplished. The system calls are captured by using
EasyHook library[3]. After investigating data, this technique is separated
into three `Functions`: *LoadZipLibrary*, *ReadAllFilesInDir* and *CompressFiles*.

---

[2] https://attack.mitre.org/groups/G0022.
[3] https://easyhook.github.io/.

Each of these Functions has several system call sequences. For example, *ReadAllFilesInDir* has *CreateFileW*, *ReadFile*, *SetFilePointer*, *FindFirstFileA*, *FindNextFile* and *CloseFile* system call sequence. Assume that the process executing these actions has the reputation value of *0.5*; the content of the file in this call has the privacy level of ConfidentialContent; and no previous content modification attack is detected. By combining these information and previous data collected in the system, the suspect situation will be detected with the inference of DLPSuspect. The corresponding inference flow is shown in Fig. 2:

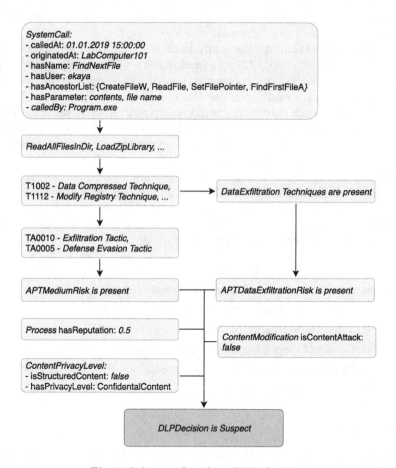

Fig. 2. Inference flow for a DLP decision.

After a *SystemCall* is captured, its properties are extracted. It's important to note that the historical data is also taken into account and the *SystemCall* is evaluated together with its ancestor *SystemCalls*. Using the *SystemCall*'s properties, the corresponding *Functions*; (*LoadZipLibrary* and *ReadAllFilesInDir*) are inferred. The inferring engine will further decide that these *Functions* are also part of some *Techniques* (*T1002*, *T1112*). At this point, two inferring decisions are made: One for deciding which *Tactics* are present, and the other for deciding if there's a *Technique* related to *DataExfiltration* is present. Those decisions point out which *APTRisks* are in action in the system. Meanwhile the evaluations for the *Process*'s reputation level, the classification of the content modification and the privacy level of the content is done in parallel. By combining the risk state, with the other classification results in the inference of the final decision for the DLP system for the specific *SystemCall* is made, which is *Suspect* in this case. A *Suspect SystemCall* can either be blocked, or allowed reporting the situation to system admin, which depends on the implementation of the DLP system.

4   Conclusion and Future Work

APTs' distributed, complicated, multi-step and targeted behaviors are effective against current DLP solutions. In order to mitigate the data exfiltration threats of APTs, DLP solutions need a Semantic Web based inference approach that correlates low-level details of an event with the behaviors of an APT. This study proposes an ontology based approach for such a DLP solution against APTs. The main elements of the ontology and their relationships are defined, and a case study is presented. The study presents a point of view for developing an ontology for a better DLP against APTs. As a future work, the relationships between ontology components will be defined more in detail after testing the available options for a relationship. For example, inferencing a `Function` using `SystemCalls` has different options such as utilizing regular expressions, using ordered list ontologies [21], data properties that are acquired through machine learning. The ontology will also have a layered structure with a meta-ontology on the top and a detailed ontology at the bottom. The meta-ontology will be especially used to allow the auto-generation of the inference rules in order to maximize the sharing of knowledge among systems and provide a better classification.

Acknowledgment. This work was supported by TUBITAK, the Scientific and Technological Research Council of Turkey (Grant No. 117E100).

References

1. More, S., Matthews, M., Joshi, A., Finin, T.: A knowledge-based approach to intrusion detection modeling. In: IEEE Symposium on Security and Privacy Workshops, pp. 75–81. IEEE, San Francisco (2012). https://doi.org/10.1109/SPW.2012.26
2. Rashid, A., et al.: Detecting and Preventing Data Exfiltration. Lancaster University, Academic Centre of Excellence in Cyber Security Research, Security Lancaster Report (2013)
3. Kafka, F.: ESET's guide to deobfuscating and devirtualizing FinFisher (2018). https://www.eset.com/me/whitepapers/wp-finfisher/. Accessed 30 June 2019

4. Canfora, G., Medvet, E., Mercaldo, F., Visaggio, C.A.: Detecting android malware using sequences of system calls. In: Proceedings of the 3rd International Workshop on Software Development Lifecycle for Mobile, pp. 13–20. ACM, Bergamo (2015). https://doi.org/10.1145/2804345.2804349
5. Ravi, C., Manoharan, R.: Malware detection using windows Api sequence and machine learning (0975–8887). Int. J. Comput. Appl. **43**(17), 12–16 (2012)
6. Alneyadi, S., Sithirasenan, E., Muthukkumarasamy, V.: A survey on data leakage prevention systems. J. Network Comput. Appl. **62**, 137–152 (2016)
7. Shabtai, A., Rokach, L., Elovici, Y.: A Survey of Data Leakage Detection and Prevention Solutions, 1st edn. Springer-Verlag, New York (2012). https://doi.org/10.1007/978-1-4614-2053-8
8. Choi, J., Choi, C., Lynn, H.M., Kim, P.: Ontology based APT attack behavior analysis in cloud computing. In: 10th International Conference on Broadband and Wireless Computing, Communication and Applications (BWCCA), pp. 375–379. IEEE, Krakow (2015). https://doi.org/10.1109/BWCCA.2015.69
9. Woo, S., On, J., Lee, M.: Behavior ontology: a framework to detect attack patterns for security. In: 27th International Conference on Advanced Information Networking and Applications Workshops (WAINA), pp. 738–743. IEEE, Barcelona (2013). https://doi.org/10.1109/WAINA.2013.42
10. Zhu, Y.: Attack pattern ontology: a common language for cyber security information sharing. Master Thesis, TUDelft - Delft University of Technology (2015)
11. Grègio, A., Bonacin, R., De Marchi, A.C., Nabuco, O.F., De Geus, P.L.: An ontology of suspicious software behavior. Appl. Ontology **11**(1), 29–49 (2016)
12. Jacob, G., Debar, H., Filiol, E.: Behavioral detection of malware: from a survey towards an established taxonomy. J. Comput. Virol. **4**(3), 251–266 (2008)
13. Väisänen, T., Trinberg, L., Pissanidis, N.: I accidentally malware - what should I do. is this dangerous? Overcoming inevitable risks of electronic communication. NATO Cooperative Cyber Defence Centre of Excellence, Tallinn, Estonia (2016)
14. Kott, A., Wang, C., Erbacher, R.F. (eds.): Cyber Defense and Situational Awareness. ADIS, vol. 62. Springer, Cham (2014). https://doi.org/10.1007/978-3-319-11391-3
15. Singh, S., Sharma, P.K., Moon, S.Y., Moon, D., Park, J.H.: A comprehensive study on APT attacks and countermeasures for future networks and communications: challenges and solutions. J. Supercomputing **75**(8), 4543–4574 (2016)
16. Milajerdi, S.M., Gjomemo, R., Eshete, B., Sekar, R., Venkatakrishnan, V.N.: HOLMES: real-time APT detection through correlation of suspicious information flows. In: The 40th IEEE Symposium on Security and Privacy, pp. 447–462. IEEE, San Fransisco (2019)
17. Blasco, J., Hernandez-Castro, J.C., Tapiador, J.E., Ribagorda, A.: Bypassing information leakage protection with trusted applications. Comput. Secur. **31**(4), 557–568 (2012)
18. Mustafa, T.: Malicious data leak prevention and purposeful evasion attacks: an approach to Advanced Persistent Threat (APT) management. In: Saudi International Electronics, Communications and Photonics Conference, pp. 1–5. IEEE, Fira (2013). https://doi.org/10.1109/SIECPC.2013.6551028
19. Moon, D., Im, H., Kim, I., Park, J.H.: DTB-IDS: an intrusion detection system based on decision tree using behavior analysis for preventing APT attacks. J. Supercomputing **73**(7), 2881–2895 (2017)

20. Gupta, S., Sharma, H., Kaur, S.: Malware characterization using windows API call sequences. In: Carlet, C., Hasan, M.A., Saraswat, V. (eds.) SPACE 2016. LNCS, vol. 10076, pp. 271–280. Springer, Cham (2016). https://doi.org/10.1007/978-3-319-49445-6_15

21. Drummond, N., et al.: Putting OWL in order: Patterns for sequences in OWL. In: 2nd OWL Experiences and Directions Workshop (OWLED), Athens, Georgia, USA (2006)

22. Canzanese, R., Mancoridis, S., Kam, M.: System call-based detection of malicious processes. In: International Conference on Software Quality, Reliability and Security, pp. 119–124. IEEE, Vancouver (2015). https://doi.org/10.1109/QRS.2015.26

Subtype Identification of Parkinson's Disease Using Sparse Canonical Correlation and Clustering Analysis of Multimodal Neuroimaging

Ji Hye Won[1,2] (ID), Mansu Kim[1,2], Jinyoung Yoon[3,4],
and Hyunjin Park[2,5(✉)]

[1] Department of Electrical and Computer Engineering,
Sungkyunkwan University, Suwon, Korea
jihyelol00@gmail.com
[2] Center for Neuroscience Imaging Research,
Institute for Basic Science, Suwon, Korea
[3] Department of Neurology, Sungkyunkwan University School of Medicine,
Seoul, Korea
[4] Neuroscience Center, Samsung Medical Center, Seoul, Korea
[5] School of Electronic and Electrical Engineering,
Sungkyunkwan University, Seoul, Korea
hyunjinp@skku.edu

Abstract. Parkinson's disease (PD) is a progressive neurodegenerative disorder with heterogeneity, which indicates that there are subtypes within PD. Identification of subtypes in PD is important because it may provide a better understanding of PD and improved therapy planning. Our aim was to find and characterize the subtypes of PD using multimodal neuroimaging. We computed structural neuroimaging and structural connectivity information from 193 patients. The structural connectivity information was computed through connectivity analysis derived from tractography of diffusion tensor imaging. A three-way sparse canonical correlation analysis was applied to reduce the dimension of three modalities into three latent variables. A clustering analysis with four clusters using the resulting latent variables was conducted. We regarded each cluster as subtypes of PD and showed that each subtype had distinct patterns of correlation with important known clinical scores in PD. The clinical scores were unified Parkinson's disease rating scale, mini-mental state examination, and standardized uptake value of putamen calculated using positron-emission tomography. The distinct correlation patterns of subtypes supported the existence of subtypes in PD and showed that the subtypes could be effectively identified by clustering a few features obtained with dimensionality reduction.

Keywords: Parkinson's disease · Sparse canonical correlation analysis · Clustering analysis

© Springer Nature Switzerland AG 2019
E. Garoufallou et al. (Eds.): MTSR 2019, CCIS 1057, pp. 126–136, 2019.
https://doi.org/10.1007/978-3-030-36599-8_11

1   Introduction

Meta-analysis of neuroimaging data can summarize a vast amount of research findings across a large number of participants and various experimental settings. Such an approach further enables statistically valid generalizations on the neural basis of psychological processes for healthy subjects and diseased patients. Thus, quantitative meta-analysis is a powerful technique to obtain a synoptic view of distributed neuroimaging findings.

Parkinson's disease (PD) is the second most common neurodegenerative disorder. PD is characterized by a various range of motor and non-motor symptoms such as cognitive impairment [1]. PD patients show heterogeneity in terms of symptoms, imaging, and other clinical markers, which implies there are different subtypes of the disease under the broad term of PD. Accurate identification of PD subtypes might provide insights into different pathophysiology of the subtypes, which could contribute to personalized therapy planning in the context of precision medicine. PD pathophysiology can be assessed with various neuroimaging modalities. Diffusion tensor imaging (DTI) allows the study of white fiber integrity influenced by the neurodegenerative process. Fractional anisotropy (FA) and the mean diffusivity (MD) are commonly used derived measures from DTI and they have been used as biomarkers of structural damage [2]. Besides FA and MD, which can be regarded as structural information, we can extract relevant fiber information from DTI through a tractography algorithm and obtain structural connectivity information. Many studies have shown changes in the structural connectivity and demonstrated their use as potential biomarkers in neurodegenerative diseases [3, 4]. These three imaging modalities might provide an opportunity to identify subtypes of PD.

Many dimensionality reduction algorithms have been developed to deal with high dimensional data such as neuroimaging. The classical well-known approach includes principal component analysis and multi-dimensional scaling [5]. The canonical correlation analysis (CCA) is a flexible method capable of dimensionality reduction, where one seeks to find a linear combination of features that maximize the correlation between two high-dimensional data. Sparse CCA (SCCA) is more suitable for dimension reduction as the user can impose sparsity constraint on the canonical vectors. The SCCA finds a sparse linear combination of features that lead to maximizing the correlation between two high-dimensional data [6].

Cluster analysis (CA) is suitable to study subtypes when the prior information of the data is unknown [7]. There are many clustering approaches including the k-means and hierarchical clustering. The algorithms seek clusters (subgroups) where between-cluster differences are large and within-cluster differences are small. The CA is a data-driven approach where the characteristics of the subgroups arise from the data not from prior assumptions.

In this study, we first computed three types of information from DTI, then dimensionality of these three modalities was reduced using an extended version of SCCA for three modalities, three-way SCCA (TSCCA). Subsequently, we applied cluster analysis techniques to identify PD subtypes. The characteristics of the subtypes were quantified with correlation with important clinical variables of PD. Existing studies of exploring subtypes in PD considered clinical scores based on self-completed questionnaires of PD patients [8, 9]. However, our study is one of the first studies to explore subtypes in PD using neuroimaging data. Our approach is better as the imaging data is more objective and less biased than self-reported completed questionnaires.

2   Methods

2.1   Data Description

Subjects. This study was approved by the Institutional Review Board of Samsung Medical Center and performed according to the principles of Helsinki declaration. All enrolled subjects provided written informed consent. We recruited 193 PD patients aged 36–87 (average 65.93 ± 9.76 [standard deviation], 89 males and 104 females). We prospectively recruited drug naïve, early-stage PD patients at Movement Disorders Clinic of Samsung Medical Center from 2015 to 2016. PD was diagnosed using the United Kingdom Parkinson's Disease Society Brain Bank criteria. The early stage of PD was defined as disease duration of fewer than 4 years and the Hoehn and Yahr (HY) stage less than 3. Subjects who had structural brain lesions including territorial stroke or white matter changes (age-related white matter change score ≥ 2 on brain MRI), other known neurodegenerative diseases, psychiatric disorders requiring medication, cognitive, or musculoskeletal problems mimicking parkinsonism were excluded.

Neuroimaging Data. Our data consist of several modalities, such as FA and MD from DTI, and betweenness centrality from tractography of DTI. DTI was collected using a 3.0 T MRI scanner (Philips 3T Intera Achieva). Scans were collected with the following parameters: 128×128 acquisition matrix; $1.72 \times 1.72 \times 2$ mm^3 voxels; reconstructed to $1.72 \times 1.72 \times 2$ mm^3; 70 axial slices; 22×22 cm^2 field of view; TE 60 ms, TR 7696 ms; flip angle 90°; slice gap 0 mm; b-factor of 600 s/mm2; 45 diffusion directions. Axial sections were acquired parallel to the anterior commissure-posterior commissure line.

Clinical Scores. Several clinical scores, including unified Parkinson's disease rating scale (UPDRS) part 3 score and the Korean mini-mental status exam (MMSE-K) were collected. Standardized uptake value (SUV) of putamen was also used. These values were used for correlation analysis to identify the subtypes of PD. Parkinsonian motor symptoms were evaluated with the UPDRS part 3. Part 3 covers the motor evaluation of disability and includes ratings for tremor, bradykinesia, and rigidity. MMSE-K was performed to check general cognition in all enrolled subjects. MMSE-K is the Korean version of the mini-mental status exam. ^{18}F positron emission tomography was to measure presynaptic dopamine loss. We computed the SUV of putamen as the ratio between region uptake value of putamen from the dominant side and those of the cerebellum.

2.2   DTI Processing

Preprocessing. Preprocessing of DTI data, including skull-stripping, head motion and eddy current correction was performed using FSL software (FSL, http://fsl.fmrib.ox.ac.uk/fsl/fdt). We adopted the automated anatomical labeling (AAL) atlas defined on the MNI space to specify the regions of interest (ROIs) via image co-registration.

Calculation of FA and MD. Diffusion tensor analysis toolkit of FSL was used to compute voxel-wise maps of FA and MD. Regional FA and MD values were computed by the sample mean of voxel-wise FA and MD maps for each ROI.

Tractography. The probabilistic tractography algorithm implemented in FSL was adopted to extract the fiber connection in 90 ROIs. We used the Bedpost tool in FSL to allow the modeling of crossing fibers. The probtrackX was used to generate a connectivity distribution between each ROI to a specified target region. Fiber tracking ended when fiber direction changed rapidly. Tractography was performed in the native space for each patient. All 90 ROIs were used as seeds. Each brain region was selected as the seed region and its connectivity probabilities to the other 89 regions were calculated.

Connectivity Analysis. Matrices representing the fiber-to-fiber connectivity derived from the tractography process were used for the connectivity analysis. Graph nodes were the 90 ROIs and the edges were defined as the fiber probability connecting a pair of regions. A weighted and undirected network model was adopted. The constructed graph is commonly referred to as the structural connectivity matrix. We computed the betweenness centrality (BC), the fraction of all shortest paths in the network that contain a given node, to quantify the relative importance of the nodes.

2.3   Three-Way Sparse Canonical Correlation Analysis (TSCCA)

Herein, we use the boldface lowercase letter to denote a vector, and the boldface uppercase letter to denote a matrix. Given datasets $X \in \mathbb{R}^{n \times p}$, $Y \in \mathbb{R}^{n \times q}$, and $Z \in \mathbb{R}^{n \times r}$, with n samples, where X denotes p features of the FA values, and Y denotes q features of MD values, and Z denotes r features of BC values. We applied the TSCCA to reduce the dimension of neuroimaging data. TSCCA is an extended SCCA method that can handle three datasets, where three pair-wise SCCAs are performed simultaneously [10, 11]. The formulation is defined as follows:

$$\max_{u,v,w} u^T X^T Y v + v^T Y^T Z w + w^T Z^T X u \tag{1}$$

$$s.t.\ u^T X^T Y v \le 1, v^T Y^T Z w \le 1, w^T Z^T X u \le 1, \|u_1\| \le c_1, \|v_1\| \le c_2, \|w_1\| \le c_3,$$

where u, v and w were the corresponding canonical loading vectors. We can rewrite the objective functions for TSCCA as follows:

$$\min_{u,v,w} -u^\mathrm{T}X^\mathrm{T}Yv - v^\mathrm{T}Y^\mathrm{T}Zw - w^\mathrm{T}Z^\mathrm{T}Xu + \beta_u\|u_1\| + \beta_v\|v_1\| + \beta_w\|w_1\|, \qquad (2)$$

where β_u, β_v, and β_w were regularization parameters. The l_1 penalty, controlled by β_u, β_v, and β_w, was applied to induce sparsity and prevent overfitting [11].

Parameter Selection. For tuning the parameters (i.e., β_u, β_v, and β_w), we applied the nested five-fold cross validation algorithm:

$$\mathrm{CV} = \frac{1}{5}\sum_{i=1}^{5} \frac{1}{3}\left(corr(X_i u_{-i}, Y_i v_{-i}) + corr(X_i u_{-i}, Z_i w_{-i}) + corr(Y_i v_{-i}, Z_i w_{-i})\right), \quad (3)$$

where X_i, Y_i, and Z_i denoted the i-th subset of the test set and u_{-i}, v_{-i}, and w_{-i} denoted the estimated loading vectors from the datasets except for the i-th subset (training set, X_{-i}, Y_{-i}, and Z_{-i}). The optimal parameters were selected by maximizing CV in (3). We repeated the parameter selection procedure 1000 times and choose the parameters showing the largest averaged CV.

Calculation of Latent Variables. The elements of the loading vector represent weights of ROIs contributing to maximize correlation among three data. Inner product between loading vector and imaging data was computed to obtain latent variable for each modality. Each high-dimensional data was reduced to a scalar (90 to 1).

2.4 Clustering Analysis and Verification of the Subtypes

We applied the k-means clustering using the latent variables. We chose an appropriate number of clusters using the elbow method, which examines the ratio of variance explained as a function of the number of clusters. The elbow method was tried from 1 to 5 to find optimal k. Our study lacked ground truth regarding subtypes thus we verified subtypes in an indirect fashion. We verified the subtypes by conducting an analysis of variance (ANOVA) test and correlation analysis using the clinical scores for each subtype.

3 Results

3.1 TSCCA Results

We applied TSCCA to the 90 regional FA, MD and BC from 193 patients. We observed that 25 ROIs from FA, 19 from MD, and 31 from BC had non-zero weights for the loading vectors (Fig. 1). In FA, there were Inferior frontal gyrus, triangular part (L), Rolandic operculum(L), Rolandic operculum(R), Supplementary motor area(L), Supplementary motor area(R), Olfactory cortex(L), Olfactory cortex(R), Superior frontal gyrus, medial(R), Gyrus rectus(L), Anterior cingulate and paracingulate gyri(R), Median cingulate and paracingulate gyri(L), Median cingulate and paracingulate gyri (R), Hippocampus(L), Hippocampus(R), Amygdala(L), Calcarine fissure and surrounding cortex(R), Lingual gyrus(R), Fusiform gyrus(L), Fusiform gyrus(R), Angular gyrus(R), Paracentral lobule(L), Thalamus(R), Superior temporal gyrus(R), Inferior temporal gyrus(L) and Inferior temporal gyrus(R). In MD, there were Precental gyrus (L), Precental gyrus(R), Inferior frontal gyrus, orbital part(L), Rolandic operculum(L), Rolandic operculum(R), Gyrus rectus(R), Anterior cingulate and paracingulate gyri(R), Posterior cingulate gyrus(R), Hippocampus(L), Hippocampus(R), Parahippocampal gyrus(L), Parahippocampal gyrus(R), Lingual gyrus(R), Middle occipital gyrus(R), Inferior occipital gyrus(R), Postcentral gyrus(R), Thalamus(L), Thalamus(R), and Inferior temporal gyrus(R). In BC, there were Inferior frontal gyrus, opercular part(R), Inferior frontal gyrus, triangular part(R), Rolandic operculum(L), Rolandic operculum (R), Superior frontal gyrus, medial(L), Superior frontal gyrus, medial orbital(L), Gyrus rectus(L), Gyrus rectus(R), Insula(R), Anterior cingulate and paracingulate gyri(R), Median cingulate and paracingulate gyri(R), Hippocampus(L), Hippocampus(R), Cuneus(L), Lingual gyrus(L), Inferior occipital gyrus(R), Fusiform gyrus(L), Post-central gyrus(L), Supramarginal gyrus(R), Angular gyrus(L), Angular gyrus(R), Paracentral lobule(R), Caudate nucleus(L), Caudate nucleus(R), Lenticular nucleus, pallidum(L), Lenticular nucleus, pallidum(R), Thalamus(L), Thalamus(R), Superior temporal gyrus(R), Temporal pole: superior temporal gyrus(R), and Inferior temporal gyrus(R). The selected regions from the three modalities tend to be similar and com-plementary. The weights were sorted in terms of magnitude and the top five regions were as follows. In FA, we identified right and left rolandic operculum, right thalamus, right superior temporal gyrus, and right fusiform gyrus. In MD, there were left and right hippocampus, left and right rolandic operculum, and right thalamus. In BC, we observed left and right rolandic operculum, right inferior temporal gyrus, right superior temporal gyrus, and right hippocampus.

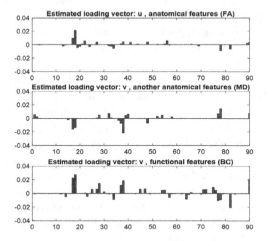

Fig. 1. Comparison of estimated loading vectors. The first row corresponds to the FA, the second row corresponds to the MD, and the third row corresponds to the BC. The x-axis represents 90 ROIs and the y-axis represents the values of loading vectors. Non-zero elements of the loading vector represent selected regions contributing to the TSCCA.

3.2 Clustering Analysis of Subtypes

The elbow method suggested that the optimal number of clusters was four. K-mean clustering with four clusters was performed. Three latent variables were clustered to four subtypes as shown in Fig. 2(a). If we projected three latent variables to two variables, there were small overlaps between clusters and this serves as additional evidence of using all three latent variables is desirable (Fig. 2(b)).

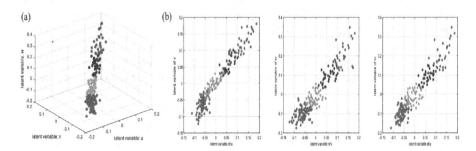

Fig. 2. (a) Clustering results using three latent variables. (b) Projected plots using only two variables in three axes of the (a).

3.3 Verification Results of the Subtypes

We conducted ANOVA test to compare how clinical scores differed among subtypes. The only significant difference between the subtypes (p-value < 0.05) was MMSE-K (F (3,189) = 3.19, p-value = 0.0247). We performed post-hoc t-tests for all possible combination pairs from four subtypes to investigate the difference in MMSE-K. There was a significant difference between subtypes 1 and 2 (p-value = 0.0128) and between subtypes 2 and 3 (p-value = 0.0491).

Table 1 is the results of the correlation analysis of latent variables and clinical scores for each subtype. We observed that each subtype showed distinct patterns of correlation with clinical scores. Following are the correlation patterns with p-values less than 0.05. Subtype 1 showed a negative correlation with the SUV of putamen and a positive correlation with MMSE-K, subtype 2 showed a positive correlation with the SUV, and negative correlation with the UPDRS, subtype 3 only showed a positive and relatively high correlation with the MMSE-K, and subtype 4 showed an only positive correlation with SUV. In conclusion, we observed distinct correlation patterns of subtypes and this serves as an indirect validation of the subtypes.

Results of Table 1 are plotted in Figs. 3, 4 and 5. Figure 3 shows the correlation plot of latent variables from **u** and clinical scores. Figures 4, and 5 are correlation plots between the latent variable created from **v** and **w**, respectively, and clinical scores for four subtypes. We confirmed that the trends (the dashed slopes) for the three clinical scores of Figs. 3, 4 and 5 differ for each subtype (distinguishable with color; column).

Table 1. The results of the correlation analysis between the three latent variables and clinical scores for four subtypes. The correlation results are expressed as [correlation coefficient, p-value], and the elements with p-value < 0.05 are shown in bold.

Subtypes	Latent value	SUV of putamen	MMSE-K	UPDRS
Subtype 1	Latent value of u	[−0.168, 0.342]	**[0.359, 0.037]**	[−0.094, 0.595]
	Latent value of v	[−0.177, 0.317]	[0.262, 0.134]	[−0.035, 0.845]
	Latent value of w	**[−0.35, 0.043]**	[0.239, 0.174]	[−0.183, 0.301]
Subtype 2	Latent value of u	[0.053, 0.627]	[-0.078, 0.475]	[−0.062, 0.573]
	Latent value of v	[−0.003, 0.975]	[0.166, 0.128]	[0.123, 0.264]
	Latent value of w	**[0.223, 0.04]**	[0.025, 0.821]	**[−0.283, 0.009]**
Subtype 3	Latent value of u	[0.02, 0.917]	**[0.428, 0.021]**	[0.191, 0.32]
	Latent value of v	[−0.055, 0.777]	[0.219, 0.254]	[0.195, 0.311]
	Latent value of w	[0.051, 0.761]	[0.273, 0.152]	[0.357, 0.057]
Subtype 4	Latent value of u	[0.04, 0.793]	[0.027, 0.862]	[−0.012, 0.939]
	Latent value of v	[0.135, 0.377]	[0.061, 0.69]	[0.081, 0.595]
	Latent value of w	**[0.303, 0.043]**	[0.073, 0.635]	[−0.037, 0.807]

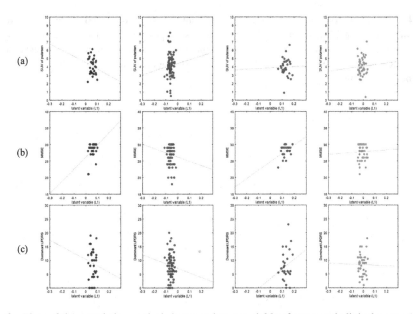

Fig. 3. Plots of the correlation analysis between latent variables from u and clinical scores (e.g., SUV of putamen, MMSE-K, and UPDRS) for four subtypes. The first row corresponds to the SUV of putamen, the second row corresponds to the MMSE-K, and the third row corresponds to the UPDRS. Each column separated by color (blue, red, magenta, and green) corresponds to four subtypes. (Color figure online)

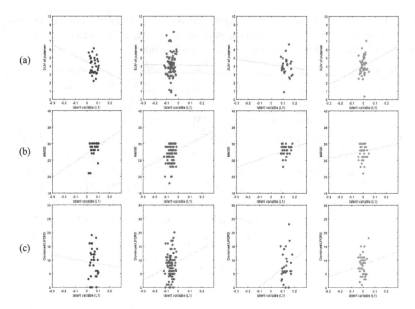

Fig. 4. Plots of the correlation analysis between latent variables from v and clinical scores (e.g., SUV of putamen, MMSE-K, and UPDRS) for four subtypes. The first row corresponds to the SUV of putamen, the second row corresponds to the MMSE-K, and the third row corresponds to the UPDRS. Each column separated by color (blue, red, magenta, and green) corresponds to four subtypes. (Color figure online)

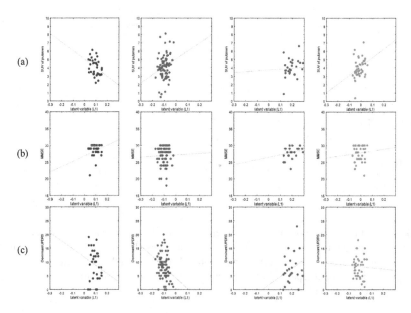

Fig. 5. Plots of the correlation analysis between latent variables from w and clinical scores (e.g., SUV of putamen, MMSE-K, and UPDRS) for four subtypes. The first row corresponds to the SUV of putamen, the second row corresponds to the MMSE-K, and the third row corresponds to the UPDRS. Each column separated by color (blue, red, magenta, and green) corresponds to four subtypes. (Color figure online)

4 Discussions

Our study identified four subtypes of PD using three neuroimaging modalities derived from DTI. Each subtype showed distinct patterns of correlation with important clinical scores in PD. Our methodology of using TSCCA for dimensionality reduction and clustering using the latent variable was effective at identifying the subtypes.

The MMSE-K score was significantly different among the subtypes. The MMSE-K measures the severity and progression of cognitive impairment for Koreans [12]. We could infer that each subtype has different levels of cognition. The selected regions (i.e., non-zero weights) of the loading vectors included thalamus and hippocampus. These are regions involved in cognitive impairment [13, 14]. The non-zero weights of the loading vectors from FA and MD were almost always of opposite sign for rolandic operculum, hippocampus, thalamus, etc. This confirmed anti-proportionate tendency between FA and MD. Overall, the selected regions from the TSCAA were consistent with existing studies [15]. Additional neuroimaging modalities besides from those derived from DTI might add complementary information, which could be handled with four-way or five-way SCCA, to reveal better-refined subtypes.

There are limitations to our study. We used the AAL atlas with 90 ROIs. There are atlases with more ROIs, which could lead to higher-dimensional observations. Our approach could be tested with the higher-dimensional data. We performed an indirect validation of subtypes using clinical scores including SUV of putamen, MMSE-K, and UPDRS. Better validation is possible with a dataset with additional clinical scores. The Parkinson's Progression Markers Initiative (PPMI) database includes additional scores of degrees of depression, sleep quality, olfactory function, etc. and using the database is left for future work. Our results were derived from clustering the latent variables from neuroimaging data. Bi-clustering approaches might allow us to consider both latent variables and the clinical scores at the same time in the clustering stage. This might improve the information content of the clustering and thus lead to better-defined subtypes.

In addition to SUVs, MMSE-K, and UPDRS, one study acquired and analyzed motor fluctuations, posture, and dyskinesia during activity of daily living data from wearable sensors [16]. Combining such diverse and refined big data related to PD with our proposed method might enhance precision medicine. Meaningful research would be possible if we extend four-way or five-way SCCA with the measurements of other sources from wearable sensors.

Acknowledgments. This study was supported by the Institute for Basic Science (grant number IBS-R015-D1), the National Research Foundation of Korea (grant number NRF-2019R1H1A2079721), the Ministry of Science and ICT of Korea under the ITRC program (grant number IITP-2019-2018-0-01798), and IITP grant funded by the Korean government under the AI Graduate School Support Program (No. 2019-0-00421).

References

1. Foltynie, T., Brayne, C., Barker, R.A.: The heterogeneity of idiopathic Parkinson's disease. J. Neurol. **249**, 138–145 (2002)
2. Atkinson-Clement, C., Pinto, S., Eusebio, A., Coulon, O.: Diffusion tensor imaging in Parkinson's disease: review and meta-analysis. NeuroImage Clin. **16**, 98–110 (2017). https://doi.org/10.1016/j.nicl.2017.07.011
3. Lo, C.-Y., Wang, P.-N., Chou, K.-H., Wang, J., He, Y., Lin, C.-P.: Diffusion tensor tractography reveals abnormal topological organization in structural cortical networks in Alzheimer's disease. J. Neurosci. **30**, 16876–16885 (2010). https://doi.org/10.1523/JNEUROSCI.4136-10.2010
4. van den Heuvel, M.P., Mandl, R.C.W., Stam, C.J., Kahn, R.S., Hulshoff Pol, H.E.: Aberrant frontal and temporal complex network structure in schizophrenia: a graph theoretical analysis. J. Neurosci. **30**, 15915–15926 (2010). https://doi.org/10.1523/JNEUROSCI.2874-10.2010
5. Burges, C.J.C.: Dimension reduction: a guided tour. Found. Trends® Mach. Learn. **2**, 275–364 (2009). https://doi.org/10.1561/2200000002
6. Rosa, M.J., et al.: Estimating multivariate similarity between neuroimaging datasets with sparse canonical correlation analysis: an application to perfusion imaging. Front. Neurosci. **9**, 366 (2015). https://doi.org/10.3389/fnins.2015.00366
7. van Rooden, S.M., Heiser, W.J., Kok, J.N., Verbaan, D., van Hilten, J.J., Marinus, J.: The identification of Parkinson's disease subtypes using cluster analysis: a systematic review. Mov. Disord. **25**, 969–978 (2010). https://doi.org/10.1002/mds.23116
8. Lawton, M., et al.: Developing and validating Parkinson's disease subtypes and their motor and cognitive progression. J. Neurol. Neurosurg. Psychiatry **89**, 1279–1287 (2018). https://doi.org/10.1136/jnnp-2018-318337
9. Fereshtehnejad, S.-M., Romenets, S.R., Anang, J.B.M., Latreille, V., Gagnon, J.-F., Postuma, R.B.: New clinical subtypes of Parkinson disease and their longitudinal progression. JAMA Neurol. **72**, 863 (2015). https://doi.org/10.1001/jamaneurol.2015.0703
10. Witten, D.M., Tibshirani, R.J.: Extensions of sparse canonical correlation analysis with applications to genomic data. Stat. Appl. Genet. Mol. Biol. **8** (2009). https://doi.org/10.2202/1544-6115.1470. Article 28
11. Hao, X.: Alzheimer's disease neuroimaging initiative: mining outcome-relevant brain imaging genetic associations via three-way sparse canonical correlation analysis in Alzheimer's disease. Sci. Rep. **7**, 44272 (2017). https://doi.org/10.1038/srep44272
12. Kim, D.-E., et al.: Single photon emission computerized tomography and neuropsychological tests that predict a good response to donepezil therapy for Alzheimer's Disease. Dement. Neurocognitive Disord. **14**, 106 (2015). https://doi.org/10.12779/dnd.2015.14.3.106
13. Yildiz, D., et al.: Impaired cognitive performance and hippocampal atrophy in Parkinson disease. Turkish J. Med. Sci. **45**, 1173–1177 (2015)
14. Prakash, K.G., Bannur, B.M., Chavan, M.D., Saniya, K., Sailesh, K.S., Rajagopalan, A.: Neuroanatomical changes in Parkinson's disease in relation to cognition: An update. J. Adv. Pharm. Technol. Res. **7**, 123–126 (2016). https://doi.org/10.4103/2231-4040.191416
15. Gattellaro, G., et al.: White matter involvement in idiopathic Parkinson disease: a diffusion tensor imaging study. AJNR Am. J. Neuroradiol. **30**, 1222–1226 (2009). https://doi.org/10.3174/ajnr.A1556
16. Borzì, L., et al.: Home monitoring of motor fluctuations in Parkinson's disease patients. J. Reliab. Intell. Environ. **5**, 145–162 (2019). https://doi.org/10.1007/s40860-019-00086-x

Predictive Data Transformation Suggestions in Grafterizer Using Machine Learning

Saliha Sajid[1,2], Bjørn Marius von Zernichow[2], Ahmet Soylu[2(✉)], and Dumitru Roman[1,2]

[1] University of Oslo, Oslo, Norway
salihasa@student.matnat.uio.no, dumitrur@uio.no
[2] SINTEF AS, Oslo, Norway
{saliha.sajid,bjornmarius.vonzernichow,ahmet.soylu,
dumitru.roman}@sintef.no

Abstract. Data preprocessing is a crucial step in data analysis. A substantial amount of time is spent on data transformation tasks such as data formatting, modification, extraction, and enrichment, typically making it more convenient for users to work with systems that can recommend most relevant transformations for a given dataset. In this paper, we propose an approach for generating relevant data transformation suggestions for tabular data preprocessing using machine learning (specifically, the Random Forest algorithm). The approach is implemented for Grafterizer, a Web-based framework for tabular data cleaning and transformation, and evaluated through a usability study.

Keywords: Data preprocessing · Data transformation · Transformation suggestions

1 Introduction

With the increasing amount of data being generated every day, organizations rely on reliable data quality to ensure that data analysis is done accurately and without any predispositions. Ideally it is preferred to perform analysis on clean data which is free of irrelevant values, but in real life, that kind of data is seldom available [11]. For data analysis, data scientists need to preprocess data to ensure that the data is in the right format and conforms to a certain set of rules. Through a series of interviews with data professionals, it was revealed that a majority of their time is spent on time-consuming data transformation tasks in the data preprocessing phase [8].

Data transformation, as part of preprocessing phase, plays a critical role in ensuring data quality before analysis [6]. Data transformation is a domain specific problem that focuses on the statistical properties, semantics, and structure of data and typically domain experts have the knowledge required to apply the

© Springer Nature Switzerland AG 2019
E. Garoufallou et al. (Eds.): MTSR 2019, CCIS 1057, pp. 137–149, 2019.
https://doi.org/10.1007/978-3-030-36599-8_12

right transformations on data. Several commercial tools and frameworks exist for data preprocessing, offering a large number of data cleaning and transformation actions. In addition to commercial tools, most common frameworks and languages for data analysis such as Pandas[1], scikit-learn[2] and R[3] also come with several useful methods for data preprocessing tasks. However, it can be challenging for data scientists to choose from a large number of transformations and interactively view the changes made to the dataset. This time- and cost-consuming process could be made more efficient by automatically recommending users suitable data cleaning and transformation actions in an interactive graphical user interface (GUI).

In this paper, we propose an approach for the generation of relevant data transformation suggestions for tabular data preprocessing. Our approach is based on providing user interactions as input to a recommender system built using machine learning (ML) techniques (more specifically, the Random Forest algorithm). Random Forest [1], an ensemble learning method for classification, constructs a number of decision trees and provides output by aggregating the predictions of the ensemble. The ability of the Random Forest to formulate rules and predict output by going through the characteristics of training data motivates the work in this paper to investigate its benefits for the problem at hand. Our approach offers a GUI providing users with the most relevant data transformation suggestions and enabling users to transform data by choosing one of the suggested transformations. Our proposed approach was implemented for Grafterizer [16] – a tabular data transformation and Linked Data generation tool, developed as part of the DataGraft platform [14,15], and evaluated through a usability study.

The rest of the paper is structured as follows. Section 2 provides background knowledge on data transformation, while Sect. 3 presents the related work. Section 4 describes our solution approach and Sect. 5 reports on its evaluation findings. Finally, Sect. 6 concludes the paper.

2   Tabular Data Transformations

Data transformation is a process of changing the format or structure of the data. It may be done for tasks such as extracting meaningful knowledge, enrichment, or fixing incorrect data to prepare it for analysis.

We categorize tabular transformations as *table-based*, *format-based*, and *string-based*. The set of transformations chosen for the purpose of this paper represents a subset of a potentially large number of transformations that can be applied to a tabular dataset. This subset of transformations was selected based on various relevant sources (*e.g.*, [12,16] and Trifacta[4]), and consists of basic and intuitive transformations that may not require any help from an expert. These

---

[1] https://pandas.pydata.org.

[2] https://scikit-learn.org.

[3] https://www.r-project.org.

[4] https://www.trifacta.com.

Table 1. Table-based transformations.

Scope	Name	Description
Row	Convert row to header	Convert the selected row to header
Row	Drop row	Drop the selected row
Row	Keep row	Keep the selected row
Column	Delete column	Delete the selected column
Column	Keep column	Keep the selected column
Column	Rename column	Rename the selected column

transformations can be made in a short number of steps, making it possible for the user to see the result when performed on a data object (*i.e.*, row, cell, and column).

Table-based transformations transform a dataset on the structural level. These transformations do not individually impact the data in rows and columns, but instead they change the formation of the dataset. They include feature extraction methods such as removing excess rows and columns, which may be unnecessary for analysis. Table 1 lists the selected table-based transformations.

Format-based transformations change the format of each individual cell in the selected data object without having much impact on the structure of the entire dataset. For instance, "count data by group" adds a column to the dataset containing the number of corresponding values existing in the source column. Table 2 for lists the selected format-based transformations.

Table 2. Format-based transformations.

Scope	Name	Description
Column	Normalise	Normalise numeric values
Column	Count data by group	Generate a new column with summed count of unique values of selected column
Column	Format date	Convert date to the given format
Column	To uppercase	Convert data to uppercase
Column	To lowercase	Convert data to lowercase
Cell	Round to nearest	Round the selected number to nearest integer

String-based transformations are applied to strings or text in the selected data object. This group of transformations can be used on a cell, column, and a row. It includes methods, such as filtering and modifications, applied to the individual strings in the dataset. Table 3 lists the selected string-based transformations.

Table 3. String-based transformations.

Scope	Name	Description
Row	Set row to *null*	Set the whole selected row to *null*
Column	Set column to *null*	Set the whole selected column to *null*
Column	Fill	Fill *nulls* in the column with the given input
Column	Split column	Split column using custom separator
Cell	Set cell to *null*	Set the value of selected cell to *null*
Cell	Extract	Extract values matching the selected text into a new column
Cell	Replace	Replace values matching the selected text with the given input in the corresponding column
Cell	Remove special characters	Remove special characters from the corresponding column

3 Related Work

There is a significant amount of research done in the area of data transformation, including several commercial tools and libraries that can be used both programmatically and visually through GUIs. In what follows, we discuss the most notable ones.

Tableau[5] is an interactive data analysis and visualisation platform that allows users to view data in understandable format and helps in generating customized dashboards. In addition to identifying problems in the data, Tableau analyses the given data to recommend transformations that may be of interest to the user. In also provides visual data profiling and a graphical list of steps taken to transform data in the form of a flowchart. Talend Data Preparation[6] is a tool that comes with a user-friendly interface to transform data before the analysis. It provides capabilities to filter, modify and enrich data by providing transformations intelligently. HoloClean[7] [13], a statistical inference engine to impute, clean, and enrich data is a weakly supervised ML system which makes use of data integrity constraints, quantitative statistics, value correlations, and external reference data to build a probabilistic model for data cleaning tasks. HoloClean identifies incorrect data values and conflicting tuples in a dataset but suffers from the lack of a convenient user interface.

Trifacta Wrangler is a powerful tool which comes with many data manipulation functionalities including restructuring, cleaning, and enrichment of data. A predictive model computes a ranked set of suggestions in the form of suggestion cards based on user's selection and historical data in an attempt to interpret the data transformation intent [7]. Trifacta also allows users to modify these

---

[5] https://www.tableau.com.

[6] https://www.talend.com/products/data-preparation.

[7] http://www.holoclean.io.

suggestions to identify which ones suit best, in addition to providing the user the ability to modify a particular suggestion. Though Trifacta provides transformations through predictive interactions, our work bases itself on creating a diverse set of transformations provided to the user based on historical data. OpenRefine[8], an open source tool, enables users to apply basic and advanced transformations on datasets, including normalization of numerical data and filtering of text. NADEEF [5] is a generalized data cleaning system which relies on rules to clean data, allowing users to specify data quality rules including functional dependencies for the given dataset. These rules are then used to find and repair violations in the given data. KATARA [4] is a data cleaning system which uses a knowledge base and human help. It can be used to clean various datasets by providing a table as input, and a knowledge base to interpret table semantics. It identifies incorrect data and the possible repairs for it, and uses the help of humans to disambiguate the table semantics and to annotate the data.

Despite substantial research in data preprocessing and use of ML, the above mentioned tools come with certain limitations. Though some of the tools provide graphical user interfaces, it is not always clear whether these tools make use of ML for providing data cleaning and transformation suggestions. HoloClean, on the other hand, uses ML to identify and correct anomalies in the given dataset but does not come with an interactive user interface to visualize the transformations performed on the dataset. OpenRefine, NADEEF, and KATARA rely on human input to clean data for analysis. Though Trifacta comes with a userfriendly interface providing data transformation suggestions based on user interactions, it is unclear which algorithm it uses to generate data transformation suggestions.

4   Approach for Data Transformation Suggestions

Our approach to develop a system for generating data transformation suggestions falls within the broader area of recommender systems [3,9]. We base our approach on feeding the features of the selected data object as input to a ML algorithm, in our case a Random Forest classifier [1]. The classifier then generates the most appropriate transformation by creating a set of decision trees and choosing the output that has most votes [10]. We use the features of the given dataset (*i.e.*, metadata) and the data object selected by the user as input to the Random Forest.

The former group of features contains the attributes of the dataset, including the number of variables and total observations. The latter group contains the properties of the data object selected by the user at a certain instant. That would include the selected row, column, or cell of the dataset and properties of the data it contains. Tables 4 and 5 show a detailed description of dataset features required and the type of data these could be extracted from.

---

[8] http://openrefine.org.

Table 4. Features of a given dataset.

Feature	Scope
Number of attributes	Entire dataset
Number of observations	Entire dataset
Percentage of missing values	Entire dataset
Percentage of categorical attributes	Entire dataset
Percentage of numeric attributes	Entire dataset
Percentage of boolean attributes	Entire dataset
Percentage of date attributes	Entire dataset
Percentage of *null* attributes	Entire dataset

Table 5. Features of selected data item.

Feature	Description	Scope
Data type	Number, string, boolean, and date	Column, cell
Data object selected	Row, column, and cell	Entire dataset
Number of numeric values	Number of numeric values in the selected data (zero or more)	Row
Number of boolean values	Number of values with *boolean* data type in the selected data (zero or more)	Row
Number of string values	Number of values with *string* data type in the selected data (zero or more)	Row
Number of date values	Number of values with *date* data type in the selected data (zero or more)	Row
Number of categories	Number of unique categories in the selected data (one or more)	Column
Number of *nulls*	Number of *null* values in the selected data (zero or more)	Row, column
Special characters	Check if any special characters exist in the selected data	Cell

4.1 Architecture and Process

The proposed architecture is depicted in Fig. 1. The application takes tabular data in CSV format as input and allows users to select a row, column or a cell. Relevant transformation suggestions are then generated based on user interaction and the properties of dataset. The different steps involved in the generation of tabular data transformation suggestions include:

1. **Input dataset:** As the first step for data preprocessing, the user is prompted to input a tabular dataset in CSV format into the system. The imported dataset is made visible to the user on the GUI in the form of a table.

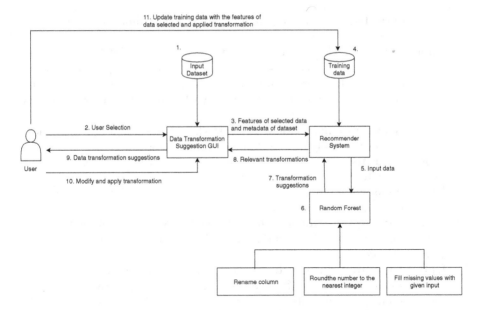

Fig. 1. Architecture of prototype for tabular data transformation suggestions.

2. **User selection:** The user can then select either a row, column or cell to transform the underlying data.
3. **Features of selected data and metadata of the dataset:** As the user selects data to be transformed, the features of the entire dataset along with the features of data object selected are fetched and saved as test data to be sent to the recommender system.
4. **Training data:** Training data consists of several entries comprised of dataset features and the applied transformations. These entries are part of historical data used to train the ML model to predict the transformations for test data.

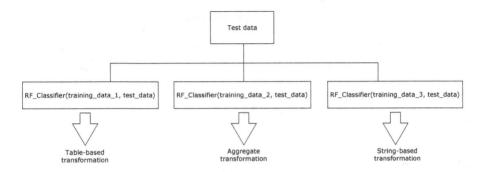

Fig. 2. Generation of multiple data transformation suggestions.

5. **Input data:** Both test and training data are sent as input to the Random Forest.
6. **Random Forest:** The Random Forest trains on historical data to learn the mappings between the features of the selected data and applied transformations. To include diversity in the transformations generated, we use the same test data to build predictive models with three different training sets (see Fig. 2).
7. **Transformation suggestions:** At most three transformations are generated as a result of applying the Random Forest algorithm.
8. **Relevant transformations:** The resulting transformations are then sent to the user interface.
9. **Data transformation suggestions:** The data transformation suggestions are shown to user.
10. **Modify and apply transformation:** The user selects one of the transformations and applies it to the dataset. The dataset is then updated with the applied changes.
11. **Update training data:** After the user selected and applied a transformation to the dataset, the features of selected data object that led to the generation of that particular transformation along with the target variable are added to the respective training dataset (see Fig. 3).

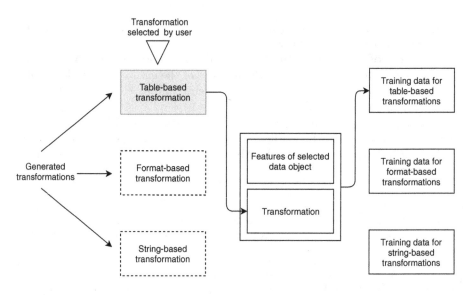

Fig. 3. Updating training data.

4.2   Implementation

A prototype was implemented by reusing a user-friendly interface for tabular data visualization, taken from two of the authors' previous work [17].

Angular 2[9], an open source Web application framework based on TypeScript[10] was used as development framework for implementing the prototype for data transformation suggestions. For generation of transformation suggestions, we used `random-forest-classifier`[11], which is an open source Javascript library under MIT license.

A screenshot of application prototype is shown in Fig. 4. It includes (1) a component for file import in tabular format, (2) tabular representation of data, (3) characteristics of the dataset, (4) features of corresponding column of selected data object, (5) a set of generated transformations, (6) fields for user input, and (7) the steps taken to transform data.

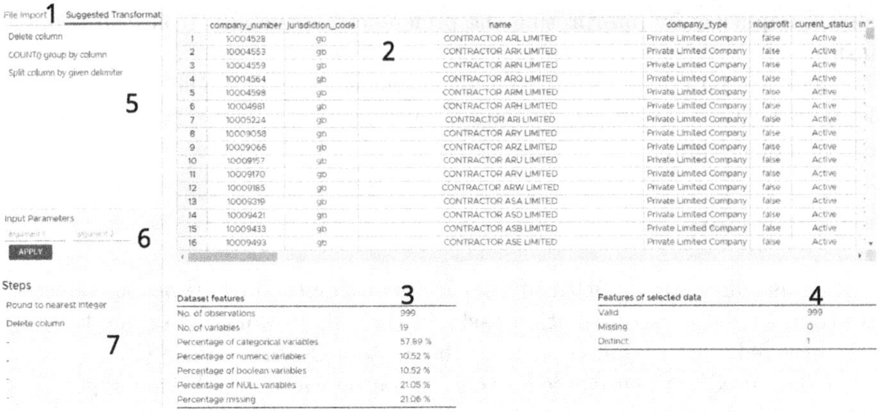

Fig. 4. Screenshot of the application prototype.

The dataset characteristics contain basic statistical features of data to help the user view the dimensions and the different data types included in the dataset. These statistical features include the number of observations, number of variables, percentage of categorical variables, percentage of numeric variables, percentage of boolean variables, percentage of null variables, and percentage missing variables.

The features of corresponding column of selected data object include the number of values that are not null, undefined or NaN[12], the number of null and undefined values, and the number of distinct values.

At the initialization of the application, we use training data generated beforehand to generate transformations. For inducing diversity, training data is divided into three categories. These three categories do not necessarily include data transformations for all three data objects, *i.e.*, row, column and cell. The ML

---

[9] https://angular.io.

[10] https://www.typescriptlang.org.

[11] https://www.npmjs.com/package/random-forest-classifier.

[12] https://en.wikipedia.org/wiki/NaN(Not-A-Number).

classifier therefore returns null for the corresponding category if the user selection has not been mapped to an appropriate transformation. To ensure that no irrelevant transformations are suggested to the user, we implemented two checks, as follows. (1) Initially, due to lack of sufficient training data, the Random Forest classifier may not generate the appropriate transformations. A check for irrelevant transformations ensures that no incorrect transformations with respect to the data object selected and its data type are suggested to the user. Also (2) if there are no transformations returned, we generate transformations randomly based on the data type and the type of data object selected. This check is implemented to ensure that at least one recommendation is provided.

Once the transformation has been applied, the system needs feedback for the generation of future transformations. The recommendation system collects feedback implicitly by interpreting the preferences of the user from the applied transformation and adds an entry containing features of the dataset, features of the selected data object and the applied transformation to the training data. Adding more examples in the training dataset increases the performance of the prediction algorithm.

5 Evaluation

We ran a usability study with 15 target users testing the prototype. All selected users conduct data transformation tasks in their daily work. After the testing, users answered a set of questions from the System Usability Scale (SUS) [2].

The data used as the use case for this evaluation was a sample from OpenCorporates[13], which is an open database of companies and company-related data. The dataset is in CSV format and consists of 999 rows and 19 columns. This dataset includes textual, numerical and boolean data in addition to dates. There are several transformations that can be applied to tabular data for preprocessing. For the purpose of this evaluation, however, only a few have been selected and implemented as shown in Table 6.

For the evaluation, each participant was provided with a list of transformations implemented in the prototype, type of data they can be applied to, and the information about external input, if any. The participants were then required to choose the dataset containing information about companies for preprocessing. Each participant was allowed to perform necessary preprocessing of the dataset by selecting rows, columns and cells, and applying transformations on those data objects. In addition to the predefined test data, personal preferences were automatically inferred for each user of the prototype by analyzing the transformations applied.

Each participant of the usability testing ranked each of the 10 SUS questions with a scale from 1 to 5. An SUS score was calculated individually for each participant's responses. For calculating the SUS score, for each of the odd numbered questions, 1 is subtracted from the response, and for each of the even numbered questions, 5 is subtracted from the response.

---

[13] https://opencorporates.com.

Table 6. Selected data transformations.

Function name	Data type	Scope
deleteColumn	Any	Column
keepColumn	Any	Column
renameColumn	Any	Column
convertRowToHeader	N/A	Row
deleteRow	N/A	Row
setToNULL	Any	Cell
normalize	Number	Column
countGroupByColumn	Number, String, Boolean	Column
upperCase	String	Column
lowerCase	String	Column
roundToNearest	Number	Cell
setRowToNULL	N/A	Row
setColumnToNULL	Any	Column
fillMissingValues	Any	Column
extract	String	Cell
replace	Number, String, Boolean, NULL	Cell
splitColumn	String	Cell
removeSpecialCharacters	String	Cell

The values calculated were added up and the sum was multiplied by 2.5 to obtain the overall value of SUS in a range of 0 to 100. Even though the score is on the scale of 0–100, it is not percentage. We obtained an average score of 72 which lies above 50th percentile.

Based on feedback from the users who did hands-on testing of prototype, we could draw the following conclusions: (1) the users found the application easy to use, (2) data transformations are often repeated on similar data objects, (3) the users prefer a wide variety of data transformations to choose from, (4) editable transformations should be implemented, which can provide flexibility while transforming data, and (5) more intelligent detection of data types such as zip codes and URLs ease data transformation process.

6   Conclusions

In this work, we developed an approach for the use of ML to recommend data transformation suggestions based on user interactions, and analyzed the usefulness of the approach for users of data cleaning and transformation tools. The proposed approach based on the Random Forest algorithm was implemented and tested on a company dataset. By tracking the user interactions performed by the selection of data objects in the tabular dataset, the application prototype recommends relevant data transformations. The implementation was evaluated with a usability study and found efficient by the users. Future work includes detection and support for non-primitive data types (*e.g.*, geographical), a multi-label classification model to generate multiple possible target variables, and a friendlier user interface that would help users transform data with ease.

Acknowledgements. The work in this paper was partly funded by the EC H2020 projects euBusinessGraph (Grant nr. 732003), EW-Shopp (Grant nr. 732590), and TheyBuyForYou (Grant nr. 780247).

References

1. Breiman, L.: Random forests. Mach. Learn. **45**(1), 5–32 (2001)
2. Brooke, J.: SUS-A quick and dirty usability scale. In: Usability Evaluation in Industry, vol. 189, no. 194, pp. 4–7 (1996)
3. van Capelleveen, G., Amrit, C., Yazan, D.M., Zijm, H.: The recommender canvas: a model for developing and documenting recommender system design. Expert Syst. Appl. **129**, 97–117 (2019)
4. Chu, X., Morcos, J., Ilyas, I.F., Ouzzani, M., Papotti, P., et al.: Katara: a data cleaning system powered by knowledge bases and crowdsourcing. In: Proceedings of the ACM SIGMOD International Conference on Management of Data (SIGMOD 2015), pp. 1247–1261 (2015)
5. Dallachiesa, M., Ebaid, A., Eldawy, A., Elmagarmid, A., et al.: NADEEF: a commodity data cleaning system. In: Proceedings of the ACM SIGMOD International Conference on Management of Datav (SIGMOD 2013), pp. 541–552 (2013)
6. Famili, A., Shen, W.M., Weber, R., et al.: Data preprocessing and intelligent data analysis. Intell. Data Anal. **1**(1–4), 3–23 (1997)
7. Heer, J., Hellerstein, J.M., Kandel, S.: Predictive interaction for data transformation. In: Proceedings of the 7th Biennial Conference on Innovative Data Systems Research (CIDR 2015) (2015)
8. Kandel, S., Paepcke, A., Hellerstein, J.M., Heer, J.: Enterprise data analysis and visualization: an interview study. IEEE Trans. Visual Comput. Graphics **18**(12), 2917–2926 (2012)
9. Melville, P., Sindhwani, V.: Recommender systems. In: Sammut, C., Webb, G.I. (eds.) Encyclopedia of Machine Learning and Data Mining, pp. 1056–1066. Springer, Boston (2017). https://doi.org/10.1007/978-1-4899-7687-1
10. Oshiro, T.M., Perez, P.S., Baranauskas, J.A.: How many trees in a random forest? In: Perner, P. (ed.) MLDM 2012. LNCS (LNAI), vol. 7376, pp. 154–168. Springer, Heidelberg (2012). https://doi.org/10.1007/978-3-642-31537-4_13
11. Rahm, E., Do, H.H.: Data cleaning: problems and current approaches. IEEE Data Eng. Bull. **23**(4), 3–13 (2000)
12. Raman, V., Hellerstein, J.M.: Potters wheel: an interactive framework for data cleaning and transformation. In: Proceedings of the 27th International Conference on Very Large Data Bases (VLDB 2001), pp. 381–390 (2001)
13. Rekatsinas, T., Chu, X., Ilyas, I.F., Ré, C.: Holoclean: holistic data repairs with probabilistic inference. Proc. VLDB Endow. **10**(11), 1190–1201 (2017)
14. Roman, D., et al.: DataGraft: simplifying open data publishing. In: Sack, H., Rizzo, G., Steinmetz, N., Mladenić, D., Auer, S., Lange, C. (eds.) ESWC 2016. LNCS, vol. 9989, pp. 101–106. Springer, Cham (2016). https://doi.org/10.1007/978-3-319-47602-5_21

15. Roman, D., et al.: DataGraft: one-stop-shop for open data management. Semant. Web **9**(4), 393–411 (2018)
16. Sukhobok, D., et al.: Tabular data cleaning and linked data generation with Grafterizer. In: Sack, H., Rizzo, G., Steinmetz, N., Mladenić, D., Auer, S., Lange, C. (eds.) ESWC 2016. LNCS, vol. 9989, pp. 134–139. Springer, Cham (2016). https://doi.org/10.1007/978-3-319-47602-5_27
17. von Zernichow, B.M., Roman, D.: Usability of visual data profiling in data cleaning and transformation. In: Panetto, H., et al. (eds.) OTM 2017. LNCS, vol. 10574, pp. 480–496. Springer, Cham (2017). https://doi.org/10.1007/978-3-319-69459-7_32

Knowledge Graph Embeddings over Hundreds of Linked Datasets

Michalis Mountantonakis[1,2](✉) [ID] and Yannis Tzitzikas[1,2] [ID]

[1] Institute of Computer Science, FORTH-ICS, Heraklion, Greece
{mountant,tzitzik}@ics.forth.gr
[2] Computer Science Department, University of Crete, Heraklion, Greece

Abstract. There is an increasing trend of using Linked Datasets for creating embeddings from URI sequences, since such embeddings can be exploited for several tasks, i.e., for machine learning problems, tasks related to content-based similarity, and others. Existing techniques exploit either a single or a few datasets (or RDF graphs) for creating URI sequences for one or more entities. However, there are not available approaches, where data from multiple datasets are combined, for enriching the URI sequences for a given entity. For this reason, we introduce a prototype, called `LODVec`, that exploits `LODsyndesis` knowledge graph, which is the largest knowledge graph including all inferred equivalence relationships. `LODVec` exploits this graph for creating URI sequences for millions of entities by combining data from 400 datasets, whereas it offers several configurable options for creating such URI sequences that are based on metadata (e.g., provenance). Moreover, it uses as input the produced URI sequences for creating URI embeddings through *word2vec* model. We evaluate the gain of exploiting several datasets (instead of a single or few ones) and the impact of cross-dataset reasoning for machine-learning based tasks (i.e., classification and regression), and we compare the effectiveness of several configurations and machine learning models.

Keywords: URI embeddings · Multiple datasets · Machine learning

1 Introduction

There is an increasing trend of exploiting LOD (Linked Open Data) for creating embeddings for URIs (Uniform Resource Identifiers), which can be exploitable for a number of tasks. Indicatively, they can be exploited (i) for machine learning-based tasks [17], such as classification, regression, etc., (ii) for similarity-based tasks [4], e.g. "Give me the top-K related entities to a given one", (iii) for link prediction purposes [14], and others. There have been proposed several novel methods [17] taking as input RDF (Resource Description Frameworks) knowledge graphs and producing URI sequences for a set of given entities, i.e., sequences starting from a focused entity (or URI) that contains a path of URIs which is reachable from that entity. These sequences are given as input for producing URI embeddings which can be exploited in the aforementioned tasks.

© Springer Nature Switzerland AG 2019
E. Garoufallou et al. (Eds.): MTSR 2019, CCIS 1057, pp. 150–162, 2019.
https://doi.org/10.1007/978-3-030-36599-8_13

However, current approaches exploit usually a single dataset for creating URI embeddings for one or more URIs (or entities). Moreover, many approaches are difficult to be configured by non-experts, since they do not provide an interactive service. Our objective is to make it feasible to exploit hundreds of RDF datasets simultaneously, for creating URI sequences and URI embeddings for any given entity (i.e., a URI). Concerning our research hypothesis, we assume that it is better to exploit multiple datasets for creating URI sequences and embeddings, instead of using one or few datasets, whereas we assume that there is not a single knowledge graph that can outperform all the others for any possible task.

Generally, it is not easy to combine all the available information for a given entity, since (a) data are scattered in different places, and (b) datasets use different URIs and models for representing their entities and schema elements, respectively [13]. For example, each of the three datasets of Fig. 1 uses a different URI for representing the movie "Inception" and the schema element "actor", while these datasets are located in different places. Indeed, for combining information from several datasets, one should collect the desired data and find the equivalences in instance and schema level. For achieving this target, it is required to compute the transitive and symmetric closure of equivalence relationships, such as owl:sameAs and owl:equivalentProperty, which is quite expensive [11].

For tackling the above difficulties, we exploit LODsyndesis knowledge graph [11], which contains two billion triples from 400 datasets of 9 different domains, and it has pre-computed the transitive and symmetric closure of the equivalence relationships in instance and schema level. Due to cross-dataset reasoning, its' indexes offer direct and fast access to all the available information for any entity. In this way, it is feasible to create URI sequences for the same entity from multiple datasets, therefore, the number of possible URI sequences that can be created is highly increased (as we shall see in Sect. 4). For example, suppose that the required task is to predict the exact rating of a movie, e.g., "Inception" (see Fig. 1), and for this reason we plan to create embeddings from URI sequences for using them in such a machine learning task. In Fig. 1, by using only one dataset, say *DBpedia* (http://dbpedia.org/), we can find data such as the genres of this movie. However, it does not contain information about the awards won by this movie, e.g., in Fig. 1 such data occur in *Wikidata* (http://wikidata.org/). On the contrary, LODsyndesis (see the lower side of Fig. 1), (a) precomputes the equivalences in schema (e.g., dbp:actor≡wkd:actor≡frb:played) and instance level (e.g., dbp:Inception≡wkd:Inception≡frb:Inception), (b) collects all the available triples containing an entity (e.g., Inception) either as a subject or as an object (by following both direct and indirect edges), and (c) records data provenance (see the label near to each node in Fig. 1). Therefore, by using LODsyndesis, it is feasible to create URI sequences by using all the three datasets of Fig. 1.

For exploiting the above characteristics, we introduce a research prototype, i.e., LODVec, that (i) takes as input one or more entities (as URIs or in plain text), (ii) it offers several configurable options for creating URI sequences and embeddings for these entities from hundreds of datasets through LODsyndesis, and

(iii) it produces URI sequences based on user's selections. Moreover, LODVec (iv) converts the produced sequences into vector representations (i.e., embeddings) by exploiting *word2vec* approach [8,9] through *dl4j* API (https://deeplearning4j. org/). Finally, it can (v) exploit the produced vectors for several purposes, e.g., for performing classification and regression tasks by using *WEKA* API [20]. For testing the proposed approach, we report experimental results for machine learning classification and regression tasks by using two datasets containing movies and music albums, i.e., the target of classification task is to classify whether a movie or a music album has a high or low rating, whereas the target of regression task is to predict their exact rating. We introduce experiments showing the impact of using multiple datasets and cross-dataset reasoning in terms of effectiveness, whereas, we compare the performance of different configurations.

The rest of this paper is organized as follows: Sect. 2 introduces the background and related work. Section 3 provides the problem statement, the algorithm for creating URI sequences and all the steps and functionalities that our approach supports, whereas Sect. 4 includes the experimental evaluation about the effectiveness of our approach. Finally, Sect. 5 concludes the paper.

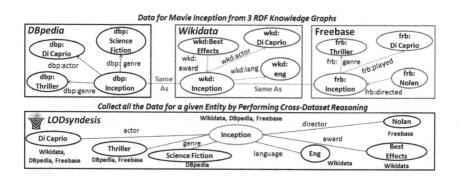

Fig. 1. Running example containing 3 knowledge graphs and LODsyndesis

2 Background and Related Work

2.1 Background

Linked Data. Resource Description Framework (RDF) [1] is a model that can be represented as a graph, and uses Uniform Resource Identifiers (URIs), or anonymous nodes to denote resources, and literals to denote constants. Every statement in RDF can be represented as a triple. A triple is a statement of the form subject-predicate-object $\langle s, p, o \rangle$, and it is any element of $T = (U \cup B) \times (U) \times (U \cup B \cup L)$ where U, B and L are the sets of URIs, blank nodes and literals, respectively. Any finite subset of T corresponds to an RDF graph (or dataset). We divide the URIs in three disjoint sets, entities E (e.g., "Inception"), properties P (e.g., actor) and RDF classes C (e.g., Drama Movie). In this paper, we focus only on triples containing an entity as subject, and an RDF class or an entity as object, therefore we consider triples in $T' = U \times P \times (E \cup C) \subseteq T$.

Word2Vec. It is a shallow two-layer neural network model for producing word embeddings [8,9]. It takes as input a text, and it produces a vector with several (usually hundreds of) dimensions for each unique word appearing in the text. The target of *word2Vec* [8,9] is to group the vectors of similar words closely in the vector space. In this paper, we will exploit this model for creating vectors for entities, by using the skip-gram model, which is a method that uses a specific word for predicting a target context, since "it produces more accurate results for large datasets" (https://deeplearning4j.org/docs/latest/deeplearning4j-nlp-word2vec). Our target is to use this model for placing similar entities (e.g., similar movies) to a close position in the vector space.

2.2 Related Work

Knowledge Graph Embedding Approaches. *RDF2Vec* [17] is an approach that takes as input an RDF knowledge graph, produces URI sequences based on several strategies, such as random graph walks, and uses *word2vec* for creating vectors. They have also proposed strategies for performing biased graph walks [3], which are based on a number of metrics and statistics, such as the frequency of properties, objects, pagerank and others. They have tested these strategies for multiple tasks, such as classification and regression, by using two datasets *Wikidata* and *DBpedia*, whereas they have used the *GloVe* model [15] for creating RDF embeddings by exploiting global patterns. The authors in [5] used several bibliographic RDF datasets and *word2vec* for enriching the data of scientific publications with information from multiple data sources, while in [6] the authors exploited enriched ontology structures for producing RDF embeddings which were used for the task of Entity Linking. In [14], the authors combined embeddings from *DBpedia* and social network datasets for performing link prediction, whereas in [4] Wikipedia knowledge graph was exploited for finding the most similar entities to a given one for a specific time period. Concerning other graph-based models, such as TransH [19] and TransR [7], they use algorithms for creating entity and relation graph embeddings, i.e., the relationships between two entities are represented as translations in the embedding space.

Feature Extraction Approaches Combining Data from Several Datasets. In [10], the authors proposed a tool that can send SPARQL queries in several endpoints for creating features. However, it does not produce embeddings and it cannot collect all the data for a given entity (i.e., cross-dataset reasoning is required). Moreover, RapidMiner Semantic Web Extension [16] creates features by integrating data from a lot of datasets. However, it performs the integration task by traversing owl:sameAs paths on-the-fly (through SPARQL queries, which can be time-consuming), and not by exploiting pre-constructed indexes.

Novelty & Comparison with Other Approaches. To the best of our knowledge, this is the first work providing an interactive tool which can easily create URI embeddings for any set of entities by combining data from hundreds of datasets simultaneously. Since current approaches do not take into account the equivalences in schema and instance level, they have been mainly tested on a single dataset. At this point our objective is (a) to offer a simple way for creating URI sequences for multiple datasets, and (b) to investigate whether the creation of even simple URI sequences and embeddings from different datasets can improve the effectiveness of several tasks (e.g., machine-learning tasks). Concerning the limitations of our approach, for the time being we do not support methods for creating longer URI sequences (e.g., through random walks [2]), and algorithms that have been successfully applied to knowledge graphs (e.g., [7,19]).

3   LODVec: The Proposed Approach

Section 3.1 introduces the problem statement, Sect. 3.2 shows some useful notations and metadata, and Sect. 3.3 describes all the steps of LODVec.

3.1   Problem Statement

Creating URI Sequences. The input is a set of entities $E' \subseteq E$, and the first target for each $e \in E'$ is to create a finite set of URI sequences $Seq_U(e)$. Each URI sequence $s \in Seq_U(e)$ is of the form $\langle e, p, o \rangle$ where $p \in P$ and $o \in (C \cup E)$. In this paper, we exploit the neighborhood of an entity e by following both direct and indirect edges, therefore each URI sequence corresponds to a single triple containing e either as a subject or as an object. Our target is to collect all the produced $Seq_U(e)$ for each $e \in E'$, i.e., we construct the set $Seq_U E' = \bigcup_{e \in E'} Seq_U(e)$, where $Seq_U E' \subseteq T'$.

From URI Sequences to URI Embeddings. The target is to map each entity e to a vector space $v(e)$ by using the set $Seq_U E'$, and *word2vec* algorithm (by using skip-gram model). We expect that if two entities e and e' are similar, then their produced vectors $v(e)$ and $v(e')$ will be close to the vector space.

Output Exploitation. Our target is the output vectors to be directly exploitable for machine learning classification and regression tasks, and for finding the top-K similar entities to a given entity e. Concerning the first case, one should also provide as input the corresponding categorical or continuous variable $Y(e)$ for a given entity e. On the second case, there is no need for additional input.

3.2   Metadata and Notations

First, we denote as $D = \{D_i, ..., D_n\}$ a set of datasets, and as $triples(D_i)$ the set of triples for a given dataset D_i (e.g., DBpedia). Table 1 represents a set of notations and metadata that can aid users to select what type of URI sequences will be created. The first one corresponds to the datasets containing a triple t, while the second one indicates which datasets contain at least one triple for an entity e. The third one denotes the datasets that contain at least one triple, for one or more entities $e \in E'$. The fourth is used for showing how many of the entities in E' can be found in a single dataset D_i (i.e., a number in range $[0, |E'|]$), whereas the fifth and the sixth formulas denote all the properties of an entity e and of all the entities E', respectively. The seventh formula shows the number of entities, for whom there is at least one triple that contain a property p. Formula 8 shows all the objects of a triple whose subject is e and predicate is p (e.g., all the actors of a movie). The last formula shows the frequency (popularity) of a URI in the whole graph, i.e., how many triples contain a URI u.

Table 1. Notations-Metadata

ID	Notation or Metadata	Formula
1	Provenance of Triple t	$prov(t) = \{D_i \in D \mid t = \langle s, p, o \rangle, t \in triples(D_i)\}$
2	Provenance of Entity e	$dsets(e) = \{D_i \in D \mid \exists \langle e, p, o \rangle \in triples(D_i)\}$
3	Provenance of Entities E'	$dsets_{E'} = \bigcup_{e \in E'} dsets(e)$
4	Coverage of a Dataset given E'	$covD(D_i, E') = |\{e \in E' \mid D_i \in dsets(e)\}|$
5	Coverage of Properties given E'	$covP(p, E') = |\{e \in E', \mid \exists \langle e, p, o \rangle \in T'\}|$
6	Properties of an Entity e	$Prop(e) = \{p \in P \mid \langle e, p, o \rangle \in T'\}$
7	Properties of Entities E'	$Prop_{E'} = \bigcup_{e \in E'} Prop(e)$
8	Objects of an entity-prop. pair	$Obj(e, p) = \{o \in U | \langle e, p, o \rangle \in T'\}$
9	Frequency of a given URI u	$freq(u) = |\{t \in T' \mid t = \langle s, p, o \rangle, s = u \ or \ o = u\}|$

3.3   The Steps and Algorithm for Creating URI Sequences

Here, we describe the functionality and all the steps of LODVec (see Fig. 2).

Steps 1–4. Input & Configuration. The first step (see Fig. 2) is to receive the input entities E' (we support over 400 million entities), which can be given (a) as a list of URIs (e.g., dbp:Inception), (b) as a list of entities in plain text (e.g., "Inception"), or (c) just a URI that represents an RDF class or a category (e.g., dbc:Films_about_dreams)! In the latter case, LODVec retrieves automatically the desired URIs. By exploiting LODsyndesis, LODVec can optionally show to the user (i) the datasets containing the input entities (i.e., $dsets_{E'}$), in descending order according to their $covD(D_i, E')$, and (ii) the list of available properties for the given entities, i.e., $Prop_{E'}$, in descending order according to their $covP(p, E')$ (i.e., Steps 2 and 3). In Step 4 of Fig. 2, the user selects which configuration will be used, i.e., the input of Algorithm 1. In particular, one can select the datasets D_{sel} that will be used ($D_{sel} \subseteq dsets_{E'}$), the desired properties $Prop_{sel}$ ($Prop_{sel} \subseteq Prop_{E'}$) and whether all the possible sequences or the top-K ones will be created. For creating the top-K URI sequences, one should give as input

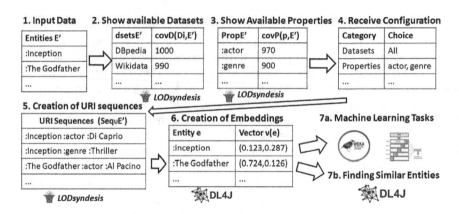

Fig. 2. The steps of LODVec approach.

the exact number K (i.e., a positive integer), and the method to sort the triples according to the frequency of each triple's object (i.e., in ascending, descending or random order).

Step 5. Algorithm for Creating URI Sequences. Algorithm 1 creates URI sequences for a set of entities E'. It iterates over all the input entities and for each entity e (lines 2–3), it initializes its corresponding set of URI sequences and a frequency map (it is used for creating only the top-K sequences). The next step is to traverse each direct or indirect property p of entity e (i.e., $Prop(e)$) that belong also to the desired properties given by the user (i.e., $Prop_{sel}$). The indexes of LODsyndesis store in the same place all the objects for each entity-property pair (e.g., movie-actor) [11]. Therefore, for each p we traverse all the possible objects, and we check if at least one dataset containing that triple, belongs to the desired datasets D_{sel} (lines 4–5). In such a case, we check the cardinality variable, i.e., if the user desires to find all the possible URI sequences, we add the URI sequence (i.e., triple) to $Seq_u(e)$ (lines 6–7). Otherwise, we add the triple and its object's frequency, i.e., $freq(o)$ (retrieved by sending a request to LODsyndesis REST services [12]), to the frequency map (lines 8–9). After traversing all the desired triples for the entity e, if the user wants to create the top-K URI sequences, we sort the values according to the given sortType (lines 10–11), e.g., if sortType equals "desc", we will sort the K triples, which are found in the left side of $freqMap(e)$, in descending order with respect to their object's frequency. We iterate over the sorted map (i.e., $sortSeq(e)$), that contains in its left side (i.e., $Left$) a URI sequence and in its right side the $freq(o)$, and we add to $Seq_u(e)$ the top-K results (lines 12–15). Finally, we add the $Seq_u(e)$ to $Seq_U E'$, whereas after all the iterations, Algorithm 1 returns all the URI sequences.

The time complexity of Algorithm 1 is $\mathcal{O}(|triples_{E'}|)$, since in the worst case we read all the triples for the entities E'. The space complexity is $\mathcal{O}(Seq_U E')$, since we keep in memory all the produced sequences. We do not load in memory

---

Algorithm 1. Creating URI $sequences$ for a set of entities E'

Input: Entities E', properties $Prop_{sel}$, datasets D_{sel}, cardinality crd ({ "All" |
   "Top-K" }), Integer K, sortType ({ "asc"| "desc"| "rand" })
Output: URI Sequences $Seq_U E'$ for all the entities E'
1 $Seq_U E' \leftarrow \emptyset$
2 **forall** $e \in E'$ **do**
3      $Seq_U(e) \leftarrow \emptyset, freqMap(e) \leftarrow \emptyset$
4   **forall** $p \in (Prop(e) \cap Prop_{sel})$ **do**
5   **forall** $o \in Obj(e,p), prov(\langle e,p,o\rangle) \cap D_{sel} \neq \emptyset$ **do**
6   **if** $crd \equiv$ "All" **then**
7                  $Seq_U(e) \leftarrow Seq_U(e) \cup \{\langle e,p,o\rangle\}$
8   **else if** $crd \equiv$ "Top-K" **then**
9                  $freqMap(e) \leftarrow freqMap(e) \cup \{\langle e,p,o\rangle, freq(o)\}$
10   **if** $crd \equiv$ "Top-K" **then**
11         $sortSeq(e) \leftarrow mergeSortByValue(freqMap(e))_{sortType}$
12   **forall** $\langle e,p,o\rangle \in Left(sortSeq(e))$ **do**
13             $Seq_U(e) \leftarrow Seq_U(e) \cup \{\langle e,p,o\rangle\}$
14   **if** $|Seq_U(e)| \equiv K$ **then**
15   **break**
16     $Seq_U E' \leftarrow Seq_U E' \cup Seq_U(e)$
17 **Return** $Seq_U E'$

---

the triples of each entity, since we use random access methods for reading the desired part of the indexes. Finally, for creating the top-K sequences for each entity e we also use a sorting algorithm whose time complexity is $\mathcal{O}(n * log_n)$.

Steps 6–7. Creation of Embeddings & Exploitation. The next step (Step 6 of Fig. 2) is to exploit the produced set $Seq_U E'$ for creating one vector per entity e. Indeed, we use the *word2vec* implementation of *dl4j* library, which produces as output a vector $v(e)$ for each $e \in E'$. These vectors can be exploited for (i) machine-learning and (ii) similarity tasks. Regarding task (i), the vectors can be downloaded in ".arff" format for performing classification and regression through *WEKA* API (Step 7a of Fig. 2), while LODVec offers a service for producing automatically such results. Concerning task (ii), they can be downloaded in ".txt" format, which is directly accessible from *dl4j* API. Finally, LODVec offers a service for finding the top-K related entities to a given one (Step 7b of Fig. 2).

Demo & Video. A demo video of LODVec is accessible in the following link: https://youtu.be/qR9RFZVs4TY. An online demo (i.e., a JAVA web application) that allows anyone to create URI embeddings for over 400 million entities is available in https://demos.isl.ics.forth.gr/lodvec.

4   Experimental Evaluation

In Sect. 4.1, we evaluate the impact of cross-dataset reasoning and of using multiple datasets, for four machine-learning tasks, while Sect. 4.2 shows a small example for the task of finding similar entities. All the experiments were performed on a single machine with an *i5 core*, 8 GB *RAM*, and 1 TB *disc space*. Moreover, the indexes and services of LODsyndesis, which are used in our approach, are hosted in a single machine of *okeanos* cloud computing service (https://okeanos. grnet.gr/) with *8 cores*, 8 GB *RAM*, and 60 GB *disc space*.

4.1   Machine Learning Tasks - The Gain of Using Multiple Datasets

Movies & Music Albums Datasets. We use the Metacritic Movies and Music Albums datasets (derived from [18]) containing the DBpedia URIs of 2,000 movies and of 1,600 music albums. Both datasets contain an average rating of all time reviews for each movie and music album. Concerning movies, 1,000 of them have high rating (>60), and the remaining 1,000 ones have low rating (<40). Regarding music albums, 800 of them have high rating (>79), and the other 800 ones have low rating (<63). The goal of (binary) classification is to predict whether a movie or a music album has a high or a low rating, whereas the target of regression is to find the exact rating of each movie and music album.

Word2Vec Parameters. For building our *word2vec* model, we use the skip-gram model of *dl4j* library, we exclude URIs existing <5 times in the produced sequences ($minWordFrequency = 5$), we use 10 iterations and we select the window size parameter to be 2 ($windowSize = 2$). For each entity e, we produce a single vector $v(e)$ with 100 dimensions ($layerSize = 100$), and we expect that movies and albums with similar rating will be placed closely in the vector space.

Machine Learning Models & Metrics. The vectors produced by LODVec are given as input in WEKA API [20], for performing classification and regression, by using a 10-fold cross validation [20]. Regarding classification (CF), we use the default implementation of *Naive Bayes* (NB) and *Support Vector Machine* (SMO) of WEKA. For each model, we measure the accuracy percentage (percentage of correct predictions), i.e., the goal is to maximize that percentage. Concerning regression (Reg), we use the default implementation of *Linear Regression* (LR) and *Support Vector Machine for Regression* (SMOreg) of WEKA, and we measure the root mean squared error (RMSE), i.e., the target is to minimize the RMSE value. Finally, we measure the accuracy and the RMSE for the trivial *Vote* method, that selects randomly a class and a rating for each entity.

Results for Both Tasks and Datasets. Tables 2 and 3 show several statistics and experiments for movies and music albums, respectively. In each Table, the first column shows the used RDF datasets, the second the properties, the third one the cardinality, the fourth one the average URI sequences per entity, and the fifth one the total creation time of all URI sequences. The columns 6 and 7 show the accuracy of the classification task (SF) and the last two columns the RMSE value for the regression task (Reg), by using different models.

Results for Movies. In rows 2–9 of Table 2, we show experiments by using all the possible properties and by creating all the possible URI sequences, however, in each case we use a different subset of datasets. We can see how the average

Table 2. Classification and regression experiments on Movies dataset

Datasets	Prop.	crd	$|Seq_U(e)|$ average	Creation time	NB (CF)	SVM (CF)	LR (Reg)	SMOreg (Reg)
Freebase (FR)	All	All	112.0	4.3 min	79.71%	82.02%	16.37	16.56
DBpedia (DB)	All	All	23.8	4.0 min	68.42%	71.14%	20.02	20.71
Wikidata (WK)	All	All	22.5	4.2 min	66.88%	67.66%	20.81	21.40
DB, WK	All	All	38.3	4.4 min	68.62%	74.92%	19.18	19.90
DB, FR	All	All	132.0	4.5 min	79.75%	82.51%	16.11	16.35
FR, WK	All	All	129.0	4.6 min	81.20%	83.32%	16.25	16.55
DB, FR, WK	All	All	144.7	4.7 min	82.11%	84.10%	16.01	16.31
All 14 $dsets(E')$	All	All	**170.1**	5.7 min	**82.41%**	**84.70%**	**15.57**	**15.65**
FR	type	All	5.5	3.5 min	67.49%	71.40%	19.18	19.59
All 14 $dsets(E')$	type	All	18.3	4.0 min	67.53%	72.92%	18.90	19.42
All 14 $dsets(E')$	ct+tp	All	30.9	4.7 min	73.13%	74.90%	18.80	19.04
All 14 $dsets(E')$	All	30 asc	30.0	120 min	66.95%	72.50%	19.58	20.05
All 14 $dsets(E')$	All	30 rand	30.0	6.0 min	69.24%	73.10%	19.86	20.26
All 14 $dsets(E')$	All	30 desc	30.0	120 min	71.43%	75.86%	19.07	19.46

number of URI sequences increases as we add more datasets (see the fourth column of Table 2), e.g., by using *DBpedia* we created 23.8 URI sequences per movie, whereas with all the datasets we created on average 170.1 URI sequences. Moreover, as we add more datasets, the total time for creating all the URI sequences did not increase so much, i.e., by using only *DBpedia* we needed 4 min (i.e., 0.12 seconds per entity), whereas by using all datasets the corresponding time was 5.7 min (i.e., 0.17 seconds per entity).

Classification and Regression Results. First, for the trivial *Vote* method, we obtained 50% accuracy, whereas the *RMSE* value was 23.1. The single dataset with the highest accuracy and the lowest RMSE was *FreeBase* (http://freebase. com), i.e., we obtained 82% accuracy through *SVM* model, whereas its RMSE value was 16.37 (through *LR* model). The corresponding percentages for *DBpedia* and *Wikidata* were much smaller. However, by taking each pair of these 3 datasets, the accuracy increased, and the RMSE value decreased in all cases (versus using only one dataset from each pair). Certainly, by using only *FreeBase*, we achieved better results comparing to use both *DBpedia* and *Wikidata*, which seems rational, since from *Freebase* we created a large number of sequences. However, by combining *Freebase* with either *DBpedia* or *Wikidata*, or by using all 3 datasets (these combinations are feasible due to cross-dataset reasoning), we obtained better results. By using all the 14 available datasets (out of 400 datasets) having data about these movies, we achieved the highest accuracy (84.7%) and the lowest RMSE (15.57). However, we should note that 8 of these 14 datasets offered very few URI sequences for this task. Finally, *SVM* outperformed *NB* in all classification cases, while *LR* was more effective in regression tasks.

Other Configurations. In rows 10–15 of Table 2, we show indicatively some experiments with different configurations. By creating URI sequences containing only the property *rdf:type*, we obtained better results by using all datasets in comparison to use only *Freebase*, while by creating sequences that contain both *rdf:type* and *dcterms:subject* (ct+tp) the results improved. Regarding experiments containing the top-K sequences, by creating only the top-30 URI sequences according to objects frequency for each movie in descending order (i.e., triples with the 30 most popular objects per movie), we achieved the highest accuracy and the lowest RMSE. On the contrary, a random order was more effective versus an ascending one. Concerning the creation time of *desc* and *asc*, is it slower versus the other configurations (i.e., 3.6 seconds per entity), since we send several requests to LODsyndesis [12] for retrieving the frequency of objects.

Results for Music Albums. Table 3 shows experiments by creating all the URI sequences, each time by using a different subset of datasets. By using only *DBpedia* (see the fourth column), we created on average 16.3 URI sequences per album, whereas by using all the datasets, we created 35.9. Concerning the creation time of URI sequences, it is again low (i.e., 0.11 seconds per entity).

Classification and Regression Results. For the trivial *Vote* method, we obtained 50% accuracy, whereas the *RMSE value* was 13.95. The single dataset having the best performance was *DBpedia* (see Table 3), whereas *Freebase* was not so accurate for this task. Therefore, even by selecting to use exactly one dataset for both movies and music albums (i.e., the same dataset in both cases), we will not be able to obtain good results for both tasks. Similarly to movies, as we add more datasets, the results are better for both regression and classification, except for the pairs containing the dataset *Wikidata*. By including all the 5 available datasets for music albums, we obtain the highest accuracy (i.e., 71.31%) and the lowest *RMSE* value (i.e., 12.41). Finally, similarly to the case of movies, the best model was the *SVM* for classification and the *LR* for regression.

Table 3. Classification and regression experiments on Music Albums dataset

Datasets	Prop.	crd	$|Seq_U(e)|$ average	Creation time	NB (CF)	SVM (CF)	LR (Reg)	SMOreg (Reg)
Freebase (FR)	All	All	9.2	2.1 min	52.75%	56.57%	13.74	14.08
DBpedia (DB)	All	All	16.3	2.3 min	64.01%	68.21%	12.75	13.07
Wikidata (WK)	All	All	6.7	1.9 min	60.38%	61.37%	13.89	14.68
DB, WK	All	All	20.5	2.3 min	63.42%	67.61%	12.85	13.10
DB, FR	All	All	25.5	2.3 min	64.30%	68.64%	12.60	13.03
FR, WK	All	All	16.0	2.2 min	54.10%	57.65%	14.00	14.50
DB, FR, WK	All	All	29.8	2.4 min	64.73%	69.02%	12.55	13.01
All 5 $dsets(E')$	All	All	**35.9**	2.5 min	**67.21%**	**71.31%**	**12.41**	**12.72**

Table 4. Top-5 related movies to "Wall-E" movie by using different datasets

Datasets	Position 1	Position 2	Position 3	Position 4	Position 5
DB	Pink Panther 2	**Ratatouille**	Shrek 2	Rain Mant	**Space Chimps**
DB, FR	**Finding Nemo**	**Toy Story 2**	**Incredibles**	**Toy Story**	Princess and the Frog
All	**Finding Nemo**	**Ratatouille**	**Incredibles**	**Toy Story 3**	**Toy Story**

4.2 Finding Similar Entities

LODVec can produce the top-K similar entities for a given one, since it uses *word2vec* from *dl4j* API. Table 4 shows an indicative example, i.e., finding the 5 most similar movies (from the set of 2,000 movies) to the animated movie "WALL-E", by creating all the URI sequences and by using (a) only *DBpedia*, (b) *DBpedia* and *Freebase* and (c) all datasets. For evaluating the results, we typed in *Google Search Engine* the keywords "WALL-E related movies", and we retrieved a list with related movies that "People also search for WALL-E". By using only *DBpedia*, 2 of 5 movies were in the list of related movies (the bold ones in Table 4), whereas by using both *Freebase* and *DBpedia*, 4 of 5 movies were at that list. Finally, by exploiting all the datasets, all the 5 movies were part of the list.

5 Conclusion

There is a lack of approaches that create URI embeddings from multiple RDF datasets. For this reason, we introduced a prototype called LODVec that exploits the semantically enriched indexes of LODsyndesis knowledge graph, and offers configurable options for creating URI sequences and embeddings through *word2vec* algorithm, for over 400 million entities from 400 RDF datasets. The produced embeddings can be exploited in several tasks. In our case, we evaluated the gain of using multiple datasets (and cross-dataset reasoning) for four machine-learning tasks, e.g., for classifying whether a movie has a high or low rating. Indicatively, by using data from *DBpedia* we created 23.8 URI sequences per movie, while by combining information from 14 datasets, the corresponding number was 170.1. We identified even 13% increase in the accuracy of predicting if a movie is highly rated by using multiple datasets, instead of using only *DBpedia*. As a future work, we plan (a) to create longer URI sequences, (b) to create vectors through other models, such as *GloVe* [15], and (c) to apply graph-based techniques, such as [3,19]. Finally, our goal is to train the whole knowledge graph for retrieving the top-K similar entities for any given entity quickly.

Acknowledgements. The research work was supported by the Hellenic Foundation for Research and Innovation (HFRI) and the General Secretariat for Research and Technology (GSRT), under the HFRI PhD Fellowship grant (GA. No. 166).

References

1. Antoniou, G., van Harmelen, F.: A Semantic Web Primer, 2nd edn. The MIT Press, Cambridge (2008)
2. Cochez, M., Ristoski, P., Ponzetto, S.P., Paulheim, H.: Biased graph walks for RDF graph embeddings. In: WIMS, p. 21. ACM (2017)
3. Cochez, M., Ristoski, P., Ponzetto, S.P., Paulheim, H.: Global RDF vector space embeddings. In: d'Amato, C., et al. (eds.) ISWC 2017. LNCS, vol. 10587, pp. 190–207. Springer, Cham (2017). https://doi.org/10.1007/978-3-319-68288-4_12
4. Dietze, S., Mohapatra, N., Iosifidis, V., Ekbal, A., Fafalios, P.: Time-aware and corpus-specific entity relatedness, pp. 33–39 (2018)
5. Hajra, A., Tochtermann, K.: Linking science: approaches for linking scientific publications across different LOD repositories. IJMSO **12**(2–3), 124–141 (2017)
6. Inan, E., Dikenelli, O.: Effect of enriched ontology structures on RDF embedding-based entity linking. In: Garoufallou, E., Virkus, S., Siatri, R., Koutsomiha, D. (eds.) MTSR 2017. CCIS, vol. 755, pp. 15–24. Springer, Cham (2017). https://doi.org/10.1007/978-3-319-70863-8_2
7. Lin, Y., Liu, Z., Sun, M., Liu, Y., Zhu, X.: Learning entity and relation embeddings for knowledge graph completion. In: AAAI Conference (2015)
8. Mikolov, T., Chen, K., Corrado, G., Dean, J.: Efficient estimation of word representations in vector space. arXiv preprint arXiv:1301.3781 (2013)
9. Mikolov, T., Sutskever, I., Chen, K., Corrado, G.S., Dean, J.: Distributed representations of words and phrases and their compositionality. In: Advances in Neural Information Processing Systems, pp. 3111–3119 (2013)
10. Mountantonakis, M., Tzitzikas, Y.: How linked data can aid machine learning-based tasks. In: Kamps, J., Tsakonas, G., Manolopoulos, Y., Iliadis, L., Karydis, I. (eds.) TPDL 2017. LNCS, vol. 10450, pp. 155–168. Springer, Cham (2017). https://doi.org/10.1007/978-3-319-67008-9_13
11. Mountantonakis, M., Tzitzikas, Y.: High performance methods for linked open data connectivity analytics. Information **9**(6), 134 (2018)
12. Mountantonakis, M., Tzitzikas, Y.: LODsyndesis: global scale knowledge services. Heritage **1**(2), 335–348 (2018)
13. Mountantonakis, M., Tzitzikas, Y.: Large scale semantic integration of linked data: a survey. ACM Comput. Surv. **52**, 103 (2019)
14. Nechaev, Y., Corcoglioniti, F., Giuliano, C.: Type prediction combining linked open data and social media. In: CIKM, pp. 1033–1042. ACM (2018)
15. Pennington, J., Socher, R., Manning, C.: Glove: global vectors for word representation. In: Proceedings of EMNLP Conference, pp. 1532–1543 (2014)
16. Ristoski, P., Bizer, C., Paulheim, H.: Mining the web of linked data with rapidminer. J. Web Semant. **35**, 142–151 (2015)
17. Ristoski, P., Rosati, J., Di Noia, T., De Leone, R., Paulheim, H.: RDF2Vec: RDF graph embeddings and their applications. Semant. Web **10**(4), 721–752 (2019)
18. Ristoski, P., de Vries, G.K.D., Paulheim, H.: A collection of benchmark datasets for systematic evaluations of machine learning on the semantic web. In: Groth, P., et al. (eds.) ISWC 2016. LNCS, vol. 9982, pp. 186–194. Springer, Cham (2016). https://doi.org/10.1007/978-3-319-46547-0_20
19. Wang, Z., Zhang, J., Feng, J., Chen, Z.: Knowledge graph embedding by translating on hyperplanes. In: AAAI Conference on Artificial Intelligence (2014)
20. Witten, I.H., Frank, E., Hall, M.A., Pal, C.J.: Data Mining: Practical Machine Learning Tools and Techniques. Morgan Kaufmann, San Francisco (2016)

Changing the Subject: Dynamic Discussion Monitoring in Twitter

Marçal Mora-Cantallops$^{(\boxtimes)}$ (ID) and Salvador Sánchez-Alonso (ID)

University of Alcalá, Alcalá de Henares, Madrid, Spain
{marcal.mora,salvador.sanchez}@uah.es

Abstract. In recent years, Twitter has become increasingly popular both as a social networking service (where users express their opinions) and as a tool for information retrieval. Many events that are commented, debated or argued online, however, are dynamic and unpredictable in nature, resulting in the need to derive the corresponding dynamic computational methodologies to track and to extract such changing topics, events and relevant content in a timely and unattended manner. In this paper, we propose a framework to accomplish two objectives: periodically obtaining the relevant topics of discussion among authorities and adapting the tracked keywords or hashtags accordingly to retrieve the most relevant possible information in each time window. The application of this framework to a case study reveals how our proposed approach is able to accurately and dynamically track the conversation around an event. Our method could therefore be applied to query Twitter in many domains, such as politics, sport events, marketing campaigns or media engagement, among others.

Keywords: Information retrieval · Twitter · Dynamic · Topic monitoring

1 Introduction

The adoption of Social Networking Services (SNS) (also referred as social media) has been growing steadily over the last years, with an estimated 3.5 billion active users and 45% penetration globally[1]. Many users have drifted away from mainstream media as its credibility scores have dropped across all venues and have embraced the new possibilities offered by the social media as a source of information, as news shared by contacts or friends seems to improve the level of trust; this effect is amplified when the contact sharing the story is perceived as an "opinion leader" [1].

Therefore, trends in social media have become highly relevant to understand public opinion and perception [2]. They can be useful to track public conversations and debates, to assess a product performance or to understand human

---

[1] https://wearesocial.com/global-digital-report-2019.

© Springer Nature Switzerland AG 2019
E. Garoufallou et al. (Eds.): MTSR 2019, CCIS 1057, pp. 163–174, 2019.
https://doi.org/10.1007/978-3-030-36599-8_14

behavior, among many others. To be able to know where public attention is at a particular moment becomes a critical problem for researchers and practitioners alike as trending topics can both describe the opinion of a large community and provide the means to analyze it.

Not all SNS serve the same purpose, though. Twitter is a social networking service that has emerged as the reference in micro-blogging platforms [3]. It combines some unique features such as a very simple interface and a character limit in its postings, making it convenient for information retrieval and automatic processing purposes. Users post short messages (up to 280 characters currently) called tweets and are able to interact with the tweets posted by others (replying to them, quoting or retweeting them). Huge amounts of data are generated every day that can provide valuable information for many different domains, such as political communication, consumer behaviors, marketing campaigns and disaster management, among others. This data is freely and publicly available both through its site and its API (application programming interface), allowing for a near real-time monitoring of users' preferences, opinion and behavior. User messages often include hashtags as a way of explicitly marking the relevant topics, easing such monitoring and analysis.

User behavior and occurrences, however, are unpredictable and dynamic in nature. Not only many events can't be accurately predicted (e.g. natural disasters or accidents) but also it's even harder for researchers and analysts to anticipate the wording that will be used by users in their hashtags. It could be argued that a constant manual monitoring could mitigate such issues, adding any new relevant words to the tracking as soon as they are noticed. This approach, however, presents two main caveats:

– Late response, as there might be a (relevant) delay between the new topic emerging and the start of its tracking, losing what could potentially be relevant information or interactions.
– Human supervision, which might not be possible at all times (e.g. at night), resulting in either inefficient resource allocation or the inability to detect and track relevant changes at any time.

In this paper, we propose a dual framework to accomplish two objectives: periodically obtaining the relevant topics of discussion (in a predefined scope) while adapting the tracked hashtags accordingly in order to be able to retrieve the most relevant possible information in each time window in an unattended and timely manner, minimizing information loss and human intervention. Our framework uses two algorithms. A first algorithm is devoted to monitor a group of authorities; as a result, a list of hashtags under discussion is obtained. The second algorithm then uses the most relevant topics to reset the data stream filter, extracting and storing the related posts. This way, we maximize the probability of capturing and tracking the most relevant hashtags at a given point in time.

The remainder of this paper is organized as follows: related works are outlined in the following section. The proposed approach is described in detail in the methodology section, while a test case study is presented in Sect. 4. Finally, conclusions are discussed in Sect. 5.

2   Background

2.1   Social Media

Social media (or SNS) are web-based services that allow individuals to create a profile, articulate a list of connections to other users, view and traverse such connections between users, and share content [4]. SNS users tend to interact with other users to whom they already have some kind of social tie; therefore, online conversation through these platforms may more closely resemble opportunities for everyday conversation [5] about any topic than a more structured online forum where most users are strangers to each other. According to previous research, young people already show a clear preference for online engagement and organization; politically engaged young people integrate social media use into their existing organizations and political communications [6]. Many works have studied the effect of social media, specially Twitter, as a facilitator in political campaigns [7] and protests [8] worldwide.

One important aspect to consider is how information spreads in online social networks. Mønsted et al. [9] found that the best explanation was a complex contagion model, implying that information diffusion is affected not only by the number of exposures to a piece of information, but also by the exposure to multiple sources and their social influence. Users tend to follow other users that become their sources in this media environment; those perceived as leaders of opinion become more influential and the information diffused by them, more "viral" [1]. Thus, the dominant mode of information acquisition is through "incidental news", "news content encountered on mobile devices while visiting social media sites, in a process that is derivative of social media interactions rather than deliberately sought for" [10].

Therefore, while social media is rapidly becoming the main source of information for many citizens, the spread of information is irregular, difficult to predict in nature and incidental. Methods that aim to track and retrieve such conversations are required to be flexible and dynamic enough to be able to follow them and minimize information loss.

2.2   Topic Tracking

To be able to properly track opinion over time has been one of the main concerns by the public opinion analysts for a long time [11]. With the advent of Twitter, public opinion can be tracked continuously and in real time. The high volume of information and the myriad different topics that are being talked in any particular time, however, stand in the way of direct tracking. One way to overcome such limitation is to look at the Twitter hashtags (keywords or terms starting with "#"), which are the most common feature for users to connect and relate to within a larger networked discourse [12]. Posts that contain hashtags are prone to contain more informational value than non-hashtagged tweets, as they are related with longer messages, additional hashtags and hyperlinks [13]. Moreover, hashtag use is not limited to one's own network, as Enli and Simonsen found; journalists and politicians, for example, use them to reach outside their personal networks [14], demonstrating that their use of social media is closely connected to their professional practice.

Accurate and appropriate hashtag tracking is, therefore, crucial for discourse and conversation analysis in Twitter. But, in terms of information life cycle, it is difficult to predict what hashtag is going to be adopted by the community in a given discussion and whether it will alternate with custom or modified tags, so dynamic tracking is also key. In spite of this, most studies opt for a static approach. To cite a few examples, in [15], the authors used Twitter data to monitor a constitutional referendum in Italy. Even though they recorded tweets during five weeks, the extracted keywords were static: five hashtags that were manually selected by the authors. Another similar case is found in [16], where #WorldEnvironmentDay is tracked to understand public opinion about the subject, but user variants that might be widely used or hashtags in other languages were discarded. When Takahashi et al. [17] analyzed communication on Twitter during a natural disaster (a typhoon), they used four fixed hashtags, even though the typhoon lasted for five days. Missing data and losing track of the conversation when hashtags remain static is inevitable, as Tsakalidis et al. [18] acknowledge in their work about the EU 2014 election trends, even when they "aggregated tweets written in the respective language that contained a party's name, its abbreviation, its Twitter account name and some possible misspells" and "excluded several ambiguous keywords in an attempt to reduce the noise". In all cases, major candidate or party names along with generic terms were used, leaving little space to unusual terms, unexpected events or minor candidates, losing potentially relevant information. It is also worth noting how different languages, abbreviations, misspells or ambiguous keywords are problematic.

A few works have addressed real-time Twitter analysis with topic detection. Choi and Park [19] proposed a method to detect emerging topics on Twitter using High Utility Pattern Mining (HUPM), which takes frequency of appearance and utility of words into account. Although their method works well to detect topics in known datasets, it is not designed to dynamically use the resulting topics for extraction. A similar issue appears in the work of Adedoyin-Olowe et al. [20]; their work aims to detect relevant events from a collection of Tweets but, again, this is done in post-processing. There is no live adaptation where, for example, an event is detected and immediately followed by the Tweet extractor. This dynamic adaptation is found in Gaglio et al. [21], who proposed a system able to progressively refine its query to include new relevant terms, reflecting the emergence of new topics of trends. In their conclusions, they also noted how "other systems were unable to capture the social aspects of the observed events [...] every time the users left the main topic and started to talk about unexpected events". Their work, however, presents another limitation that might be relevant in some contexts: it requires an initial set of keywords to track and term selection depends on the collected tweets, not taking into account the authority of the users tweeting them. Our proposed solution will aim to overcome this situation.

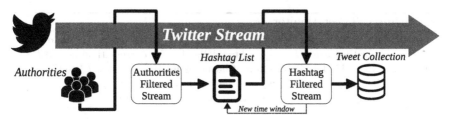

Fig. 1. Twitter is monitored using a initial set of accounts that are considered "authorities" in the topic of discussion or analysis. The acquired tweets are analyzed to extract the relevant terms. Terms are weighted, so for every time period an ordered list of topics of discussion is obtained, sorted by relevance. At the start of each time window, the N top terms are passed into the extraction script, updating the applied filter into the second stream. The collected tweets are stored for later analysis.

3   Methodology

The proposed solution is intended to be used as an automatic and unattended tool for tracking the conversation that is generated around a particular area or topic, although manual tuning is still possible at any moment in case running changes are needed. A general overview of the process is represented in Fig. 1, following four main steps, namely: (1) Selection of authorities, (2) Monitoring authorities, (3) Hashtag selection and (4) Conversation tracking.

3.1   Selection of Authorities

Users that, according to a certain criteria defined by the researcher, lead the conversation or are relevant in the topic of analysis are considered "authorities". To study the debate of news stories, for example, one would follow the media, the experts and the influential users in that matter. In a sport event, the list of authorities could be composed by not only by the team's accounts but also by relevant journalists and analysts.

Having a good list of authorities is a prerequisite for the proposed approach. This list will be followed using the Twitter API and will prevent the topic tracking from drifting to potentially undesired scopes.

3.2   Monitoring Authorities

Once a list of authorities is defined, the Twitter API stream can be filtered by following these users. In particular, the stream will contain and deliver posts that are either created or retweeted by any of the authorities, are replies to any Tweet created by any of the authorities or are retweets of any of their Tweets.

Every time a Tweet matching the filter is received, the script will proceed to process it, as described in Algorithm 1. This script has two main purposes: to generate the weighted collection of hashtags and to control whether a new time window has started.

Algorithm 1. Tweet Monitor

Input: A Tweet delivered from the authorities stream (matching the followed authorities) **and** $C_t \longleftarrow$ Hashtag collection for current time period t

Output: $C_t' \longleftarrow$ Updated collection of hashtags for time window t (if still in the same time window) **or** a new collection of hashtags for time window $t + 1$ (C_{t+1}) (in case it is a new time window)

begin

    /* Check whether it is a new time window   */

    if *new time window* **then**

        Save C_t to file   /* Store C_t for later processing */

        Clear C_t /* C_t is now C_{t+1} */

    /* Process the received Tweet from the stream   */

    for *each Hashtag* **in** *Tweet* **do**

        if *Hashtag* **not in** C_t **then**

            Add Hashtag to C_t with weight w

        else

            Increase $C_t[Hashtag]$ w units

The collection of hashtags C_t is, in essence, an ordered list of hashtags found on all the posts recovered during a single time window. For each Tweet received, the script extracts all its hashtags (identified by their # symbol). Each hashtag can be assigned a weight w; the weight function may be, again, defined by the user. Depending on the intent, the weight function could take many forms. For instance, one might decide to simply count the number of times a hashtag appears, but it is also possible to weight a hashtag according to the posting user number of followers (assuming that it might have more impact or relevancy), the logarithm of that number (to avoid being too influenced by dominant users) or more complex functions.

The time window t must be defined by the user and it allows to adapt the monitoring to different paces. A long range tracking (a marketing campaign, for instance) might require a hourly or daily tracking, while shorter events (e.g. an sports event or a natural disaster) could need a window of only a few minutes. Regardless of the time window used, the Tweet Monitor script saves the collection of hashtags for each time period.

3.3 Hashtag Selection

Before proceeding to monitor the hashtags used by the authorities, a selection step is required. Here, an approach mixing "hot" and "emerging" topics is suggested.

To obtain the list of hashtags to be tracked to monitor the derived conversation in Twitter, the following steps are completed:

1. If desired, a list of stop words can be added to remove common everyday spurious hashtags (such as #goodmorning or #happymonday).

2. Every time period, the script looks at the hashtag collection for that window and extracts the top M hashtags in absolute terms by their weight. These are supposed to be the topics that are being strongly discussed and posted by the authorities.
3. Every time period, the hashtags for the corresponding window (C_t) are compared to the previous window C_{t-1} in order to obtain the E hashtags with the biggest increase (note that this might be extended up to the n previous periods). These are potential emerging topics, that might not yet be on the peak of the discussion but are rapidly growing.
4. The top M and E hashtags are combined into the final list, consisting of N (at maximum $M + E$) hashtags, as represented in Fig. 2.

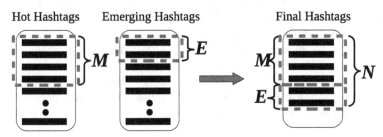

Fig. 2. The list with the top N hashtags combines the biggest terms of discussion (M) with the fastest growing ones (E). For each case, M and E can be adapted to the researcher needs.

3.4 Conversation Tracking

Once the final list of hashtags is obtained, a separate stream can be set to track such hashtags. The Twitter API stream, in this case, delivers all Tweets (from the provided stream, which is in turn a sample of all public Tweets) that match any of that hashtags in their texts (and ignoring case). These Tweets can be processed or stored for a later analysis. Tracked hashtags are dynamically changed in each time period; they are renewed with a new list coming from the previous step, allowing for the unattended and dynamic tracking of the topics present in the authorities discussion.

4 Experimental Results

4.1 Case Study

In order to analyze and provide a few insights on the proposed methodology, a case study has been used. In particular, the conversation around the 2019 Eurovision Song Contest was tracked during the event, between 20:00 CEST on the 18th of May and 02:00 on the following day. As known, Eurovision is an event that is broadcast internationally and attracts a large number of interactions in Twitter, as "users offer their own running commentary on the universally shared media text of the event as it unfolds live" [22]. For this case, the weight function

w was defined as the number of followers that the tweeting user had (therefore, the more followers, the more relevance in the discussion) and the time window t was set at two minutes (given that each performance lasts for 3–4 min).

The following subsections will focus on the hashtag collections generated by the Tweet Monitor; the selection of the top N hashtags and their extraction is considered straightforward after that step. A N of 25, with 20 hot (M) and 5 emerging (E) hashtags will be assumed for this case.

4.2   Authorities

For this case study, the official Eurovision Twitter accounts of every participating country's public broadcaster were used as authorities. Although there were up to 41 participant countries (26 of which performed at the final event), only active and verified accounts specific to Eurovision were included. The selection included a total of 20 accounts, composed by the official Eurovision account (@eurovision) and 19 official accounts managed by each country's broadcasting company, where available. These include, among others, @kaneurovision from Israel, @bbceurovision from the UK, @sbseurovision for Australia, @yleeurovision for Finland and @eurovision_tve for Spain.

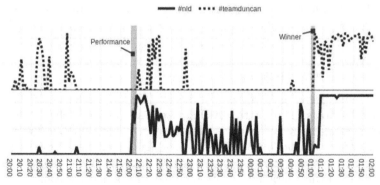

Fig. 3. Ranked position of each two hashtags supporting the same performance (#nld and #teamduncan) in each time window

4.3   Results

A total of 1814 different hashtags were obtained during the six hour extraction. After extracting the top 25 hashtags in each time period, 429 unique hashtags remain. Each hashtag is then ranked according to its weight during the time window. The first visible result is that, although the official hashtags (#eurovision, #daretodream) are consistently in the top 3 (and, therefore, constantly tracked) there are other variations that are also often present in the conversation, such as #esc2019 or #eurovision2019.

Unpredictable Topics. As previously noted, most studies start by monitoring a fixed list of hashtags. That list may include all expected words (in this case, the official hashtags, both for the festival and for each country). Therefore, for a country like The Netherlands, which was the contest winner, one could have expected to track #nld and, maybe, the name of their song (#arcade). But the fan community adopted a different hashtag, #teamduncan, composed with the singer's (Duncan Laurence) first name. As can be seen in Fig. 3, this hashtag is highly relevant not only right after the performance, but also before the contest started (when the official hashtag was not online yet) and after the winner was announced, responding more quickly than the conventional tag.

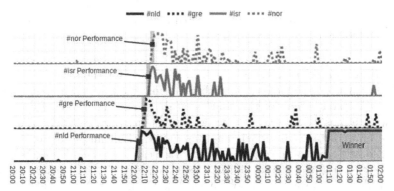

Fig. 4. Ranked position (in the top 25) of each hashtag related to four consecutive performances (#nld, #gre, #isr and #nor) in each time window

Events. On one hand, to obtain a more efficient extraction, it is interesting to track each hashtag only when it is relevant enough. On the other, some events might happen spontaneously or are hard to predict. Figure 4 is a good example of this. First, it must be noted that these four consecutive performances by as many countries get into the top hashtags right in the moment (and not before) when the authorities start talking about them during their respective performances. Second, some events (such as the performance by #isr) reach a peak when they happen, are on the conversation for a while, decay and disappear from the list (note that Israel was not a favorite in this edition). This also shows how irrelevant topics are "forgotten" promptly. Third, the case of the #nld, one of the favorites and final winner, where discussion lasts for longer, then goes down during the voting and goes back to the top when the winner is announced.

Languages. This method is also able to track variations of the same topic in different languages (in case they are relevant enough). In the case of Eurovision, the Polish word #eurowizja was also among the top 25 hashtags in 43 out of 181 time windows. Other example can be found in the calls for boycott (the festival took place in Israel, raising controversy due to the situation with Palestine) with #boicoteurovision2019 and #boycotteurovision2019 showing similar levels of usage.

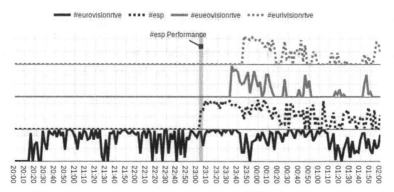

Fig. 5. Ranked position of each hashtag related to #eurovisionrtve among the top 25 in each time window

Misspellings or Alternatives. Alternative words for the same concepts are also found in a good amount. Spanish fans, for example, used #esp, #spain or even #lavenda (name of the song) to talk about their song. In a similar way, Swedish fans used #swe or #sweden interchangeably. Not only some hashtags are unpredictable, but their alternatives or misspellings created by users might also be problematic. A paradigmatic case can be seen in Fig. 5, where the hashtags related to the Spanish Public Television (RTVE). The official hashtag, #eurovisionrtve, is prominent over the whole festival, often among the top three. However, after the Spanish performance, two misspelled related hashtags appear in the conversation: #eueovisionrtve and #eurivisionrtve (note how the "e" is next to the "r" and the "i" is next to the "o" in the Spanish keyboard). Although some misspellings might be anecdotal, both these hashtags were relevant (among the top 25) in many time windows until the end of the festival; not tracking them would derive in a definite loss of information.

5   Conclusions

Even relatively simple events such as the Eurovision Song Contest derive in complex conversations. In our study, more than 1800 different hashtags were generated by the authorities (official and verified accounts) in the subject, with 429 unique different hashtags among the top 25 topics in at least one time window. Previous studies analyzed Eurovision using only a few static hashtags; [22], for instance, tracked only three keywords (#eurovision, #esc and #sbseurovision), missing interesting information only traceable through misspelled hashtags or user generated tags that must be detected in real time. We have shown how our unattended approach could enrich this kind of extractions, adding a dynamic tracking of the conversation among the relevant accounts to capture the resulting public discussion. In particular, it should be noticed how #esc was not even relevant as a hashtag for the 2019 edition, as users ended using #esc2019 instead.

Thus, the proposed methodology is able to track hashtags in an unattended and dynamic manner, capturing the hashtags used by the authorities of the community of interest and adapting them as the conversation changes or moves, even if dramatically, while being robust against disruptions and avoiding the requirement of an initial set of words; term selection depends exclusively on the terms used by the authorities and is also able to take their relevance into account.

This method is limited by a few restrictions, however. First, it requires a fairly accurate identification of the authorities, users that are relevant in the discussion. In political contexts or in many events, they should be arguably straightforward to identify (political leaders, influencers, etc.) but there might be some scopes where this leadership is less clear. Second, the determination of the time window and the weight function is also important for its behavior; they should be determined for each case using proper testing, which is not always possible as the event might be unique. In any case, similar events might be useful to tune the algorithm.

Future work will look at how to dynamically adapt the list of authorities, as not all the users driving the conversation might be included in the initial list; in this way, it would be possible to add new members or replace the less active ones after identifying the most influential users in a particular time window [23]. Another venue for further research is appropriate parameter setting in each situation, as to be able to correctly set the time window, the weight function and the number of hashtags to be followed is also critical for the method's generalization.

References

1. Turcotte, J., York, C., Irving, J., Scholl, R.M., Pingree, R.J.: News recommendations from social media opinion leaders: effects on media trust and information seeking. J. Comput. Commun. **20**, 520–535 (2015). https://doi.org/10.1111/jcc4.12127
2. Fang, Y., Chen, X., Song, Z., Wang, T., Cao, Y.: Modelling propagation of public opinions on microblogging big data using sentiment analysis and compartmental models. Int. J. Semant. Web Inf. Syst. **13**, 11–27 (2017). https://doi.org/10.4018/ijswis.2017010102
3. Gadek, G., et al.: Topological and topical characterisation of Twitter user communities. Data Technol. Appl. **52**, 482–501 (2018). https://doi.org/10.1108/DTA-01-2018-0006
4. Boyd, D.M., Ellison, N.B.: Social network sites: definition, history, and scholarship. J. Comput. Commun. **13**, 210–230 (2007). https://doi.org/10.1111/j.1083-6101.2007.00393.x
5. Hampton, K.N., Shin, I., Lu, W.: Social media and political discussion: when online presence silences offline conversation. Inf. Commun. Soc. **20**, 1090–1107 (2017). https://doi.org/10.1080/1369118X.2016.1218526
6. Vromen, A., Xenos, M.A., Loader, B.: Young people, social media and connective action: from organisational maintenance to everyday political talk. J. Youth Stud. **18**, 80–100 (2015). https://doi.org/10.1080/13676261.2014.933198
7. McGregor, S.C., Mourão, R.R., Molyneux, L.: Twitter as a tool for and object of political and electoral activity: Considering electoral context and variance among actors. J. Inf. Technol. Polit. **14**, 154–167 (2017). https://doi.org/10.1080/19331681.2017.1308289

8. Jost, J.T., et al.: How social media facilitates political protest: information, motivation, and social networks. Polit. Psychol. **39**, 85–118 (2018). https://doi.org/10.1111/pops.12478

9. Mønsted, B., Sapieżyński, P., Ferrara, E., Lehmann, S.: Evidence of complex contagion of information in social media: an experiment using Twitter bots. PLoS ONE **12** (2017). https://doi.org/10.1371/journal.pone.0184148

10. Boczkowski, P., Mitchelstein, E., Matassi, M.: Incidental news: how young people consume news on social media. In: Proceedings of the Hawaii International Conference on System Sciences, pp. 1785–1792 (2017). https://doi.org/10.24251/hicss.2017.217

11. Green, D.P., Gerber, A.S., Boef, S.L. De.: Tracking opinion over time: a method for reducing sampling error. Public Opin. Q. **63**, 178–192 (2002). https://doi.org/10.1086/297710

12. Bruns, A. and Burgess, J.: Twitter hashtags from ad hoc to calculated publics. Hashtag publics: the power and politics of discursive networks, pp. 13–28 (2015)

13. D'heer, E., Verdergem, P., De Grove, F.: #MissingData: a methodological inquiry of the hashtag to collect data from Twitter. Selected Papers AoIR 2016 17th Annual Conference of the Association of Internet Research (2016)

14. Enli, G., Simonsen, C.A.: 'Social media logic' meets professional norms: Twitter hashtags usage by journalists and politicians. Inf. Commun. Soc. **21**, 1081–1096 (2018). https://doi.org/10.1080/1369118X.2017.1301515

15. Fano, S., Slanzi, D.: Using Twitter data to monitor political campaigns and predict election results. In: De la Prieta, F., et al. (eds.) PAAMS 2017. AISC, vol. 619, pp. 191–197. Springer, Cham (2018). https://doi.org/10.1007/978-3-319-61578-3_19

16. Reyes-Menendez, A., Saura, J.R., Alvarez-Alonso, C.: Understanding #worldenvironmentday user opinions in Twitter: a topic-based sentiment analysis approach. Int. J. Environ. Res. Public Health. **15**, 2537 (2018). https://doi.org/10.3390/ijerph15112537

17. Takahashi, B., Tandoc, E.C., Carmichael, C.: Communicating on Twitter during a disaster: an analysis of tweets during Typhoon Haiyan in the philippines. Comput. Human Behav. **50**, 392–398 (2015). https://doi.org/10.1016/J.CHB.2015.04.020

18. Tsakalidis, A., Papadopoulos, S., Cristea, A.I., Kompatsiaris, Y.: Predicting elections for multiple countries using Twitter and polls. IEEE Intell. Syst. **30**, 10–17 (2015). https://doi.org/10.1109/MIS.2015.17

19. Choi, H.J., Park, C.H.: Emerging topic detection in Twitter stream based on high utility pattern mining. Expert Syst. Appl. **115**, 27–36 (2019). https://doi.org/10.1016/j.eswa.2018.07.051

20. Adedoyin-Olowe, M., Gaber, M.M., Dancausa, C.M., Stahl, F., Gomes, J.B.: A rule dynamics approach to event detection in Twitter with its application to sports and politics. Expert Syst. Appl. **55**, 351–360 (2016). https://doi.org/10.1016/j.eswa.2016.02.028

21. Gaglio, S., Lo Re, G., Morana, M.: A framework for real-time Twitter data analysis. Comput. Commun. **73**, 236–242 (2016). https://doi.org/10.1016/j.comcom.2015.09.021

22. Highfield, T., Harrington, S., Bruns, A.: Twitter as a technology for audiencing and fandom. Inf. Commun. Soc. **16**, 315–339 (2013). https://doi.org/10.1080/1369118x.2012.756053

23. Mahmoudi, A., Yaakub, M., Abu Bakar, A.: New time-based model to identify the influential users in online social networks. Data Technol. Appl. **52**, 278–290 (2018). https://doi.org/10.1108/DTA-08-2017-0056

Proposal of a Metadata Application Profile for Technical Reports

Morgana Andrade[1](✉) ⓘ and Ana Alice Baptista[2] ⓘ

[1] Espirito Santo Federal University, Vitória, Espírito Santo, Brazil
morganaandrade@hotmail.com
[2] University of Minho, Guimarães, Portugal

Abstract. Technical reports may be elaborated to serve multiple objectives and they constitute important sources of information for researchers and organizations. However their discovery and retrieval may be compromised due to particular characteristics related to the way they are described. A metadata application profile is recognized for providing increased interoperability and semantics between information systems, favouring discovery. In this article we report on the process of developing an application profile for technical reports and present the respective profile. This application profile includes elements from metadata vocabularies already consolidated in the context of scholarly publication and also elements from a specific metadata vocabulary developed within the scope of this work, *techrap*. The final product of this study are the constraints matrices with 7 classes and 89 properties. The results of this work are useful for metadata librarians and managers of online digital respositories.

Keywords: Technical report · Metadata application profile · Linked data

1 Introduction

A technical report may be defined as a "[…] a document that formally reports on the results or progress of research and development or that describes the state of a technical or scientific issue" [1]. It may be classified as: "technical-scientific, of travel and participation in events, of traineeship, of technical visit, administrative, for special and progressive purposes" and is drawn up for the function or under the responsibility of an organization or person [2, 3]. The first records of publication and use of reports as a means of scholarly communication date back to the period of 1909–1915, by the National Aeronautics and Space Administration - NASA [3].

Technical reports, identified by some authors as grey literature, may contribute to the development of teaching and research activities [4] but, due to their characteristics, they require specific treatment for their management and retrieval [5]. According to González de Gomez and Machado [6], access to this type of resources may be hampered in part by: the independence with which they are developed, i.e., the research activities described in a report may have been developed within an institution to which the authors are not bound; confidentiality issues; intellectual property rights; dissemination and reproduction restrictions [3, 7].

© Springer Nature Switzerland AG 2019
E. Garoufallou et al. (Eds.): MTSR 2019, CCIS 1057, pp. 175–186, 2019.
https://doi.org/10.1007/978-3-030-36599-8_15

Currently, technical reports and other types of grey literature are being stored using a variety of information systems, mainly in scholarly digital repositories (SDR). Of the 3,519 SDR in the world, 35% store this type of publication [8].

González de Gomez and Machado [6] have shown concern about how these documents are described and how this influences their organization and retrieval. They have proposed a set of metadata elements for describing reports based on MARC 21. On the other hand, Zou et al. [9] suggest elements for metadata schemas based on Functional Requirements for Bibliographic Records (FRBR). Turner, Liddy, Bradley, and Wheatley [10] developed a model for locating grey literature documents relating to public health interventions. They presented metadata elements that describe the organization, intervention type, methods (date/duration, setting and target population), outcomes and documents (document type and bibliographic elements).

Taking as a basis relevant literature on metadata and Linked Data, especially the one related to technical reports, in this paper we propose a Metadata Application Profile (MAP) for technical reports in the context of SDR. We consider both the physical and thematic representation. The creation and availability of MAP contributes to the uniformization and interrelation of resource descriptions, enhancing the semantic interoperability between different information systems. The results of this work are useful for metadata librarians and SDR managers.

This paper is structured as follows: Sect. 2 provides an overview of MAPs and Resource Description Framework (RDF); Sect. 3 presents the methodological procedures for the development of the MAP. The MAP for technical reports (TechRAP), is presented in Sect. 4. Section 5 presents the final considerations.

2 Metadata Application Profiles

The large amount of existing metadata schemas and vocabularies has created the conditions for the emergence of developments aimed at their creation, relation, recording, access, use and reuse. Among these are the MAP [11].

In this article, the term "application profile" is used such as defined by Heery and Patel [12]: "[…] schemas which consist of data elements drawn from one or more namespaces, combined together by implementors, and optimised for a particular local application". Although in the present case we are not thinking about a "particular local application", it seems to us that this is still the most interesting definition of MAP as it focuses on the final scheme and does not include intermediate documents resulting from other phases of the MAP development process as, for example, the Singapore Framework does.

From the literature it is possible to draw the history of the concept of application profile. It is clear that the article by Heery and Patel [12] was a milestone for the definition of the concept currently adopted by the DCMI community (http://repositorio. ufes.br/handle/10/11414). In Semantic Web applications, the use of a MAP is recommended at least when it is necessary to use properties drawn from different metadata vocabularies, including own vocabularies [12, 13], as long as these vocabularies are defined in RDF and follow the generic model for metadata records (DCAM) [12, 14].

For clarification, in this paper we distinguish between attribute and property in the following way: we use the term attribute to designate a characteristic of a resource (e.g., author, first name,…), while the term property is used to designate a RDF property (e.g., http://purl.org/dc/terms/creator, http://xmlns.com/foaf/0.1/firstName,…). In simple terms, we call property an RDFized version of an attribute.

3   Research Design

The aim of this research was to propose a metadata application profile for technical reports in the context of Semantic Web and SDR. The research started with a literature review to identify appropriate metadata schemas and application profiles for technical reports/grey literature. From September to December 2018, bibliographical searches were carried out in order to identify MAPs for technical reports. We used the Scopus and Web of Science databases and the GoogleScholar and Google search engines using the following terms: "metadata schema", "metadata vocabulary", "application profile" and "dictionary metadata" associated with "technical report" and "grey literature". The results of the search pointed to the absence of specific studies with that purpose. The search was also performed with the terms: "report or grey literature" and "representation", "report or grey literature" and "access point". We have identified studies about the metadata representation of grey literature, which includes the reports. However, these studies have not proposed a specific application profile [6, 9, 10, 15], which led us to create one.

The work of developing the AP for technical reports was carried out in four stages: (a) identification of the attributes needed to describe a technical report – mainly the study of Andrade, Shintaku and Barros [15]; (b) comparative analysis of data obtained by Andrade, Turner et al. [10] and Shintaku and Barros [15]; (c) data modeling; and (d) development of the MAP – this article reports on this part of the work.

We have based our work in the previous study of Andrade, Shintaku and Barros [15] as these authors have advanced in the identification of elements related to the descriptive and thematic representation of technical reports and by the gap of studies on the subject. Their study has identified 58 terms. We then analized and further reworked and arranged these terms, resulting in 7 classes and 60 properties, as showed in Fig. 1.

Although Dublin Core Terms is the most used metadata schema due to reasons widely presented in the literature, Andrade, Shintaku and Barros [15] found that its properties do not cover all technical report elements. The development of the data model showed the need to add properties that could reflect on the quality and coherence of the representation on the reports. Inclusions were carried out based on the authors' experience, either in RDF and/or in Library Science.

The representation of the attributes identified by Andrade, Shintaku and Barros in a semantic web environment, in this case in scholarly digital repositories, requires the use of properties drawn from more than one metadata schemas. Conversely, schemas such as Marc21, which is widely used for technical report bibliographic description, have characteristics which makes their use difficult in our context, such as problems associated with cataloging rules (data structure) and the difficulty in representing hierarchies [16, 17]. And since there is no specific schema for technical reports that includes all the

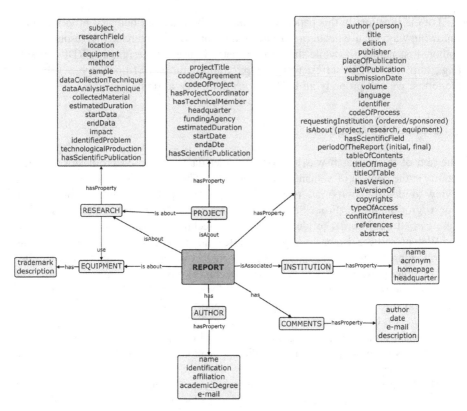

Fig. 1. Attributes related to technical reports (Source: Adapted from Andrade, Shintaku and Barros [15])

attributes identified by Andrade, Shintaku and Barros, the need to develop a metadata application profile is justified.

The MAP for technical reports, called TechRAP, aims to include metadata properties and rules that meet the needs of users of "a particular community with common application requirements" [18], namely, the community of SDR. For this purpose, Me4MAP was adopted [19].

Me4MAP is a method based on the Singapore Framework, which "[…] is the framework for designing metadata applications for maximum interoperability and for documenting such applications for maximum reusability" [20]. In this sense, the development of an application profile should include the following steps: identification of requirements; development of the domain model; and elaboration of the Description Set Profile (DSP) that, in this case, will be replaced by the elaboration of the constraints matrices. We have taken this option because DSPs are underused, even within DCMI, and the constraint matrices are more intelligible for humans.

After the definition of the detailed data model, Excel spreadsheets, called the Constraints Matrices, were elaborated, where information about cardinality and encoding schemes was included. Cardinality refers to specifying how many times a metadata property may or may not appear in a description. The cardinality of a property may vary according to a particular context: a property may be mandatory in one profile and optional in another one. Or, a given property may be repetitive to allow more than one description or to allow different description options for a value. For example, when reporting an author's nationality, it is possible to repeat the property to say that (s)he has two or three nationalities, or repeat the property to encode the same value in two different ways: one using a string and another using an IRI.

4 TechRAP – Metadata Application Profile for Technical Report

The constraint matrix was elaborated based on the model proposed by Malta [19], but with two changes. In the header we include information about the respective class using the *rdf:type* property, and we include information regarding the Optionality, Min and Max, into a single column: Cardinality. The matrix includes the following information [19]:

(a) Label: property denomination;
(b) Property: the RDF property (the IRI);
(c) Range: the range of the property, where it is defined if the value is a Literal (L) or non-Literal (NL);
(d) Value string: is there a value string, yes or no?. The value string is "a Literal, optionally associated with either a syntax encoding scheme IRI or a value string language" [21];
(e) SES IRI: the IRI of the syntax encoding scheme, in case there is one. "The encoding scheme provides contextual information or parsing rules that aid in the interpretation of a term value". The syntax encoding scheme "indicates that the value is a string formatted in accordance with a formal notation" (for example, yyyy-mm-dd) [22];
(f) Value IRI: when the IRI identifies an actual value (yes/no). It is "an identifier that that identifies the actual value" [23];
(g) VES IRI: the IRI of the VES. The Vocabulary Encoding Scheme is a list of controlled term (Medical Subject Heading, Library of Congress Subject Heading). This is the identifier for term this list" [21, 23];
(h) Related description: to indicate (yes/no) if there is a related description, in this case a related matrix, and
(i) Usage: how the property may be used at instance level.

In the elaboration phase of the matrix, based on our expertise, some properties not mentioned in the study by Turner et al. [10] or Andrade, Shintaku and Barros [15] were added because they contribute to the consistency and quality of reporting. They are: *techrap:scheduledActivities, techrap:outcomesAnalysis, techrap:researchFieldActivity, techrap:guidelines, techrap:conclusion, techrap:hasIssue, schema:result, schema: scheduledTime, schema:reportNumber, onco:sampleSize, bibo:status, bibo:pages, frapo:hasGrantNumber, frapo:hasProjectIdentifier, dcite:geoLocation, dcterms:type, dcterms:format, dcterms:audience, and dcterms:source.*

Once this was done, we proceeded with the vocabulary alignment, that is, we analyzed metadata schemes to identify properties corresponding to the attributes. To that end, we used the Linked Open Vocabulary (LOV), "a high-quality catalog of reusable vocabularies for the description of data on the Web" [24]. To select a particular class/property, three aspects were considered: (a) use according to context; (b) property widely used by the metadata community; and (c) number of datasets that use the vocabulary. It is worth noting that a class/property was created only when: (a) no class/property was identified for a given attribute(s); or (b) to avoid using a large number of metadata schemas.

The creation of new properties (16) occurred with the development of a new vocabulary called "techrap". The namespace "techrap" was created using RDFS (http://opendata.dsi.uminho.pt/publications/techrap) and stored at http://hdl.handle.net/1822/61308. The Resource Description Framework Schema (RDFS) "is a semantic extension of RDF. It provides mechanisms for describing groups of related resources and the relationships between these resource" [25].

As a result of this work, several vocabularies were used (Table 1), where 7 classes and 89 properties come from. Table 2 presents the Technical Report constraints matrice. All constraints matrices can be acessed at link: http://hdl.handle.net/1822/61402.

Table 1. The namespace used

Vocabulary	Namespace
bibo	http://purl.org/ontology/bibo/
dbo	http://dbpedia.org/ontology
dcite	https://schema.datacite.org/meta/kernel-4.1
dcterms	http://purl.org/dc/terms
fabio	http://purl.org/spar/fabio
foaf	http://xmlns.com/foaf/0.1
frapo	http://purl.org/cerif/frapo/
onco	http://opendata.dsi.uminho.pt/health/onco-schema
rdf	http://www.w3.org/1999/02/22-rdf-syntax-ns#
rdfs	http://www.w3.org/2000/01/rdf-schema
schema	http://schema.org
techrap	http://opendata.dsi.uminho.pt/techrap

The constraints matrices are shown in consonance with results of studies that sought to identify properties that represent technical reports, as is the case of Gonzalez de Gomez & Machado's studies; Zou et al. [9], cited by Turner, et al. [10] and Andrade, Shintaku and Barros [15] as it seeks to identify properties that optimize the discovery and reuse of such resources.

Table 2. Constraints matrices

Description: Technical report			rdf:type=http://purl.org/spar/fabio/TechnicalReport					Use: A report of a technical nature		
Label	Property	Range	Value string	SES IRI	Value IRI	VES IRI	Related description	Cardinality	Type	Usage
Abstract	dcterms: abstract	L	Y	—	N	—	N	1..*	String	A summary of the resource
Author	dcterms:creator	NL	N	—	Y	https://orcid.org/	Author	1..*	IRI	The responsible for making the resource
Conflit of Interest	onco:conflit OfInterest	L	Y	—	N	—	N	0-1	String	Conflit of interest
Coverage	dcterms: coverage	NL	Y	—	Y	http://purl.org/dc/ terms/TGN	N	0...*	IRI	The spatial topic of the resource
Date	dcterms: created	L	Y	http:// purl.org/ dc/terms/ W3CDTF	N	—	N	1	Date	Date of creation of the resource
Date of publication	dcterms: issued	L	Y	http:// purl.org/ dc/terms/ W3CDTF	N	—	N	1	Date	Date of formal publication of the resource
Date submission	dcterms:date Submitted	L	Y	http:// purl.org/ dc/terms/ W3CDTF	N	—	N	1	Date	Date of submission of resource
Edition	bibo:edition	L	Y	—	N	—	N	1	String	The edition of a document
Final considerations	techrap: conclusion	L	Y	—	N	—	N	1	String	Final proposition of reasoning

(continued)

Table 2. (*continued*)

Description: Technical report				rdf:type=http://purl.org/spar/fabio/TechnicalReport			Use: A report of a technical nature		
Format	dcterms:format	NL	Y	http://www.iana.org/assignments/media-types/	Y	N	1..*	IRI	The file format
Funding code	frapo:hasGrant Number	L	Y	—	N	Project	0-1	String	A data property specifying the grant number of a grant provided by a funding agency
Guidelines	techrap:guideline	L	Y	—	N	N	0-1*	String	Recommended action
Has version	dcterms:has Version	NL	N	—	Y	N	0-1*	IRI	A related resource that is a version, edition
Identifier	dcterms:identifier	NL	Y	—	Y	N	1..*	IRI	An unambiguous reference to the resource within a given context
Interested Group	dcterms:audience	L	Y	—	N	N	1*	String	A class of entity for whom the resource is intended or useful
Is Version Of	dcterms:isVersionOf	NL	N	—	Y	N	0-1	IRI	A related resource of which the described resource is a version, edition, or adaptation
Language	dcterms:language	L	Y	http://purl.org/dc/terms/ISO639-2	N	N	1*	String	A language of the resource

(*continued*)

Table 2. (continued)

			rdf:type=http://purl.org/spar/fabio/TechnicalReport				Use: A report of a technical nature			
Description: Technical report										
	Property	L/NL	Y/N	URI	Y/N	URI	Y/N	Type	Card.	Description
Legend	schema:caption	L	Y	—	N	—	N	String	0...*	Legend of an illustration or table
Licence	dcterms:rights	NL	N	—	Y	http://creativecomons.org/	N	IRI	1	Rights held in and over the resource
Pagination	bibo:pages	L	Y	—	N	—	N	String	1	Page range of a document
Period of the report	dbo:period	L	Y	http://purl.org/dc/terms/W3CDTF	N	—	N	Date	1	Period initial and final of report
Process number	frapo:hasReferenceNumber	L	Y	—	N	—	N	String	0-1	A reference number for that item
Publisher	dcterms:publisher	NL	Y	—	Y	http://id.loc.gov/authorities/names.html	N	IRI	1..*	An entity responsible for making the resource available
Purpose	techrap:isAbout	NL	Y	—	Y	http://vocabularies.coar-repositories.org/documentation/resource_types/2.0.draft/	N	IRI	1	The purpose of this report is to project, research or equipment
References	dcterms:references	NL	Y	—	Y	—	N	IRI	1	A related resource that is referenced, cited by the described resource
Report number	schema:reportNumber	L	Y	—	N	—	N	String	1	The number or unique designator assigned to a report by the publishing Organization

(continued)

Table 2. (continued)

Description: Technical report			rdf:type=http://purl.org/spar/fabio/TechnicalReport					Use: A report of a technical nature	
Requesting institution	techrap: requesting Institution	NL	Y	Y	http://id.loc.gov/ authorities/names. html	Institution	1*	IRI	Name of requesting institution
Research Field	techrap:research Field	L	Y	N		N	1	String	Research domain
Status	bibo:status	L	Y	N		N	1	String	Status of a resource
Subject	dcterms:subject	NL	Y	Y	http://id.loc.gov/ authorities/subjects. html	N	1..*	IRI	The topic of the resource
Summary	dcterms: tableOfContents	L	Y	N		N	1	String	A list of subunits of the resource
References	dcterms: references	NL	Y	Y		N	1	IRI	A related resource that is referenced, cited by the described resource
Technical team	dcterms: contributor	NL	N	Y	https://orcid.org/	N	1..*	IRI	An entity responsible for making contributions to the resource
Title	dcterms:title	L	Y	N		N	1..*	String	A name given to the resource
Type	dcterms:type	NL	N	Y	http://vocabularies. coar-repositories.org/	N	1	IRI	The nature or genre of the resource
Type of access	dcterms:access Rights	NL	N	Y	http://vocabularies. coar-repositories.org	N	1	IRI	Declares the degree of openness of a resource
Volume	bibo:volume	L	Y	N		N	1	String	Volume of a resource

Note: NL – Non Literal, L – Literal, Y – Yes, N – No

It is believed that in this way, the contributions resulting from the field of activity of these researchers may contribute greatly to the description of technical reports. As these contributions are incorporated in the form of metadata properties and described by an application profile, the chances of optimizing the discovery and reuse of these resources is increased.

5   Conclusions

This article reports on the procedures for the development of a MAP for technical reports (TechRAP) in which classes and properties have been identified that may contribute to the discovery of this type of documents and optimize semantic interoperability for use and reuse. As a result seven constraints matrices were developed, holding 7 classes and 89 properties with respective encoding schemes, when they exist. Although there are metadata schemes such as Marc21, DC Terms or Funding Research Administration and Projects Ontology (Frapo) that can be used to represent technical reports, the use of the a single schema is not enough to describe specific aspects of these reports. By adopting different schemas to enrich the representation of the document and by using MAP, it is expected to ensure interoperability and semantics between information systems and so increase findability the resources in a domain-specific collection.

Currently, it is expected that this study may contribute to the visibility of this type of literature and also to related initiatives in the context of Semantic Web.

As future work we suggest the validation of the MAP and its test in the production environment and the development of ShEx schemas for data validation purposes.

We look forward to the outcome of the work of the DCMI Application Profiles Interest Group in order to apply it in TechRAP.

Acknowledgment. This work has been supported by FCT – Fundação para a Ciência e Tecnologia within the Project Scope: UID/CEC/00319/2019 and Universidade Federal do Espírito Santo.

References

1. Associação Brasileira de Normas Técnicas: Informação e documentação: relatório técnico e/ou científico. Apresentação. ABNT, Rio de Janeiro (2015)
2. Universidade Federal do Paraná: Relatórios. Ed. UFPR, Curitiba (2000)
3. Campello, B.L: Relatórios técnicos. In: Campello, B.S., Cendón, B.V., Kremer, J.M. (Org.) Fontes de informação para pesquisadores e profissionais. Ed. UFMG, Belo Horizonte (2000)
4. Kremer, C.D., Kovaleski, J.L., De Carvalho, H.G.: A memória técnica organizacional como prática de gestão do conhecimento em uma indústria metalúrgica de médio porte. In: Anais KMBrasil do Congresso Brasileiro de Gestão do Conhecimento (2008)
5. Abeckaer, A., Bernardi, A., Hinkelmann, K., Kühn, O., Sintek, M.: Toward a technology for organizational memories. IEEE Intell. Syst. **13**, 40–48 (1998)
6. González De Gómez, M.N., Machado, R.: A ciência invisível: o papel dos relatórios e as questões de acesso à informação científica. DataGramaZero - Rev Cienc. Inf. **8**(5) (2007)

7. Población, D.A.: Literatura cinzenta ou não convencional: um desafio a ser enfrentado. Ciência da Informação **21**, 243–246 (1992). http://revista.ibict.br/ciinf/article/view/438
8. Directory of Open Access Repositories: Content types in OpenDOAR repositories-Worldwide. University of Nottingham, Nottigham (2018)
9. Zou, X., Siyi, X., Li, Z., Jiang, P.: Constructing metadata schema of scientific and technical report based on FRBR. Comput. Inf. Sci. **11**(2), 34–39 (2018)
10. Turner, A.M., Liddy, E.D., Bradley, J., Wheatley, J.A.: Modeling public health interventions for improved access to the gray literature. J. Med. Libr. Assoc. **93**(4), 487–494 (2005)
11. Baker, T., et al.: Principles of metadata registries: a white paper of the DELOS Working Group on Registries (DELOS Network of Excellence on Digital Libraries) [s.d.], https://pdfs. semanticscholar.org/01ea/e200c915fbb38faf2584e87230bb15d2d683.pdf
12. Heery, R., Patel, M.: Application profiles: mixing and matching metadata schemas. Ariadne **25**, 27–31 (2000). http://www.ariadne.ac.uk/issue25/app-profiles/
13. Hillmann, D.: Using Dublin Core. Metadata Dublin Core® Metadata Initiative (2005). http:// dublincore.org/documents/usageguide/. Accessed 03 Feb 2019
14. Baker, T.: A common grammar for diverse vocabularies: the abstract model for Dublin core. In: Fox, E.A., Neuhold, E.J., Premsmit, P., Wuwongse, V. (eds.) ICADL 2005. LNCS, vol. 3815, p. 495. Springer, Heidelberg (2005). https://doi.org/10.1007/11599517_71
15. Andrade, M.C., Shintaku, M., Barros, P.P.: Proposta de elementos de metadados para representação e recuperação de memória técnica: o caso da Rede Ufes-Rio Doce. Cad. BAD **1**, 41–58 (2018)
16. Coyle, K.: Future considerations: the functional library systems record. Library Hi Tech. **2** (22), 166–174. https://doi.org/10.1108/07378830410524594
17. Fusco, E.: Aplicação dos FRBR na modelagem de catálogos bibliográficos digitais. Cultura Acadêmica, São Paulo (2011)
18. Lynch, C.A.: The changing role in a networked information environment. Libr. Hi Tech. **15** (1/2), 30–38 (1997). https://doi.org/10.1108/07378839710306981
19. Malta, M.C.: Contributo metodológico para o desenvolvimento de perfis de aplicação no contexto da Web Semântica (Tese). Universidade do Minho, Guimarães (2014)
20. Nilsson, M., Baker, T., Johnston, P.: The Singapore Framework for Dublin Core Application Profiles, 14 January 2008. http://dublincore.org/documents/singapore-framework/. Accessed 11 Feb 2019
21. Powell, A., Nilsson, M., Naeve, A., Johnston, P., Baker, T.: DCMI Abstract Model. DCMI. http://www.dublincore.org/specifications/dublin-core/abstract-model/
22. Dublin Core Metadata Inititative. DCMI grammatical principles (20017). www.dublincore. org/specifications/dublin-core/grammatical-principles
23. Coyle, K.: DCAM explained (2008). http://kcoyle.net/dcam.html
24. Vandenbussche, P.-Y., Atemezing, G.A., Poveda-Villalón, M., Vatant, B.: Linked open vocabularies (LOV): a gateway to reusable semantic vocabularies on the web. Semant. Web **1**, 1–5 (2014). http://www.semantic-web-journal.net/system/files/swj1127.pdf
25. W3C: RDF Schema 1.1. W3C recommendation, 25 February 2014. http://www.w3.org/ TR2014/REC-rdf-schema-20140225

Applying Predictive Models to Support skos:ExactMatch Validation

Riccardo Albertoni[(✉)] [ID]

Istituto di Matematica Applicata e Tecnologie Informatiche "Enrico Magenes",
Consiglio Nazionale delle Ricerche (IMATI-CNR),
Via De Marini, 6, 16149 Genoa, Italy
albertoni@ge.imati.cnr.it

Abstract. The paper investigates the use of Machine Learning (ML) to support experts validating skos:exactMatch links. It trains ML techniques provided by RapidMiner with manually validated links and shows how to use the obtained predictive models for saving expert efforts. The obtained results are preliminary but encouraging: the trained predictive models reduce up to 70% the number of manual checking required from experts, leaving only 10% of the wrong links unnoticed. Cutting the 70% of the expert burden is crucial, especially when dealing with the validation of large sets of links.

Keywords: Linkset correctness · Quality · Expert validation · Predictive models

1 Introduction

Artificial Intelligence (AI) is a multidisciplinary, long-standing research field which is recently having a hype. It promises to solve the unprogrammable tasks, to reduce the time required to program complex solutions, to make products more customizable. In particular, the advancement of Machine Learning (ML) is producing a paradigm-shift in solving problems which moves the focus from the logic of a solution to the observation of examples[1].

Following the belief that ML tools will soon become as disruptive as spreadsheets in everyday activities, this paper investigates the reuse of well-known ML technology to ease manual validation of automatically generated links. In general, the expert validation is a painstaking, error-prone and tedious activity. Any support aimed at easing the burden of validation is precious.

This paper starts from the validation carried out in the eENVPlus project (CIP-ICT-PSP No. 325232). In eENVPlus, domain experts were required to validate automatically generated *skos:exactMatch* links between the thesauri included in Linked Thesaurus Framework for the Environment (LusTRE) [1]. Distinguishing between correct and incorrect *skos:exactMatch* is particularly important in LusTRE, as user navigations and service results are enriched with translations and concepts which are reachable

---

[1] https://developers.google.com/machine-learning/crash-course/ml-intro.

© Springer Nature Switzerland AG 2019
E. Garoufallou et al. (Eds.): MTSR 2019, CCIS 1057, pp. 187–193, 2019.
https://doi.org/10.1007/978-3-030-36599-8_16

through these links [2], and the wrong *skos:exactMatch* links would bring to wrong enrichments. This paper trains state-of-art ML techniques made available by Rapid-Miner with a subset of manually validated links, and it shows how the obtained predictive models can reduce the number of manual checks required during the validation.

2 Related Work

Link correctness is addressed by a certain number of works, most of those focus on *owl:sameAs* links. Raad et al. [3] use network metrics to check the correctness of *owl:sameAs*. CEDAL [4] provides a time-efficient method to detect inconsistent *owl:sameAs* arising from transitive closure, Papaleo et al. [5] detect logical conflicts of *owl:sameAs* links in RDF data. Paulheim [6] exploits RapidMiner multidimensional outlier detections to identifying wrong links between datasets.

Besides the works aiming at automatically identify wrong *owl:sameAs*, there are crowdsourcing-based methodologies to share the validation efforts on a larger group of experts (see [7] and [8]). None of the previous specifically address *skos:exactMatch* links, nor they learn from data of previous validations. At the best of our knowledge, Rico et al. [9] have proposed the most related approach. They exploit binary classifiers to check wrong mapping in the data extraction from Wikipedia to DBpedia. However, they rely on features which are not directly applicable to the *skos:exactMatch* links considered in this paper.

3 LusTRE and Link Validation

The eENVplus project has spent considerable efforts reviewing the available environmental thesauri and checking those not yet available as linked data [10]. As a result of such a review, we have designed LusTRE [1], in which ThiST [11] and EARTh [12] are published as Linked Data using the Simple Knowledge Organization System (SKOS) and connected to popular thesauri such as GEMET, AGROVOC [13] and EUROVOC.

LusTRE provides different kinds of links between the concepts, as the concepts belonging to separate thesauri might be equivalent (*skos:exactMatch*), almost equivalent (*skos:closeMatch*), more specific (*skos:broadMatch*), less specific (*skos:narrowMatch*), or related (*skos:relatedMatch*).

The links are generated with a two-step procedure. Firstly, SILK [14] (http://silkframework.org/) is applied to discover new links, and then the SILK results are validated by domain experts to verify their accuracy. SILK discovers candidate links relying on user-parameterized similarity comparison. For LusTRE, a link between two concepts is added if the similarities between their preferred labels (i.e., *skos:prefLabel*), or alternative labels/synonyms (i.e., *skos:altLabel*) are greater than a given threshold. The set of discovered candidate links are then provided to experts in the form of spreadsheets (see Fig. 1). In the spreadsheet, each link is represented as a row with the URI of the mapped concepts (subject and object of the link are in columns *s* and *o* respectively), with their preferred labels (columns *sPrefLabel* and *oPrefLabel*), their broader (columns *sBT* and *oBT*) and related concepts (columns *sRT* and *oRT*). The 'NaN' value appears in correspondence of not available broader or related concepts; multiple broader and related terms for the same concept are separated by the symbol '|'. Concept definitions are not included as they were not available for most of the considered thesauri.

Considering the spreadsheet, the experts can catch the meaning of linked concepts, so that they can confirm if each link is a correct *skos:exactMatch*. If needed, they can get more information about the represented concepts resolving their links. Experts might also reject the links if wrong, or suggest to downgrade the links to another kind of matching (e.g., *skos:closeMatch*, *skos:broadMatch*, *skos:relatedMatch*).

	sBT	sRT	sPrefLabel	s		o	oPrefLabel	oBT	oRT
61	analysis	trace-element analyses| standard rocks| flame ...	quantitative analysis	../ThIST/ analisiquantitativa	http://eurovoc.europa.eu/6272		quantitative analysis	research method	NaN
62	Arctic region| Denmark	Laurentia| glacial rebound| Atlantic Ocean	Greenland	../ThIST/gronland	http://eurovoc.europa.eu/1188		Greenland	Nordic Council countries| North America	regions of Denmark
63	Asia	NaN	Far East	../ThIST/estremooriente	http://eurovoc.europa.eu/956		Far East	NaN	NaN
64	Asia	Gobi Desert	Mongolia	../ThIST/mongolus	http://eurovoc.europa.eu/1968		Mongolia	Far East	NaN
65	Asia	Indian Ocean| Indian Peninsula| Indian Shield	Sri Lanka	../ThIST/srilanka	http://eurovoc.europa.eu/4246		Sri Lanka	SAARC countries| South Asia	NaN

Fig. 1. Excerpt of the validation spreadsheet proposed to the experts

The following section introduces how we applied the ML techniques to distinguish between correct and incorrect *skos:exactMatch*. In particular, we consider the set of links from ThIST to EARTh, Agrovoc, DBpedia, Eurovoc, which overall includes 4236 links.

4   Methods and Experiment Setting

We model the task of distinguishing between correct and incorrect *skos:exactMatch* as a binary classification. Our binary classification labels links into two classes: **Exact-Match** indicating the correct *skos:exactMatch* and **Not ExactMatch** which includes the erroneous links as well as all the other SKOS mappings (e.g., *skos:closeMatch*, *skos:broaderMatch*).

To train the classifier, we need to select a set of features characterizing the links. As discussed, experts have assessed the correctness of links relying on their knowledge and also the annotations provided in the spreadsheet. The expert knowledge is not easily representable, but we can elaborate on the annotations (i.e., preferred label, broader and related terms) to compare the context in which the concepts are defined.

4.1 Features

We consider three types of features: the presence of the annotations, text similarity and composed text similarity applied to the annotations.

We deploy two text similarity metrics: the *nhammingSim*, which is the hamming normalized similarity available in the package textdistance[2], and *wmdistance*, which is the cosine on the Word2Vec embedding [15] implemented in the gensim package[3]. In particular for the latter, we use a third-party word2vec trained model[4] which includes word vectors for a vocabulary of 3 million words and phrases trained on roughly 100 billion words from a Google News dataset.

As observable in Fig. 1, many of the concepts involved in the links have multiple broader and related concepts (e.g., *Arctic region* and *Denmark* in row 62), and their preferred labels, their broader and related terms are often composed labels (e.g., *Arctic region, glacial rebound*). To deal with multiple and composed labels, we split and flatten them in sets of single words and we apply specific functions[5]. Given two sets of single words indicated as X and Y (e.g., for the subject's broader in row 62, $X = \{$Arctic, Region, Denmark$\}$) and one of the text-similarity metrics indicated as *sim*, we define the functions (1) and (2).

$$Max(X, Y, sim) = max_{i,j}\big(sim\big(x_i, y_j\big)\big) \tag{1}$$

$$SummingMax(X, Y, sim) = \sum\nolimits_i max_j\big(sim\big(x_i, y_j\big)\big) \tag{2}$$

The function *Max* (1) returns the maximum pairwise similarity. The function *SummingMax* (2) sums the maximum similarity for each x_i.

In this way, we get 8 features for each kind of annotation. For example, considering broader terms, we have: *sBT_missing* and *oBT_missing* which are true when the subject and the object broader terms are not available; *BT_wmdistance, BT_Mwmdistance, BT_SMwmdistance,* which are obtained comparing the concepts' broader terms by applying *wmdistance* directly and in the functions *Max* and *SummingMax; BT_nhammingSim, BT_MnhammingSim, BT_SMnhammingSim* which are obtained by applying *nhammingSim* alone and in the functions *Max* and *SummingMax*. The procedure adopted to prepare the overall 24 features (8 for preferred labels, 8 for broader terms and 8 for related terms) are available as a Jupyter Python Notebook[6].

---

[2] https://pypi.org/project/textdistance/.

[3] https://radimrehurek.com/gensim.

[4] https://drive.google.com/file/d/0B7XkCwpI5KDYNlNUTTlSS21pQmM/.

[5] This strategy works for languages such as English, Italian, Spanish which uses spaces/hyphen for dividing compound words. It may not work for German and Dutch where compound words are represented differently.

[6] https://github.com/riccardoAlbertoni/LinkCorrectness/blob/master/PreparingFeaturesForLinksetCorr ectness.ipynb.

4.2   Predictive Models and Results

This paper investigates the applicability of ML for validating *skos:exactMatch* links, not the definition of new ML algorithms. As a consequence, instead of implementing the classifiers from scratch, we decided to use the RapidMiner Framework [16]. RapidMiner is an extensible and open source ML framework which offers a collection of state-of-the-art ML algorithms. The RapidMiner Studio provides an intuitive GUI which impressively reduce the efforts required to define and compare distinct ML techniques. Exploiting RapidMiner, we build six predictive models (M1–M6), in which, we trained three classifiers (i.e., a Decision Tree for M1 and M4, a Gradient Boosted trees for M2 and M5, a Deep Learning network for M3 and M6). We use a training set that contains 172 examples out of 4236 (half **exactMatch** and half **Not exactMatch**) using all the negative examples in a 10-fold cross-validation. In the training of M1, M2, M3, we consider both the missing attributes and similarity features, for the training of M4, M5, M6, we consider only the similarity features.

Table 1. Classification performance.

	Correct ExactMatch	Wrong ExactMatch	Wrong Not ExactMatch	Correct Not ExactMatch	Precision ExactMatch	Recall ExactMatch	Precision NotExactMatch	Recall NotExactMatch	% Link to Doublecheck	% of missed not ExactMatch
M1	2899	17	1251	69	99.42%	69.86%	5.23%	80.23%	31.16%	19.77%
M2	2976	10	1174	76	99.67%	71.71%	6.08%	88.37%	29.51%	11.63%
M3	2895	14	1255	72	99.52%	69.76%	5.43%	83.72%	31.33%	16.28%
M4	3040	19	1110	67	99.38%	73.25%	5.69%	77.91%	27.79%	22.09%
M5	2924	9	1226	77	99.69%	70.46%	5.91%	89.53%	30.76%	10.47%
M6	2916	15	1234	71	99.49%	70.27%	5.44%	82.56%	30.81%	17.44%

Table 1 shows the classification performance of the models tested on the whole set of links. All the models offer very good precision for **ExactMatch**, acceptable and good recall for **ExactMatch** and **Not ExactMatch**, but very low precision for **Not ExactMatch**. The models are not good enough for being used as a replacement of experts. However, we can use them for reducing the number of links the experts need to validate manually. We can ask the experts to doublecheck only the set of links classified as **Not ExactMatch** instead of the whole set of links. For example, if we apply the model M5, experts would need to focus on only the 30.76% of the initial links (i.e., 1333 instead of 4236 links) getting the chance to find the 89.53% of the wrong *skos: exactMatch*. This strategy seems quite advantageous: it would provide an error rate of about 10%, reducing the number of manual checking of 70%. Similar advantages can be obtained using the other models.

5   Conclusion

This paper shows that predictive models might ease the validation of *skos:exactMatch* correctness reducing the number of links to doublecheck manually. The results are preliminary but promising and deserve further investigations. We have not elaborated on which is the better similarity or ML technology to apply, but we have shown that even a quick and dirty approach can help to reduce the validation efforts. Each time one of the thesauri is updated in LusTRE, the links need to be revalidated, and there is room for applying the above predictive models. Considering 7 min on average for checking a link in LusTRE, the proposed models can make the maintainer spend two hours and half instead of more than eight hours. Perhaps, it is not a life-changing improvement but it eases the work of maintainers, and it can result extremely useful when dealing with a greater number of link. As future work, we want to investigate if other similarity measures would have worked better, if there is a minimal number of wrong and correct links to ensure acceptable performances, and to evaluate the applicability of such an approach in contexts other than LusTRE.

Acknowledgment. The author thanks RapidMiner GmbH for granting an education license of their studio tool and the EU project eENVPlus for providing data about the validation of links.

References

1. Albertoni, R., de Martino, M., Podestà, P., Abecker, A., Wössner, R., Schnitter, K.: LusTRE: a framework of linked environmental thesauri for metadata management. Earth Sci. Inf. **11** (4), 525–544 (2018)
2. Albertoni, R., De Martino, M., Podestà, P.: Quality measures for skos: ExactMatch linksets: an application to the thesaurus framework LusTRE. Data Technol. Appl. **52**(3), 405–423 (2018)
3. Raad, J., Beek, W., van Harmelen, F., Pernelle, N., Saïs, F.: Detecting erroneous identity links on the web using network metrics. In: Vrandečić, D., et al. (eds.) ISWC 2018. LNCS, vol. 11136, pp. 391–407. Springer, Cham (2018). https://doi.org/10.1007/978-3-030-00671-6_23
4. Valdestilhas, A., Soru, T., Ngomo, A.C.N.: CEDAL: time-efficient detection of erroneous links in large-scale link repositories. In: Proceedings of the International Conference on Web Intelligence, Leipzig, Germany. pp. 106–113 (2017)
5. Papaleo, L., Pernelle, N., Saïs, F., Dumont, C.: Logical detection of invalid SameAs statements in RDF data. In: Janowicz, K., Schlobach, S., Lambrix, P., Hyvönen, E. (eds.) EKAW 2014. LNCS (LNAI), vol. 8876, pp. 373–384. Springer, Cham (2014). https://doi.org/10.1007/978-3-319-13704-9_29
6. Paulheim, H.: Identifying wrong links between datasets by multi-dimensional outlier detection. In: WoDOOM 2014, Co-located with ESWC 2014, Anissaras/Hersonissou, Greece, pp. 27–38 (2014)
7. Acosta, M., Zaveri, A., Simperl, E., Kontokostas, D., Auer, S., Lehmann, J.: Crowdsourcing linked data quality assessment. In: Alani, H., et al. (eds.) ISWC 2013. LNCS, vol. 8219, pp. 260–276. Springer, Heidelberg (2013). https://doi.org/10.1007/978-3-642-41338-4_17
8. Zaveri, A., et al.: User-driven quality evaluation of DBpedia. In: I-SEMANTICS 2013, Graz, Austria, 4–6 September 2013, pp. 97–104. ACM (2013)
9. Rico, M., Mihindukulasooriya, N., Kontokostas, D., Paulheim, H., Hellmann, S., Gómez-Pérez, A.: Predicting incorrect mappings. In: Proceedings of the 33rd Annual ACM Symposium on Applied Computing - SAC 2018, pp. 323–330. ACM Press, USA (2018)

10. Albertoni, R., De Martino, M., Podestà, P.: Environmental thesauri under the lens of reusability. In: Kő, A., Francesconi, E. (eds.) EGOVIS 2014. LNCS, vol. 8650, pp. 222–236. Springer, Cham (2014). https://doi.org/10.1007/978-3-319-10178-1_18

11. Carusone, A., Olivetta, L.: Thesaurus Italiano di Scienze della Terra. Ist. Poligrafico dello Stato (2006)

12. Albertoni, R., De Martino, M., Di Franco, S., De Santis, V., Plini, P.: EARTh: an environmental application reference thesaurus in the linked open data cloud. Semant. Web. **5**, 165–171 (2014)

13. Caracciolo, C., et al.: The AGROVOC linked dataset. Semant. Web. **4**, 341–348 (2013)

14. Volz, J., Bizer, C., Gaedke, M., Kobilarov, G.: Discovering and maintaining links on the web of data. In: Bernstein, A., et al. (eds.) ISWC 2009. LNCS, vol. 5823, pp. 650–665. Springer, Heidelberg (2009). https://doi.org/10.1007/978-3-642-04930-9_41

15. Mikolov, T., Chen, K., Corrado, G., Dean, J.: Efficient estimation of word representations in vector space. In: 1st International Conference on Learning Representations, ICLR 2013, Scottsdale, Arizona (2013)

16. Hofmann, M., Klinkenberg, R.: RapidMiner: Data Mining Use Cases and Business Analytics Applications. Chapman & Hall/CRC (2013)

Ontology Based Anomaly Detection for File Integration

Özgü Can[(✉)] and İbrahim Uzum

Department of Computer Engineering, Ege University, 35100 Bornova-Izmir, Turkey
ozgu.can@ege.edu.tr, ibrahim.uzum@windowslive.com

Abstract. File integration systems enable file transfers between different systems in order to automate routine business processes. Therefore, the standardization in data exchange between different organizations or decentralized subsidiaries of an organization is achieved. However, abnormal situations may occur during the file integration process. In order to protect the persistence of integration channels, the abnormal files must be detected. For this purpose, anomaly detection is used to trace integrations continuously and to detect abnormal files instantly. In this study, an ontology based anomaly detection approach is proposed in order to detect abnormal situations in real time file integration systems. Thus, a file integration that is achieved on an electronic system will be traced and information will be given to the system administrator if any abnormalities occur during the integration process. Therefore, an abnormal situation that can stop the current file flow on file integration systems will be detected.

Keywords: Anomaly detection · Ontology · Semantic web · File integration

1 Introduction

File integration systems allow organizations to store information on multiple databases, to retrieve data from different sources and to gather data in a unified way. Therefore, file integration systems have an important role in today's information organizations. Also, it is important to maintain privacy, data integrity and availability by ensuring continuity in systems that provide access to information. In particular, the creation of a consciousness structure by timely detection of possible unexpected behaviors within systems has a critical precaution in security-based systems. Anomaly detection is the problem of finding patterns in data that do not conform to expected behavior [1]. Anomaly detection systems detect irregularities in information systems and alert them to relevant or authorized individuals in the organization. The main task of such systems is to detect and to report unexpected movements. Anomaly detection on file integration based systems could detect anomalies in the following ways: (i) to detect anomalies that occur in terms of size and integration time, (ii) to

© Springer Nature Switzerland AG 2019
E. Garoufallou et al. (Eds.): MTSR 2019, CCIS 1057, pp. 194–199, 2019.
https://doi.org/10.1007/978-3-030-36599-8_17

control and to intercept the file contents, (iii) to avoid violations of data integrity in the file, (iv) to provide the continuity and availability of integration channels.

File integration systems provide data and business process automation through file transfers that are based on specific standards between distributed systems. Information systems could manage their routine business processes and business logic in these type of infrastructures. Abnormalities that are detected in integration-based systems are usually data integrity-based symptoms such as XML with corrupted content, entity expansion, coercive parsing, content replacement, and server-side request forgeries [1]. These symptoms could be detected as oversized files or integration time anomalies. Abnormalities in file size and file transfer time increase the bandwidth load and make the integration channels unavailable which results with file transfer delays. Since there are many databases on several file integration technologies and distributed information systems, developing a technology-specific database-dependent method is not an efficient solution in order to detect anomalies in file integrations. Hence, the anomaly detection system should be independent of the technology and present a knowledge base. For this purpose, an ontology based solution is proposed in order to create a more general, extensible, standards-based and reusable structure. The paper is organized as follows: the related work is summarized in Sect. 2, the proposed ontology and a case study are presented in Sect. 3 and finally, Sect. 4 concludes and specifies the future work.

2   Related Work

Ontology based anomaly detection studies in the literature mostly focus on detecting intrusions in network and operating systems. In [2], an attack ontology is developed by using the taxonomy of attacks for intrusion detection systems and the developed attack ontology is used to extract semantic relations between computer attacks and intrusions. An ontology-based wireless intrusion detection system for wireless sensor networks is developed in [3]. The developed system applies the proposed ontology to a patrol intrusion detection system that is used to detect anomalies. In [4], ontologies are used in order to develop an intrusion detection application. The goal of creating these ontologies is to allow users to model an intrusion detection application at the conceptual level and in terms of concepts from the application domain. An attack pattern ontology and a framework for network traffic anomalies detection within a distributed multiagent intrusion detection system architecture is presented in [5]. In [6], an anomaly management framework for smarthomes is proposed. In order to use the framework in all heterogeneous environments, the proposed framework uses ontologies to represent anomaly information. Also, a recent survey study on network anomaly detection system is presented in [7]. In [8], it is stated that anomalies of business process that lead to losses for the company are regarded as fraud. Therefore, an ontology-based process modeling is proposed in order to model and capture the business process anomalies. Ontology-based anomaly detection approach is also studied for maritime domain. In [9], the maritime domain is represented with an ontology and the developed ontology is used to detect anomalies and threats that occur in the maritime domain. Similarly, in [10] an ontology is proposed in order to enable experts in the maritime domain to specify rules governing abnormal ship behaviour.

Consequently, ontology-based approaches are used to detect abnormal situations in diverse application domains. However, as presented above, it is concluded that currently none of the ontologies and anomaly detection approaches focus on the file integration domain. In this work, an ontology-based approach is used to detect anomalies in file integration systems. For this purpose, a knowledge base for the file integration domain is created and expressed in a semantically rich ontology. Thus, the goal of this study is to provide an ontology that represents the file integration domain. Therefore, abnormal transfers could be detected by using the proposed semantic model.

3   An Ontology for File Integration

An ontology is an explicit specification of a conceptualization [11]. Hence, ontology is the modeling of information by using a common terminology and defining relationships between concepts. The file integration ontology aims to detect abnormal situations in file integration systems. Therefore, a reusable, generalized and an operation-independent knowledge base for the file integration domain will be created. As seen in Fig. 1, the proposed file integration basically consists of the following concepts: `CommunicationModel`, `FileTransfer`, `Integration`, `IntegrationImportance`, `Platform`, `Server` and `WorkType`.

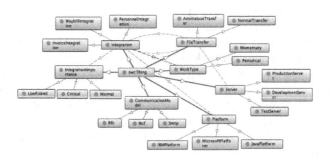

Fig. 1. Concepts of the file integration ontology

The `CommunicationModel` represents the network communication model of the file integration. File integration systems can use different technologies for communication infrastructure. Hence, `CommunicationModel` has sub-classes: `RfcCommunication`, `WcfCommunication` and `SmtpCommunication`. `FileTransfer` is used to represent the incoming file transfers that occur on an integration basis. `AnomalousTransfer` shows file transfers of abnormal quality and NormalTransfer shows normal file transfers. Integration represents the type of integration (data flow) between two system. InvoiceIntegration represents an invoice integration between two system, PersonnelIntegration represents the integration of personnel information, and WaybillIntegration represents the integration of railway transport. IntegrationImportance represents the importance of an integration and has subclasses of Normal, LowRisked and Critical. Critical integrations have the greatest priority in organizations. Server represents servers that perform file transfers on the system. File transfers take place on servers, and servers allow files to flow online between systems. TestServer represents the servers that are used for testing and ProductionServer represents the servers in the live environment. Platform represents the integration technology on which file integrations are developed and has subclasses of MicrosoftPlatform and JavaPlatform. The WorkType represents the instantaneous or periodic operation type of the integration. Thus, the instant triggers are represented with the Momentary sublass and periodic triggers are represented with the Periodical subclass. Besides the given ontological concepts, the object attributes of the file integration domain are as follows: happensAt, belongsTo, developedAt, communicatesAt, hasImportance, communicatesAs, hasImportance, worksAs and has. happensAt is the relationship between the FileTransfer and Server classes. It shows the relationship that a file transfer takes place on a terminal server. belongsTo is the relationship between the FileTransfer and Integration classes. belongsTo states that a file transfer belongs to a B2B integration. developedAt is the relationship between the Integration and Platform classes. developedAt notifies the technological platform that the B2B integration is developed on. communicatesAs is the relationship between the Integration and CommunicationModel classes. communicatesAs indicates that the B2B integration communicates through a communication model. hasImportance is the relationship between the Integration and IntegrationImportance classes. hasImportance specifies that the B2B integration has a particular integration importance. worksAs is the relationship between the Integration and WorkType classes. worksAs states that the B2B integration works as a business type. has is an attribute that represents the relationship between the Integration and FileTransfer classes. has indicates that the B2B integration has file transfers. Also, data attributes are described as follows: successRatioLimit represents succession limit ratio; code is used for the code of integration, and authorizedPersonName represents the authorized person. These data properties are related with the Integration class. The FileTransfer class has fileName, fileSize, transferNumber, startTime, finishTime, duration, fileType, reTransmitted and status data properties to represent the information of the integrated file and the transfer process. Server class has an ipAddress as a data attribute in order to represent the IP address of the server.

The file integration process has a tuple of *(Server, IntegrationPlatform, FileTransfer, Integration, IntegrationPlatform)*. The proposed semantic model has the following atomic concepts and roles:

- Atomic concepts are `CommunicationModel`, `FileTransfer`, `Integration`, `IntegrationImportance`, `Platform`, `Server` and `WorkType`.
- The atomic role `happensAt` links a `FileTransfer` and a `Server`.
- The atomic role `belongsTo` links a `FileTransfer` and an `Integration`.
- The atomic role `developedAt` links an `Integration` and a `Platform`.
- The atomic role `communicatesAs` creates a link between an `Integration` and a `CommunicationModel`.
- The atomic role `hasImportance` creates a link between an `Integration` and an `IntegrationImportance`.
- The atomic role `worksAs` links an `Integration` and a `WorkType`.
- The atomic role `has` links an `Integration` and a `FileTransfer`.

The file integration model rules have the following forms:

- $\forall FileTransfer\ happensAt(FileTransfer, Server),$
  $Server \sqsubseteq happensAt.FileTransfer$
- $\forall FileTransfer\ belongsTo(FileTransfer, Integration),$
  $Integration \sqsubseteq belongsTo.FileTransfer$
- $\forall Integration\ developedAt(Integration, Platform),$
  $Platform \sqsubseteq developedAt.Integration$
- $\forall Integration\ communicatesAs(Integration, CommunicationModel),$
  $CommunicationModel \sqsubseteq communicatesAs.CommunicationModel$
- $\forall Integration\ hasImportance(Integration, IntegrationImportance),$
  $IntegrationImportance \sqsubseteq hasImportance.Integration$
- $\forall Integration\ worksAs(Integration, WorkType),$
  $WorkType \sqsubseteq worksAs.Integration$
- $\forall Integration\ has(Integration, FileTransfer),$
  $FileTransfer \sqsubseteq has.Integration$

A SPARQL query [12] that is used to find an integration which has the shortest average processing time is shown in Fig. 2. The query result is also seen in Fig. 2.

Fig. 2. A SPARQL query example

4   Conclusion

The real-time file integration is widely used by organizations in order to improve their business processes. The integration is the first step toward transforming data into meaningful and valuable information. Therefore, anomalies that occur in file integrations must be instantly detected and reported to the system administrators. Hence, the presence of anomaly detection mechanisms is critical for integration systems. In this study an ontology-based approach is proposed in order to provide extensibility and reusability within the file integration domain. The goal of this study is to reveal a semantic expressiveness for anomaly detection in file integrations. As a future work, the proposed model will be implemented by using Apache Jena framework [13] and the performance of the file integration system will be evaluated.

References

1. Chandola, V., Banerjee, A., Kumar, V.: Anomaly Detection : A Survey. J. ACM Comput. Surv. (CSUR) **41**(3), 15 (2009). Article No. 15
2. Abdoli, F., Kahani, M.: Ontology-based distributed intrusion detection system. In: 14th International CSI Computer Conference (CSICC), pp. 65–70. IEEE, Tehran (2009)
3. Hsieh, C., Chen, R.-C., Huang, Y.-F.: Applying an ontology to a patrol intrusion detection system for wireless sensor networks. Int. J. Distrib. Sensor Netw. **10**(1), 634748 (2014). 14 pages
4. Hung, S.-S., Liu, D.S.-M.: A user-oriented ontology-based approach for network intrusion detection. Comput. Stand. Interfaces **30**(1–2), 78–88 (2008)
5. Kolaczek, G., Juszczyszyn, K.: Attack pattern analysis framework for multiagent intrusion detection system. Int. J. Comput. Intell. Syst. **1**(3), 215–224 (2008)
6. Pardo, E., Espes, D., Le-Parc, P.: A framework for anomaly diagnosis in smart homes based on ontology. Proc. Comput. Sci. **83**, 545–552 (2016)
7. Moustafa, N., Hua, J., Slay, J.: A holistic review of network anomaly detection systems: a comprehensive survey. J. Netw. Comput. Appl. **128**, 33–55 (2019)
8. Sarno, R., Sinaga, FP.: Business process anomaly detection using ontology-based process modelling and multi-level class association rule learning. In: International Conference on Computer, Control, Informatics and its Applications (IC3INA), pp. 12–17. IEEE, Bandung (2015). https://doi.org/10.1109/IC3INA.2015.7377738
9. Roy, J., Davenport, M.: Exploitation of maritime domain ontologies for anomaly detection and threat analysis. In: International WaterSide Security Conference, pp. 1–8. IEEE, Carrara (2010). https://doi.org/10.1109/WSSC.2010.5730278
10. Vandecasteele, A., Napoli, A.: An enhanced spatial reasoning ontology for maritime anomaly detection. In: 7th International Conference on System of Systems Engineering, pp. 247–252. IEEE, Genoa (2012)
11. Gruber, T.R.: A translation approach to portable ontologies. Knowl. Acquis. **5**(2), 199–220 (1993)
12. SPARQL Query Language for RDF. https://www.w3.org/TR/rdf-sparql-query. Accessed 30 June 2019
13. Apache Jena. https://jena.apache.org. Accessed 30 June 2019

Schema-Based Visual Queries over Linked Data Endpoints

Kārlis Čerāns[✉], Lelde Lāce, Aiga Romāne, Jūlija Ovčiņņikova,
Mikus Grasmanis, Artūrs Sproģis, and Agris Šostaks

Institute of Mathematics and Computer Science,
University of Latvia, Riga, Latvia
karlis.cerans@lumii.lv

Abstract. We present the option to use the schema-based visual query tool
ViziQuer over realistic Linked Data endpoints. We describe the tool meta-
schema structure and the means for the endpoint schema retrieval both from an
OWL ontology and from a SPARQL endpoint. We report on a store of the
endpoint-specific schemas and the options to support the schema presentation to
the end-user both as a class tree within the environment and as external visual
diagram.

Keywords: Visual query tool · RDF · SPARQL · Linked data · Data schema

1 Introduction

Visual query composition paradigm (cf. [1–5]) along with facet-based [6, 7] and
controlled natural language based [8] approaches is a promising venue enabling end-
user involvement in query composition over SPARQL endpoints (cf. [1]).

Since the visual query composition is based on creating query patterns from the data
classes and their connecting properties, the *a priori* knowledge of the schema of the data
to be queried is helpful to support the query construction. The dynamic on-the-fly data
schema extraction from a SPARQL endpoint, as used in the facet-based [7] and language based [8] approaches, could be used also in visual query composition. Although
probably appreciated by a casual tool end user and by-passing the size limitations of the
schema-based approach, the on-the-fly approach would not allow to provide an overall
data structure presentation; it would be expected to have difficulties with context-
sensitive query creation guidance and the general performance efficiency, as well.

We focus here on the schema-based approach to the query formulation and answer
the question, how to create and present to the end-user the schema describing a given
existing Linked Data endpoint. The data schema we are to retrieve includes the class and
their connecting property information as well as the data types and the property cardinalities. A principal component of the schema computation is observing the sub-class
information among the data classes that enables compact data schema presentation in a
tree or graph-like form, important e.g. for reducing the relevant source and target class
sets for a given property (cf. [2] for a visual illustration of the problem), or enabling a
tree-shaped presentation of the endpoint's class structure within the query tool.

© Springer Nature Switzerland AG 2019
E. Garoufallou et al. (Eds.): MTSR 2019, CCIS 1057, pp. 200–206, 2019.
https://doi.org/10.1007/978-3-030-36599-8_18

We describe here the following novel solutions for Linked data endpoint structure examination and visual query creation over those:

- a pipeline for enabling schema-based visual query creation over a Linked Data endpoint (involving schema generation, storing, adjustment, export as OWL ontologies and visual presentation);
- a store of generated and manually curated schemas for specific Linked data endpoints, ready for loading into the visual query tool *ViziQuer*[1] [9, 10];
- hierarchical class tree component in the *ViziQuer* tool allowing to start query creation from a tree-shaped schema presentation.

We explain also, for the first time, the data meta-schema holding information structure enabling the visual query management in *ViziQuer* and report on a proof of concept experiment with a group of students visually querying a Linked Data endpoint.

2 Visual Tool Data Meta-Schema

Figure 1 provides an overview of the basic data structure used for storing the data schema information in *ViziQuer* [9]. There are entities: classes, properties and data-types in the data model, identified by their full names (IRIs) and equipped with local names, optionally with prefixes. Every role comes with a list of its applicability contexts ("schema roles"), consisting of source and target classes. For every attribute there is a datatype and a list of source classes. The minimum and maximum cardinalities can be specified both at the property level and at the level of the property within schema; the strongest of the cardinalities must apply. The entities can be annotated.

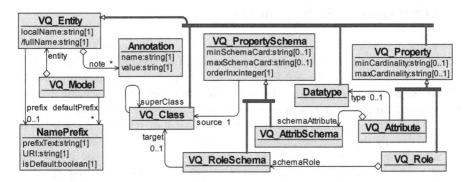

Fig. 1. Visual tool data meta-schema (*ViziQuer*)

We use the knowledge graph with the structure shown in Fig. 1 as the core meta-data model in the visual tool and provide its interoperability with RDFS/OWL ontology format via explicit import and export operations. Direct use of RDFS/OWL with

---

[1] http://viziquer.lumii.lv/.

property domain and range for the property applicability is problematic for properties applicable to multiple classes since a property domain assertion just states that the property cannot be applied outside the class (not that the property can be applied in the class' context).

The mapping of the visual data schema to OWL that we offer can be achieved using two approaches: either the annotation-based one, or mapping the set of property applicability assertions in the data schema to a single OWL property domain assertion with the union of all classes where the property is applicable to (the target classes correspond to the property range class, or to the target class in the all values from restriction). Both the data schema generation from an OWL ontology (ontology "import") and the OWL ontology export from the visual tool data schema can be performed using either of these approaches.

The navigation graphs [11] used recently by *Optique VQs* [12] provide a richer unidirectional way (corresponding to ontology import) of interpreting an OWL ontology as a class and property connectivity graph forming a visual tool schema. The navigation graphs are based on observing any property-based links among the classes found in the ontology (including domain/range, as well as all values from, some values from and cardinality restrictions); it would be useful to extend the OWL ontology import in *ViziQuer* to include the various axiom formats used in navigation graph generation.

Technically, the construction of the *ViziQuer* data schema from an OWL ontology would not include the subclass closure and superclass closure steps of navigation graph construction [11], instead the closures are computed during the tool runtime.

Still, one of the principal data schema acquisition means in *ViziQuer* is by examining the SPARQL endpoint structure itself (cf. Sect. 3), possibly less relevant and therefore not supported within *Optique VQs* approach.

3 Visual Query Enabling Pipeline

The visual queries in *ViziQuer* are created within a context of a project that requires a loaded data schema to enable the query composition (the specification of a SPARQL endpoint is necessary, if the queries are to be directly executed, as well). So, the pipeline of enabling the visual queries starts with obtaining the data schema that is a JSON-structured file, corresponding to the conceptual structure of Fig. 1.

The data schema can be created from an OWL ontology (cf. Sect. 2), or it can be obtained directly from a SPARQL endpoint by a series of schema-level queries.

Several sources, including [2, 13, 14], describe systematic approaches of SPARQL endpoint schema retrieval. Our schema retrieval approach stands out among the others by aiming at full data schema coverage in accordance to Fig. 1 model, including the subclass and cardinality information. The principal (consolidated) steps of the schema extraction involve:

(1) Find all classes and their instance counts and all pairs of intersecting classes;
(2) Based on intersecting classes graph compute the superclass relation;
(3) Find property source and target class information;
(4) Compute minimum and maximum (check, if 1) cardinalities.

The schema extraction process (involving the sub-class and cardinality computation and property assignment to the domain and range classes) can be somewhat lengthy. Having the schema creation process detached from the actual query composition allows to overcome the eventual computational problems of the schema creation.

There is fully viable option of the data schema extraction by the data end user by the schema extractor accompanying the *ViziQuer* tool (the schema extractor can be run on a local computer as JAVA-based web-service).

Furthermore, the created data schemas can be manually tuned, they can be stored and shared; some of the *ViziQuer* schemas for popular SPARQL endpoints are available on its Schema Store[2]. A possible option would be also for a SPARQL endpoint maintainer to create and publish the visual tool schema for the endpoint to foster visual exploration of the endpoint data.

The manual tuning of the automatically generated schemas can be aimed towards improving the visual query creation experience (e.g. by tuning the schema prefix names, or, more radically, by re-grouping and/or excluding classes and their properties that are not considered relevant for the endpoint schema presentation and querying).

The automated data schema generation has been performed for several SPARQL endpoint including, among others, Scholarly data[3], UNESCO[4] (SKOS) and Linked GeoData[5]. Endpoints like *DBPedia* and *wikidata* have not been tried for size considerations.

An important aspect of the visual query enabling is also the presentation of the data schema structure to the end user. The availability of the data schema in the ViziQuer tool format allows exploring it in a tree-like fashion during the query generation (cf. Sect. 4). The option to export the data schema to OWL enables using the OWL ontology support software (e.g. the VOWL ontology visualizer[6] or OWLGrEd[7] ontology editor) to obtain visual presentation of the data schema. The LD_VOWL [11] and LODSight [12] approaches may allow to obtain a visual presentation of the endpoints' data schema, helping the end user orientation, as well.

4   Visual Query Environment

Figure 2 shows a visual query environment fragment in the *ViziQuer* tool with loaded Scholarly data schema. Two important parts are shown: the visual query pane with two queries (each starting at an orange rectangle), and the data schema tree. The generated SPARQL query and its execution results are available within the environment, as well.

The visual queries in Fig. 2 can be described in the natural language, as follows: *"List titles of all papers from the eswc 2017 conference, together with their author*

---

[2] http://viziquer.lumii.lv/schema-store/index.html.

[3] http://www.scholarlydata.org/sparql.

[4] http://vocabularies.unesco.org/sparql.

[5] http://geo.linkeddata.es/sparql.

[6] http://vowl.visualdataweb.org/.

[7] http://owlgred.lumii.lv/.

count (sort descending)" and "*Find top 10 situations with persons publishing most papers at a single conference*". Both queries rely on the nested query concept (visually introduced using a black circle at an edge end) letting to compute the subquery (possibly including aggregation) in the context of each host query node instance separately. The query notation has been described in detail in [5] and [10].

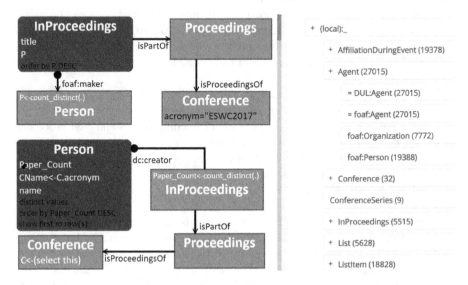

Fig. 2. Visual query environment fragment

The schema tree shows the hierarchy of data schema classes; each class node can be doubly clicked to start a query composition from that class. The current design decision is to make the top-level hierarchy arranged by the namespaces used in the data model; the sub-class structure for each class is shown within its corresponding namespace fragment. The classes and properties from the local namespace are typically shown without the name prefix. The Scholarly schema example can be viewed fully by loading it into the tool from the *ViziQuer* schema store.

A preliminary user study with the query environment has been performed with 17 master's degree students attending the Knowledge Engineering course at University of Latvia, without prior knowledge of the data endpoint structure, with essentially no prior experience with ViziQuer. There has been well over 75% success rate for each of the simple queries (e.g. "*Find all papers published at ESWC2017 conference together with their author count*", or "*Find all conferences together with number of published papers within proceedings of a conference*"). For more complicated queries the result quality varies comparably with result quality variation for query composition success over simple schemas (e.g. the query composition over an in-house hospital data schema, reported in [10]), so a conclusion can be reached that realistic Linked data endpoints may be reachable via the visual query approach, offered by *ViziQuer*.

5   Conclusions

We have shown that schema-based visual query environments, including the *ViziQuer* tool can be used to query SPARQL endpoints, encountered within Linked Data. The full data schema (including sub-class relations) retrieval described here has been successfully applied to a number of data endpoints, still it is work in progress to adjust to handling of different SPARQL endpoints, as they have been made available.

The data schema store at the *ViziQuer* tool home page offers the data schemas ready to be used for visual query composition over the designated Linked Data endpoints. The schema store is expected to be growing both by automatically retrieved and manually curated data schemas. The option to save the data schema as OWL ontology allows to further analyze and visualize it using OWL ontology support software.

The schema retrieval service is open source, as is the *ViziQuer* tool itself, its download and public instance running links are available from the *ViziQuer* tool home page.

References

1. Soylu, A., Giese, M., Jimenez-Ruiz, E., Vega-Gorgojo, G., Horrocks, I.: Experiencing OptiqueVQS: a multi-paradigm and ontology-based visual query system for end users. Univ. Access Inf. Soc. **15**(1), 129–152 (2016)
2. Zviedris, M., Barzdins, G.: ViziQuer: a tool to explore and query SPARQL endpoints. In: Antoniou, G., et al. (eds.) ESWC 2011. LNCS, vol. 6644, pp. 441–445. Springer, Heidelberg (2011). https://doi.org/10.1007/978-3-642-21064-8_31
3. Kapourani, B., Fotopoulou, E., Papaspyros, D., Zafeiropoulos, A., Mouzakitis, S., Koussouris, S.: Propelling SMEs business intelligence through linked data production and consumption. In: Ciuciu, I., et al. (eds.) OTM 2015. LNCS, vol. 9416, pp. 107–116. Springer, Cham (2015). https://doi.org/10.1007/978-3-319-26138-6_14
4. Haag, F., Lohmann, S., Siek, S., Ertl, T.: QueryVOWL: visual composition of SPARQL queries. In: Gandon, F., Guéret, C., Villata, S., Breslin, J., Faron-Zucker, C., Zimmermann, A. (eds.) ESWC 2015. LNCS, vol. 9341, pp. 62–66. Springer, Cham (2015). https://doi.org/10.1007/978-3-319-25639-9_12
5. Čerāns, K., et al.: Extended UML class diagram constructs for visual SPARQL queries in ViziQuer/web In: Voila!2017, CEUR Workshop Proceedings, vol. 1947, pp. 87–98 (2017)
6. Vega-Gorgojo, G., Giese, M., Heggestoyl, S., Soylu, A., Waaler, A.: PepeSearch: semantic data for the masses. PLoS ONE **11**(3), e0151573 (2016). https://doi.org/10.1371/journal.pone.0151573
7. Khalili, A., Meroño-Peñuela, A.: WYSIWYQ—what you see is what you query. In: Voila! 2017, CEUR, vol. 1947, pp. 123–130 (2017). http://ceur-ws.org/Vol-1947/paper11.pdf
8. Ferré, S.: Sparklis: an expressive query builder for SPARQL endpoints with guidance in natural language. Semant. Web **8**, 405–418 (2017)
9. Čerāns, K., et al.: ViziQuer: a web-based tool for visual diagrammatic queries over RDF data. In: Gangemi, A., et al. (eds.) ESWC 2018. LNCS, vol. 11155, pp. 158–163. Springer, Cham (2018). https://doi.org/10.1007/978-3-319-98192-5_30
10. Čerāns, K., et al.: ViziQuer: a visual notation for RDF data analysis queries. In: Garoufallou, E., Sartori, F., Siatri, R., Zervas, M. (eds.) MTSR 2018. CCIS, vol. 846, pp. 50–62. Springer, Cham (2019). https://doi.org/10.1007/978-3-030-14401-2_5

11. Soylu, A., et al.: OptiqueVQS: a visual query system over ontologies for industry. Semant. Web **9**(5), 627–660 (2018)
12. Soylu, A., Kharlamov, E.: Navigating OWL 2 ontologies through graph projection. In: Garoufallou, E., Sartori, F., Siatri, R., Zervas, M. (eds.) MTSR 2018. CCIS, vol. 846, pp. 113–119. Springer, Cham (2019). https://doi.org/10.1007/978-3-030-14401-2_10
13. Weise, M., Lohmann, S., Haag, F.: LD-VOWL: extracting and visualizing schema information for linked data. In: Voila!2016, pp. 120–127, October 2016
14. Dudáš, M., Svátek, V., Mynarz, J.: Dataset summary visualization with LODSight. In: The 12th Extented Semantic Web Conference (ESWC2015). http://lod2-dev.vse.cz/lodsight/lodsight-eswc2015-demopaper.pdf

Track on Metadata and Semantics for Open Repositories, Research Information Systems, and Data Infrastructures

Data Science from a Perspective of Computer Science

Sirje Virkus[1(✉)] and Emmanouel Garoufallou[2]

[1] Tallinn University, Tallinn, Estonia
sirje.virkus@tlu.ee
[2] Alexander Technological Educational Institute of Thessaloniki,
Thessaloniki, Greece
mgarou@libd.teithe.gr

Abstract. Data science is a new field which has gained considerable attention from different disciplines. The purpose of this paper is to present the results of the study that explored the field of data science from the computer science perspective. Analysis of research publications on data science was made on the basis of papers published in the Web of Science database. There has been continuous increase in articles on data science in the field of computer science from the year 2012. The main document types are conference proceedings, followed by journal articles, editorial material, book chapters and reviews. The top five countries publishing are USA, England, India, China and Germany. The most cited article has got 3501 citations. The analysis revealed that the data science field is quite interdisciplinary by nature. In addition to the field of computer science the papers belonged to 45 other research areas. The limitations of this research are that this study only analyzed research papers in the Web of Science database and therefore only covers a certain amount of scientific papers published in the field of computer science. Therefore, several relevant studies are not discussed in this paper that are not reflected in the Web of Science database.

Keywords: Data science · Computer science · Bibliographic analysis

1 Introduction

Data science has emerged in response to the increased amount of data and is a relatively new field which has gained considerable attention from different disciplines including mathematics and statistics, computer science, engineering, information science, business economics, education and educational research, physics, telecommunications and medical informatics.

Kelleher and Tierney [1, p. 1] define data science as "a set of principles, problem definitions, algorithms, and processes for extracting non-obvious and useful patterns from large data sets". They also mention that data science also takes up other challenges such as the capturing, cleaning, and transforming of unstructured social media as well as web data, and the use of big data technologies to store and process large data sets. In addition, questions related to data ethics and regulation are also included [1, p. 2].

© Springer Nature Switzerland AG 2019
E. Garoufallou et al. (Eds.): MTSR 2019, CCIS 1057, pp. 209–219, 2019.
https://doi.org/10.1007/978-3-030-36599-8_19

Data science has many approaches, aspects and dimensions. Various definitions of data science have different emphases and they reflect different aspects and dimensions. Although different opinions exist, there appears to be some consensus that data science is an emerging, interdisciplinary field that concerns identifying and extracting valuable patterns from big data, converting data into information and knowledge through data analysis and mining [2, p. 1244]. Provost and Fawcett [3] note that the goal of data science is to discover relationships, trends and patterns extracted from large data sets to gain valuable knowledge in order to support decision making and conclude that each of us sees the field from a different perspective and thereby forms a different conception.

Virkus and Garoufallou [4] have analyzed the concept of data science, its definitions, business value, development and related activities as well as skillset of data scientists. Therefore, this paper will not focus on these aspects as these are discussed thoroughly before.

The purpose of this paper is to present the results of the study that explored the field of data science from a computer science perspective on the basis of papers published in the Web of Science database. The structure of this paper is organized as follows: the second section describes the research methodology adopted. In the third section, the results of the bibliographic analysis of the data science from the computer science perspective are presented, in the fourth section conclusions are presented.

2 Methodology

Analysis of research publications on data science was made on the basis of papers published in the Web of Science database. Web of Science™ Core Collection provides access to the world's leading citation databases and its authoritative, multidisciplinary content covers over 12,000 of the highest impact journals worldwide, including Open Access journals and over 150,000 conference proceedings across more than 250 disciplines with coverage to 1900 [5]. Therefore, it seemed reasonable to start exploring this emerging field on the basis of this database.

The following research questions were proposed: What are the main tendencies in publication years, document types, countries of origin, source titles, authors of publications, affiliations of the article authors, the most cited articles related to data science in the field of computer science and the disciplinary affiliation of published papers?

Searches were carried out in the database by topic in June 2019 using the term 'data science'. The search strategy discovered 1145 publications. The following categories were explored: (1) the years in which the documents were published; (2) the document types of the publication; (3) the countries of origin; (4) the sources in which the papers were published, (5) the authors of the publications, (6) affiliations of the article authors, (7) the most cited articles, and (8) disciplinary affiliation of publications. A statistical descriptive analysis of these categories of data are presented.

The limitations of this research are that this study only analyzed research papers in the Web of Science database and therefore only covers a certain amount of scientific papers published in the field of computer science. In addition, only publications with the term 'data science' in the topic area of the Web of Science database were analyzed.

Therefore, several relevant studies are not discussed in this paper that are not reflected in the Web of Science database or were related to other relevant keywords [4].

3 Data Science from the Computer Science Perspective

In the Web of Science database 2536 publications were received under the topic area 'data science' in the period 1980–2019. The highest contribution comes from the computer science research community. 45.15% (1145) of publications come from the subject area of computer science, followed by engineering 18.14% (460), mathematics 7.49% (190), science technology and other topics 5.44% (138), business economic 4.61% (117), education and educational research 3.83% (97), information science and library science 3.39% (86), physics 2.8% (71), telecommunications 2.92% (74), medical informatics 2.76% (70), operations research and management science 2.6% (67), and materials science 2.52% (64). Table 1 illustrates the percentage of articles by subject area.

Table 1. The subject areas of the publications.

Subject area	Number of publications	Percentage of public- cations
Computer Science	1145	45.15
Engineering	460	18.14
Mathematics	190	7.49
Science Technology and Other Topics	138	5.44
Business Economics	117	4.61
Education/Educational Research	97	3.83
Information Science and Library Science	86	3.39
Telecommunications	74	2.92
Physics	71	2.8
Medical Informatics	70	2.76
Operations Research/Management Science	67	2.6
Materials Science	64	2.52

Next, the analysis of the bibliographic information of the 1145 articles in the subject area of computer science is analysed. The first paper on data science in the field of computer science was published in 2004. Table 2 shows the number of papers per year since the year 2004. It appears that there has been continuous increase in articles from the year 2012. The number of articles has significantly increased since 2013 reaching to 322 articles published in 2018.

Table 2. Years of data science publications

Year	Number of publications	Percentage of publications
2019	90	7.86
2018	322	28.122
2017	278	24.279
2016	227	19.825
2015	140	12.227
2014	53	4.629
2013	19	1.659
2012	4	0.349
2011	1	0.087
2010	1	0.087
2009	2	0.175
2008	3	0.262
2006	2	0.175
2005	2	0.175
2004	1	0.175

The main document types are conference proceedings 704 (61.49%), followed by journal articles 362 (31.62%), editorial material 65 (5.68%), book chapters 47 (4.11%), reviews 16 (1.4%), books 6 (0.52%), book reviews 2 (0.18%), letters 1 (0.09%) and news items 1 (0.09%) (Table 3).

Table 3. Document types.

Document type	Number of publications	Percentage of publications
Proceedings Paper	704	61.49
Article	362	31.62
Editorial material	65	5.68
Book chapter	47	4.11
Review	16	1.4
Book	6	0.52
Book Review	2	0.18
Letter	1	0.09
News Item	1	0.09

Table 4 reveals the main sources of publications in which relevant articles are published. The top nine sources, which account for 19.8% of the articles are the *Lecture Notes in Computer Science* (4.2%), *IEEE International Conference on Big Data* (3.3%), *Statistical Analysis and Data Mining* (2.4%), *Big Data* (2.0%), *Studies in Big Data* (1.8%), *2018 IEEE International Conference on Big Data* (1.7%), *2016 IEEE International Conference on Big Data* (1.5%), *Advances in Intelligent Systems and*

Computing (1.5%) and *Procedia Computer Science* (1.5%). These are followed by *Communications in Computer and Information Scie*nce (1.4%), *IEEE Access* (1.4%), *2017 IEEE International Conference on Big Data* (1.3%), *Proceedings of the International Conference on Data Science and Advanced Analytics* (1.3%), *Journal of the American Medical Informatics Association* (1.1%), *2018 IEEE 5th International Conference on Data Science and Advanced Analytics DSAA* (1.0%). The top fifteen sources of publication account for a total of 314 articles, the other articles are divided between the other 790 sources. This indicates that the field of data science and its core journals in the field of computer science is not yet fully developed.

Table 4. The main sources of publications

Document types	Number of publications	Percentage of publications
Lecture Notes in Computer Science	48	4.2
IEEE International Conference on Big Data	38	3.3
Statistical Analysis and Data Mining	28	2.4
Big Data	23	2.0
Studies in Big Data	20	1.8
2018 IEEE International Conference on Big Data	19	1.7
2016 IEEE International Conference on Big Data	17	1.5
Advances in Intelligent Systems and Computing	17	1.5
Procedia Computer Science	17	1.5
Communications in Computer and Information Science	16	1.4
IEEE Access	16	1.4
2017 IEEE International Conference on Big Data	15	1.3
Proceedings of the International Conference on Data Science and Advanced Analytics	15	1.3
Journal of the American Medical Informatics Association	13	1.1
2018 IEEE 5th International Conference on Data Science and Advanced Analytics DSAA	12	1.0

The Table 5 shows the main countries of publications. The main countries are USA, England, India, China, Germany, Canada, Italy, Spain, Australia, Netherlands, Japan and France. It is evident from the analysis that USA is the leading continent in the field of data science from the computer science perspective publishing 440 (38.4%) papers in the field of data science. From European countries, England (106; 9.3%), Germany (67; 5.9%), Italy (53; 4.6%), Spain (49; 4.3%) and Netherlands (36; 3.1%) are the main countries where the publications come in the field of data science from the computer science perspective. From other regions, from Asia India and China both has 74 publications (6.5%) and Japan 33 (2.9%) publications. Canada has 59 (5.2%) and Australia 42 (3.7%) publications.

Table 5. The main countries of publications.

Country	Number of publications	Percentage of publications
USA	440	38.4
England	106	9.3
India	74	6.5
China	74	6.5
Germany	67	5.8
Canada	59	5.2
Italy	53	4.6
Spain	49	4.3
Australia	42	3.7
Netherlands	36	3.1
Japan	33	2.9
France	30	2.6
Russia	22	1.9
Austria	21	1.8
Sweden	21	1.8
Brazil	19	1.7
Switzerland	18	1.6
Taiwan	18	1.6
South Korea	16	1.4
Norway	14	1.2
Portugal	14	1.2
Greece	13	1.1
Poland	13	1.1
Finland	12	1.0

The top five authors are Carson K. Leung (16 publications; 1.4%) from the University of Manitoba (Manitoba, Canada), Abir Hussain (9; 0.8%) from the Liverpool John Moores University (Liverpool, England), Yuri Demchenko (8; 0.7%) from the University of Amsterdam (Amsterdam, Netherlands), Thomas Zimmermann (8; 0.7%) from the University of California, Los Angeles (Los Angeles, USA) and from the Microsoft Research Redmond, Ravi Vatrapu (7; 0.6%) representing the Copenhagen Business School (Copenhagen, Denmark) and Westerdals Oslo School of Arts Communication and Technology (Oslo, Norway) (see Table 6).

Bernard Chen (USA), Alfredo Cuzzocrea (Italy), Robert DeLine (USA), Karina Gibert (Spain), Fan Jiang (Canada), Tim Menzies (USA), Adam G. M. Pazdor (Canada), Foster Provost (USA), Jeffrey S. Saltz (USA), Kalyan Veeramachaneni

Table 6. The main authors of publications.

Author	Number of publications	Percentage of publications
Carson K. Leung (Canada)	16	1.4
Abir Hussain (England)	9	0.8
Yuri Demchenko (Netherlands)	8	0.7
Thomas Zimmermann (USA)	8	0.7
Ravi Vatrapu (Denmark/Norway)	7	0.6
Bernard Chen (USA)	6	0.5
Alfredo Cuzzocrea (Italy)	6	0.5
Robert DeLine (USA)	6	0.5
Karina Gibert (Spain)	6	0.5
Fan Jiang (Canada)	6	0.5
Tim Menzies (USA)	6	0.5
Adam G. M. Pazdor (Canada)	6	0.5
Foster Provost (USA)	6	0.5
Jeffrey S. Saltz (USA)	6	0.5
Kalyan Veeramachaneni (USA)	6	0.5
Heng Zhang (USA)	6	0.5

(USA) and Heng Zhang (USA) each published six publications (each 0.5%) (see Table 6).

Table 7 shows the top affiliations of the authors. The main contributions come from the Massachusetts Institute of Technology (MIT) (19; 1.7%) and the University of Washington (19; 1.7%), followed by the University of Manitoba (18; 1.6%), the Microsoft Research Redmond (17; 1.5%), the New York University (NYU) (17; 1.5%), Carnegie Mellon University (CMU) (12; 1.1%), Syracuse University (12; 1.1%), the University of Chicago (12; 1.1%) and the University of Maryland (11; 1.0%).

Table 8 shows the top 10 cited articles. The most cited article is "The quantified self: fundamental disruption in big data science and biological discovery" by Swan [6] with 3501 citations (average citations per year 233.4%) in the journal *Big Data*. This is followed by article "Data science and its relationship to big data and data-driven decision making" by Provost and Fawcett [3] with 204 citations (average citations per year 29.1%) also in the journal *Big Data* and "Data Science and Prediction" by Dhar [7] with 179 citations (average citations per year 25.6%) in the *Communications of the ACM*. Margolis et al. [8] paper "The National Institutes of Health's Big Data to Knowledge (BD2 K) initiative: capitalizing on biomedical big data" in the *Journal of the American Medical Informatics Association* has received 106 citations (average citations per year 17.7%), the paper "Big Data with cloud computing: an insight on the computing environment, MapReduce, and programming frameworks" by Fernandez et al. [9] in the *Wiley Interdisciplinary Reviews-Data Mining and Knowledge Discovery* 102 citations (average citations per year 17.0%) and the paper "MedRec: using Blockchain for medical data access and permission management" by Azaria et al. [10]

Table 7. The main affiliation of publications

Organization	Number of publications	Percentage of publications
MIT	19	1.7
University of Washington	19	1.7
University of Manitoba	18	1.6
Microsoft RES	17	1.5
NYU	17	1.5
CMU	12	1.1
Syracuse University	12	1.1
University of Chicago	12	1.1
University of Maryland	11	1.0
University of Amsterdam	10	0.9
University of California San Diego	10	0.9
University of Illinois	10	0.9
University of Manchester	10	0.9
Institute of the Italian National Research Council (CNR)	9	0.8
Stanford University	9	0.8
University of California Berkley	9	0.8
University of Minnesota	9	0.8
University of Technology Sydney	9	0.8
Chinese Academy of Sciences	8	0.7
Drexel University 8	0.7	
Georgia Institute of Technology	8	0.7
Ohio State University	8	0.7
Technical University of Munich	8	0.7
University of California, Los Angeles	8	0.7
Universitat Politècnica de Cataluny	8	0.7

Table 8. The top 10 cited articles.

Authors of the paper	Number of publications	Percentage of publications
Swan [6]	3501	233.4
Provost and Fawcett [3]	204	29.1
Dhar [7]	179	25.6
Margolis et al. [8]	106	17.7
Fernandez et al. [9]	102	17.0
Azaria et al. [10]	100	25.0
Demchenko et al. [11]	87	12.4
Dobre and Xhafa [12]	77	12.8
Rokach [13]	58	14.5
Emmert-Streib et al. [14]	51	12.8

100 citations (average citations per year 25.0%) in the proceedings of the 2nd International Conference on Open and Big Data (OBD) in Vienna, Austria in August 2016.

The analysis also revealed that the data science field is quite interdisciplinary by nature (Table 9). In addition to computer science, the papers belonged to 45 other research areas. 634 (55.4%) publications belonged to the research area of Computer Science. 251 (21.9%) of publications belonged both to the Computer Science research area and Engineering research area. 53 (4.6%) of publications belonged to the Computer Science and Telecommunications research area. 51 (4.5%) of publications belonged to the Computer Science and Mathematics research area. 44 (3.8%) of publications belonged to the Computer Science and Information Science and Library Science research area. 37 (3.2%) of publications belonged to the Computer Science and Medical Informatics research area. 26 (2.3%) of publications belonged to the Computer Science and Education and Educational Research area. 22 (1.9%) of publications belonged to the Computer Science and Operations Research and Management Science research area. 18 (1.6%) of publications belonged to the Computer Science and Robotics research area. 15 (1.3%) of publications belonged both to the Computer Science and Automation and Control Systems and Computer Science and Health Care Sciences and Services research areas. 14 (1.2%) of publications belonged both to the Computer Science and Business and Economics and Computer Science and Mathematical and Computational Biology research areas. 10 (0.9%) of publications belonged both to the Computer Science and Environmental Sciences and Ecology and Computer Science and Social Sciences and other topics research areas.

Table 9. Disciplinary affiliation.

Research areas	Number of publications	Percentage of publications
Computer Science (CS)	634	55.4
CS and Engineering	251	21.9
CS and Telecommunications	53	4.6
CS and Mathematics	51	4.5
CS and Information Science and Library Science	44	3.8
CS and Medical Informatics	37	3.2
CS and Education and Educational Research	26	2.3
CS and Operations Research and Management Science	22	1.9
CS and Robotics	18	1.6
CS and Automation and Control Systems	15	1.3
CS and Health Care Sciences and Services	15	1.3
CS and Business and Economics	14	1.2
CS and Mathematical and Computational Biology	14	1.2
CS and Environmental Sciences and Ecology	10	0.9
CS and Social Sciences – other topics	10	0.9

In addition to these research areas, the other topic areas included Nursing (8 publications), Imaging Science & Photographic Technology (7), Neurosciences & Neurology (7), Astronomy & Astrophysics (6), Geography (5), Public Administration (5), Science & Technology - Other Topics (5), Agriculture (4), Biochemistry & Molecular Biology (4), Biotechnology & Applied, Microbiology (4), Communication (4), Physics (4), Psychology (4), Radiology, Nuclear Medicine & Medical Imaging (4), Remote Sensing (4), Government & Law (3), Mathematical Methods in Social Sciences (3), Social Issues (3), Chemistry (2), Geology (2), Instruments & Instrumentation (2), Optics (2), Public, Environmental & Occupational Health (2), Transportation (2), Cardiovascular System & Cardiology (1), Life Sciences & Biomedicine -Other Topics (1), Linguistics (1), Music (1), Pharmacology & Pharmacy (1), Philosophy (1) and Physical Geography (1).

The detailed content analysis of the 1145 publications in the area of data science related to computer science will be reported elsewhere.

4 Conclusions

During the last decade, many authors have published books and articles in the field of data science, the term has been included in the title of conferences, workshops and journals, academic institutions have developed programs to educate and train data scientists, and companies have started to recognize the importance of data scientists and hire them. Since it is a new field there is still both excitement and confusion about it.

In the Web of Science database 2536 publications were received under the topic area 'data science' in the period 1980-2019 in June 2019. The highest contribution to data science comes from the computer science research community (45.15%).

The first paper in the area of data science, reflected in the Web of Science database related to the topic area of computer science, was published in 2004. The number of articles have increased significantly over the last few years. It appears that there has been continuous increase in articles from the year 2012. The main document types are conference proceedings, followed by journal articles, editorial material, book chapters, reviews, books, book reviews, letters and news items. The top three sources that publish data science papers from the computer science perspective are the *Lecture Notes in Computer Science*, *IEEE International Conference on Big Data* and *Statistical Analysis and Data Mining*.

The top five countries publishing are USA, England, India, China and Germany. It is evident from the analysis that USA is the leading continent in the field of data science from the computer science perspective. From European countries, England, Germany, Italy, Spain, Netherlands, France, Austria, Sweden and Switzerland are leading in the field of data science from the computer science perspective. The most cited articles have got 3501, 204 and 179 citations.

The analysis also revealed that the data science field is quite interdisciplinary by nature. In addition to computer science, the papers belonged to 45 other research areas: for example, Engineering, Telecommunications, Mathematics, Information Science and Library Science, Medical Informatics, Education and Educational Research, Operations Research and Management Science, Robotics, Automation and Control Systems,

Health Care Sciences and Services, Business and Economics, Mathematical and Computational Biology, Environmental Sciences and Ecology, Social Sciences and other topics and many other research areas.

It is hoped that the findings of this research will help computer science educators and practitioners understand the educational challenges triggered by the advent of the data-driven society and the opportunities of the field of data science. However, this study only analysed publications with the term 'data science' in the topic area of the Web of Science database, but the future research could expand the field of research and explore publications also reflected by Scopus and Google Scholar and add other relevant keywords.

References

1. Kelleher, J.D., Tierney, B.: Data Science. MIT Press, Cambridge (2018)
2. Wang, K.: Twinning data science with information science in schools of library and information science. J. Documentation **74**(6), 1243–1257 (2018)
3. Provost, F., Fawcett, T.: Data science and its relationship to Big Data and data-driven decision making. Big Data **1**(1), 51–59 (2013)
4. Virkus, S., Garoufallou, M.: Data science from a library and information science perspective. Data Technologies and Applications (accepted for publication) (2019)
5. Virkus, S.: Knowledge management and information literacy: an exploratory analysis. In: Kurbanoğlu, S., Boustany, J., Špiranec, S., Grassian, E., Mizrachi, D., Roy, L., Çakmak, T. (eds.) ECIL 2016. CCIS, vol. 676, pp. 119–129. Springer, Cham (2016). https://doi.org/10. 1007/978-3-319-52162-6_12
6. Swan, M.: The quantified self: fundamental disruption in big data science and biological discovery. Big Data **1**(2), 85–99 (2013)
7. Dhar, V.: Data science and prediction. Commun. ACM **56**(12), 64–73 (2013)
8. Margolis, R., et al.: The National Institutes of Health's Big Data to Knowledge (BD2 K) initiative: capitalizing on biomedical big data. J. Am. Med. Inform. Assoc. **21**(6), 957–958 (2014)
9. Fernández, A., et al.: Big Data with Cloud Computing: an insight on the computing environment, MapReduce, and programming frameworks. Wiley Interdisc. Rev. Data Mining Knowl. Discovery **4**(5), 380–409 (2014)
10. Azaria, A., Ekblaw, A., Vieira, T., Lippman, A.: Medrec: using blockchain for medical data access and permission management. In: 2016 2nd International Conference on Open and Big Data (OBD), pp. 25–30. IEEE (2016)
11. Demchenko, Y., Grosso, P., De Laat, C., Membrey, P.: Addressing big data issues in scientific data infrastructure. In: 2013 International Conference on Collaboration Technologies and Systems (CTS), pp. 48–55. IEEE (2013)
12. Dobre, C., Xhafa, F.: Intelligent services for big data science. Future Gener. Comput. Syst. **37**, 267–281 (2014)
13. Rokach, L.: Decision forest: twenty years of research. Inf. Fusion **27**, 111–125 (2016)
14. Emmert-Streib, F., Dehmer, M., Shi, Y.: Fifty years of graph matching, network alignment and network comparison. Inf. Sci. **346**, 180–197 (2016)

Track on Metadata and Semantics for Digital Libraries, Information Retrieval, Big, Linked, Social and Open Data

Extending Faceted Search with Automated Object Ranking

Kostas Manioudakis[1,2] and Yannis Tzitzikas[1,2(✉)]

[1] Institute of Computer Science, FORTH, Heraklion, Greece
manioudaki@ics.forth.gr
[2] Computer Science Department, University of Crete, Heraklion, Greece
tzitzik@ics.forth.gr

Abstract. Faceted Search is a widely used interaction scheme in digital libraries, e-commerce, and recently also in Linked Data. Nevertheless, object ranking in the context of Faceted Search is not well studied. In this paper we propose an extended version of the model enriched with parameters that enable specifying the characteristics of the sought object ranking. Then we provide an algorithm for producing an object ranking that satisfies these parameters. For doing so various sources are exploited including preferences and statistical properties of the dataset. Finally we present an implementation of the model, the GUI extensions that were required, as well as simulation-based evaluation results that provide evidence about the reduction of the user's cost.

1 Introduction

Faceted Search (FS) is the de facto query paradigm in e-commerce for more than one decade [14,16]. It is widely used in digital libraries, in the semantic web and in Linked Data. FS is essentially a *session-based* interactive method for *gradual query formulation* (commonly over a multidimensional information space) through *simple clicks* that offers to the user an *overview* of the result set (groups and count information) and *never leads to empty result sets*. At each state of the interaction the user explores the *focus*, i.e. the set of objects that satisfy the various constraints/filters that the user has specified up to that point. These objects are *unranked*, e.g. when the user explores a catalogue for buying a new laptop, or *ranked*, e.g. when the user explores the available hotels which are ordered with respect to price, user ratings or other criteria (default or specified by the user in the form of preferences as in the case of PFS [19]). The focus is ranked also in cases FS is applied after a keyword search query, e.g. as in Google Scholar. Although object ranking in FS is already used in commercial systems, the scientific literature on this topic is relatively short. Most of the research, has focused on methods only for facet ranking, i.e. for deciding in what order to place the facets. In this paper we focus on the *ranking of objects*. We propose an extension of the FS model that is enriched with parameters for specifying the desired properties of object ranking. These parameters allow

© Springer Nature Switzerland AG 2019
E. Garoufallou et al. (Eds.): MTSR 2019, CCIS 1057, pp. 223–235, 2019.
https://doi.org/10.1007/978-3-030-36599-8_20

tackling the problem of too big or too small answers and can specify how refined the sought ranking should be, as well as how long the answer should be. Then we describe methods and algorithms for deriving such object rankings. In the sequent we describe how we have realized the model. To grasp the idea, the left side of Fig. 1 sketches the GUI of a typical FS containing three facets and a focus comprising 8 objects partitioned into 2 buckets, the first containing 6 objects and the second 2 objects. The right side sketches the GUI according to the extended model that we introduce, where the user has asked for 10 objects, and a more refined ranking, specifically that no bucket should contain more than 3 objects. We can see that more objects have appeared (approximate results) and the focus respects the Maximum Block (MB) constraint of 3.

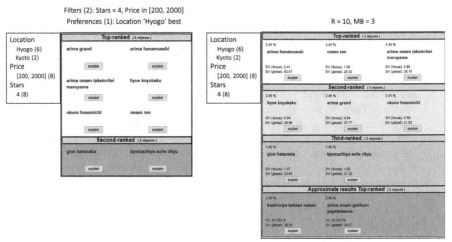

Fig. 1. Impact of automatic ranking on search results. The approximate results satisfy the preference and one of the 2 filters.

In a nutshell, the main contributions of this paper are: (a) the extension of the model with object ranking-related parameters, (b) the formulation of the corresponding object ranking problem, (c) the discussion on the ability to solve the problem, (d) the algorithm SmartFSRank for providing a solution, (e) the proposal of how to extend the GUI of FS systems for making evident and clear the object ranking, (f) the description of the model's implementation, and (g) some promising simulation-based evaluation results. The rest of this paper is organized as follows: Sect. 2 describes the context and related work. Section 3 introduces the extended model. Section 4 provides the algorithms for realizing the extended model. Section 5 describes the extensions of the GUI and the implementation, Sect. 6 discusses related systems and some evaluation results. Finally, Sect. 7 concludes the paper.

2   Context and Related Work

2.1   Background

Faceted Search. *Faceted Exploration* (or *Faceted Search*) is a widely used interaction scheme for Exploratory Search. It is the de facto query paradigm in e-commerce [14,16]. It is also used for exploring RDF Data (e.g. see [18] for a recent survey, and [10] for a recent system). In a short (and rather informal) way we could define it as a *session-based interactive method for query formulation (commonly over a multidimensional information space) through simple clicks that offers an overview of the result set (groups and count information), never leading to empty result sets.*

PFS: Preference-enriched Faceted Search. *Preference-enriched Faceted Search* [19], for short PFS, is an extension of FS that supports *preferences*. PFS offers actions that allow the user to order facets, values, and objects using *best, worst, preferTo* actions (i.e. relative preferences), *aroundTo* actions (over a specific value), and other criteria. Furthermore, the user is able to *compose* object related preference actions, using *Priority, Pareto, Pareto Optimal* (i.e. skyline) and other. The distinctive features of PFS is that it allows expressing preferences over attributes whose values can be hierarchically organized (and/or multi-valued), it supports preference inheritance, and it offers scope-based rules for resolving automatically the conflicts that may arise. As a result the user can restrict his focus by using the faceted interaction scheme (hard constraints) that lead to non-empty results, and rank according to preference the objects of his focus. PFS has been used in various domains, also in the context of spoken dialogue systems [12]. Recent extensions of SPARQL with preferences ([13,15]) will facilitate the implementation of PFS over RDF data.

2.2   Related Work

There is related work from several areas including FS systems, Databases, and Learning to Rank approaches.

In Faceted Search Systems. The idea of automatic ranking in faceted search is not new, and there are various approaches for automatic ranking in faceted search systems, discussed in the survey [18]. Most of the research, has focused on methods only for *facet ranking*, i.e. for deciding in what order to place the facets. In most cases (e.g [7,8]), the proposed methods are based on the frequency of facet values. The approach in [20] dynamically ranks the properties depending on the query. Moreover, they define different measures on qualitative and numeric facets, and also suggest ranking the values of each property by their frequency in descending order. Other metrics have also been utilized such as navigational cost [5]. In [6] a set-cover ranking method is used. Ranking the facets can be also useful for ordering the objects.

Object ranking, is already used in commercial systems. For instance, the hotel platform booking.com offers a ranking method based on various properties. However, the scientific literature on this topic is relatively short. In [14] (Chapter 9) a method based on property values is briefly described through an e-shopping example. According to PFS, and the system Hippalus [11], the user can specify the ranking of objects through preference actions. In the context of PFS, [17] introduced a method for quantifying the degree of match between an object and the user's preference actions. This is mainly for making evident to the user how good the top-ranked objects are. In the same context of PFS, [12] introduces selectivity and entropy, that can be used for ranking the objects.

In Databases. The problem of automated ranking has also been studied in the context of databases. For instance, [1] aims at tackling the Many Answers Problem, which arises when a query returns too many result tuples without any ordering. That work proposes a framework that adopts the popular Information Retrieval ranking method of cosine similarity on TF-IDF weights. An alternative approach for the Many Answers Problem was proposed in [4] that is based on Probabilistic Information Retrieval. In that work, they investigate attributes not specified in the query and calculate two scores: a *global score* which captures the global importance of unspecified attribute values and a *conditional score* which captures the strengths of dependencies (or correlations) between specified and unspecified attribute values. These scores are estimated automatically from a workload of *past queries* and with data analysis. A user evaluation showed better quality in comparison to methods of [1].

Learning to Rank Approaches. In the field of Information Retrieval apart from the classical retrieval models, lately various methods that utilize Machine Learning have been developed [9]. These processes involve creating a ranking function by training a machine learning model on user data, collected from past queries (e.g. number of clicks on each item, explicit user ratings, etc). A Learning to Rank approach for faceted search is proposed in [3]. In that work, a weighted TF-IDF scoring formula calculated on facets is adopted. Queries and documents are represented as sets of facet-value pairs, and learning methods are employed to determine the optimal weights of the formula, given a user query and a set of previously judged documents (from explicit and implicit user feedback).

3   The Extended Model

Representation of Data. We assume a set of objects Obj described by a set of facets $F_1, \ldots, F_k$. The values of these facets can be categorical, numerical, as well as values from a taxonomy. Moreover facets can be multi-valued. Overall this representation framework captures to most widely (and successful) applications of FS (for e-commerce, booking application, bibliographic search, etc).

Plain FS Interaction. The user during the FS formulates interactively a set of hard constraints (filters), denoted by hc. The focus is actually the extension of the hc, denoted by $E(hc)$ $(E(hc) \subseteq Obj)$.

FS with Preferences. If PFS is supported and the user has expressed a set of preferences, i.e. a set of *soft constraints* denoted by sc, then they are exploited for ranking the elements of $E(hc)$ with respect to the preference relation $\succ_{sc}$.

The Focus. In general we can consider that the focus at each state of the interaction is a *bucket order*, $L = \langle b_1, \ldots, b_z \rangle$, i.e. a sequence of blocks $b_1 \ldots b_z$, each being a subset of Obj which are pairwise disjoint ($b_i \cap b_j = \emptyset$). Note that z could be 1, meaning that the focus consists of a single block with objects not ranked (or ranked arbitrarily for reasons of presentation). Note that this formulation captures both FS and PFS, which uses preferences to rank the objects.

User Session. A user session us is a series of actions, $s = \langle a_1, \ldots, a_n \rangle$ where each a_i is a hard or soft constraint.

Parameters of the Extended Model. We propose extending the model with two parameters

- MB: Maximum Block size. E.g. if $MB = 1$ then the system should return a linear order of objects, if $MB = 2$ the answer should not contain ties between more than 2 objects.
- R: number of requested objects.

With these two parameters several requirements can be tackled:

- Too many objects: R forces the system to rank the objects for returning the best R objects.
- Too few objects: R forces the system to also return approximate objects
- Arbitrary order: MB forces the system to rank the objects so that no block has more than MB objects, and in this way the rank is not arbitrary

Characterizing a Bucket Order L. Let L be a bucket order $L = \langle b_1, \ldots, b_z \rangle$, i.e. a possible ranked answer, and let $objects(L)$ denote the set of objects that occur in L. We could characterize L according to various criteria:

- **HCsat.** We could say that L satisfies the hard constraints hc, if $objects(L)$ are exactly those that satisfy hc, i.e. $objects(L) = E(hc)$.
- **SCsat.** We could say that L satisfies the soft constraints sc (i.e. it respects the preference order), if $L \supseteq \succ_{sc|E(hc)}$. This means that autoranking is used only for ranking the objects in each block of the preference order (it never "violates" the blocks, it just adds relationships, and these relationships do not create any cycle).
- **MBsat.** We could say that L satisfies a *maximum allowable block size MB*, if $|b_i| \leq MB$ for each $1 \leq i \leq z$.
- **Rsat.** We could say that L satisfies R, if L contains exactly R objects.

It is not hard to see that it is not always possible to find an L that satisfies all of the above constraints. For instance if the objects that satisfy the hc are less than R, i.e. $|E(hc)| < R$, then the system should either return less objects (sacrificing Rsat), or should try to return R objects by extending $E(hc)$ with the $R - |E(hc)|$ in number "closest" objects (sacrificing HCsat).

On the other extreme, if those that satisfy the hc are more than R, then the system should rank them and return the best of them. This is another case of an L that is not HCsat, since it contains less objects than those satisfying hc. A problem statement that includes more requirements follows:

Definition 1 (Problem Statement). Given a user session us with hard and soft constraints, a parameter R specifying the number of desired objects, a parameter MB specifying the maximum allowable block size, compute and return to the user the "best" (wrt HCsat, SCsat, MBSat, Rsat) answer L. $\square$

What remains is to clarify what "best" means. A first objective is to produce one or more L that satisfy all the criteria if possible. In case there are more than one, then we need a method to select one of them. To this end, dataset statistics and other metrics (as we have seen in the related work) can be used. For example we could promote frequently or rarely occurring values. If there is no L that satisfies all hard constraints, then we need to find one that "better approximates" a bucket order that satisfies them all. We will elaborate on this issue in the next section.

4   The SmartFSRank Ranking Method

Here we define an algorithm that provides a solution to the problem statement (as defined in Definition 1). In general the algorithm exploits PFS, if supported, and it tries to satisfy R by ranking and approximate matching, and MB through ranking based on statistical properties of the data. Note that the algorithm can be applied even if PFS is not supported (in that case we have one block, i.e. $z = 1$). In brief, the algorithm SmartFSRank, Algorithm 1, first tries to satisfy hc (line 1), and then sc (Part 1, line 2) by exploiting the PFS-based ranking method. Then it tries to satisfy R (Part 2, lines 5–7), and finally MB (Part 3, lines 8–13). In Part 2, if R is greater than the size of the current focus, then more objects (not satisfying hc) have to be added and this should be based on the approximate satisfaction of the hard constraints. This selection is done by **AppendBlocks** that is analyzed in 4.1. In Part 3, the block breaking for

---

Algorithm 1: SmartFSRank
Input: Obj, hc, sc, MB, R
Output: A ranked answer that satisfies hc, sc, MB and R.

1: $A = E(hc)$;   ▷ The objects satisfying the hc
2: /** Part (1): Apply the PFS method to satisfy sc */
3: Compute $(A, \succ_{sc \,|A})$ which is a series of blocks Result $= \langle b_1, \ldots, b_Z \rangle$.
4: /** Part (2): Satisfy R */
5: **if** $|A| < R$ **then**   ▷ need to add more objects
6:     $Result = Result.\textbf{AppendBlocks}(R - |A|)$;   ▷ Add new blocks to the answer
7: **end if**
8: /** Part (3): Satisfy MB */
9: **for** each $b \in Result$ **do**
10:     **if** $|b| > MB$ **then**   ▷ If block b does not satisfy MB
11:         Replace b by **BreakBlock**(b, MB, sc, hc)
12:     **end if**
13: **end for**

---

satisfying MB can be based on frequency, and similarity to soft constraints, as defined in [17], and it is done by **BreakBlock(b)** that is analyzed in 4.2.

4.1 AppendBlocks

The idea is to score each object according to its distance from the hc. Having such a scoring function, a method to realize AppendBlocks is to score each object not in $E(hc)$ and return the $R - |E(hc)|$ objects that have the highest score. This method guarantees that it will return the objects which maximize the score, i.e. those that better approximate the information need, as expressed by the hc. As regards the scoring, below we detail a method based on facet types. Let $hc = c_1 \wedge \ldots \wedge c_n$, where each c_i is a constraint like $F_i = t_i$, e.g Stars = 4. If o_j is an object, with o_{ji} we denote the value of o_j on the facet F_i. In Table 1 we define the score per conjunct based on the facet type. The first column corresponds to the case where a conjunct is satisfied, while the second presents the formulas used when a conjunct is not satisfied. In both cases the scores are in the interval $[0, 1]$. In the last row, corresponding to the case where the terminology is structured as a taxonomy, we define a similarity measure that reflects the distance in the taxonomy. For a term $x \in F_i$, let $up(x) = \{ t \in F_i \mid x \leq_i t\}$. We define the similarity between two terms x and y, as the Jaccard similarity of their greater nodes, specifically: $sim_{tax}(x, y) = \frac{|up(x) \cap up(y)|}{|up(x) \cup up(y)|}$ and then define $score_{taxonomy}(F_i = t_i, o_j) = sim_{tax}(t_i, o_{ji})$.

Table 1. Formulas for calculating $score_{hc}$ per conjunct

score type	o_j satisfies c_i	o_j does not satisfy c_i
$score_{flatterminology}(F_i = t_i, o_j)$	1	0
$score_{numeric}(F_i = t_i, o_j)$	1	$1 - \frac{|t_i - o_{ji}|}{\max_{o_m \in Obj}\{|t_i - o_{mi}|\}}$
$score_{interval}(F_i \in [a,b], o_j)$	1	$score_{numeric}(F_i = \frac{a+b}{2}, o_j)$
$score_{taxonomy}(F_i = t_i, o_j)$	$sim_{tax}(t_i, o_{ji})$	$sim_{tax}(t_i, o_{ji})$

Back to the running example of Fig. 1, we can now see how the scores of the approximate results were calculated, regarding the constraint Stars = 4. They both have Stars = 5, so their score [1] according to the numeric case of the above table is: $score_{numeric}(Stars = 4, 5) = 1 - \frac{|4-5|}{4-0} = 1 - \frac{1}{4} = 0.75$

Definition 2 (HCscore). We can define the consolidated score of an object o with respect to $hc = c_1 \wedge \ldots \wedge c_n$, as: $score_{hc}(o_j) = \frac{1}{n} \sum_{i=1}^{n} score_{type(c_i)}(o_j)$ where $type(c_i) \in \{flatterminology, numeric, interval, taxonomy\}$.

This formula can be considered as the *baseline*. It expresses how close o_j is with respect to a point that satisfies hc. The exact algorithm for AppendBlocks is Algorithm 2. It returns the bucket order to be appended.

---

[1] Assuming that the range of the facet Stars, in the dataset, is the set $\{0,1,2,3,4,5\}$.

Algorithm 2. AppendBlocks
Input: Num, hc
Output: A bucket order to be appended

1: $CO = Obj \setminus E(hc)$;   ▷ The candidate objects
2: **for** each $o \in CO$ **do**
3:    $o.score = score_{hc}(o)$;   ▷ compute the score of o wrt hc
4: **end for**
5: $Sort(CO, score, descending)$;   ▷ sort CO wrt $score$ attribute in desc. order
6: Let $B = \langle b_1, \ldots, b_F \rangle$ the resulting blocks   ▷ after the previous sorting
7: $c = 0$; $i = 1$; $A = \epsilon$;
8: **while** $c < Num$ **do**   ▷ While the objective of Num objects is not reached
9:     $A = A.appendBlock(b_i)$; $i + +$; $c = c + |b_i|$;
10: **end while**
11: Return A;

4.2   BreakBlock

For breaking each block that does not satisfy MB an idea is to score each object of the block according to its *discrimination value*. Rare elements are harder to find, therefore it could be reasonable to promote objects that have rare values, i.e. those with higher discrimination value. On the other hand, frequent values may correspond to popular values, therefore it could be also reasonable to promote frequent values, i.e. those that appear in several objects. As we shall see in the section about GUI, the GUI allows the user to specify whether rare or frequent values are preferred. In any case we have to define and compute the discrimination value. Having such a formula we can apply it to each object of any block that does not satisfy MB to order its objects. Then, such blocks will break to smaller ones satisfying MB. We can define the *discrimination value* (dV) of a tuple $o_j = (o_{j1}, \ldots, o_{jk})$ by taking the average inverse frequency, i.e.: $dV_w(o_j) = \frac{1}{k} * \sum_{i=1,k} \frac{1}{freq_w(o_{ji})}$. Note that frequency can be defined in various ways, this is why the above formula uses $freq_w$ where $w \in \{g, ga, E\}$. Specifically the frequency of a value $t \in F_i$, can be defined *globally* $(freq_g)$, or with respect to the objects that *have value in facet* F_i $(freq_{ga})$, or in the *current focus* E $(freq_E)$. Formally:

$$freq_g(o_{ji}) = \frac{|\{o_x \in Obj \mid o_{xi} = o_{ji}\}|}{|Obj|} \tag{1}$$

$$freq_{ga}(o_{ji}) = \frac{|\{o_x \in Obj \mid o_{xi} = o_{ji}\}|}{|\{o_y \in Obj \mid o_{yi} \neq \epsilon\}|}, \tag{2}$$

$$freq_E(o_{ji}) = \frac{|\{o_x \in E \mid o_{xi} = o_{ji}\}|}{|E|}. \tag{3}$$

Note that if $o_{ji} = \epsilon$, i.e. null, then $freq_{\{g,E\}}(o_{ji}) =$ number of objects having null (just like an ordinary value). In general it makes sense to consider a *series* of "tie breaking" methods, for making sure that all ties can be broken so that MB is eventually satisfied. Each such method can be assigned a level, meaning that if the application of the level i method does not break a tie, then the level $i + 1$ method is applied. The exact algorithm for BreakBlock is Algorithm 3.

Algorithm 3. BreakBlock
Input: $b, MB, level, hc, sc$, where b does not satisfy MB.
Output: A bucket order of the objects of b that satisfies MB.

1:   $A = objects(b)$;   ▷ the objects occuring in b
2:   **for** each $o \in A$ **do**
3:      $o.dv = DV(o, level)$;   ▷ compute the discrimination value of o at $level$
4:   **end for**
5:   $Sort(A, dv, descending)$;   ▷ sort A wrt dv attribute in desc. order
6:   Let $B = \langle b_1, \ldots, b_F \rangle$ the resulting blocks   ▷ after the previous sorting
7:   **for** each $b_i \in B$ **do**
8:      **if** $|b_i| > MB$ **then**   ▷ if b_i still does not satisfy MB
9:          $Bnew = $ **BreakBlock**$(b_i, MB, level + 1, sc, hc)$;   ▷ recursive call with +1 level
10:     **end if**
11:     Replace in B the block b_i by the series of blocks $Bnew$
12:   **end for**
13: Return B;

It first breaks the block b with respect to the discrimination value in the focus (i.e. $freq_E$). If MB is still not satisfied, it uses $freq_g$ (recursively only for that block). Specifically we assume the following series of levels: $Levels = \langle dv_E, dv_G, lexicographic \rangle$. At level 3 we assume the lexicographic order wrt the name of the object. This ensures that the algorithm terminates. The algorithm returns a bucket order that certainly satisfies MB. One key point is that a cost is paid only if needed i.e. only for the blocks that do not satisfy MB.

5   Extensions of the Graphical User Interface

In general we have identified the following GUI issues: (a) how to make evident the automatic ranking, (b) how to enable the user to change the ranking (e.g. frequent vs rare), (c) how to make clear the objects that do not satisfy the hard constraints, (d) how to provide ranking explanation (both for hc and sc). For the implementation of the extended FS model that we propose in this paper, we decided to use Hippalus which is a publicly accessible web system that implements the PFS interaction model. The information base that feeds Hippalus is represented in RDF/S[2] using a schema adequate for representing objects described according to dimensions with hierarchically organized values. Below

---

[2] http://www.w3.org/TR/rdf-schema/.

we describe how we tackled the above questions by showing screenshots from our implementation. The bucket order is presented by separating buckets with a line label "Top-ranked", "Second-ranked", etc. so that the preference-based ranking is made clear to the user. The objects within a preference-based bucket are ordered based on the automatic method presented in this paper (instead of an arbitrary one). The settings provided are the following (see also Fig. 2):

1. Enable / disable Rsat
2. Specify the value of R parameter
3. Enable / disable inner bucket ordering
4. Enable / disable MBsat
5. Specify the value of MB parameter
6. Select policy about discrimination value: prefer rare values, common values or no preference

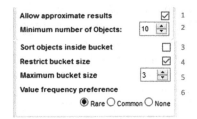

Fig. 2. The automatic ranking settings as provided in the GUI

Figure 2 displays the settings used in the running example (Fig. 1). As regards *ranking explanation*, (a) the GUI shows the scores for each object (consolidated $score_{hc}, dv_E, dv_G$, and similarity to soft constraints, as a percentage) as shown in the right side of Fig. 1, and (b) the GUI provides a button labeled "explain" on each object, that when pressed, it displays the $score_{hc}$ per facet, as well as the soft constraints and which of them are satisfied by the object.

6   Evaluation

Comparison with Related Systems. In comparison to the existing work, at first we should say that the data space we assume supports hierarchically organized values. As regards the proposed ranking framework, it is the first that considers hard constraints (the typical functionality of FS), soft constraints (including preference inheritance in the hierarchically organized values), as well as statistical-based object ranking. It does not require log or training data, therefore it can be widely applied. Probably the closest work to ours is [3] however they rely on machine learning techniques and user data, while we focus on the query constraints and the statistical properties of the dataset. To make clear the key differences between our system and the most related systems that were mentioned in Sect. 2, Table 2 provides a list of features and marks those systems that provide them.

Simulation-based Evaluation. The main purpose of automatic ranking, is to assist the user in finding the desired object. One way to measure this gain, is to consider the number of constraints required, until the desired object is ranked in the top-K positions of the focus (for various values of K). The better the automatic ranking is, the less constraints are required. To this end, we have started a simulation based evaluation, since this can be more objective and less

Table 2. Comparison with related systems

	Our Tool	GRAFA [10]	Basu et al. [2]	van Belle [3]
Facet hierarchies	Yes	No	Yes	No
Approximate matching	Yes	No	No	Yes
Blocks of desired size	Yes	No	No	No
Preferences	Yes	No	No	No
Needs training data	No	No	No	Yes

laborious than evaluation with users. So far we have made experiments using one dataset, which contains information about 382 hotels and has 18 facets. We considered each of these 382 hotels as a possible ideal top result. We run 2 tests. In the first one, we simulated users that try to find that hotel by sequentially applying hard constraints that match the object's description (the conjuncts correspond to the object's facet-value pairs). In the second one, instead of hard constraints the user formulated only soft constraints. Specifically, for each facet-value pair of the target object a soft constraint of type *"best"* was applied (e.g *prefer Stars...4 best*). The initial ordering of the objects was a random one, but the same in each simulated session. Below we report the average and maximum number of constraints needed in each of three cases: (1) No automatic ranking, (2) Automatic ranking based on discrimination value, preferring rare values, (3) Automatic ranking based on discrimination value, preferring common values. For cases (2) and (3) the maximum block size (MB) is 1, so that there aren't any ties in the ranking. Tables 3 and 4 show the simulation results.

Table 3. Hard constraints session simulation results

Automatic Ranking	Preference on DV	Avg. HC (K = 1)	Max HC (K = 1)	Avg. HC (K = 2)	Max HC (K = 2)	Avg. HC (K = 3)	Max HC (K = 3)
Disabled	–	4.55	19	3.08	15	2.51	14
Enabled	Rare	4.85	19	3.29	18	2.62	15
Enabled	Common	**4.11**	**18**	**2.92**	**10**	**2.45**	**10**

Although we plan to continue evaluation on more datasets and with more complex simulated user sessions, the results so far show that preferring *common* values is better than searching without automatic ranking. This holds for all metrics that are measured in Tables 3 and 4. On the contrary, if preference is given on rare values, we get worse results than those with arbitrary ranking. The above provide positive evidence for the benefits of MB and of BreakBlocks, specifically they reduce the average cost up to to 9.18% (HC, K = 1) and the maximum cost up to 50% (SC, K = 3). As regards the benefits from R, it is not hard to see that whenever a new approximate object is added, it reduces the number of constraints the user would have to formulate (for getting that

Table 4. Soft constraints session simulation results

Automatic Ranking	Preference on DV	Avg. SC (K = 1)	Max SC (K = 1)	Avg. SC (K = 2)	Max SC (K = 2)	Avg. SC (K = 3)	Max SC (K = 3)
Disabled	–	4.26	16	2.99	14	2.46	14
Enabled	Rare	4.43	16	3.14	14	2.57	14
Enabled	Common	**3.99**	**14**	**2.89**	**11**	**2.43**	**7**

object). Therefore the gain from adding $R - |A|$ objects is the number of distinct descriptions of these objects, so the gain ranges $[1, R - |A|]$.

Efficiency. Although scalability is not currently our focus, we should note that the time complexity of the ranking methods is $O(N * K)$ where N, K are the number of objects and facets. For the dataset we used, which contained 382 objects, the average time to apply a hard constraint increased from 2 ms (without automated ranking) to approximately 20 ms (with automated ranking), which is not noticeable by the user.

7   Concluding Remarks

We proposed an extended model for FS for improving the exploration experience of the users in various contexts. Specifically, we proposed a set of parameters for specifying the desired properties of *object ranking*, and then, through SmartFSRank, we factorized the problem to sub-tasks that can be tackled more easily. Finally, we showed the model's implementation and the required GUI extensions. The evaluation results of the extended model through simulation are promising, i.e. they provide evidence that the proposed model reduces the user cost for finding the desired object, specifically it reduces the average cost up to 9.18% and the maximum cost up to 50%. Apart from continuing the simulation-based evaluation, an interesting extension would be to consider diversification requirements, as well as to investigate indexes and algorithms for scalability i.e. for enabling FS with automated ranking over very big datasets.

Acknowledgement. This work was partially supported by the project AI4EU (EU H2020, Grant agreement No 825619).

References

1. Agrawal, S., Chaudhuri, S., Das, G., Gionis, A.: Automated ranking of database query results. In: Proceedings of CIDR (2003)
2. Basu Roy, S., et al.: Minimum-effort driven dynamic faceted search in structured databases. In: Proceedings of the 17th CIKM. ACM (2008)
3. van Belle, A.: Learning to rank for faceted search: bridging the gap between theory and practice (2017). https://berlinbuzzwords.de/sites/berlinbuzzwords.de/files/media/documents/bb2017.pdf

4. Chaudhuri, S., Das, G., Hristidis, V., Weikum, G.: Probabilistic ranking of database query results. In: Proceedings of the Thirtieth VLDB (2004)
5. Li, C., et al.: Facetedpedia: Dynamic generation of query-dependent faceted interfaces for wikipedia. In: Proceedings of the 19th ICWWW. ACM (2010)
6. Dakka, W., Ipeirotis, P., Wood, K.: Automatic construction of multifaceted browsing interfaces. In: Proceedings of the 14th CIKM (2005)
7. Hahn, R., et al.: Faceted wikipedia search. In: Abramowicz, W., Tolksdorf, R. (eds.) BIS 2010. LNBIP, vol. 47, pp. 1–11. Springer, Heidelberg (2010). https://doi.org/10.1007/978-3-642-12814-1_1
8. Harth, A.: VisiNav: Visual web data search and navigation. In: Bhowmick, S.S., Küng, J., Wagner, R. (eds.) DEXA 2009. LNCS, vol. 5690, pp. 214–228. Springer, Heidelberg (2009). https://doi.org/10.1007/978-3-642-03573-9_17
9. Liu, T.Y.: Learning to rank for information retrieval. Found. Trends Inf. Retrieval **3**(3), 225–331 (2009)
10. Moreno-Vega, J., Hogan, A.: GraFa: Scalable faceted browsing for RDF graphs. In: Vrandečić, D., et al. (eds.) ISWC 2018. LNCS, vol. 11136, pp. 301–317. Springer, Cham (2018). https://doi.org/10.1007/978-3-030-00671-6_18
11. Papadakos, P., Tzitzikas, Y.: Hippalus: Preference-enriched faceted exploration. In: EDBT/ICDT Workshops, vol. 172 (2014)
12. Papangelis, A., Papadakos, P., Stylianou, Y., Tzitzikas, Y.: Spoken dialogue for information navigation. In: SIGDial (2018)
13. Pivert, O., Slama, O., Thion, V.: SPARQL Extensions with Preferences: a Survey. In: ACM Symposium on Applied Computing (2016)
14. Sacco, G.M., Tzitzikas, Y. (eds.): Dynamic Taxonomies and Faceted Search: Theory, Practice, and Experience. The Information Retrieval Series, vol. 25. Springer, Berlin (2009). https://doi.org/10.1007/978-3-642-02359-0
15. Troumpoukis, A., Konstantopoulos, S., Charalambidis, A.: An extension of SPARQL for expressing qualitative preferences. In: d'Amato, C., et al. (eds.) ISWC 2017. LNCS, vol. 10587, pp. 711–727. Springer, Cham (2017). https://doi.org/10.1007/978-3-319-68288-4_42
16. Tunkelang, D.: Faceted search. Synthesis lectures on information concepts, retrieval, and services (2009)
17. Tzitzikas, Y., Dimitrakis, E.: Preference-enriched faceted search for voting aid applications. IEEE Trans. Emerg. Top. Comput. **7**(2), 218–229 (2019)
18. Tzitzikas, Y., Manolis, N., Papadakos, P.: Faceted exploration of RDF/S datasets: a survey. J. Intell. Inf. Syst. **48**(2), 329–364 (2017)
19. Tzitzikas, Y., Papadakos, P.: Interactive exploration of multidimensional and hierarchical information spaces with real-time preference elicitation. Fundamenta Informaticae **20**, 1–42 (2012)
20. Vandic, D., et al.: Dynamic facet ordering for faceted product search engines. IEEE Trans. Knowl. Data Eng. **29**(5), 1004–1016 (2017)

C-Rank: A Concept Linking Approach to Unsupervised Keyphrase Extraction

Mauro Dalle Lucca Tosi$^{(\boxtimes)}$ and Julio Cesar dos Reis

Institute of Computing, University of Campinas, Campinas, SP, Brazil
maurodlt@hotmail.com, jreis@ic.unicamp.br

Abstract. Keyphrase extraction is the task of identifying a set of phrases that best represent a natural language document. It is a fundamental and challenging task that assists publishers to index and recommend relevant documents to readers. In this article, we introduce C-Rank, a novel unsupervised approach to automatically extract keyphrases from single documents by using concept linking. Our method explores Babelfy to identify candidate keyphrases, which are weighted based on heuristics and their centrality inside a co-occurrence graph where keyphrases appear as vertices. It improves the results obtained by graph-based techniques without training nor background data inserted by users. Evaluations are performed on SemEval and INSPEC datasets, producing competitive results with state-of-the-art tools. Furthermore, C-Rank generates intermediate structures with semantically annotated data that can be used to analyze larger textual compendiums, which might improve domain understatement and enrich textual representation methods.

Keywords: Keyphrase extraction · Complex networks · Semantic annotation

1 Introduction

Keyphrases are expressions intended to represent the content of a document and highlight its main topics. They may be single or multi-termed and may be provided by the author, which is uncommon in most of the non-scientific texts. Keyphrases are used by potential readers to decide whether or not the topics approached in the document are relevant to them. Furthermore, they may be used to recommend articles to readers, analyze research trends over time, among other NLP tasks [1]. However, the automatic keyphrase extraction is a challenging task as it varies from domains, suffers from the lack of context, and its result keyphrases may be formed by multiple words [1]. Therefore, despite the improvements achieved in the last years, it still is an active research topic that deserves further studies.

The keyphrase extraction task can be performed based on different approaches. Hasan and Ng [5] segmented the keyphrase extraction task in Supervised, that demands an annotated training set; and Unsupervised, that does not depend on annotated data, which is the line followed in this article.

© Springer Nature Switzerland AG 2019
E. Garoufallou et al. (Eds.): MTSR 2019, CCIS 1057, pp. 236–247, 2019.
https://doi.org/10.1007/978-3-030-36599-8_21

The unsupervised methods can be developed to extract the keyphrases of a document based on different inputs other than the document text itself. The background data varies according to the method and can consider web-pages, specific-domain documents and general scientific texts [7]. Although the best results have been achieved by most of the methods using background data, it may demand information, training time or both, that the user does not necessarily possess. Therefore, approaches that do not require training nor other data to be inputted by the user should be investigated.

A predefined-domain-independent knowledge resource could improve the extraction results without requesting further data nor training from users. Babelnet[1] [11] is a wide-coverage multilingual semantic network automatically constructed that has about 16 million entries, which are called synsets. Each synset represents a given concept or a named entity and contains all its synonyms and translations in different languages. Despite the amount of relevant information contained in Babelnet, its usage would be limited without the Babelfy [10], which is a graph-based approach to simultaneously perform Entity Linking (EL) and Word Sense Disambiguation (WSD) on Babelnet.

In this article, we propose C-Rank as a novel approach to automatic perform unsupervised keyphrase extractions from free-text documents. For the best of our knowledge, it is the first method to explore concept linking to improve results in this task. C-Rank does not demand training nor other data provided by the user as it performs its linkages through Babelfy using as resources the BabelNet [11], Wikipedia[2] and WordNet [9] knowledge. C-Rank parses the inputted document text, runs Babelfy and constructs a co-occurrence graph with the annotated concepts as vertices. Next, it weights the vertices using their centrality in the graph, selects the top-ranked as candidates and modifies them using heuristic factors. Finally, C-Rank identifies vertices that belong to the same keyphrase and merge them, re-rank all the candidates and outputs the result. We extensively evaluate our approach with distinct gold standard datasets and demonstrate the effectiveness and benefits in our defined solution.

This article is organised as follows: Sect. 2 presents keyphrase extraction related works. Afterwards, Sect. 3 introduces C-Rank, our model to automatically extract keyphrases from documents. Section 4 reports on the used benchmark datasets in addition to the achieved results. Whereas Sect. 5 discusses our findings and compares C-Rank with existing methods, Sect. 6 concludes the article exhibiting the final considerations.

2   Related Work

This section presents unsupervised keyphrase extraction techniques and compares their approaches to obtain the phrases that best describe the content of a textual document. A survey conducted by Hasan and Ng [5] segmented unsupervised methods in four categories "Graph-based Ranking", that considers the

---

[1] https://babelnet.org/.
[2] http://www.wikipedia.org.

co-occurrence of the phrases in a text as graph edges, in which its vertices represent the keyphrases, that are ranked based on the graph structure; "Topic-Based Clustering", which constructs a graph with the document topics as vertices and its relations as edges, then clusters it to identify the main topics discussed in the analyzed document; "Simultaneous Learning", considering that keyphrase extraction and text summarization tasks can benefit from each other and be performed simultaneously, combining "Graph-based Ranking" with other summarization techniques to improve results; and "Language Modeling", that uses a background textual set to rank the relevance of a phrase in the analysed document, which is then compared with the same metric gathered in the background set.

Despite achieving some of the best results, "Language Modeling" approaches require external data to be inputted by the user. Therefore, they will not be covered in this paper. In addition to the four categories, Hasan and Ng also observed that many techniques merge their approaches with heuristics to push forward their results. Table 1 presents some of the best-unsupervised keyphrase extraction techniques that do not demand a background textual set to be provided by the user.

Table 1. Unsupervised keyphrase extraction techniques.

Models	Graph-based	Topic-based clustering	Heuristics	Year
Text-Rank [8]	X	-	X	2004
BUAP [12]	X	-	X	2010
Topic-Rank [4]		X	X	2013
C-Rank	**X**	-	**X**	2019

Mihalcea and Tarau [8] presented the Text-Rank algorithm as a way to represent a text as a graph. First, they tokenize their text and annotate it with part-of-speech tags. Second, Text-Rank creates a syntactic filter and uses the tokens that pass by it as graph vertices, that are connected by undirected and unweighted edges representing their co-occurrence in the text. Third, the technique ranks the graph vertices with a variation of Google's PageRank algorithm [13] and selects the best-ranked as the document keywords. Finally, the algorithm identifies sequences of those tokens in the text and treats them as multi-word keywords, recognized as part of the final result along with the other candidates that are represented by a single token.

On the other hand, instead of constructing a graph with individual words as vertices, Ortiz *et al.* [12] developed *BUAP* that identifies the most frequent sequences of words in a document as vertices of a graph and weights them using the PageRank algorithm. Then, BUAP outputs 15 keyphrases formed by the top-3 multi-term candidates, the top-ranked single-words, and up to 3 of their expanded-forms, if there are acronyms among them.

Bougouin, Boudin and Daille [4] developed the *TopicRank* algorithm. First, it tokenizes, part-of-speech tags the text and clusters it into topics, weighted with the same ranking algorithm used in Text-Rank [8]. In the end, *TopicRank* outputs the most common keyphrases of the principal topics as a result.

The proposed approach in this paper, C-Rank, different from other state-of-the-art unsupervised keyphrase extraction approaches, does not request further data to be provided by the user. It relies on predefined background knowledge to leverage the meaning of terms in the extraction process. Instead of gather knowledge from statistical techniques, which demand a compendium that encompasses domain knowledge, C-Rank extracts information from a wide-coverage semantic-network.

3 C-Rank

C-Rank is an unsupervised algorithm that automatically extracts keyphrases from single documents without the support of a background textual collection. In this sense, the user needs to insert only the text from which the system should extract the keyphrases. It combines the knowledge of the document itself and contained inside BabelNet [11], collected through Babelfy [10]. C-Rank works in three stages illustrated in Fig. 1, and detailed in the following subsections. The first stage pre-processes the input document and annotate it with BabelNet concepts. The second stage takes those concepts as vertices and generates a co-occurrence graph, which is ranked and trimmed based on heuristics and its centrality, producing candidate keyphrases. The third and final stage identifies candidates that belong to the same phrase, which are merged and re-ranked, generating the final keyphrases list as output.

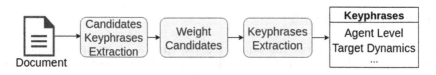

Fig. 1. C-Rank stages.

3.1 Extraction of Candidate Keyphrases

The first stage receives as input a textual document that is initially parsed to have its concepts linked with Babelnet, named here concept linking, resulting in a set of paragraphs annotated with babel synsets as illustrated in Fig. 2.

Babelfy[3] is the adopted approach to link the document concepts with Babelnet, semantic annotating them. Despite receiving whole texts to process and

---

[3] http://babelfy.org/.

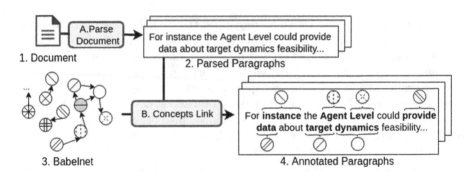

Fig. 2. C-Rank first stage: extraction of candidate keyphrases.

annotate, some constraints occurred during the use of the Babelfy, as a maximum length of the input text and the service inability to process some special characters.

In order to overcome these limitations, we parsed the input document - process A, Fig. 2 - segmenting it in sets of paragraphs with at most 5000 words, and removing all non-letter characters, except for "!", ".", "?", "-" and "", which are important as they segment sentences and words.

Afterward, the process B - Fig. 2 - links the parsed paragraphs using Babelfy, which identifies the correspondences between concepts and babel synsets. It can also determine multi-word concepts and its sub-concepts. For example, in "semantic network" the following synsets are linked "semantic", "network", and "semantic network". In our approach, we only use the multi-word concept annotation because the sub-concepts would always appear more in the document and they would be positively biased in C-Rank next stages.

3.2   Weight Candidates

The second stage receives the annotated paragraphs as input, generating a weighted directed co-occurrence graph based on it. This is ranked and trimmed with heuristics to output a graph of candidate keyphrases (*cf.* Fig. 3).

In order to construct the graph, process C (in Fig. 3) uses the paragraphs linked concepts as vertices and their co-occurrence to generate the direct edges, that connects directly subsequent vertices represented as solid arrows in Fig. 3; and indirect ones, linking concepts within a predefined window width, explored in Sect. 4.2, which are represented by dotted arrows.

The graph has their vertices weighted based on the number of times their concepts appear inside the document. This also occurs with the edges, that are weighted based on the distances between the concepts which its vertices represent (*cf.* Eq. 1), in which $weightEdge_{i,j}$ is the weight of the edge that connects vertice i with vertice j; $In(j)$ refers to the set of edges that arrive at j; $window$ is the predefined window width; and $distance(i,j)$ stands for the co-occurrence distance in text between the concepts that the vertices i and j represent.

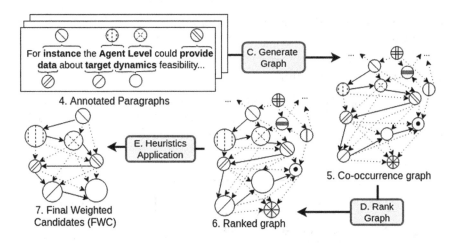

Fig. 3. C-Rank second stage: weight candidates.

$$weightEdge_{i,j} = \sum_{i \in In(j)} 1 - log_{window} distance(i,j) \qquad (1)$$

Process D (in Fig. 3) ranks the vertices of the co-occurrence graph to obtain the candidate keyphrases. It uses the centrality degree value normalized by the maximum possible degree of a node. Although being a simple measure, the degree centrality achieves higher results in the identification of keyphrase on graph-based approaches, compared to other traditional ranking techniques [2].

C-Rank second stage also applies four heuristics into the graph, which were studied on a training set and are analyzed in Sect. 4.2. However, one must previously determine how to label each concept of the graph before applying the heuristics, because the same idea can be expressed divergently. As an example, "Artificial Intelligence" and "AI", both represent the same concept, despite being written differently. We label each concept based on its first occurrence in the document because we understand that it may cover the concept extended form instead of its initials, considering that usually, in a text, a concept is introduced before its abbreviation.

The first heuristic identifies the Part-of-speech (POS) of each candidate label and discards those that have any word different from a noun, a verb or an adjective, which are the most common keyphrase POS tags. The second one cuts the 87% lower-ranked candidates (LRC) if the analyzed document is long - has more than 1000 words - in order to reduce noise. The third heuristic re-ranks the candidates favoring those formed by multiple words, as they are more likely to be chosen to become keyphrases; it uses $c_w = c_w^{\frac{1}{len(c)}}$, in which c_w represents the candidate weight and $len(c)$ its number of words. The fourth and final heuristic discards all candidates that first appeared after a *CutOff* threshold of the text, defined to 18% for long documents, as keyphrases usually are introduced at the beginning of a text.

3.3   Keyphrase Extraction

C-Rank third stage (Fig. 4) receives the Final Weighted Candidates graph (FWC), identifies the concepts that belong together in the same keyphrase and outputs a re-ranked list of the input document keyphrases.

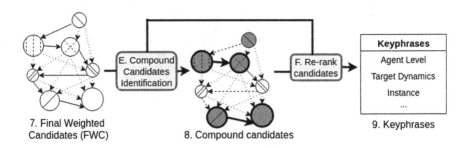

Fig. 4. C-Rank third stage: keyphrase extraction.

A "Compound Candidates" is the given definition of the candidates that belong to the same keyphrase, which are formed by the union of two different concepts. As in Fig. 4, the vertices with dotted patterns, which are labeled as "agent" and "level", despite being subsequently in the text, representing a single thought, were linked separately in stage one, Fig. 2. The compound candidates identification mitigates this issue and merges these concepts together, allowing them to be multi-word concepts.

The compound candidates identification considers the vertices relations in the graph to determine whether two terms represent a single concept and, therefore, belong together in the same keyphrase. To conclude that two candidates are compound, their subsequent co-occurrence must occur multiple times, which will vary depending on the text length. Therefore, compound candidates must be linked through a direct edge weighting at least $2 + (totalWords_d/1000)$, being $totalWords_d$ the number of words in the document d. This minimum weight ensures that the compound candidates appear at least twice in short texts and require a higher frequency in larger ones.

Next, the third stage weights the compound candidates to have a comparison metric to re-rank them based on the other candidate keyphrases. Process F in Fig. 4, calculates the normalized edges weight that connects the compound candidates (cf. Eq. 2), in which $NE_{i,j}$ refers to the normalized edge that links vertice i with vertice j; $w(Out(i))$ is the sum of all edges weights outgoing vertice i; and $w(In(j))$ is the sum of all edges weights incoming vertice j. Then, Process F calculates the ranking weight of the compound candidates as expressed by Eq. 3. It has $CC_{i,j}$ as the ranking value of the compound candidate formed by the vertices

i and j, and v_i, v_j are the weight of the vertices i and j from the FWC. At last step, Process F normalizes the compound candidates by their sum as presented by Eq. 4, in which $NCC_{i,j}$ is the normalized $CC_{i,j}$; and outputs a sorted list of the input document keyphrases $Keyphrases_d$, generated by the union of the Final Weighted Candidates and the top-ranked Compound Candidates. However, the NCC values difference decrease because of the normalization and after its union with the FWC they tend to cluster, standing out over the rest of the data. To overcome this issue, we join only 6 top-ranked Compound Candidates with the Final Weighted Candidates, a value defined from observations and tests over the keyphrases data-sets, thus $Keyphrases_d = FWC \cup NCC_{1:6}$.

$$NE_{i,j} = \frac{indirectEdge_{i,j}}{w(Out(i)) + w(In(j))} \tag{2}$$

$$CC_{i,j} = (v_i + v_j) * \left(\frac{NE_{i,j}}{\sum_{k \in NE} k}\right) \tag{3}$$

$$NCC_{i,j} = \frac{CC_{i,j}}{\sum_{t \in NE} t} \tag{4}$$

4   Experimental Evaluation

This section presents the analysis performed for C-Rank development and its evaluation, along with the protocols utilized during the corresponding experiments. We first introduce the used datasets, then report on the refinement performed in the heuristics values followed by the achieved results with *C-Rank* compared to other unsupervised keyphrase extraction techniques discussed in Sect. 2. C-Rank was developed on python and is available online[4].

4.1   Datasets

We use two standard benchmark datasets to evaluate the results achieved during and after C-Rank development and compare them with other keyphrase extraction approaches, which explored the same datasets.

The first is the SemEval2010 [7] dataset, divided in a trial, a train and a test set containing 40, 100 and 144 documents, respectively. Each one is an academic article belonging to one of four distinct ACM classifications. All the records are annotated with two sets of keyphrases as the author-assigned, which were part of the original document; and the reader-assigned, that were manually annotated by Computer Science students.

The INSPEC is the second dataset [6], composed of 3 sets of documents, a training set containing 3000 text files, a validation set with 1500 and a test set consisting of 500. Despite having a similar number of keyphrases assigned per document, the INSPEC dataset, different from the SemEval, is composed by academic abstracts, which makes its files shorter.

---

[4] https://github.com/maurodlt/C-Rank.

4.2   Parameters Refinement

During C-Rank development several variables were defined. To determine the best possible values for those variables, we performed different analyses considering the SemEval training set, which lead us to our defined heuristics and parameters. These were explored to evaluate *C-Rank* in the test set of the datasets (*cf.* Subsect. 4.3).

The co-occurrence window was the first variable defined in C-Rank development. Table 2 shows the results variance when the co-occurrence window changes and highlight in bold its optimal value.

Table 2. Micro-average F-scores achieved extracting the Top-5, Top-10, and Top-15 keyphrases on the SemEval2010 trainning dataset varying the graph co-occurrence window.

Co-occurrence window	Top-5 (%)	Top-10 (%)	Top-15 (%)	Average (%)
2	15,23	19,98	20,49	18,6
3	**15,83**	**20,58**	**20,76**	**19,1**
4	15,83	20,48	20,81	19,0
5	15,83	20,53	20,95	19,1
10	15,63	20,26	20,95	18,9
100	14,96	19,82	21,08	18,6

Moreover, two heuristic variables values were defined, *LRC* and *CutOff* Threshold. Both of them were varied and provided optimal results when set to 87% and 18% respectively. Another analyzed C-Rank parameter was the centrality measure used to rank the co-occurrence graph. Table 3 shows the results when this metric changes.

In order to evaluate the Concept Linking usage and the proposed heuristics, Table 4 exhibits the variances of results applying our defined contributions. It clearly shows the improvement achieved when implementing the proposed techniques of concept linking and our elaborated heuristics.

4.3   Results

A final evaluation was performed to determine the effectiveness of *C-Rank* results achieved in both SemEval and INSPEC test datasets, which allows comparing *C-Rank* among other keyphrase extraction approaches. Table 5 presents the obtained results and Table 6 shows the comparison with other unsupervised keyphrases extraction techniques.

Table 3. Micro-average F-scores achieved extracting the Top-5, Top-10, and Top-15 keyphrases on the SemEval2010 trainning dataset varying the co-occurrence graph centrality measure.

Centrality measures	Top-5	Top-10	Top-15	Average
Closeness centrality	15,29	18,95	19,62	18,0
Betweenness centrality	15,36	19,49	20,76	18,5
Eigenvector	12,37	15,95	17,43	15,3
Pagerank	15,83	19,87	20,58	18,8
Degree centrality	**15,83**	**20,58**	**20,76**	**19,1**

Table 4. Micro-average F-scores achieved extracting the Top-5, Top-10, and Top-15 keyphrases on the SemEval2010 trainning dataset applying our proposed contributions.

Contributions	Top-5	Top-10	Top-15	Average
Using concept linking & heuristics	**15,83**	**20,58**	**20,76**	**19,1**
Using only concept linking	8,56	11,58	12,69	10,9
Using only heuristics	11,15	14,58	15,42	13,7
Without concept linking & heuristics	7,07	9,55	10,68	9,1

Table 5. Micro-average precision, recall and f-score on the extraction of Top-5, Top-10, and Top-15 keyphrases on the SemEval2010 and the Inspec test datasets.

	Top-5			Top-10			Top-15		
	P.	R.	F1.	P.	R.	F1.	P.	R.	F1.
SemEval	28	9,6	14,2	24,2	16,5	**19,6**	20,3	20,7	20,5
Inspec	32	16	21,2	23,1	23,5	**23,3**	17,1	25,9	20,6

Table 6. Comparison among micro-average precision, recall, and f-score achieved by extracting 10 keyphrases on the SemEval2010 and the INSPEC test datasets.

	SemEval			INSPEC		
	Precision	Recall	F-score	Precision	Recall	F-score
Text Rank	7,9	4,5	5,6[†]	14,2	12,5	12,7[†]
BUAP	17,8	12,4	14,4[†]	-	-	-
Topic-Rank	14,9	10,3	12,1[†]	27,6	31,5	27,9
C-Rank	24,2	16,5	**19,6**	23,1	23,5	**23,3**

[†] Indicates statistical significance improvement using a 2-sided paired t-test at $p < 0.05$.

5   Discussion

For the best of our knowledge, the algorithms not relying on user data and yielding the best results were outperformed by C-Rank with statistical significance in the SemEval 2010 dataset.

Our approach explored external background knowledge from Babelnet, which is an important characteristic. We found a relevant impact with the use of the concept linking in the keyphrase extraction (*cf.* Table 4). The Concept Linking approach is a novel aspect of our algorithm that might be further explored in the keyphrase extraction and other NLP tasks. It not just brings background knowledge that assists in the keyphrases identification, but further produces intermediate structures with concepts and entities semantically annotated that can be used to improve domain understatement and enrich other textual representation structures.

During the graph construction, the results varying the maximum co-occurrence distances between concepts (*cf.* Table 2) showed that the variance between results is low. Therefore, if performance is an issue, despite the lower f-scores, setting the co-occurrence window to 2 is equivalent of using only the direct-edges during all the algorithm, which would decrease the computational cost without much impact in the resultant values.

Despite the variance of the results, the heuristic values do not impact the algorithm performance. The centrality measure, on the other hand, can significantly decrease the results. As demonstrated by Boudin [3] and corroborated in Table 3, despite being simple, the degree centrality achieves higher results than other popular metrics usually used in keyphrase extraction algorithms, as the Pagerank. Considering the achieved results, further investigations on the use of concept linking in related NLP tasks could support and complement current solutions.

6   Conclusion

Keyphrase extraction plays a key role in the interpretation and analyses of textual documents. Existing proposals heavily rely on training datasets and external input. In this paper, we introduced *C-Rank*, an unsupervised keyphrase extraction algorithm that explored concept linking and graph-based techniques. Our approach enables the analysis of single documents and does not demand a textual compendium to be inserted by users. Our technique explored background knowledge from a wide-coverage semantic-network in a novel approach to obtain candidate Keyphrase and rank them. It used the concepts linked with the network as vertices of a co-occurrence graph, which is ranked based on heuristics and centrality measures. The conducted experiments showed the benefits of the elaborate features in the technique. The evaluation revealed that *C-Rank* outperformed, with statistical significance, all the unsupervised techniques that do not demand extra information to be provided by users on the SemEval2010 benchmark dataset. As future work, we plan to evaluate C-Rank against different types of data, other than scientific-related articles. Furthermore, we will investigate the C-Rank intermediate semantic structures produced in tasks related to the identification of domain topics based on a set of textual documents.

Acknowledgements. This work was financially supported by the São Paulo Research Foundation (FAPESP) (grants #2017/02325-5 and #2013/08293-7) (The opinions expressed in here are not necessarily shared by the financial support agency.) and the Coordenação de Aperfeiçoamento de Pessoal de Nível Superior - Brasil (CAPES) - Finance Code 001.

References

1. Augenstein, I., Das, M., Riedel, S., Vikraman, L., McCallum, A.: SemEval 2017 task 10: ScienceIE - extracting keyphrases and relations from scientific publications. In: Proceedings of the 11th International Workshop on Semantic Evaluation (SemEval-2017), pp. 546–555. Association for Computational Linguistics (2017)
2. Beliga, S., Meštrović, A., Martinčić-Ipšić, S.: An overview of graph-based keyword extraction methods and approaches. J. Inf. Organ. Sci. **39**(1), 1–20 (2015)
3. Boudin, F.: A comparison of centrality measures for graph-based keyphrase extraction. In: International Joint Conference on NLP, pp. 834–838 (2013)
4. Bougouin, A., Boudin, F., Daille, B.: TopicRank: graph-based topic ranking for keyphrase extraction. In: International Joint Conference on Natural Language Processing (IJCNLP), pp. 543–551 (2013)
5. Hasan, K.S., Ng, V.: Automatic keyphrase extraction: a survey of the state of the art. In: Proceedings of the 52nd Annual Meeting of the Association for Computational Linguistics (volume 1: Long Papers), vol. 1, pp. 1262–1273 (2014)
6. Hulth, A.: Improved automatic keyword extraction given more linguistic knowledge. In: Proceedings of the 2003 Conference on Empirical Methods in Natural Language Processing, pp. 216–223. Association for Computational Linguistics (2003)
7. Kim, S.N., Medelyan, O., Kan, M.Y., Baldwin, T.: Automatic keyphrase extraction from scientific articles. Lang. Resour. Eval. **47**(3), 723–742 (2013)
8. Mihalcea, R., Tarau, P.: TextRank: bringing order into text. In: Proceedings of the 2004 Conference on Empirical Methods in Natural Language Processing, pp. 404–411 (2004)
9. Miller, G.A., Beckwith, R., Fellbaum, C., Gross, D., Miller, K.J.: Introduction to WordNet: an on-line lexical database. Int. J. Lexicogr. **3**(4), 235–244 (1990)
10. Moro, A., Raganato, A., Navigli, R.: Entity linking meets word sense disambiguation: a unified approach. Comput. Linguist. **2**, 231–244 (2014)
11. Navigli, R., Ponzetto, S.P.: BabelNet: the automatic construction, evaluation and application of a wide-coverage multilingual semantic network. Artif. Intell. **193**, 217–250 (2012)
12. Ortiz, R., Pinto, D., Tovar, M., Jiménez-Salazar, H.: BUAP: an unsupervised approach to automatic keyphrase extraction from scientific articles. In: Proceedings of the 5th International Workshop on Semantic Evaluation, pp. 174–177. Association for Computational Linguistics (2010)
13. Page, L., Brin, S., Motwani, R., Winograd, T.: The PageRank citation ranking: bringing order to the web. Technical report 1999–66, Stanford InfoLab, November 1999. previous number = SIDL-WP-1999-0120

Scholarly Resources Structuring: Use Cases for Digital Libraries

Fidan Limani$^{(\boxtimes)}$, Atif Latif, and Klaus Tochtermann

Leibniz Information Centre for Economics, Kiel, Germany
{f.limani,a.latif,k.tochtermann}@zbw.eu
https://www.zbw.eu/

Abstract. With the growing generation of links between scholarly resources, information infrastructures such as Digital Libraries (DL) are compelled to explore the potential of data (re)usability. Coupled with the need for increased (research) transparency and reproducibility, linked scholarly resources offer major convenience to researchers in their daily research work. In this way, it is easier for them to get the different research artifacts – be it publication, dataset, workflow, etc. – that form the complete research picture and (re)use any/all of its parts in their work. In this paper, we explore the potential from harnessing such links for a DL environment, model them based on an emerging standard, and represent and publish them via the Semantic Web technology stack. Moreover, to highlight our unique approach for realization of scholarly link collection, we present few use cases to illustrate the potential for a DL environment. Through this study we claim that by adoption of links as new resources, DLs can extend their collection and/or services for their users.

Keywords: Scholarly links · Digital Library · Semantic Web

1 Introduction

Research data (RD) is shaping into one of the emerging scholarly research artifacts with considerable traction in the research community. The RD data generation and sharing potential [1] is putting it on par with traditional research artifacts, such as research publications. Moreover, it is becoming more common for scholarly-relevant organizations, such as government agencies, funding bodies, research events (conferences, journals, etc.), to accept and disseminate RD in addition to (or even independently, as is the case with data papers) research publications. Additionally, initiatives[1] that increase RD impact and enable the development of accompanying services and its (re)use are also becoming a common research practice.

---

[1] FAIR principles: https://www.force11.org/group/fairgroup/fairprinciples.

Leibniz Information Centre for Economics.

E. Garoufallou et al. (Eds.): MTSR 2019, CCIS 1057, pp. 248–259, 2019.
https://doi.org/10.1007/978-3-030-36599-8_22

Sharing RD is meant to support reproducibility and provide reusability [2]. However, to get the real impact of RD in sense of reuseability, it is critical to accept and promote RD along with other notable complementary research artifacts. Research publications, as one such resource type, could provide the context required to reproduce and reuse RD, as well as use RD in ways not originally envisioned by the authors. This is but one example that demonstrates the benefits of providing relevant resource artifacts as a linked, "research bundle"; other research artifacts can similarly provide benefits when combined with relevant research resources.

In parallel to researchers as producers of RD, changing research practices are affecting the expectations that users (as consumers) have for information infrastructures such as Digital Libraries (DL). As new research artifacts become available, DLs have an opportunity to strive for a more comprehensive research picture that includes different aspects of a research besides publications, and exploring new use cases the benefit that this brings to them.

Due to the prominence of RD, having already explored scenarios of integrating heterogeneous resources with research publications and scientific blogs (see [3]), we now turn to publications-to-data links as complementary resources for DLs. Our aim in this paper is to structure links via suitable vocabularies and, as a follow up, explore potential use cases for DLs based on these link collections.

2   Research Motivation and Use Cases

With the emergence of new research artifacts, users require a more holistic view of a research body of work. In this fashion, the general motivation for this work is to provide users of a DL with the experience of a single, complementary, "research bundle", provided in a "one-stop shop" fashion. We focus on research publications and RD as key components of this research unit.

2.1   Research Artifact Links

Providing links between research resources as a way to enable reproducibility and credit researchers for sharing their data (see [4]), to mention but a few, is already recognized and supported in the research community. This enables the development of services based on the links between different research resource types (publications, data, software, etc.). Figure 1 illustrates an instance of a link model that we adopt to represent and base our use cases on. The link instance can bring different aspects of a research into (a single) view; model extensions as new research artifacts become available is also possible.

2.2   Research Motivation

Motivated by data reuse or reproducibility, in a typical scenario, given a publication, the user wants to also access the supplementing RD. Note that the reverse "discovery path" could also work: given a RD, she would try to identify research

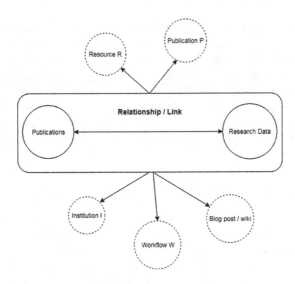

Fig. 1. A link model bringing multiple research artifacts together

or data paper(s) that help contextualize the dataset for a better understanding of its applicability, limitations, etc. Moreover, in order to apply the existing or test a new approach to a wider RD collection, she might be interested in additional RD collections.

An environment that handles different research artifacts could rely on the links between artifacts to provide a complementary research picture to its users. Such complementarity is what we want to enable by providing a semantic structure to the links.

The research motivation, then, requires that we support (meta)data integration of heterogeneous collections (of research artifacts), including publication, RD, and links between them, and represent them in a common model with a query capacity to support the use case scenarios, part of which are demonstrated in Sect. 6.

2.3   Motivating Technology

Linked Data (LD)[2] provides a conceptual and technological fit for our research undertaking – typifying the links between scholarly resources. Based on established vocabularies, links are structured to provide precise meaning. Moreover, being represented in RDF, the model is easily extendable, as new attributes that describe this research context evolve, or new RDF vocabularies become available. Lastly, since it is to be expected that research resources be represented differently across projects, LD is especially handy for (meta)data integration of heterogeneous data sources. In the modeling effort of the link collections, we will

---

[2] http://linkeddata.org/.

consider a variety of vocabularies that reflect the metadata requirements, and are well-established, open, well maintained and documented.

3   Related Work

The availability of different research artifacts is presenting new opportunities to scholarly research infrastructures and many initiatives are already under way to provide a more complete (and complementary) research picture by bringing these deliverables together. The research resources linking is just one approach to this effect.

Mayernik et al. [5] report on the challenges and opportunities for linking resources across institutional repositories. Burton et al. [6] present the Scholix initiative: a framework that supports linking resources between providers (hubs) of scholarly literature. In another work, Hoekstra et al. (see [7]) explore linking from FigShare[3] articles to external resources, such as DBpedia, DBLP, etc., and publish the links as Linked Open Data (LOD). At a more general level, projects like Research Object[4] and RMap[5] bring research deliverables of different types in a common unit that parties can act upon. In this way, they recognize and handle a broader research perspective via its corresponding artifacts, from workflow to software to presentation slides, etc., as means to provide a richer scientific context for users. Moreover, being extensible enables them to accommodate new artifacts, depending on the requirements (see [8] for such an example).

Kramer et al. (see [9]) focus on relating semantified (RDF represented) datasets to relevant resources (publications, organizations, studies, people, etc.) in the domain of social sciences, and describe 5 use cases that benefit from this undertaking. Moreover, Wiljes et al. (see [10]) apply Linked Open Data principles to represent the research data artifacts of an institutional repository. This provided an effective approach to handling RD heterogeneity, RD contextualization (considering available institutional publications), and enrichment capabilities to external collections (such as DBpedia). Relying on the (Semantic) Web technologies, Kauppinen et al. [11] introduce a vocabulary (the Linked Science Core Vocabulary) that enables structuring research resources (data, publications, workflows, processes, etc.) to be better (semantically) represented and used (accessed, referenced, linked, etc.). Finally, Fathalla et al. [12] in their work bring fine-grained access to the constituting parts of survey articles, as one of the research output in scholarly communication. Via an ontology designed for this purpose, they show the benefits for researchers during the literature search on a certain topic.

4   Dataset Selection

In this section, we present the link collection from the 2 sources selected for this paper; we further describe the resources in terms of their metadata features

---

[3] https://figshare.com/.

[4] http://www.researchobject.org/.

[5] https://rmap-hub.org/.

required to denote these resources in a common representation model. In selecting the dataset we were guided by 2 aspects: (1) dataset that supports use cases important to DL and (2) one that provides a large collection to support various scenarios. In following, we briefly present both link collections:

1. Intra-institutional link collection: Modest in size, consists of resources from a single domain (economics) – originally not linked with each other – part of the same DL ecosystem and governed by a single institution. This selection enables us to explore use cases that especially exploit the benefit of linked resources in a DL. In this case, we rely on a link collection that we create for the purpose of this paper; it involves publications and datasets as resources for the link.
2. Public link collection: A richer collection (cross-domain, large in size, etc.) is especially important to study research aspects or benefits that generalize over different DL settings. Such a link collection that spans multiple research domains and enables us to implement interesting use case scenarios – cross-disciplinary ones included, typically out of scope for individual DLs, is what we rely on for this dataset selection.

Following is a brief description of both collections together with the rationale for using them in this work.

(a) DL publication-to-data links

The ZBW[6] has two subject portals that deal with publications and research data, respectively. Although part of the same institution, there are no established links between resources from the two collections. Researchers are encouraged to submit their publications and data in these repositories, but there is no (explicit) linking of the two required or provided. We apply a simple approach to establish links between these resources automatically, and use them to demonstrate one of our use cases in this paper. Let's see a short description of each subject portal, and the linking approach for these two collections:

- EconBiz[7]: a subject portal focusing on publications from the domain of economics and business administration. Its collection consists of many types of publications, such as conference or journal papers, books chapters, master and PhD thesis and working papers, etc. Currently the collection stores more than 10 million publications across participating databases, with a minimal collection of datasets (not considered in our experiment), accompanied with a set of services for discovery and recommendation to support researchers.
- JDA[8]: targets RD from journals in the domain of economics and management, including different formats: PDF, text, tabular, scripts or implementation code, etc. As a service, it supports journals as a platform for storage, dissemination, and access control for their datasets. At the time of harvest the JDA collection contains 106 datasets from 6 different journals.

---

[6] https://www.zbw.eu.

[7] https://www.econbiz.de/.

[8] http://www.journaldata.zbw.eu/.

– Publications-to-Dataset linking: Our aim is to link publication and dataset that stem from the same research work. In case an author has a publication in EconBiz and a dataset in JDA, we do the matching based on the degree of overlap between the publication and dataset title (often, a "replication data/code/script", etc., string is added to the dataset title). The result from our simple matching processes resulted with 70 JDA entries to EconBiz publications, thus this represents 70 data-to-publication links to use.

(b) Public link collection: The Scholexplorer Service
For the purpose of this work we use the link collection from OpenAIRE's Data Literature Interlinking service, Scholexplorer[9]. This service currently interlinks more than 1.3 million publications and 8.2 million datasets, all via more than 56 million bi-directional links, spanning multiple disciplines. It is worth noting that there are two types of links stored in this collection: dataset-to-publications and dataset-to-dataset links, from different data providers, all modelled according to common link metadata schema, which we introduce later in the paper.

5   Domain Modeling: Publications, Datasets and Links

Many initiatives that model research resources linking are emerging (see Sect. 3), and based on our resource features we choose Scholix [13] as a representation framework. In this section we briefly present the metadata requirements of our 2 datasets, and proceed to represent the resulting model via existing (machine-readable) structured vocabularies for an even wider access and distribution.

5.1   Publications and Datasets: Metadata Requirements

In terms of metadata, research resources span from having minimal to extensive metadata descriptions. As a result, when modeling the resources there is a need to balance between use case requirements (based on available metadata) and model capability. At times we struggle with providing the minimum-required metadata, and at times we have to leave certain elements out of the model in order to reach this balance. Next, we describe the decisions which we took for our datasets modeling and links collection.

(a) Publications and Datasets: Metadata features
This selection contains the common descriptive metadata, such as title, creators, identifier, publisher, publication date, license information, etc. For practical reasons – no immediate support for current use cases foreseen, for example – we leave few elements that can be found in both collections out of our "metadata model". While important to the respective communities, these elements represent fine-grained descriptions and fall outside our current research scope. The metadata features that we consider from both collections determine the use case scenarios that are able to be implemented; as more metadata become available

---

[9] http://scholexplorer.openaire.eu/index.html.

for both resource types, the number of possible use cases will increase correspondingly. In addition to the properties in Scholix, we also include:

- Subject term: denotes the subject of a resource; it presents a terminology linking capacity for our datasets – a nice feat to explore use cases that involve both research publications and RD.
- Number of files (applies to RD only): designates the number of files that constitute a dataset. We identify use case scenarios where such aspect is important to a user.

When determining the final set of metadata to consider, we balanced between getting as close as possible to a standardized model, as well as selecting metadata specific for the disciplines and communities. The former provides modeling breadth, especially when considering future dataset extensions, whereas the latter provides modeling depth to the use cases we implement.

(b) Links: Metadata description approach
We model the links based on the **link information model** from Scholix[10]. The model captures common attributes for research resources (publications and datasets) and links between them, which makes it relatively easy for communities to apply (see Table 1). The properties in bold are mandatory, whereas the rest are optional – a good (minimalist) take for available metadata that would adopt this model.

Table 1. Link and Resource properties from Scholix model

Link	Resource (source and target)
Link Publication Date (1)	**Object Identifier (1)**
Link Provider (1..N)	**Object Type (1)**
Relationship Type (1)	Object Title (0..1)
License URL (0..1)	Object Publisher (0..1)
	Object Creator (0..N)
	Object Publication Date (0..1)

Let's briefly treat the **link** attributes of this model, which is different from the resources it links (publications and datasets): date of link publication and its provider(s) (there can be more than 1 provider for a link) are self-explanatory; relationship type of the link specifies the nature of the resources being linked (does one derive from, cite, is part of, etc., the other resource?); license URL provides license information for the link (excluding the resources being linked). The link attributes could provide different cases for users, such as data provenance and information quality (depending who the provider is), certain relationship of linked resources, licensing arrangements, etc.

---

[10] http://www.scholix.org.

The links in the model are one-directional, and we rely on the Relationship Type property for that. The values for these properties are adopted from DataCite[11]'s controlled vocabulary for its `relationType` sub-property. Before Scholix v3, there was an Inverse Relationship Type property included in the schema to denote a bi-directional link, but an ontology that describes relationships could easily infer and support such a feature for a link if necessary.

We largely adopt Scholix's information package, with a slight extension based on the requirements discussed in (a), which pertains to resources attributes. We next represent the resources from our collections into something more semantical.

5.2   Getting Semantical: RDF Modeling

As described in Sect. 4, metadata attributes of the resources we deal with – publications, datasets, and links – are generally of descriptive nature, which supports functionalities such as discovery, (resource) identification, etc. Since we focus on (semantic) structuring of links, our goal was to reuse established vocabularies instead of creating ones from scratch. Due to the availability and maturity of vocabularies that describe datasets and publications, it was straightforward to select and structure (in RDF) these resources; for the specifics of link structuring, starting with the link itself, i.e., denoting that a resource is of type link, we combined few vocabularies to support the link metadata attributes proposed by the Scholix framework.

Regardless of resource type, the common, general attributes are captured well by the Dublin Core Metadata Initiative (DCMI)[12] and the Bibliographic Framework Initiative[13]. The former provides for usual descriptive metadata properties such as title, publisher, creator, subject, date, and size & duration; whereas the latter enables to specify the type of the resource – publication or dataset. Note that the "size and duration" property from DCMI terms supports the description of the dataset in terms of size, as introduced as a requirement in Sect. 5.1 (a).

Some of the resources in our collection contain structured identification attributes, including the scheme, identifier, and the role it plays in an identification scenario (primary vs alternative resource identification, for example). DataCite ontology [14], developed based on the metadata standard of the same name, addresses the identification aspects for all the resources of our model.

In addition to the descriptive vocabularies listed above, the Citation Typing Ontology[14] is used to represent the "link" part of the model. Its properties enable us to define the citing and the cited entities, as well as the relationship that these entitites are linked by, such as "cited/cites as data source" or "cited as related", etc. Its additional attributes for publication date and license are based on DCMI, whereas the Europeana Data Model [15] supports the link attribute required to define the entity that provides the link.

---

[11] https://schema.datacite.org/.

[12] http://www.dublincore.org/specifications/dublin-core/dcmi-terms/.

[13] https://www.loc.gov/bibframe/.

[14] https://sparontologies.github.io/cito/current/cito.html.

There is always the option to extend existing vocabularies/ontologies or develop a custom one for the problem at hand. However, amid multiple competing/different link models available, a standardized version has yet to come. Thus, we rely on existing vocabularies that not necessarily are conceptualized with linking research resources as a key driver, but nonetheless are a good fit to link model requirements.

6 Links Harvesting and Storage: The Workflow

This section describes the workflow which we made use of in this study. It is a three stage approach which starts with resources harvesting, modeling and conversion to RDF, and ends with storage of resulting links (see Fig. 2). In order to share the technical environment and processing of our datasets, following is a brief description of the activities that constitute all the parts of the workflow.

- **Link collections:** We establish the intra-institutional link collection (EconBiz-JDA) via the REST API of the corresponding repositories. For the Scholexplorer collection we use the (JSON) data dump available in the Zenodo research repository [16] (the Scholexplorer REST API was unavailable at the time of harvest). Due to its large size, the collection is organized in several (compressed) files that contain link batches of approximately 2.5 GB each, of which we include only a subset sufficient for this work.
- **Link harvesting:** For the generation of first link collection, we search the EconBiz collection for a match (mainly based on the title) with every dataset available in JDA. With this approach, we were able to identify 70 links. Scholexplorer, on the other hand provides the bulk of the links and is more straightforward to harvest. The subset that we use consists of over 2.3 Million links.
- **Link modeling and storage:** We convert link collections to RDF based on the vocabularies presented in 4.2. For the RDFizing process we rely on Apache Jena[15]. We store the datasets in separate named graphs, as this provides easier future management of the collection, such as update, maintenance, but also provision of a more granular access.

7 Use Cases: Explored Scenarios

In general terms, the use cases revolve around (fine-grained) search and, as applicable, involve different metadata elements that describe links, publications and research data, such as: publication date, resource provider, persistent identifier, resource type of the resource and dataset size, etc.

---

[15] https://jena.apache.org/.

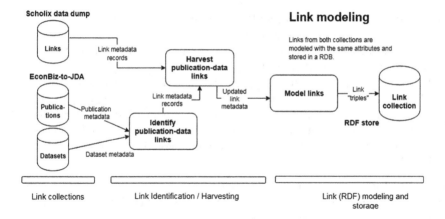

Fig. 2. From datasets to central link collection: a workflow

From Publications to Data: Find RD that support or are relevant to a publication. This can be a data paper or data that revolves around the subject of the paper to certain extent (a narrower, related, etc., subject term).

We start with the scenario where the user retrieves the RD that directly support (as a primary source of data) the research paper at hand. If the user wants to further specify the result, she can refine the query to include the most re-used RD in the collection (based on the number of times it has been cited). On the other hand, if the results are scarce or the user wants to broaden the search, she could also retrieve all the RD by the same author of the paper. In another scenario, a user can retrieve the "trending" RD (RD being cited the most in a more recent time frame) – and their corresponding publications – for a quick impression of what her community is currently working on. In a final scenario for this part, the user can rely on the "subject terms" to search for a field of interest across link providers for a more interdisciplinary search scenario (search for a fish type to see its fishing quotas, market fluctuations in a certain period, as well as the impact from climate conditions on its habitat).

Importantly, the DL collection we are working with primarily supports publications, thus in presented scenarios we assume the user first selects a publication and then proceeds to find RD. This aspect can easily be reversed (start with RD of interest, and find publications and/or RD) and practical to the DL especially if its collection reaches a critical mass of RD.

From Data to (Even More) Data: In this set of scenarios, the user starts with a RD and wants to find relevant/related RD within and across research domains.

Having collected (a set of) RD, a researcher wants to identify related RD from the same subject (or field) that she could re-use (for reproducibility) or combine it with her own or additional RD for new research purposes. In this case, the "subject term" metadata element plays an important role as it enables us to search across collections from different institutions that provided their links (and consequently, publications and RD). As mentioned, the available metadata in our collection provide many filtering capabilities for this scenario such as: restricting links based on certain time frame, the type of resources they linked to and the institution that publishes them, etc.

Moreover, users want to see which are the related disciplines of the "trending" RD. Usually every linked resource has a metadata about the entity that cover certain research fields. In this way, a researcher who wants to search for RD of interest from few research fields, such as economics and social sciences, can explore what "trending" RD from one discipline could be matched with others in the other discipline.

Generic Use Case Scenarios: This set of scenarios provides more general information, which, although not the first use case of choice, could turn useful to the researchers; examples include:

- List resources that are linked by the same publisher, publication date, domain, and other relevant metadata.
- Based on links that cite my research artifacts (publications or RD), who is using my RD? In what scenarios and context (information you get after reading a citing paper or RD, for example)? This question would apply both to individual researchers and institutions.
- Show me the potential of relevant resources based on a certain criteria such as: classification terms for the subject of coverage, resources type, number of files that constitute a resource, etc.

We used Apache Jena framework (and its Fuseki server) to realize the mentioned use cases (either programmatically, or via its SPARQL editor); for the reproducibility of use case scenarios, we provide RDF dump to interested parties.

8   Conclusion

In this work we showcased the links between scholarly resources as value drivers to information infrastructures such DLs. We harvested more than 2.7 million links from 2 different link collections, and structured them in a common representation model via Semantic Web technologies. As a result, we were able to explore many use case scenarios that fit in a DL environment.

With the initial results in, we plan to test our workflow with the complete link collection from Scholexplorer, as well as other available collections. Another follow up includes enrichment of links and resources being linked for a richer research/knowledge context for users. An issues that we identified during our work was the metadata inconsistencies for the different resources (identification schemes, metadata variety, etc.), which we need to consider especially when expanding our scope (and RDF link collection).

In our future work, in addition to publications and datasets, we plan to "package" resources via linking. Moreover, being that we use a graph representation for the harvested links, we would like to experiment with alternative graph representation strategies, such as the Label Property Graph (LPG), and explore more analysis-driven scenarios over the resulting link collection. These analyses are especially important as the link collection grows and includes new resource types. Finally, during the RDF modeling part of the work, at times, it felt like there is a lack of an ontology that would represent the link model adopted in the study, and we see this as a beneficial follow up to this work.

References

1. Borgman, C.L.: The conundrum of sharing research data. J. Am. Soc. Inf. Sci. Technol. **63**(6), 1059–1078 (2012)
2. Kratz, J., Strasser, C.: Data publication consensus and controversies. F1000Research **3**, 94 (2014)
3. Limani, F., Latif, A., Tochtermann, K.: Bringing scientific blogs to digital libraries. In: WEBIST, pp. 284–290 (2017)
4. Burton, A., et al.: The data-literature interlinking service: towards a common infrastructure for sharing data-article links. Program **51**(1), 75–100 (2017)
5. Mayernik, M.S., Phillips, J., Nienhouse, E.: Linking publications and data: challenges, trends, and opportunities. D-Lib Mag. **22**(5/6), 11 (2016)
6. Burton, A., et al.: The Scholix framework for interoperability in data-literature information exchange. D-Lib Mag. **2/3**, 12 (2017)
7. Hoekstra, R., Groth, P., Charlaganov, M.: Linkitup: semantic publishing of research data. In: Presutti, V., et al. (eds.) SemWebEval 2014. CCIS, vol. 475, pp. 95–100. Springer, Cham (2014). https://doi.org/10.1007/978-3-319-12024-9_12
8. Stocker, M.: From data to machine readable information aggregated in research objects. D-Lib Mag. **23**(1), 1 (2017)
9. Kramer, S., Leahey, A., Southall, H., Vompras, J., Wackerow, J.: Using RDF to describe and link social science data to related resources on the web (2012)
10. Wiljes, C., et al.: Towards linked research data: an institutional approach (994) (2013)
11. Kauppinen, T., Baglatzi, A., Keßler, C.: Linked science: interconnecting scientific assets, pp. 383–400 (2016)
12. Fathalla, S., Vahdati, S., Auer, S., Lange, C.: Towards a knowledge graph representing research findings by semantifying survey articles. In: Kamps, J., Tsakonas, G., Manolopoulos, Y., Iliadis, L., Karydis, I. (eds.) TPDL 2017. LNCS, vol. 10450, pp. 315–327. Springer, Cham (2017). https://doi.org/10.1007/978-3-319-67008-9_25
13. RDA/WDS Scholarly Link Exchange Working Group. Scholix metadata schema for exchange of scholarly communication links (version 3). D-Lib Magazine (2017)
14. Peroni, S., Shotton, D., Ashton, J., Barton, A., Gramsbergen, E., Jacquemot, M.-C.: DataCite2RDF: mapping DataCite metadata schema 3.1 terms to RDF, February 2016
15. Isaac, A., et al.: Europeana data model primer (2013)
16. La Bruzzo, S., Manghi, P.: OpenAIRE scholeXplorer service: Scholix JSON Dump, March 2018

OntoPPI: Towards Data Formalization on the Prediction of Protein Interactions

Yasmmin Cortes Martins[1(✉)], Maria Cláudia Cavalcanti[2(✉)],
Luis Willian Pacheco Arge[1(✉)], Artur Ziviani[1(✉)],
and Ana Tereza Ribeiro de Vasconcelos[1(✉)]

[1] National Laboratory of Scientific Computing, Petrópolis, Brazil
{yasmmin,l.willian,ziviani,atrv}@lncc.br
[2] Military Institute of Engineering, Rio de Janeiro, Brazil
yoko@ime.eb.br

Abstract. The Linking Open Data (LOD) cloud is a global data space
for publishing and linking structured data on the Web. The idea is to
facilitate the integration, exchange, and processing of data. The LOD
cloud already includes a lot of datasets that are related to the biological area. Nevertheless, most of the datasets about protein interactions
do not use metadata standards. This means that they do not follow
the LOD requirements and, consequently, hamper data integration. This
problem has impacts on the information retrieval, specially with respect
to datasets provenance and reuse in further prediction experiments. This
paper proposes an ontology to describe and unite the four main kinds
of data in a single prediction experiment environment: (i) information
about the experiment itself; (ii) description and reference to the datasets
used in an experiment; (iii) information about each protein involved in
the candidate pairs. They correspond to the biological information that
describes them and normally involves integration with other datasets;
and, finally, (iv) information about the prediction scores organized by
evidence and the final prediction. Additionally, we also present some
case studies that illustrate the relevance of our proposal, by showing
how queries can retrieve useful information.

Keywords: Protein interaction ontology · Biological dataset · Linked
open data · Prediction experiment

1 Introduction

The construction of the Semantic Web has been an important effort towards the
reuse of data and text resources. It involves, for instance, the introduction of
semantic annotations on these resources, using the Resource Description Framework (RDF[1]). The idea is to use URIs (Uniform Resource Identifiers) to identify
such resources, building a global data space containing billions of described data

---

[1] http://www.w3.org/rdf.

© Springer Nature Switzerland AG 2019
E. Garoufallou et al. (Eds.): MTSR 2019, CCIS 1057, pp. 260–271, 2019.
https://doi.org/10.1007/978-3-030-36599-8_23

as a navigable Web of Data [1]. The Linking Open Data (LOD)[2] initiative is one of the main efforts that has been contributing to the growth of the Web of Data. It provides a set of best practices that should be adopted by data publishers to facilitate data linking. One of them is organizing the data according to the concepts of their corresponding domains, using controlled vocabularies or ontologies.

The biological area figures among those domains that have been described along the last years with the semantic web technology. From this biological area, we can derive the Protein-Protein Interaction (PPI) [5] area that indicates functional and physical associations between proteins. PPI have an important role in biological processes that orchestrate up level functions in the organisms. In the PPI area, the databases that provide this kind of information have different ways to export the data. Most export as tab separated values, whereas other common formats are psi-mi xml, mitab, and xml/mitab [14]. Nevertheless, each database has its own metadata to describe data, which makes it difficult to exchange them. Typically, these formats cannot express how the dataset was generated, the evidences used, or the scores derived from each characteristic computed from the candidate interaction pairs. In the literature, there are some efforts in this direction [2,7,10,15], but they do not cover all the desired specifications to represent the PPI's experiment process. Some of these works cover specific biological areas involved in the process and others only describe machine learning experiments or metadata designed to pipelines and data flow. Others focus on protein feature's annotation, but do not describe the provenance of the annotations. For instance, they do not register the score decisions that were generated by different computational methods used to detect protein interactions.

In this paper, we aim at building a lightweight ontology, a formal explicit specification of a shared conceptualization [16]. Thus, we propose the OntoPPI ontology to overcome the aforementioned limitations (as discussed in further detail in Sect. 5). OntoPPI has classes and properties to deal with PPI data provenance; protein information annotations (including the integration through identifiers from other databases like Gene Ontology (GO),[3] KEGG,[4] and Pfam[5]) to explain the interactions and filter the network formed by the interactions to turn the visualization easier. OntoPPI also reports scores obtained from each evidence, which helps to analyze and evaluate the interactions. All these items contribute to a better understanding and communication between scientists that study and use such protein interactions. We have used OntoPPI to annotate three predicted PPI datasets, test the data flow, and execute scenarios to illustrate the data that can be retrieved.

The remainder of the paper is organized as follows. Section 2 brings a brief contextualization about protein interactions and the types of experiments to

---

[2] http://www.w3.org/wiki/SweoIG/TaskForces/CommunityProjects/
LinkingOpenData.
[3] http://geneontology.org/.
[4] https://www.kegg.jp/.
[5] https://pfam.xfam.org/.

detect them. OntoPPI classes and properties are introduced in Sect. 3. Section 4 discusses query examples of how to use the data annotated with OntoPPI to achieve important information about the experiments. Related work is discussed in Sect. 5 and OntoPPI is positioned in relation to them. Finally, we conclude the paper and discuss future works in Sect. 6.

2   Background

PPI are physical contacts with molecular docking that occur in a cell or in an live organism [5]. There are several types of functional associations between biomolecular entities (genes, proteins, metabolites). These associations, or PPI, can be detected in two different ways: computationally and experimentally.

The computational alternative, also known as PPI prediction, is based on probabilistic methods and can be performed addressing many candidate protein pairs at zero cost. On the other hand, the experimental alternative must be performed in specialized laboratories, and involves a laborious and costly protocol. Moreover, this alternative can deal with just a few protein pairs at a time [3].

Among such methodologies, the most promising ones take advantage of multiple evidences, i.e., they can use specific information about the proteins to infer an association between them. Some of these methodologies use machine learning algorithms (e.g. classifiers) and take into account their results, as evidences, to come up with interaction prediction results. Section 3 presents the OntoPPI ontology, which was designed to describe results of PPI prediction methods when classifiers and multiple evidences are involved.

In summary, prediction experiments involve: (i) pre-processing of the PPI datasets, for training the algorithms; (ii) acquisition of information about the proteins of the candidate pairs to be used as evidences; (iii) features generation for each candidate pair by calculating probabilities using those algorithms; and (iv) the final score generation for the candidate pairs.

3   OntoPPI Overview

In this paper, we introduce OntoPPI, an ontology built to formalize and standardize the PPI prediction experiment process. OntoPPI general schema is illustrated in Fig. 1. This schema reused some classes and properties from two already existent ontologies: Biopax and Biomanta.

Biopax [6] covers a lot of concepts and it is very complex. Biopax represents biological pathways at the molecular and cellular level and aims at facilitating the exchange of pathway data. However, Biopax has some classes such as *Entity* and *Interaction*, and the data property *participant* that can be reused by OntoPPI to represent the same concepts in our domain. Biomanta [13] is the closest ontology as compared with OntoPPI because it has metadata designed with focus on the PPI domain. However, so far it does not cover all the data flow involved in an experiment. The class reused from Biomanta was the *PredictedObservation*, there are some object properties in Biomanta, but the range is attached to instances of specific detection methods (experimental validation techniques used in laboratory) in Biopax.

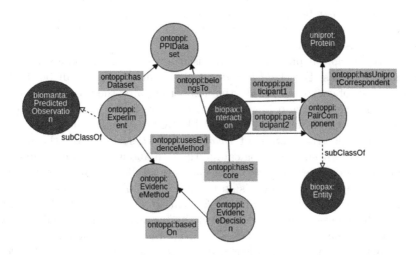

Fig. 1. OntoPPI classes and their object properties showing their relationships.

OntoPPI includes the *ontoppi:Experiment* class, which is a subclass of the *biomanta:PredictObservation* class. The *Experiment* class is associated (*ontoppi:usesEvidenceMethod*) with the *ontoppi:EvidenceMethod* class, which represents the methods that can be used for an experiment. However, it is important to highlight that the *Experiment* class aims to represent computational and experimental experiments. In addition, the *Experiment* class is associated (*ontoppi:hasDataset*) with the *ontoppi:PPIDataset* class, representing datasets used in both kinds of experiments.

A typical PPI dataset contains a set of candidate protein pairs. Each protein in OntoPPI is represented in the *ontoppi:PairComponent* class, which is a subclass of *biopax:Entity* and corresponds to (*ontoppi:hasUniprotCorrespondent*) a protein identifier from Uniprot database[6]. To represent the candidate protein pair, we reused the *biopax:Interaction* class, which is associated with two components (*ontoppi:PairComponent*). Each candidate pair is associated with a PPI dataset. This association is represented by the *ontoppi:belongsTo* property. Finally, *biopax:Interaction* is also associated with *ontoppi:hasScore* and with *ontoppi:EvidenceDecision* class to represent the results of evidence methods. Additionally, *ontoPPI:EvidenceDecision* class is attached (*ontoppi:basedOn*) with the *ontoppi:EvidenceMethod* class.

Considering the experiment process and the concepts reused from the mentioned ontologies, OntoPPI data flow starts with the descriptors about experiment configuration. *Experiment* class, in this context, means a PPI experiment that can use one or a set of datasets to evaluate protein pair candidates.

---

[6] https://www.uniprot.org.

The *Experiment* class properties are *hasOwner*, *hasContactEmail*, and *has-Description*. *hasOwner* property informs who is responsible for the data provided and for the experiment. *hasContactEmail* property has the information about contact email that can be used to inform the status of experiment execution. *has-Description* property shares the domain with *PPIDataset* and *EvidenceMethod* classes, and is used for describing these classes.

The *hasDescription* property can be used to give details about the experiment, such as goals. For the *PPIDataset* class, this property can be used to describe details of each dataset, like the number of pairs, the proportion of negative and positive ones, and how the datasets were formed (original database where the pairs came from (for instance, STRING[7])). Finally, this property can also be used to describe details of *EvidenceMethod*, such as how the method calculates its score from the biological information about the protein pairs.

The object properties of *Experiment* class are *hasDataset* and *usesEvidence Method*. The range of *hasDataset* is an instance of *PPIDataset* class. The range of *usesEvidenceMethod* is an instance of *EvidenceMethod* class. *PPIDataset* represents a PPI Dataset given for evaluation that normally contains pairs known to interact and others to train as false examples. Each line of the false and positive files contains two database identifiers, one for each protein. One example is the identifier from a database named Uniprot,[8] which has information about the protein and annotations/linkage to other databases to enrich the information. *PPIDataset* class has two datatype properties: (i) *hasFolder* property represents the address where pre-processing step can find the files mentioned before starting the experiment; and (ii) *hasPrefix* property represents a pattern to identify the false and positive file names with the pairs.

The *EvidenceMethod* class is used to represent the different methods to calculate and analyze the possible interactions between proteins. Some examples of such methods can be categorized according to their approach: sequence co-occurrence blocks [11]; semantic similarities [9] between GO terms; interaction between conserved substructures in the protein structure (known as domain families) [12]; and others. This class also has the *hasType* property, which indicates the kind of evidence. The evidence methods can be classified into the following types: evolutionary relationship; functional features; network topology; sequence-based signatures; structure-based signatures; and text mining.

The *PairComponent* class represents a protein involved in a protein pair. The *PairComponent* class has the following properties: *hasGO_cc_annotation*, *hasGO_bp_annotation*, *hasGO_mf_annotation*, *hasPfam_annotation*, *hasKo_annotation*, and *hasUniprotCorrespondent* (unique object property, the others are datatype properties). The *hasGO_cc_annotation* property can be used to annotate all GO terms in the cellular component branch that the protein has. The *hasGO_bp_annotation* property can be used to annotate all GO terms in the biological process branch. The *hasGO_mf_annotation* property can be used to annotate all GO terms in the molecular function branch assigned to the protein.

---

[7] https://string-db.org.
[8] https://www.uniprot.org/.

The *hasPfam_annotation* property can be used to annotate all the pfam database[9] identifiers (i.e., protein families) assigned to the protein. The *hasKo_annotation* property can be used to annotate enzyme identifiers of metabolic pathways stored in the KEGG database[10]. The *hasUniprotCorrespondent* property links the pair component with their correspondent in the Uniprot database. The range of this property is an instance of the class *Protein*, found in the Uniprot ontology.[11]

The *Interaction* class from Biopax was reused as its definition is the same for our domain and we add some properties to it. Two properties were adapted from an already existent property in Biopax for this class, i.e. *participant*. The two properties added were *participant1* and *participant2*, while their range is an instance of *PairComponent*. The goal of this change is to improve the efficiency of query results because an interaction always involves two components. The results using only one *participant* implied in a duplication for the results of interaction scores because of the second participant, which was solved defining the two properties. The *Interaction* class also has the following properties: *belongsTo* and *hasScore*. The *belongsTo* property is a link between the interaction and the PPI dataset where it came from, so its range is an instance of *PPIDataset*. The *hasScore* property has as range an instance of the *EvidenceDecision* class and links the interaction with the probabilities generated by the evidence methods. The *EvidenceDecision* class allows establishing the relationship between the interaction and all score results that it has according to each evidence method. The *EvidenceDecision* class has the object property *basedOn* and the datatype property *predictedValue*. The *basedOn* property has an instance of the class *EvidenceMethod*, and links to the evidence method that generated the respective score. Finally, the *predictedValue* property can be used to attribute the score value (between 0 and 1).

4   Experiments and Query Scenarios

In order to evaluate the proposed ontology, we present some queries that retrieve all the important sub-products (inputs and outputs) of an experiment execution performed using three distinct PPI datasets as inputs. The experiment was executed using a workflow for PPI prediction.

The triplification process was developed in the Python[12] programming language. At the end, it generates files in the Turtle RDF format divided in four parts: (i) description of the experiment setting with the evidence methods to be used; (ii) description and reference to the datasets used in an experiment; (iii) description of the protein information; and (iv) description of score results. The data is stored in an RDF triple store called Arc2[13] for PHP[14] (language for

---

[9] https://pfam.xfam.org/.
[10] https://www.kegg.jp/.
[11] http://purl.uniprot.org/core/.
[12] https://www.python.org/.
[13] https://github.com/semsol/arc2.
[14] https://php.net/.

the web server). This triple store uses a MySQL[15] database to store the data and it offers an interface to submit SPARQL [8] queries.

The complete data extracted from the workflow execution over the three mentioned PPI datasets used in the experiment is available at the website[16], where it is possible to run the example queries mentioned in this section.

Each dataset has 200,000 candidate pairs, in which 50% are positive (do interact) and 50% are negative (do not interact) examples. These datasets have been submitted to the PPI prediction workflow mentioned before. This workflow has as input a configuration file in the JSON format, which is used to start the triplification process, containing the experiment title, description, owner, and owner's contact email, as well as a list of the datasets information, containing the description, folder, and prefix.

All the negative examples of the PPI datasets were retrieved from STRING (scores between 100 and 200). The positive examples of the first dataset were retrieved from DIP[17], HPRD[18] and a part of Biogrid[19]. The second and the third datasets have positive interactions from Biogrid. It is important to note that there are no duplicated pairs, i.e., these are disjunct datasets.

In the query examples presented in this section we use the same prefix pattern[20] and, for simplification, we omitted them in the queries' expressions. We organize the pair component and the resulting URIs according to their original datasets (the three PPI datasets) to get no conflict of ids in the database (this means that the URIs are composed of the object to be described, like interaction_1), and also the dataset identification like (interaction_dataset_1_1). The idea of the following queries is to investigate the results of the experiment. Given a specific protein, the scientist can navigate through the data to get the protein features used in the experiment and also the similar interactions (forming a cluster) and the resulting predicted interactions for this cluster.

The first query example (Query 1) aims at getting the annotations about a specific pair component. It obtains detailed information about the protein whose Uniprot identifier is $P98196$[21]. This protein is synthesized from the gene $ATP11A$ and it is a phospholipid-transporting ATPase IH, which has a catalytic activity and catalyzes the hydrolysis of ATP coupled to the transport of

---

[15] https://www.mysql.com/.

[16] https://ypublish.info/portalppi/#/exploration.

[17] https://dip.doe-mbi.ucla.edu/dip/Main.cgi.

[18] http://www.hprd.org/.

[19] https://thebiogrid.org/.

[20] prefix ppi: <https://www.ypublish.info/protein_interaction_domain_ontology#>
   prefix annot: <https://www.ypublish.info/protein_annotation_information#>
   prefix prov: <https://www.ypublish.info/provenance_information#>
   prefix result: <https://www.ypublish.info/prediction_results_information#>
   prefix rdf: <http://www.w3.org/1999/02/22-rdf-syntax-ns#>
   prefix biopax: <http://www.biopax.org/release/biopax-level2.owl#>.

[21] https://www.ypublish.info/protein_annotation_information#protein_dataset_1_P98196.

Table 1. Features and their respective annotations for protein *P*98196.

Features	Terms
Cellular component	GO_0005765, GO_0005769, GO_0005783, GO_0005802, GO_0005886, GO_0016020, GO_0016021, GO_0035579, GO_0043231, GO_0055037 and GO_0070821
Molecular function	GO_0000287, GO_0004012 and GO_0005524
Biological process	GO_0043312 and GO_0045332
PFAM	PF16209 and PF16212
KO	K01530

aminophospholipids[22]. Depending on the quality of the protein's annotations, provided by specialists of Uniprot, each protein feature (mainly, gene ontology terms) can have a lot of terms as result for queries such as Query 1. The higher quality of protein annotations increases the information about proteins and leads to a better use of the evidence methods to predict interactions.

Query 1. Get the pair component detailed information

```
1: select * where {
2:    annot:protein_dataset_1_P98196 ppi:hasGO_cc_annotation ?go_cc.
3:    annot:protein_dataset_1_P98196 ppi:hasGO_bp_annotation ?go_bp.
4:    annot:protein_dataset_1_P98196 ppi:hasGO_mf_annotation ?go_mf.
5:    annot:protein_dataset_1_P98196 ppi:hasPfam_annotation ?pfam.
6:    annot:protein_dataset_1_P98196 ppi:hasKo_annotation ?ko.
7: }
```

Query 1 results (summarized in Table 1) show that protein *P*98196 was particularly well annotated. It shows many annotated terms and their provenance. For instance, *GO_0005765* term comes from the cellular component branch of the Gene Ontology.

Once we have access to the biological annotations of the proteins under investigation, we can get the interactions that have some of these annotations in common. This can be used to retrieve protein clusters (functional modules) and filter the interactions. Therefore, in the case of protein *P*98196, Query 2 uses one of its annotated terms (*GO_0005765*) to filter and retrieve all the interactions that have this term in common, forming a protein cluster of interest.

The results for Query 2 are the URI of interactions as well as the URIs of the proteins involved in these interactions. Additionally, in all these interactions, the proteins are localized in the same cellular component, i.e., the lysosomal membrane. In general, proteins that share gene ontology terms and these terms

---

[22] https://www.uniprot.org/uniprot/P98196.

Query 2. Filter the interaction network applying some biological information

1: select distinct ?interaction ?protein1 ?protein2 where {
2:    ?interaction rdf:type biopax:Interaction.
3:    ?interaction ppi:belongsTo prov:dataset1.
4:    ?interaction ppi:participant1 ?protein1.
5:    ?protein1 ppi:hasGO_cc_annotation ?go_cc1.
6:    ?interaction ppi:participant2 ?protein2.
7:    ?protein2 ppi:hasGO_cc_annotation ?go_cc2.
8:    filter (regex(?go_cc1, 'GO_0005765', 'i') && regex(?go_cc2, 'GO_0005765', 'i')).
9: }

---

are far from the branch root (annotation is more specific) may have high semantic similarity. This fact can indicate a high probability of protein interaction.

Investigating further, after running some of the *Evidence Methods*, the scientist is able to analyze the scores obtained for new predicted protein interactions that are in the same cluster of protein *P98196*. In Query 3, we select the interactions from the first dataset and their scores. We then link the *evidenceDecision* instance to the respective *EvidenceMethod* to identify the origin of the predicted value. Additionally, Query 3 includes a constraint (filter) to retrieve just the interactions as well as their score and information about the evidence involved whose score of *prov:evidenceMethod7* (final score given by the combination of the others) was greater than 0.8. Besides the chosen score of the evidence method, we added the same constraint of Query 2 (filter).

Query 3. Get the interactions that have scores greater than 0.8 for the evidence method PredRep (prov:evidenceMethod7) which is the combination of all others.

1: select distinct ?interaction ?protein1 ?protein2 ?info_evidence ?score where {
2:    ?interaction rdf:type biopax:Interaction.
3:    ?interaction ppi:belongsTo prov:dataset1.
4:    ?interaction ppi:participant1 ?protein1.
5:    ?interaction ppi:participant2 ?protein2.
6:    ?protein1 ppi:hasGO_cc_annotation ?go_cc1.
7:    ?protein2 ppi:hasGO_cc_annotation ?go_cc2.
8:    ?interaction ppi:hasScore ?ed.
9:    ?ed ppi:basedOn prov:evidenceMethod7.
10:    ?ed ppi:predictedValue ?score.
11:    prov:evidenceMethod7 ppi:hasDescription ?info_evidence.
12:    filter (?score > 0.8 && (regex(?go_cc1, 'GO_0005765', 'i') && regex(?go_cc2, 'GO_0005765', 'i'))).
13: }

The results for Query 3 are the URI of interactions, the URIs of the two involved proteins, the details about the evidence method used as filter and the interactions score. The description of *prov:evidenceMethod7* is "stacking of multiple prediction methods". The scientist can use this kind of query to study the interactions according to the evidence method that he/she has some preference. Query 2 retrieved 258 interactions that are in the same cluster of protein $P98196$. Analyzing these results, note that 208 interactions have 1 as score value. This shows that most of the interactions of this cluster had an interaction confirmation aside from the fact that they share functional annotations. Although the other 50 were in the same cluster, they were predicted as false interactions taking into account other protein characteristics.

There are much more possible query expressions that can be used to retrieve useful information from the dataset described by OntoPPI, including those who answer specific biological questions. One of these questions concerns inferring biological functions for poorly annotated proteins. A simple way to do that is using their respective interaction partners who have a reliable number of functional annotations. We can filter the proteins with few or zero annotations and choose the interactions whose scores are above some threshold like 0.8 and then compare with the partner's annotations. It is important to highlight that besides the computational interpretation of the problem, in order to reach a final conclusion, we have also to apply the biological interpretation and analysis.

5   Related Work

There are some initiatives that already explore the organization, integration, and formalization of PPI data. In [10], the authors developed a framework to integrate data about reference PPI datasets and data sources of protein biological information. They created an interesting vocabulary that includes classes such as *experiment, interaction* (with the score attribute) and information about features. However, this vocabulary lacks some important information related to the PPI entire process. The experiment class attributes are oriented to experimental methods and do not allow the description of the dataset information. The score of interactions is available, but it is not possible to know which evidence method was used to predict them.

In [2], the authors enriched a database of PPI with Gene ontology terms annotated for each protein involved in the interactions. They also built a framework where the user can navigate through data using remote SPARQL queries, providing also a public website to retrieve the information able to do topological analysis in the network. Similarly to the related work, this work lacks scores discrimination by evidence method and does not provide data about the provenance of the predicted PPI network.

In [7], three vocabularies were created (*mex-core, mex-algorithm,* and *mex-performance*) to describe all information involved in a machine learning experiment. Similar to OntoPPI, it includes concepts such as datasets and experiment. However, PPI datasets have not the same meaning, since they represent datasets about protein interaction pairs. The concept of dataset in *mex-core* means the dataset with all the final features given to the classifier. Besides, the other two vocabularies aim at representing machine learning methods, algorithms and performance, which is not the case for OntoPPI experiments. In our case, we may use machine learning methods in our experiments, but we are not focused on registering their performance details, such as the parameter values used. Instead, we focus on the protein interaction scores.

In [15], the authors describe metadata related to execution pipelines, such as datasets' transformations and data provenance. Although OntoPPI is also concerned about experiments' data provenance, it is focused in the specific characteristics of PPI experiments.

OntoPPI was created to overcome the limitations of these related works, allowing the registry of experiment and datasets details. Furthermore, it provides a manner to express biological information used for each pair component and associates the information of what evidence method generated the interaction scores. Such kind of information helps the scientist on learning the details of a given experiment and the provenance of a predicted interaction.

6   Conclusion and Future Work

This paper presented the OntoPPI, an ontology to formalize and standardize the protein interaction prediction process. OntoPPI was developed to combine information about PPI prediction experiments, including previous annotation about the components of the candidate pairs as well as the scores for each pair and the methods and evidences based on which they were obtained.

We carefully developed this ontology reusing and looking for other related ontologies. We have also defined new terms (for classes and properties) according to the specific literature. These terms cover the whole process of protein interactions discovery.

A use case adopting real predicted datasets previously annotated is described. It illustrates the use of all OntoPPI elements, and showed some ways to filter and analyze the interaction network using SPARQL queries. We showed how the scientist can investigate starting from the information of a protein of interest, forming a cluster with its similar properties and then confirming the interaction relationship in 208 from 258 interactions in that cluster.

We have built a light weight ontology but it still does not have restrictions on classes and axioms to improve the reasoning capacity to help a deeper analysis. Future works include adding rules using the annotations properties to enhance the information and biological classification of interactions. In addition, we intend to work on the integration of the annotations about experiment provenance [4] along the steps of the prediction methods used to describe all the steps that originate the intermediate files. Another foreseen improvement is to enrich OntoPPI with other protein information, i.e., to add information extracted from reference datasets.

Acknowledgements. This work was partially funded by CAPES, CNPq, and FAPERJ.

References

1. Bizer, C., Heath, T., Berners-Lee, T.: Linked data - the story so far. Int. J. Semant. Web Inf. Syst. **5**(3), 1–22 (2009)
2. Cannataro, M., Guzzi, P.H., Veltri, P.: Using ontologies for querying and analysing protein-protein interaction data. Procedia Comput. Sci. **1**(1), 997–1004 (2010)
3. Chang, J.W., Zhou, Y.Q., Ul Qamar, M., Chen, L.L., Ding, Y.D.: Prediction of protein-protein interactions by evidence combining methods. Int. J. Mol. Sci. **17**(11), 1946 (2016)
4. Cuevas-Vicenttín, V., et al.: ProvONE: a PROV extension data model for scientific workflow provenance. DataOne Project (2014)
5. De Las Rivas, J., Fontanillo, C.: Protein-protein interactions essentials: key concepts to building and analyzing interactome networks. PLoS Comput. Biol. **6**(6), e1000807 (2010)
6. Demir, E., et al.: The biopax community standard for pathway data sharing. Nat. Biotechnol. **28**(9), 935 (2010)
7. Esteves, D., et al.: MEX vocabulary: a lightweight interchange format for machine learning experiments. In: Proceedings of the 11th International Conference on Semantic Systems, pp. 169–176. ACM (2015)
8. TWSW Group: Sparql 1.1 overview (2013). https://www.w3.org/TR/sparql11-overview/. Accessed 02 Dec 2015
9. Guzzi, P.H., Mina, M., Guerra, C., Cannataro, M.: Semantic similarity analysis of protein data: assessment with biological features and issues. Brief. Bioinform. **13**(5), 569–585 (2011)
10. Kazemzadeh, L., Kamdar, M.R., Beyan, O.D., Decker, S., Barry, F.: LinkedPPI: enabling intuitive, integrative protein-protein interaction discovery. In: Proceedings of the 4th Workshop on Linked Science 2014 - Making Sense Out of Data (LISC 2014) co-located with the 13th International Semantic Web Conference (ISWC 2014), Riva del Garda, Italy, 19 October 2014, pp. 48–59 (2014)
11. Li, Y., Ilie, L.: Sprint: ultrafast protein-protein interaction prediction of the entire human interactome. BMC Bioinform. **18**(1), 485 (2017)
12. Mosca, R., Céol, A., Stein, A., Olivella, R., Aloy, P.: 3DID: a catalog of domain-based interactions of known three-dimensional structure. Nucleic Acids Res. **42**(D1), D374–D379 (2013)
13. Newman, A., Hunter, J., Li, Y.F., Bouton, C., Davis, M.: BioMANTA ontology: the integration of protein-protein interaction data (2008)
14. Perfetto, L., et al.: Causaltab: Psi-mitab 2.8 updated format for signaling data representation and dissemination. BioRxiv, p. 385773 (2018)
15. Sicilia, M.Á., García-Barriocanal, E., Sánchez-Alonso, S., Mora-Cantallops, M., Cuadrado, J.-J.: Ontologies for data science: on its application to data pipelines. In: Garoufallou, E., Sartori, F., Siatri, R., Zervas, M. (eds.) MTSR 2018. CCIS, vol. 846, pp. 169–180. Springer, Cham (2019). https://doi.org/10.1007/978-3-030-14401-2_16
16. Studer, R., Benjamins, V.R., Fensel, D.: Knowledge engineering: principles and methods. Data Knowl. Eng. **25**(1–2), 161–197 (1998)

Create Dashboards and Data Story with the Data & Analytics Frameworks

Petito Michele[3,4] , Francesca Fallucchi[1,2(✉)] ,
and Ernesto William De Luca[1,2]

[1] DIII, Guglielmo Marconi University, Rome, Italy
{f.fallucchi, ew.deluca}@unimarconi.it
[2] DIFI, Georg Eckert Institute, Brunswick, Germany
{fallucchi, deluca}@gei.de
[3] Università di Pisa, Pisa, Italy
michele.petito@unipi.it
[4] Guglielmo Marconi University, Rome, Italy
m.petito@unimarconi.it

Abstract. In recent years, many data visualization tools have appeared on the market that can potentially guarantee citizens and users of the Public Administration (PA) the ability to create dashboards and data stories with just a few clicks, using open and unopened data from the PA. The Data Analytics Framework (DAF), a project of the Italian government launched at the end of 2017 and currently being tested, has the goal to improve and simplify the interoperability and exchange of data between Public Administrations, thanks to its big data platform and the integrated use of data visualization tools and semantic technologies. The DAF also has the objective of facilitating data analysis, improving the management of Open Data and facilitating the spread of linked open data (LOD) thanks to the integration of OntoPiA, a network of controlled vocabularies and ontologies, such as "IoT Events", an ontology for representing and modelling the knowledge within the domain of the Internet of Things. This paper contributes to the enhancement of the project by introducing a case study created by the author, concerns tourism of Sardinia (a region of Italy). The case study follows a process in the DAF in 5 steps, starting from selection of the dataset to the creation phase of the real dashboard through Apache Superset (a business intelligence tool) and the related data story. This case study is one of the few demonstrations of use on a real case of DAF and highlights the ability of this national platform to transform the analysis of a large amount of data into simple visual representations with clear and effective language.

Keywords: Data & Analytics Framework · Data visualization · Dashboard · Business intelligence · Open data

1 Introduction

Public sector is rich of data. In recent years, the open data dataset in Italy has increased considerably: in 2018 there were about 15,000 and in 2019 the number is increased to over 25,000 [1]. Unfortunately this dataset growth has not been accompanied by an

© Springer Nature Switzerland AG 2019
E. Garoufallou et al. (Eds.): MTSR 2019, CCIS 1057, pp. 272–283, 2019.
https://doi.org/10.1007/978-3-030-36599-8_24

improvement in the quality of open data portals that represent only simple catalogs. The analysis and implementation phase of the dashboards can only take place using third-party tools, thus not favoring the sharing of knowledge and the birth of new ideas. But the biggest problem concerns the fragmentation of data that limits the analysis and the interpretation of national social and economic phenomena [2, 3]. Therefore, in order to make the most of the data potential, it is necessary to abandon the silo approach and adopt a systemic vision that favors access and data sharing.

In this scenario, the big data platform DAF [4] designed by the *Digital Transformation Team* [5], has the challenge to provide a single point of access for government data and support increased public participation, collaboration and cooperation. The DAF is an infrastructure of the Italian Government established in September 2016, represents Italy's latest effort to valorize public information assets. The objective of the DAF is to overcome these difficulties by using big data platforms to store in a unique repository the data of the PAs, implementing ingestion procedures, promoting standardization and interoperability. So, thanks to a framework for distributed applications such as Apache Hadoop [6], the DAF allows the exploitation of enormous public sector data that describes the realities of citizens and businesses to generate insights and information hidden in it [7, 8].

Furthermore, the DAF promotes semantic interoperability, according to the new European Interoperability Framework (EIF) [9]. To enhance interoperability DAF make use of an ecosystem of ontologies and controlled vocabularies (OntoPiA) [10]. Every dataset in DAF is accompanied by metadata that describes the dataset and its internal structure. It will be the user's responsibility to define the ontological information and controlled vocabularies associated with the data structure, through the meaning of the semantic tags. A tagging system will allow to drive the user to the correct use of controlled vocabularies and to ensure that all datasets can be effectively connected together.

In this paper, we will focus in particular on DAF data visualization technologies, providing a comparative analysis with other tools and platforms on the market (see Sect. 2). In Sect. 3 we will present the general architecture of the Data & Analytics Framework and OntoPiA, the network of ontologies and controlled vocabularies. Section 4 focuses on the process of building a dashboard through Apache Superset. Finally, a case of use of the DAF will be presented for the construction of a dashboard starting from a dataset on tourism in the Sardinia Region (see Sect. 5). We conclude the paper with some future developments.

2 Related Works

Research supports an increasing focus on visual imagery, in all its forms, as a way of communicating with and engaging with online audiences. *Data visualization*[1] allows PA to obtain useful trends and information with maximum simplicity and speed. The DAF project embraces this approach by integrating Superset [11], a business

---

[1] The science of visual representation of 'data', which has been abstracted in some schematic form, including attributes or variables for the units of information.

intelligence tool for data representation. There are many other tools in the same category such as Microsoft Power BI [12], Tableau [13], Google Data Studio [14] e Ploty. ly [15] that offer the possibility of use in the cloud via API and that could allow integration with the DAF, even if with important limitations.

Public Tableau [13] allows the creation of complex dashboards with great flexibility, without requiring specific technical skills. But the use of the free version is allowed only through a desktop application.

Google Data Studio [14] is very intuitive but does not allow the use of more than one dataset within the same dashboard. It has few data connectors (only for MySql [16], and for PostgreSQL [17]) and the quality of the dashboards is not comparable to that of the competitors in the sector.

Plot.ly [15] allows the creation and sharing of quick interactive dashboards. But it only accepts datasets with a maximum size of 5 MB and the published graphics must be public (for them to be private it is necessary to pay a subscription). Among the open source categories we have instead distinguished three data visualization tools: Superset [11], Metabase [18] and Redash [19]. All these projects meet the requirements [20] that an OGD[2] visualization tool should possess. Superset and Redash are very similar. Both are powerful and give the possibility to connect to a large number of data sources. In addition, they have a powerful interface for writing and executing SQL queries.

Once saved, queries can also be used as a basis for the creation of dashboards. Superset supports a larger number of authentication systems than Redash. For example, it includes LDAP[3], the system used for the unique authentication of all modules in the DAF. Although Redash is an excellent project in rapid evolution, Superset [11] has been chosen for three main reasons: the presence of LDAP authentication, the high number of views, and the support of the Python language (used throughout the DAF project).

Superset [11] is an open source product hosted on the Apache Foundation Github[4] platform and is developed using Flask [21] a very lean Python framework [22] for web development. The part that generates the interactive graphs instead makes use of NVD3 [23] a javascript library built on D3.js [24]. Any dashboard created with Superset consists of a series of graphs (called slices). Each of these can be resized, moved relative to the others, or shown in full screen. In addition, each dataset represented in a graph can also be exported in CSV or JSON format or through SQL queries. The "slices" are created starting from a table available in the many data sources that Superset is able to manage. Superset provides two main interfaces: the first is the Rich SQL IDE (Interactive Development Environment) called *Sql Lab*[5] with which the user can have immediate and flexible access to data or write specific SQL queries, the second is a data exploration interface that allows the conversion of data tables into rich visual insights.

---

[2] Open Government Data. http://www.oecd.org/gov/digital-government/open-government-data.htm.

[3] Lightweight Directory Access Protocol. http://foldoc.org/ldap.

[4] Superset Github repository. https://github.com/apache/incubator-superset.

[5] https://superset.incubator.apache.org/sqllab.html.

3 Data & Analytics Framework (DAF)

DAF has a complex architecture which integrates different components [25]. Figure 1 shows a simplified view of two relevant related characteristics: the interoperability between the components mediated by the use of microservices and the use of docker container[6] technology that isolates the components for greater security.

The *Dataportal* is the main point of access to the DAF and its functionalities. It is characterized by a public section [26] and a private section [27]. In the public section (accessible via https://dataportal.daf.teamdigitale.it/) anyone can browse the *data stories*[7] and dashboards associated with the data in the national catalog. The private section is accessed only after login, thus allowing only accredited users to exploit the functionality of querying, analyzing and sharing data.

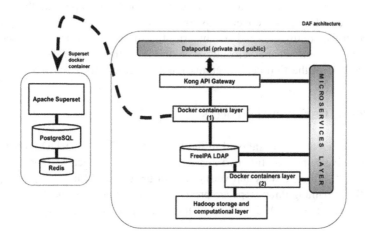

Fig. 1. Logical architecture of the DAF

The Dataportal communicates with the rest of the system through the *Kong API Gateway* [28] and the *MICROSERVICE LAYER*. The docker container layer represented in point 1 of Fig. 1, manages the analysis, cataloging and display of data. This layer encapsulates some docker containers, including *Superset* [29], *Metabase* [18], *Jupyter* [30] and *CKAN* [31]. The latter implements a component called a harvester, which allows the DAF to collect all datasets within the DAF. In addition, CKAN performs data catalog functions and allows the download of datasets. *Jupyter* is instead a very useful tool for data scientists, as it allows to perform operations such as data cleaning and transformation, numerical simulations, statistical modeling, machine learning and to run Scala and Python applications on the big data platform of DAF

---

[6] https://www.docker.com/resources/what-container.

[7] Data stories are an extension of the dashboards, which allow you to express what you can see from the views.

thanks to integration with Apache Spark. On the left side of Fig. 1, the *Superset* docker container is shown: as you can see, in this container there are also databases as *PostgreSQL* [17], used to store the tables and *Redis* [32] to manage the cache. Centralized authentication is guaranteed by the *FreeIPA LDAP* [33], an open source solution for integrated identity management. The point 2 of Fig. 1 shows a second layer of docker containers consisting of the platforms *OpenTSDB* [34], *Livy* [35] and *Nifi* [36]. Finally, in the lower part we find the *Hadoop storage and computational layer* [37] that contains the entire storage platform provided by Hadoop (HDFS [38], Kudu [39] and HBase [38]).

The microservices layer, described in the previous study [40], provides the semantic microservices and allow the implementation of semantic technologies, namely the standardization, production, and publication of LOD. These processes can be achieved thanks to the presence of *OntoPiA* [10] a network of remote ontologies and vocabularies, published on Github. *OntoPiA* allows the DAF to provide the catalog of controlled vocabularies. Moreover it favors the function of semantic tagging and the reuse of controlled ontologies and vocabularies by companies and PAs. The network is based on the standards of the Semantic Web and it is aligned with the so-called Core Vocabulary [41] of the European Commission's ISA2 program.

4 Building Dashboard Process

The process of creating a dashboard in the DAF, inspired by the KDD model [42], is structured in five steps. The first two phases are described in Sect. 4.1 and concern the selection (step 1), the analysis and verification of the quality of the dataset (step 2). In Sect. 4.2 the remaining three steps are presented: configuration of local tables (step 3), creation of slices (step 4) and creation of the dashboard and data story (step 5).

4.1 Selection and Dataset Analysis (Step 1–2)

In the first step you look for the dataset to analyze. This activity can be carried out in two ways: through the *public portal* [26], as anonymous visitor, or from the *private portal* [27]. Using the search form you can search with keywords or browse through the categories that describe the domain. Once the dataset has been identified, we move on to the second step consisting in carrying out a first analysis of the data to evaluate a part of the quality characteristics foreseen by the ISO/IEC 25024 [43] and described in action no. 9 of the *National guidelines for the enhancement of public information*[8].

4.2 Superset's Tables Configuration and Visualization (Step 3–5)

The last three steps of the DAF dashboard creation process are mainly realized in Superset. Before proceeding to the realization of the slices, it is necessary to modify the settings of the fields (or columns in the Superset jargon) of the table. This means that it

---

[8] https://lg-patrimonio-pubblico.readthedocs.io.

will be necessary to verify the correct assignment of the field types (INT, BIGINT, CHAR, DATETIME etc.), establish the dimensions on which to perform the aggregations and define the relative metrics.

Once the step of settings of local tables is finished, it is possible to proceed with the realization of the first slice (step 4). Superset has no less than 34 different types of graphics[9].

The last step is the realization of the dashboard which consists of a personalized composition of the individual slices.

5   Case Study

The case study we created in the DAF on February 4, 2018 during the *Open Sardinia Contest*[10], concerns the development of a dashboard and the related data story based on the Sardinia Region's tourism dataset. Specifically, we describe the 5 steps of the process for creating a dashboard illustrated in the previous paragraph. In particular, the phenomenon to be studied and the analysis of the relative dataset will be introduced (see Sect. 5.1), the whole development activity in Superset will be illustrated (see Sect. 5.2), concerning the configuration of the dataset, the realization of the slices and the dashboard. In Sect. 5.3 the case of data story associated with the dashboard is presented.

5.1   Sardinia Tourism Dataset

The tourism industry in general occupies an important place in the economy of a country and tourism activities are a potential source of employment, so it is good to know the volume of tourism and its characteristics. This is important for the local government to answer questions such as:

- What is the origin of tourism between June and September?
- What is the tourist period preferred by the Germans in the Olbia area?
- What is the accommodation capacity in the south of the island?
- Which types of accommodation are present?

This allows the local government to decide how and where to spend public money. For example, with regard to the first question, if a high percentage of German tourism is highlighted, the Mayor could establish the installation of tourist road signs in German or provide German language courses for City employees. Regarding the second question, if you find that the German tourism is concentrated mainly in the months of September and June, the local administrator may choose for example to enhance tourist services in the areas and months involved, extending the opening hours of offices or municipality health districts.

---

[9] https://superset.incubator.apache.org/gallery.html#visualizations-gallery.

[10] Contest dedicated to open data, promoted by the Sardinia Region and held in the period from 16/10/2017 to 21/01/2018. http://contest.formez.it/.

In the open data catalog of the Sardinia Region (published on dati.regione.sardegna. it) it is possible to find the datasets related to the *movements of the clients in the hospitality establishments in the years between 2013 and 2016*. The data derive from the communications for statistical and obligatory purposes by law, which the accommodation facilities do to the Sardinia Region. Finally, the Region transmits the data to ISTAT (The Italian National Institute of Statistics), according to the current legal requirements.

The following datasets (in CSV format) are those selected for the case study:

(1) Tourist movements in Sardinia by municipality;
(2) Tourist movements in Sardinia by province;
(3) Tourist movements in Sardinia by macro type of accommodation facility;
(4) Capacity for accommodation facilities in Sardinia.

The CSV (1–3) collect the *arrivals* (number of hosted customers) and the *visit duration* (number of nights spent) of tourists in Sardinia, divided by the tourist's origin and type of accommodation. The CSV (4) collects the capacities of the receptive structures of the Sardinia Region. The capacity measures the consistency in terms of number of accommodation facilities and related beds and rooms.

Through data portal it is possible to perform a series of operations including downloading the dataset (in JSON format [44] and limited to 1000 records), obtaining the endpoint API, access the analysis tools and display dashboards related. It is also possible to access to CKAN [31], a module integrated in DAF which allows to see all metadata associated to the current dataset.

5.2   Sardinia Tourism Dashboard

After selecting the dataset, it is possible to open Superset very intuitively by clicking on a button on the web interface. At this point we have reached the third step of the process of creating the dashboard described in paragraph 4. In this phase the Superset tables must be configured for a specific slice. As an example, let's consider the type of slice *Table view* named "Arrivi e presenze totali per provenienza turista", one of slices created for this use case.

The datasource's configuration form of *Table view* (see Fig. 2) is divided into three tabs (*Detail, List Columns* and *List Metrics*) and allows the modification of the table parameters. The initial tab shows some basic information such as the table name and the associated slices. The second tab displays the fields in the table, for example, province, macro-typology, arrivals, etc. The first and third columns respectively contain the name of the field (e.g. province, macro-typology, arrivals, etc.) and the type of data contained (STRING, INT, DATETIME, etc.).

	Column	Verbose Name	Type	Groupable	Filterable	Count Distinct	Sum	Min	Max	Is temporal
Q ☑ ✎	provincia	None	STRING	✓	✓	□	□	□	□	□
Q ☑ ✎	macrotipologia	None	STRING	✓	✓	□	□	□	□	□
Q ☑ ✎	arrivi	None	INT	□	□	□	✓	□	□	□
Q ☑ ✎	presenze	None	INT	□	□	□	✓	□	□	□
Q ☑ ✎	processing_dtlm	None	STRING	✓	✓	□	□	□	□	□
Q ☑ ✎	descrizione	Provenienza	STRING	✓	✓	□	□	□	□	□
Q ☑ ✎	_anno_mese		DATETIME	✓	✓	□	□	□	□	✓
Q ☑ ✎	anno		INT	✓	✓	□	□	□	□	✓
Q ☑ ✎	mese		INT	✓	✓	□	✓	□	□	✓

Record Count: 9

Fig. 2. Edit table form

Superset automatically assigns the correct properties in relation to the type of data declared, but you can decide to change them or increase the details. Special attention should be paid to DATETIME columns. Formatting and orders by day, month and year can change. Superset allows you to customize them thanks to all the combinations that can be created with the management of dates in Python. In the specific case of the table in Fig. 2, the format "% Y-% m-% d% H:% M:% S" was used for the calculated field "_anno_mese", i.e. a timestamp useful for a time based analysis on month/year. The "_anno_mese" field is not a standard field, but is dynamically generated by the function "Expression = concat (cast (year as string), '-', cast (month as string), '-01 00:00:00')" and from the option "Datetime Format = % Y-% m-% d% H:% M:% S": this sets the timestamp format according to the Python datetime string pattern. Here the syntax can vary depending on the database used: the DAF uses Apache Impala [45] the engine for Hadoop SQL queries [37]. If you use SQLite [46] (the default Superset database) the setting to use would be "Expression = year || '-' || month "and" Datetime Format = % Y-%d". This happens because SQLite accepts a date format of type Year + Month that does not exist in Impala. The only way to get the same result in Impala is to use a timestamp format and concatenate the "year" and "month" fields with the string '-01 00:00:00'.

Now let's consider the "year" field: on this the "Is temporal" option has been set which tells Superset to treat the values to describe variable phenomena over time. On this same field, "Datetime format = % Y" was set, in order to tell Superset to treat the values as years. If in the ingestion phase (as happened in this case) the field should be of an incorrect type (for example INT) it is possible to use the option "Database expression = date_part ('year', '{}')" to perform the conversion from INT to DATETIME. The Impala function "date_part" in addition to casting from INT to DATETIME, extracts the year from the timestamp.

Once the dimensions have been established, i.e. the fields on which to group, the metrics (SUM, AVG, etc.) to be applied to these groupings must be defined (third and last tab of Fig. 2). For this specific case we created "Origin" field and the "sum_arrivi" and "sum_presenze" metrics were defined and assigned using the SUM(arrivals) and

SUM(visits-duration) functions. The result is a "Table view" with the list of arrivals and visits duration divided by geographical area of origin of the tourist.

After completing the table configuration phase, we move on to the fourth step of creating the slices. Superset has no less than 34 different types of graphics. Now suppose we want to create a graph that shows the average number of tourists in Sardinia and at the same time a graph that shows the trend of visit duration over time. This is achievable thanks to a slice view as *Big number with trendline*. Using the "_anno_mese" field on the abscissa axis and on the ordinates the "_presenzamedia" metric will get the result as shown in the last graph on the right of the Fig. 3 (point 1).

Many other options can be applied on the slice: for example, in the *Filters section* you can add one or more values to exclude in the results. For more complex filters, you can use *Where clause* option, which allows you to write conditions directly in SQL. There is also the possibility to create complex tables (such as pivot tables) or create dynamic selectable filters that can be used directly by the user on the dashboard.

Once we have finished the first slice, we will already be able to proceed with the creation of the dashboard (fifth step of the process), which initially will naturally contain only one slice. The layout of the Superset dashboards is very flexible: slices can be easily resized by drag and drop. Between one slice and another you can insert a box containing text or html to better describe the graph. For the realization the *tourist movements dashboard in Sardinia from 2013 to 2016* (Fig. 3) were used 13 slices. For reasons of space, in Fig. 3 only part of the realized dashboard[11] is shown.

5.3   Sardinia Tourism Data Story

With the data story we try to provide an interpretation of a phenomenon from the data. This narration was published in the *Public Data Portal* and can be accessed from the *Menu > Community > Story*.

Thanks to the filters the user can analyze the data by year, province, macro-typology, origin and month. For example, analyzing the datasets as a whole (i.e. without setting filters) it is possible to observe how Sardinian tourism has grown steadily both in terms of visit duration and arrivals during the four years of survey (2013–2016): 10 million arrivals in total with an average stay of 3.14 days which generated 47.9 million of nights in the accommodation facilities of the island (see Fig. 3 point 1).

From the point of view of the foreign tourist, the most important numbers are those of the Germans (5.91 million) and the French (3.95 million), while the major visit duration from Italy, as shown in the Fig. 3 (point 2), they are those of the residents of Lombardy (6.45 million) and Lazio (2.92 million). These data, filtered for 2016, are compatible with an ANSA article [47] that stated that 2016 "was a record year for Sardinian tourism: 2.9 million arrivals with an average stay of 4.6 days which generated 13.5 million of nights in the accommodation facilities of the Island".

As shown in Fig. 3 (point 3) tourism is mainly distributed in the provinces of Olbia-Tempio, Cagliari and Sassari with preference for hotel facilities in 74% of cases.

---

[11] The complete dashboard is accessible online at http://bit.ly/storia-turismo-sardo-story.

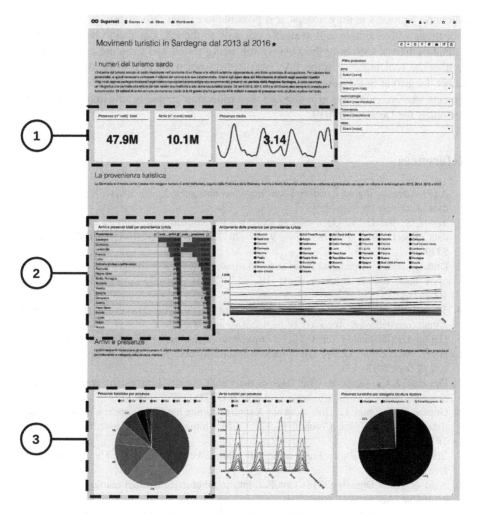

Fig. 3. A section of the dashboard of tourist movements in Sardinia

6 Conclusion

In this document we presented the shortcomings of the some data visualizing tools on the market with respect to the potential of open source tools integrated into the DAF, a project requested by the Italian Government to overcome the difficulties of channeling data stored in local public administrations into a single container (data lake). We have therefore introduced the DAF architecture and the semantic functionality of OntoPiA. In particular, we introduced Superset, a data visualization tool which has a central role in the creation of dashboards. Finally, a dashboard use case was presented using some datasets from the Sardinia Region present in the DAF. The use case represents not only one of the first experimental uses of the DAF but also the demonstration of how, following a process in only 5 steps, it is possible to extract information from large data collections with a simple tool available not only to the PA, but also to businesses and ordinary citizens. Currently the DAF is still being tested and there are critical issues, such as the reluctance of some PAs who still do not want to provide their data and accept the arrival of the new platform. But in general the number of public and private subjects who are using it is growing and the production release is now imminent as it is scheduled for December 2019.

References

1. AgID Advance digital transformation. https://avanzamentodigitale.italia.it/it/progetto/open-data. Accessed 10 Aug 2019
2. Temiz, S., Brown, T.: Open data project for e-government: case study of Stockholm open data project. Int. J. Electron. Gov. **9**, 55 (2017). https://doi.org/10.1504/IJEG.2017.1000 5479
3. Drakopoulou, S.: Open data today and tomorrow: the present challenges and possibilities of open data. Int. J. Electron. Gov. **10**, 157 (2018). https://doi.org/10.1504/IJEG.2018. 10015213
4. Team Transformation D GitHub - italia/daf: Data & Analytics Framework (DAF). https://github.com/italia/daf. Accessed 10 Sept 2018
5. Digital Transformation Team (2019). https://teamdigitale.governo.it. Accessed 1 Jun 2018
6. HDFS Architecture Guide. https://hadoop.apache.org/docs/r1.2.1/hdfs_design.html. Accessed 12 Sept 2018
7. Desouza, K.C., Jacob, B.: Big Data in the Public Sector: Lessons for Practitioners and Scholars. Adm. Soc. (2017). https://doi.org/10.1177/0095399714555751
8. Gomes, E., Foschini, L., Dias, J., et al.: An infrastructure model for smart cities based on big data. Int. J. Grid Util. Comput. **9**, 322 (2018). https://doi.org/10.1504/IJGUC.2018.100 16122
9. European Interoperability Framework (EIF). https://ec.europa.eu/isa2/eif_en. Accessed 10 Dec 2018
10. Agid & Team Digitale (2018) OntoPia. https://github.com/italia/daf-ontologie-vocabolari-controllati. Accessed 10 Nov 2018
11. Apache Superset. https://superset.incubator.apache.org. Accessed 19 Aug 2018
12. Sabotta, C.: Introducing Microsoft BI Reporting and Analysis Tools. In: Microsoft (2015). http://msdn.microsoft.com/en-us/library/d0e16108-7123-4788-87b3-05db962dbc94
13. Tableau. Free Data Visualization Software. Tableau Public (2011)
14. Google Data Studio. https://datastudio.google.com/. Accessed 15 Sept 2018
15. Plotly. Modern Visualization for the Data Era – Plotly (2017). https://plot.ly/
16. MySql. https://www.mysql.com/i. Accessed 15 Sept 2018
17. PostgreSQL. PostgreSQL: The world's most advanced open source database (2014). http://www.postgresql.org/. http://www.postgresql.org/
18. Metabase. https://www.metabase.com/. Accessed 16 Sept 2018
19. Redash. https://github.com/getredash/redash. Accessed 15 Sept 2018
20. Graves, A., Hendler, J.: Visualization tools for open government data. In: Proceedings of the 14th Annual International Conference on Digital Government Research - dg.o 2013, p. 136 (2013)
21. Ronacher A Flask MicroFramework. http://flask.pocoo.org/. Accessed 10 Sept 2018
22. Python. https://www.python.org/. Accessed 15 Sept 2018

23. NVD3 Project. http://nvd3.org/. Accessed 15 Sept 2018
24. van Dierendonck, R., van Tienhoven, S., Elid, T.: D3.JS: Data-Driven Documents (2015)
25. Team Transformation D Data & Analytics Framework (DAF) - Developer Documentation. https://daf-docs.readthedocs.io/. Accessed 15 Sept 2018
26. DAF - Public Dataportal. https://dataportal.daf.teamdigitale.it. Accessed 5 Jan 2019
27. DAF Private Dataportal. https://dataportal.daf.teamdigitale.it/#/login. Accessed 5 Jan 2019
28. Kong. https://konghq.com/. Accessed 15 Sept 2018
29. Apache Software Foundation, Apache Superset Contributors. Apache Superset — Apache Superset documentation (2018). https://superset.incubator.apache.org/
30. Jupyter Project. Project Jupyter | Project (2016). http://jupyter.org/about.html
31. CKAN (2018). https://github.com/ckan/ckan. Accessed 12 Sept 2018
32. Redis. https://redis.io. Accessed 15 Sept 2018
33. FreeIPA LDAP. https://www.freeipa.org/. Accessed 19 Sept 2018
34. StumbleUpon. OpenTSDB - A Distributed, Scalable Monitoring System (2012)
35. Apache Livy. https://livy.incubator.apache.org/. Accessed 19 Sept 2018
36. The Apache Software Foundation. Apache NiFi (2017)
37. Apache hadoop. https://hadoop.apache.org/. Accessed 3 Feb 2018
38. Apache HBase (2015). https://hbase.apache.org/. Accessed 12 Sept 2018
39. Apache Kudu. https://kudu.apache.org/. Accessed 11 Sept 2018
40. Fallucchi, F., Petito, M., De Luca, E.W.: Analysing and visualising open data within the data and analytics framework. In: Garoufallou, E., Sartori, F., Siatri, R., Zervas, M. (eds.) MTSR 2018. CCIS, vol. 846, pp. 135–146. Springer, Cham (2019). https://doi.org/10.1007/978-3-030-14401-2_13
41. (SEMIC) SIC Core Vocabularies. https://joinup.ec.europa.eu/collection/semantic-interoperability-community-semic/core-vocabularies. Accessed 1 Dec 2018
42. Fayyad, U., Piatetsky-Shapiro, G., Smyth, P.: The KDD process for extracting useful knowledge from volumes of data. Commun. ACM (1996). https://doi.org/10.1145/240455.240464
43. ISO/IEC ISO/IEC 25024:2015 Systems and software engineering — Systems and software Quality Requirements and Evaluation (SQuaRE) — Measurement of data quality. Int. Stand. ISO/IEC 250242015. https://www.iso.org/obp/ui/#iso:std:iso-iec:25024:ed-1:v1:en. Accessed 14 Sept 2018
44. Sriparasa, S.S.: JavaScript and JSON Essentials (2013)
45. Apache Impala. https://impala.apache.org/. Accessed 15 Sept 2018
46. SQLite. https://www.sqlite.org/. Accessed 15 Sept 2018
47. Ansa. Turismo: 2,9mln arrivi in Sardegna 2016 (2018). http://bit.ly/AnsaTurismo2016. Accessed 15 Dec 2018

Method for the Assessment of Semantic Accuracy Using Rules Identified by Conditional Functional Dependencies

Vanusa S. Santana[1]([⊠]) and Fábio S. Lopes[2]([⊠])

[1] Graduate Master Program IPT – Institute of Technological Research,
São Paulo, Brazil
vanusa.santana1@yahoo.com.br
[2] Mackenzie Presbyterian University, São Paulo, Brazil
flopes@mackenzie.br

Abstract. Data is a central resource of organizations, which makes data quality essential for their intellectual growth. Quality is seen as a multifaceted concept and, in general, refers to suitability for use. This indicates that the pillar for the quality evaluation is the definition of a set of quality rules, determined from the criteria of the business. However, it may be impossible to manually specify the quality rules for the evaluation. The use of Conditional Functional Dependencies (CFDs) allows to automatically identifying context-dependent quality rules. This paper presents a method for assess data quality using the CFD concept to extract quality rules and identify inconsistencies. The quality of the database in the proposed method will be evaluated in the semantic accuracy dimension. The method consolidates the process of knowledge discovery with data quality assessment, listing the respective activities that result in the quantification of semantic accuracy. An instance of the method has been demonstrated by applying it in the context of air quality monitoring data. The evaluation of the method showed that the CFDs rules were able to reflect some atmospheric phenomena, emerging interesting context-dependent rules. The patterns of the transactions, which may be unknown by the users, can be used as input for the evaluation and monitoring of data quality.

Keywords: Data quality · Conditional functional dependence (CFD) · Data quality assessment

1 Introduction

Quality is presented as a multifaceted concept and, in general, refers to all the characteristics of a product that support its ability to satisfy needs [5]. In 1963, the importance of data quality was already emphasized with the phrase "garbage in, garbage out". In subsequent years, data became a central resource of organizations, and quality problems became more complex as a result of evolution. Data-driven decisions can be observed in almost every aspect of society. With the emerging universe of Big Data-related technologies, data has gained even more relevance by providing the ability

© Springer Nature Switzerland AG 2019
E. Garoufallou et al. (Eds.): MTSR 2019, CCIS 1057, pp. 284–297, 2019.
https://doi.org/10.1007/978-3-030-36599-8_25

to collect and analyze data of unprecedented breadth and depth, bringing new insights into work, human relationships and society in a way general.

Several studies have been published in the literature to guide activities related to data quality. ISO 25012: 2008 [15] presents the dimensions of quality, such as accuracy, consistency, traceability, among others. There is also a vast literature in the area of quality, with proposals for methods for the assessment and improvement of data quality, describing the phases, strategies, techniques, dimensions and applicability of each method [6, 10, 17]. Despite these studies, the area of data quality still presents challenges to be solved. Lack of quality prevails because of the huge volume of data generated, the speed of incoming data, and especially the large variety of heterogeneous data. This fact makes essential to understand the dimensions of quality and how they can be evaluated. According to [18], in practice, some dimensions can be measured by the number of errors. However, the problem is to determine what an error is, since it requires a set of clear, context-dependent criteria.

In the literature, it is suggested to find these rules through Conditional Functional Dependencies (CFDs) that are functional dependencies applied only to a subset of data, according to the context in which they are [19]. According to the authors, it may be impossible to specify quality rules manually. So, an alternative is to learn the rules from the data itself, using real-world data, which mirrors business transactions and corresponding data. This approach can be used in data quality management to suggest possible context-dependent quality rules and to identify inconsistencies. The automatic identification of rules is one of the suggestions of future work of [2] and also was proposed in the study of [3] that uses association rules extracted from transactions of systems in production to find data quality problems. However, using CFDs to support data quality activities involves using a knowledge discovery method. The published work on CFDs focuses on improving algorithm performance, while quality methods generally suggest a manual approach to rules. A method with their respective techniques and set of activities has not yet been proposed in the literature, which defines a logical process for quality assessment using CFD. There remains a need to detail how this can be done in a real-world system and how CFD identified rules can be used to automate data quality assessment.

In this paper, we propose a method for assess data quality, using rules identified by CFDs, which consolidates literature approaches for data quality with the process of identifying contextual dependency rules through CFD. The data quality assessment was based on data quality methods, processes and metrics proposed in the literature. The observation should be evaluated quantitatively according to the semantic accuracy dimension. The study was applied using data from the Air Quality System of CETESB, which is the agency of the state government of São Paulo, Brazil, responsible for the control, supervision, monitoring and licensing of pollution-generating activities, with the fundamental concern of preserving and recovering water quality, air and soil. The quality rules in the context of air pollutants were identified by an automated method, as proposed by [8].

2 Related Work

2.1 Data Quality

Quality, in general, refers to all the characteristics of a product that support its ability to satisfy needs, or fitness for use [5]. Lack of quality may indicate a defect in the specification of requirements, since quality relates to compliance of customer requirements and expectations.

Each quality dimension captures a specific aspect of quality [5]. For each data type one dimension may be more relevant than another, and one dimension can be evaluated from several perspectives. Thus, data quality improvement activity begins with the definition of the quality dimensions that will be evaluated through the analysis of the context and business rules. In this article, we approach the assessment of the semantic accuracy dimension. Accuracy means how much the data represents the real world, the extent to which data is correct, reliable, and error-free [21]. There are two types of structural accuracy: syntactic and semantic. While the syntactic accuracy can be measured by a distance function, semantic accuracy is improved with knowledge of the domain where the corresponding actual value is known, allowing to evaluate whether the value v is true. Thus, semantic accuracy is usually more complex to calculate [5]. Despite this complexity, establishing metrics for data quality assessment is a key activity. According to [14], data quality metrics are required for two main reasons. First, metric values are used to support data-based decision making. In this case, well-founded data quality metrics are required to indicate the extent to which decision makers should rely on data values. Secondly, metric values are used to support cost-effective data quality management. In this context, improving data quality should apply if the benefits of high quality information do not outweigh the associated costs.

In [13], evaluation strategies are divided as application-independent and application-dependent, in which domain knowledge is required to verify logic errors. For the authors, data quality assessment and monitoring are the keys to solving quality problems. Also, an essential part of improving data quality is addressing data inconsistency issues that arise from rule violations. Data inconsistency is usually the result of rules violation. Quality rules are constraints that validate data relationships and can be verified through automated processes. They are the mainstay for quality assessment and, if properly designed, allow the identification and accurate classification of problems in the data [17].

Deriving a complete set of integrity constraints that accurately governs an organization's policies and domain semantics is a primary task for improving data quality. These rules determine the relationships between a restricted set of attribute values that are expected to be true in a given context. However, the rules are often unknown or insufficiently documented, so it may be useful to retrieve rules from transactions in production systems. Deviations from these patterns can signal data quality problems [3]. Conditional functional dependency is one of the alternatives to derive the patterns in the data and associations between attributes, as discussed below.

2.2   Conditional Functional Dependencies

The work of [8] proposes a data-based tool that can be used to manage the data quality of an organization to suggest possible context-dependent quality rules and to identify inconsistencies. This study searches for CFDs, that is, functional dependencies applied only to a subset of data, according to the context in which they are found. For example, an organization may have rules such as: (a) all new customers will receive a 15% discount on their first purchase and (b) preferred customers will receive a 25% discount on all purchases. These semantic quality rules can be expressed as the following CFDs:

$$\varphi 1a : [status = 'NEW', numPurchases = 1] \rightarrow [discount = 15\%]$$
$$\varphi 1b : [status = 'PREF'] \rightarrow [discount = 25\%]$$

CFDs define a restricted semantics in which, for a set of attributes X, Y, the CFD $X \rightarrow Y$ indicates that the values in X must (only) occur with the corresponding values in Y. A CFD φ on R can be represented by $\varphi: (X \rightarrow Y, Tp)$, where X, Y are sets of attributes in R and $X \rightarrow Y$ is a functional dependency (FD). Tp is a pattern of φ, with attributes in X and Y. For each attribute B in $(X \cup Y)$, the value of B for a tuple in Tp, tp [B], is a constant of the domain of B or '-', representing a variable value. In the CFDs rules, the discount (DISC attribute) functionally depends on the status (STAT attribute) and customer purchase number (NUM-PUR attribute). However, the discount is not applicable to all customers. The rule is only applied to a subset of clients, namely new (STAT = 'NEW') or preferred clients (STAT = 'PREF').

A CFD improves functional dependencies by allowing constant values to be associated with dependency attributes. In particular, CFDs are able to capture semantic relationships between data values. It was analyzed whether a statistical method to determine outliers could solve the problem of the domain under study and signal quality problems. However, a central aspect of this research is that we need to validate not only one attribute, but a whole transaction. In the context of air pollutant data, the value of an attribute can be admitted into the domain, but it becomes uncommon in comparison to other attributes. CFDs help in this case, once the rules capture the relationships between the attributes, showing which data depend on others. When associating constants, we have the expected values for a given attribute in relation to the other attributes of the transaction.

According to [11], the work of [8] was a pioneer in studying the discovery of CFDs by algorithms, since previous works assumed that the CFDs would be projected manually. Rule discovery is indeed a critical aspect of data quality tools. It is unrealistic to manually design CFDs for use in data cleansing. Thus, it is necessary to have algorithms that automatically discover or learn CFDs from a sample basis [11]. The authors present the CFDMiner algorithm for the discovery of CFDs with patterns expressed only in constants whose output contains neither redundant attributes nor redundant patterns.

In recent years, several studies have been published on the discovery of CFDs and their use for detection of inconsistencies, repair and improvement of data quality [9, 22, 23]. According to [1] data mining can play a key role in ensuring data quality, whose rules can be efficiently reused in the data cleansing process. The work of [20] also conducts an experiment on datasets from medical applications domain, to detect inconsistencies. In this article, the authors pointed out that there is little discussion in the literature for improving data consistency and most recent work focus on record matching and duplicate detection. The automated quality assessment can use rules discovery tools [10]. However, before attempting to extract useful knowledge of the data, it is important to understand that just applying algorithms for data analysis is not sufficient for a successful data mining project. It is necessary to employ a knowledge discovery process (KDD), which defines a sequence of steps that must be followed to discover knowledge (eg patterns) in the data. KDD focuses on understanding patterns and seeks to extract high-level knowledge from low-level data in the context of large data sets. The method proposed in this article joins the activities of knowledge discovery with the quality evaluation process.

3   Method Design

The proposed method has 10 distinct activities, showed in Fig. 1. The Data Set Definition specifies the set of data that will be evaluated. The process-oriented approach or the specific basis can be used. In this article, the experiment covers some specific bases of CETESB, since starting the quality process in a smaller project increases the chances of success, since it produces results in a short period of time. In order to test the method proposed in this paper, the CETESB data sets were used, according to Table 1.

Table 1. Datasets used in the experiment.

#	Dataset	# Samples	Period
1	Hourly average of atmospheric pollutant	3884	01/01/2018 to 06/30/2018
2	Hourly average of atmospheric pollutant	4413	07/01/2018 to 12/31/2018

This dataset contains atmospheric pollutant values collected per hour. Dataset 1 contains the records that were used to extract the rules and the dataset 2 records for rules validation. These databases are public and available on the Qualar System website [7]. Regarding to the experiment in this article, in order to obtain a reliable collection of CFDs, we considered only the transactions that were previously validated by CETESB as correct. Transactions with null data were also removed from the database.

The activity of Definition of Dimensions of Interest establishes which characteristic of quality will be measured. In this article, the dimension of interest is semantic accuracy, since its assessment and improvement is related to the mapping of conditional functional dependencies. Once the dimensions have been defined, the Base Preprocessing activity is performed in order to process the data so that the results of the algorithm execution are more relevant. In the CETESB database, there are several attributes that store the pollutant values with numerical data, generating a wide variety of possible values. To treat this situation and allow the algorithm to return a smaller number of rules, allowing them to be evaluated more clearly, the values were grouped into classes. For this, it was necessary to calculate the sample amplitude, the number of classes by with Sturges Distribution and the amplitude of the class interval, to determine the limits of each class. It was decided to create an attribute for each pollutant that represented the distribution of classes in a code of type *string*, since a distribution with a binary indicator would generate many attributes, making the execution of the algorithm impracticable.

For example, considering that the "Hourly Average" value of pollutant MP_{10} is 15, this would categorize the value into a "100000000000" string, as the value fits into the first class (0 | —— 60). This activity was performed for all pollutants. An example is shown in Table 2.

Table 2. Class distribution – Inhalable Particles

MP_{10} – Inhalable particles (µg/m3)		
Order	Class	Class Code
1	0 |-------- 60	100000000000
2	60 |-------- 120	010000000000
3	120 |-------- 180	001000000000
4	180 |-------- 240	000100000000
5	240 |-------- 300	000010000000
6	300 |-------- 360	000001000000
7	360 |-------- 420	000000100000
8	420 |-------- 480	000000010000
9	480 |-------- 540	000000001000
10	540 |-------- 600	000000000100
11	600 |-------- 660	000000000010
12	660 |-------- 720	000000000001

Then the process calls the Rule Evaluation Metrics Definition activity that will be used to identify the degree of interest of the rule, according to the data domain. For example, one can minimum threshold of support and confidence. These metrics help you extract rules that are more interesting.

The activity Choice of the CFD Mining Algorithm consists of defining which algorithm will be used in the method for discovering patterns and functional dependencies. The algorithm chosen in this work was CFDMiner. However, this paper proposes a generic method that can be applied in other domains. There are other algorithms, such as CTANE, that could be used in this activity. Once this is done, the Execution of the Mining Algorithm is performed in the database previously treated in activity 3.

The execution activity generates a set of rules, which must be evaluated by a specialist. This is the purpose of the Validation of rules by Expert Domain Analysis activity. The domain expert analyzes and interprets the extracted patterns. The extracted rules are validated to see if, in fact, they represent the rules of the context and to consolidate the discovered knowledge.

The validity rules follow for the activity of Translation of Quality Rules for SQL queries. It is necessary to translate the violation of these rules into SQL queries, which will be used to retrieve inconsistent records.

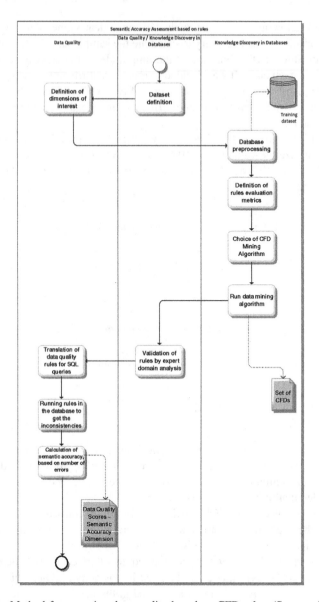

Fig. 1. Method for assessing data quality based on CFD rules. (Source: Author)

The queries constructed in the previous activity are applied in new databases, in the activity of Running of the Rules in the Database to get the Inconsistencies, to find out the records that violates the rules. It is worth noting that once these rules have been documented, they can be used for continuous monitoring of data quality.

Finally, the Calculation of Semantic Accuracy, based on Number of Errors, consists in quantifying the semantic accuracy based on the number of errors and the number of records evaluated. For this step, the DQA method of [18] and the proposed formulas [12] are used.

4   Results and Discussion

After executing the algorithm, it was calculated some measures of significance and interestingness of the rule, such as support, confidence and lift. The definition of support and minimum confidence to filter the results of the algorithm depends on the criteria of each domain. These metrics aim to help filter which rules are more relevant. However, in the scenario proposed here, a large part of the rules had low lift indices, although they had significant support and confidence. Thus, it was essential for this work to complement the analysis of the rules according to the theoretical knowledge of the domain. Due to the high number of rules, only a few were selected for analysis. For the choice of rules, two criteria were adopted: (i) rule with the highest number of support (ii) search for rules that reflected atmospheric phenomena known in the literature.

In general, the concentration levels of pollutants suspended in the atmosphere are strongly related to weather conditions [4, 7, 16]. The dynamics and movement of the air masses is a decisive factor of the weather conditions of a place. A stable atmosphere limits the dispersion of pollutants and favors pollution peaks. It is possible to observe that the highest concentrations of pollutants are obtained in the winter period, when atmospheric conditions are unfavorable to the dispersion and removal of pollutants and that the time is a factor that influences the value of the pollutant. The winds are part of the dispersion of the pollutant. If the wind increases in the atmosphere, the concentration of the pollutant decreases.

Chemical reactions also alter the concentration of pollutants as they produce other compounds. For example, nitrogen oxide and hydrocarbons, under the action of solar radiation, can react producing the photochemical oxidants, especially ozone. The concentration of nitrogen dioxide increases when the hydrogen oxide reaches its maximum, while the maximum of the ozone is around noon, after the maximum of nitrogen dioxide and only after the concentration of nitrogen monoxide is notably decreased. In this way, hydrogen dioxide and solar energy contribute to the formation of ozone, while hydrogen oxide is responsible for its destruction, and then only after noon, plenty of solar energy and nitrogen dioxide the dynamic equilibrium of the chemical reaction towards an increase in ozone.

Table 3. CFD rules – Nitrogen Oxide and Ozone

Rules - Nitrogen Oxide and Ozone
φ: [Code_Wind_Direction, Code_Ozone, Indicator_Hour_13_18] => Code_Nitrogen_Oxide, (010000000000, 000010000000, 1 ‖ 100000000000) **Rule Description:** Nitrogen oxide depends on the direction of wind, ozone and time. If the wind direction is greater than 74 ° and less than 148 ° (class 2 equivalent), the ozone is greater than 61 µg / m3 and less than 75 µg / m3 (class 5 equivalent) and the time is between 1:00 pm and 6:00 pm , then the nitrogen oxide will be greater than 2 ppb and less than 30 ppb (class 1 equivalent)
φ: [Code_Ozone, Code_Temperature] => Code_Nitrogen_Oxide, (001000000000, 000100000000 ‖ 100000000000) **Rule Description:** Nitrogen oxide depends on ozone and temperature. If the ozone is greater than 33 µg / m 3 and less than 47 µg / m 3 (equivalent class 3) and the temperature is higher than 14 ° C and less than 16 ° C (class 4 equivalent), then the nitrogen oxide will be greater than 2 ppb and less than 30 ppb (class 1 equivalent)
φ: [Code_UltraViolet, Code_Ozone, Code_Wind_Speed, Code_Humidity] => Code_Nitrogen_Oxide, (100000000000, 010000000000, 001000000000, 000000000100 ‖ 100000000000) **Rule Description:** Nitrogen oxide depends on ultraviolet radiation, ozone, wind speed and humidity. If the ultraviolet radiation is greater than 0 W / m2 and less than 4 W / m2 (Class 1 equivalent), the ozone is greater than 19 µg / m3 and less than 33 µg / m3 (Class 2 equivalent), the wind speed is greater than 0.68 m / s and less than 1.02 m / s (equivalent class 3) and the humidity is greater than 83% and less than 89% (class 10 equivalent), then the nitrogen oxide will be greater than 2 ppb and less than 30 ppb (class 1 equivalent)
φ: [Code_Ozone, Month] => Code_Nitrogen_Oxide, (000010000000, 5 ‖ 100000000000) **Rule Description:** Nitrogen oxide depends on the ozone and the month. If the ozone is greater than 61 µg / m3 and less than 75 µg / m3 (equivalent class 5) and the month is 5, then the nitrogen oxide will be greater than 2 ppb and less than 30 ppb (class 1 equivalent)
φ: [Code_UltraViolet, Code_Ozone, Code_Temperature] => Code_Nitrogen_Oxide, (100000000000, 010000000000, 000010000000 ‖ 100000000000) **Rule Description:** Nitrogen oxide depends on ultraviolet radiation, ozone and temperature. If the ultraviolet radiation is greater than 0 W / m2 and less than 4 W / m2 (Class 1 equivalent), the ozone is greater than 19 µg / m3 and less than 33 µg / m3 (class 2 equivalent) and the temperature is greater than 16 ° C and less than 18 ° C (class 5 equivalent), then nitrogen oxide will be greater than 2 ppb and less than 30 ppb (class 1 equivalent)

By means of the processes of discovery of CFDs instantiated in this article, were found some rules that relate the oxide of nitrogen, nitrogen dioxide, nitrogen monoxide and some conditions like the temperature and the schedule with the ozone, according to Table 3. As explained above, the values of pollutants were distributed into classes in which a code representing the distribution class was assigned. The rule description in Table 3 is a textual description based on the meaning of the class. In the transaction shown in Table 4, the ozone has a low value (class 1), while the values of nitrogen oxide, nitrogen monoxide and nitrogen dioxide are still high. It is worth noting that values were measured in the morning, at a time when solar radiation, ultraviolet radiation and temperature were low.

Table 4. Transactions with low ozone (class 1)

#	Month	Indicator_Hour_0_6	Indicator_Hour_7_12	Indicator_Hour_13_18	Indicator_Hour_19_24	Code_Ozone	Code_Nitrogen_Oxide	Code_Nitrogen_Monoxide
1	6	0	1	0	0	100000000000	000000000001	000000000001

#	Code_Nitrogen_Dioxide	Code_Wind_Direction	Code_Wind_Speed	Code_Humidity	Code_Temperature	Code_UltraViolet	Code_Radiation
1	000000001000	000000000010	100000000000	000000001000	000100000000	100000000000	100000000000

A query was made in the sample in which the ozone values are higher, according to Table 5. It was found that the transaction pattern was changed (i) the high values occurred in the afternoon (Indicator_Hour_13_18 with value equal true) (ii) the values of nitrogen oxide, nitrogen monoxide and nitrogen dioxide decreased notably, concentrating on the (iii) the values of temperature, ultraviolet radiation and solar radiation are high (iv) velocity and direction of the lower wind.

Table 5. Transactions with high ozone (values from class 9)

#	Month	Indicator_Hour_0_6	Indicator_Hour_7_12	Indicator_Hour_13_18	Indicator_Hour_19_24	Code_Ozone	Code_Nitrogen_Oxide	Code_Nitrogen_Monoxide
1	2	0	0	1	0	00000000001	100000000000	100000000000
2	2	0	0	1	0	000000001000	100000000000	100000000000
3	2	0	0	1	0	000000000100	100000000000	100000000000
4	5	0	0	1	0	000000000100	100000000000	100000000000
5	5	0	0	1	0	000000001000	100000000000	100000000000
6	5	0	0	1	0	000000000010	100000000000	100000000000
7	5	0	0	1	0	000000001000	100000000000	100000000000
8	5	0	0	1	0	000000000010	100000000000	100000000000
9	5	0	0	1	0	000000001000	100000000000	100000000000

#	Code_Nitrogen_Dioxide	Code_Wind_Direction	Code_Wind_Speed	Code_Humidity	Code_Temperature	Code_UltraViolet	Code_Radiation
1	001000000000	010000000000	001000000000	010000000000	000000000001	000000100000	000000000100
2	001000000000	010000000000	001000000000	010000000000	000000000010	010000000000	001000000000
3	000100000000	010000000000	000001000000	010000000000	000000000010	001000000000	000100000000
4	010000000000	000000000001	001000000000	000100000000	000000000100	000010000000	000000100000
5	001000000000	010000000000	001000000000	000010000000	000000100000	000100000000	000001000000
6	010000000000	000000000001	001000000000	000100000000	000000000100	000100000000	000001000000
7	001000000000	010000000000	001000000000	000100000000	000000010000	000100000000	000001000000
8	010000000000	000100000000	001000000000	000100000000	000000000100	001000000000	001000000000
9	010000000000	010000000000	001000000000	010000000000	000000000010	001000000000	000100000000

A very implicit rule is the relationship between solar radiation and ultraviolet radiation with temperature and time. Some examples are shown in Table 6.

Table 6. CFD rules – Temperature and Radiation

Rules - Temperature and Radiation
φ:[Indicator_Hour_19_24, Code_Temperature] => Code_Radiation, (1, 000100000000 ‖ 100000000000)   **Rule Description:** Solar radiation depends on the time and temperature. If the time is between 19h and 24h and the temperature is greater than 14°C and less than 16°C (class 4 equivalent), than the solar radiation will be greater than 0 and less than 94W/m2 (class 1 equivalent)
φ: [Code_Wind_Direction] => Code_Radiation, (000000000010 ‖ 100000000000)   **Rule Description:** Solar radiation depends on wind direction. If the wind direction is greater than 740° and less than 814° (class 11 equivalent), then the solar radiation will be greater than 0 and less than 94 (class 1 equivalent).
φ: [Indicator_Hour_19_24] => Code_UltraViolet, (1 ‖ 100000000000)   **Rule Description:** Ultraviolet radiation depends on the time. If the time is between 19h and 24h, then ultraviolet radiation will be greater than 0 and less than 4W/m2 (class 1 equivalent)
φ: [Month, Code_Radiation, Code_Temperature] => Code_UltraViolet (2, 100000000000, 000001000000 ‖ 100000000000)   **Rule Description:** Ultraviolet radiation depends on the month, solar radiation, and temperature. If the month is 2, the solar radiation is greater than 0 and less than 94W/m2 (class 1 equivalent), and the temperature is greater than 18°C and less than 20°C (class 6 equivalent), then the radiation ultraviolet will be greater than 0 and less than 4W/m2 (class 1 equivalent).

By consulting in the sample, a date with the value of high solar radiation (last class equivalent), it can be observed that the high values of solar radiation imply high temperatures. The algorithm also captured the relationship of solar radiation and ultraviolet radiation with wind. Through a research on the dynamics of the winds, it was verified that, in fact, it has a relation with the temperature. The winds, displacements of the atmospheric air, appear with the movement of some parts of the atmosphere, caused by the differences of the atmospheric pressure due to changes of the temperature. It was also possible to note that in fact there is an inverse correlation of solar radiation with the direction of the wind.

After the mining rules analysis, as proposed in the method, the next step is to translate them to SQL statements that express the violation of the rules and apply those queries in the database to retrieve the number of records with error. The result of this activity is shown in Table 7.

Table 7. CFD Query Violation

CFD	Attribute	Violation of the Rule SQL query translation	Nº of records that violates the rule	Nº of records pointed out by CETESB as error
[Indicator_Hour_19_24, Code_Temperature] => Code_Radiation, (1, 000100000000 || 100000000000)	Code_Radiation	SELECT COUNT(0) FROM ##DataTableAssessment WHERE Indicator_Hour_19_24 = 1 AND Code_Temperature = '000100000000' AND Code_Radiation <> '100000000000'	0	0
[Code_Wind_Direction] => Code_Radiation, (000000000010 || 100000000000)	Code_Radiation	SELECT COUNT(0) FROM ##DataTableAssessment WHERE Code_Wind_Direction = '000000000010' AND Code_Radiation <> '100000000000'	0	0
[Indicator_Hour_19_24] => Code_UltraViolet, (1 || 100000000000)	Code_UltraViolet	SELECT COUNT(0) FROM ##DataTableAssessment WHERE Indicator_Hour_19_24 = 1 AND Code_UltraViolet <> '100000000000'	13	0
[Code_Wind_Direction, Code_Ozone,Indicator_Hour_13_18] => Code_Nitrogen_Oxide, (010000000000, 000010000000, 1 || 100000000000)	Code_Nitrogen_Oxide	SELECT COUNT(0) FROM ##DataTableAssessment WHERE Code_Wind_Direction = '010000000000' AND Code_Ozone = '000010000000' AND Indicator_Hour_13_18 = 1 AND Code_Nitrogen_Oxide <> '100000000000'	0	0
[Code_Ozone,Code_Temperature] =>Code_Nitrogen_Oxide, (001000000000, 000100000000 || 100000000000)	Code_Nitrogen_Oxide	SELECT COUNT(0) FROM ##DataTableAssessment WHERE Code_Ozone = '001000000000' AND Code_Temperature = '000100000000' AND Code_Nitrogen_Oxide <> '100000000000'	0	0
[Code_UltraViolet, Code_Ozone, Code_Wind_Speed, Code_Humidity] => Code_Nitrogen_Oxide, (100000000000, 010000000000, 001000000000, 000000000100 || 100000000000)	Code_Nitrogen_Oxide	SELECT COUNT(0) FROM ##DataTableAssessment WHERE Code_UltraViolet = '100000000000' AND Code_Ozone = '010000000000' AND Code_Wind_Speed = '001000000000' AND Code_Humidity = '000000000100' AND Code_Nitrogen_Oxide <> '100000000000'	3	0
[Code_UltraViolet,Code_Ozone, Code_Temperature] => Code_Nitrogen_Oxide, (100000000000, 010000000000, 000010000000 || 100000000000)	Code_Nitrogen_Oxide	SELECT COUNT(0) FROM ##DataTableAssessment WHERE Code_UltraViolet = '100000000000' AND Code_Ozone = '010000000000' AND Code_Temperature = '000010000000' AND Code_Nitrogen_Oxide <> '100000000000'	9	6
[Code_Pressure, Indicator_Hour_13_18] => Code_Inhalable_Particles, (000000001000, 1 || 100000000000)	Code_Inhalable_Particles	SELECT COUNT(0) FROM ##DataTableAssessment WHERE Code_Pressure = '000000001000' AND Indicator_Hour_13_18 = 1 AND Code_Inhalable_Particles <> '100000000000'	1	0
[Code_Wind_Direction,Code_Wind_Speed, Code_Temperature] => Code_Inhalable_Particles, (010000000000, 000001000000, 000000100000 || 100000000000)	Code_Inhalable_Particles	SELECT COUNT(0) FROM ##DataTableAssessment WHERE Code_Pressure = '000000001000' AND Indicator_Hour_13_18 = 1 AND Code_Inhalable_Particles <> '100000000000'	0	0

To illustrate the calculation of the semantic accuracy and the artifact produced with the quality scores, we will consider that all the records pointed to as violation of the rules in Table 7 are really a transaction error. In this way, we have the values represented by attribute in Table 8. Based on the metrics presented in the work of [18] and [12], the individual scores of each attribute are calculated. The total of the semantic accuracy dimensional score in the assessed database was also calculated by dividing the sum of all individual scores by the number of all tested properties. If the importance of the variables in the organization is known, the scores can be multiplied by a weighting factor. In the example, the 99.85% value represents the percentage of data in the tested dataset that does not violate any known conditional functional dependencies. It can be said, then, that the database has semantic accuracy of 99.85%.

Table 8. Calculation of semantic accuracy

Attribute	# samples	Records with error	Score $(1-(DQRV/T))$	%
Code radiation	4413	0	$(1-(0/4413)) = 1$	100%
Code ultraviolet	4413	13	$(1-(13/4413)) = 0{,}9970$	99,7%
Code nitrogen oxide	4413	12	$(1-(12/4413)) = 0{,}9972$	99,72%
Code_inhalable_particles	4413	1	$(1-(1/4413)) = 0{,}9997$	99,97%
Total $\sum(\mathbf{IQ} - \mathbf{Score})/\mathbf{P}$ (Pipino et al. [18]) (Furber e Hepp [12])			0,9985	99,85%

5 Conclusion and Future Work

The execution of the method for assessment of data quality in the CETESB context showed relevant results. It was observed that the method proposed in this research makes it possible to combine the data quality assessment activities with the methods of knowledge discovery. It was possible to confirm that the CFD rules identification process is able to capture interesting rules and that, in fact, represent the domain. The analysis showed that many of these rules corresponded to phenomena known in the context of atmospheric pollution.

Conditional functional dependencies have a syntax that can clearly represent context rules to document dependencies between attributes. This syntax also makes it easier to translate the rules for commands and queries that look for records that violate the rules.

One of the disadvantages observed in the mining process of the conditional functional dependencies was the high number of rules. The analysis of so many rules is an onerous process. Despite this, the use of a process of knowledge discovery emerges rules that would be unknown by business users, as well as stimulate discussions about the possible deviation of the standard and problem of data quality. CFD helps filter out the attention points, some assumptions, and assumptions for a data quality project. Since CFD identifies a rule applied to a subset, similar rule mining was observed, only with the differentiation of constants. Although they are complementary rules, this situation can be a disadvantage, because the rules can configure as contradictory, generating errors in the evaluation of data quality.

CFDs discovered by the mining algorithm can signal potential quality problems and aid in the process of data quality assessment. It is necessary to validate if the signaling is even a quality problem or if it would be a false positive. But in a system, such as CETESB, nonstandard transactions may be the first sign that there is a problem to check. In this way, system crashes can be discovered and corrected earlier.

The application of the method confirmed that the treatment of the variables is primordial in the process of data mining. In this work, instead of assigning a string code to the Time indicator, just as done to Average, a binary indicator was assigned. However, this binary allocation generated non-interesting rules. This situation questions the hypothesis that it is possible to extract rules automatically independent of previous knowledge of the context. In fact, without understanding the importance of variables and their correct treatment, we may incur many redundant rules, which are not interesting or attributes that do not have any strong correlation with each other. Thus, it is emphasized that the process of knowledge discovery requires human interaction with domain experts.

The preparation phase took up a good part of the time. Preprocessing also generated demands, such as adding a method for class distribution. In the literature, when suggesting using this tool in the activities of data quality, knowledge discovery activities are not listed, being able to err in the project when having this effort underestimated. The complex mining process requires the development of an ideal environment for analysis.

For further work, it would be interesting to analyze if it is possible to use the rules generated to impute data, extending the proposed method for a missing data filling approach. Another question would be to evaluate if the method improves according to the algorithm used, detailing how the algorithm influences the results of the method and if it is possible to observe more accurate results using other mining algorithms. It would also be interesting to extend the method by proposing continuous quality monitoring activities. The documented rules can serve as input for a method of improving data quality and for creating a Classification System that consolidates the different rules for the same variable.

References

1. Abdo, A.S., Rashed, K.S., Hatem, M.A.: Enhancement of data quality in health care industry: a promising data quality approach. In: Handbook of Research on Machine Learning Innovations and Trends, pp. 230–250. IGI Global (2017)
2. Abdullah, U., Sawar, M.J., Ahmed, A.: Design of a rule-based system using Structured Query Language. In: Eighth IEEE International Conference on Dependable, Autonomic and Secure Computing DASC 2009, pp. 223–228. IEEE (2009)
3. Alpar, P., Winkelsträter, S.: Assessment of data quality in accounting data with association rules. Expert Syst. Appl. **41**(5), 2259–2268 (2014)
4. Aria. Teoria da Poluição Atmosférica. <http://www.ariadobrasil.com.br/pollutant_dispersal. php/>. Accessed 18 Feb 2019
5. Batini, C., Scannapieco, M.: Data and Information Quality. DSA. Springer, Cham (2016). https://doi.org/10.1007/978-3-319-24106-7
6. Batini, C., et al.: A comprehensive data quality methodology for web and structured data. Int. J. Innovative Comput. Appl. **1**(3), 205–218 (2008)
7. Cetesb website. Qualar. <http://cetesb.sp.gov.br/ar/qualar/>. Accessed 16 July 2018
8. Chiang, F., Miller, R.J.: Discovering data quality rules. Proc. VLDB Endowment **1**(1), 1166–1177 (2008)
9. Du, Y., et al.: Discovering context-aware conditional functional dependencies. Front. Comput. Sci. **11**(4), 688–701 (2017)
10. English, L.P.: Improving Data Warehouse and Business Information Quality: Methods for Reducing Costs and Increasing Profits. Wiley, Hoboken (1999)
11. Fan, W., et al.: Discovering conditional functional dependencies. IEEE Trans. Knowl. Data Eng. **23**(5), 683–698 (2011)

12. Furber, C., Hepp, M.: SWIQA – A semantic web information quality assessment framework. In: European Conference on Information Systems (ECIS) (2011)
13. Guo, A., Liu, X., Sun, T.: Research on key problems of data quality in large industrial data environment. In: Proceedings of the 3rd International Conference on Robotics, Control and Automation (ICRCA 2018), pp. 245–248. ACM, New York (2018)
14. Heinrich, B., et al.: Requirements for data quality metrics. J. Data Inf. Qual. **9**(2), 32 (2018). Article 12
15. IEC 25012: 2008 Software engineering-Software product Quality requirements and evaluation (SQuaRE) - data quality model (2008)
16. Lira, T.S.: Modelagem e previsão da qualidade do ar na cidade de Uberlândia – MG. Tese (doutorado) Universidade Federal de Uberlândia, Programa de Pós-Graduação em Engenharia Química (2009)
17. Maydanchik, A.: Data Quality Assessment. Technics Publications, Basking Ridge, 322 p. (2007)
18. Pipino, L.L., Lee, Y.W., Wang, R.Y.: Data quality assessment. Commun. ACM **45**(4), 211–218 (2002)
19. Saha, B., Srivastava, D.: Data quality: the other face of big data. In: 2014 IEEE 30th International Conference on Data Engineering (ICDE), pp. 1294–1297. IEEE (2014)
20. Salem, R., Abdo, A.: Fixing rules for data cleaning based on conditional functional dependency. Future Comput. Inf. J. **1**(1–2), 10–26 (2016)
21. Wang, R.Y., Strong, D.M.: Beyond accuracy: What data quality means to data consumers. J. Manag. Inf. Syst. **12**(4), 5–33 (1996)
22. Zhou, J., et al.: A method for generating fixing rules from constant conditional functional dependencies. IEEE Trans. Knowl. Data Eng. 6–11 (2016)
23. Zhang, C., Yufeng, D.: Conditional functional dependency discovery and data repair based on decision tree. In: International Conference on Fuzzy Systems and Knowledge Discovery, pp. 864–868 (2015)

A Semantic Representation
of the Citation Structure

Marcin Skulimowski[✉][ID]

Faculty of Physics and Applied Informatics, University of Lodz,
Pomorska 149/153, 90-236 Lodz, Poland
marcin.skulimowski@uni.lodz.pl

Abstract. A scientific citation is usually represented as a relation between two publications without any precise meaning and inner structure. In fact, the structure of a citation, which is usually not represented explicitly, can be quite complicated. In our previous papers, we have proposed so-called expanded citations which allow representing the structure of a citation in a machine-readable way. In this short paper, we present and discuss selected structures of citations. In particular, we consider their meaning and possible application.

Keywords: Citation relationship · Semantic publishing · Digital libraries

1 Introduction

A citation is a relation between two scientific publications[1]. We can visualize it as an arrow from a node representing a citing publication to a node representing a cited publication. A collection of articles and citations between them form a directed graph called a *citation graph* or *citation network* [1]. A citation network analysis provides useful data for many research information systems. However, a citation is more than merely a relationship between two papers without any precise meaning and inner structure. Consequently, there is a vast amount of literature on the creation and analysis of citation content data (e.g. [2,3]). For example, the *citation context* can provide us with knowledge about the reasons for a citation. This knowledge allows us to add meaning to an arrow representing a citation. To this end, we can use the CiTO ontology, enabling *characterization of the nature or type of citations* [4]. In our opinion, we can do something more. After reading two papers (citing and cited), we can add meaning to relations between parts of papers (e.g. concepts, definitions, figures) linked by a citation. It is possible because we know which parts (entities) from a cited paper are *used* in a citing paper and how they are *used*. Moreover, we can name relations between

---

[1] Our considerations apply to any scientific publication. Throughout this paper, the publications are also referred to as papers, articles or books. We do not distinguish between them.

© Springer Nature Switzerland AG 2019
E. Garoufallou et al. (Eds.): MTSR 2019, CCIS 1057, pp. 298–303, 2019.
https://doi.org/10.1007/978-3-030-36599-8_26

papers and entities from these papers. In this way, the *structure of a citation* emerges. The structure which is usually known to a reader but is not represented explicitly and machines cannot process it. Until recently, such a representation has not been possible. Nowadays, however, using semantic technologies, we can represent the *structure of a citation* in a machine-readable way. We have proposed such a representation based on the so-called *expanded citations* in our previous papers [5,6].

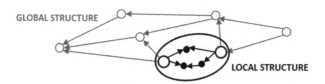

Fig. 1. The global and local structure of a citation network ($\bigcirc$ - publications, $\bullet$ - entities from publications).

There is a vast amount of literature on citation networks and their *global* structure (see, e.g. [7]). In this paper, we are interested in the *local* properties of a citation network. Namely, we are going to present and shortly analyze the structures of individual citations containing not only papers but also entities from them (Fig. 1). The paper is organized as follows. Section 2 gives a brief overview of expanded citations. In Sect. 3, we analyze selected structures of citations. In particular, we discuss their meaning and consider whether the structures can be useful in the evaluation of scientist's work. The paper ends with a short discussion and the outline of future work.

2   Expanded Citations

A bibliographic citation links two articles (see Fig. 2a). Egghe and Rousseau [1] state: *the fact that a document is mentioned in a reference list indicates that in the author's mind there is a relationship between a part or the whole of the cited document and a part or the whole of the citing document.* Most studies have focused on a relationship between entire papers [1,4,7]. The point is that using expanded citations we can represent in a machine-readable form a relationship between parts of papers. Consequently, instead of one relation (*cites*) between two papers, we consider more relations between these papers and also between parts of them called *concepts* (see Fig. 2b). A *concept* we define as any entity (part) of a paper named with a URI (Uniform Resource Identifier) [5]. We assume that it is possible to assign a URI to each entity from a scientific publication (for details - see [5]). In the rest of this paper, a concept from a publication X we denote by C_X.

We are now ready to introduce the main definition of this paper (see [6] and references therein). Let A and B be two publications. We say that a citation

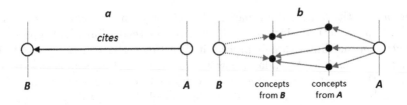

Fig. 2. A citation A *cites* B (a) and its exemplary structure (b).

$A \to B$ (A *cites* B) is *expandable* if there exist concepts C_A and C_B, relations r, r_A, r_B represented by object properties from some ontology O and the following RDF (Resource Description Framework) triples:

$$B \, r_B \, C_B. \quad C_A \, r \, C_B. \quad A \, r_A \, C_A. \tag{1}$$

We call the set of triples (1) an *expanded citation*. Moreover, an *expanded citation* created for a standard citation we call its *expansion*.

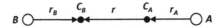

Fig. 3. An expanded citation.

Note that, using one expanded citation we can describe in RDF one "path" between nodes A and B representing articles (Fig. 3). Consequently, to represent a citation structure that can be made up of several "paths", we may need a few *expansions* (compare Figs. 2b and 3). Moreover, note that in order to create expanded citations, we need terms from appropriate ontologies to add semantics to relations between publications and concepts. An example of such an ontology is CiTO [4].

3   Citations and Their Structures

Let us now consider three examples of citations and their structures[2].

(I) Citing entity: DOI 10.2478/plc-2013-0010
Cited entity: ISBN 10 0195070038
Citation context: *This process is called "knowledge construction" (e.g. Rogoff, 1990).*
The author refers to the concept of *knowledge construction* introduced in the cited article. We present in Fig. 4-I an expansion for this citation.

---

[2] For simplicity, we do not use URIs in our examples. We also do not use object properties from any particular ontology.

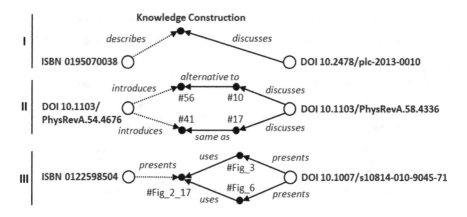

Fig. 4. The structures of citations from examples A-C.

(II) Citing entity: DOI 10.1103/PhysRevA.58.4336
Cited entity: DOI 10.1103/PhysRevA.54.4676
Citation contexts: *Grot, Rovelli and Tate [13] introduced a regularized self-adjoint operator and considered the full expression (10) for possible application to more general states having both positive and negative momenta but vanishing in the proximity of* $p = 0$.
Grot, Rovelli, and Tate [13] (...) produce a "regularized" self-adjoint time operator T_ε *with eigenstates (...),* $\langle p|T\pm\rangle_\varepsilon = ... (17)$.
Formulas (10) and (17) from the citing paper are in well-defined relations with formulas (56) and (41) from the cited paper. Hence, we represent the structure of this citation by two expanded citations - see Fig. 4-II.

(III) Citing entity: DOI 10.1007/s10814-010-9045-7
Cited entity: ISBN 10 0122598504
Citation contexts: *Fig. 3 Ground plans Ground plans of prehispanic houses from Oaxaca redrawn and adapted from the following sources: (...)(Flannery and Winter 1976, Fig. 2.17)(...) Fig. 6 Two extensively and meticulously excavated houses.(...) Flannery and Winter 1976, Fig. 2.17(...).*
Figures 3 and 6 use figure 2.17 from the cited paper. The structure of this citation is presented in Fig. 4-III.

The structures of citations presented in Fig. 4 do not exhaust all possibilities of connection between two papers. Let us consider what structures, in general, are possible in this case. We limit ourselves to structures of citations with at most *two expansions*. All possible structures, in this case, are presented in Fig. 5. The citation presented above in example (I) has structure **1** (*1-chain*). Citations having this structure are often used in *Introduction, Related Works* or *Discussion* sections. Note that, in structure **1**, paper A refers directly to C_B. If C_B is somehow used in A, then there may exist a concept C_A in some relation with C_B. A citation has then structure **2** (*2-chain*). Structure **3** (*diamond*) corresponds to the situation when A directly refers to two concepts from B. However, these con-

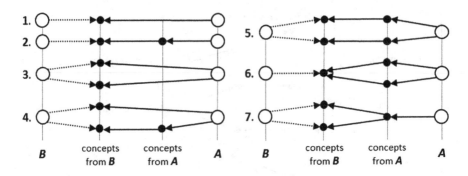

Fig. 5. The structures of citations with at most 2 expansions.

cepts are not "linked" to any concepts from A. In turn, structures **4** (*pentagon*) and **5** (*hexagon*) contain concepts from A related to concepts from B. Structure **5** contains two concepts from A. This structure appeared already in the above example (II). In structure **4**, a concept from B is related to a concept from A. Moreover, another concept from B is only *discussed* or *mentioned* in paper A. It is important to note that two expansions of a citation may *overlap*. For example, they may contain the same concept. In structure **6** two different concepts from A are linked to the same concept from B. By analogy to *bibliographic coupling* [7] we can say that the two concepts from A are *conceptually coupled* because they both are linked to the same concept from B. Figures #Fig_3 and #Fig_6 from our example (III) are *conceptually coupled* (see Fig. 4-III). In structure **7** a concept from A is linked to two concepts from B. In this case, by analogy to *co-citation* [7], we can say that two concepts from B are *co-used* by a concept from A. It seems reasonable to assume that all structures **1–7** may appear in practice. So one may ask the question: *how can we use them?* Let us now consider whether the structures of citations can be useful in the evaluation of scientist's work.

Nowadays, in the evaluation of a scientist's work, only the presence of a citation is taken into account [1]. The structure (meaning) of a citation is ignored. However, the structure may contain important information. It is reasonable to assume that for authors particularly valuable are those publications of others in which concepts (e.g. propositions, approaches, formulas) from their publications are somehow *used*, i.e. they are related to (new) concepts from citing publications. We may say that such *used* concepts *contribute to the progress of science*. On the contrary, citations of the form: *In the literature, there are many examples of...* placed in the *Introduction* section are of less value. Nowadays, these citations are treated equally. The knowledge of a *citation structure* enables us to distinguish between them. Without considering the details of the structures, we can assume that *the more concepts (from a citing paper) in a citation structure, the higher the value of a citation*. Using this "rule", we can sort the structures presented in Fig. 5 (in importance increasing order) by their values as follows: $1, 3, 2, 4, 7, 6, 5$. Note that the above considerations are valid, assuming that citations are *positive* or at least *neutral*. However, this is not necessarily the case. There are also *negative* citations which may indicate problems or flaws in the work or an opposing viewpoint. For example, in paper A, two counterexamples to a statement proposed in B can be given. This negative citation has structure **6**, which is very valuable according to the above list. Thus, for negative citations, the proposed "rule" of citation evaluation does not apply.

4 Discussion and Future Work

Expanded citations allow representing the structure of a citation in a machine-readable way. This possibility opens new perspectives for processing (searching and visualizing) of scientific domains and the evaluation of a scientist's work (see [6] and references therein). However, the picture is still far from completeness. Further studies are needed to estimate how large is the class of expandable citations. Does the size of this class depend on the scientific domain? In order to create an expanded citation, we need appropriate ontologies. Consequently, future work should also determine ontologies and terms from them useful in expanded citations. Another critical issue for future studies is to determine the extent to which machines can support the creation of expanded citations. The results obtained in the automatic classification of citation function using CNNs (Convolutional Neural Networks) and NLP (Natural Language Processing) suggest that machine support in the creation of expanded citations cannot be ruled out [8].

References

1. Egghe, L., Rousseau, R.: Introduction to Informetrics: Quantitative Methods in Library, Documentation and Information Science. Elsevier Science Publishers, Amsterdam (1990)
2. Kogalovsky, M., Krichel, T., Lyapunov, V., Medvedeva, O., Parinov, S., Sergeeva, V.: Open citation content data. In: Garoufallou, E., Sartori, F., Siatri, R., Zervas, M. (eds.) MTSR 2018. CCIS, vol. 846, pp. 355–364. Springer, Cham (2019). https://doi.org/10.1007/978-3-030-14401-2_34
3. Ding, Y., Zhang, G., Chambers, T., Song, M., Wang, X., Zhai, C.: Content-based citation analysis: the next generation of citation analysis. J. Assoc. Inf. Sci. Technol. **65**(9), 1820–1833 (2014)
4. Peroni, S., Shotton, D.: FaBiO and CiTO: ontologies for describing bibliographic resources and citations. J. Web Semant. **17**, 33–43 (2012)
5. Skulimowski, M.: On expanded citations, In: Proceedings of the 14th International Conference on Knowledge Technologies and Data-driven Business, i-KNOW, pp. 38:1–38:4. ACM (2014)
6. Skulimowski, M.: The flows of concepts. In: Proceedings of the International Conference on Knowledge Management and Information Sharing, KMIS, vol. 3, pp. 292–298 (2015)
7. Fang, Y., Rousseau, R.: Lattices in citation networks: an investigation into the structure of citation graphs. Scientometrics **50**, 273–287 (2001)
8. Bakhti, K., Niu, Z., Yousif, A., Nyamawe, A.S.: Citation function classification based on ontologies and convolutional neural networks. In: Uden, L., Liberona, D., Ristvej, J. (eds.) LTEC 2018. CCIS, vol. 870, pp. 105–115. Springer, Cham (2018). https://doi.org/10.1007/978-3-319-95522-3_10

Track on Metadata and Semantics for Agriculture, Food and Environment (AgroSEM 2019)

Hydrographic Datasets in Open Government Data Portals: Mitigation of Reusability Issues Through Provenance Documentation

Monica De Martino[1]([⊠]) [iD], Sergio Rosim[2] [iD], and Alfonso Quarati[1] [iD]

[1] Institute of Applied Mathematics and Information Technology, CNR, Genova, Italy
{demartino,quarati}@ge.imati.cnr.it
[2] INPE - Instituto Nacional de Pesquisas Espaciais, São José dos Campos, Brazil
sergio.rosim@inpe.br

Abstract. The paper provides a quantitative and qualitative snapshot on hydrographic datasets currently published in Open Government Data (OGD) portals aiming at investigating their reusability according to W3C recommendations and FAIR principles. Highly reputed OGD portals have been considered and searched for hydrographic datasets and their metadata. The resulting datasets have been analysed according to their compliance with reusability principles. In particular, we considered three metrics: data format machine readability; licence availability and openness; metadata provenance provision. The analysis highlights that OGD portals still have to solve some issues, in particular, a lack of detailed provenance. To promote the provision of provenance metadata of hydrographic datasets, enabling their comprehension and reuse, we illustrated a practice to improve their reusability by supplying workflow provenance metadata according to W3C PROV recommendation. We provide an illustrative example by documenting and publishing the generation of flooding areas maps produced by the Brazilian National Institute for Space Research (INPE).

Keywords: Hydrography · Open data · Reusability · Provenance

1 Introduction

Hydrographic data is essential in the study of natural hazards and hydro meteorological disasters such as floods and their impact on agriculture. Agriculture depends on water, which means that changes in rainfall patterns and intensity, droughts, and floods significantly impact crop production. The report "Water for agriculture in the Americas"[1], published by the Inter-American Institute for Cooperation on Agriculture estimated that just 19% of these events produced losses of almost USD 20 billion in Latin America and the Caribbean. To face

---

[1] http://repositorio.iica.int/bitstream/11324/6148/2/BVE17109367i.pdf.

© Springer Nature Switzerland AG 2019
E. Garoufallou et al. (Eds.): MTSR 2019, CCIS 1057, pp. 307–319, 2019.
https://doi.org/10.1007/978-3-030-36599-8_27

natural hazards requires prompt responses from the governmental and decision making bodies both to prevent and/or recover from their consequences. To be effective such reactions have to rely on the availability, sharing, and promptness of territorial datasets such as hydrographic one [1,2]. The term *hydrographic datasets* herein refers to a set of relevant terrain descriptors such as drainage networks, basins, flood risk areas, watersheds, catchments, rivers, and channels.

Open Government Data (OGD) is data produced or provided by governments which can be freely used, reused and redistributed by anyone [3]. In 2011 the Open Data for Resilience Initiative[2] started to apply the Open Data (OD) practices [4] to face vulnerability to natural hazards and the impacts of climate change. The initiative supports the World Bank Regional Disaster Risk Management Teams[3] in building long-term ownership of OD projects that are tailored to meet specific needs and goals of stakeholders.

Although the amount of OGD, as well as the number of consumers, is continuously growing, their fruition is still challenging due to their heterogeneity and quality [5–8]. To address this issue several international initiatives (e.g. GODI[4], OECD[5], the Open Data Monitor[6] and the Open Data Barometer[7]) promote the evaluation and ranking of portals under different perspective. These activities concentrate on open data platforms and highlight that important improvement should be made to enhance openness, interoperability, and usability in many countries, with few exceptions regarding countries such as UK, Canada, and the US traditionally renown for the maturity of their OGD ecosystems.

International initiatives such as, W3C Data on the Web Best Practices (W3C-DWBP[8]) related to the publication and usage of data on the Web and FAIR[9] Guiding Principles for scientific data management and stewardship, provide recommendations on data publication, accessibility, interoperability and reuse on the Web. For example, W3C recommends the machine readability of data formats, and the FAIR reusability principle includes metrics such as the availability of usage openness licenses and the provision of metadata provenance. These principles and guidelines should be adopted by OGD portals to improve their reusability. For instance, more care should be placed on data format to avoid interoperability and integration issues. In particular, the use of a structured and machine-readable file format such as RDF[10] is recommended as it enables more effective discovery of datasets as well as the inter-linking of datasets from multiple sources. Metadata should adopt the standard DCAT, a RDF vocabulary designed by the W3C to facilitate interoperability between data catalogs

---

[2] https://opendri.org/about/#sharing-data-anchor.
[3] https://www.worldbank.org/en/topic/disasterriskmanagement.
[4] https://index.okfn.org.
[5] https://www.oecd.org.
[6] https://opendatamonitor.eu.
[7] https://opendatabarometer.org.
[8] https://www.w3.org/TR/dwbp.
[9] https://www.go-fair.org/fair-principles.
[10] https://www.w3.org/RDF.

published on the Web[11] [7,9]. Provenance metadata is a key requirement for data reuse. According to W3C PROV[12]: "Provenance is information about entities, activities, and people involved in producing a piece of data or thing, which can be used to form assessments about its quality, reliability or trustworthiness". The use of provenance metadata is recommended both by FAIR in "R1.2. (meta)data are associated with their provenance" and W3C-DWBP in "Best Practice 5: Provide data provenance information". To be machine-readable, provenance should be express by means of shared ontologies like the W3C's Provenance Ontology (PROV-O)[13]. For their relevance in understanding and prevent natural hazard is particularly important to preserve the meaning of hydrography data sources by describing the provenance of the activities related to data creation and transformation [1], as well their input and output, following a sequential workflow pattern [10].

The paper provides a preliminary and quantitative analysis of currently available hydrographic datasets in OGD. Nineteen OGD portals ranked by the Barometer framework have been studied. We discuss the compliance of the datasets with respect to some reusability dimensions as recommended by FAIR and W3C-DWBP initiatives. In particular, we considered three metrics: machine-readable data formats, availability and openness of license, metadata provenance. The result of our investigation highlights that OGD hydrographic datasets still have some issues to comply with reusability principles. Moved by this consideration, we supply an example of provenance metadata documentation, according to the PROV data model, related to the generation of a thematic map of potential flood areas in South America with the HAND tool provided by INPE. To improve dataset comprehension and reusability we deliver the provenance documentation along with the documented datasets on the Open Data portal datahub.io[14].

The paper is organized as follows. Section 2 introduces the OGD portals, the methodological approach and the outcome of our investigation. Section 3 discusses the analysis of the hydrographic datasets with respect to reusability metrics. Section 4 provides practice for documenting workflow provenance metadata of the South America flood map. Section 5 presents the conclusions.

2   Materials and Methods

2.1   Identification of Open Data Portals

We focus our study on a set of the OGD portals having a worldwide coverage of scientific open data. In particular, we have selected the OGD portals ranked by The Open Data Barometer, which looks at how leading governments are performing a decade into the Open Data movement and outlines what needs to happen for the movement to progress forward. The report of last edition

---

[11] https://www.w3.org/TR/vocab-dcat.
[12] https://www.w3.org/TR/prov-overview.
[13] https://www.w3.org/TR/prov-o.
[14] https://datahub.io.

looks specifically at 30 Governments that have made concrete commitments to champion OD, either by adopting the Open Data Charter[15], or by signing up to the G20 Anti-Corruption Open Data Principles[16]. The report divides the 30 Governments into three groups, based on their performance: (1) *champions*; (2) *contenders*; (3) *stragglers*. For our analysis we selected the portals belonging to the champions and contenders groups.

2.2   Criteria Definition

Domain Criteria. A common approach to search for data within a portal is by keywords. Thus the first step is to identify a list of keywords connected to the studied domain. According to W3C-DWBP ("Best Practice 15: Reuse vocabularies, preferably standardized ones") and FAIR ("Reusable principle, R1. meta(data) are richly described with a plurality of accurate and relevant attributes"), the choice of the keywords should not be user dependent. Controlled vocabularies (i.e. thesauri and code lists) encoded in Simple Knowledge Organization System SKOS [11] should to be used as a semantic layer which facilitates data search [12]. Good quality vocabularies [13] provide a key to disclosing the potential of OGD, by supplying common terms for marking up metadata and data in a consistent and coherent way [14].

We exploited the multilingual linked thesaurus framework LusTRE[17] which provides a unique point of access to several Environmental thesauri and code lists. Among them, we used the well known multilingual thesauri covering areas for Environment, Food, and Agriculture: GEMET[18], [15], ThiST and AGROVOC[19]. They are encoded in SKOS and are published and linked according to the Linked Data Best Practices[20]. This allows cross-navigating between thesauri enlarging the space of concepts that can be browsed and used for data discovery. A query involving a concept returns all the information related to it, i.e. preferred label, alternative label and semantic relations. Example of relations are: *skos:broader* and *skos:narrower* to define hierarchical properties, *skos:related* to associate two concepts, and *skos:exactMatch, skos:closeMatch* to define equivalent concepts belonging to separate linked thesauri. To ease OGD multilingual search, we exploited the translation facility provided by LusTRE allowing access to the translation available in GEMET and AGROVOC.

Table 1 shows for each selected keyword: the associated top concept in a thesaurus (first column), the concept description and the exploited thesaurus (second column), and examples of concepts in the linked thesauri which have semantic relations (the circles icons) with the keyword related concept (third

---

[15] https://opendatacharter.net/principles.
[16] http://www.g20.utoronto.ca/2015/G20-Anti-Corruption-Open-Data-Principles. pdf.
[17] http://linkeddata.ge.imati.cnr.it.
[18] www.eionet.europa.eu/geme.
[19] http://aims.fao.org/vest-registry/vocabularies/agrovoc.
[20] http://www.w3.org/DesignIssues/LinkedData.html.

column). Semantic related concepts suggest the user further associated keywords to be used in his/her search. For example, *flood* concept in GEMET, has a *exactMatch* with *flood* in AGROVOC where it has a *narrower* relation with the concept *irrigation channels*. Thus *irrigation channels* could be further selected to refine the query. Let us note that the set of selected keywords is not exhaustive to discover all the hydrographic datasets. As a guideline, the OGD portals should provide a semantic keyword search by exploiting LusTRE, or similar vocabulary-based tools, transparently and automatically.

Table 1. The selected hydrographic concepts, their description, and their semantic relations with other concepts in the linked thesauri. The circles icons represent the semantic relations in the specified thesaurus. (●exactMatch, ○ closeMatch, ◐broader, ◑ narrower).

Keywords	Description and source	Related concepts
Drainage	The discharge of water from a soil by percolation, the process by which surface water moves downwards through cracks, joints and pores in soil and rocks (in GEMET). (●EARTh), (●AGROVOC)	*watersheds* (●AGROVOC), *hydrological processes* (◐EARTh)
Basins	Area having a common outlet for its surface runoff (in INSPIRE feature concept dictionary)	*watersheds* (◑ThiST)
Catchment	Area having a common outlet for its surface runoff (in EARTh). (●GEMET), (●AGROVOC)	*Flood* (◐GEMET), *Natural disasters, High water* (◑AGROVOC)
Watershed	The dividing line between two adjacent river systems, such as a ridge (in GEMET)	*watershed divide* (●EARTh). *Drainage channels, Irrigation canals, Navigable Canals* (◑AGROVOC)
Flood	A great flow along a watercourse or a flow causing inundation of lands not normally covered by water (in GEMET). (●EARTh), (●AGROVOC)	*Drainage channels, Irrigation channels, Navigable Canals* (◑AGROVOC)
Canals	An artificial open waterway used for transportation, waterpower, or irrigation (in EARTh). (●AGROVOC)	*Drainage canals, Irrigation canals*, and *Navigable canals* (◑AGROVOC)
River	A stream of water which flows in a channel from high ground to low ground and ultimately to a lake or the sea, except in a desert area where it may dwindle away to nothing. (in GEMET) (●EARTh)	*streams* (◐EARTh), *watercourse* (◐GEMET), *waterfall* (◑GEMET)

Reusability Criteria. To investigate the compliance of hydrographic datasets with reusability recommendations promoted by W3C-DWBP and FAIR, we identified three dimensions: data format, licence, and provenance. In particular, we focused on the metrics: format machine readability (W3C-DWBP Best Practice 12), clear and accessible open usage licence (FAIR R1.1), and provision of detail provenance (FAIR R1.2).

2.3   Data Search and Collection

Table 2 summarizes the hydrographic datasets search outcome. For each OGD portal, it reports the total number of datasets, the number of hydrographic datasets and the number of distribution files (excluded Russia and Ukraine because of language issue, and India which does not provide the overall searched data). The amount of hydrographic datasets is very varied, ranging from 35,973 (US) to 8 (Argentina) and only seven portals provide over a thousand data. The ratio of hydrographic datasets with the overall portal datasets is 51% for Australia, between 10% and 18% for (South Korea, New Zealand, United States, and Brazil), all the others have less than 10%. For the distribution files, the quantity is normally higher than the number of datasets of the portal: commonly a dataset is associated with several files downloadable in different formats. Australia and the USA supply large distributions 52,166 and 47,825 respectively. Some portals may supply distribution only by contacting the data provider.

Table 2. Total number of datasets, number of hydrographic datasets and number of file distributions in the OGD portals listed according to Open Data Barometer.

Country	Portal	#datasets	#hydro	%hydro	#distribution
Canada	open.canada.ca	82,339	3,824	5%	6,520
UK	data.gov.uk	52,259	2,829	5%	1,067
Australia	data.gov.au	77,485	39,572	51%	52,166
France	data.gouv.fr	36,582	4,087	11%	11,727
South Korea	data.go.kr	29,259	367	1%	621
Mexico	datos.gob.mx	44,727	161	0%	165
Japan	data.go.jp	24,915	300	1%	486
New Zealand	data.govt.nz	6,733	1,170	17%	5,902
Germany	govdata.de	22,941	252	1%	619
U.S.A	data.gov	232,436	35,973	15%	47,825
Uruguay	datos.gub.uy	2,153	9	0%	28
Colombia	datos.gov.co	10,231	146	1%	761
Brazil	dados.gov.br	6,690	1,043	16%	2,842
Italy	data.gov.it	24,811	76	0%	244
Argentina	datos.gob.ar	893	8	1%	18

3 Reusability Analysis of Hydrographic Datasets

As to reusability criteria, for each OGD portal, we collected information about data format, license, and provenance.

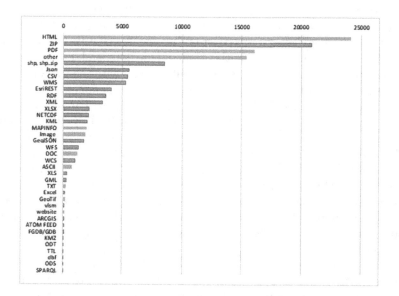

Fig. 1. Distribution of data formats. Blue is for machine-readable formats. (Color figure online)

W3C recommends "Make data available in a machine-readable standardized data format that is easily parseable including but not limited to CSV, XML, HDF, JSON and RDF serialization syntaxes like RDF/XML, JSON-LD, or Turtle". We collected overall information on formats. According to [17], we mapped them with the list of machine-readable formats provided by the OpenDataMonitor project[21]. In addition, for geographic data formats (i.e. GeoJeson, WFS, WCS, GML), we considered other different references available in literature such as the normalized list of machine-readable formats on github[22]. Figure 1 summarises the distribution of hydrographic datasets according to their formats: blue histograms refer to machine-readable format and yellow to not machine-readable ones. HTML and PDF are the most widely used formats. As an overall evaluation, little more than half of the datasets have a machine-readable format (52%), and among these, apart from ZIP, CSV and JSON are the most used. Let us note that although RDF is the W3C recommended standard format, scoring as four stars format in the rating scheme for OGD proposed by Tim Berners Lee,

---

[21] https://github.com/opendatamonitor/odm.restapi/blob/master/odmapi/def_formatLists.py#L5-L39.

[22] https://github.com/okfn/opendatasurvey/issues/585.

it is only used by about 3% of the hydrographic datasets examined. In particular, Colombia provides almost all of its distribution in RDF. Concerning the not machine-readable formats, HTML and PDF are the most widely used formats, few other not machine-readable (e.g. Image format, TXT, doc) distributions are less frequent.

We inspected the datasets against the existence of the license and their openness. To investigate this information, we mapped the licenses to the list of licenses reviewed by the Open Definition[23]. Most of the portals quantify datasets respect to specifics licenses, i.e. Canada, the United Kingdom and France associate OGL[24] to almost all data sets. UK specifies all datasets with the US Government license. Almost all portals specify the different Creative Commons[25] (CC) (Australia provides all data sets with cc-by). Few datasets (Brazil) are licensed under the Open Data Commons Open Database License[26] (ODbl). Only two portals (New Zealand, Uruguay) specify all datasets with "Other license" and France, Brazil and Italy quantify few datasets with "no specified" license. Summarising the most used licences for the number of datasets, OGD is the most frequent: is adopted by 46,090 datasets, 52% (we included also the 35,973 datasets licensed with U.S.GOV). Creative Common license family accounts for 41,147 datasets, %46. A small number of datasets are licensed with "Other Open", 1%. There is a small number of datasets 2% associated with "Other licence" explicitly state any license.

An important aspect concerning data reusability is the availability of provenance metadata to describe the history of a dataset and its origin[27]. From the direct analysis of portals metadata, few provenance details are provided: usually they are limited to the publisher/organization and the maintainer/contactPoint names. All the OGD portals we have analyzed provide easily accessible information on the Organization and in the case of large portals such as Australia, an immediate summary of the distribution of data series for different organizations is available. Unfortunately, it is not the same for information about provider and contact point which usually are stored at the metadata level of the single data set thus requiring a more complex exploration process. Anyway, no detailed properly provenance is provided for dataset distributions. A similar result is confirmed by Marchello et al. [16], analyzing a set of portals they argue "Despite the importance of access traceability, accountability, and accuracy of data none of the portals properly provides provenance information". According to FAIR, detailed information on the source of the data is needed (e.g. information to understand how the data was generated). From our analysis, none of the selected portals provide this information.

---

[23] https://opendefinition.org/licenses.

[24] http://www.nationalarchives.gov.uk/doc/open-government-licence.

[25] https://creativecommons.org/licenses.

[26] https://www.opendatacommons.org/licenses/odbl/.

[27] https://www.w3.org/TR/dwbp.

4   Provenance Metadata for Flood Maps in South America

To contribute at the diffusion of best practices towards the documentation of datasets provenance, we exemplify the description of data entities and processes involved in the generation of thematic maps of potential flooding areas, aimed at improving their reuse in the study of environmental events.

We focus on data produced by INPE, which developed tools to create hydrographic datasets of every Earth region: the distributed hydrologic modeling platform TerraHidro[28], which generates drainage networks and basins from a SRTM-DEM, and the Height Above the Nearest Drainage (HAND) algorithm, which predicts the location and spatial extent of potential inundation. To generate a potential flood areas map in South America, firstly, the drainage network is extracted by TerraHidro from the SRTM-DEM [1] with resolutions of 90 m. Then the flood area map is generated from the drainage network by HAND.

HAND outcome is sensitive to three factors which may affect its reuse: DEM resolution, the density of channels in the drainage network (provided by a stream initiation threshold value) and the different water altimetry track which determine the areas with a higher potential flood. To make HAND results effectively reusable we provide such information along with other provenance data. The provenance for the execution of HAND, is provided according to the W3C PROV data model, and metadata are encoded into RDF, serialized as Turtle (ttl). The provenance diagram in Fig. 2 summarizes the PROV-O elements involved in the HAND execution. The diagram uses the graphical notation introduced in [18] to depict the elements of the PROV model.

HAND ingests three datasets (i.e. a DEM, a drainage network and a local drain directions grid) to produce a raster map in TIF format (*HANDCalulation1*). A vector transformation is yielded by *:HANDvectorCalculation1* activity, based on a water altimetry value (*:waterAltimetry1*). PROV excerpts related to this activity, the entity *:HANDvector1* generated by agent *HNDscientist1* follow. We published the complete provenance of drainage network dataset[29] and flooding area dataset[30], in machine readable format, along with the other data metadata on the DataHub portal.

```
:HANDvectorCalculation1
   a prov:Activity;
   prov:value "HANDvector";
   dcterms:description "Generation of vector map of contour
   lines of potential flood areas from raster file" ;
   prov:used   :HANDGrid1;
   prov:used   :waterAltimetry1;
   prov:wasAssociatedWith :HNDscientist1 .
```

---

[28] http://www.dpi.inpe.br/terrahidro.
[29] https://old.datahub.io/dataset/southamerica-drainage-network-from-srtm-90m.
[30] https://old.datahub.io/dataset/south-america-flood-areas-from-srtm-90-m.

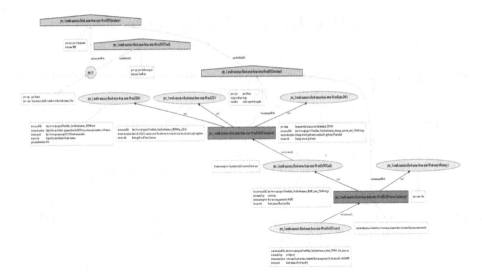

Fig. 2. Provenance diagram of the flood workflow available on DataHub. Entities are depicted as yellow ovals, Activities as blue rectangles, and Agents as orange pentagons. (Color figure online)

```
:HANDvector1
  a prov:Entity;
  dcterms:title "South America Flood Area Map";
  dcterms:description "vector map of contour lines of potential
  flood areas generated by the raster file with HAND";
  dcat:downoladURL "http://www.dpi.inpe.br/TerraHidro_Data/
  SouthAmerica_Hand_2500000_10m_shape.zip";
  dcat:mediaType "text/shp+zip" ;
  prov:wasGeneratedBy :HANDvectorCalculation1 ;
  prov:generatedAtTime "2019-05-25 15:30 UST".

:waterAltimetry1
  a prov:Entity;
  prov:value "10m".

:HNDscientist1 a prov:Agent;
  vcard:hasMember "dblp:Sergio_Rosim";
  vcard:title     "INPE, Brazil"@en.
```

Figure 3 shows the drainage network and the areas of potential flood map of South America produced. Assuming that the predictor of flood is directly related to the river stage height, different colors indicate the different flood areas respect to assigned water altimetry track (in meter). While their metadata (included provenance both in ttl and pdf formats) is published and stored by datahub.io, their management is carried out by INPE and stored in a centralized repository.

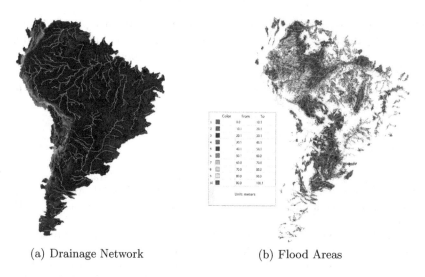

(a) Drainage Network   (b) Flood Areas

Fig. 3. South America drainage network and map of flood area levels. The legend shows the area colour associated to each water altimetry increased by 10 m: red indicates the first surface potentially to be flooded (higher risk) and blue color the last one (lower level). (Color figure online)

5   Conclusion

We provided an overview of hydrographic datasets available in highly reputed OGD portals, and presented a reusability analysis with respects to the compliance with standard initiatives. We provided guidelines aimed to improve reusability by documenting provenance metadata. Our analysis reveals that hydrographic datasets amount to about 14% of the overall published datasets for the OGD portals considered. Almost all datasets have associates an open licences (CC or OGL). Concerning the format, only 52% are machine readable and very few in RDF. A critical reusability issue concerns the provision of provenance metadata which currently includes very limited organization and data publisher information. To this end, we exemplified the documentation of workflow provenance for the creation of potential flood areas maps in South America.

From our study we address the following recommendations to portal providers: (i) to adopt a common standard compliance approach to data description (i.e. mapping the metadata to standard DCAT, DCAT-AP), (ii) to exploit concepts from known controlled vocabularies for keywords facilitating data interoperability, (iii) to restrict metadata values to a predefined list of options (e.g. file format, licence descriptions) and (iv) to enrich metadata information with provenance metadata. By doing so, the portal may guarantee a quality level compatible with standards which, in return, ensure that hydrographic data can be used more effectively and thereby representing a significant step towards preventing catastrophes from happening.

As for future work, we prioritize the evaluation of further portals including other quality dimensions. In particular, we will focus on the use of Satellite Earth Observation Open Data provided by ESA Copernicus Programme and their integration with INPE data to manage the natural disaster. Provenance metadata and processing workflows will be investigated and encoded in machine-readable format for the realization of concrete applications.

References

1. Rosim, S., Namikawa, L.M., de Freitas Oliveira, J.R., De Martino, M., Quarati, A.: Workflow provenance metadata to enhance reuse of South America drainage datasets. In: International Conference on eDemocracy & eGovernment, pp. 16–23 (2018)
2. Geiger, A.C.P., Von Lucke, J.: Open data could have helped us learn from another mining dam disaster. Sci. Data **6**(56), 1–2 (2019)
3. Geiger, A.C.P., Von Lucke, J.: Open government and(linked)(open)(government) (data). JeDEM-eJournal eDemocracy Open Gov. **4**(2), 265–278 (2012)
4. Eight principles of open government data. Open Government Working Group (2007). https://opengovdata.org/. Accesed 29 May 2019
5. Sadiq, S., Indulska, M.: Open Data: quality over quantity. Int. J. Inf. Manage. **37**(3), 150–154 (2017)
6. Safarov, I., Meijer, A.J., Grimmelikhuijsen. J.: Utilization of open government data: a systematic literature review of types, conditions, effects and users. Inform. Polity **22**, 1–24 (2017)
7. Máchova, R., Lnénicka, M.: Evaluating the quality of open data portals on the national level. J. Theor. Appl. Electron. Commer. **12**(1), 21–41 (2017)
8. Quarati, A., De Martino, M.: Open Government Data usage: a brief overview, IDEAS. In: 23rd International Database Engineering & Applications Symposium, pp. 229–236 (2019)
9. Umbrich, J., Neumaier, S., Polleres, A.: Quality assessment evolution of open data portals. In: Proceedings IEEE International Conference on Open and Big Data, pp. 1–8. IEEE, Rome (2015)
10. Van Der Aalst, W.M.P., ter Hofstede, A.H.M., Kiepuszewski, B., Barros, A.P.: Distribuited and parallel databases. Work. Patterns **14**(1), 5–51 (2003)
11. Miles, A., Bechhofer, S.: W3C Recommendation: Simple Knowledge Organization System Reference (2009). http://www.w3.org/TR/skos-reference
12. Albertoni, R., De Martino, M., Podestà, P., Abecker, A., Wössner, R., Schnitter, K.: LusTRE: a framework of linked environmental thesauri for metadata management. Earth Sci. Inform. J. **11**(4), 525–544 (2018)
13. Quarati, A., Albertoni, R., De Martino, M.: Overall quality assessment of SKOS thesauri: an AHP-based approach. J. Inf. Sci. **43**(6), 816–834 (2017)
14. Albertoni, R., De Martino, M., Quarati, A.: Documenting context-based quality assessment of controlled vocabularies. IEEE Trans. Emerg. Top. Comput. **1** PrePrints, 1 (2018)
15. Albertoni, R., De Martino, M., Di Franco, S., De Santis, V., Plini, P.: EARTh: an environmental application reference thesaurus in the linked open data cloud. Semantic Web **5**(2), 165–171 (2014)

16. Marcelo, J.S.O., Rodrigues de Oliveira, H., Oliveira, L.A., Farias, L.: Open government data portals analysis: the Brazilian case. In: Kim, Y., Liu, M. (eds.) Proceedings of the 17th International Digital Government Research Conference on Digital Government Research 2016, pp. 415–424. ACM, NY (2016). https://doi.org/10.1145/2912160.2912163
17. Neumaier, S., Umbrich, J., Polleres, A.: Automated quality assessment of metadata across open data portals. J. Data Inf. Qual. (JDIQ) **8**(2), 2–29 (2016)
18. Sahoo, S., Lebo, T, McGuinness, D., PROV-O: the PROV Ontology, W3C Recommendation (2013). http://www.w3.org/TR/2013/REC-prov-o-20130430/

An Architecture for Enabling IoT Edge Devices to Allow Scalable Publishing of Semantic Linked Data

Mark Burkley$^{(\boxtimes)}$

Ubiworx Systems, Limerick, Ireland
mark@ubiworx.com
http://www.ubiworx.com

Abstract. The Internet of Things (IoT) is growing exponentially and is creating enormous sets of data that often reside in proprietary formats and storage containers. Linked Data and the Semantic Web has been around for a long time but adoption by industry has been slow. Linked Data research tends to have an academic biasand real world applicability is often neglected. Based on our experience with ubiworx, an IoT framework used inseveral real world projects, we propose an architecture using intelligent edge gateways, scalable cloud micro-services and semantic adaption layers to bridge the gap between legacy sensor data acquisition and publishing linked data to ontologies such as Semantic Sensor Network (SSN) and Smart Appliances REFerence ontology (SAREF). In combination, the edge gateway paradigm and the layered cloud micro-services paradigm intersect to provide an accelerated path to publishing linked sensor data while achieving the scalability required by the explosive growth of the IoT and doing so with the best efficiency of resources. Dynamically creating Linked Data serialisations from rapidly changing sensor data sets is a key enabler for adoption of linked data principals in the IoT space.

1 Introduction

The Internet of Things (IoT) has seen explosive growth in recent years but the Semantic Web of Things (SWoT) has not been adopted well by industry despite being heavily researched. Exposing sensor data to the web is moving at a slow pace and is happening in an ad-hoc fashion according to the W3C [1]. The Generic Sensor API is standardising the open web platform but while there we have web APIs that allow machines to communicate effectively, they are using "more or less ad-hoc data structures" [2] to achieve this. Practical solutions are missing and this is leading to an emergence of proprietary solutions and protocols. Our research indicates that one reason for this is the lack of an assurance that large volumes of IoT data can be published as Linked Data and queried by structured query tools such as SPARQL [3]. This paper proposes an architecture to bridge this chasm and present dynamic and distributed sensor data and

© Springer Nature Switzerland AG 2019
E. Garoufallou et al. (Eds.): MTSR 2019, CCIS 1057, pp. 320–331, 2019.
https://doi.org/10.1007/978-3-030-36599-8_28

derived analytics through RDF. The features of our architecture are scalability, reliability, workload distribution and efficiency which combine to achieve this goal.

There are a number of key attributes and components required to build a scalable IoT architecture that can support semantic metadata at scale. Abstraction as always is fundamental to ensuring system layers properly hide the complexities of underlying subsystems and each layer in the architecture must ensure this requirement is met. Figure 1 depicts the layers in our proposed architecture. Already in place are legacy sensors, actuators and control nodes based on constrained devices such as MCUs. An intelligent edge gateway is also required to aggregate data, perform edge analytics and control and to provide device management and security services. A cloud proxy is required to mirror the edge devices and provide APIs. Finally a semantic adaption layer is required to bridge the gap from proprietary API to open Linked Data generic sensor ontologies such as SSN [4] but also domain specific ontologies such as the Smart Appliance REFerence (SAREF) [5] ontology.

1.1   Layering, Abstraction and Scalability

Scalability in Semantic Web of Things (SWoT) applications seems often to be an after thought or to not have been considered at all. It is vital to properly design

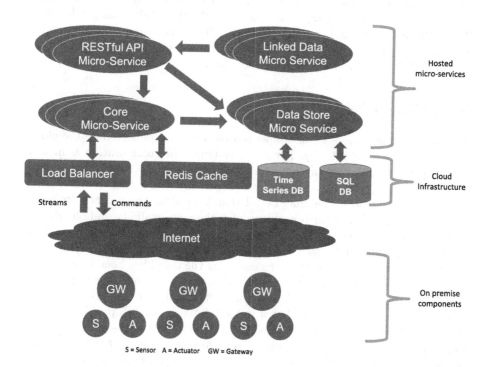

Fig. 1. System architecture with cloud micro services

and build functional layers that isolate layers above and below from unnecessary details. It is obviously not desirable for example to have to know the ZigBee PANID for a temperature sensor in a building to perform a SPARQL query returning data from that sensor. Conversely it is asking too much of the same ZigBee temperature sensor to be able to participate in a LD network and create RDF/XML responses or have knowledge of the SAREF ontology. Intermediate layers are needed to abstract the details away. In additional to functional abstraction, it is important to hide topological aspects such as network connectivity and protocols. A common paradigm used to create scalable web services is to use a micro-services architecture which will be discussed in the cloud proxy section of this paper.

A key blocker to semantic web enabling of existing sensor networks is the development cost of adding support for LD ontologies to constrained edge devices. By creating a layered architecture, this problem can be moved to the cloud where an abstraction layer can be created specifically to bridge the data-set to a standard linked data ontology. The details of specific sensor protocols, edge to cloud protocols and cloud data storage are hidden through abstraction and at the upper layer through a standardised RESTful API. The semantic enabling layer simply needs to conform to the published RESTful API.

In addition to the heterogeneous nature of the IoT we also have the problem of having many ontologies. The Linked Open Vocabularies (LOV) community is driving a conversation around the creation and use of shared metadata (shared vocabularies) [7]. IoT ontologies include SSN, SAREF, IoT-ontology, IoT-lite, SPITFIRE, IoT-S, SA and oneM2M. LOV4IoT lists currently references over 400 ontologies [9]. Creating an abstraction layer allows support for more ontologies to be added more easily from existing data sets.

2   Intelligent Edge Devices

Early IoT systems consisted of simple sensors directly connected to the cloud with no intermediate gateway. For some systems this configuration is in fact still adequate. Standalone smart meters or other simple applications that simply need to report a small number of values per day over Sigfox or other WAN with limited bandwidth this may be all that is needed. Many other use cases are however quickly faced with problems of scale, manageability and security. A connected car may have over a thousand sensors. It isn't practical or efficient for each sensor to maintain its own connection to the cloud and to send all recorded data to the cloud. Consequently in recent years the trend has been to introduce intelligent edge gateway devices to perform more of the IoT functionality at source or at the network "edge" instead of in the cloud. This has primarily been driven through the realisation that a potential "data deluge" problem existed which would overload cloud analytics. In any non trivial IoT system the edge device or edge gateway layer becomes a requirement to abstract details of sensor connectivity from higher application layers and to insulate constrained sensor devices from higher layer complexities such as managing metadata, network security, discovery and provisioning. In our proposed architecture we differentiate between data flowing from sensors to gateways ("southbound") and from gateway to cloud ("northbound") by using the terms "sensor" and "actuator" only for devices physically connected to the gateway and "stream" and "command" for data sent from gateway to cloud and vice versa. This is depicted in Fig. 2.

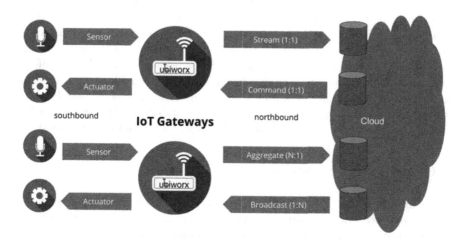

Fig. 2. Southbound and Northbound interfaces with data flow terminology

The role of the edge gateway is multifaceted. In the context of this paper, two of the more important aspects are autonomy and metadata creation.

2.1 Autonomy

An gateway at the network edge, in a vehicle or in a building, can aggregate and relay data for many sensors and provide a single portal for discovery and manageability of these sensors. In many cases instantaneous sensor sample data does not need to be recorded or sent to the cloud and is only required to inform an immediate action. For example a temperature sensor may activate a heating or air conditioning system or a PID loop controller may require feedback values several times per second. These immediate readings are not required to be stored long term and so uploading all the data to the cloud would simply result in most of it being immediately discarded. A data deluge can be the result of improperly reducing the data set to be transmitted. In addition, edge gateways may have intermittent or unreliable internet connectivity. It is vitally important that edge gateways can continue to operate autonomously and perform local control functions and analytics even without cloud connectivity. Sample data recorded should be stored for later relaying to the cloud when connectivity is restored.

2.2 Metadata Creation

Our architecture provides standardised metadata for all things known to a gateway. Metadata for a sensor may include units, manufacturer, accuracy and high and low limits. These are all synchronised with the cloud proxy for use by higher level APIs. The metadata set is extensible as it is transferred as a JSON payload over HTTP in our architecture. New fields can be added with newer software versions without impacting existing deployments. Defining a standardised set of metadata parameters enables the abstraction and encapsulation of sensor details and allows the higher layer APIs to perform queries and other operations across multiple sensors without regard for the physical operation of the sensors. The edge device therefore acts as a proxy for the sensors and provides a uniform data transmission protocol to enable faster and more reliable system integration. System designers can focus on the important domain specific details of the data acquisition and analytics without being encumbered with details of what protocol needs to be implemented to reliably transfer the data to the cloud.

3 Cloud Proxy Services

Adding intelligence at the edge is not without its challenges. Devices at the network edge are not typically directly accessible from the internet, and this is often intentional. IoT devices on a premises such as a home or business are usually deliberately hidden from the internet behind a gateway that does NAT or has a firewall or both. Even when edge devices are made visible to the internet, they may not be consistently locatable due to having a dynamic IP address, or may have intermittent connectivity. Our architecture proposes a cloud proxy approach where a hosted cloud based service is used to represent an edge gateway. This approach has a number of significant advantages which will be discussed in this section. By having RESTful API representations of physical sensors at a location that is consistent and with high levels of security and availability, the reliability and utility of the IoT system increases significantly.

Scalability is a critical characteristic of a viable IoT system. While the machine to machine aspects of scalability are easier to manage and predict, there are also human interactions to consider. APIs are used by applications on smart devices for example and the load on these APIs will vary as human interactions with their smart devices vary further driving the need to scale.

3.1 Cloud Protocols

As with sensor protocols, there are several competing standards for sensor to cloud and gateway to cloud protocols. In their survey of IoT communication protocols, Dizdarević et al. [8] document several protocols and discuss the advantages and disadvantages of each. MQTT is a popular choice of protocol since it is lightweight and implementable on constrained devices. AQMP is designed to be broadly applicable but is considered a heavyweight protocol. DDS promises real time data scalable data services using publish/subscribe similarly to MQTT. CoAP is a web transfer protocol specifically designed for constrained devices. Many devices also simply use RESTful HTTP requests [6] to send requests to cloud applications. This latter approach provides the easiest fit to existing web infrastructure as requests from IoT devices look no different to intermediate routers, firewalls, load balancers, etc, than normal human web traffic. This does add more burden to the device side as HTTP is a more complex protocol than MQTT or CoAP but it does have very significant advantages when it comes to scaling a cloud solution as will be shown later.

It should be noted thought that most of these IoT "protocols" can be more accurately described as transport layers (e.g. MQTT) since they don't typically specify any payload format. Users and application developers may agree to exchange data using MQTT and may agree the topics to publish to each other but without agreement as to the content of the messages, interoperability will be limited to sending trivial data values. A more useful approach is to use an encoding serialisation such as JSON, which works the most seamlessly with web applications, to include data and metadata in one message.

3.2   Micro-services

A current trend in cloud computing is the growing application of the micro-services architectural style [10]. This is "an approach to developing a single application as a suite of small services, each running in its own process and communicating with lightweight mechanisms, often an HTTP resource API" [11]. Each micro-service runs independently in its own container, which could be a virtual machine or a file system container such as docker [12], and has in its own HTTP interface and internal API for inter-service communication. A further evolution is to have "serverless" functional model such as AWS Lambda [13].

Micro-service or serverless instances can be scaled up or down as required and costs are only incurred for processing power and bandwidth that is actually used. A group of server instances is referred to as a "cluster". Cloud computing hosts such as Google cloud, Microsoft Azure and Amazon Web Services (AWS) provide "load balancers" to distribute incoming requests across multiple running service instances. Load balancers also monitor workload on each running instance and can be configured to automatically create or destroy service instances to ensure the requested load is met with the correct amount of compute resources at the most efficient cost. A new instance of a service is brought into service dynamically by the load balancer as load increases to share the work load. Conversely, when load reduces, the load balancer can shut down instances to save resources. Back end storage is provided and is also scalable. AWS provides "Aurora" which is a scalable MySQL database and the elastic file system ("EFS") which is a scalable mounted file system.

3.3 Service Instances

In keeping with our architectural principals of modularity and layered abstraction, the cloud proxy subsystem is composed of a number of discrete services. Referring back to Fig. 1 which shows the server micro service architecture, the services provided are:

– core service
– data storage
– External API
– Linked Data Platform

3.4 Core Service

As discussed, edge gateways are assumed to be not directly accessible via the internet. For this reason, our architecture always requires gateways to initiate contact with cloud services. Gateways have their own access portal and each gateway has individual security credentials to access this portal. Requests to the data portal are sent to a load balancer which distributes requests to core service instances. The core service accepts connections from edge devices and manages the context for an edge device. It provides database services for provisioning and configuration of things and associated metadata. A core instance may be handling sessions for hundreds of gateways at any one time. The load balancer will try to route requests from the same gateway to the same core instance. This fact can be used by the core instance to cash database metadata such as sensor configuration.

3.5 Data Storage

A scalable SQL database (AWS Aurora) is used to store metadata about gateways, interfaces, nodes, sensors and actuators. Sample data should not be stored in a SQL database as the volume of sample data will quickly lead to performance issues. Instead it can be directly stored to a time series database such as InfluxDB, or in the case of ubiworx it is stored to a proprietary log file backend called HistDB which is stored on Amazon EFS. HistDB is used to store sample data, either as sensor data streams or actuation commands.

A Redis [14] cache is used to ensure queries for a specific sensor are consistently handled by the same instance. Separating metadata from sample data provides an efficient use of resources since both datasets have quite different requirements. It would be difficult to consolidate both sets of requirements with a single data store. In any case, from the user perspective this detail is hidden as both the gateway portal API and the public API present an API that contains a mix of both datasets.

3.6   External API

The external API service is the interface between the rest of the world and the IoT system. This API can be published for developers to use for smart apps or cloud services. For example, the ubiworx API [15] contains all the necessary details required to build queries and to parse the responses. Knowledge can be built up in stages by querying for gateways, then interfaces, nodes, sensors and finally data. Data can be requested as discrete samples or can be summarised. For example a query could request an hourly average of all temperature values in the last week.

4   Linked Data Service

The final layer in our architecture is the Linked Data translation layer. This layer confirms to a Linked Data Platform (LDP) layeras defined [16]. This layer provides semantic web of things interoperability with the linked data network.It maps propriety RESTful APIs to standard ontologies such as SSN and SAREF. In keeping withourabstraction goal, the LDP service layer encapsulates details of cloud micro-services and SQL/NoSQL data storage and hides these from Linked Data consumers. Reciprocally, it hides details of semantic web ontologies from IoT services running in the cloud and on gateways. By providing a separate adaption layer such as this, it becomes easier to add support for new ontologies or encodings.

The LDP layer builds on the capabilities of the underlying RESTful API to combine time invariant and time variant metadata together as required to dynamically create Linked Data query responses. Like the other services, it operatesusing a data "pull" strategy where the request for data are initiated by external entities. For efficiency the pull request creates the data response dynamically.

4.1   Dynamic Linked Data Generation

Linked Data initiatives assume linked data and its representation is static. However in IoT, particularly with respect to sensor data, is very dynamic. The "things" themselves in IoT are also dynamicas devices are commissioned and configured or reconfigured regularly. What is needed is a method to dynamically translate Linked Data queries to RTDB queries dynamically.

The LDP service layer operates by directing linked data queries to the external LDP API. The queries are handled bya service instance which in turn queries the IoT API server instances. The responses are dynamically created serialised RDF in RDF/XML, turtle or JSON-LD linked data objects. It is also perfectly feasible to have multiple LDP service layers where each one implements a specified ontology, for example SSN or SAREF. The ontological specific implementation is contained entirely in this layer which is implemented above the external core and data storage APIs which allows multiple implementations to exist simultaneously and independently.

The implementation of each LDP service is responsible for gathering data and metadata for a sensor. The metadata is obtained by querying the core internal API. This query responds with all known metadata about a sensor, such as limits, units and scaling. It also returns the UUID of the node the sensor belongs to. A further call to retrieve the node metadata can then be made to retrieve the manufacturer and other details.

The real-time portion of the query is found by querying thedata storageinstance which manages the sensor in question. The query can be a single point of data, or it can be a summary for a particular time range. For example, the average value of a data point in the last hour, or the difference over 24 h, Indeed it could be a multi-row response, such as the total values for each of the days in the preceding month.

To retrieve details of a specific sensorfrom the ubiworx RESTful API, we could request the following URL: https://staging.ubiworx.com/v2/sensors/7516bc49 which returns

```
{
  "result": {
    "id": "7516bc49",
    "object": "sensor",
    "gateway": "02aab131",
    "node": "675ab02b",
    "name": "temperature",
    "scale": 1,
    "offset": 0,
    "max": 100,
    "min": -50,
    "units": "degrees C",

       .
       .
       .

  }
}
```

Since we would like to know more about the node the sensor belongs to, we can use the UUID for the node from the sensor query and ask about the node:

```
https://staging.ubiworx.com/v2/nodes/675ab02b
{
  "result": {
    "id": "675ab02b",
    "object": "node",
    "interface": "aa31b739",
    "name": "Entrance Hall Temperature",
    "type": "Oregon Scientific THGR810",

       .
       .
       .

  }
}
```

Finally we can retrieve the most recent data sample for the sensor by retrieving the URL: https://staging.ubiworx.com/v2/sensors/7516bc49/data which returns the following result:

```
{
    "result": [{"time":"2019-03-31T15:52:21.871725Z","val":18.2,"seq":251921}]
}
```

The LDP micro-serviceis a NodeJS application that issues these requests on our behalf. It can cache the results for better performance. It the task is to provide SAREF Linked Data then we canconstructa `saref:Temperature` Linked Data object.

Using http://ontology.tno.nl/examples/saref/temperaturesensor.ttl as a guide to create a measurement from SAREF: http://ontology.tno.nl/saref/ we can construct a turtle serialisation of the data retrieved from the ubiworx RESTful API to return the following response:

```
# baseURI: http://ontology.tno.nl/saref/tempsensor
# imports: https://w3id.org/saref

@prefix geo: <http://www.w3.org/2003/01/geo/wgs84_pos#> .
@prefix owl: <http://www.w3.org/2002/07/owl#> .
@prefix rdf: <http://www.w3.org/1999/02/22-rdf-syntax-ns#> .
@prefix rdfs: <http://www.w3.org/2000/01/rdf-schema#> .
@prefix saref: <https://w3id.org/saref#> .
@prefix saref-ts: <http://ontology.tno.nl/saref/tempsensor#> .
@prefix time: <http://www.w3.org/2006/time#> .
@prefix xsd: <http://www.w3.org/2001/XMLSchema#> .

<http://ontology.tno.nl/saref/tempsensor>
  rdf:type owl:Ontology ;
  owl:imports <https://w3id.org/saref> ;

saref-temp:BuildingSpace_EntranceHall
  rdf:type saref:BuildingSpace ;
  rdfs:label "Entrance Hall"^^xsd:string ;
  geo:lat "39.531445"^^xsd:string ;
  geo:long "2.729344"^^xsd:string ;
  saref:hasSpaceType "Entrance Hall"^^xsd:string ;

saref-temp:SenseTemperature rdf:type saref:Service ;
  rdfs:label "Sense temperature"^^xsd:string ;
  saref:hasInputParameter saref-temp:Temperature ;
  saref:hasOutputParameter saref-temp:Temperature ;
  saref:isOfferedBy saref-temp:TemperatureSensor_TEMP01 ;
  saref:represents saref-temp:SensingFunction ;
```

```
saref-temp:SensingFunction
  rdf:type saref:SensingFunction ;
  rdfs:label "Sensing function"^^xsd:string ;
  saref:hasCommand saref-temp:GetSensingDataCommand ;
  saref:hasSensorType "Temperature"^^xsd:string ;

.
saref-temp:Temperature
  rdf:type saref:Temperature ;
  rdfs:label "Temperature"^^xsd:string ;
  saref:hasValue "18.2"^^xsd:string ;
  saref:hasTimestamp "2019-03-31T15:52:21.871725Z"^^xsd:dateTime ;

.
saref-temp:TemperatureSensor_TEMP01
  rdf:type saref:TemperatureSensor ;
  rdfs:label "Temperature sensor TEMP01"^^xsd:string ;
  saref:IsUsedFor saref-temp:Temperature ;
  saref:hasCategory saref:Sensor ;
  saref:hasDescription "Temperature sensor TEMP01"^^xsd:string ;
  saref:hasFunction saref-temp:SensingFunction ;
  saref:hasManufacturer "Oregon Scientific"^^xsd:string ;
  saref:hasModel "THGR810"^^xsd:string ;
  saref:isLocatedIn saref-temp:BuildingSpace_EntranceHall ;
  saref:offers saref-temp:SenseTemperature ;
```

5   Discussion and Conclusion

This paper has presented the case for a layered architecture to create scalable Linked Data IoT systems. An intelligent edge gateway device with cloud proxying micro services are fundamental components of any non trivial Linked Data IoT system and this paper has shown how this architecture has evolved since the beginning of the IoT paradigm. The paper has discussed the functions of an intelligent edge gateway and the advantages in using micro-services for scalability both functionally and in terms of volume of sensors.

Edge gateway devices will not be required for every IoT use case but for most use cases, particularly those in the industrial segment, they will become a cornerstone of the solution. The need for more and more data to be processed locally will be the primary driver in the move towards intelligence at the edge but security and manageability concerns will also play a part. Linked Data ontologies are key enablers of IoT interoperability but their complexity and connectivity demands have made it difficult to implement them at the edge. The architecture we have presented here is a way to bridge the gap between edge and cloud.

Vertical silos of data are still very much apparent in the current IoT landscape and there is little evidence of a desire to change this yet. The IoT vision of everything interconnected will require breaking down these silos. Better interoperability of IoT systems is needed before IoT can deliver on its promise to bring everything together in a connected world. Connecting the many adhoc IoT initiatives to the Linked Data cloud will facilitate this.

References

1. W3C. https://www.w3.org/
2. Champin, P.A.: RDF-REST: a unifying framework for web APIs and linked data. In: CEUR Workshop Proceedings, pp. 10–19 (2013)
3. SPARQL Query Language for RDF. https://www.w3.org/TR/rdf-sparql-query/
4. Semantic Sensor Network Ontology. https://www.w3.org/TR/vocab-ssn/
5. Daniele, L., Solanki, M., den Hartog, F., Roes, J.: Interoperability for smart appliances in the IoT world. In: Groth, P., et al. (eds.) ISWC 2016. LNCS, vol. 9982, pp. 21–29. Springer, Cham (2016). https://doi.org/10.1007/978-3-319-46547-0_3
6. Laine, M.: Restful Web Services for the Internet of Things (2012)
7. Bauer, M., Davies, J., Girod-Genet, M., Underwood, M.: Semantic Interoperability for the Web of Things. Research Gate (2016)
8. Dizdarević, J., Carpio, F., Jukan, A., Masip-Bruin, X.: A survey of communication protocols for internet of things and related challenges of fog and cloud computing integration. ACM Comput. Surv. **51**(6), 116 (2019)
9. Gyrard, A., Bonnet, C., Boudaoud, K. and Serrano, M.: LOV4IoT: a second life for ontology-based domain knowledge to build semantic web of things applications. In: Proceedings - 2016 IEEE 4th International Conference on Future Internet of Things and Cloud, FiCloud 2016, pp. 254–261 (2016)
10. Saransig, A., Tapia, F.: Performance analysis of monolithic and micro service architectures – containers technology. In: Mejia, J., Muñoz, M., Rocha, Á., Peña, A., Pérez-Cisneros, M. (eds.) CIMPS 2018. AISC, vol. 865, pp. 270–279. Springer, Cham (2019). https://doi.org/10.1007/978-3-030-01171-0_25
11. Fowler, M.: Microservices: A Definition of This New Architectural Term. http://martinfowler.com/articles/microservices.html. Accessed 22 Aug 2016
12. Docker. https://www.docker.com/
13. AWS Lambda Serverless Computing. https://aws.amazon.com/lambda/
14. Redis in memory data cache. https://redis.io/
15. Ubiworx API. https://ubiworx.com/documentation/api/ubiworx-REST-api.html
16. LDP. https://www.w3.org/TR/ldp/

WASOS: An Ontology for Modelling Traditional Knowledge of Sustainable Water Stewardship

Andreas Vlachidis[1](✉) and Mark Everard[2]

[1] Department of Information Studies, University College London, Gower Street, London WC1E 6BT, UK
a.vlachidis@ucl.ac.uk
[2] Geography and Environmental Management, University of the West of England, Coldharbour Lane, Bristol BS16 1QY, UK
mark.everard@uwe.ac.uk

Abstract. Recent work and publications concerning sustainable water stewardship in Rajasthan (India) highlight how contemporary challenges are eroding traditional, communal approaches to water stewardship through mechanised extraction beyond the renewable capacities of ecosystems. Our work is focused on developing a formal ontology for modelling the knowledge of traditional water stewardship in India's drylands by capturing the key constitutional elements of regenerative methods. Our method follows an iterative evolving prototype process for delivering the first version of the Ontology for Sustainable Water Stewardship (WASOS). The ontology contains a moderate number of high-level classes and properties that represent the water management decision-making process. By making key relationships visible, we aim to support decision-making in complex catchments particularly where there are contested urban and rural claims on water.

Keywords: Ecoinformatics · Water stewardship · Ontology · Ecosystem · India

1 Introduction

The purpose of this paper is to capture the traditional water stewardship knowledge that has enabled societal progress over four-and-a-half thousand years in India's drylands. This is achieved by modelling of ontologies, in order to inform and guide water management in the face of modern challenges (population, urbanisation, industrialisation and climate change). This project aims to model the key constitutional elements of decision-making systems in terms of entities, attributes and relationships that can potentially protect or restore ecosystem processes to support human wellbeing into the longer-term future. It also serves to assess the feasibility of the use of ontologies (formal conceptual structures) in the context of water stewardship at landscape scale, with the aim of exploring the potential of ontologies for embedding sophisticated statements of environmental knowledge particular to practices and methods underpinning sustainable water stewardship.

© Springer Nature Switzerland AG 2019
E. Garoufallou et al. (Eds.): MTSR 2019, CCIS 1057, pp. 332–339, 2019.
https://doi.org/10.1007/978-3-030-36599-8_29

Recent work and publications concerning sustainable water stewardship in Rajasthan (India) highlight how contemporary challenges are eroding traditional, communal approaches to water stewardship focused on sustainable and equitable management of water resources recharged only during episodic monsoon rainfall [1]. Expertise from the contrasting disciplines of water management and ontology modelling can support the aims of systematising 'traditional wisdoms'. It is evident that bio-ontologies can enable the modelling, discovery and unified querying of multidimensional and heterogeneous environmental data resources while benefiting automatic procedures for collection, selection, annotation and indexing of data [2, 3]. Ontologies have already greatly benefited the agricultural domain providing definitions for crops and crop products, agricultural management, and agricultural and environmental policy [4]. We envisage that ontologies can be similarly applied to the water management domain to formally express and integrate traditional knowledge of water stewardship, informing water management decision making process towards a sustainable form of development that makes a wise use of scarce water resources.

2 Background

2.1 Background on Decision-Making Challenges and Issues in Dryland India

Groundwater is a critically important resource for Indian dryland systems. This is due to the fact that episodic monsoon rainfall occurs only in a short window of time, and the high temperatures and evaporation rates throughout the rest of the year result in substantial evaporation rapidly drying soil moisture and surface water bodies. Over millennia, rural communities have adapted innovative physical structures, community governance arrangements and water use habits to subsist in these challenging conditions [5]. However, in India in general, and in Rajasthan and adjacent Indian dryland states in particular, a pervasion of modern, mechanised technologies are driving over-abstraction of groundwater well beyond natural regeneration rates [1]. Understanding the dynamics of decision-making processes around water is a pressing priority as a contributor to wiser and more sustainable management of scarce water resources.

2.2 Background on the Role of Ontologies in Environmental Decision-Making

As ecological and environmental sciences expand their scope to larger, interdisciplinary and collaborative networks, the potential role of informatics offers increasing promise for facilitating the use and exploration of scientific data and information [6]. Ecoinformatics can deliver this potential by making evident often formerly subliminal conceptual processes and enabling generation of new knowledge, discovery, integration and analysis of biological, environmental, and socioeconomic data through the use of innovative tools and computational methods [7]. Ontologies constitute the main digital artefact in the stack of the Semantic Web (SW) technologies for the formal representation of the semantics and conceptual arrangements of data. Ontology-driven data integration can significantly improve the semantic interoperability, analysis and synthesis of data whereas the Web Ontology Language (OWL) is capable of modelling concepts of complex domains and enhance the interoperability of multiple sources of data [8].

The interdisciplinary characteristics of the environmental sciences and the breadth of research questions associated with the field, which can span from gene to biosphere, create the need for effective access and sharing of data and information resources. The heterogeneity and disparity of such resources is a hindrance to their discovery, integration and analysis. Collaborative systems and information sharing tools should be capable of enabling scientists to access, trust and understand the shared load of information without inflicting biases or misconceptions.

Several examples in the domain of environmental studies have employed ontologies for describing the semantics of observational data sets. The InWaterSense project has developed a set of ontologies (i.e. core, regulation and polluters) for modelling observational data types of water quality, regulations and other water domain knowledge (e.g., water-relevant contaminants, bodies of water, etc.) [9]. The Science Environment for Ecological Knowledge (SEEK) has developed the Extensible Observation Ontology (OBOE) [10] as a formal and generic conceptual framework for describing the semantics of observational data sets based on the concepts of Observation, Measurement, Unit, Characteristic, and (Ecological) Entity. The OntoAgroHidro ontology of the Embrapa's research network represents knowledge about the impacts of climatic changes and agricultural activities on water resources [6]. The Consortium of Universities for the Advancement of Hydrologic Science has developed the Cuahsi Ontology [11] for describing hydrologic concepts, whereas the Semantic Web for Earth and Environmental Terminology (SWEET) developed by NASA Jet Propulsion Laboratories contains over 6,000 science concepts organized in 200 ontologies represented in OWL [12].

3   Method

An abundance of ontology engineering methodologies is available in the scientific literature. Early attempts to develop an ontology engineering methodology date as back to the mid-1990s. They articulate several steps as important for building an ontology, including identification of the ontology's purpose, ontology coding, integration of existing ontologies, ontology evaluation and ontology documentation. The Methontology approach [13] is an early example demonstrating the added value brought in the ontology development process by an iterative, evolving prototype approach.

Our work is focused on capturing the key constitutional elements of regenerative water stewardship methods in terms of entities, attributes and relationships. The first version of the WASOS ontology is aimed at formally expressing the key constitutional elements of decision-making systems and water stewardship governance in Rajasthan with a direct effect on water sustainability, rather than attempting to capture all relevant entities of the water management domain. Therefore, concepts and relationships relating to water quality, environmental and ecological domain were not the primary focus of the ontology design. The abundance of ontology models for capturing ecological and environmental knowledge, as already discussed, represent a significant resource and channel for directing and informing further tasks of ontology reuse and alignment, which will be considered and addressed by the future versions of the ontology.

Our work is mainly informed by the Methontology approach and is primarily focused on the development-oriented tasks of specification, conceptualisation and implementation. The design of the ontology was driven by a team of three experts (information scientist, environmentalist and a water stewardship expert) who regularly met and discussed the aims and scope of entities and relationships.

4   The WASOS Ontology

The alpha version WASOS[1] ontology contains a moderate number of high-level classes and properties which were concluded after a several design iterations and discussion between experts. It contains 44 class declarations, 14 object property declarations and 202 axioms in total. This alpha version is a 'work in progress' that sets the foundations of an ontology aimed at capturing the knowledge of traditional water stewardship methods. Therefore, the range and scope of the entities as discussed below constitute an initial understanding of the domain which, to the best of our knowledge, has not been modelled before using formal languages.

4.1   Ontology Classes

Activity: the class comprises of actions carried out by *Person* that result to a permanent change of the state of a tangible (e.g. Physiographic Feature) or intangible (e.g. Policy) matter. An *Activity* has a temporal duration which can be short-lived or on-going. Subclasses are; *Water Harvesting, Issue Right, Remove Right, Issue Penalty*.

Administration Area: The class comprises of instances of geographical areas of political administration connected to local or national government. Such areas are administer by instances of *Governance Unit* which in their turn are composed of instances of *Person*. Subclasses are; *Block, District, Stage, Village*.

Financial Resources: The class comprises of resources of monetary value which are made available to support actions relating to water stewardship. Subclasses are; *Government Fund, International Donation*.

Governance Unit: The class comprises of all different types of instances of governance including elected or appointed units of local or national level that can take the form of councils, boards, and offices. Subclasses are; *Block Development Office, Block Panchayat, Gram Panchayat, Informal Governance Unit, Vidhan Parishad, Zilla Parishad*.

Measurement: This class comprises of measurement actions relevant to water stewardship which determine properties and values by a systematic procedure.

---

[1] The alpha version of the WASOS ontology is available from the Github repository at https://github.com/avlachid/WASOS.

Person: The class comprises of instances of real persons which relate, contribute, participate or can be broadly associated with water stewardship. Subclass are; *Villager, Worker, Government Unit Member, Head of Administration, Block Development Officer, CEO, Pradhan, Sarpanch*

Physiographic Feature: The class comprises of real world instances of identifiable features of the natural world. The class contains two main subclasses, *Water body* and *Land Feature* which in turn contain the subclasses *River, Pond, Pool, Nullah* (ravine) and *Mountain, Field, Forest*, respectively.

Policy: The class comprises of instances of statements, plans and procedures that can take the form of formal documentation. Sub classes are; *Agreement, Civil Sanction, Consent, Requirement.*

4.2   Ontology Properties

The ontology contains a small set of object properties focused on modelling the relationships between the classes *Person, Administrative Area* and *Governance Unit Person*. The properties identify relationships in connection to the composition of administrative areas, governance of such areas and member participation to governance. Larger administrative areas are composed of smaller administrative areas,

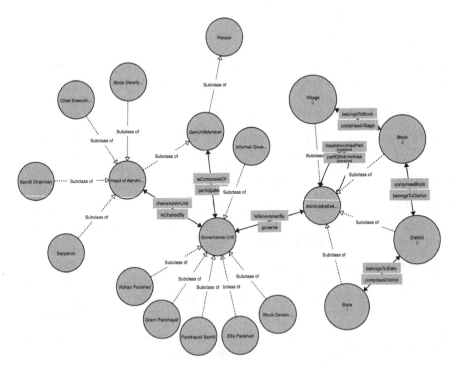

Fig. 1. WASOS ontology: a graph of classes and properties focused on modelling the relationships between Person, Administrative Area and Governance Unit. Dotted lines represent subclass relations, solid black lines represent object properties.

whereas each area is governed by a governance unit which is made of members and is chaired by a head of administration. Figure 1 presents the object properties and the respective domain and range classes, including subclass relationships.

5   Discussion

Key success criteria for regeneration of water resources supporting socio-economic wellbeing in rural Rajasthan included a fully systemic approach to water stewardship, in which decision-making and ongoing management implements water management solutions that work with natural catchment processes supporting landscape and water use on a sustainable basis [1]. Recognition of these success criteria is essential if reversal of former declines in linked socio-ecological systems is to influence water resource decisions across broader and more complex catchments subject to competing rural and urban demands. It is therefore important that the decision-making apparatus, including institutions and individual, decision-making frameworks and key criteria are understood and transparently articulated, hence the value of their representation in the form of an ontology.

Key elements represented in the ontology presented here include administrative levels (village, block, district and state), how they relate in terms of input from environmental criteria (such as water bodies) and how they interact through decision-making forums. Ensuring that this network of institutions and decision-making links is represented in decisions can support more sustainable and equitable policy and practical outcomes, and may be transferrable with adaptation more widely across India and other dryland global regions. An integrated approach to catchment management is essential not merely for addressing directly water-related goals but in support of linked goals such as the contribution of sustainable water systems to food security and health [14].

6   Conclusions and Future Work

The ontology delivers a first (alpha) version of formal semantics dedicated to capturing the knowledge of traditional water stewardship methods whilst providing a transparent representation of power and decision-relevant interactions, which may be applied to environmental decision-making situations. Using ontologies for representing the water management decision-making process and by making key relationships visible, we aim to support decision-making in complex catchments particularly where there are contested urban and rural claims on water, both in India (Rajasthan) and beyond. The current version constitutes a proposition to further discussion and development of a more comprehensive ontology of the domain of traditional water stewardship.

We envisage that further development of our preliminary approach could support sustainable management of water in arid and semi-arid environments, promoting attainment of the UN Sustainable Development Goals. Future steps include the expansion of the ontology to cover the range of entities relating to the domain of water stewardship such as buildings and infrastructure, subclasses of physiographic features, events and activities and the definition of a comprehensive set of object properties that implement the relationships between ontology classes. In addition, we are planning to incorporate into the ontology elements of the Agrovoc[2] thesaurus in order to provide vocabulary specialisations and to investigate the possibilities of re-using classes from other domain ontologies identified in Sect. 2.2. We are also planning for a thorough evaluation of the ontology in real case study by means of quantitative and qualitative metrics, such as accuracy, completeness, adaptivity using established evaluation methods [15].

References

1. Everard, M.: Community-based groundwater and ecosystem restoration in semi-arid north Rajasthan (1): socio-economic progress and lessons for groundwater-dependent areas. Ecosyst. Serv. **16**, 125–135 (2015)
2. Lokers, R., Van Randen, Y., Knapen, R., Gaubitzer, S., Zudin, S., Janssen, S.: Improving access to big data in agriculture and forestry using semantic technologies. In: Research Conference on Metadata and Semantics Research, pp. 369–380 (2015)
3. Keet, C.M.: Ontology design parameters for aligning agri-informatics with the semantic web. In: Research Conference on Metadata and Semantic Research, pp. 239–244 (2009)
4. Athanasiadis, I.N., Rizzoli, A.E., Janssen, S., Andersen, E., Villa, F.: Ontology for seamless integration of agricultural data and models. In: Research Conference on Metadata and Semantic Research, pp. 282–293 (2009)
5. Pandey, D.N., Gupta, A.K., Anderson, D.M.: Rainwater harvesting as an adaptation to climate change. Curr. Sci. **85**(1), 46–59 (2003)
6. Bonacin, R., Nabuco, O.F., Pierozzi Junior, I.: Ontology models of the impacts of agriculture and climate changes on water resources: scenarios on interoperability and information recovery. Future Gener. Comput. Syst. **54**, 423–434 (2016)
7. Michener, W.K., Jones, M.B.: Ecoinformatics: supporting ecology as a data-intensive science. Trends Ecol. Evol. **27**, 85–93 (2012)
8. Ding, L., Michaelis, J., McCusker, J., McGuinness, D.L.: Linked provenance data: a semantic web-based approach to interoperable workflow traces. Future Gener. Comput. Syst. **27**, 797–805 (2011)
9. Ahmedi, L., Jajaga, E., Ahmedi, F.: An ontology framework for water quality management. In: Corcho, Ó., Henson, C.A., Barnaghi, P.M. (eds.) SSN@ISWC, pp. 35–50 (2013)
10. Madin, J., Bowers, S., Schildhauer, M., Krivov, S., Pennington, D., Villa, F.: An ontology for describing and synthesizing ecological observation data. Ecol. Inform. **2**, 279–296 (2007)
11. Tarboton, D.G., et al.: Data interoperability in the hydrologic sciences, the CUAHSI hydrologic information system. In: Proceedings of the Environmental Information Management Conference, Santa Barbara, CA, pp. 132–137 (2011)
12. Raskin, R.G., Pan, M.J.: Knowledge representation in the semantic web for earth and environmental terminology (SWEET). Comput. Geosc. **31**(9), 1119–1125 (2005)
13. Fernández-López, M., Gómez-Pérez, A., Juristo, N.: Methontology: from ontological art towards ontological engineering. In: Proceedings of the Ontological Engineering AAAI-97 Spring Symposium Series. Presented at the AAAI-97 Spring Symposium Series, Facultad de Informática (UPM), Stanford University, EEUU (1997)

---

[2] http://aims.fao.org/vest-registry/vocabularies/agrovoc.

14. Everard, M.: Repurposing business around the meeting of human needs. Environmental Scientist, September 2017, pp. 40–45 (2017)
15. Hlomani, H., Stacey, D.: Approaches, methods, metrics, measures, and subjectivity in ontology evaluation: a survey. Semant. Web J. **1**(5), 1–11 (2014)

Track on Metadata and Semantics for Digital Humanities and Digital Curation (DHC2019)

Digital Transformation of Research Processes in the Humanities

Ernesto William De Luca[1,2(✉)] ⓘ and Riem Spielhaus[1,3] ⓘ

[1] Georg Eckert Institute for International Textbook Research,
Brunswick, Germany
{deluca, spielhaus}@gei.de
[2] Università degli Studi Guglielmo Marconi, Rome, Italy
[3] Georg-August-Universität Göttingen, Göttingen, Germany

Abstract. This paper presents the transdisciplinary work on digital tools in the field of textual analysis. The availability of digitized or digital born textual sources provides opportunities for automatized analyses and new forms of support for researchers by information technology. However, this can only be successful under the condition that humanists and other researchers who want to use digital tools for their analyses and tool developers enter in a thorough reflection on the processes involved in textual analysis in order to provide detailed descriptions of each step in the research.

Keywords: Research process · Digital transformation · Digital Curation · Digital Humanities

1 Introduction

This paper presents the transdisciplinary work on digital tools in the field of textual analysis. The availability of digitized or digital born textual sources provides opportunities for automatized analyses and new forms of support for researchers by information technology. However, this can only be successful under the condition that humanists and other researchers who want to use digital tools for their analyses and tool developers enter in a thorough reflection on the processes involved in textual analysis in order to provide detailed descriptions of each step in the research.

Meanwhile, textbooks are appealing research objects lending themselves to manifold deductive and inductive textual analyses and comparisons concerning subjects, historical periods, states, regions, or languages.

As a non-university research institution, the Georg Eckert Institute for International Textbook Research (GEI) conducts and facilitates fundamental research into textbooks and educational media from the perspective of history and cultural studies. For this purpose, the GEI provides research infrastructures such as its renowned research library with an international collection of school textbooks and various dedicated digital information services. Hence, the institute develops and manages both digital and social research infrastructures.

In the Digital Humanities (DH), the investigation of research questions is supported by a range of increasingly sophisticated digital methods such as automatic image and

E. Garoufallou et al. (Eds.): MTSR 2019, CCIS 1057, pp. 343–353, 2019.
https://doi.org/10.1007/978-3-030-36599-8_30

text analysis, linguistic text annotation, or data visualization. Digital tools and services combined with the increasing amount of resources available through digital libraries such as the German Digital Library or Europeana and international research infrastructures such as CLARIN or DARIAH have the potential to provide substantial digital support for textbook analysis. In this work, we present the current state of the art of the development of digital infrastructures for digital humanities in the field of international textbook research.

Textbook research in the analogue era often involves searching and finding relevant sources to answer a specific research question, identifying relevant text passages, tables and other visualizations etc. in those sources and finally observing and describing those passages, relevant for the respective research question.

While the research of educational media can also refer to how textbooks were produced and how they are used and understood in classrooms, and such research can surely be supported by digital means as well, this paper concentrates on the approaches to textbooks that focus on their content and structure. Such analyses are made in order to investigate whether and how certain issues, communities or (pedagogical) concepts are presented (see [16]).

Tools of the Digital Humanities have shown to be successful in supporting research on books. For instance, the Georg-Eckert-Institute provides several tools for research on educational media, textbooks and curricula. The GEI library offers different services, such as the digital curriculum workstation (*Curricula Workstation*), the database of approved textbooks in Germany (*GEI.DZS*) and the digital historical textbook library (*GEI-Digital*) that allow searching and researching digitalized curricula, textbooks and other educational media. At the moment, we are realizing a research toolbox [8], which will allow the analysis of heterogeneous digital corpora. For instance, it will support researchers in performing interdisciplinary research questions; analyzing the data from different perspectives, they can use the relevant findings provided in their original services (like *GEI-Digital* or *Curricula Workstation*).

In the following, we discuss the challenges of interdisciplinary cooperation in the rising field of Digital Humanities (in Sect. 2) and present a formalized research process for text analysis that indicates opportunities for a digital-driven research process supported by digital tools (see Sect. 3). Section 4 shows two concrete Use Cases which analyse the representations of 'Crisis' and 'Extremism' in textbooks and are put into a research design context. Afterwards we explain the possibilities of providing data and their potential for digital curation (see Sect. 5). We conclude the paper with a discussion and some recommendations given in Sect. 6.

2 Interdisciplinary Research

Digital Humanities aims at linking different subjects, such as historical information technology, information science and computational linguistics. It encompasses the use of digital resources in the humanities and related disciplines, computer-based methods, tools and applications.

The field is currently socio-politically framed, strongly project-related and led to the establishment of structures in the university landscape which are located either in the humanities or in the computer science. In some cases the Digital Humanities are covered with two chairs at the same university with different disciplinary foci.

Digital Humanities are not a new auxiliary science, nor do the digital humanists – as of yet – use fundamentally new research methods, yet its activities might well lead to the development of new approaches and methods in the future. The research is based on different research fields such as quantitative and qualitative text analysis, different search methods, text mining, subject-specific databases, corpus linguistics, visualization of complex data structures and offer user-oriented/user-centred representations of the data, which can then be further analysed hermeneutically in the humanities.

Different approaches, which help in the analysis of the data have already been implemented and offered, e.g. for a personalized access to cultural artifacts [3] or to open data [4, 10, 12]. Methods for analyzing social networks [5, 20], to evaluate popularity [7] or to support logistics during Humanitarian Assistance and Disaster Relief [11] have also been provided and can be adapted for Digital Humanities issues.

The significance of Digital Humanities for the humanities is its adjustment, re-definition and use of the already established methods of computational linguistics, machine learning and information retrieval. These methods are currently strongly focused on the text level. They try to support hermeneutic work of humanities scholars dealing with digital media, so that they can compare the sources with their insights and hypotheses with computer-aided analyses and research with novel possibilities of interaction, existing infrastructures, and novel methods for searching or visualizing larger amounts of data (see our work on CMDI [13] and [14]).

A first challenge is related to the conceptual level of the term "Digital Humanities." We observe, efforts are being made to represent the "counterpart" of the term "big data" (in computer science) and to establish "Digital Humanities" in the humanities community with a different buzz word (or hype).

In general, the humanities are engaging increasingly with digital methods. Over the years, for example, the research field of linguistics, related to the one of computer science has become more and more specific. Thus, the terms "applied linguistics", "linguistic data processing", "computational linguistics", "text technology" have been established and in the end determined their connection to "Digital Humanities". However, the basic methods used have not considerably changed.

At the moment, we find it difficult to identify the existence of digital humanists as such, but would rather speak of two disciplinary approaches converging: the *computer science* and the *humanities* approaches, which in their combination enable digital and hermeneutic processing (Digital Humanities), but then have their own characteristics in their individual disciplines. Thus, experts mostly still define themselves in the terms of their original disciplinary research, yet, making contributions to this newly created research field of Digital Humanities.

Search engines are a contemporary example for this challenge. Many methods of computer science, psychology and linguistics have been implemented to make different sources digitally available:

– An index is created and maintained (information about documents is structured).
– The user initiates the search queries and the search engine processes them (results are found and sorted).
– The results are presented in a meaningful way, so that users can interact with them.

Search engines provide the sources in a way that a systematized, practical procedure for the users is available. This enables hermeneutic work, since the users can independently analyse and interpret the identified sources, draw conclusions and develop own theses or questions.

As a basis for interdisciplinary cooperation, we review and formalize the research processes, which combine digital methods (developed by computer scientists), and hermeneutical work (experiences and expertise of humanists) for text analysis purposes.

3 Research Processes for Text Analysis in the Humanities

In order to develop an appropriate research design, humanists need an overview of the existing curricula, textbook and other educational media that might be relevant to answer a specific research question and they need access (preferably in full text) to those sources, they want to include in their analysis. On this basis a corpus can be created, subsamples selected and analyzed, what leads to a subdivision of the text analysis process into three steps: corpora creation, corpora selection and corpora analysis (see Fig. 1). For each step, the research question and the related settings play an important role. Digital tools can support all three steps, as we discuss in the following.

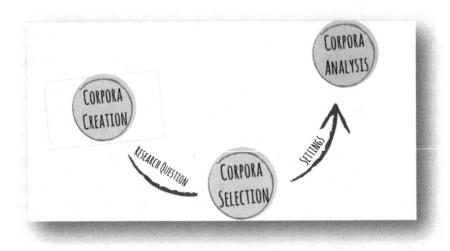

Fig. 1. Overview of the research process for text analysis in the humanities

For the corpora creation (see Fig. 2), researchers need to review, find and select sources to create a corpus for a specific analysis or study. In general, the different sources which are required to answer a research question can be located in different places, such as libraries or digital libraries. These data sources can be very heterogeneous, because they could be developed e.g. manually, automatically and standardized. Furthermore, they could be foreseen for internal use only (such as research data) or provided for external use.

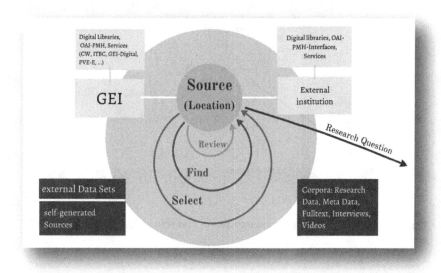

Fig. 2. Corpora creation in the research process for text analysis in the humanities

An important approach in textbooks studies is to investigate how often or in which contexts and with what content specific terms or topics such as 'Religion' [21], 'Crisis' [18], 'Migration' [19] or 'Extremism' [6] are presented. A first step thereby often is to find the passages that deal with a specific subject in order to analyze them thoroughly afterwards. Digital search tools lend themselves to perform this process both, faster as well as more efficiently and thoroughly than manual techniques.

Figure 3 presents the process of creating digital samples in order to support humanists in analyzing and specifying their research questions. During this process the research question or search terms can be reformulated or the sample can be refined, both leading to new or different hits, which can be parametrized for deeper analysis.

Figure 4 shows the relevant passages as hits. They can be texts, photos and other visualizations, info-boxes or whole chapters. The findings can lead to a reformulation of the research question or a revision of the sample drawn for a specific analysis, but in the best case, it is large enough but not too big to start the next research step: the analysis. A next step for a textual analysis includes the coding of identified passages and sentences and the deep description of reoccurring semantic and syntactic patterns. This can include frequencies, co-occurrences, passive and active constructions or prepositions used with the analyzed term(s) [9].

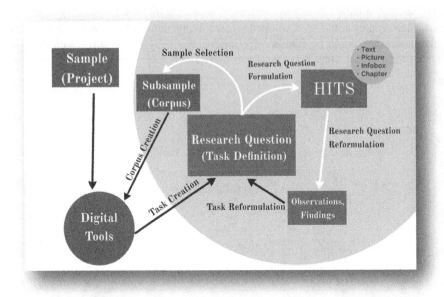

Fig. 3. Corpora selection in the research process for text analysis in the humanities

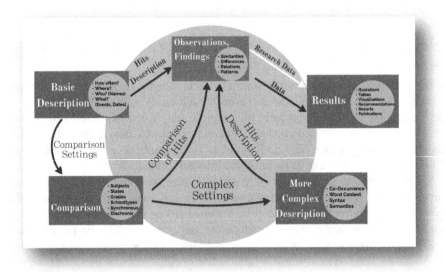

Fig. 4. Corpora analysis in the research process for text analysis in the humanities

An important method for textbook analysis is comparison, for instance concerning countries, year or decade of publication, publishing houses or school subjects. Hence, visualizations of hits found per line, passage, page or textbook should support researchers in finding similarities and differences as well as dominant patterns and relevant exceptions in the representation of a specific issue. In many cases, humanists depend on the possibility to try out different units of analysis before they make a striking observation or find a meaningful pattern. Consequently, different options to both systematize and compare are needed.

4 Analyzing Representations of 'Crisis' and 'Extremism' as Use Cases for Research Designs

After discussing the use of digital tools for textbook analysis we concentrate on the description of two use cases from the field of textbook studies on 'Crisis' and 'Extremism'.

In a conceptual paper, Otto, Sammler and Spielhaus [18] suggest two basic approaches (inductive and deductive) at different levels of comparison for investigations of crisis discourses in school textbooks. On the one hand, the concept of crisis and other terms grouped in a semantic field itself, and on the other hand individual events or phenomena – like the world economic crisis 1929, the Cuban crisis 1962 – defined as crises in the research design would be relevant here. Both approaches enable comparisons across school subjects, grades, countries and languages in order to establish the regional specificity and historicity of the understandings of crisis. This allows addressing the question as to whether the concept of crisis has become a central topos in social self-descriptions beyond the Western context. Based on the relevant text passages and images referring directly or indirectly to crises, humanists can discuss on an empirical basis whether crisis discourses and the description of social change in crisis narratives are really globalized, how the concept of crisis is used in different regions of the world, and which events and phenomena are interpreted as crises [18].

In another analysis of textbooks from four countries in different world regions (Germany, Kenya, India and the United States), Tobias Ide investigates how 'Terrorism' is portrayed in textbooks [17]. 'Extremism' and pedagogic approaches to Prevent Violent Extremism in German textbooks where analyzed by Eleni Christodoulou and Simona Szakácz with the help of digital tools. The research team asked how often terms like 'Extremism' and 'Terrorism' are mentioned in contemporary German curricular texts for History and Social Studies, and how these terms are distributed across curricula for different states, school types and school subjects? In which general thematic and semantic contexts do they appear? They were able to show that the keywords 'Extremism' and 'Terrorism' and their derivate terms appear infrequently in the curricula for the two subjects, "indicating their low level of importance in the curricula". The highest frequency of the term 'Extremism' found in a single curricular text was 7 occurrences in a document of 157 pages, and of the word 'Terrorism' was 6 occurrences in a document of 62 pages with a total corpus of 3078 pages of curricular documents. The word 'Extremism' appears 60 times in 26 of a total number of 87 documents, and the word 'Terrorism' 60 times in 29 out of 87 documents. A comparison to other or more frequent terms was also fruitful. Most often were the concepts 'Democracy' (788 times), 'Revolution' (607 times), and 'Rule' (Herrschaft) (514 times) mentioned in the full corpus of 87 documents. Compared to these terms, 'Extremis' and 'Terrorism' appeared insignificant in frequency [6].

5 Research Processes for Digital Curation

Research processes require not only data creation, but also data curation, which has become more and more important, if we want to make information available. *Digital Curation* involves maintaining, preserving and adding value to digital data throughout its lifecycle. The active management of data reduces risks to their long-term value and mitigates the threat of digital obsolescence. Meanwhile, digital repositories provide curated data to a wider research community, increasing the intrinsic value of the Cultural Data and making it available for further high quality research. Humanists are increasingly engaged with curating and making accessible digital materials.

Different Methodologies have been presented [1, 2, 15] that may automate and optimize functions, such as categorization, classification, clustering and digitalizing Big Cultural Data. This new line of research should study, first of all, the meaning of Data Curation, which are the actions to be performed and which actions may be automated and supported by digital instruments. The first action consists of describing and representing the information with appropriate standards to describe metadata and controlling it over a long term. Furthermore, all metadata and associated digital material should be represented in appropriate formats. The second action consists in building a preservation strategy that is important to plan for preservation throughout the data lifecycle.

The actions involved in curating (collaborating, supervising, and participating) need to include both researchers from digital science and humanities in order to supervise data creation activities and to assist in the creation of the standards to be used [1].

6 Discussion and Recommendations

As shown above, the functionalities implemented for Digital Humanities (such as automatic search, frequency analysis or sentiment analysis) hold opportunities and limitations for textual analysis. They demand and promote the openness of researchers to all areas associated with Digital Humanities. Digital transformation of the research processes in the humanities and neighbouring disciplines provides researchers with accessible sources in digital form and enables new statistics-based findings (i.e. Distant Reading). However, before these tools can be successfully applied, an intensive interdisciplinary exchange is necessary that reflects the different steps and methods of the hermeneutical analysis. Digital Humanities tools do not only enable searching and analysing large data corpora in limited time, but will also facilitate asking new research questions for instance concerning relations within and between different texts and genres. This can be relevant for the field of textbook studies, for instance when we ask whether norms promoted by education laws, international paradigms or pedagogical concepts are appearing in textbooks.

The limits for Digital Humanities are given by the different subject-related views of specific problems, since prioritizations of tasks can be different depending on the discipline.

Hence, communication between the researchers from different disciplines with sometimes contradicting notions of what research is all about is a prerequisite to develop a common understanding of research processes. As we see it, this communication has to be understood as an act of translation(s) and bridge building. While a genuine interest in the research aims in the different fields of the humanities is necessary on the side of computer scientist and tool developers, humanists can be struggling with a number of issues in this process, which are related to trust. In our interdisciplinary cooperation we figured three substantial challenges in this regard:

First, the work with digitalised or digitally born text sources can lead to a feeling of fuzziness or elusiveness, since the corpora are not approachable as a material corpus. Files and lists of sources on the screen cannot be visited like a library, a collection of manuscripts or handled like a bookshelf in the office. An effect of the digitization of sources is the urge to get a better sense of the sources that were included in the analysis. Researchers have to be able to comprehend and to explain, which sources have been included in their analysis. Answer/Solution: as clear a documentation as possible about the sources used.

Second, how can humanists trust automatic searches/readings, if they do not fully understand how they work? Answer/Solution: Training and test data can be used in order to prove the expert's knowledge. Comparison of automated and manual classifications and annotations based on a gold standard given by a researcher from the humanities [21].

Third, within the heterogeneous views in the humanities and between them and the computer science, we can observe different understandings of knowledge, as well as their evaluation that allude to different epistemological assumptions and prerequisites. Thus, many humanities scholars approach encyclopedias with a hermeneutic of suspicion concerning power relations inscribed into them over centuries of knowledge production; if these are used for the automatic understanding of texts, this threatens to counteract any skeptical reading. Hence, using vocabularies and encyclopedias for semantic enrichment of classifications, can risk the perpetuation of dominant knowledge that manifests itself in encyclopedias. Answer/Solution: none, so far.

In conclusion, we suggest an open discussion between humanities and computer science, which should drive the digital transformation of research processes, in order to better understand the challenges and find common solutions.

In this paper, we formalized the first steps to be done for the corpora creation, selection and analysis that can help in better understanding the research processes involved in textual analysis and develop digital tools to support research in the humanities.

References

1. Arcidiacono, G., De Luca, E.W., Fallucchi, F., Pieroni, A.: The use of lean six sigma methodology in digital curation. In: Proceedings of the First Workshop on Digital Humanities and Digital Curation (DHC 2016). In Conjunction with the 10th Conference on Metadata and Semantics Research (MTSR 2016) (2016)
2. Arcidiacono, G., Martini, I., De Luca, E.W.: Sharing knowledge engineering for digital humanities. In: Proceedings of the First Workshop on Digital Humanities and Digital Curation (DHC 2016), 22 November 2016, Göttingen, Germany. In Conjunction with the 10th Conference on Metadata and Semantics Research (MTSR 2016) (2016)
3. Beccaceci, R., Fallucchi, F., Giannone, C.F., Spagnoulo, F., Zanzotto, F.M.: Education with "living artworks" in museums. In: CSEDU 2009 - Proceedings of the 1st International Conference on Computer Supported Education, vol. 1, pp. 346–349 (2009). ISBN: 978-989811182-1
4. Bianchi, M., Draoli, M., Fallucchi, F., Ligi, A.: Service level agreement constraints into processes for document classification. In: ICEIS 2014 - Proceedings of the 16th International Conference on Enterprise Information Systems, vol. 1, pp. 545–550 (2014). ISBN: 978-989758027-7
5. Cena, F., Dattolo, A., De Luca, E.W., Lops, P., Plumbaum, T., Vassileva, J.: Semantic adaptive social web. In: Ardissono, L., Kuflik, T. (eds.) UMAP 2011. LNCS, vol. 7138, pp. 176–180. Springer, Heidelberg (2012). https://doi.org/10.1007/978-3-642-28509-7_17
6. Christodoulou, E., Szakács, S.: Preventing Violent Extremism through Education: International and German Approaches. Georg Eckert Institute, Braunschweig (2018)
7. De Luca, E.W., Fallucchi, F., Giuliano, R., Incarnato, G., Mazzenga, F.: Analysing and visualizing tweets for U.S. president popularity. Int. J. Adv. Sci. Eng. Inf. Technol. 9(2), 692–699 (2019). https://doi.org/10.18517/ijaseit.9.2.8284. ijaseit.insightsociety.org
8. De Luca, E.W., Fallucchi, F., Ligi, A., Tarquini, M.: A research toolbox: a complete suite for analysis in digital humanities. In: Track Digital Humanities and Digital Curation of the 13th Metadata and Semantics Research Conference, Rome, Italy, 28–31 October 2019 (2019)
9. Abdou, E.D.: Copts in Egyptian history textbooks: towards an integrated framework for analyzing minority representations. J. Curriculum Stud. 50(4), 476–507 (2018)
10. Fallucchi, F., Alfonsi, E., Ligi, A., Tarquini, M.: Ontology-driven public administration web hosting monitoring system. In: Meersman, R., et al. (eds.) Lecture Notes in Computer Science (Including Subseries Lecture Notes in Artificial Intelligence and Lecture Notes in Bioinformatics), vol. 8842, pp. 618–625. Springer, Heidelberg (2014). https://doi.org/10.1007/978-3-662-45550-0_63
11. Fallucchi, F., Tarquini, M., De Luca, E.W.: Knowledge management for the support of logistics during humanitarian assistance and disaster relief (HADR). In: Díaz, P., Bellamine Ben Saoud, N., Dugdale, J., Hanachi, C. (eds.) ISCRAM-med 2016. LNBIP, vol. 265, pp. 226–233. Springer, Cham (2016). https://doi.org/10.1007/978-3-319-47093-1_19
12. Fallucchi, F., Petito, M., De Luca, E.W.: Analysing and visualising open data within the data and analytics framework. In: Garoufallou, E., Sartori, F., Siatri, R., Zervas, M. (eds.) MTSR 2018. CCIS, vol. 846, pp. 135–146. Springer, Cham (2019). https://doi.org/10.1007/978-3-030-14401-2_13
13. Fallucchi, F., De Luca, E.W.: Connecting and mapping LOD and CMDI through knowledge organization. In: Garoufallou, E., Sartori, F., Siatri, R., Zervas, M. (eds.) MTSR 2018. CCIS, vol. 846, pp. 291–301. Springer, Cham (2019). https://doi.org/10.1007/978-3-030-14401-2_27

14. Fallucchi, F., Steffen, H., De Luca, E.W.: Creating CMDI-Profiles for textbook resources. In: Garoufallou, E., Sartori, F., Siatri, R., Zervas, M. (eds.) MTSR 2018. CCIS, vol. 846, pp. 302–314. Springer, Cham (2019). https://doi.org/10.1007/978-3-030-14401-2_28

15. Fogarty, D.: Lean six sigma and big data: continuing to innovate and optimize business processes. J. Manage. Innov. **1**(2), 2–20 (2015)

16. Fuchs, E., Bock, A. (eds.): Palgrave Handbook of Textbook Studies. Palgrave MacMillan, Basingstokeet (2018)

17. Ide, T.: Terrorism in the textbook: a comparative analysis of terrorism discourses in Germany, India, Kenya and the United States based on school textbooks. Camb. Rev. Int. Aff. **30**(1), 44–66 (2017)

18. Otto, M., Sammler, S., Spielhaus, R.: "Krisen" als Seismographen gesellschaftlichen Wandels und Gegenstand schulischer Bildungsmedien. In: Handbuch Krisenforschung. Campus Verlag. in Print (2019)

19. Otto, M., Niehaus, I., Georgi, V.: Schulbuchstudie Migration und Integration. Die Beauftragte der Bundesregierung für Migration, Flüchtlinge und Integration, Berlin (2015)

20. Plumbaum, T., Wu, S., De Luca, E.W., Albayrak, S.: User modeling for the social semantic web. In: CEUR Workshop Proceedings, vol. 781, pp. 78–89 (2011). http://ceur-ws.org/

21. Štimac, Z.: Religion – Sprache – Politik. Reformation in ausgewählten Schulbüchern Südosteuropas. In: Luther und die Reformation in internationalen Geschichtskulturen. Perspektiven für den Geschichtsunterricht. Roland Bernhard, Felix Hinz und Rober Maier (eds.). Göttingen: V&R unipress 2017, pp. 233–254 (2017)

Curatr: A Platform for Semantic Analysis and Curation of Historical Literary Texts

Susan Leavy[(✉)], Gerardine Meaney, Karen Wade, and Derek Greene

University College Dublin, Dublin, Ireland
{susan.leavy,gerardine.meaney,karen.wade,derek.greene}@ucd.ie

Abstract. The increasing availability of digital collections of historical and contemporary literature presents a wealth of possibilities for new research in the humanities. The scale and diversity of such collections however, presents particular challenges in identifying and extracting relevant content. This paper presents *Curatr*, an online platform for the exploration and curation of literature with machine learning-supported semantic search, designed within the context of digital humanities scholarship. The platform provides a text mining workflow that combines neural word embeddings with expert domain knowledge to enable the generation of thematic lexicons, allowing researches to curate relevant sub-corpora from a large corpus of 18th and 19th century digitised texts.

Keywords: Text mining · Digital humanities · Corpus curation

1 Introduction

The interpretability of the algorithmic process and the incorporation of domain knowledge are essential to the use of machine learning and text mining in the semantic analysis of literature. The absence of these factors can inhibit adoption of machine learning approaches to text mining in the humanities, due to issues of accuracy and trust in what is often regarded as a 'black-box' process [6,13, 15]. This paper presents *Curatr*, an online platform that incorporates domain expertise and imparts transparency in the use of machine learning for literary analysis. The system supports a corpus curation workflow that addresses the requirements of scholars in the humanities who are increasingly working with large collections of unstructured text and facilitates the development of sub-corpora from large digital collections.

Selection, curation and interpretation is central to knowledge generation in the humanities [18,36]. This process is supported in *Curatr* with conceptual search functionality that uses neural word embeddings to build conceptual lexicons specific to a given theme or topic. These thematic lexicons can then be used to mine relevant texts to form curated literary collections that may be saved, further modified, or exported as sub-corpora. The platform was developed based on a collection of 35,918 English language digital texts from the British Library[1].

---

[1] British Library Labs: https://www.bl.uk/projects/british-library-labs.

E. Garoufallou et al. (Eds.): MTSR 2019, CCIS 1057, pp. 354–366, 2019.
https://doi.org/10.1007/978-3-030-36599-8_31

An evaluation of *Curatr* was conducted in conjunction with an associated project examining the relationship between societal views of migration, ethnicity, and concepts concerning contagion and disease in 19th century Britain and Ireland. In order to explore the cultural representation of migrants, the study focused on their representation within historical fiction which comprises 16,426 texts of the British Library digital collection. Given the largest communities of migrants to London during the late 19th century were Irish and Jewish, this study focused on their portrayal in relation to prevailing concepts of contagion, disease and migration. Lexicons related to these themes were generated through recommendations derived from word embedding models and text were retrieved based on relevance of the texts. The findings were evaluated in terms of the overall requirements of a humanities scholar along with the relevance of the texts uncovered. We describe this case study in more detail in Sect. 4.

2 Related Work

2.1 Text Mining in the Humanities

The work builds on a range of literature that demonstrates requirements for digital humanities platforms. Close reading functionality to provide context is an essential aspect of humanities research, as evidenced in the provision of close reading functionality along with quantitative analysis in systems developed by Hinricks et al. [16] and Vane [34]. Domain knowledge was combined with automated text classification to provide more accurate retrieval results in a system developed by Sweetnam and Fennel [1] to explore early-modern English texts. A system based on semantic search was demonstrated by Kopaczyk et al. [20] for the analysis of Scottish legal documents from the 16th century. Other systems, such as that proposed by Jockers [18], have focused primarily on the use of machine learning methods for text analysis.

In a study of the update of machine learning in industry, Chiticariu et al. [6] noted a gap in the volume of academic research on machine learning, compared with lower levels of uptake within industry and found the causes of this pertained to training data, interpretability and incorporation of domain knowledge. Similarly, the relatively low uptake of machine learning methods in the digital humanities has been attributed to issues pertaining to interpretation and trust [13,15,33]. Imparting domain knowledge into the process of text analysis through interpretation and annotation is also central to humanities research [17,36]. The *Curatr* platform addresses these specific requirements of digital humanities research by incorporating domain knowledge and transparency within a text mining workflow.

2.2 Concept Modelling with Word Embeddings

Word embedding refers to a family of methods from natural language processing that involve mapping words or phrases appearing in large text corpora to dense, low-dimensional numeric representations. Typically, each unique word in the corpus vocabulary will be represented by its own vector. By transforming textual data in this way, we can use the new representation to capture the semantic similarity between pairs or groups of words. Word embedding methods have been used in digital humanities research to generate semantic lexicons for a range of purposes including detecting language change over time [14], extracting social networks from literary texts [35], sentiment analysis [31], and semantic annotation [21]. An interactive strategy whereby a user incrementally creates a lexicon based on recommendations for similar words as recommended by a word embedding model has been demonstrated in a number of works [10,27].

A variety of different approaches have been proposed in the literature to construct embeddings. The word embedding algorithm used in this research is *word2Vec* [22], which generates distributed representations of words that can be used to interpret their meaning. This approach captures the concept from distributed semantics that the meaning of a word "can be determined by the company it keeps" [11]. Word co-occurrence is identified over an entire corpus and each word along with the words found beside it in the text are represented by a vector. The similarity of terms can then be derived based on whether they are used alongside similar words, or in a similar context. This approach to generating lexicons has been shown to be useful where the language of a particular corpus is highly specific [5] and where existing general-purpose lexicons are not appropriate and is therefore particularly relevant to digital humanities. It has also been pointed out that pre-processing and methods of representing text can have particular significance within a digital humanities context [4,12]. These decisions are a crucial aspect of the evaluation of results within humanities scholarship. Given that using word embedding in text analysis has been critiqued for its lack of transparency [30], it is crucial within a digital humanities context to impart transparency into the text mining workflow.

3   Curatr Design

3.1   Platform Overview

Curatr implements a text mining framework involving conceptual search using word embeddings to dynamically build a semantic lexicon specific to a given literary corpus. The humanities researcher begins with seed terms and these are expanded using neural word embedding through an interactive online interface to produce semantic lexicons. The *Curatr* system also provides for keyword search, filtering based on metadata, ngram frequencies, and categorisation based on the original British Library topical classifications (Fig. 2). The information retrieval component of the system involves the indexing of texts and using the open source Apache Solr engine[2].

---

[2] http://lucene.apache.org/solr/.

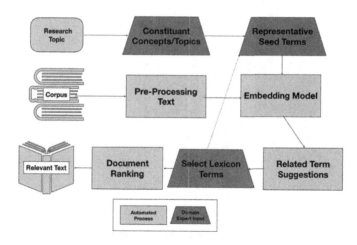

Fig. 1. *Curatr* workflow for digital humanities text mining.

3.2 Concept Lexicon Generation

The conceptual search workflow outlined in Fig. 1 enables the compilation of seed terms associated with a given concept or topic by the humanities researcher. *Curatr* allows for the expansion of these terms to form a lexicon of semantically similar words based on associations suggested from the querying of a neural word embedding model developed from the corpus. Word embedding models were generated from the complete English language corpus using the *word2vec* approach [22] yielding real-valued, low-dimensional representations of words based on lexical co-occurrences. The use of word embeddings rather than more complex language models were deemed appropriate due to the lack of structure in the text and OCR errors introduced through the process of digitisation. The specific embedding variant used in this work is a 100-dimensional Continuous Bag-Of-Words (CBOW) *word2vec* model, trained on the full-text volumes of the corpus. To address the levels of transparency required in digital humanities scholarship regarding approaches to text representation and parameter settings and their potential effects on results, decisions regarding text processing options and parameter strategies in generating the neural word embedding models are available to the user.

Based on the embedding model, the top 20 words found to be similar to the seed words are recommended to expand the current lexicon. The user selects the subset of recommendations to be included in the conceptual lexicon. This inclusion of a "human in the loop" ensures that the process of generating a lexicon is informed by domain knowledge of the user. Multiple iterations of this semantic search allow the researcher to refine the lexicon and augment the conceptual category on each iteration, simulating the process of knowledge generation from close reading and annotation.

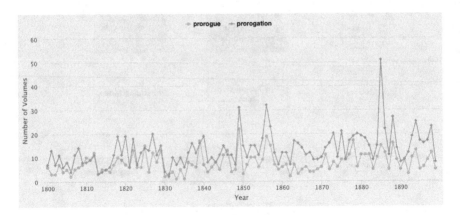

Fig. 2. Sample *Curatr* n-gram frequency analysis.

3.3 Corpus Curation

The finalised semantic lexicons are used as a basis for ranked volume retrieval from the indexed library corpus. Texts are ranked according to the frequency of occurrence of terms from each generated lexicon relative to the document length. This process uncovers documents that pertain to the given conceptual category. These document rankings may then be saved by the user for later use.

Curatr also facilitates the amendment of the sub-corpus to remove non-relevant texts. Based on the results of this search, the user may revise the contents of the conceptual lexicon and rerun the text mining process. Along with the provision of a close reading interface for examining individual texts, the platform also enables the export of curated sub-corpora to download for further analysis.

4 Case Study Evaluation

The case study involved an exploratory investigation of historical cultural attitudes towards migration in Britain and their associations with concepts of contagion and disease from the set of 16,426 texts in the corpus [19,26]. Poverty-induced migration from Ireland to Britain during the Great Famine (1845–1851) is cited as generating a fear of transmission of contagious disease [23]. The association of fear of contagion with historical sentiments towards migrants, according to Cohn however, requires more systematic study and more nuanced interpretation of both historical and cultural archives [8]. The aim of this exploratory study is to uncover new texts and literary representations that are less well known to researchers and which might challenge current understandings of the relationship between migration and concepts of contagion and disease.

Evaluating the usefulness of retrieved documents in the context of humanities research does not always align with standard information retrieval precision metrics. This is particularly pertinent in the preliminary exploratory phase of humanities research, where new and diverse texts are sought by the researcher and their relevance to the research topic is often not immediately apparent [7]. However, a prime advantage of text mining in the humanities is the potential to uncover novel and diverse texts that could challenge prevailing theory. This research therefore draws on Bates et al. [3], who examined what constitutes relevance of a document in the context of humanities research defining two aspects of relevance in humanities research, *content relevance* and *utility relevance*. Content relevance determines whether the search terms in the query relate to the content retrieved while utility relevance evaluates the usefulness in the context of the research topic. Given that a humanities researcher requires texts that inform their topic, texts deemed to be most relevant in terms of utility are often not those with the highest content relevance, but are those that alter the judgement and challenge existing theories of the researcher. Document unfamiliarity is therefore an attribute that 'may be presumed to swamp all other considerations' [3, p. 702]. Unfamiliarity of a text was defined by Barry et al. [2] in terms of content, source or stimulus. *Content novelty* describes how the content of a text itself provides new knowledge to a researcher. *Source novelty* refers to whether the text is written by a previously unknown author or publisher. *Stimulus novelty* indicates whether the text itself is new to the researcher. Brought together the framework outlines capture the complexity of judgements of value and relevance of text mining for the humanities.

The key thematic strands of the case study were identified and associated seed terms defined. The themes pertained to 'migration', 'illness', 'contagion', and Irish and Jewish ethnic identities. The word embedding model was queried to uncover words used in a similar context to the seed terms in the fiction corpus (see Fig. 3). The results were selectively added based on contextual knowledge and interpretation on the part of the humanities researcher through an interactive lexicon building interface. The resulting expanded semantic lexicons were then used as a basis for ranking the documents to uncover texts that capture the key themes of the study. See Table 1 for examples of lexicons generated in this way.

Analysis of the recommended terms suggested new associations in the fiction corpus. For example, terms pertaining to the theme of civil unrest *(rebels, dynamiters, conspirators, incendiarism, anarchistic, nihilists, revolutionary, sedition, informers, radicals)* make up a substantial portion of the lexicon pertaining to 'ethnic identity'. As a result of these suggestions, aligning with the iterative theory-building approach of research in the humanities, the suggested words enriched the original conceptualisation of the research theme of ethnic identity to incorporate relationships with political ideology. Additionally, the expanded lexicons indicated points where conceptual ontologies overlap. Suggested terms in *Curatr* also provided indications of relevant but unfamiliar or archaic terminology. For instance, in this study the term 'distemper', which is more commonly applied to animal illnesses nowadays, appears as a term that is relevant to the concept of contagion within these works. OCR (optical character recognition) and spelling errors and variants were also uncovered using this method.

Table 1. Examples of top recommended words for different conceptual lexicons.

Lexicon	Seed terms	Recommended words
Ethnic identity	irish, fenian, papist, jewish, jew	jews, fenianism, hibernian, usurer, celtic, rebels, invincibles, whiteboys, incendiary, brogue, chartists, irishman, catholics, ringleaders, rabbis
Migration	immigrant, alien, interloper, migrant	civilisers, doavn trodden, self governing, circumcised, peoples, separatists, cousinhood, usurpers, interloper, aliens, intruder, middlemen, ryots, kinless, alien
Contagion	infect, epidemic, inoculate, contagion, contaminate, vaccinate	infection, contagion, infectious, infected, fever, contagious, epidemic, plague, epidemic, disease, epidemics, fever, malarial, endemic, malady
Disease	disease, smallpox, cholera, fever, pestilence	scarlet fever, epidemics, morbus, cancers, tumour, incurable, malaria, sickness, cancer, brain, diseases, distempers, typhus, anaemia, heart disease

Table 2. Texts retrieved before and after query expansion, for concepts related to 'illness' and 'contagion'.

Prior to query expansion	Post query expansion
1894 The Captain's Youngest, Frances H. Burnett	1891 The Year of Miracle, Fergus Hume
1888 The Devil's Die, Allen Grant	1897 The Sign of the Red Cross, Evelyn E. Green
1894 The Azrael of Anarchy, Gustave Linbach	1855 Old Saint Paul's, William H. Ainsworth
1891 The Year of Miracle, Fergus Hume	1894 The Azrael of Anarchy, Gustave Linbach
1870 Unawares, Frances Mary Peard	1847 A Tale of the Irish Famine, Unknown
1893 Doctor, or Lover?, Faber Vance	1885 The Legend of Samandal, James Fer
1888 A Crown of Shame, Florence Marryat	1855 The Wood-Spirit, Ernest C. Jones
1875 Ashes to ashes, Hugh R. Haweis	1888 The Devil's Die, Grant Allen
1865 Not Proven, Christina B Cameron	1898 Vanya, Orlova Olga
1892 The Medicine Lady, Elizabeth T Meade	1897 A Literary Gent, J.C. Kernahan

4.1   Finding and Discussion

Drawing upon the framework of retrieval value outlined by Bates et al. [3] and Barry et al. [2], the top 10 retrieved texts in each category were analysed in terms of novelty to the humanities researcher involved in the project. The qualitative difference in text retrieved before and after the query expansion phase was also examined. Texts in the corpus were ranked according to the frequency by which the curated conceptual lexicons were mentioned, relative to the length of the documents. The iterative process whereby the researcher returns to edit the conceptualisation of the key thematic trends of the research topic through editing the semantic lexicons aligns with the process of grounded theory research and

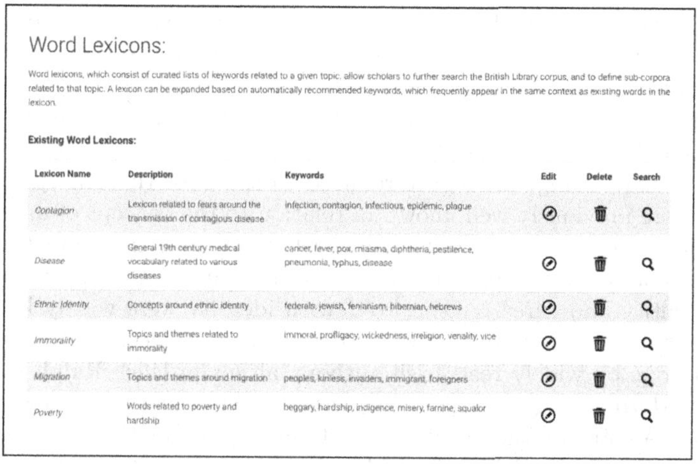

Fig. 3. The *Curatr* lexicon management interface.

Table 3. Texts retrieved before and after query expansion, for a concept related to 'migration'.

Prior to query expansion	Post query expansion
1898 For Lilias, Rosa Nouchette Carey	1881 Gifts and Favours Doctor Olloed, Unknown
1875 The Golden Shaft, George C. Davies	1871 Ierne, William R. Trench
1876 The Youth of the Period, James F.S. Kennedy	1863 Sackville Chase, Charles J. Collins
1876 Her Dearest Foe, Alexander	1894 Ivanda or the Pilgrim's quest, Claude A. Bray
1886 A Modern Telemachus, Charlotte M. Yonge	1894 Doctor Izard, Anna K. Green
1887 Major Lawrence, Emily Lawless	1865 The Crusader or the Witch of Finchley, Unknown
1857 Guy Fawkes, William H. Ainsworth	1864 The Bee-Hunters, Gustave Aimard
1846 The Moor, the Mine and the Forest, William Heatherbred	1850 Helen Porter, Thomas P. Prest
1865 The Notting Hill Mystery, Charles Felix	1852 Idone, James H. L. Archer
1897 Owen Tanat, Alfred N. Palmer	1886 A Mysterious Trust, Edmund Mitchell

necessitated a close reading of the results by humanities researchers to evaluate the value of the retrieved documents.

Source Novelty. A striking pattern among the texts retrieved with the expanded query set was the relative obscurity of some of the authors. In analysing the top ten texts retrieved using the seed terms alone, five of the migration category and four of illness category were immediately familiar to the researchers (Tables 2 and 3). However, after the list was expanded based on suggestions from neural word embedding, this figure reduced to three for the concept of illness, and none were previously well known in relation to the concept of migration.

A similar trend is evident in the texts retrieved using the semantic lexicons of ethnic identity where only one of the authors in the top ten texts related to Irish identity and three relating to Jewish identity were widely known (see Table 4). The texts retrieved based on the semantic lexicon of Irish ethnicity contained none by widely read Irish authors, although Ulick Ralph Burke and Albert Stratford George Canning do merit an entry in the database of Irish Literature[3]. A work by the prolific English author Fergus Hume was retrieved, as were works by the British authors Mabel Collins and Edith Cuthell, the latter novel being its author's only work based in an Irish setting. This identification of a number of writers less prominent in the canon, but who wrote on topics relating to the key themes of the case study, demonstrate how the expansion of query terms in this context has the potential to uncover relevant texts which might otherwise be overlooked.

Stimulus Novelty. In this case study the texts retrieved presented a number of works that represented not only less well-known authors of the 18th and 19th centuries, but also less well-known texts written by more prominent authors. In relation to the texts retrieved using the conceptual lexicon of illness for instance, the majority of retrieved titles were not commonly known and none pertaining to Irish identity attracted significant bibliographic or critical commentary. The text marked as most relevant to Irish identity, *Sweet Irish Eyes*, was written by an English author and was their only Irish-themed work. Thee expanded list of query terms also uncovered slightly older texts pointing to the potential of word embedding to compile a semantic lexicons that are less biased towards contemporary linguistic norms.

The most relevant of the retrieved set of texts pertaining to Jewish identity was that by British novelist Hall Caine. This work is referred to in studies of the Gothic (e.g. Mulvany-Roberts [24]), but there is very little reference to this novel and its portrayal of Jewish characters. It is notable that Anglo-Jewish writers (Zangwill and Farjeon[4]) feature prominently alongside one of Dickens' best known novels. Charles Dickens' *Oliver Twist* and Israel Zangwil's *Dreamers of the Ghetto*, which appear on the list of novels pertaining to Jewishness, were the only two novels on the list that have previously attracted sustained scholarly attention. For example, Udelson [32], Rochelson [28,29] and Murray [25] have all written on Zangwill, though he is far less well known to the public than Dickens.

---

[3] Ricorso: Database of Irish writers http://www.ricorso.net.

[4] Farjeon features more prominently in histories of Australian literature as he emigrated there.

Table 4. Texts retrieved for the 'Irish' and 'Jewish' conceptual lexicons.

Irish lexicon	Jewish lexicon
1897 Sweet Irish Eyes, E. Cuthell	1890 The Prophet. A parable, T. H. H. Caine
1893 The Harlequin Opal, F. Hume	1897 A Rogue's Conscience, D. C. Murray
1875 The Autobiography of a Man-o-War's Bell, C. R. Low	1864 The Hekim Bashi, H. Sandwith
1883 The Wild Rose of Lough Gill, P. G. Smyth	1874 Jessie Trim, B. L. Farjeon
1880 Loyal and Lawless, U. R. Burke	1853 The Turk and the Hebrew, Unknown
1867 Baldearg O'Donnell, A. A. G. Canning	1865 The Crusader or the Witch of Finchley, Unknown
1893 The Great War of 189-. A forecast, F. Villiers	1895 Maid Marian and Crotchet Castle, T. L. Peacock
1896 The Idyll of the White Lotus, M. Collins	1898 Dreamers of the Ghetto, I. Zangwill
1886 Our Radicals. A tale of love and politics, F. Burnaby	1838 Oliver Twist, C. Dickens
1891 The Last Great Naval War, A. N. Seaforth	1869 Count Teleki: A story of modern Jewish life, UN
1890 Heir and no Heir Canning, A. S. G. Canning	

Content Novelty. While uncovering authors and titles that were previously less familiar to a researcher is beneficial, its value is ultimately dependent on the relevance of the content. Close analysis showed that the expanded set of query terms retrieved books that were less specific to the topics than those retrieved using the manually generated set of seed terms suggesting new associations and challenging the researcher's understanding of the key themes. For instance, in relation to the concept of illness, a text pertaining to the Irish Famine and texts addressing political issues were returned. The most relevant to the concept of illness using an expanded lexicon was Evelyn Everett Green's novel, *The Sign of the Red Cross*. The content of this novel describes details of a plague in London and was critiqued at the time for its graphic nature [9]. The novel *Old Saint Paul's* was concerned with the plague in London and provides a wealth of information relevant to the topic. While these novels are not among the most well known currently, their graphic account of plague in London provides a wealth of insight regarding the historical conceptualisation of illness in Britain. The content of texts retrieved pertaining to Irish and Jewish ethnic identities were highly relevant to the topic and uncovered texts that are less well known, thus presenting new opportunities to examine cultural representations of ethnicity.

For instance, the theme of seafaring in the titles pertaining to Irish identity is an association that was new to the researchers. The content that was returned in relation to the concept of migration returned more titles that addressed migration in the broader sense in connection with international political events, in contrast with the narrower focus of the results retrieved using seed terms alone.

5 Conclusion

This research presents an approach whereby machine learning and text analysis is used within a text mining workflow designed for digital humanities research. The corpus curation workflow in *Curatr* is supported by neural word embedding and through an interactive online platform, ensures transparency and incorporates domain knowledge. The approach demonstrates how machine learning techniques may be used to enhance the curation process for humanities scholars. Evaluation of the system demonstrated that domain-specific conceptual modelling with neural word embedding is effective in uncovering texts that capture given concepts. Texts retrieved using the *Curatr* text mining workflow were particularly useful in the context of exploratory humanities research. The system uncovered works that had not previously attracted sustained scholarly attention, and which presented opportunities to uncover new insights in relation to the given research topic. In future work the addition of new sources to the platform would further enrich this process. Through the exploratory text mining workflow supported by *Curatr*, humanities scholars are enabled to challenge prevailing methods of canonisation of historical fiction.

Acknowledgements. This research was partially supported by Science Foundation Ireland (SFI) under Grant Number SFI/12/RC/2289.

References

1. Bailey, E., et al.: CULTURA: supporting enhanced exploration of cultural archives through personalisation. In: the Proceedings of the 2nd International Conference on Humanities, Society and Culture, ICHSC. ICHSC (2012)
2. Barry, C.L.: User-defined relevance criteria: an exploratory study. J. Am. Soc. Inf. Sci. **45**(3), 149–159 (1994)
3. Bates, M.J.: The Getty end-user online searching project in the humanities: report no. 6: overview and conclusions. Coll. Res. Libr. **57**(6), 514–523 (1996)
4. Camacho-Collados, J., Pilehvar, M.T.: On the role of text preprocessing in neural network architectures: an evaluation study on text categorization and sentiment analysis. arXiv preprint arXiv:1707.01780 (2017)
5. Chanen, A.: Deep learning for extracting word-level meaning from safety report narratives. In: Integrated Communications Navigation and Surveillance (ICNS), p. 5D2-1. IEEE (2016)
6. Chiticariu, L., Li, Y., Reiss, F.R.: Rule-based information extraction is dead! Long live rule-based information extraction systems! In: Proceedings of the 2013 Conference on Empirical Methods in Natural Language Processing, pp. 827–832 (2013)

7. Clarke, C.L., et al.: Novelty and diversity in information retrieval evaluation. In: Proceedings of the 31st Annual International ACM SIGIR Conference on Research and Development in Information Retrieval, pp. 659–666. ACM (2008)

8. Cohn, S.K.: Pandemics: waves of disease, waves of hate from the plague of athens to aids. Hist. Res. **85**(230), 535–555 (2012)

9. Dempster, J.A.: Thomas Nelson and Sons in the late nineteenth century: a study in motivation. Part 1. Publ. Hist. **13**, 41 (1983)

10. Fast, E., Chen, B., Bernstein, M.S.: Empath: understanding topic signals in large-scale text. In: Proceedings of the 2016 CHI Conference on Human Factors in Computing Systems, pp. 4647–4657. ACM (2016)

11. Firth, J.R.: A synopsis of linguistic theory, 1930–1955. In: Studies in Linguistic Analysis (1957)

12. Flanders, J., Jannidis, F.: The Shape of Data in Digital Humanities: Modeling Texts and Text-based Resources. Routledge, Abingdon (2018)

13. Frank, A., Bögel, T., Hellwig, O., Reiter, N.: Semantic annotation for the digital humanities. Linguist. Issues Lang. Technol. **7**(1), 1–21 (2012)

14. Hamilton, W.L., Clark, K., Leskovec, J., Jurafsky, D.: Inducing domain-specific sentiment lexicons from unlabeled corpora. In: Proceedings of the EMNLP 2016, vol. 2016, p. 595. NIH Public Access (2016)

15. Hampson, C., Munnelly, G., Bailey, E., Lawless, S., Conlan, O.: Improving user control and transparency in the digital humanities. In: 2013 International Conference on Culture and Computing (Culture Computing), pp. 196–197. IEEE (2013)

16. Hinrichs, U., et al.: Trading consequences: a case study of combining text mining and visualization to facilitate document exploration. Digit. Sch. Humanit. **30**(suppl_1), i50–i75 (2015)

17. Jackson, H.J.: Marginalia: Readers Writing in Books. Yale University Press, New Haven (2002)

18. Jockers, M.: Detecting and characterizing national style in the 19th century novel. In: Digital Humanities, Stanford, CA (2011)

19. Kinealy, C.: This Great Calamity: The Great Irish Famine: The Irish Famine 1845–52. Gill & Macmillan Ltd., Dublin (2006)

20. Kopaczyk, J.: The Legal Language of Scottish Burghs: Standardization and Lexical Bundles (1380–1560). Oxford University Press, Oxford (2013)

21. Leavy, S., Pine, E., Keane, M.T.: Industrial memories: exploring the findings of government inquiries with neural word embedding and machine learning. In: Brefeld, U., et al. (eds.) ECML PKDD 2018. LNCS, vol. 11053, pp. 687–690. Springer, Cham (2019). https://doi.org/10.1007/978-3-030-10997-4_52

22. Mikolov, T., Chen, K., Corrado, G., Dean, J.: Efficient estimation of word representations in vector space. arXiv preprint arXiv:1301.3781 (2013)

23. Morash, C.: The Hungry Voice: The Poetry of the Irish Famine. Irish Academic Press, Newbridge (2009)

24. Mulvey-Roberts, M.: The Handbook of the Gothic. Springer, Heidelberg (2016)

25. Murray, J.: The social enterprise law market. Md. L. Rev. **75**, 541 (2015)

26. Nelkin, D., Gilman, S.L.: Placing blame for devastating disease. Soc. Res. **55**, 361–378 (1988)

27. Park, D., Kim, S., Lee, J., Choo, J., Diakopoulos, N., Elmqvist, N.: ConceptVector: text visual analytics via interactive lexicon building using word embedding. IEEE Trans. Visual Comput. Graph. **24**(1), 361–370 (2018)

28. Rochelson, M.J.: "They that walk in darkness": Ghetto tragedies: the uses of Christianity in Israel Zangwill's fiction. Victorian Lit. Cult. **27**(1), 219–233 (1999)

29. Rochelson, M.J.: A Jew in the Public Arena: The Career of Israel Zangwill. Wayne State University Press, Detroit (2010)

30. Subramanian, A., Pruthi, D., Jhamtani, H., Berg-Kirkpatrick, T., Hovy, E.: SPINE: sparse interpretable neural embeddings. In: Thirty-Second AAAI Conference on Artificial Intelligence (2018)

31. Tang, D., Wei, F., Yang, N., Zhou, M., Liu, T., Qin, B.: Learning sentiment-specific word embedding for twitter sentiment classification. In: Proceedings of the 52nd Annual Meeting of the Association for Computational Linguistics (Volume 1: Long Papers), vol. 1, pp. 1555–1565 (2014)

32. Udelson, J.H.: Dreamer of the Ghetto: The Life and Works of Israel Zangwill. University of Alabama Press, Tuscaloosa (1990)

33. Van Cranenburgh, A., van Dalen-Oskam, K., van Zundert, J.: Vector space explorations of literary language. Lang. Resour. Eval. (2019)

34. Vane, O.: Text visualisation tool for exploring digitised historical documents. In: Proceedings of the 19th International ACM SIGACCESS Conference on Computers and Accessibility, pp. 153–158. ACM (2018)

35. Wohlgenannt, G., Chernyak, E., Ilvovsky, D.: Extracting social networks from literary text with word embedding tools. In: Proceedings of the Workshop on Language Technology Resources and Tools for Digital Humanities, pp. 18–25 (2016)

36. Wolfe, J.: Annotations and the collaborative digital library: effects of an aligned annotation interface on student argumentation and reading strategies. Int. J. Comput.-Support. Collab. Learn. 3(2), 141 (2008)

Extraction of Character Profiles from the Gutenberg Archive

Mattia Egloff[1]⬥, Davide Picca[1]⬥, and Alessandro Adamou[2](✉)⬥

[1] University of Lausanne, Lausanne, Switzerland
{mattia.egloff,davide.picca}@unil.ch
[2] Data Science Institute, NUI Galway, Galway, Ireland
alessandro.adamou@insight-centre.org

Abstract. Online text repositories such as Gutenberg.org have been increasing in number, size and adoption. This growing availability prompts new investigations for insights into the knowledge emerging from the content of e.g. literature and drama. However, the process relies upon the repositories' ability to fulfill FAIR principles. We present the preparatory work on the semantic analysis of drama literature in Gutenberg, aiming at the extraction and profiling of fictional characters and their narrative roles. Our preliminary analysis matches such characters and their corresponding profiles in knowledge bases such as DBpedia and Wikidata.

Keywords: Data reconciliation · Profiling · Fictional literature

1 Introduction

Recently, text corpus repositories have been gaining particular attention in Digital Humanities. Textual corpora are becoming increasingly available on the Web through services such as LiberLiber.it, Europeana and Gutenberg.org. However, many databases mentioned above are not always built in line with the guidelines suggested by the FAIR (Findable, Accessible, Interoperable, and Reusable) principles. This misalignment makes access and the exploitation of these resources difficult and laborious.

Taking into account the FAIR indications, in this paper we present an ongoing work aiming at enriching texts from the Gutenberg.org repository, in accordance with the four principles mentioned before. Specifically, this work is a preliminary analysis of the metadata available in linking open data resources such as DBpedia and Wikidata with respect to description of fictional characters in literary.

By relying on semantic techniques (especially SPARQL queries and constructs) to link Digital Libraries and semantic archives, in this project we analyse the options for matching:

1. authors and books of Project Gutenberg (from now on PG) to DBpedia;
2. the characters present in the books (extracted using Natural Language Processing (NLP) techniques from the PG texts) to DBpedia and Wikidata.

E. Garoufallou et al. (Eds.): MTSR 2019, CCIS 1057, pp. 367–372, 2019.
https://doi.org/10.1007/978-3-030-36599-8_32

This investigation is the first step of a larger ongoing project aiming at identifying the psychological profiles of fictional characters in order to enrich the Gutenberg digital repository with metadata according to the FAIR principles. Also, in general, it enables the creation of ad-hoc datasets for NLP research using the information present in knowledge bases.

2   Related Work

Personality identification is a large field that has been only partly explored [3]. While personality identification from texts has been gaining popularity [1, 8], it mostly concentrates on profiling blog authors [7,9]. With the increasing uptake of digital humanities, the focus on personality studies from text has expanded to include the understanding of characters in literature. Recent work in this respect has gone in the direction of analysing literature and film scripts. Some such works attempt to explore character definitions by looking at the relationships between them. For example, [12] addresses the problem of inferring the polarity of relationships between people in narrative summaries. On the same line we also find authors such as [4], who focused on inferring character roles and on the problem of modeling their relationships. Others like Flekova et al. [6] focused on the automatic detection of character personalities using a range of semantic features, including WordNet and VerbNet sense-level information and word vector representations to predict the personality of protagonists in novels based on the Five-Factor Model. Bamman et al. [2] present latent variable models for unsupervised learning of latent character types in English novels. Smith et al. [11] have instead extended their work in order to explicitly learn character types in a dataset of Wikipedia film plot summaries.

3   Setting and Data Sources

Characters in fictional literature may be identified either through their appearance in corresponding works, or through creator-creation relationships with literary authors (e.g. Sherlock Holmes being *created by* Sir Arthur Conan Doyle). We therefore identified authors and authored books in Gutenberg, DBpedia and Wikidata, resulting in the figures presented in Table 1. These take into account the misalignment between Gutenberg.org, which considers different editions individually and does not group editions of the same work, and DBpedia and Wikidata, which on the contrary do not contemplate editions in general.

Table 1. Vital statistics of literary works and authors.

	Gutenberg	DBpedia	Wikidata
#Authors	20,457	221,855	106,979
#Literary works	59,634	245,547	139,472

We singled out a Gutenberg sub-corpus of 2,006 plays and 10,615 works of fiction from existing corpora metadata - or "bookshelves" in Gutenberg jargon.

3.1 Corpus-Dataset Linkage

Our research is driven by a set of initial observations upon the landscape of literary data from these sources (not yet taking national libraries into account):

1. recent improvements in cross-linking between DBpedia and Wikidata;
2. the uptake of third-party linking of those datasets with VIAF authority files[1] and Library of Congress IDs[2];
3. guidelines for reconciling Gutenberg catalogues with Library of Congress;[3]
4. the emergence of software projects for managing data alignments with VIAF.[4]

4 Analytical Approach

This preliminary work addresses: (a) the issue of providing an avenue for improving the exploitability of the Gutenberg archive; and (b) the use case of extracting character profiles from literary fiction and drama, starting with establishing links to already existing character profiles.

Issue (a) is primarily addressed through a suite of Python libraries for the management of Humanities data called Digital Humanities ToolKit (DHTK) [10]. One of the features of the DHTK module for text is to provide an interface with textual repositories so that their metadata can be accessed using the SPARQL query language. This is applied to Gutenberg text corpus metadata and a SPARQL service is published for internal consumption.

Addressing the use case as per issue (b) follows the workflow in Fig. 1:

1. Obtain a selection of corpora through available literary categories and genres (represented in Gutenberg as "bookshelves" and subjects). Selection criteria are currently focused on drama and fictional literature.
2. Prepare texts for NLP tagging: this process involves extracting character names from plays by exploiting the structure of their dialogues and scripts.
3. Processing prepared texts with POS tagging to identify parts of speech that may represent characters in the narrative. This is currently being carried out using the standard NLP pipelines of Spacy and Stanford NLP.
4. Analysis of links that bind literary works and authors together.
5. Matching characters detected in Gutenberg with DBpedia/Wikidata used as knowledge bases, as detailed in Sect. 4.1.
6. Extraction of salient properties that describe characters in those datasets.

---

[1] VIAF linking properties: `dbo:viafId` (DBpedia) and `wpprop:P214` (Wikidata).

[2] LoC linking properties: `dbo:lccnId` (DBpedia) and `wpprop:P244` (Wikidata).

[3] https://www.gutenberg.org/wiki/Cataloging_Guidelines#Check_the_author.28s.29, http://id.loc.gov/authorities/names/n79022935.html.

[4] See e.g. VIAPy - https://pypi.org/project/viapy/.

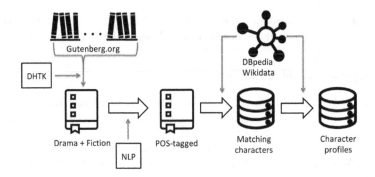

Fig. 1. Character extraction workflow.

4.1 Written Work Matching Heuristics

One of the hurdles to the construction of character profiles lies in the identification of written works in Gutenberg that match those appearing in datasets that feature character traits. While one could, in principle, rely upon national library datasets and follow the trail of authority records, properties that represent the narrative setting are mostly found in general-purpose, non specifically biographical data sources, as are Wikidata and DBpedia. Besides the "public interest bias" that affects the literary works represented in these datasets, matching also proves to be a challenge. Our current approach is detailed below:

1. Retrieve Gutenberg-DBpedia matches using DHTK, which employs cascaded heuristics based firstly on the URL of the book's Wikipedia page as found in Gutenberg, then failing that, on author and title matching.
2. Follow any `owl:sameAs` links in DBpedia that land on Wikidata entities, and extract from them the labels of the works and authors.
3. String-match said authors' labels with author names and Gutenberg aliases.
   (a) If a match is found, perform the same for the work title against the works of the authors in DBpedia or Wikidata.
   (b) Otherwise, fall back to only matching the title, ignoring authors.
4. As a last resort, use the characters found earlier by mining the texts in order to match them with characters stated to occur in DBpedia or Wikidata.

5 Preliminary Results and Discussion

Through matching names, aliases, labels and cross-links of authors and literary works, and with the support of basic biographical or publication data, we have produced a linkset available online[5]. We surmise from this linkset that our Gutenberg sub-corpus covers 7,344 of the authors and 2,553 of the books present in DBpedia, about 35% and 5% of the respective totals (which, recall,

---

[5] Gutenberg linkset in Turtle format, https://dhtk.unil.ch/static/sameas.ttl.

include non-fiction authors). The disparity between names/labels in DBpedia and Gutenberg has proven to be the most limiting factor in this preliminary work. We also observe that the vast majority of character names were identified using the Spacy NLP pipeline than the Stanford one.

5.1 Issues

Our initial analysis also allowed us to identify, from the linked datasets in use, the main obstacles to interoperability (the I in FAIR) which, if dealt with, would facilitate our case study in character profiling. We list the core ones below:

1. Inconsistent usage of the type `dbo:FictionalCharacter` in DBpedia: it is used to type both actual characters and *lists* of characters.
2. Several DBpedia entities have been found to be of types `dbo:Book` and `dbo:FictionalCharacter` at the same time.
3. Lack of features distinguishing characters in literature from those in film, TV, comics or fictionalised versions of real people.
4. High variability in the predicates that identify characters.

Surprisingly, and owing to our intuition from Sect. 3, there is stronger linking of characters to their authors, than to the works in which they appear.

6 Conclusion and Future Work

We have performed a preliminary analysis relying on semantic techniques and linked datasets for extracting existing character profiles. This required an enrichment of the Gutenberg digital archive in the direction of FAIR principles.

Correctly linking Gutenberg's eBooks to their metadata will also enable machine learning from the text to different variables:

1. books: subjects (even though some are mentioned in Gutenberg metadata), descriptions, plot summaries etc.
2. book content: characters, their roles etc.
3. authors: the network of author influences, geographical origins etc.

We envision a number of dimensions for research in NLP and machine learning to contribute to our case study, in particular:

1. detection of character roles, in a work or across works, by mining character networks;
2. creation of ad-hoc datasets related to specific literary domains or knowledge graphs of fictional narrative;
3. resolution of logical inconsistencies in knowledge bases, such as using the same RDFS/OWL classes for typing entities as well as lists thereof.

Our main direction for future work will be the move towards the psychological profiling of characters, to be modelled in accordance with an existing ontology based on the LEMON linguistic model [5].

References

1. Argamon, S., Dhawle, S., Koppel, M., Pennebaker, J.W.: Lexical predictors of personality type. In: Proceedings of Interface and the Classification Society of North America (2005)
2. Bamman, D., Underwood, T., Smith, N.A.: A Bayesian mixed effects model of literary character. In: Proceedings of the 52nd Annual Meeting of the Association for Computational Linguistics, vol. 1, Long Papers, pp. 370–379 (2014)
3. Celli, F., Lepri, B., Biel, J.I., Gatica-Perez, D., Riccardi, G., Pianesi, F.: The workshop on computational personality recognition 2014. In: Proceedings of the 22nd ACM International Conference on Multimedia, pp. 1245–1246. ACM (2014)
4. Chaturvedi, S., Srivastava, S., Daume III, H., Dyer, C.: Modeling evolving relationships between characters in literary novels. In: Proceedings of the 30th AAAI Conference on Artificial Intelligence (2016)
5. Egloff, M., Lieto, A., Picca, D.: An ontological model for inferring psychological profiles and narrative roles of characters. In: Palau, J.G., Russell, I.G. (eds.) Digital Humanities 2018, DH 2018, Book of Abstracts, El Colegio de México, UNAM, and RedHD, Mexico City, Mexico, June 26–29, 2018, pp. 649–650. Red de Humanidades Digitales A. C. (2018). https://dh2018.adho.org/en/an-ontological-model-for-inferring-psychological-profiles-and-narrative-roles-of-characters/
6. Flekova, L., Gurevych, I.: Personality profiling of fictional characters using sense-level links between lexical resources. In: Màrquez, L., Callison-Burch, C., Su, J., Pighin, D., Marton, Y. (eds.) Proceedings of the 2015 Conference on Empirical Methods in Natural Language Processing, EMNLP 2015, Lisbon, Portugal, September 17–21, 2015, pp. 1805–1816. The Association for Computational Linguistics (2015). http://aclweb.org/anthology/D/D15/D15-1208.pdf
7. Gill, A.J., Nowson, S., Oberlander, J.: What are they blogging about? Personality, topic and motivation in blogs. In: Proceedings of the Third International Conference on Weblogs and Social Media, ICWSM 2009, San Jose, California, USA, May 17–20, 2009 (2009). http://aaai.org/ocs/index.php/ICWSM/09/paper/view/199
8. Mairesse, F., Walker, M.A., Mehl, M.R., Moore, R.K.: Using linguistic cues for the automatic recognition of personality in conversation and text. J. Artif. Intell. Res. **30**, 457–500 (2007). https://doi.org/10.1613/jair.2349
9. Nowson, S., Oberlander, J.: Identifying more bloggers: towards large scale personality classification of personal weblogs. In: Glance, N.S., Nicolov, N., Adar, E., Hurst, M., Liberman, M., Salvetti, F. (eds.) Proceedings of the First International Conference on Weblogs and Social Media, ICWSM 2007, Boulder, Colorado, USA, March 26–28, 2007 (2007). http://www.icwsm.org/papers/paper4.html
10. Picca, D., Egloff, M.: DHTK: the digital humanities toolkit. In: Adamou, A., Daga, E., Isaksen, L. (eds.) Proceedings of the Second Workshop on Humanities in the Semantic Web (WHiSe II) Co-Located with 16th International Semantic Web Conference (ISWC 2017), Vienna, Austria, October 22, 2017. CEUR Workshop Proceedings, vol. 2014, pp. 81–86. CEUR-WS.org (2017). http://ceur-ws.org/Vol-2014/paper-09.pdf
11. Smith, N.A., Bamman, D., OConnor, B.: Learning latent personas of film characters. In: Proceedings of the 51st Annual Meeting of the Association for Computational Linguistics (2013)
12. Srivastava, S., Chaturvedi, S., Mitchell, T.: Inferring interpersonal relations in narrative summaries. In: Proceedings of the 30th AAAI Conference on Artificial Intelligence (2016)

Fine-GRAINed Process Metadata

Kerstin Jung$^{(\boxtimes)}$ ⓘ, Markus Gärtner ⓘ, and Jonas Kuhn ⓘ

Institute for Natural Language Processing, University of Stuttgart,
Stuttgart, Germany
{kerstin.jung,markus.gaertner,jonas.kuhn}@ims.uni-stuttgart.de

Abstract. We describe the process metadata of GRAIN, a complex language data corpus, as a show case for application of metadata in the Digital Humanities. While the creation of language resources usually involves some automatic processing ranging from format conversion to labeling of structural features, data selection, inspection and interpretation are important manual steps, which tend to be neglected in the description of scientific workflows. GRAIN makes use of a format which (i) maps all workflow steps to flexible triples of $\{input, operator, output\}$ and (ii) treats manual and automatic steps equally. Moreover, the process metadata has been semi-automatically generated and allows for a straightforward visualization describing the creation of the resource.

Keywords: Process metadata · Natural language processing · Linguistic annotation

1 Introduction

Text and speech corpora are collections of language data which are applied in studies from various disciplines in the field of linguistics and the social sciences among others. Not only since the rise of the Digital Humanities have devices from (automatic) natural language processing found their way into creation of corpora, i.e. collecting and selecting primary data and enhancing it with discipline-specific labels (noun, verb, president of X, etc.) and structural markers (subject of, student of, etc.). However, in the creation process, automatic workflow steps stand on a par with manual steps e.g. for extraction, interpretation and correction. Both, manual and automatic steps implement significant decisions with respect to comparability of the resulting corpus resource and studies conducted on it.[1]

While existing metadata schemes for the description of the resulting resource, e.g. Dublin Core[2] or CMDI[3], reflect only few or very specific workflow aspects, traditional workflow tools such as Kepler[4] and Galaxy[5] tend to focus on fully

---

[1] Cf. [2] for the impact of a minor decision in the data creation process on several downstream tasks.
[2] http://dublincore.org/.
[3] https://www.clarin.eu/content/component-metadata.
[4] https://kepler-project.org/.
[5] https://galaxyproject.org/.

© Springer Nature Switzerland AG 2019
E. Garoufallou et al. (Eds.): MTSR 2019, CCIS 1057, pp. 373–378, 2019.
https://doi.org/10.1007/978-3-030-36599-8_33

automatic processes and neglect the impact of possible manual steps. Thus, approaches such as RePlay-DH [3] and the TEI LAUDATIO customization[6] reflect manual and automatic workflow steps for the resource description.

The case study we want to discuss here is GRAIN, a structurally and linguistically annotated language data corpus which takes an innovative approach between size and quality of the annotations. While the corpus and its annotation layers have been released in 2018, one crucial aspect has been discussed only marginally in respective publications [1,4,7]: GRAIN comes with a large set of process metadata, which has been semi-automatically generated. This contribution thus restricts the description of the corpus and the theoretical implications of the applied process metadata scheme to the amount necessary for understanding and focuses on creation and content of the process metadata for GRAIN.

2   The GRAIN Corpus of Linguistic Annotations on Radio Interviews

GRAIN [7] is a language data corpus and part of the SFB732 Silver Standard Collection. The primary data of GRAIN consists of German radio interviews (speech) and their transcripts edited by the broadcasting station (text).

Traditionally, linguistic annotations are often created in a bootstrapping approach [5, 103f.]: An annotation scheme is set up, which defines possible structures and category labels, as well as guidelines describing the cases for which a structure or label is applicable. An example would be a set of part-of-speech tags (regular noun, proper name, adjective, verb, etc.) which are to be applied on text parts of the size of a word[7]. Guidelines will then comprise for example the distinction between regular noun and proper name in this annotation (How to treat generic trademarks like *thermos* or *band-aid*?). The annotation scheme and guidelines are applied on some data by several annotators and the result is evaluated with respect to inter-annotator-agreement and confusion of labels. Based on this evaluation, annotation scheme and guidelines are refined and the process repeats. Once the annotation scheme and guidelines become stable the whole dataset can be annotated. Existing annotation schemes can be applied or adapted to the data at hand. In cases where manually annotated data of high quality (gold-standard) is already available, automatic tools can be trained on the data to learn the annotation scheme and annotate unseen data.

Since a gold-standard annotation by (i) several annotators, evaluation of differences, discussion and resolution of diverging annotations, or (ii) manual correction of automatic processed data, is only feasible for a certain size of the dataset, GRAIN, as a large dataset with respect to primary data and number of annotation layers[8], takes two approaches to annotation quality. 20 interviews have been chosen to be enhanced with some additional gold-standard annotation

---

[6] https://github.com/korpling/LAUDATIO-Metadata/.

[7] The definition of 'word' is highly discussed among linguists, this contribution thus opts for a colloquial understanding of the term.

[8] About 140 interviews of 9–10 minutes each with up to 24 annotation layers.

```
                                    {"result": ["20140927.tokenized.pos.xml",
                                                "20140927.tokenized.pos-times.xml"],
{"result": [],                       "input": ["20140927.tokenized.pos.xml"],
 "input": [],                        "workflowSteps":[
 "workflowSteps":[                     {"description": "syntax annotation",
   {"description": "",                  "mode": "manual",
    "mode": "",                         "operators":[
    "operators":[                          {"name": "D802",
      {"name": "",                          "version": "",
       "version": "",                       "parameters": "",
       "parameters": "",                    "components":[
       "components":[                          {"name": "QuAn",
         {"name": ",                            "version": "2017",
          "version": "",                        "type": "tool"},
          "type": ""                          {"name": "Annotation Guidelines",
         }]                                     "version": "21.03.2016",
      }]                                        "type": "guidelines"},
   }]                                         {"name": "Tiger Guidelines",
 }                                             "version": "24.06.2003",
                                               "type": "guidelines"}]}]}]}
         (a)                                          (b)
```

Fig. 1. (a) Empty JSON form of the process metadata scheme. (b) Manual workflow step of an annotator creating a syntactic annotation.

layers (e.g. part-of-speech tags and referential information status [6]) and for some annotation layers, the interviews have been processed by different tools for the same layers, e.g. syntax of three constituency parsers and of four dependency parsers providing confidence estimations based on their agreement. The size and variety of its annotations suggests GRAIN as a show case for the application of process metadata as a crucial device.

3   Process Metadata for GRAIN

GRAIN applies the process metadata scheme presented in [4]. An empty JSON[9] form containing all possible features is shown in Fig. 1(a). *result* denotes the files created by the described *workflowSteps*, based on the files listed in *input*. Details of the workflow step are given by *mode* (automatic, manual, semi-automatic), *description* and respective *operators*. Operators are identified by *name* and *version* where applicable, and may need a description of *parameters* or additional *components*, e.g. to make automatic operators language-specific. Components in turn are identified by *name* and *version*, and their *type* can be stated (e.g. model, lexicon, guidelines). In JSON, the squared brackets denote lists, making multiple contents possible there, e.g. several input files, workflow steps, components, etc.

The scheme is based on the assumption that each workflow step can be mapped onto a triple {*input, operator, output*} with two important rules: The first one is that the user keeps the sovereignty over the (granularity of all) workflow steps: each application of a tool can be an entry on its own, or some tools can be combined into one entry, e.g. by wrapping around a classic pipeline approach,

---
[9] http://www.json.org/.

or by parallel processing of several tools. In the same vein, it is the decision of the user, if an additional knowledge base, e.g. a lexicon file applied with a tool is mapped to a component of the operator or to the input.

```
{"result": ["20171014.1.0.0.0.dparse-it-conll09"],
 "input": ["20171014.3.61.0.0.mtag-mt-conll09"],
 "workflowSteps":[
   {"description":"IMSTrans parser",
    "mode": "automatic",
    "operators":[
      {"name": "../operators/imstrans-dparser-1.0.0.sh",
       "version": "1.0.0 (IMSTrans parser)",
       "parameters": "-format CoNLL09 -model IMSTrans/v1_2015/TIGER_2.2.model",
       "components":[
         {"name": "IMSTrans/v1_2015/TIGER_2.2.model",
          "description": "Trained on 80% of TIGER dependency treebank, version 2.2",
          "version": "3.61 (Mate-tools)",
          "type": "model"}]}]}]}
```

Fig. 2. Automatic workflow step of IMSTrans parser creating a syntactic analysis.

As a second rule manual workflow steps are equal in priority and mapping to automatic ones. This is a crucial aspect dedicated to work in the Digital Humanities since data exploration, interpretation and extraction steps are the groundwork for most language-driven studies. Thus the operator describes a tool (e.g. IMSTrans parser), its version (e.g. 1.0.0), command line parameters (e.g. -format CoNLL09) and internal components (e.g. a trained model) as in Fig. 2 as well as an annotator (e.g. anonymized such as D802), in a specific knowledge state (e.g. a date/after tutorial Y), with parameters (e.g. annotation with headphones), and components (e.g. applying guidelines in a specific version), see Fig. 1(b) for an example. Each workflow step is labeled by a mode, indicating if it refers to manual, automatic or semi-automatic work. Figure 1(b) describes a manual annotation step, creating a syntactic annotation based on two sets of annotation guidelines.[10] Note, that the annotator uses a tool to (manually) enter the annotations, however the mode of the step is still manual. Again, also the sovereignty over which features apply or can be omitted is with the user.

In GRAIN, the process metadata entries have been created in two ways. For the manual annotations entries have been made by the annotators as soon as they committed a workflow step to the version control system.[11] A commented empty JSON-like form was the template for each commit message. The automatic steps have been conducted by means of a pipeline, including consistency checks, where every step automatically generated a respective JSON form, which was stored together with the result file, see Fig. 2 as described above.

---

[10] The manual syntactic annotation is not in the GRAIN release, but work in progress.
[11] In the creation of GRAIN, git (https://git-scm.com/) was applied.

4   Visualization

The large number of workflow steps[12] in GRAIN (Fig. 3) and the fact that the annotation process is not just a linear pipeline, calls for a visualization approach to be able to inspect the tracked process metadata, get an overview of workflows for different interviews and see on which files the process heavily depends.

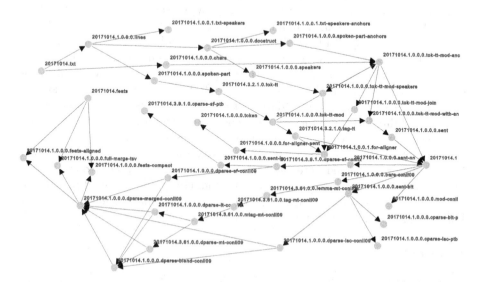

Fig. 3. Excerpt of full workflow for one specific interview. Filenames are modified for readability and some nodes have been manually moved away from gravity centers to provide a figure respecting the paper margins.

Based on the {*input*, *operator*, *output*}-triple the visualization makes use of two centers of gravity[13], one for the files being only used as input (gravity center to the left) and one for the files being only used as output (gravity center to the right). That way, the typical mid-center graph, by default applied by graph databases such as Neo4j[14], is transformed into a visualization showing creation and dependencies of the annotation steps.

Figure 3 shows an excerpt of the full workflow for one specific interview. Each node constitutes an input and/or output file, each edge reflects a workflow entry. By an on-mouse-over event of the edge, i.e. when the cursor is moved on the edge, the entry in the JSON form is shown. The whole (unconnected) graph multiplies this for 140 interviews and is only relevant in interactive inspection.

---

[12] About 6350 JSON structures with process metadata for the automatic part.
[13] https://bl.ocks.org/mbostock/1021841, https://d3js.org.
[14] https://neo4j.com/.

5   Conclusion and Outlook

We described the process metadata of GRAIN as a showcase for extensive documentation of workflow processes in the creation of large and complex language data corpora. Its main features are the equal treatment of both manual and automatic processing steps – a crucial device for application in the Digital Humanities – and the simple visualization purposes based on the mapping of each workflow step to the triple of {input, operator, output}. While the scheme has been set up with different applications in mind, it has so far only been tested with GRAIN. However, the RePlay-DH Client[15] makes use of a similar scheme. Further application of both schemes will give more insights into which features might have to be refined or are still missing. While the suggestion of a common vocabulary for specific process metadata features would have to be discussed, enhancing several corpora with such process metadata will also allow to visually compare workflows and highlight typical annotation steps or applied tools, providing guidance and insight for resource creators and prospective users alike.

As is often the case, the pipeline for automatic workflow steps in GRAIN is a manually assembled heterogeneous collection of scripts and tools. Due to its formation process and usage resembling common practices found in software engineering, transforming it and building on readily available solutions (such as build engines, e.g. Gradle[16]) could also proof beneficial.

References

1. Eckart, K., Gärtner, M., Kuhn, J., Schweitzer, K.: Nützlich und nutzbar für die linguistische Forschung: Sprachtechnologische Infrastruktur. In: Lobin, H., Schneider, R., Witt, A. (eds.) Digitale Infrastrukturen für die germanistische Forschung, chap. 6, pp. 115–148. de Gruyter, Berlin/Boston (2018). https://doi.org/10.1515/9783110538663-007
2. Elming, J., Johannsen, A., Klerke, S., Lapponi, E., Martinez Alonso, H., Søgaard, A.: Down-stream effects of tree-to-dependency conversions. In: Proceedings of NAACL-HLT 2013, pp. 617–626. Association for Computational Linguistics, Atlanta, Georgia (2013)
3. Gärtner, M., Hahn, U., Hermann, S.: Supporting sustainable process documentation. In: Rehm, G., Declerck, T. (eds.) GSCL 2017. LNCS (LNAI), vol. 10713, pp. 284–291. Springer, Cham (2018). https://doi.org/10.1007/978-3-319-73706-5_24
4. Jung, K., Gärtner, M.: Approaches to sustainable process metadata. In: Simov, K., Eskevich, M. (eds.) Proceedings of CLARIN Annual Conference 2019, Leipzig, Germany (2019)
5. Lemnitzer, L., Zinsmeister, H.: Korpuslinguistik. Narr Francke Attempo, Tübingen (2015)
6. Riester, A., Baumann, S.: The RefLex Scheme - Annotation Guidelines, SinSpeC. Working Papers of the SFB 732, vol. 14, University of Stuttgart (2017). http://dx.doi.org/10.18419/opus-9011
7. Schweitzer, K., et al.: German radio interviews: the grain release of the SFB732 silver standard collection. In: Calzolari, N., et al. (eds.) Proceedings of LREC 2018. Miyazaki, Japan (2018). ISBN 979-10-95546-00-9

---

[15] https://github.com/RePlay-DH/replay-dh-client.
[16] https://gradle.org/.

Formal Ontology in a Relativistic Setting

Guido Vetere$^{(\boxtimes)}$

Università Guglielmo Marconi, Rome, Italy
g.vetere@unimarconi.it

Abstract. Ontologies are supposed to address the problem of making information systems' conceptual models shareable and understandable. Most often, however, ontologies are nothing but structured lexical resources, which bring with them the classic problem behind natural language meanings: how to make sure that names and predicates are consistently interpreted all through the information sphere? Here is where formal ontology comes to play. In fact, the 'ontological level' [1,3] is where, thanks to formal constraints (meaning axioms), unintended models (spurious interpretations) should be cut off. Yet, interpreting well-founded, highly formalized ontologies is far from trivial, and does not come for free. What makes ontology so difficult in practice? How to make concepts understandable and alleviate the burden of mapping strict ontological specifications with business data? This short paper will provide a brief overview on common issues when working with formal ontology and how to address them in practice, and will give some hint on effective usages of highly formalized shared conceptual models for business information systems.

Keywords: Formal ontology · Meaning theories · Vagueness · Relativity · Conceptual modelling

1 Introduction

After more than twenty-five years of research on formal ontology in information systems[1], most of today's business ontologies still look like old time "thesauri", i.e. lexical resources with some, quite informal, semantics-oriented structuring. Yet, as envisioned in [1], highly formalized *ontological commitments* could significantly improve business conceptualizations, especially when they are designed as models for information integration and data exchange. In fact, ontological commitments are kind of *meaning stipulations* which should reduce *unintended models* (i.e. spurious interpretations) when different users happen to interpret imported conceptual models in their specific contexts.

Broadly speaking, formal ontology, introduced by Edmund Husserl and developed through the tradition of Twentieth Century's metaphysics [4], can be seen as a meta-level characterization of descriptive first-order languages. For instance,

---

[1] https://iaoa.org/fois/.

© Springer Nature Switzerland AG 2019
E. Garoufallou et al. (Eds.): MTSR 2019, CCIS 1057, pp. 379–384, 2019.
https://doi.org/10.1007/978-3-030-36599-8_34

one could mark a concept (say, Person) as `RIGID` (a prominent ontological meta-property) to characterize the fact that:

$$\forall x.(Person(x) \rightarrow \text{NEC}(Person(x))) \tag{1}$$

That is: a `RIGID` concept is one that inheres to individuals for their entire life and in every context (possible world), whereas a `NON-RIGID` concept such as *Student* does not. The benefit of taking this kind of constraints into account is twofold: on the one hand, meta-level properties lead to better conceptualizations [5]; on the other hand, the interpretation of formally characterized concepts is more strongly constrained, and therefore less prone to misunderstandings. The stage at which systems designers are expected to tackle the problem of keeping interpretations under control is in fact commonly called *ontological level*. Despite progresses in theoretic research, one can say that, by the industry, this level is still approached with little awareness [6]. As a matter of facts, the standard ontology specification language (W3C's Ontology Web Language) does not feature any specific ontological pattern (e.g. *parthood, dependence, rigidity*), but only Description Logics constructs. While this gives users and communities the freedom of choosing the amount of formality they want to buy, the weakness of ontology languages has probably contributed to a general *ontological decommitment* even among those who make intensive use of automated reasoning based on logic formalisms. Also, cross-domain, well-founded general ontologies (*upper ontologies*), which may drive a principled development of conceptual models worldwide, struggle reach a large adoption. Proposals like DOLCE, SUMO[2], UFO[3] or BFO[4] seem to be still confined to specialist niches.

2   The Problem of Interpretation

To the extent that informative transactions can be regarded to as *linguistic acts*[5], information systems are similar to linguistic ones. For instance, a database update resembles an *assertion*, while a query is fundamentally a *question*. It is commonplace that, in order to be successful, receivers must interpret linguistic utterances by deciphering the meanings intended by producers. This encoding-decoding process relies on the availability of a body of shared semantic rules (indeed, the *code*). However, according to philosophers like Quine, the way this kind of processes take place by humans, and the results they actually produce, are basically inscrutable [8]. Although informative transactions usually rely on meaning stipulations governed by accountable organizations, the problem of inscrutability affects information systems as well. In fact, a shared recognition of *intended models* resulting from the application of semantic rules (interpretation), requires conditions which often appear to be very difficult to meet.

---

[2] http://www.adampease.org/OP/.

[3] https://ontology.com.br/.

[4] http://basic-formal-ontology.org.

[5] https://plato.stanford.edu/entries/speech-acts/.

Generally speaking, information systems could be *centralized* (i.e. a single system owns or controls resources and information flows) or *decentralized* (i.e. resources are distributed and nobody has full control over informations flows). Similarly, semantic integration patterns may be *decentralized* (i.e. each system has its own ontology possibly mapped to ontologies of other agents) or **centralized** (i.e. each system uses the same ontology by mapping it to local information resources) [2]. Notice that, while the (semantic) Web was envisioned as a physically and conceptually decentralized system, today's *infosphere* features a small number of giant centralized systems.

Through the centralization spectrum, a number of human and social factors impact the concrete ability of users, developers, content providers and stakeholders alike to reach consensus about *intended models* of shared conceptualizations. These factors include:

- **Epistemic**: accessibility of *truthmakers* (facts that make propositions true);
- **Hermeneutical**: availability of explicit interpretation criteria;
- **Pragmatical**: operative purposes, e.g. normative or descriptive;
- **Organizational**: presence of organized and coordinated workflows;
- **Socio-cultural**: impact of collective specificities such as linguistic habits and trust attitudes;
- **Political**: influence relationships among individuals and groups.

Depending on these factors, the concrete use of ontological specifications may vary significantly, as well as the effectiveness of formal meta-level categories as interpretation heuristics.

Studies on vagueness (the inherent indeterminacy of predicates like good or relevant), and how to handle it, have been quite extensively carried out in the last decade [7]. However, the problem of granting ontologies the very same interpretation across different and independent user communities goes beyond vagueness. There is in fact a more general phenomenon, known as the *inscrutability of reference* [8], which potentially affects every predicate, be it vague or not. Transposed to information systems, *inscrutability* can be summarized as follows: there's no control on how a conceptual model may be used in a context which is out of the *sphere of influence* of those who conceived it.

As a matter of facts, while it is true that formal meta-level categories such as *rigidity* or *sortality* (i.e. the property of carrying an identity criterion) may limit the radical arbitrariness of interpretation, thus mitigating *inscrutability*, such categories remain largely underdeveloped in business information systems at the time being. At a first sight, formal ontology fails to establish itself as a tool for semantic integration.

3   Using Formalized Ontologies

Formal ontology guidelines provided by OntoClean [5] may help drawing high quality, *upper level* ontologies. Still, such kind of formality could be completely disregarded when it comes to using ontologies in business scenarios, that is, interpreting them within some specific socio-technical context. In fact, industry people who are supposed to use the ontology could turn out to be unprepared to work with formal notions such as *identity criteria* or *possible worlds*. In these cases, formal constraints are not much handy to drive ontology interpretations, e.g. by mapping business databases, and this can also explain why formal ontology, as a discipline, is not so widespread among business communities. Yet, high quality upper levels, such as DOLCE [9], usually benefit of such kind of meta-level axiomatisation. As a consequence, users of high-quality ontologies (e.g. based on such upper levels) could find themselves in the situation of applying, even implicitly, metaphysical distinctions they are barely aware of. This leads to the conclusion that specific attention should be paid to support the application of well-founded ontologies in business scenarios.

Most of business conceptual models tacitly rely on natural language for their interpretation. As a matter of facts, even for concepts yielding strong formal ontological commitments, semantic judgements are mostly based on name labels. Unfortunately, linguistic knowledge is metaphysically opaque. To see this, consider the phenomenon of *regular polysemy* [10]. A noun as common as book in a sentence as plain as *"The book is interesting, but it is too heavy"* brings together two very different categories: INFORMATION (the book's content) and ARTEFACT (the book's body). The former is non-physical (e.g. the content of Dante's *Divine Comedy*, which is not placed in any time-space location), while the latter is physical (e.g. the thick copy of Dante's *Divine Comedy* on the shelf right now).

Using ontologies is a linguistic practice, but the very nature of natural language is ontologically problematic. Moreover, while language is cognitively pervasive, metaphysics is a specialistic niche. For these reasons, working with formalized ontologies appears to be full of difficulties for non trained people. Here follows a brief discussion on how to alleviate such difficulties.

4   Some Practical Guideline

In principle, due to *inscrutability*, there's no way to make concepts (linguistic predicates) "hermeneutically compelling", i.e. such to commit everybody on the very same interpretation and what is more, as is well known after Tarski and Goedel, *truth* is not definable at the conceptual level. At the end, for every concept, there's no way to avoid interpretations that deviate from the meaning the modellers intended. Reducing the source of these errors is therefore a matter of good practices, or even good luck.

4.1   Tips for Ontology Authors

In most of business socio-technical systems, the best an ontologist can do is to adopt a good metaphysical (foundational) layer and provide the proper documentation support to the domain conceptual model he or she draws upon that layer. A suitable foundational layer supplies basic categorical distinctions, without which one could not even properly speak of ontology. Good documentation, on the other hand, is the only reasonable way to foster *intended interpretations* of potentially obscure conceptualizations.

A good documentation (e.g. for *Human*) should include:

- **Quality comments**: Comments should follow a *genus-differentia* model[6], e.g. "Humans are rational animals"
- **Examples**: Instances of the defined concept should be exemplified, e.g. "Humans include Plato, Socrates, and Aristotle".
- **Competence questions**: One or more questions may help clarifying whether the kind of entity the user has in mind falls under the concept by spotting typical properties that were not mentioned in the main definition, e.g. "Is the entity an organism capable of social, linguistic behaviour?" [11]

4.2 Tips for Ontology Users

For each concept in the business ontology, in order to evaluate whether a certain kind of things can be classified onto a given concept, the user should be able to address a number of basic questions:

- **Classification:** "Is the thing I've in mind an instance of this concept?"
- **Deduction:** "What are the consequences of classifying a thing (pair) under this concept (relation)?"
- **Consistency:** "If the thing (pair) at hand fits more than one concept (pair), are these concepts (relations) compatible?"

For example, if the user of a shared ontology has to decide whether her local concept of Customer can be included in the borrowed concept of Human, she has to ask herself whether, for any customer instance, is it true that the entity is an organism. Now, the local conceptualization (e.g. a database schema) may have collapsed physical and legal customers into the same structure, thus leading to a negative answer and calling for some local adaptation.

Notice how the distinction involved here, i.e. between organisms and social entities, is ultimately a metaphysical one, since has to do with spatio-temporal qualities. Yet, for ordinary users, appeal to common sense may be much more effective than formal specifications.

5 Conclusion

Formal ontology is a powerful tool for conceptual modelling, but does not offer guarantees on the concrete use of shared conceptualizations. High quality documentation can do much more than metaphysics when it comes to mitigating the inscrutability of interpretation acts. This motivates and encourages the adoption

---

[6] Aristotle. Metaphysics. I.8.

of rich documentation guidelines when designing shared ontologies. On the other hand, users of shared conceptualizations must diligently check all the clues an ontology provides, whether by axiomatisation or documentation, to avoid interpretations potentially conflicting with those of others, still knowing that the risk is inevitable.

Ontology engineering methodologies have manly focused on development processes [12], paying little attention to the problem of concept-level interpretability. However, constraining interpretation is the essence of the entire ontological endeavour. This short paper has highlighted the relevance of this aspect, and suggested concept-level documentation guidelines as a suitable approach. Further research may refine and enrich the sketch provided here.

References

1. Guarino, N.: The ontological level. In: Casati, R., Smith, B., White, G. (eds.) Philosophy and the Cognitive Science, pp. 443–456. Hölder-Pichler-Tempsky, Vienna (1994)
2. Vetere, G., Lenzerini, M.: Models for semantic interoperability in service-oriented architectures. IBM Syst. J. **44**(4), 887–903 (2005)
3. Guarino, N.: The ontological level: revisiting 30 years of knowledge representation. In: Borgida, A.T., Chaudhri, V.K., Giorgini, P., Yu, E.S. (eds.) Conceptual Modeling: Foundations and Applications. LNCS, vol. 5600, pp. 52–67. Springer, Heidelberg (2009). https://doi.org/10.1007/978-3-642-02463-4_4
4. Dejnozka, J.: The Ontology of the Analytic Tradition and its Origins: Realism and Identity in Frege, Russell, Wittgenstein, and Quine. Rowman and Littlefield Publishers, Lanham (1996)
5. Guarino, N., Welty, C.: Evaluating ontological decisions with ontoclean. Commun. ACM. **45**(2), 61–65 (2002)
6. Vetere, G.: Formal ontology to the proof of facts. In: Ontology Makes Sense - Essays in honor of Nicola Guarino, PP. 152–164. IOS Press (2019). https://doi.org/10.3233/978-1-61499-955-3-152
7. Alexopoulos, P., Villazon-Terrazas, B., Pan, J.Z.: Towards vagueness-aware semantic data. In: Bobillo, F., et al. (eds.), CEUR Workshop Proceedings : 9th International Workshop on Uncertainty Reasoning for the Semantic Web, URSW 2013 (2013)
8. van Orman Quine, W.: Ontological Relativity and other Essays. Columbia University Press, New York City (1969)
9. Gangemi, A., Guarino, N., Masolo, C., Oltramari, A., Schneider, L.: Sweetening ontologies with DOLCE. In: Gómez-Pérez, A., Benjamins, V.R. (eds.) EKAW 2002. LNCS (LNAI), vol. 2473, pp. 166–181. Springer, Heidelberg (2002). https://doi.org/10.1007/3-540-45810-7_18
10. Pustejovsky, J.: The Generative Lexicon. MIT Press, Cambridge (1995)
11. Bezerra, C., Freitas, F., Santana da Silva, F.: Evaluating ontologies with competency questions, pp. 284–285. https://doi.org/10.1109/WI-IAT.2013.199 (2013)
12. Noy, N.F., McGuinness, D.L.: Ontology Development 101: A Guide to Creating Your First Ontology. Stanford Knowledge Systems Laboratory Technical Report KSL-01-05 and Stanford Medical Informatics Technical Report SMI-2001-0880 (2001)

A Research Toolbox: A Complete Suite for Analysis in Digital Humanities

Ernesto William De Luca[1,2] , Francesca Fallucchi[1,2(✉)] ,
Alessandro Ligi[3], and Massimiliano Tarquini[1]

[1] Georg Eckert Institute, 38100 Braunschweig, Germany
{deluca, fallucchi, mtarquini}@gei.de
[2] Guglielmo Marconi University, via Plinio 44, 00193 Rome, Italy
[3] MoodMe, 1400 Nivelles, Belgium

Abstract. The Georg Eckert Institute conducts applied, interdisciplinary research into textbooks and educational media, owning an important digitalized document corpus. Current Digital Libraries technologies don't allow its researchers to fully exploit the potential offered by Natural Language Processing technologies, thus a new platform, based on open source solution, has been realized with the aim to offer a set of tools to the researchers, allowing them to adapt the research process to the single case without predefining a workflow. The system offers functionalities that allow text digitalization, OCR, language recognition, digital libraries management, topic modelling, word counting, text enrichment and specific reporting elements, all in a flexible and high scalable architecture.

Keywords: Digital Humanities · Digital Libraries · Natural Language Processing

1 Introduction

Researchers in Digital Humanities domain are used to conduct their researches following their inspiration thus in a very unstructured way. Finding correlations, discovering patterns and understanding what lies behind the lines is often the method and either the goal of their job. Nowadays this work is done not only on physical paper but rather on their digital representation, then exploiting the power of Digital Libraries (DL) tools. Anyhow, DLs are mostly oriented in managing the documents lifecycle (from the digitalization process to the archiving and long term document preservation) rather than on the specific uses that a researcher could do of the related information, in particular from an analytical perspective. Some aspects of researcher's job deal mostly on formal methods in text analysis on a specific Document Corpus - such as using statistical algorithms, classifying the information or enriching the analysed texts with comments - that are obviously not present in current DL platforms as their purposes are way more generic. All these analytical methods could strongly benefit from the use of automated procedures and/or tools that are capable of analysing documents providing fast metrics that can ease the job of discovering correlations and cause-effect relations. From this need, we created a system which, without giving up the typical

E. Garoufallou et al. (Eds.): MTSR 2019, CCIS 1057, pp. 385–397, 2019.
https://doi.org/10.1007/978-3-030-36599-8_35

functionalities of a DL, could offer a set of tools that a researcher might use on a document corpus according to his/her specific needs. This is the genesis of the Research Toolbox of the Georg Eckert Institute (GEI), a Corpus Management system that is designed to help a specific class of users: researchers in Digital Humanities.

The paper is furthermore structured as in the following: In Sect. 2 we analyse the context of this work. In Sect. 3 we analyse the state of the art of the main Corpus Management tools used in Digital Humanities. In Sect. 4 we describe the methodological approach of the research activity and how it can be formalized in term of formal steps and processes. In Sect. 5 the architecture and the functionalities of Research Toolbox are described. In Sect. 6 the conclusions and further works are described.

2 Context

GEI conducts applied, multidisciplinary research into textbooks and educational media, focusing on cultural and historical aspects. At the GEI the Digital Information and Research Infrastructures department (DIRI) works in close and continuous collaboration with the Research Library and all the other departments. Doing so, it provides the digital infrastructure services which are of primary importance for supporting the research activities that are promoted by the Institute. As a result of this, after properly taking into account subject-specific issues, DIRI has systematically developed a number of tools for supporting the researchers who work in the field of Digital Humanities. Nevertheless, the development of these tools has followed specific needs without providing a broad and efficient vision, which is necessary to cover specific research needs.

Researchers are used to work with "paper" books; during their job, they usually take manual notes and highlight the most relevant text sentences. Moreover, researchers actively work with multiple different documents at the same time, searching for specific information. This same approach is expected to be available also when working into digital environment. It is increasingly necessary for researchers to be put in the best conditions to carry out their own work. To achieve this purpose, an adequate support by automatic information processing tools is offered them. At the same time, in order to adapt the tools to the user requirements, it is important to receive a feedback from researchers; in this way all tools and infrastructures can be properly improved. The department therefore upholds the GEI's "circular model" and simultaneously gets benefits from it. In [1] GEI researchers present the transdisciplinary work on digital tools in the field of textual analysis.

The result of all the considerations described above led to a thorough examination of the different needs expressed by the GEI researchers in Digital Humanities. In particular, most of their requests referred to the adoption of a new approach for exploring digitized documents. For achieving such a purpose, however, new technologies and related tools had to be provided. After assessing the technological solutions currently available, DIRI took the decision of designing and implementing a new, comprehensive web portal for managing digital documents.

In this document we will describe the Research ToolBox which has been carefully designed to provide to backoffice operators, librarians and researchers of the GEI a unique and comprehensive digital document management system. This research-oriented platform will give GEI users the opportunity to manage text from paper to digital format, add information by using different Natural Language Processing tools and, eventually, explore the enriched text contents.

3 State of the Art

Digital Humanities is not a new scientific branch as digital humanists use well known research methods; nevertheless its activities might well lead to the development of new approaches and methods in the future. It is based on a set of different research fields such as quantitative and qualitative text analysis, corpus linguistics, different search methods, text mining, subject-specific databases, visualization of complex data structures and offer user-oriented/user-centred representations of the data, which are specifically tuned and applied in the domain of the humanities. This multidisciplinary approach, that is oriented to data analysis, has been already implemented and used, e.g. for a personalized access to cultural artifacts [2] or to open data [3–5]. Methods for analyzing social networks [6], to evaluate popularity [7] or to support logistics during Humanitarian Assistance and Disaster Relief [8] have been studied and developed thus becoming applicable to Digital Humanities issues. The real innovation of Digital Humanities deals in the peculiar adjustment, re-definition and use of the already established methods of computational linguistics, machine learning and information retrieval for the humanities. As these methods are currently strongly focused on the text level, they support hermeneutic work of humanities scholars whenever dealing with digital media. By means of using Digital Humanities methods, scholars can compare the sources with their insights and hypotheses with the help of computer-aided analyses and research, using the ultimate possibilities of interaction, exploiting existing infrastructures and state-of-the-art methods for searching, visualizing and correlating larger amounts of data (see our work on CMDI in [9, 10]).

Before going into the development of a new platform, a comparative analysis on the most used Corpus Management Tools has been performed in order to assess if reusing an existing solution it would have been more appropriate to reach the previously described goals. In particular, we analysed the main Corpus Management Tools.

A corpus manager (also known as corpus browser or corpus query system) is a complex software platform which provides users with convenient functions for the ingestion of big annotated text datasets (corpora) and the effective searching of linguistic information inside a corpus. It implies both a search engine and a query language are provided.

The two most famous and widely used platforms have been analysed: Sketch Engine and CWB. Sketch Engine[1] is the ultimate tool to explore how language works. Its algorithms analyze authentic texts of billions of words (text corpora) to identify

---

[1] Sketch Engine Homepage. https://www.sketchengine.eu/.

instantly what is typical in language and what is rare, unusual or emerging usage. It is also designed for text analysis or text mining applications. The tool present some lacks such as pre-defined POS tagging tagset, unable to manage a standard corpus mark-up structure and no text lookup in user-defined subcorpora or text subsets NoSketch engine[2] is the limited open source version of Sketch Engine but this tool neither contains any corpora, nor linguistic resources; the usage of external tools to prepare corpora is required. CWB Corpus WorkBench[3] is an open source solution composed by a collection of tools for managing and querying large text corpora (ranging from 10 million to 2 billion words) with linguistic annotations. Its central component is the flexible and efficient query processor Corpus Query Processor[4,5]. It presents some missing functionalities such as corpus POS tagging must be done previously with other tools, not manageable standard corpus mark-up structure, no text lookup in user-defined subcorpora or text subsets.

4   Methodological Approach

In this Section we describe the theoretical workflow model that corresponds to current workflow that is used by the researchers and that is implemented in the Research Toolbox. Note that the Research Toolbox is (intentionally) not designed as a workflow system because it would like to offer a set of tools that permit a flexible configuration of the sequence of the job steps. Nevertheless, during the design of the system, we beard in mind the way of working that researchers described and that can be ideally described as follows.

4.1   Digitization Process

The very first step should deal with digitization of paper textbooks. This operation implies managing the whole set of book metadata in accordance with a defined standard. In general metadata allow users to uniquely identify any bibliographic resource. However, whereas paper texts have a fixed set of metadata, whenever dealing with digital resources, the overall amount may seriously increase. In particular, information about the address where digital resources can be accessed and the description of the most relevant file features must be provided.

Assuming that issues related to choosing the most suitable standard have already been solved[6], it is important to highlight that bibliographic metadata can be fruitfully used by researchers to infer new information. This can be possible by exploiting the possibility to set semantic links between elements whose access is open (i.e. freely available) within the entire web space. Such technology takes the name of Linked Open

---

[2] NoSketch engine: https://nlp.fi.muni.cz/trac/noske.

[3] CWB Corpus Workbench homepage: http://cwb.sourceforge.net/.

[4] CWB/CQPweb: http://cwb.sourceforge.net/cqpweb.php.

[5] Corpus WorkBench: http://www.ims.unistuttgart.de/forschung/projekte/CorpusWorkbench.html.

[6] Clarin-CMDI: http://www.clarin.eu.

Data (LOD) and implies the implementation of a complete framework based on RDF (Resource Description Framework) datasets and related ontologies. The relevance of this approach for academic research becomes clearer if considering all the possible relations that carefully selected (meta)data are able to set. As an example, researchers could establish relations between the name of the author of a specific textbook (or a part of a collective book) and external information like his/her biography, bibliography, education, hobbies or travels. Those data, which in the web may appear as scattered and totally unrelated, when linked together could provide useful information about possible involvement of the said author in political or social activities which could bias his/her work in some ways. This is just an example; much more information may be inferred by using LOD in different creative ways.

In spite of the leading role of metadata, a still more important role is covered by the text content. Taking for granted that all the books which were selected for the researches have already been digitized and made available into the digital library environment, text content should be extracted from all the digitized pages by using an OCR software. Subsequently, the resulting text should undergo a careful proofreading. This step is crucial. In case this operation is passed by, the risk of producing incorrect results due to serious text errors could be high. Results from keyword-driven search could be seriously affected and, consequently, become unreliable. A different, partly easier scenario, regards the conversion into plain text of an already available digital file which has been saved into a specific, proprietary format (e.g. PDF, DOC, etc.). In most cases the file conversion process does not affect the text integrity or its layout and, in general, it does not require users to make step-by-step operations because it runs in batch mode. However, in case the original file contained complex text structure (e.g. nested tables) or was affected by font encoding issues, a manual editing intervention could be required.

4.2 From Single Texts to a Structured Corpus: The Digitalization Process

Until now we have described the mandatory steps to produce a number of texts whose metadata and contents are made accessible. Yet, this is not sufficient. All files are still unrelated; they represent single entities and their content can be searched only by opening any single document per time. Therefore, to make text research more effective and easier, the next step is moving from a set of strewn documents towards the concept of linguistic corpus. A corpus is an articulated structure in which all texts are collected into a unique complex file. However, creating a corpus to better meet GEI research aims, it does not simply mean merging all the selected files together. On the contrary, specific characteristics of the bibliographic resources should be taken into account and carefully evaluated. GEI holds the largest and most complete collection of textbooks, that represent the library that is mostly used as a basis for researches and from which the corpora are created.

Leaving aside the issues tied to the corpus representativeness and balance, which should be faced by researchers during the text selection activity, the first aspect to consider is strictly related to the type of school and educational purpose the original textbooks were adopted for. Because the German education system is currently managed by any single federal *Länder*, across Germany the same textbook may be adopted in different schools belonging to different education levels. Knowing this information is fundamental to perform text analysis and data comparison with a scientific approach. For instance, researchers should be able to selectively retrieve information from the corpus on the basis of textbook usage. However, as textbook adoption may vary in accordance with the changes different Länder may put forth in their own education system, information regarding usage cannot be provided by the textbook itself. In this field metadata and content are of no use. This problem may be solved by adopting two different approaches. The first one relies on the ability of the digital library framework to manage metadata as LOD datasets to create RDF structures. In this way, given that school administration has published their own data on the web, all the relevant information on textbooks usage can be easily taken by enquiring the public administration open data. The query results will be subsequently transmitted to the corpus management system and properly used. Since this approach requires getting data from external resources, a preliminary feasibility study should be made to understand whether open data from public institutions can really encounter the project research requirements. A totally different solution should be taken if no open data from school administration are available and the information on textbook have to be collected in other ways. Since a corpus is a completely new digital object and, as such, has no direct relations with the library infrastructures managing the original paper books or their digital versions, all the metadata which identify and describe the various textbook have to be included into the corresponding corpus section as a document header. Regarding this task, it is relevant to remark that it can be accomplished only after a specific markup standard has been chosen (e.g. TEI - Textbook Encoding Initiative).

Text Manipulation

When creating a corpus, mark-up and annotation represent two very important tasks to enhance the information a simple plain text provides. In particular, the term mark-up refers to the set of external elements which can describe the structure of a text (i.e. titles, pages, chapters, paragraphs, lines, pictures, notes, etc.), while annotation refers to additional linguistic information such as lemmas, Part-of-Speech, phrase structures, semantic roles, etc. Regarding research purposes, mark-up is fundamental because it allows users to select specific parts of text, skipping all what may be considered irrelevant like, for instance, chapter titles, tables or image captions. In general mark-up requires the adoption of a standard; for this reason, it is manually performed by expert users. In some cases, however, the general structure of a text can be automatically derived by its index. As mentioned before, a corpus is not a simple sequential merging of different plain text files. Research projects can take advantage of the useful information that corpora provide only after some change in their linguistic structure is made. In particular, the whole text should undergo a preliminary, mandatory process called tokenization. This procedure aims at overriding the standard orthographic rules by dividing what should be considered a complete string from other text elements like punctuation marks. In corpus linguistics it represents a mandatory step because only in this way users can perform reliable quantitative analysis, text statistics and text mining. Although in general this procedure is performed automatically after a set of linguistic rules have been defined, there may be cases in which the support of an electronic dictionary or, at worst, a manual intervention is required. A typical example is the reconstruction of an entire token which has been divided into two parts by syllabication rules. In German such cases may cause problems because no generic rules can be provided to automatically disambiguate the first part of a wrap word from prefixes with hyphens which may appear at the end of a line.

Text Enrichment

After the changes made by the tokenization process, further linguistic information may be added to the texts, which lead to the creation of the corpus. This is part of the annotation process; it may take different steps in relation to the complexity of the information required. Although there is virtually no limit to the features one may tie to the corpus tokens, for research purposes taking advantage of lemmatization and semantic tagging should be sufficient. Yet, more detailed information like Part-of-Speech tagging may be added in a second moment if required.

The term "lemmatization" refers to the process of re-conducting a morphologically complex structure to its canonical form (also called citation form or dictionary form). This information is very important for text search activity. By using citation forms, researchers and corpus users may find all the contexts surrounding a specific word regardless of the various morphologic patterns it may assume. Because of the corpus dimensions and the type of data involved, lemmatization is never carried out manually. Usually this task is performed automatically by using morphological analysers and electronic lexicons.

For better defining the semantic areas the different tokens belong to or infer general semantic information from a particular text selection, additional word sense information should be added. In spite of the various data-driven ontologies freely available on the Internet, one of the most reliable resource for German language is GermaNet, which has been adopted to create the sense-annotated corpus TüBa-D/Z Treebank. Since most of GEI research projects deal with school textbooks, the generic ontologies currently available might not be sufficient to map the whole semantic area the different books cover. In such case, the chosen ontology should be integrated with new information taken from the selected textbook.

Corpus Management and Enquiry Tool

Corpora are very powerful tools for text and data-driven research. However, in order to effectively exploit all the information they contain, a corpus management tool should be used. Since users are primarily interested in extracting linguistic information (i.e. phrase contexts) related to text patterns, the most important instrument a corpus management tool should provide is a comprehensive search engine. Although a corpus represents a single digital entity, in order to improve usability, the queries should not be forced to run exclusively on the whole corpus. On the contrary, users should be given the opportunity to select the corpus areas in which the search is performed. Doing so, users may focus their research on specific text areas instead of simply getting results from the entire corpus with no distinction. Obviously, this can be possible only if the corpus has already been provided with specific mark-up structure. Otherwise, manual post-processing activities may be necessary.

From the technical perspective, both the corpus and its management system should operate online and should limit the visualization of the source texts in case it was covered by copyright. According to the user selection, search results should be visualized in a KWIC (keyword in context) format or as a simple block of text. The system should also give the opportunity to select which metadata, mark-up or linguistic information are returned.

Finally, to further support research activities, the corpus management system should be able to concurrently run a specific query on different parallel corpora and, subsequently, help compare the results by highlighting the matching text patterns. The program should also compute all the most relevant statistical information both from the corpus as a whole and from the user's selection. In particular, graphical representation concerning the quantity of texts the corpus is made of, tokens, types and type/token ratio should be provided. In addition, the ability of producing frequency lists calculated on the basis of different parameters (i.e. keyword and its context, Zipfs' law, semantic features) and their related graphs, may represent a helpful resource for researchers. In Fig. 1 the over described process is shown as a workflow.

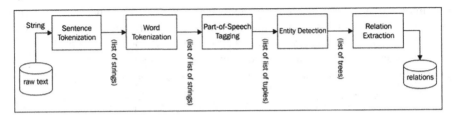

Fig. 1. Corpus management workflow.

4.3   Implementation Approach

In order to effectively manage the text search activities, a number of Digital Humanities and Natural Language Processing (NLP) libraries and tools have been realized. Moreover, since a bunch of digitized and processed text files taken as a whole represent a text corpus, specific tools for managing big corpora have been developed. As for linguistic issues, despite any natural language analysis is strictly related to a specific theory, NLP tools must be neutral to this and accept any kind of suitable dataset. All texts can be analysed in accordance with the following standard linguistic structures: lexicon, morphology, syntax, semantics, discourse.

Lexicon
For exploring the lexicon of a text, a tokenizer, a lemmatizer and a Part-of-Speech tagger are required. Tools like Named Entity Recognizers can be very useful, but are not mandatory.

- Tokenization is the process of dividing a string of input characters into lexemes. As a consequence of this, the tokenization process may break the orthographic rules currently in use in a language. Tokenizers can be rule based or use a statistical approach.

- Lemmatization usually returns the base or dictionary form of a word, which is known as the lemma. This can be achieved by using a morphologically enriched machine-readable vocabulary.
- POS taggers are used to attach grammar class labels to words. It can be done by using a machine-readable vocabulary and subsequent disambiguation rules or by trained stochastic processing based on Hidden Markov Models.
- Named entity recognition (NER) is used to determine which text item is a proper name.

Morphology

A morphological analyzer is a program that analyzes a given input token and returns its morphological information (e.g. gender, number, tense, etc.) as an output. Morphological analysis can be performed in three ways: morpheme-based morphology (item and arrangement approach), lexeme-based morphology (item and process approach), and word-based morphology (word and paradigm approach). In general morphological analyzers are based on Finite State Transducers technology.

Syntax

Chunkers (also known as Shallow Parsers) are used for labelling segments of sentences with syntactic correlated keywords like Noun Phrase and Verb Phrase (NP or VP). These tools first identify the POS tagged constituent parts of sentences and then group them together to form higher order units (i.e. phrases).

Syntactic analyzers are able to uncover the grammatical structure of a sentence. These tools parse the input string of tokens and show the relations established between the different lexical element that compose it in terms of dependency relationship, type of phrase structure and position in the sentence. All syntax analysis programs require a fine-grained grammar description of a language, so they are not available in case linguistic resources are missing.

Semantics

Semantic processing determines the possible meanings of a sentence by examining the semantic interactions between the words the sentence is made of. This level of processing can incorporate the semantic disambiguation of words with multiple senses which cannot be solved at syntactic level (Word sense disambiguation) or the assignment of the proper semantic role of a word in a sentence (semantic role labeling). All the above functions can be achieved by using language-specific lexical ontologies like WordNet.

Discourse

Discourse analysis focuses on the properties of the text to convey meaning by making cohesive and coherent connections between sentences. The most used applications are:

- Anaphora resolution - a method for resolving references to earlier or later items in the discourse.
- Topic modeling - a statistical method for uncovering the cluster of words that frequently occur together in a collection of texts.
- Co-occurrences - the extraction of words that frequently appear together in a specific context.

- Zipf's law - a statistical method which analyses the rank and frequency of the words in a text to help understand the usage of the lexicon and discover hapax legomena, which are usually tied to errors, neologisms or rare words.
- Sentiment analysis - extracts sentiments about a specific topic. Tools for sentiment analysis use a sentiment lexicon and a sentiment pattern database to provide positive and negative ratings to the words which are taken into account.

In general, to carry out a specific task, the usage of various standalone NLP modules is required. In order to work together, they are usually connected into pipelines. They all take a standard input, do their own annotation, and produce a standard output which in turn is the input for the next module. Pipelines follow a data centric architecture, therefore any module can be modified or replaced to implement different configurations.

Corpus Management Tools

In Fig. 2 the linguistic analysis approach is shown together with the tools that are used to implement it inside Research Toolbox.

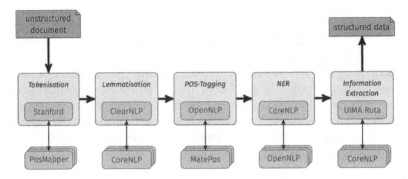

Fig. 2. The linguistic analysis approach and its implementing tools.

5   Proposed Solution

5.1   Functional Goals

The platform Research Toolbox has been realized aim to accomplish also the following functional goals:

- implementing the previously described methodological approach
- creating an integrated environment that provides a set of independent tools but in which each tool can benefit of the synergy provided by a common platform
- thus allowing researcher in the domain of Digital Humanities to perform their research activities with the level of flexibility that they need and without obliging them in a predefined workflow that might reduce their creativity and effectiveness.

The challenge about combining these goals consists in providing a set of functionalities that are not blocked into a workflow. Once created a project and associated a document corpus, the system automatically performs a set of basic analysis on the corpus (such as all the information retrieval and search functionalities) and for each document (such as language detection, OCR, text extraction). The researcher can freely decide to apply any of the analysis and annotation tools that are included into the systems. He can start from topic modelling or from NLP functions, searching for occurrences or either tagging a document or part of it, thus choosing the "tool" to be used according to the goal of the research and the obtained results. The system allows sharing among different users of any of the managed objects (documents, tags, corpus, analysis, reports etc.).

5.2 Architecture of the Solution

The technical architecture of Research Toolbox is composed by the classical three level system for web applications as shown in Fig. 3. The presentation layer is dedicated to the preparation and management of the user interface, and it's managed by an application server.

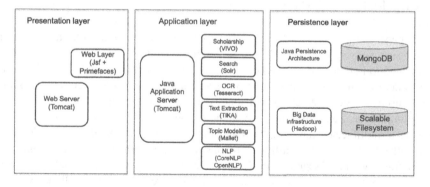

Fig. 3. Component architecture of research toolbox.

In this first design the web server is Apache Tomcat[7] (that plays the role also of application server), but the architecture is designed to be fully scalable by means of substituting the web server with a dedicated one (i.e. Apache Web server). From the application development perspective, presentation layer is developed using standard technologies like Java Server Faces[8] together with the framework Primefaces[9].

The application layer is composed as a java application, deployed inside Tomcat container, that coordinates a set of components dedicated to:

---

[7] Apache Tomcat: http://tomcat.apache.org/.

[8] Java Server Faces: https://www.oracle.com/technetwork/java/javaee/javaserverfaces-139869.html.

[9] Primefaces homepage: https://www.primefaces.org/.

- full text search engine, to provide search capability for the documents that are treated by the system. The integrated component is Apache SoLR[10]
- a solution for extracting text from images (OCR), managed by the component Tesseract[11]
- a solution to manage documents (PDF, Word etc.), extracting text, managed by the component TIKA[12]
- A set of components that perform Natural Language Processing (NLP) algorithms, each one selected and dedicated to particular functionalities, such as CoreNLP[13] and OpenNLP[14]
- A solution including scholarship functionalities (VIVO)[15]
- A component for Topic modeling and documents classification (Mallet)[16].
- A component for graphic reporting[17]

The persistence layer is composed by:

- the orchestration, in data management, provided by Java Persistence Layer
- A solution for Big Data management (Hadoop)[18]
- a highly scalable NoSQL database (MongoDB)[19].

6   Conclusion and Further Works

In this paper we present Research Toolbox, a system which could offer a set of tools that a researcher might use on a document corpus according to his/her specific needs. It is designed to help a specific class of users, the researchers in Digital Humanities. We start to describe the theoretical workflow model that corresponds to current workflow that is used by the researchers and that is implemented in the Research Toolbox. Straddling national and disciplinary boundaries, our research-oriented platform brings together a multifaceted range of tools and materials from academic works. The platform gathers information regarding textbooks from around the world and presents it in a user-friendly and research-oriented manner. In this way, the, widely dispersed community of textbook researchers and practitioners are able to access all the available information conveniently. The research-oriented platform is organized as a modular infrastructure in order to simplify access to the different functions the system may offer. Functionality will be improved by the addition of machine learning algorithms. A basic

---

[10] Solr homepage: http://lucene.apache.org/solr/.

[11] Tesseract homepage: https://github.com/tesseract-ocr/tesseract.

[12] Apache TIKA: https://tika.apache.org/.

[13] Stanford CoreNLP: https://stanfordnlp.github.io/CoreNLP/.

[14] Apache OpenNLP: https://opennlp.apache.org/.

[15] VIVO homepage: https://duraspace.org/vivo/.

[16] Mallet homepage: http://mallet.cs.umass.edu/classification.php.

[17] d3.js.

[18] Apache Hadoop homepage: https://hadoop.apache.org/.

[19] MongoDB homepage: https://www.mongodb.com/.

prototype has been implemented and it is currently available for GEI researchers to be tested. All this is supported by a user friendly interface which will enable data exchange, advanced integrated processing, smart annotation functionalities and advance query engine, etc. The Research Toolbox has been released in a beta version and it's currently under test and improvement by the GEI researchers. The first results are encouraging as the flexibility of the platform goes beyond the limitations of the current market solutions.

References

1. De Luca, E.W., Spielhaus, R.: Digital transformation of research processes in the humanities. In: Garoufallou, E., De Luca, E.W. (eds.) 13th Metadata and Semantics Research Conference, MTSR 2019, pp. 1–14 (2019)
2. Beccaceci, R., Fallucchi, F., Giannone, C.F., Spagnoulo, F., Zanzotto, F.M.: Education with 'living artworks' in museums. In: Proceedings of the 1st International Conference on Computer Supported Education, CSEDU 2009, vol. 1 (2009)
3. Fallucchi, F., Alfonsi, E., Ligi, A., Tarquini, M.: Ontology-driven public administration web hosting monitoring system. In: Meersman, R., et al. (eds.) OTM 2014. LNCS, vol. 8842, pp. 618–625. Springer, Heidelberg (2014). https://doi.org/10.1007/978-3-662-45550-0_63
4. Bianchi, M., Draoli, M., Fallucchi, F., Ligi, A.: Service level agreement constraints into processes for document classification. In: Proceedings of the 16th International Conference on Enterprise Information Systems, ICEIS 2014, vol. 1 (2014)
5. Fallucchi, F., Petito, M., De Luca, E.W.: Analysing and visualising open data within the data and analytics framework. In: Garoufallou, E., Sartori, F., Siatri, R., Zervas, M. (eds.) MTSR 2018. CCIS, vol. 846, pp. 135–146. Springer, Cham (2019). https://doi.org/10.1007/978-3-030-14401-2_13
6. Plumbaum, T., Wu, S., De Luca, E.W., Albayrak, S.: User modeling for the social semantic web. In: Proceedings of the Second International Conference on Semantic Personalized Information Management: Retrieval and Recommendation, vol. 781, pp. 78–89. CEUR-WS. org (2011)
7. De Luca, E., Fallucchi, F., Giuliano, R., Incarnato, G., Mazzenga, F.: Analysing and visualizing tweets for U.S. president popularity. Int. J. Adv. Sci. Eng. Inf. Technol. 9(2), 692–699 (2019)
8. Fallucchi, F., Tarquini, M., De Luca, E.W.: Knowledge management for the support of logistics during Humanitarian Assistance and Disaster Relief (HADR). In: Díaz, P., Bellamine Ben Saoud, N., Dugdale, J., Hanachi, C. (eds.) ISCRAM-med 2016. LNBIP, vol. 265, pp. 226–233. Springer, Cham (2016). https://doi.org/10.1007/978-3-319-47093-1_19
9. Fallucchi, F., De Luca, E.W.: Connecting and mapping LOD and CMDI through knowledge organization. In: Garoufallou, E., Sartori, F., Siatri, R., Zervas, M. (eds.) MTSR 2018. CCIS, vol. 846, pp. 291–301. Springer, Cham (2019). https://doi.org/10.1007/978-3-030-14401-2_27
10. Fallucchi, F., Steffen, H., De Luca, E.W.: Creating CMDI-profiles for textbook resources. In: Garoufallou, E., Sartori, F., Siatri, R., Zervas, M. (eds.) MTSR 2018. CCIS, vol. 846, pp. 302–314. Springer, Cham (2019). https://doi.org/10.1007/978-3-030-14401-2_28

The Null Result Portal

Lydia Müller$^{(\boxtimes)}$ (ORCID), Dirk Goldhahn$^{(\boxtimes)}$, and Gerhard Heyer$^{(\boxtimes)}$

NLP Group, Computer Science Institute, University of Leipzig,
Augustusplatz 10, 04109 Leipzig, Germany
{lydia, dgoldhahn, heyer}@informatik.uni-leipzig.de

Abstract. Null results occur in every discipline and research field. While positive results are usually published null results are underrepresented in the literature. Nevertheless, they can contribute to knowledge of the field as much as positive results. There are already a few attempts to make null results publicly available such as special issues on null results or journal dedicated to null results. However, the response of the research community is often low in means of submitted papers. We here present the Null Result Portal. It provides the possibility to publish null results with a much lower effort compared to a paper. Null results can be discussed by and with the community. Authors may decide to stay anonymous. Furthermore, the portal provides search functionality to foster the collection of null results. It hereby contributes to make null results less underrepresented and more acknowledged by the research community. Discussions with the research community furthermore ensure that potential methodological issues or problems with the used data may be detected. The Null Result Portal is available online.

Keywords: Null result · Portal · Meta data

1 Introduction

In every discipline and field, scientific studies may not be successful. This usually means that the desired outcome, i.e. the research hypothesis, is not supported by the data. Often, nonetheless that there is evidence for the hypothesis, statistical tests turn out to be insignificant with respect to an accepted significance level.

The reasons for insignificant results are manifold. The data may not be appropriated for the research question, e.g. the sample size is too small to obtain significant results or the data is too noisy. The method might not be appropriated, e.g. it is not sensitive enough or does not fit to the data characteristic (such as underlying distribution of the data). The hypothesis may even simply not apply. And, as a special case, if the aim was to reproduce a result of a previous study, the already published result may be a type I error.

"Positive" results are usually published. Usually, it depends on the expected impact of the result how prominent it is published. As a consequence, most journals are full of significant and impacting results and thus, do not reflect the current knowledge of the scientific community. This problem is known for long and often termed 'file drawer problem' or publication bias. Rosenthal [1] already stated in 1979 that likely 95% of

© Springer Nature Switzerland AG 2019
E. Garoufallou et al. (Eds.): MTSR 2019, CCIS 1057, pp. 398–403, 2019.
https://doi.org/10.1007/978-3-030-36599-8_36

the results are not published and provides a method to calculate to which extend future null results can be accepted for a significant hypothesis. However, null results are nonetheless useful. They can show that certain hypotheses and assumptions do not hold. Null results may demonstrate that a data set does not fulfill certain assumptions. It can be demonstrated that a certain approach will not lead to the expected outcome. Null results can also show that a published result may cannot be reproduced. How-ever, they are still less frequently published than "positive" result.

In this publication, we describe the Null Result Portal. It is designed to be a venue for null results that would other-wise be discarded. It allows to publish null results alongside their meta data. Null results can be publicly mined and registered users may comment on null results to discuss possible reasons for insignificance.

2   Null Result Portal

The problem that null results are less likely published than "positive" results drew more and more attention over the last years. Many editorials and opinion are written about this topic [2, 3] and discuss the usefulness of null results for the community [4]. Some even tackle the problem by providing special issues or journals dedicated to null results. However, the motivation of the authors to publish null results appear to be low leading to few papers for such venues [3].

There are several reasons why researchers do not publish null results. One is that it is a common believe that papers reporting null results will be less likely accepted for publication than papers with positive results [5]. Nevertheless, there are a few venues for null results. Landis et al. [3] report that for their special issue on null results only 31 proposals were submitted. 15 of them were selected for a full manuscript but the final special issue comprised only 4 articles. The editors speculate about the reasons and ended up with two likely causes: (1) the authors thought that their null results were worthless and (2) the recognition of methodological deficiencies by other researchers. Ioannidis discusses that researchers aim to publish in high impact journals and thus focus on strongly significant results which will impact further re-search [2]. Conse-quently, null results are not published or not even written up somewhere to be able to spend more time on high impact results.

Based on our experiences and those published in literature, we designed a concept for the platform to publish and search null results. In the following, we discuss the main points of the concept. We organized the points in collecting and searching null results. While only registered users may contribute to collect null results, everybody is able to search within the Web portal. As a last point, we describe additional features of the concept.

Fig. 1. Null result in editor (left) and on the public website (right).

2.1 Collecting Null Results

Low Effort to Publish a Null Result. The process of writing a paper to publish a result is often time consuming. The motivation of researcher to do this for a null result appears to be low. Therefore, the Null Result Portal is conceptionally not a journal and does not incorporate a review process. In fact, it is designed as a multi-author blog.

We do not predefine the structure of the blog entry but added some meta data which has to be provided by the author. This includes a description for the null result, the hypothesis tested, and the result. Additional information and data can be added if available. While the meta data is supposed to be short (e.g., as the abstract of a paper), the body of the entry can be used to report more detailed information about the null result. Figure 1 shows the editor's view and public website view of a null result in the Null Result Portal. Meta data and the null result content and title are edit on the same page for simplicity. The null result is shown alongside with its meta data on the public website.

Open Discussions Instead of Reviews. Areview process of a paper aims at strengthening the statement of a paper and to identify and correct methodological issues before publication. We relocate the review process to the stage after publication. Registered users may comment on null results and thus discuss any aspect of the null result. Comments or suggestions may be picked up by the author to improve the results. However, by opening up the discussion to all users also other users than the authors may con-tribute by performing suggested additional analyses.

Null Results can be Edited and Even Deleted. We are aware of the fact that discussions of the null result may lead to changes in the result. Therefore, it is possible to edit the null result to keep it up to date with the discussion. Discussions may even lead to the insight that with another methodology or different data, the result could be significant. We thus offer the possibility to delete the null result to publish it elsewhere.

Anonymity. While users have to be registered to write and comment on the Null Result Portal, we do not require them to uncover their identity. Any personal information (such as E-Mail) is kept confidential and the display name may or may not represent the person's identity. Thus, authors who do not want to be associated with their null result may still contribute with their null results to the community's knowledge. This option might be most important for young research having only a limited number of research papers and grants. A long list of null results associated with their names may thus unfavorable when apply for new positions or research grants. However, also young researchers can provide valuable contributions to the community's knowledge.

2.2   Searching Null Results

Categories and Tags. The author may attach a null result to a category or provide tags (i.e. keywords) for the null result. An anonymous user may browse the collection of null results by categories or tags.

Quick Search. A search bar allows to find null results for a given search term. This will conduct a search in the title, contents, and meta data information (i.e. description, hypothesis, result) of the null results.

Facetted Search. A facetted search allows the user to narrow down the list of null results of interest. Search terms for the meta data fields and content and title can be specified separately, results can be filtered by category, tag and date. The resulting list may be sorted by relevance or date.

2.3   Additional Features

Limited Access Content. We provide the possibility to restrict the access to a null result to only a subset of the registered users. Thus, authors who would like to have the opinion of other authors but do not want to make the null result publicly available yet, can write up their null result and share it with the desired users. This restriction can be changed and removed at any time.

Private Communication. Since users might be anonymous, i.e. their true identity is not revealed to other users, it is not always possible to contact another author and, e.g., ask question about a null result or to ask for data. Thus, we added a very simple mailing system for private communications on the platform. Users can write emails with optional attached data to other users. The recipient will be informed by email using the email address provided upon registration.

Deleting Accounts. We consider the possibility that users may want to delete their null result portal account. The EU General Data Protection Regulation states that every user is entitled to be forgotten. Therefore, user can delete their private information, posts, and comments. However, we provide the possibility to delete the private information and the account while leaving the posts and comments in the portal. When using this option, a non-functional anonymous account is created and the posts and comments of the original account are associated with this account. Note that such an account cannot be used for login to the system.

3 Implementation Details

The Null Result Portal is implemented on the basis of the WordPress software. Several customizations (publicly available) are integrated to add or limit functionality as desired. We furthermore implemented additional functionality as part of our own WordPress child theme (a collection of templates and stylesheets to customize the appearance of a WordPress installation) or as plugins. We deployed several security relevant plugins to ensure that private data is kept privately and cannot be accessed by unauthorized persons.

We limit the roles available in WordPress to essentially 2 roles. Authors may contribute with null results to the portal, comment on posts, use the private communication system, and edit their private information. Administrators in addition make changes to the functionality and design of the website, curate the posts and comments, and administrate the users. An implicit third role is the website visitor which can only search for null results on the portal's public website.

The WordPress software has by default a public area and an administration area. The public area presents the con-tent to the users without the need to be registered or logged in. The administration area provides an interface to add or modify content and to administrate the website. We kept this separation but modified it to our needs. Comments, by default possible without registration, are limited to registered and logged in users. This not only limits the ability to write spam comments but ensures that the commentator can be contacted by the author for further discussion. The administration area is strongly limited in its functionality for the authors. Authors may add posts, edit or delete their posts, review comments associated with their posts, edit and delete their comments, write private messages, or change their account information.

4 Conclusion

Null results are as important as positive result. They, however, are underrepresented in scientific literature. The Null Result Portal tries to improve the situation by providing a platform for null results. They can be published in fast and easy manner at a much lower effort than a publication. We allow to publish anonymously to lower the inhibition level of making a null result publicly available. Open discussions allow to review and improve the methods and data used.

The Null Result Portal can be mined using several search strategies publicly. Researchers are enabled to make use of unsuccessful approaches and false hypotheses early in their work.

The Null Result Portal was made available online only recently. Therefore, we currently lack user's feedback. However, we are in the process of collecting and evaluating user's feedback to improve the Null Result Portal.

Furthermore, we will evaluate whether the portal proves to be a successful venue for null results. Success may be measured in number of registered users, number of visitors of the public website, or number of published null results.

Design choices, such as anonymity and review free publication, have to be revised once the Null Result Portal acquired users and null results. For example, the quality of anonymously published null results as opposed to null results published by users displaying their real identity could be assessed. Large differences in quality may indicate that, for example, some review mechanism is required to ensure a certain minimal quality of the null results.

Further research on why researchers decide to publish or not publish their null results can serve as a starting point to improve the current situation. These research results can then directly be incorporated in the Null Result Portal.

References

1. Rosenthal, R.: The "File Drawer Problem" and tolerance for null results. Psychol. Bull. **86**(3), 638–641 (1979)
2. Ioannidis, J.P.: Journals should publish all "Null" results and should sparingly publish "Positive" results. Cancer Epidemiol. Prev. Biomark. **15**(1), 186 (2006)
3. Landis, R.S., James, L.R., Lance, C.E., Pierce, C.A., Rogelberg, S.G.: When is nothing something? Editorial for the null results special issue of journal of business and psychology. J. Bus. Psychol. **29**(2), 163–167 (2014)
4. Munafò, M., Neill, J.: Null is beautiful: on the importance of publishing null results. J. Psychopharmacol. **30**(7), 585 (2016)
5. Iwachiw, J.S., Button, A.L., Atlas, J.: The perceived role of null results in school psychology research and publication. School Psyvhology International (2019)

Track on Metadata and Semantics for Cultural Collections and Applications

Enriching Wikidata with Cultural Heritage Data from the COURAGE Project

Ghazal Faraj[1（✉）] and András Micsik[2]

[1] Eötvös Loránd University, Pázmány Péter stny. 1/C, Budapest 1117, Hungary
ghazal.faraj@gmail.com
[2] SZTAKI DSD, Lágymányosi u. 11, Budapest, Hungary
micsik@sztaki.hu

Abstract. Creating links manually between large datasets becomes an extremely tedious task. Although the linked data production is growing massively, the interconnecting needs improvement. This paper presents our work regarding detecting and extending links between Wikidata and COURAGE entities with respect to cultural heritage data. The COURAGE project explored the methods for cultural opposition in the socialist era (cc. 1950–1990), highlighting the variety of alternative cultural scenes that flourished in Eastern Europe before 1989. We describe our methods and results in discovering common entities in the two datasets, and our solution for automating this task. Furthermore, it is shown how it was possible to enrich the data in Wikidata and to establish new, bi-directional connections between COURAGE and Wikidata. Hence, the audience of both databases will have a more complete view of the matched entities.

Keywords: Linked data · Cultural heritage · Wikidata · Link discovery · Link disambiguation

1 Introduction

The COURAGE (Cultural Opposition: Understanding the CultuRal HeritAGE of Dissent in the Former Socialist Countries) project explored the methods for cultural opposition in the socialist era (cc. 1950–1990) [1]. One of the project goals was to highlight the variety of alternative cultural scenes that flourished in Eastern Europe before 1989 in spite of rigorous government control. The project has compiled a registry of historic collections, people, groups, events and sample collection items stored in an RDF triple store. The registry is available online and has been used to create virtual and real exhibitions and learning material. It is also planned to serve as a basis for further narratives and digital humanities (DH) research [2]. The main entities of the COURAGE dataset are:

- Collections, the main focus of the research;
- Interviews with key persons of collections;
- People, groups, and organizations playing an important role in the history of the collection, for example, owners, founders, operators, collectors;

E. Garoufallou et al. (Eds.): MTSR 2019, CCIS 1057, pp. 407–418, 2019.
https://doi.org/10.1007/978-3-030-36599-8_37

- Some major events in the history of collections;
- Featured items from each collection.

The registry schema is called the COURAGE Ontology, which contains cca. 100 classes, 220 object properties, and 170 data properties [3].

Wikidata is the main storage for structured data which is related to Wikipedia, Wikisource, and others [4] thus it creates new ways for managing Wiki* data on a global scale [5]. This data is freely available online, regularly updated by volunteers worldwide and is extremely correlated and connected to other datasets. The most important advantage of using Wikidata is linking datasets with appropriate relationships that can be understandable by humans and machines.

According to the recent statistics, Wikidata contains more than 57 million entities. They have approximately 718 million statements, and over 800 million labels and descriptions which are available in 350 languages or more [6].

The production of Linked Data is growing massively these days, but the linking between these datasets needs to be improved. Typically, the following anomalies exist in the linked data world: different entities describe the same individual in different datasets, or similar statements are described differently in different datasets. The closer we get in the elimination of these anomalies, the more complete knowledge we can serve to users.

Currently, both Europeana and Wikidata collect cultural heritage (CH) data extensively. Wikidata had a campaign dedicated to collecting cultural heritage data [7]. Europeana is about digital cultural heritage in general, including metadata, illustrations, narratives, and many other aspects. Europeana data providers are encouraged to use Wikidata as a source for enriching data and to connect their vocabularies to Wikidata [8].

Following this guideline, the current paper aims to connect Wikidata and COURAGE datasets. We found that the overlapping set of resources is mostly of the types: person, group and organization, so our investigations were based on these entity classes. The research questions we address include:

- How safely can we identify matching entities in Wikidata and COURAGE?
- How can we extend Wikidata and COURAGE so that the audience of both databases gets more facts about matched entities?

The remainder of the paper is organized as follows: Sect. 2 surveys the link discovery tools and entity resolution approaches which are related to our research. Section 3 describes preliminary statistics, the requirements for the matching approach and how the matching process was carried out. Section 3 also discusses the results generated by the matching algorithm. Extending Wikidata after determining the injected properties and generating the triples file are presented in Sect. 4. Finally, we conclude the paper in Sect. 5.

2   Related Work

Wikidata was established to become a multilingual and global database which contains the entire cultural heritage data for data integration and data management. Moreover, they also aimed to become a focal point for interconnecting heritage collections and providing links to other external data sources [9, 10].

One of the main ideas about the web of data besides representing data to be understandable by a machine is to set relationships between entities across knowledge bases. These relationships may be determined automatically using link discovery tools.

There are quite a few link discovery tools mentioned in [11], but most of them seem abandoned for 3 or more years. Silk was the first link discovery tool for finding links between entities and it provides a language to specify the link types which should be discovered between datasets [12]. Silk and LIMES support more link types than other tools which just determine owl:sameAs and they provide a GUI for an interactive use [13]. KNOFUSS just supports owl:sameAs link type and string similarity approach [14]. SERIMI takes input only from SPARQL endpoints as it does not support RDF input. It is restricted to one property for matching and the thresholds must be manually determined. We tried to use some of these tools for our link discovery task, but without any success. We got farthest with LIMES, but still, it was not able to find any links applying either acceptance conditions or unsupervised learning. We think the reason for this was that Wikidata has millions of entities and querying these often results in time-out. Moreover, using the previously mentioned tools usually requires an acceptance threshold for matching, and finding the optimal threshold value requires an iterative method similar to ours.

Mix'n'match is a tool developed by Magnus Manske to let the user match entities with Wikidata ones [15]. We tried to use the tool with organization entities but unfortunately, the outcomes were not really useful (see Fig. 1). 3% of the entities were automatically matched with many false positive cases and 87.9% of the entities were unmatched. This happened partly because the sought entity did not exist in Wikidata, and partly because the search method of the tool did not find an unambiguous match.

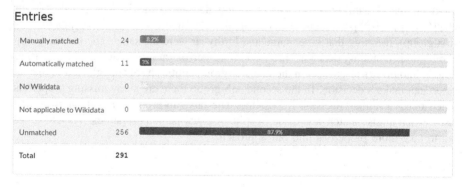

Fig. 1. Organization matching results using Mix'n'match tool

In [16] authors manage ambiguity in VIAF by clustering similar authorities and analyzing these clusters (or subgraphs). On the other hand, COURAGE and Wikidata have a very low number of duplicates, and we had to select a single best matching entity as a result. Another similar name disambiguation problem is handled in [17], but only the names are used for matching.

3 Matching Individuals

COURAGE has a scope limited in both time and region, but the entity data were created by historians with thorough quality control. The entity descriptions are available in at least two languages and they may be quite lengthy. On the contrary, Wikidata entity descriptions are typically 1–2 lines of length, while Wikipedia pages may be 1–3 times longer than COURAGE pages about the same entity.

Wikidata lacks the contribution types and roles of people in various cultural groups and collections. Basic properties such as birthplace, gender, profession, etc. are sometimes more precise in one entity than in the other. This creates a delicate situation both when matching individuals and when trying to complement the data in one dataset based on the other.

A Person entity in Wikidata is addressed by an opaque item identifier which starts with "Q" and a number. This entity is also presented in a page which consists of these main parts: label, description, a set of aliases, a set of statements and a set of external links [9]. The set of statements usually includes instance of, image, given name, family name, birthdate and birthplace properties.

In COURAGE, the Person entity also has a unique identifier and a list of statements. Person properties include given name, family name, year of birth, birthplace, profession and some other personal data.

Person and Organization Preliminary Statistics. For our investigations, we collected 1218 person entities with 3 properties: name, type, and birthyear from COURAGE. We performed a simple search based on these properties to find all possible Wikidata entities. After this, we classified the matched pairs into two groups based on the possibility of a clear matching decision (Fig. 2). We found that for 63.21% of matched person entities the matching decision can be made unambiguously (first group), meaning that type, name and birthyear were the same. The second group "Ambiguous matching decision" has 36.79% of person entities which could be further divided into three sub-groups. In the first sub-group entities have enough data so that an expert can make a decision. In the second sub-group there are many missing properties which make a human decision impossible. The last sub-group is about false-positive cases, when a false match was made in spite of equal person properties. Therefore, we had to take more properties into our approach.

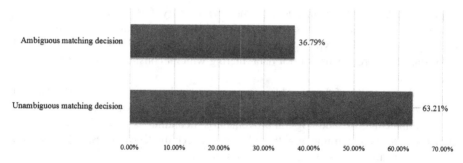

Fig. 2. Person results classification based on matching decision

For example, "Gerhard Ortinau" (Q101211) is a person entity which belongs to the first group where all specified properties exist and that made the matching decision clear. "Dragoş Petrescu" (Q18545324) belongs to the first subgroup in the second group where the birthdate property value was missing, still an expert may be able to make the matching decision based on other properties. The "Ion Dumitru" (Q23309144) entity is also in the second group since the human matching decision was ambiguous due to missing critical data in the coupled Wikidata and COURAGE entities. "Patti Smith" (Q27582022) is an example of the false positive matches. This entity was matched based on the same name and birthyear, but it turned out that it was not the same person as the birthplace was different.

As for organization entities in Wikidata and COURAGE, we used 4 properties for matching: name, type, country, and GPS. The statistics, which were calculated for 457 organizations in COURAGE, state that 58.84% of organization entity pairs belong to the first group where a matching decision could be made unambiguously. Consequently, 41.16% of the entities were in the second group (Fig. 3).

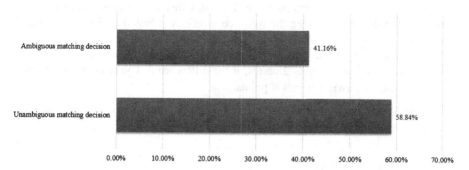

Fig. 3. Organizations results classification based on matching decision

3.1 Metrics for Similarity

After analyzing the data regarding people and organizations, we set up many suitable characteristics to identify them, such as name, type, location, birthdate, founding year, etc. Unfortunately, not all of these properties exist in both Wikidata and COURAGE datasets. Therefore, we considered two basic sets of criteria. The first set contains 5 properties that identify organizations: name, city, country, GPS and year of founding. The second set contains 3 keys that identify people: name, birthplace, and birthdate. We assumed that the 'type' property is always correct in both COURAGE and Wikidata. Therefore, we used it for data filtering without considering it as a key in the latter formulas.

In Wikidata, 52% of the possible organization matches missed geocoordinates and 31% missed city location. Furthermore, the year of foundation was unknown for 39%.

Since matching methodology improvement is a continuous process, first we made simple statistics to determine how to find correct matching decisions. Based on several experimental studies a scoring system was introduced to provide points for each candidate entity based on the matching status as below.

The metrics established for matching person entities were:

- Name: we removed the diacritics and checked the results of the comparison: if the name of Wikidata entity is exactly equal to the COURAGE entity name, it gets 4 points, containing the name it gets 2 points, and if the Levenshtein distance was at most 1 it gets 1 point. Otherwise, the comparison of the two names gets 0 points.
- Birthplace: if the birthplace of Wikidata entity exactly equals to the COURAGE entity birthplace, it gets 2 points. If one of the values is missing, the score is 1 point. Otherwise, it gets 0 points.
- Birthdate: if the year in birthdate for Wikidata entity exactly equals to the birthyear of COURAGE entity it gets 2 points, if the difference is 1 year between values it gets 1 point. Otherwise, it gets 0 points.

The metrics for matching organizations were:

- Name: similarly to persons' names.
- City and Country: if the city properties and country properties exactly equal, it gets 4 points. if just the city properties are exactly equal, it gets 2 points. If one of the values is missing, the comparison gets 1 point. Otherwise, it gets 0 points.
- GPS: if the distance between the resource locations is less than 1.6 km, it gets 3 points. If it is missing, the comparison gets 1 point. Otherwise, it gets 0 points.
- Year of foundation: if the year of Wikidata entity exactly equals to the COURAGE entity foundation year it gets 2 points, if the difference is 1 year between values it gets 1 point. Otherwise, it gets 0 points.

Regarding the scores approach, the exact equality status and the distance between resource locations may get the most points.

3.2   Matching Algorithm

The aim of our work was to develop and implement a relatively reliable matching process on person and organization entities. There was no human capacity for research of matching individuals one-by-one, and a fully automatic matching also proved to be unfeasible. Therefore, we aimed at detecting the cases where a human decision was needed but at the same time also minimizing the number of such cases.

Approach. A matching algorithm was developed in C# for the previous purpose. Firstly, we executed a SPARQL query via the COURAGE SPARQL endpoint and downloaded organization data keys which are: name, city, country, GPS and founding year. After cleaning this data, we imported it to our database. Next, we ran a C# script for each item to get all possibly related entities from Wikidata based on its type and name containment. In the beginning, we compared the name, type, city, country, GPS and founding year at once. But in order to enhance the performance, we followed sequential steps, by comparing the name and the type as a first step. After which, we moved to compare city and GPS then the country and founding year. For each exact or partial similarity with the 5 keys (name, city, country, GPS and founding year) we provided points in all conditions according to the previous rules. The number of Wikidata candidates for COURAGE entities was between 1 and 6. The previous five key points with their weights produced a total score for the match:

$$wo1 * namePoints + wo2 * cityPoints + wo3 * countryPoints + wo4 * GPSPoints + wo5 * foundingYearPoints = totalScore$$

$$(1)$$

Secondly, we downloaded person data keys which are: name, birthplace, and birthyear from COURAGE dataset. Similarly to organizations, we executed a SPARQL query and applied the same methodology on this data. The total score was calculated as:

$$wp1 * namePoints + wp2 * birthPlacePoints + wp3 * birthdatePoints = totalScore$$

$$(2)$$

During the matching algorithm, points were assigned to each metric in each matched pair and thus a matrix of matching points was built. Based on this matrix, weighted matching scores (*totalScore*) were calculated for each matched pair in the sample.

To determine the best weights two random sample sets were created with 300 matched pairs for persons and 50 matched pairs for organizations. Each pair was manually checked as matching or non-matching. Next, the scores were calculated in the sample sets for all possible weights between [0, 2] with a step increment of 0.1. After this, various indicator values for the goodness of the weights were calculated: the lower threshold *Tlo* is the largest *totalScore* value below which only non-matching pairs will be seen in this sample. The upper threshold *Tup* is the smallest *totalScore* value above which only matching pairs will be seen. Between *Tlo* and *Tup*, one finds the ambiguous pairs, which we called the human decision window. The least number of items in the window (*windowSize*) is the best. The *minError* count is generated for each threshold in the sample based on how many cases are below this threshold but they are matched, and above the threshold but are not matched. Finally, we calculated the minimum threshold *Tmin* at which the number of error cases (*minError*) is the lowest.

Findings and Results. The results of all the prior calculations indicated that the foundation year of organizations is not an important property, because whatever the weights were, we got the same size for the human decision window. Consequently, we could eliminate it from the properties list before applying the matching process on all the data.

414   G. Faraj and A. Micsik

Overall, we took the person and organization weights related to the least items in the human decision window and applied these weights and thresholds on the entire person and organization entities respectively. After which, we checked 50 random entities from the matched cases and also 50 random entities from not matched cases without facing any incorrect decision. We also checked manually the cases inside the window. The statistics of the result showed that 78.64% of person entities and 80.5% of organization entities could be safely matched automatically with Wikidata entities.

The person outcomes state that the human decision window has more than one value for the *Tlo* and the *Tup*. However, the *windowSize* inside this window is 121 (Table 1).

Table 1. Threshold calculations for matching persons

Tlo	Tup	windowSize	wName	wPlace	wYear
4.4	6.1	121	0.8	1.3	1.4
5	6.9	121	0.9	1.5	1.6
5.5	7.5	121	1	1.6	1.7
5.5	7.7	121	1	1.6	1.8
5.6	7.7	121	1	1.7	1.8

On the other hand, the organization matching result (Table 2) shows that the *Tlo* of human decision window is 9.2 and the *Tup* is 13.1. The *windowSize* is 51 (for the whole set). Consequently, the corresponding weights *wCity*, *wCountry*, *wGPS*, and *wName* values are the best weights among all weight sets.

Table 2. Threshold calculation for matching organizations

Tlo	Tup	windowSize	wCity	wCountry	wGPS	wName
9.2	13.1	51	1.9	1.8	2	1.8

4 Establishing Connections

As a next step, a list of transferable properties has been set up and triples to extend Wikidata have been compiled. We created a table of matching properties in COURAGE and Wikidata. These properties can be grouped into two categories for each entity type: properties used for matching and new properties.

First, we gathered the common properties between people and organizations to avoid duplication as shown in Table 3. Regarding other properties, they are displayed in the tables (Tables 4 and 5) below.

Table 3. General properties for both persons and organizations

Courage	Wikidata	
public#mainImage	P18/P154	Image/logo image
courage.owl#website	P856	Official website
courage.owl#place	P276	Location
Item Courage URI	P973	Described at URL

Table 4. Properties matched for person data

Courage	Wikidata	
courage.owl#hasGivenName	P735	Given name
courage.owl#hasFamilyName	P734	Family name
courage.owl#birthDate	P569	date of birth
courage.owl#birthPlace	P19	Birth Place
courage.owl#deathDate	P570	Date of death
courage:hasNickName	P1449	Nickname
courage:hasSex	P21	Sex or gender
courage:memberOf	P463	Member of
courage:ownerOf	P1830	Owner of
courage:hasCreatorRole	P6379	Has works in the collection(s)
courage:creatorOf	P170	Inverse of creator

Table 5. Properties matched for organization data

Courage	Wikidata	
courage. owl#yearOfFunding	P571	Inception
courage.owl#country	P17	Country
courage.owl#city	P131/P159	Located in the administrative territorial entity/headquarters location
courage.owl#lat, courage.owl#long	P625	Coordinate location
courage.owl#instType	P31	Instance of
courage. owl#ownerRoleOf	P1830	Owner of
courage.owl#leader	P488/P1037	Chairperson/director or manager
courage. owl#operatorRoleOf	P126	Maintained by

Based on the final transferable properties list, we generated triples in the format of the QuickStatements tool, which allows the bulk addition of Wikidata items [18]. For the implementation, an algorithm was established to generate a file which contained the needed triples to do this extension. The file has 1765 statements for person and organization entities. For person entities, we enriched 385 Wikidata entities successfully (Table 6).

Table 6. Sample of person properties in the generated file

Item	Property	Value	Source property	
Q112688	P734	Q2168571	S248	Q64784883
Q112688	P973	"http://courage.btk.mta.hu/courage/individual/n13144"		
Q112688	P1830	"http://courage.btk.mta.hu/courage/individual/n25127"	S248	Q64784883

While for organization entities we enriched 143 Wikidata entities (Table 7).

Table 7. Sample of organizations properties in the generated file

Item	Property	Value	Source property	
Q11179076	P276	Q1085		
Q11179076	P973	"http://courage.btk.mta.hu/courage/individual/n100194"	S248	Q64784883
Q11179076	P571	+1949-01-01T00:00:00Z/9	S248	Q64784883
Q11179076	P625	@50.0755381/14.4378005	S248	Q64784883

We also generated another file with different syntax to create new entities (Table 8).

Table 8. Sample of creating a new entity in the generated file

Statements				
CREATE				
LAST	Len	"Gardzienice Theatre"		
LAST	Lpl	"Teatr Gardzienice"		
LAST	P31	Q43229		
LAST	P973	http://courage.btk.mta.hu/courage/individual/n45835		
LAST	P571	+1977-01-01T00:00:00Z/9	S248	Q64784883
LAST	P131	Q5522662	S248	Q64784883
LAST	P625	@51.110556/22.8586111	S248	Q64784883
LAST	P856	http://gardzienice.org	S248	Q64784883

Our contribution was enriching and linking the person and organization entities as the dashed lines show in Fig. 4. Person and organization Wikidata entities are mapped to COURAGE entities via property P973 (Described at URL). Following this, we also created new person and organization Wikidata entities for non-matched COURAGE entities. Later, when scholars have time, they can create the Wikipedia pages for these new entities.

We found it hard to establish links other than 'has id' between Wikidata and COURAGE entities. For example, the creator and 'has works in collection' properties accept only Wikidata entities as an object. Thus, it was impossible to direct Wikidata readers' attention to artifacts authored by a person. Similarly, we could not refer to roles (owner, operator, supporter, etc.) taken by persons or groups at collections in the COURAGE registry. However, we could create member and leader links between persons and groups as they were all in Wikidata after our data injection.

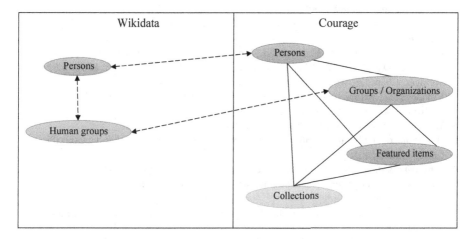

Fig. 4. Main connections inside COURAGE and with Wikidata

5   Conclusion

Our aim was to connect the linked data registry of COURAGE into a broader linked data context, for which Wikidata seemed to be the ideal candidate. The COURAGE project made an extensive research on the cultural heritage of former European socialist countries, resulting in high quality linked data about available collections on the subject and their surrounding personal networks. The common point of integration was found to be persons, groups and organizations. To match these entities in the two datasets, a score-based method has been shaped, and automated link discovery has been performed successfully on 78% of person entities and 80% of group/organization entities. For the remaining matching candidates, a human decision was needed in order to maintain the good quality of links between the datasets.

As a result, matched entities have links to the corresponding Wikidata entity in the COURAGE registry, and Wikidata users may choose to navigate to matched COURAGE entities for more information. On the other hand, the link to Wikidata on the COURAGE side provides access to many other authority IDs (e.g. VIAF, IMDB) collected in Wikidata. Furthermore, Wikidata has been enriched with data present in COURAGE registry, including official websites and connections between persons and organizations. In the future, the insertion of collections and artifacts to Wikidata may give further benefits for Wikidata users, even if these entities are for a quite specialized interest at the moment, as only a minimal number of such items exist currently in Wikidata.

Acknowledgement. The project has been supported by the European Union, co-financed by the European Social Fund (EFOP-3.6.3-VEKOP-16-2017-00002).

References

1. COURAGE project. http://cultural-opposition.eu/
2. Apor, B., Apor, P., Horváth, S. (eds.): The Handbook of COURAGE, Budapest (2018). https://doi.org/10.24389/handbook
3. Micsik, A.: Courage registry - open dataset 1.1, July 2019. https://doi.org/10.5281/zenodo.3333540
4. Erxleben, F., Günther, M., Krötzsch, M., Mendez, J., Vrandečić, D.: Introducing Wikidata to the Linked Data Web. In: Mika, P., et al. (eds.) ISWC 2014. LNCS, vol. 8796, pp. 50–65. Springer, Cham (2014). https://doi.org/10.1007/978-3-319-11964-9_4
5. Vrandečić, D., Krötzsch, M.: Wikidata: a free collaborative knowledgebase. Commun. ACM **57**(10) (2014). https://doi.org/10.1145/2629489
6. Wikidata Statistics. https://www.wikidata.org/wiki/Wikidata:Statistics
7. WikiProject Cultural heritage. https://www.wikidata.org/wiki/Wikidata:WikiProject_Cultural_heritage
8. Why data partners should link their vocabulary to Wikidata: a new case study. Europeana pro page. https://pro.europeana.eu/post/why-data-partners-should-link-their-vocabulary-to-wikidata-a-new-case-study
9. Malyshev, S., Krötzsch, M., González, L., Gonsior, J., Bielefeldt, A.: Getting the most out of Wikidata: semantic technology usage in Wikipedia's knowledge graph. In: Vrandečić, D., et al. (eds.) ISWC 2018. LNCS, vol. 11137, pp. 376–394. Springer, Cham (2018). https://doi.org/10.1007/978-3-030-00668-6_23
10. Allison-Cassin, S., Scott, D.: Wikidata: a platform for your library's linked open data. Code4Lib 40 (2018)
11. Nentwig, M., Hartung, M., Cyrille, A., Ngomo, N., Rahm E.: A survey of current link discovery frameworks. Semant. Web J. **2**(224) (2017). https://doi.org/10.3233/sw-150210
12. Isele, R., Jentzsch, A., Bizer, C.: Efficient multidimensional blocking for link discovery without losing recall. In: 14th International Workshop on the Web and Databases, WebDB, Athens (2011)
13. Ngomo, A.C.N., Auer, S.: LIMES - a time-efficient approach for large-scale link discovery on the web of data. In: IJCAI, pp. 2312–2317 (2011). https://doi.org/10.5591/978-1-57735-516-8/ijcai11-385
14. Nikolov, A., Uren, V., Motta, E.: KnoFuss: a comprehensive architecture for knowledge fusion. In: Proceedings of the 4th International Conference on Knowledge Capture, pp. 185–186. ACM (2007)
15. Mix'n'match Manual Wikimedia. https://meta.wikimedia.org/wiki/Mix%27n%27match/Manual
16. Hickey, T.B., Toves, J.A.: Managing ambiguity in VIAF. D-Lib Mag. **20**(7/8). https://doi.org/10.1045/july2014-hickey
17. Larson, R.R., Janakiraman, K.: Connecting archival collections: the social networks and archival context project. In: Gradmann, S., Borri, F., Meghini, C., Schuldt, H. (eds.) TPDL 2011. LNCS, vol. 6966, pp. 3–14. Springer, Heidelberg (2011). https://doi.org/10.1007/978-3-642-24469-8_3
18. QuickStatements help. https://www.wikidata.org/wiki/Help:QuickStatements

The Data Aggregation Lab Software

Experimentation for Linked Data Aggregation in Cultural Heritage

Nuno Freire[(✉)]

INESC-ID, Lisbon, Portugal
nuno.freire@tecnico.ulisboa.pt

Abstract. This paper describes the Data Aggregation Lab software tool, which implements the metadata aggregation workflow of Cultural Heritage, based on semantic technologies. It aims to provide a framework to support several aspects of our research, such as conducting case studies, provide reference implementations, and support technology adoption. Currently, it provides working implementations of data aggregation methods with which Europeana research has obtained positive results. These methods explore technologies such as linked data, Schema.org, IIIF, Sitemaps and RDF.

Keywords: Linked data · IIIF · Schema.org · Sitemaps · Software

1 Introduction

The data aggregation technologies used in Cultural Heritage (CH) are not widely used in other domains, and they are not the same as those employed by Internet search engines or on the Web of Data. In the CH domain, the common practice is to aggregate metadata using an agreed data model that tackles data heterogeneity between organizations and countries. In the case of Europeana, it is the Europeana Data Model (EDM). The second aspect of CH metadata aggregation is the sharing of the sets of metadata between the providers and the aggregator. The metadata is transferred to the aggregator and has to be periodically updated. This can be described as a data synchronization problem across organizations, and in CH, OAI-PMH is the established solution to address it. Nowadays, however, the motivation for OAI-PMH is low given the wider interoperability possibilities of popular Internet technologies. It is often misunderstood, and its implementations may be unreliable [1]. Internet data technologies provide a new setting that touches both data modelling and data synchronization, and may fulfil the needs of CH.

This paper describes the Data Aggregation Lab software tool (DAL), which implements the metadata aggregation workflow of CH. It provides a framework to support several aspects of our research, such as conducting case studies, provide reference implementations, and support technology adoption. Currently, it provides working implementations of the methods with which we have obtained positive.

E. Garoufallou et al. (Eds.): MTSR 2019, CCIS 1057, pp. 419–424, 2019.
https://doi.org/10.1007/978-3-030-36599-8_38

2 Related Work

Most of the published literature addresses the aspect of the publication of LD (e.g. [2]) and does not fully address the metadata aggregation approach of CH, however. The most similar work to ours is that of the Dutch Digital Heritage Network[1] project (NDE, ongoing) and the Research and Education Space project[2] (RES, 2013–2017). Technical solutions have been proposed by others, e.g. [3]. However, a standards-based approach has not yet been put into practice in CH.

3 The Data Aggregation Lab

In our context, a solution must fulfil the same functional requirements as the current aggregation solution of Europeana and to be based on standards supported by very wide usage. DAL implements a general workflow focusing on the aggregator role.

3.1 The Metadata Aggregation Workflow

In the scope of DAL, the aggregation workflow starts after a data provider has published its metadata. The activities of the workflow are comprised by data analysis and processing steps performed by data providers and aggregators. DAL provides the system to support such workflow and provides several implementations for the different steps, in some cases with alternative technological solutions. DAL's role in the workflow ends with the preparation of a dataset export to provide to the regular data ingestion and integration systems of the aggregator. Our workflow may vary slightly depending on the technology in use, but in general it consists of 7 main steps (Fig. 1):

1. Publish dataset and dataset description - The data provider creates a RDF resource describing the dataset. It contains descriptive information about the CH content covered by the dataset and technical details about how the dataset can be harvested.
2. Register dataset URI - The provider notifies the aggregator of the availability of its dataset for aggregation by providing the URI of the RDF resource created in step 1.
3. Harvest dataset - The dataset is harvested by DAL, applying the harvesting mechanism specified in step 1.
4. Profile dataset - The harvested dataset is profiled by the aggregator supported by data analysis tools. These tools analyse aspects of the dataset that are important to integrate it into the aggregator's central dataset. It allows the aggregator to detect deficiencies in the dataset (which are to be communicated to the data provider) and to assess the effort and specific tasks required for the following steps.
5. Align data model and vocabularies - The aggregator aligns the data model and vocabularies used in the data provider's dataset with EDM. This task is supported by information gathered during the profiling of the dataset and by software to support the aggregator in the alignment.

---

[1] https://github.com/netwerk-digitaal-erfgoed/.

[2] https://bbcarchdev.github.io/res/.

6. Convert dataset - The dataset is converted to EDM and the result is verified.
7. Integrate dataset - DAL interacts with the regular data ingestion and integration systems of the aggregator and provides the converted dataset.

3.2   The Aggregation Technologies

This section presents the most relevant methods for metadata aggregation implemented in DAL and the key technologies it uses for data management and processing.

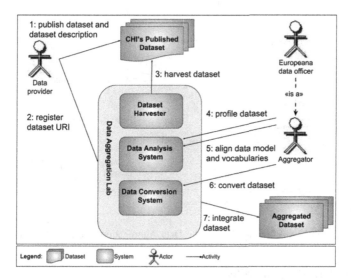

Fig. 1. High-level workflow for cultural heritage metadata aggregation.

3.2.1   IIIF

IIIF is a family of specifications that were conceived to facilitate systematic reuse of image resources in digital repositories maintained by CH institutions. It specifies several HTTP based web services [4] covering access to images, the presentation and structure of complex digital objects composed of one or more images and searching within their content. IIIF's strength resides in the presentation possibilities it provides for end-users. From the perspective of metadata aggregation, however, none of the released IIIF APIs was specifically designed to support it. The aggregation use case is nowadays being addressed by the IIIF community, resulting in the IIIF Change Discovery API, which is a work in progress, currently in its version 0.3. Nevertheless, within the output given by the IIIF APIs, there may exist enough information to allow HTTP robots to crawl IIIF endpoints and harvest the links to the digital resources and associated metadata.

DAL's implementation of harvesting IIIF sources is shown in Fig. 2. It includes a reference implementation of the IIIF Change Discovery API v0.3, and implementations of two methods from our earlier work using IIIF Collection or Sitemaps [4]. In DAL's workflow, the harvesting of IIIF sources is split in two phases: in the 1st phase, the IIIF presentation information is harvested (IIIF Manifest), from where the references to metadata are identified; the 2nd phase harvests the actual metadata required by the aggregator.

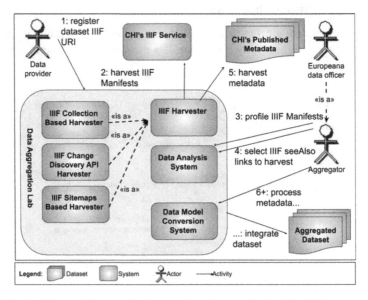

Fig. 2. The workflow applied in the Data Aggregation Lab for IIIF sources.

3.2.2   Web Crawling and Sitemaps

Sitemaps allow webmasters to inform search engines about pages on their sites that are available for crawling by search engines robots. Moreover, there are Sitemaps extensions, like Google's Image Sitemaps and Video Sitemaps, which have potential usage in metadata aggregation. DAL implements harvesting guided by Sitemaps and can apply it to IIIF sources and for Web crawling. Web crawling can be applied to the websites of digital libraries that contain structured metadata available through the HTML, either using micro data formats or references to JSON-LD and other serializations of RDF data.

3.2.3   Linked Data

Harvesting of linked data sources is supported in DAL. In this kind of data sources, it is required that the data provider indicates which RDF resources are part of the dataset for aggregation, since providers that publish linked data, typically have additional data published for other purposes. We have prepared guidelines for describing datasets for aggregation by Europeana, which include the specification of downloadable distributions, with the technical details about how the datasets can be harvested. The Europeana guidelines allow the usage of three standard vocabularies for describing datasets [5], whose key aspects for harvesting and aggregation are shown in Table 1.

Table 1. The most relevant classes and properties for describing datasets and their distributions.

Requirement	DCAT	Schema.org	VoID
Class for dataset	dcat:Dataset	schema:Dataset	void:Dataset
Title of the dataset	dcterms:title	schema:title	dcterms:title
Class for distribution	dcat:Distribution (linked with dcat: distribution)	schema: DataDownload (linked with schema: distribution)	No Distribution class. These are referenced using properties of the dataset
Dataset license	dcterms:license	schema:license	dcterms:license
Downloadable distribution	dcat:downloadURL, dcat:mediaType	schema:contentUrl, schema: encodingFormat	void:dataDump, void: feature, void: TechnicalFeature
Listing of URIs	Not supported	Not supported	void:rootResource

Namespace abbreviations used in this table: dcat = "http://www.w3.org/ns/dcat"; schema = "http://schema.org/"; void = "http://rdfs.org/ns/void#"; dcterms = "http://purl.org/dc/terms/"

3.2.4   Schema.org

Schema.org is a vocabulary developed for encouraging the publication and consumption of structured data in the Internet. Schema.org is relevant for us as it was the only Web technology we have identified, which could fulfil the requirements of the Europeana aggregation for data modelling and representation. Europeana has researched Schema.org in several aspects related to CH, notably in evaluating its usage in CH institutions [6]. DAL has extensive functionality based on Schema.org, allowing it to be harvested via any of the implemented methods, and with adapted data processing functionality, such as data profiling and data alignment with EDM.

3.2.5   RDF

A conclusion from our past studies is that the functionalities provided by DAL to data analysts need to be specialized for working within the semantic context of linked data.

The data profiling functionality in DAL is adapted to RDF data, supporting the aggregator in getting a view of the data model of the dataset. It reports statistics on the usage of classes and properties as subject, object or predicate of the RDF statements in the dataset.

The definition and maintenance of data model mappings is a key aspect for sustainable aggregation of RDF data. We are researching machine-actionable specifications of detailed mappings between models, based on the characteristics of RDF. Currently, DAL applies the conversions between Schema.org and EDM that CH data experts have prepared with us in past work. We represented the conversions as machine-actionable specifications, which allow DAL to trace the mapping and data manipulations affecting specific RDF properties and classes. When aggregators analyse the data model of a dataset, they can detect which classes and properties require attention for defining conversions. This, in conjunction with the data profiling reports, intends to help the aggregators to perform the data conversion tasks more efficiently.

4 Conclusion and Future Work

DAL is a software application that has been supporting our research in the research of metadata aggregation in CH, based on sematic technologies. At its current stage, DAL is starting to facilitate the work on technology adoption by Europeana and CH data providers by allowing the potential users to experiment with the new methods (for example the professionals responsible for metadata ingestion in Europeana) and providing an open source implementation of the methods for reuse by participants of CH aggregation networks. Future work on DAL will be guided by the technology adoption within the Europeana network. The actual adoption of IIIF and Schema.org are already taking their first steps in Europeana. Linked data aggregation has already been successfully tested throughout the complete ingestion workflow of Europeana, resulting in successful ingestion of three datasets in the production Europeana dataset. Finally, a larger scale pilot on linked data has recently started.

Acknowledgements. This work was partly supported by Portuguese national funds through Fundação para a Ciência e a Tecnologia (FCT) with reference UID/CEC/50021/2019, and by the European Commission under contract number 30-CE-0885387/00-80.e.

References

1. Van de Sompel, H., Nelson, M.L.: Reminiscing about 15 years of interoperability efforts. D-Lib Mag. **21**(11/12) (2015)
2. Simou, N., Chortaras, A., Stamou, G., Kollias, S.: Enriching and publishing cultural heritage as Linked Open Data. In: Ioannides, M., Magnenat-Thalmann, N., Papagiannakis, G. (eds.) Mixed Reality and Gamification for Cultural Heritage, pp. 201–223. Springer, Cham (2017). https://doi.org/10.1007/978-3-319-49607-8_7
3. Vander Sande, M., Verborgh, R., Hochstenbach, P., Van de Sompel, H.: Towards sustainable publishing and querying of distributed Linked Data archives. J. Doc. **74**(1), 195–222 (2018)
4. Freire, N., Robson, G., Howard, J.B., Manguinhas, H., Isaac, A.: Cultural heritage metadata aggregation using web technologies: IIIF, Sitemaps and Schema.org. Int. J. Digit. Libr. (2018)
5. Freire, N., Meijers, E., Voorburg, R., Cornelissen, R., Isaac, A., de Valk, S.: Aggregation of Linked Data: a case study in the cultural heritage domain. In: 2018 IEEE International Conference on Big Data (Big Data). IEEE (2018)
6. Freire, N., Charles, V., Isaac, A.: Evaluation of Schema.org for aggregation of cultural heritage metadata. In: Gangemi, A., et al. (eds.) ESWC 2018. LNCS, vol. 10843, pp. 225–239. Springer, Cham (2018). https://doi.org/10.1007/978-3-319-93417-4_15

Sinopia: A New Linked-Data Editing Environment Designed for Libraries

Philip E. Schreur$^{(\boxtimes)}$

Stanford University, Stanford, CA 94305, USA
pschreur@stanford.edu

Abstract. Linked Data for Production (LD4P): Pathway to Implementation is a grant funded by the Mellon Foundation to begin the implementation of the cataloging community's shift to linked data for the creation and manipulation of their metadata. Although LD4P has seven overarching goals, the heart of the project will be the creation of a cloud-based, communal editing environment called Sinopia. Sinopia will support the efforts of a cohort of academic libraries in the creation and reuse of their resource metadata as linked data structured according to the BIBFRAME ontology. And by making use of another service created by the grant called Questioning Authority (QA), cohort members will be able to bring in additional identifiers for entities contained in data stores such as the RDA Vocabularies or Wikidata. The initial release of Sinopia will be in July of 2019 with a final release due at the close of the grant in June of 2020.

Keywords: Cataloging · Linked Data · Sinopia

1 Introduction

Linked Data for Production (LD4P) is focused on the transition of basic Technical Services workflows from their current infrastructure built upon a 1960's communication format called Machine Readable Cataloging (MARC) [1] to linked open data and the Web. The second phase of LD4P, called Pathway to Implementation [2], moves from experimentation to implementation. Building upon the expertise, structure, and workflows developed during the first phase of LD4P, the four partners (Cornell, Harvard, Stanford, and the University of Iowa) are implementing a prototype environment, from metadata acquisition/creation through to discovery. An important enhancement in this phase is collaboration with the Program for Cooperative Cataloging (PCC) [3] and the Library of Congress to expand the number of libraries moving to implementation of linked data.

The choice of working with the PCC was deliberate. Within the United States, libraries work within the concept of a virtual, distributed "national library" for the creation of high-level metadata. The PCC provides the community with a forum for the development of policy and training programs for member libraries. The full buy-in of the PCC, along with their ability to provide training and support, is key to expanding the transition to linked data from the core libraries within LD4P to the broader academic library community.

E. Garoufallou et al. (Eds.): MTSR 2019, CCIS 1057, pp. 425–430, 2019.
https://doi.org/10.1007/978-3-030-36599-8_39

The heart of the project will be the development of a cloud-based linked-data editing environment called Sinopia.

2 Previous Work

There are other linked data editors in existence of which libraries can make use. Callimachus [4] is a mature editing platform making use of RDFa as a templating format in a web browser environment. Its focus, however, is on the domains of government, healthcare, pharmaceuticals, publishing, and research. The special needs of catalogers as to data structures and formatting are not addressed.

Graphity [5] (now Atomgraph) also has potential and has started an extension making use of the ontology needed by the library community, BIBFRAME [6]. However, it also has difficulty in dealing with the complex structural forms of library data.

CEDAR (Center for Expanded Data Annotation and Retrieval) [7] is a recent development by the bioinformatics community. It wishes to be an essential component of Open Science and to ensure FAIR data [8]. It too, however, has difficulty with the complexities of library data structures, cataloging rules, and graded levels of trust in data sources.

In the end, the LD4P development team decided to build upon a prototype editor developed by the Library of Congress called the LC BIBFRAME Editor. The LC BIBFRAME editor was designed to handle the complexities of bibliographic data but was never meant to be a production level system. It was also designed to meet the needs of LC. But with the LC editor as a core, the developers could expand the editor to become a truly communal editing environment that could fulfill the needs of the library community

3 Sinopia

Sinopia is the dark reddish-brown pigment used to create the preliminary sketch found on a layer of its own on the wall underneath a fresco. It's not the final image, or in our case, work environment, but it gives a very clear idea of where we are headed.

Sinopia is being developed to support four main goals of the grant:

1. The creation of a continuously fed pool of linked data expressed in BIBFRAME-based application profiles.
2. The development of an expanded cohort of libraries (the LD4P Cohort) capable of the creation and reuse of linked data through the creation of a cloud-based sandbox editing environment called Sinopia.
3. The development of policies, techniques, and workflows for the creation and reuse of linked data and its supporting identifiers as libraries' core metadata.
4. Better integration of library metadata and identifiers with the Web through collaboration with Wikidata.

These goals will be considered fulfilled if LD4P Cohort members can produce original metadata as linked data with links to external identifiers in support of internal entities, export the data they create to their discovery system of choice, develop use cases for future developments, and develop best practices to help others make this transition from MARC to linked data.

3.1 Sinopia Development

Sinopia is designed to be open source with all code available on GitHub [9]. The Sinopia wiki [10] keeps members of the LD4P Cohort up-to-date on where development is at any given point. The User Interface page [11] includes instructions on how to make use of the editor as it develops.

Development is planned in five milestones to be completed by June of 2019. Milestone 1 centered on the completion and testing of the Profile Editor. The Profile Editor allows a cataloger to develop and save a metadata profile for each format they wish to catalog (e.g., book, video recording, sound recording, computer file). The profiles are a prerequisite to any further work in Sinopia. Milestone 2 allowed a cataloger to load a profile they created into the bibliographic editor, enter data, and view the data they entered. It also allowed a cataloger to import bibliographic data from source files into the editor for viewing purposes only. Milestone 3 develops the capability for catalogers to log in with their own credentials, allowing for the capability to track responsibility for profile and metadata creation. This milestone also develops the capability for group log in. Milestone 4 focuses on URI minting capabilities for each entry created in Sinopia, including deference support. Also, via the Questioning Authorities application development, this milestone will allow catalogers to link to existing entities created by LD4P Cohort members within Sinopia and to a limited number of external sources such as Wikidata. Milestone 5 allows a cataloger to create new bibliographic data by deriving from existing data. Data export will also be available at this stage.

3.2 Developmental Complications

The development of the Sinopia editing environment has not been without complications, some political and some structural. Although catalogers, and cataloging agencies, survive by making use of metadata created by others, that metadata must be created according to the same standard so that the metadata can be reused with little or no revision. These standards are both well understood and enforceable in a MARC environment in which data creation, and trust, can be ascribed to a particular institution or association such as the PCC. The Web, and the Resource Description Framework (RDF), are much more flexible. Catalogers may make use of different ontologies to best capture their data needs (BIBFRAME, schema.org, etc.) and the cataloging standard, Resource Description and Access (RDA) [12], can be expressed in different ways in the different ontologies. As the cataloging standards body for the United States, the PCC must establish the policies to which their members will adhere. But policy development can be a difficult and lengthy process. In the meantime, Sinopia members must establish their own best practices, such as bibliographic profiles, until more authoritative standards can be developed.

In addition, there have been technical complications as well. Key to development of Sinopia was the ability to work in a shared Web environment. Because of this decision, the development team decided to work with Amazon Web services, a less familiar environment.

A further complication is that the Sinopia environment is built upon a preexisting editor developed by the Library of Congress called the BIBFRAME Editor. The BIBFRAME Editor has been optimized for work at the Library of Congress creating the need to genericize the approach for a multi-institution, open Web environment. These parallel development efforts require close coordination to ensure that any benefits are available to both teams. A Minimum Viable Product (MVP) will be available to the Cohort members by the end of July, 2019. The ability to derive and export data will be deferred to a future development cycle.

3.3   Sinopia Interface

The Sinopia editor allows data to be input/edited in two main areas following the definitions of data construction according to RDA. The first area is the Work (see Fig. 1).

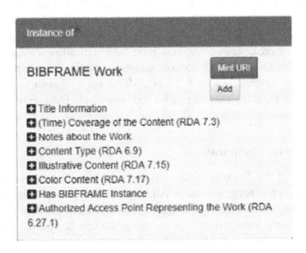

Fig. 1. BIBFRAME work editor.

The BIBFRAME Work is an amalgam of Work (a distinct intellectual or artistic creation) and Expression (a specific intellectual or artistic form that a work takes when it is realized) as defined by the conceptual model of the Functional Requirements for Bibliographic Records (FRBR) [13]. The editor allows the cataloger to enter specific data required for the description of a BIBFRAME work and links the field to cataloging rules (RDA) so that the cataloger can read the definition of what should be included in that particular element. It also allows the cataloger to add a link to the BIBFRAME Instance (see Fig. 2).

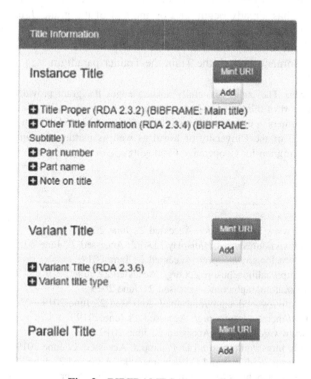

Fig. 2. BIBFRAME Instance editor.

The BIBFRAME Instance is equivalent to the FRBR Manifestation (the physical embodiment of the FRBR Work/Expression); that is, the item in hand to be cataloged. As is the case with the BIBFRAME Work, the editor allows the cataloger to enter data appropriate to the Instance with links to the cataloging rules relevant to the particular element. Data created by any member of the Cohort will be available for others in the group to use.

4 Conclusion

Libraries' transition to the Semantic Web will be key to their long term survival. Patrons are already engaging with the Web for their discovery needs and library data is often not represented there as it is encoded in a format developed in the 1960s and used exclusively by libraries and their vendors. The Library of Congress has developed an ontology called BIBFRAME which captures library data as linked data and can help the community move beyond the confines of the MARC formats. However, a new editing environment, tailored to the needs of libraries, is required before libraries can fully transition to linked data and the Semantic Web. LD4P, a Mellon-funded project, is developing such an environment called Sinopia. The Sinopia editor as a MVP will be available to members of the LD4P Cohort by the end of July 2019. Training in the use of the new editor has already begun and by the end of the grant (June 2020) Cohort members should be fully trained and a training program firmly established. The PCC and members of the Cohort will then be able to expand the circle of libraries making use of this environment through the Train-the-Trainer paradigm.

Acknowledgements. The author gratefully acknowledges the grant provided by the Mellon Foundation in support of this project. The author also acknowledges the essential development work of the four partners in the grant (Cornell, Harvard, Stanford, and the School of Library and Information Science of the University of Iowa) as well as partnerships with the Library of Congress and the Program for Cooperative Cataloging

References

1. MARC. https://www.loc.gov/marc/. Accessed 22 June 2019
2. LD4P2. https://wiki.duraspace.org/display/LD4P2. Accessed 22 June 2019
3. PCC. https://www.loc.gov/aba/pcc/. Accessed 22 June 2019
4. Callimachus. http://callimachusproject.org/. Accessed 22 June 2019
5. Graphity, https://atomgraph.com/. Accessed 22 June 2019
6. BIBFRAME. http://www.loc.gov/bibframe/. Accessed 22 June 2019
7. CEDAR. https://metadatacenter.org/. Accessed 22 June 2019
8. FAIR. https://www.go-fair.org/. Accessed 22 June 2019
9. Sinopia Github. https://github.com/LD4P/sinopia. Accessed 22 June 2019
10. Sinopia Wiki. https://github.com/LD4P/sinopia/wiki. Accessed 22 June 2019
11. Sinopia User Interface. https://ld4p.github.io/code4lib_2019/user-interface#part-one. Accessed 22 June 2019
12. RDA. http://www.rda-rsc.org/content/about-rda. Accessed 22 June 2019
13. FRBR. https://www.ifla.org/book/export/html/8914. Accessed 22 June 2019

Title Matching for Finding Identical Metadata Records in Different Languages

Yuting Song[1]([⊠]) , Biligsaikhan Batjargal[2] , and Akira Maeda[3]

[1] Research Organization of Science and Technology,
Ritsumeikan University, Kusatsu, Japan
ytsong@gst.ritsumei.ac.jp
[2] Kinugasa Research Organization, Ritsumeikan University, Kyoto, Japan
biligee@fc.ritsumei.ac.jp
[3] College of Information Science and Engineering,
Ritsumeikan University, Kusatsu, Japan
amaeda@is.ritsumei.ac.jp

Abstract. This paper proposes a title matching method for finding identical metadata records from multiple databases in different languages. To overcome the language barriers, we represent words in titles in different languages by using bilingual word embeddings that allow word similarities to be measured across languages. The proposed method can be used to link or integrate databases in different languages. We evaluate our proposed method's effectiveness on the Japanese and English ukiyo-e print databases. We also compare the performance of our method with a method that relies on machine translation.

Keywords: Title matching · Digital cultural collections · Cross-language record linkage

1 Introduction

Many cultural institutions (e.g. libraries, museums, archives, etc.) have built large digital collections to preserve art and culture and provide worldwide online access. Most of the digital objects in these collections are organized and described by metadata in their nation's local languages. This means that identical objects may exist in different digital collections with metadata in different languages. For example, ukiyo-e, a type of Japanese traditional woodblock print, have been digitized by many libraries and museums around the world, and identical ukiyo-e prints are exhibited on the internet with metadata in different languages, as shown in Fig. 1.

Fig. 1. Examples of ukiyo-e metadata records from the Edo-Tokyo Museum (left) and the Metropolitan Museum of Art (right).

E. Garoufallou et al. (Eds.): MTSR 2019, CCIS 1057, pp. 431–437, 2019.
https://doi.org/10.1007/978-3-030-36599-8_40

The task of finding identical metadata records, so-called record linkage, is an important step in integrating data from different sources or comparing data to improve metadata quality. Finding identical metadata records requires comparison of metadata values. This task is challenging in cross-lingual settings because metadata is in different languages. To overcome the language barriers, a naive solution employs machine translation (MT) to translate metadata from one language to another language, but the performance of this method highly depends on the quality of the MT.

In this paper, we focus on the titles of digital objects because titles are descriptive metadata that summarize the content. The title also distinguishes an object from other objects, which is critical for determining if two metadata records are identical. Computing the similarities between the titles in different languages is not an easy task because some corresponding titles in the target language are not literal translations of the titles in the source language. Table 1 shows some examples of title pairs[1] in Japanese (source language) and English (target language) that describe the same digital objects, but the corresponding English translations of some words in Japanese titles are not literal translations.

Bilingual word embeddings [1–3] are cross-lingual semantic representations of words; they have attracted a lot of attention because they can capture the semantic meanings of words across languages. In this paper, we show how to utilize bilingual word embeddings for cross-lingual metadata matching to find identical metadata records. We calculate title similarities in two ways: (1) representing titles as the sums of constituent word vectors, and (2) word-to-word matching based on the bilingual word embeddings. We evaluate the effectiveness of our proposed method with Japanese and English ukiyo-e print databases.

Table 1. Examples of title pairs in Japanese and English.

Title pairs	Explanations
従千住花街眺望ノ不二 (Japanese title) Fuji Seen in the Distance from Senju Pleasure Quarter	"眺望 (view)" is translated into "Seen in the Distance."
上野公園開花ノ図 (Japanese title) Blossoming Cherry Trees in Ueno Park	"開花 (blooming)" is translated into "Blossoming" and added "Cherry Trees."

2 Related Work

Over the past decade, various approaches to find identical metadata records (record linkage) have been proposed [4]. Existing approaches for record linkage mainly aim to find identical records in the same language. However, we focus on finding identical metadata records across different languages, which is called "cross-language record

---

[1] Japanese titles are from the Edo-Tokyo Museum; English titles are from the Metropolitan Museum of Art.

linkage". To overcome language barriers, some works employ bilingual dictionaries and MT to translate metadata into the same language [5, 6]. Our method solves language barrier problems by utilizing bilingual word embeddings.

3   Title Matching Based on Bilingual Word Embeddings

Our method utilizes bilingual word embeddings for title matching by representing words in the titles in different languages in the same embedding space. In this section, first, we briefly introduce word embeddings and bilingual word embeddings. Then, we explain our method of title similarity calculation for title matching.

3.1   Bilingual Word Embeddings

In recent years, word embeddings [7], distributed representations of words, have achieved impressive results in many natural language processing tasks and applications [8]. Distributed representations represent semantically similar words by similar vectors to calculate the semantic similarities of words. Since words need to be represented in cross-lingual settings, several models for learning bilingual word embeddings have been proposed and have achieved good results via some forms of bilingual supervision, such as word-level, sentence-level, and document-level bilingual parallel or comparable data [1–3]. Bilingual word embeddings are appealing because they can capture the semantic meaning of words across languages, which can be applied to cross-lingual tasks.

3.2   Title Matching

Given titles in two languages, the source language is defined as the language of the titles that are used to match the titles in the other language. The other language is the target language. For example, we use the Japanese titles to match English titles to find identical metadata records. In this case, Japanese is the source language, and English is the target language.

We can directly measure the similarity of words in different languages with bilingual word embeddings, but we still need to define how to represent titles. To this end, we introduce two ways to utilize bilingual word embeddings for title matching.

Bilingual Word Embeddings Addition (BiWE-add). In the first way, we represent titles as vectors by adding the bilingual word embeddings of their constituent words. We opt for vector addition as composition since word embedding spaces exhibit linear linguistic regularities [9]. Let b be the vector space of bilingual word embeddings. Each word w in the source language and target language can be represented by the bilingual word embeddings as $b(w)$. The vector representation of a title in the source language is represented as the sum of embeddings of constituent words, which is formulated in Eq. 1.

$$\overrightarrow{t_S} = \sum_{i=1}^{N_{t_S}} b(w_i^{t_S}) \tag{1}$$

In Eq. 1, t_S is a title in the source language, $w_i^{t_S}$ is word i in t_S, N_{t_S} is the number of words in t_S. To obtain the representation of a title in the target language, we use the weighted addition where each word's embedding is weighted with the word's inverse document frequency (IDF). Here, the document frequency is the frequency of a word in the whole set of titles. The vector representation of a title in the target language is formulated in Eq. 2.

$$\overrightarrow{t_T} = \sum_{i=1}^{N_{t_T}} idf(w_i^{t_T}) \cdot b(w_i^{t_T}) \tag{2}$$

In Eq. 2, t_T is a title in the target language, $w_i^{t_T}$ is word i in t_T, N_{t_T} is the number of words in t_T. Finally, we compute the title similarity as the cosine similarity between the vector of the title in the source language and the vector of the title in the target language:

$$S_{BiWE-add}(t_S, t_T) = cosine\left(\overrightarrow{t_S}, \overrightarrow{t_T}\right) \tag{3}$$

Word-to-Word Matching (BiWE-w2w). In the second way, we measure the title similarity through word-to-word matching between the titles in the source language and the target language. Each word $w_i^{t_S}$ in the title in the source language is used to calculate the cosine similarity with all the words in the title in the target language, and the maximum similarity score is used as the contribution of $w_i^{t_S}$ to the title similarity, which is formulated in Eq. 4.

$$S_{BiWE-w2w}(t_S, t_T) = \sum_{i=1}^{N_{t_S}} \max_{w_j^{t_T} \in t_T} cosine\left(b(w_i^{t_S}), b\left(w_j^{t_T}\right)\right) \tag{4}$$

4 Experiments

In this section, we evaluate our method of title matching to find identical metadata records of ukiyo-e prints between the Japanese and English databases.

4.1 Experimental Setup

Datasets. We collected 203 Japanese ukiyo-e metadata records from the Edo-Tokyo Museum[2] and 3,398 English ukiyo-e metadata records from the Metropolitan Museum

---

[2] http://digitalmuseum.rekibun.or.jp/app/selected/edo-tokyo.

of Art[3]. Each Japanese ukiyo-e metadata record in the Japanese dataset has at least one corresponding English ukiyo-e metadata record in the English dataset, which means they are the identical metadata records in different languages. To reduce the number of record pairs to be compared, we used the artist element in metadata records to filter the candidate record pairs.

Bilingual Word Embeddings. The monolingual English and Japanese word vectors and bilingual parallel data are needed for a model to learn the bilingual word embeddings. We used pre-trained word embeddings trained on Wikipedia articles by using Word2vec toolkits. As we introduced in Sect. 3.1, several models for learning bilingual word embeddings with the requirements of different types of bilingual parallel or comparable data exist. We utilized a model that learns the bilingual word embeddings by relying on the parallel data of bilingual words because word-level bilingual data is easily obtainable. The bilingual word pairs are composed of 9,000 common Japanese words and their English translations. The training setup of bilingual word embeddings closely follows the recommended setup of [2].

We compare our method with a method that relies on MT. In our experiments, we used the Microsoft Translator Text API[4] to translate Japanese titles into English. The Microsoft Translator Text API provides two translation models we experimented with, the statistical machine translation (SMT) model and the neural network translation (NNT) model. After translation, we used the soft-tfidf similarity metric [10] for title matching because it showed the best performance in title matching against 20 other commonly used string-based similarity metrics [11].

4.2 Results and Discussion

Table 2 shows the experimental results. We evaluated the experimental results by mean average precision (MAP) and top-k precision. Here, we defined the top-k precision as the percentage of Japanese titles that had the correct corresponding English titles in their top-k candidates. All the values of evaluation metrics fall into [0,1]. The higher the values are, the more effectively the given methods worked.

Table 2. The performances of our proposed method and other methods.

Methods	MAP	Top-1 precision	Top-5 precision
MT-SMT	0.329	0.232	0.468
MT-NNT	0.399	0.306	0.530
BiWE-add	0.216	0.160	0.265
BiWE-w2w	0.304	0.246	0.391

---

[3] http://www.metmuseum.org/.

[4] https://www.microsoft.com/en-us/translator/translatorapi.aspx.

Machine Translation vs. Bilingual Word Embeddings. Methods that rely on an MT generally outperformed our method that relies on bilingual word embeddings. The performance of our method BiWE-w2w was just 2.5% lower than MT-SMT in MAP. The results of the MT method of using NNT are better than SMT, which indicates that the performance of an MT-based method is influenced by the translation quality. The performance of our method BiWE-w2w was 1.4% higher on Top-1 precision than MT-SMT. This finding is encouraging because bilingual word embeddings can be easily applied to other low-resource language pairs when it is difficult to find a large amount of bilingual parallel data to train an MT system.

Title Matching Methods. When comparing the methods of the BiWE-add and the BiWE-w2w, the BiWE-w2w performed better. By analyzing datasets, we found that, while Japanese and English title pairs refer to the identical metadata records, some conveyed unbalanced information. For example, for the title pair "淀川 (Yodo River)" and "Moonlight on the Yodo River," the English title has the word "Moonlight" while the corresponding Japanese title does not. In this case, the BiWE-w2w performed better than the BiWE-add, since it only matched the most similar words and filters from the irrelevant words.

5   Conclusion

We presented a method of title matching to find identical metadata records across languages. We showed our method's ability to find identical metadata records of ukiyo-e prints across Japanese and English databases. In the future, we will evaluate our method with other language pairs.

References

1. Mikolov, T., Le, Q.V., Sutskever, I.: Exploiting Similarities among Languages for Machine Translation. arXiv Prepr. arXiv:1309.4168v1. pp. 1–10 (2013)
2. Artetxe, M., Labaka, G., Agirre, E.: Learning principled bilingual mappings of word embeddings while preserving monolingual invariance. In: Proceedings of the Conference on Empirical Methods in Natural Language Processing, pp. 2289–2294 (2016)
3. Vulić, I., Moens, M.F.: Bilingual distributed word representations from document-aligned comparable data. J. Artif. Intell. Res. **55**, 953–994 (2016)
4. Koudas, N., Sarawagi, S., Srivastava, D.: Record linkage: similarity measures and algorithms. In: Proceedings of the 2006 ACM SIGMOD International Conference on Management of Data, pp. 802–803 (2006)
5. Batjargal, B., Kuyama, T., Kimura, F., Maeda, A.: Identifying the same records across multiple Ukiyo-e image database using textual data in different languages. In: Proceedings of the 14th ACM/IEEE Joint Conference on Digital Libraries, pp. 193–196 (2014)
6. Song, Y., Batjargal, B., Maeda, A.: Cross-language record linkage based on semantic matching of metadata. Database Soc. Japan Engl. J. **17**, 1–8 (2019)
7. Mikolov, T., Chen, K., Corrado, G., Dean, J.: Efficient Estimation of Word Representations in Vector Space. arXiv Prepr. arXiv:1301.3781. pp. 1–12 (2013)

8. Socher, R., Bauer, J., Manning, C.D., Ng, A.Y.: Parsing with compositional vector grammars. In: Proceedings of the 51st Annual Meeting of the Association for Computational Linguistics, pp. 455–465 (2013)
9. Mikolov, T., Yih, W.-T., Zweig, G.: Linguistic regularities in continuous space word representations. In: Proceedings of NAACL-HLT 2013, pp. 746–751 (2013)
10. Cohen, W.W., Ravikumar, P., Fienberg, S.E.: A comparison of string metrics for matching names and records. In: Proceedings of the International Workshop on Data Cleaning and Object Consolidation, held at KDD, pp. 73–78 (2003)
11. Gali, N., Mariescu-Istodor, R., Fränti, P.: Similarity measures for title matching. In: Proceedings of 23rd International Conference on Pattern Recognition, pp. 1549–1554 (2017)

Track on Metadata and Semantics for European and National Projects

Metadata Integration with Labeled-Property Graphs

Vasily Bunakov[(✉)]

Science and Technology Facilities Council, Harwell OX11 0QX, UK
vasily.bunakov@stfc.ac.uk

Abstract. The work reflects on the use case developed by FREYA project that employs labeled-property graph for the integration of metadata from diverse sources. The role of persistent identifiers in metadata integration is discussed, and a solution is proposed for the dynamic characterization of the integrated graph. The result of this characterization can be considered a metadata model for the labeled-property graph and can be used for the graph exploration, the graph content monitoring, also for the graphs comparison and for the automated generation of machine interfaces (APIs).

Keywords: EU project · Metadata integration · Metadata modeling · Research information management · Persistent identifiers · Open Science

1 Introduction

The FREYA project [1] is devoted to the use of persistent identifiers (PIDs) for discovery, access and use of research resources. It is a view of FREYA that PIDs and PID services can support FAIR principles in respect to research data [2] and other research artefacts, and therefore can contribute to the foundations of Open Science. The three conceptual pillars of FREYA are:

- PID Forum – a communication hub for engagement with research stakeholders who produce, use, or are otherwise involved with persistent identifiers. The PID Forum is not just a concept but has an online presence [3].
- PID Graph – a range of implementations that demonstrate the value of persistent identifiers when they get connected; this pertains to the more traditional PID types such as for publications or data, also to the emerging PID types such as for scientific instruments or research organizations.
- PID Commons – a range of best practices and business models in support of sustainability of the project outcomes.

FREYA partners have developed a number of use cases [4] that represent various scenarios of the PIDs use and that contribute to the development of pilot IT applications in particular organizational or research discipline contexts. The graph implementations vary in terms of logical modelling or information technology used; this work is inspired by the use case of the PhD research graph [5, 6] with a special focus on

E. Garoufallou et al. (Eds.): MTSR 2019, CCIS 1057, pp. 441–448, 2019.
https://doi.org/10.1007/978-3-030-36599-8_41

metadata integration techniques and on their implications for what can be considered a metadata model for labeled-property graphs [7].

The lessons learned and the suggestions made may have value beyond the particular use case and be applicable to the use of labeled-property graphs for metadata integration in general, including for the post-integration curation of the graph and for its exposure via machine interfaces. Compared to other possible methods of the labeled-property graphs characterization, such as the use of tabular or RDF representations, the suggested approach is based on the use of "metagraphs" that are property-labeled graphs in themselves.

2   PhD Research Use Case in FREYA

The PhD research use case was devised by two FREYA partners: STFC [8] and The British Library to explore connections between STFC institutional repositories and EThOS service for theses and dissertations [9]. The ultimate goal as it was perceived when this use case development started was to allow various kinds of impact studies traced back to experiments in STFC large-scale research facilities and to STFC PhD block grants awarded to the UK universities in support of PhD studentships.

Organizational, operational and funding context of the PhD research supported by STFC is represented by Fig. 1.

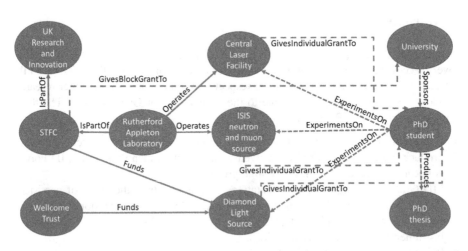

Fig. 1. Organizational, operational and funding context of the PhD research supported by STFC.

This conceptual model is in fact a representation of the STFC business model in support of the PhD research. As this conceptual model can be represented as a graph, it seemed only natural to use it not only as a representation of business processes but also as a logical model for the actual integrated IT resource. The NEO4J labeled-property graph database [10] was chosen as an IT solution for the integration of metadata from STFC repositories and EThOS, and a few other metadata sources were incorporated on the way, notably GRID.AC database was used as a source of organizational identifiers [11].

3 Metadata Sources and Metadata Integration Techniques for the PhD Research Use Case

The metadata sources used for integration are represented in Fig. 2. Metadata models, as well as methods of metadata acquisition differed for different sources: in some cases, it was bulk metadata export and import in a CSV format, and in some cases content negotiation resulted in DOIs resolution in JSON that was further parsed with NEO4J procedures.

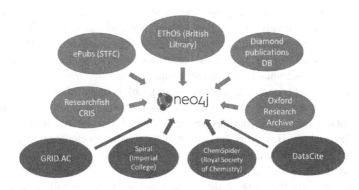

Fig. 2. Metadata sources for integration in a common PhD research graph.

The nodes in the graph were initially representations of bibliographic records in repositories, also of data records from DataCite and organizational records from GRID. AC. Then the graph was expanded with Person, University and Facility nodes and with relations exemplified by those in Table 1.

Table 1. Main relations in the integrated graph.

Relations created	Relations meaning
AwardedDegreeTo	Connects university and PhD awarded with the degree
Authored	Connects a PhD and a thesis that she authored
sameThesisAs	Connects manifestations of the same PhD thesis in different repositories
ExperimentedOn	Connects a PhD and a facility she experimented on

For matching bibliographic nodes, Levenstein distance [12] between theses titles was used, and properties were occasionally propagated using simple inference based on different manifestations of the same thesis matched. The propagated properties may include various PIDs, which is an illustration of a dual role of PIDs in metadata integration using graph technology: the PIDs can certainly facilitate metadata records matching and their integration in a common graph, also they can be propagated from one node to another in cases where the nodes relation has been established by other means than PIDs matching (or when other PIDs – not those to be propagated – were used for connecting nodes in the first instance).

The graph was initially based on repository records relevant to the PhD research supported by STFC either in the monetary form (studentship grants) or as grants-in-kind in the form of facilities beamtime awarded to PhD students as visitor scientists. Yet other opportunities of the graph enrichment were used opportunistically, too, specifically records from Imperial College London Spiral repository [13] and records from National Compound Collection [14] hosted by ChemSpider service [15]. The latter case is quite important as it paves the way for connecting more than forty thousand chemical data records to the PhD theses bibliography and full texts.

These opportunities for the graph expansion that are facilitated by available metadata sources and handy information technology come at a price though, as the graph starts to represent different perspectives: of a PhD research supported by STFC and of a PhD research in chemistry; the connections between these perspectives do exist, but the graph becomes more loosely connected.

Having a loosely connected labeled-property graph is appropriate as a new kind of information infrastructure that can support various use cases, and not necessarily those envisaged when the graph was initially designed – which universality is in the nature of any true infrastructure. However, the opportunistic graph development with metadata acquired from various sources raises a number of conceptual and practical questions, such as what is the metadata model for the resulted graph, or how this model can support reasoning over the graph shape, or the graph comparison with other graphs, or how this metadata can contribute to the development of user and machine interfaces to the graph content.

The diversity of metadata in the graph with diverse contributing metadata sources that can express different information contexts is illustrated by Fig. 3. The graph incorporates metadata acquired from the British Library EThOS service as well as from STFC institutional repositories and ChemSpider; it is a part (a subgraph) of a bigger PhD research graph that has been described in [5] and [6]. The graph represents three different contexts for the PhD research:

- the multiple nodes connected to the Diamond Light Source node on the left and to the ISIS neutron and muon source node on the right are PhD researchers supported by granting them time on one of these large-scale research facilities (grants-in-kind);
- the shorter chain on the bottom corresponds to the PhD researcher in particle physics supported by an STFC monetary grant;
- the longer chain on bottom-left has nothing to do with STFC but was supported by the University of Bristol and resulted in the ChemSpider thesis record and data record for the chemical compound explored.

This is one interconnected graph, but originating from several metadata sources (each with its own original metadata models) and with several different information

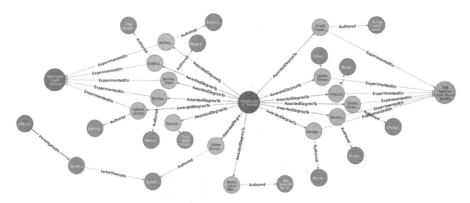

Fig. 3. Different PhD research contexts represented in the same graph.

contexts that the graph represents. So the question is what metadata can characterize the graph as a whole, and how this metadata can be used in practice?

4   Metadata for the Characterization of Labeled-Property Graphs, and Possible Uses of It

One method of presenting metadata for the entire graph could be using a tabular form. The Table 1 can be extended with counts of relations and nodes that the relations connect. The nodes themselves (different labels of them) can be counted, too, and added to the table. This will give us only a shallow characterization of the graph though, as the properties of the nodes and of relationships will remain unreported.

There is a technical difficulty, too, for managing the tabular form of the graph metadata model as the graph database engine is not an ideal fit for managing tabular data – hence some external (additional) IT solution may be required, which means not only a technological complication but also less control over the consistent reflection of the evolving graph structure (e.g. because of the new metadata sources integrated).

Another possibility would be using RDF for modeling the structure of labeled-property graphs. This approach has its benefits rooted in the universality of the RDF notation, but implies using yet another technology or two (triple store and mapping language) for the reflection over the structure of the graph database.

As an alternative to a tabular or an RDF-based model, it should be possible to express the dynamic nature of the labeled-property graph again in the form of a labeled-property graph – that can be called a "metagraph" as its purpose is to reflect on the structure of the underlying graph and to serve as its metadata model.

The "metagraph" for the aforementioned graph in Fig. 3 can look like that in Fig. 4. The numbers stand for the counts of nodes of appropriate types (with appropriate labels). The nodes properties may contain counts for the equally named properties in the original graph that is under characterization; the same principle applies to the properties of relations in the "metagraph".

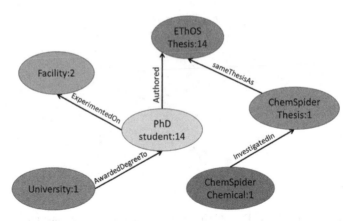

Fig. 4. "Metagraph" for the subgraph in Fig. 3. Numbers correspond to the numbers of corresponding entities in Fig. 3.

Building the "metagraph" certainly implies a reduction of information that the original graph contains, e.g. for the case presented in Fig. 3, the information is lost in the "metagraph" about what PhDs performed research on what particular facility. The good news is though that a "metagraph" can be generated using the same API or query language offered by the host graph database – so that the generation of the "metagraph" can be automated – also the "metagraph" can be managed using the same graph database technology (within the same or adjacent instance of the graph database). The automated "metagraph" generation is especially important in the situation when the original graph is being grown opportunistically via acquisition of more metadata from existing sources or from new sources (bearing different metadata schemas), or when the graph is frequently changed owing to any other reason. The "metagraph" can be autogenerated each time when the original graph is updated, and placed as "metainformation" in the same graph database, or in an adjacent instance of it.

The main cases where the "metagraph" can be useful:

- **Graph exploration:** quick characterization of the dynamic graph, and presenting its characteristics to the user as a "big picture" of what is there in the graph.
- **Monitoring graph properties:** as an example, monitoring the proliferation of various PID types used as attributes of the graph nodes and relations.
- **Graphs comparison:** the "metagraph" can be used as a hash function of a kind: if the "metagraphs" are different then it is likely that the original graphs from which they have been produced are different, too. Special cases of this check are the comparison of two versions of the same graph, also the check on the integrity of the original graph to see if it has been tampered with ("metagraph" in the role of a checksum). This use of "metagraphs" has its limitations as different graphs may reflect onto the same "metagraph", but it may be all right as a "quick and dirty" check on the graphs potential equivalence. If the "metagraph" itself grows big (owing to the underlying graph diversity), then a "metagraph of a metagraph" can

be produced recursively, so that the comparison of the initial underlying graphs starts with "metametagraphs".

- **Autogeneration of machine interfaces (APIs) to the graph.** As the "metagraph" is a fairly detailed reflection (when it includes the counts of labels and properties) of what is in the original graph, it is possible to introduce simple rules for the auto-generation of information structures in support of machine interfaces, e.g. GraphQL schemas [16]. What nodes, relations and properties of the original graph to include in the GraphQL schema can be decided based on certain minimal thresholds for the respective counts of these nodes, relations and properties in the "metagraph" – so that most popular features are fed in the schema.

5   Conclusion

Proliferation of traditional and emerging types of persistent identifiers facilitates building connected representations of research in the form of labeled-property graphs. Such graphs can be built incrementally and opportunistically using various sources of metadata that comply with different formats. The resulted labeled-property graphs do not bear any metadata model, yet there is a practical need in their characterization for the purposes of their exploration, monitoring, comparison, and access to their content via machine interfaces (APIs).

Characterization of a labeled-property graph by means of another labeled-property graph (a "metagraph") has advantages of conceptual uniformity and technological viability before alternative tabular or RDF representations.

The further exploration of the suggested approach to the labeled-property graphs characterization is going to look into a possibility to reuse and expand the existing standard and community-developed algorithms for the graph databases. The most promising case for the practical application of the suggested approach is the auto-generation of machine interfaces (APIs) to the labeled-property graphs that have been opportunistically and incrementally created from disparate sources of metadata.

Acknowledgements. This work is supported by funding from the Horizon 2020 FREYA project, Grant Agreement number 777523. The views expressed are the views of the author and not necessarily of the project or the funding agency.

References

1. FREYA project. https://www.project-freya.eu/. Accessed September 2019
2. Wilkinson, M., et al.: The FAIR guiding principles for scientific data management and stewardship. Sci. Data **3**, 160018 (2016). https://doi.org/10.1038/sdata.2016.18
3. PID Forum. https://www.pidforum.org/. Accessed September 2019
4. FREYA use cases. https://github.com/datacite/freya/issues. Accessed June 2019
5. Bunakov, V., Madden, F.: Integration of a national e-theses online service with institutional repositories. In: Presentation in the Open Repositories Conference, Hamburg, Germany, pp. 10–13, June 2019

6. Madden, F., Bunakov, V.: Using persistent identifiers to track PhD outcomes. In: Accepted by the ETD 2019, 22nd International Symposium on Electronic Theses and Dissertations – ETD 2019, Porto, Portugal (2019)
7. Labeled-property graph. https://en.wikipedia.org/wiki/Graph_database#Labeled-property_graph. Accessed June 2019
8. Science and Technology Facilities Council. http://www.stfc.ac.uk/. Accessed September 2019
9. EThOS service. https://ethos.bl.uk/. Accessed June 2019
10. NEO4J graph database. https://neo4j.com/. Accessed September 2019
11. GRID: Global Research Identifiers Database. https://grid.ac/. Accessed in June 2019
12. Levenshtein, V.: Binary codes capable of correcting deletions, insertions, and reversals. Sov. Phys. Doklady **10**(8), 707–710 (1966)
13. Spiral: Imperial College London's repository. https://spiral.imperial.ac.uk/. Accessed June 2019
14. Andrews, D., et al.: The creation and characterisation of a National Compound Collection: the Royal Society of Chemistry pilot. Chem. Sci. **7**, 3869–3878 (2016). https://doi.org/10.1039/C6SC00264A
15. ChemSpider service. http://www.chemspider.com/. Accessed June 2019
16. GraphQL schemas and types. https://graphql.org/learn/schema/. Accessed June 2019

Track on Metadata, Identifiers and Semantics in Decentralized Applications, Blockchains and P2P Systems

Timestamping Metadata Using Blockchain: A Practical Approach

Tassos Kolydas$^{(\boxtimes)}$ (iD)

National and Kapodistrian University of Athens, Athens, Greece
kolydart@music.uoa.gr

Abstract. Long-term preservation of digital information requires confidence in the credibility and ability of digital archives and systems to consistently provide accessible and usable content. Ensuring that the provided information has remained unchanged over time is a particular challenge. Trusted timestamping is an effective method that allows anyone to prove without any doubt that specific content existed at a particular date and time. A practical approach for trusted timestamping using the Ethereum blockchain is presented here. A complete metadata record is stored as transaction input data along with a document hash digest. The approach is uncomplicated, human and machine readable, self-explanatory, and modular. It supports metadata preservation and copyright protection of digital documents applying verification without disclosure. The approach aims at extending current digital archives and systems using existing, well-tested technology.

Keywords: Trusted timestamping · Ethereum blockchain · Digital preservation · Copyright protection

1 Introduction

Long-term preservation of digital information requires confidence in the credibility and ability of digital archives and systems to consistently provide accessible and usable content. Information generated today must survive long-term changes in storage media, devices, and data formats [1]. Ensuring that the provided information has remained unchanged over time is a particular challenge. Trusted timestamping is an effective method that allows anyone to prove without any doubt that specific digital content existed at a particular date and time [2]. Blockchain technology has emerged as a means of storing information on decentralized networks, secured from tampering and revision [3]. Ethereum is an open-source, globally decentralized computing infrastructure that executes programs called "smart contracts" [4]. It uses a blockchain to synchronize and store the system's state changes, along with a cryptocurrency called "ether" to meter and constrain execution resource costs [4].

A practical approach for trusted timestamping using the Ethereum blockchain is presented here. A complete metadata record is stored in transaction input data, along with a document hash digest. The approach is uncomplicated, human readable as well as machine readable, self-explanatory, and modular. It supports metadata preservation and copyright protection of digital documents without revealing the content of the documents. The approach aims at extending current archives and systems using existing, well-tested technology.

© Springer Nature Switzerland AG 2019
E. Garoufallou et al. (Eds.): MTSR 2019, CCIS 1057, pp. 451–458, 2019.
https://doi.org/10.1007/978-3-030-36599-8_42

2 Related Work and Background

Timestamping is a technique used to prove the existence of certain digital data prior to a specific point in time. When one uses a certain timestamping service, he should confirm in advance that its security level sufficiently meets his security requirements [2]. However, before the advent of blockchain technology, timestamping schemes were generally so complicated that it was not easy to evaluate their security levels accurately [2]. More recently, authenticity of information has become a core issue due to the spread of false news. Research on the subject has showed that falsehoods diffuse significantly farther, faster, deeper, and more broadly than the truth in all categories of information [5].

Blockchain technology can be used to address issues associated with information integrity in the present and near term, assuming proper security architecture and infrastructure management controls. It does not, however, guarantee reliability of information in the first place, and would have several limitations as a long-term solution for maintaining trustworthy digital records [6]. Recently, the European Union launched the International Association of Trusted Blockchain Applications, aiming to bring blockchain and distributed ledger technology into the mainstream [7]. Blockchain technology has the potential to change the practices and systems used for archival functions, both for the storage of digital resources and of the metadata describing them [3].

2.1 Overview

One of the most well-known services is *OriginStamp*, which is a trusted timestamping service that enables anyone to prove ownership of information on a specific date and time. It is provided both as a free service [8] saving data on blockchain once a day or as a paid service for instant entry [9]. It utilizes bitcoin [10], "because it has achieved the largest market capitalization and has attracted the highest number of participating computing nodes" [11], while more blockchains were added recently. A unique SHA-256 hash is generated from all content and is contained in a bitcoin transaction [12]. The free service keeps the transaction costs in the blockchain to a minimum by collecting all hashes received over a 24 h period and computing a single aggregate SHA-256 hash from the list of hashes [13]. The service exclusively stores which hashes were included in which transaction. This information allows verification of any hash using the blockchain [11]. This means that trust in a third party and/or firm cryptographic knowledge is required.

Proof of Existence is a similar solution providing only paid service to store the document proof on the bitcoin blockchain [14]. The document is certified via embedding its SHA-256 digest in the bitcoin blockchain. This is done by generating a special bitcoin transaction that encodes/contains the hash via an OP_RETURN script. Thus, no other information is provided except the document digest. The service costs much more than *OriginStamp* and has no free plan. Thus, the same limitations apply.

García-Barriocanal et al. proposed an approach in which a blockchain combined with other related technologies can be arranged in a particular way to obtain a decentralized solution for metadata supporting key functions [3]. The proof-of-concept implementation of a decentralized metadata system considers the different functions of metadata as points of departure, thus building the solution based mainly on blockchain.

Lemieux has presented a synthesis of original research documenting several cases of the application of blockchain technology, considering the different types of solutions in relation to implications for record keeping and long-term preservation of authentic records [15].

The proposed solution in this paper belongs in the first type of system – according to Lemieux – the "mirror" type, where the blockchain serves as a repository of "digital fingerprints" of the records in an originating system [15, p. 2273]. Including a documents digest, the original file content has essentially been encoded into the blockchain, and the blockchain can serve as a document registry [16, p. 37].

3   Timestamping (Meta) Data on Blockchain

3.1   Description

The method consists of storing a metadata record along with any document hash digest on the Ethereum blockchain. The record, stored as a JSON object, is inserted in the "input data" field of a zero-value transaction. Each transaction contains a single record.

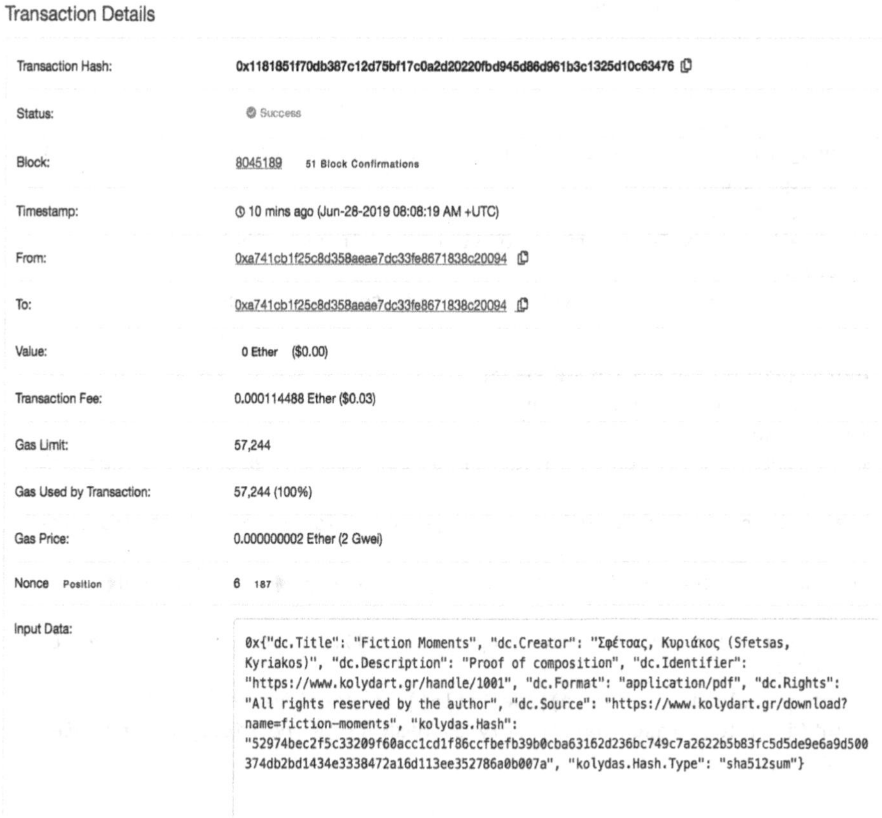

Transaction Details

Transaction Hash:	0x1181851f70db387c12d75bf17c0a2d20220fbd945d86d961b3c1325d10c63476
Status:	⊘ Success
Block:	8045189 51 Block Confirmations
Timestamp:	ⓘ 10 mins ago (Jun-28-2019 08:08:19 AM +UTC)
From:	0xa741cb1f25c8d358aeae7dc33fe8671838c20094
To:	0xa741cb1f25c8d358aeae7dc33fe8671838c20094
Value:	0 Ether ($0.00)
Transaction Fee:	0.000114488 Ether ($0.03)
Gas Limit:	57,244
Gas Used by Transaction:	57,244 (100%)
Gas Price:	0.000000002 Ether (2 Gwei)
Nonce Position	6 187

Input Data:

```
0x{"dc.Title": "Fiction Moments", "dc.Creator": "Σφέτσας, Κυριάκος (Sfetsas,
Kyriakos)", "dc.Description": "Proof of composition", "dc.Identifier":
"https://www.kolydart.gr/handle/1001", "dc.Format": "application/pdf", "dc.Rights":
"All rights reserved by the author", "dc.Source": "https://www.kolydart.gr/download?
name=fiction-moments", "kolydas.Hash":
"52974bec2f5c33209f60acc1cd1f86ccfbefb39b0cba63162d236bc749c7a2622b5b83fc5d5de9e6a9d500
374db2bd1434e3338472a16d113ee352786a0b007a", "kolydas.Hash.Type": "sha512sum"}
```

Fig. 1. Transaction viewed from EtherScan.io blockchain explorer [17].

Verifying the metadata record is as simple as retrieving the transaction content and decoding the input data from hexadecimal to UTF-8. Some blockchain explorers, like *EtherScan*, provide the function on their web applications (see Fig. 1). Validating the document requires an extra step of hashing the original bitstream and comparing it with the included digest.

The process from the digital archive's point of view includes the secure storage of each digital document *for the specific transaction* in which it is included as well as the identifier of the transaction, known as the "transaction hash". Having these two, anyone can verify the metadata record or the document's content for any changes against the timestamped content. Therefore, the responsibility for metadata creation and storage remains in the archive's system.

Creating a New Transaction:

```python
from web3 import Web3, HTTPProvider
w3 = Web3(HTTPProvider(provider)) # connect to blockchain network
    node
transaction_content = dict(
    nonce = w3.eth.getTransactionCount(address),
    gasPrice = w3.eth.gasPrice,
    gas = w3.eth.estimateGas({'to': address, 'from': address, 'value':
    0, 'data': record_hex}),
    to = address,
    value = 0,
    data=record_hex,
) # prepare transaction content
signed_txn = w3.eth.account.signTransaction(transaction_content, pk)
    # sign transaction
transaction_hash                                                      =
    w3.eth.sendRawTransaction(signed_txn.rawTransaction) # send trans-
    action
print(transaction_hash.hex()) # retrieve transaction hash
```

Retrieving a Stored Record's Element:

```python
from web3 import Web3, HTTPProvider
import json
w3 = Web3(HTTPProvider(provider)) # connect to blockchain network
    node
transaction = w3.eth.getTransaction(transaction_hash) # get transac-
    tion
inputData = transaction.input # get record from transaction input
    data
json_data = bytearray.fromhex(inputData[2:]).decode() # decode hex to
    utf-8
print(json.loads(json_data)['dc.Title']) # retrieve record element
print(json.loads(json_data)['kolydas.Hash']) # retrieve record ele-
    ment
```

The simplicity of the approach adheres to the design and philosophy of the Ethereum blockchain as described in the white paper: "An average programmer should ideally be able to follow and implement the entire specification so as to fully realize the unprecedented democratizing potential that cryptocurrency brings and further the vision of Ethereum as a protocol that is open to all" [18]. Also, the transaction input data field accepts any data. Transactions contain an optional data field that has no function by default [18]. The term "transaction" is used in Ethereum to refer to the signed data package that stores a message to be sent from an externally owned account.

3.2 Implementation

Multiple packages are available for interacting with the Ethereum blockchain. The Python package web3.py (https://github.com/ethereum/web3.py) was selected for this implementation. The code is available at https://www.kolydart.gr/download?name=mtsr-2019-kolydas-code.

Transaction. The proposed solution was used to create the transaction hash 0x11818 51f70db387c12d75bf17c0a2d20220fbd945d86d961b3c1325d10c63476. For improved security, the SHA-512 algorithm was used for the document hash value. The metadata record is available from https://www.kolydart.gr/handle/1001.

4   Evaluation

The suggested approach contains most of the well-known benefits of blockchain technology. Stored records are immutable, every transaction is timestamped, and data are interconnected in such a way that upon tampering, the structure becomes invalid.

Centralization is a process where the authority to make decisions lies in the hands of only a few. In other words, centralization is the consistent and systematic way of entrusting authority to people who are in the center of the organization [19]. Using blockchain in a decentralized network, everyone holds the same information. Interacting with anyone in the network is possible without the need for any third party. Furthermore, the proposed solution interacts directly with the blockchain and is platform-independent, without any third-party involvement. Actually, entrusting the timestamping process to a third party to store it for you on a decentralized blockchain is a kind of paradox.

Access to the data is public, and information is freely available. Each entity is responsible for the information it stores on the blockchain. At the same time, digital document content remains private, and verification of the authenticity of a document takes place without disclosing its content.

Simplicity is a key feature of the approach. The principle of least effort (PLE) is having a growing influence on library and information science research, becoming increasingly important in various subfields [20]. It postulates that people, and even well-designed machines, will naturally choose the path of least resistance or "effort." Thus, a lightweight approach implemented with a few lines of code might in many cases be preferred.

Portability and interoperability are key elements in the life cycle of metadata. Using JSON formatted data, and being able to manually verify authenticity using a single hash function is an important advantage. Also, it is possible to use different hash algorithms, depending on the circumstances, as long as it is documented in the metadata.

Document size does not affect the proposed timestamping procedure because the hash digest's string length is fixed. The size of the metadata record is the same, whether describing a small or large document. File size is a factor that could be examined during hashing when processing resources are limited, so the above-mentioned flexibility to use different hash algorithms is a major advantage over other solutions. When speed is a priority, a less resource-intensive hash function could be used to quickly compute the hash output of a large document. Alternatively, if security is a concern, a state-of-the-art collision-resistant hash function could be used – like the proposed SHA-512 – in order to make it infeasible to produce the same hash value from two different documents.

Privacy is another important aspect of the proposed method. While we all reap the benefits of a data-driven society, there is a growing public concern about user privacy [21]. Centralized organizations – both public and private – amass large quantities of personal and sensitive information [21]. Using a third-party platform that requires some kind of user registration poses a security risk when data breach incidents occur or users' data are misused. The proposed method ensures that users own and control their personal data. No interaction with third parties is involved, and storing data on the blockchain requires only the cryptographic key of a digital wallet and some ether.

The cost of the solution is variable, depending on the STARTGAS and GASPRICE values used in the transaction and also the size of the input data field [18, "Messages and Transactions"]. The cost is competitive compared to other blockchain solutions and extremely low compared to non-blockchain solutions. Since each transaction contains a single metadata record stored in real time, the solution provides a service comparable to the above-mentioned platforms *OriginStamp* and *Proof of Existence*. Using the code mentioned previously, the cost of storing the record on the Ethereum blockchain was 0.000114488 ether (about $0.025); validating the document digest is free. *Proof of Existence* requires a fixed payment of 0.00025 btc (about $2.4) per transaction [14]; validation is also free. *OriginStamp* has multiple price plans; a free plan is sufficient for uses such as creating eight timestamps and downloading the corresponding proofs each month (50 credits). Paid plans vary from $39 for 1,000 credits per month to $249 for 100,000 credits per month [9]. The Hellenic Copyright Organization has developed a non-blockchain online timestamping service that charges based on the size of the uploaded file. Prices range from €10 for timestamping a 3 MB file to €70 for a 2 GB file; the verification process costs one hundred euros (€100) [22].

The proposed solution provides added value to digital libraries and archives, which can offer copyright protection as a service to their content providers. This creates an additional incentive for digital content creators to trust their creations to digital archives since they will automatically have their copyright protected.

5   Implications

Since it is so easy to apply a trusted timestamp to your data, you *have to immediately timestamp your original content*. Otherwise, you risk having your content claimed by others who take advantage of their knowledge of the timestamping procedure and benefits. Protecting original content implies that timestamping should be performed even on works in progress.

Timestamping works in progress and re-timestamping updated info add complexity to the design of the archives because multiple transaction hashes have to be stored in order to follow intermediate states of information.

Last but not least, privacy is an important factor that must be considered. Private key management is essential in a system that relies upon cryptography, such as blockchain. This includes the generation, exchange, storage, use, and replacement of keys, which is difficult to achieve in practice [6, p. 129]. Effective key management, including system policy, user training, and organizational and departmental interactions, is a critical factor for the success of the solution.

6   Conclusion

A practical approach for trusted timestamping metadata records and digital documents has been demonstrated. Most digital library packages lack such an implementation for the moment. But interest in blockchain solutions for metadata is rapidly gaining traction. The effect that the web "fabric" had on the world during the 1990s seems comparable to the impact of the information "locking" that blockchain provides today.

Future research could explore timestamping large collections – even complete archives – in a single transaction using a *Merkle tree*, also known as a *binary hash tree*, which is a data structure used for efficiently summarizing and verifying the integrity of large sets of data [23]. This structure could be used to summarize all documents in a collection, producing an overall digital fingerprint of the entire set while providing an efficient process for verifying whether a document was included in a collection on a specific date and time.

References

1. Lorie, R. A.: Long term preservation of digital information. In: Proceedings of the 1st ACM/IEEE-CS Joint Conference on Digital Libraries, pp. 346–352 (2001). https://dl.acm.org/citation.cfm?id=379726. Accessed 29 Aug 2019
2. Une, M.: The security evaluation of time stamping schemes: the present situation and studies. In: IMES Discussion Papers Series 2001-E-18 (2001). https://citeseerx.ist.psu.edu/viewdoc/similar?doi=10.1.1.23.7486&type=ab. Accessed 30 June 2019
3. García-Barriocanal, E., Sánchez-Alonso, S., Sicilia, M.-A.: Deploying metadata on blockchain technologies. In: Garoufallou, E., Virkus, S., Siatri, R., Koutsomiha, D. (eds.) MTSR 2017. CCIS, vol. 755, pp. 38–49. Springer, Cham (2017). https://doi.org/10.1007/978-3-319-70863-8_4

4. Antonopoulos, A.M., Wood, G.: Mastering Ethereum: Building Smart Contracts and Dapps. O'Reilly Media, Newton (2018)
5. Vosoughi, S., Roy, D., Aral, S.: The spread of true and false news online. Science **359** (6380), 1146–1151 (2018)
6. Lemieux, V.L.: Trusting records: is Blockchain technology the answer? Rec. Manage. J. **26** (2), 110–139 (2016)
7. Zmudzinski, A.: European Union Launches International Association of Trusted Blockchain Applications. CoinTelegraph 03 March 2019. https://cointelegraph.com/news/european-union-launches-international-association-of-trusted-blockchain-applications. Accessed 30 June 2019
8. OriginStamp. https://originstamp.org. Accessed 30 June 2019
9. OriginStamp. https://originstamp.com. Accessed 30 June 2019
10. Nakamoto, S.: Bitcoin: A Peer-to-Peer Electronic Cash System. The Cryptography Mailing List, 31 October 2008. https://bitcoin.org/bitcoin.pdf. Accessed 30 June 2019
11. Gipp, B., Meuschke, N., Gernandt, A.: Decentralized trusted timestamping using the crypto currency Bitcoin. In: Proceedings of the iConference 2015 (υπό έκδοση), Newport Beach, CA, USA, 24–27 March 2015. http://www.gipp.com/wp-content/papercite-data/pdf/gipp15a. pdf. Accessed 30 June 2019
12. Gipp, B., Meuschke, N., Beel, J., Breitinger, C.: Using the Blockchain of cryptocurrencies for timestamping digital cultural heritage. Bulletin of IEEE Technical Committee on Digital Libraries (TCDL) **13**(1) (2017). https://www.gipp.com/wp-content/papercite-data/pdf/gipp2017a.pdf. Accessed 30 June 2019
13. Gipp, B., Breitinger, C., Meuschke, N., Beel, J.: Cryptsubmit: introducing securely timestamped manuscript submission and peer review feedback using the blockchain. In: Proceedings of the ACM/IEEE-CS Joint Conference on Digital Libraries (JCDL) (2017)
14. Proof of Existence. https://www.proofofexistence.com/. Accessed 30 June 2019
15. Lemieux, V. L.: A typology of Blockchain recordkeeping solutions and some reflections on their implications for the future of archival preservation. big data. In: 2017 IEEE International Conference – BIGDATA, (Arles 2017). https://ieeexplore.ieee.org/abstract/document/8258180. Accessed 30 June 2019
16. Swan, M.: Blockchain: Blueprint for a New Economy. O'Reilly Media, Newton (2015)
17. etherscan.io: Transaction   Details.   https://etherscan.io/tx/0x1181851f70db387c12d75bf 17c0a2d20220fbd945d86d961b3c1325d10c63476. Accessed 30 June 2019
18. A Next-Generation Smart Contract and Decentralized Application Platform. Ethereum White Paper. https://github.com/ethereum/wiki/wiki/White-Paper#ethereum. Accessed 30 June 2019
19. Kaushik, A., Choudhary, A., Ektare, C., Thomas, D., Akram, S.: Blockchain – literature survey. In: 2nd IEEE International Conference on Recent Trends in Electronics, Information & Communication Technology (RTEICT) (2017). https://ieeexplore.ieee.org/stamp/stamp. jsp?tp=&arnumber=8256979. Accessed 30 June 2019
20. Chang, Y.-W.: Influence of human behavior and the principle of least effort on library and information science research. Inf. Process. Manag. **52**(4), 658–669 (2016). https://doi.org/10. 1016/j.ipm.2015.12.011. Accessed 30 June 2019
21. Zyskind, G., Nathan, O., Pentland, A.S.: Decentralizing privacy: using Blockchain to protect personal data. In: 2015 IEEE Security and Privacy Workshops. pp. 180–184. IEEE (2015). https://ieeexplore.ieee.org/stamp/stamp.jsp?arnumber=7163223. Accessed 30 June 2019
22. Hellenic Copyright Organization: Electronic Timestamping Service. https://www.timestamp. gr/en/information. Accessed 30 June 2019
23. Antonopoulos, A.M.: Mastering Bitcoin: Programming the Open Blockchain. O'Reilly Media, Newton (2017)

Author Index

Printed in the United States
By Bookmasters